# International Conference on Information and Knowledge Engineering (IKE 2013)



Held at WORLDCOMP'13

Las Vegas, Nevada, USA
22-25 July 2013

**Editors:**

**Hamid R. Arabnia**
**Leonidas Deligiannidis**
**Ray Hashemi**
**Joan Lu**
**George Jandieri**
**Ashu M.G. Solo**
**Fernando G. Tinetti**

ISBN: 978-1-5108-9196-8

**Printed from e-media with permission by:**

Curran Associates, Inc.
57 Morehouse Lane
Red Hook, NY 12571

**Some format issues inherent in the e-media version may also appear in this print version.**



Printed by Curran Associates, Inc. (2019)

For permission requests, please contact CSREA Press
at the address below.

CSREA Press
ATTN: Hamid R. Arabnia
1060 Long Creek Drive
Watkinsville, GA 30677
USA

Phone: (706) 542-3480

hra@cs.uga.edu

**Additional copies of this publication are available from:**

Curran Associates, Inc.
57 Morehouse Lane
Red Hook, NY 12571 USA
Phone: 845-758-0400
Fax: 845-758-2633
Email: curran@proceedings.com
Web: www.proceedings.com

# PROCEEDINGS OF
# THE 2013 INTERNATIONAL CONFERENCE ON
# INFORMATION & KNOWLEDGE ENGINEERING

# IKE 2013

## Editors


**Hamid R. Arabnia**
**Leonidas Deligiannidis, Ray Hashemi**
**Joan Lu**


## Associate Editors


**George Jandieri**
**Ashu M. G. Solo**
**Fernando G. Tinetti**



*WORLDCOMP'13*
July 22-25, 2013
Las Vegas Nevada, USA
www.world-academy-of-science.org

This volume contains papers presented at The 2013 International Conference on Information & Knowledge Engineering (IKE'13). Their inclusion in this publication does not necessarily constitute endorsements by editors or by the publisher.

# Foreword

It gives us great pleasure to introduce this collection of papers to be presented at the 2013 International Conference on Information and Knowledge Engineering (IKE'13), July 22 through 25, 2013, at The New Tropicana Hotel, Las Vegas, USA.

An important mission of the World Congress in Computer Science, Computer Engineering, and Applied Computing (a federated congress to which this conference is affiliated with) includes *"Providing a unique platform for a diverse community of constituents composed of scholars, researchers, developers, educators, and practitioners. The Congress makes concerted effort to reach out to participants affiliated with diverse entities (such as: universities, institutions, corporations, government agencies, and research centers/labs) from all over the world. The congress also attempts to connect participants from institutions that have* ***teaching*** *as their main mission with those who are affiliated with institutions that have* ***research*** *as their main mission. The congress uses a quota system to achieve its institution and geography diversity objectives."* By any definition of diversity, this congress is among the most diverse scientific meeting in USA. We are proud to report that this federated congress has authors and participants from 82 different nations representing variety of personal and scientific experiences that arise from differences in culture and values. As can be seen (see below), the program committee of this conference as well as the program committee of all other tracks of the federated congress are as diverse as its authors and participants.

The program committee would like to thank all those who submitted papers for consideration. About 65% of the submissions were from outside the United States. Each submitted paper was peer-reviewed by two experts in the field for originality, significance, clarity, impact, and soundness. In cases of contradictory recommendations, a member of the conference program committee was charged to make the final decision; often, this involved seeking help from additional referees. In addition, papers whose authors included a member of the conference program committee were evaluated using the double-blinded review process. One exception to the above evaluation process was for papers that were submitted directly to chairs/organizers of pre-approved sessions/workshops; in these cases, the chairs/organizers were responsible for the evaluation of such submissions. The overall paper acceptance rate for regular papers was 31%; 6% of the remaining papers were accepted as poster papers (at the time of this writing, we had not yet received the acceptance rate for a few individual tracks.)

We are very grateful to the many colleagues who offered their services in organizing the conference. In particular, we would like to thank the members of the Program Committee of IKE'13, members of the congress Steering Committee, and members of the committees ol lederated congress tracks that have topics within the scope of IKE. Many individuals listed below, will be requested after the conference to provide their expertise and services for selecting papers for publication (extended versions) in journal special issues as well as for publication in a set of research books (to be prepared for publishers including: Springer, Elsevier, BMC, and others).

- *Dr. Alireza Abbasi; University of New South Wales (UNSW), Canberra, Australia*
- *Dr. Selim Aissi (World Congress Steering Committee); formerly, Chief Strategist - Security, Intel Corp, USA; Senior Business Leader & Head of Global Enterprise Security Architecture, Visa Corporation, USA*
- *Prof. Babak Akhgar (World Congress Steering Committee); Fellow of the British Computer Society, CITP; Professor of Informatics; Co-Director of CENTRIC (Centre of Excellence in Terrorism, Resilience, Intelligence & organised Crime research), Sheffield Hallam University, Sheffield, UK*
- *Dr. Fahad Al-Harby (EEE); The National Centre for Financial & Economic Information, Ministry of Finance, Riyadh, Saudi Arabia*
- *Prof. Nizar Al-Holou (World Congress Steering Committee); Professor and Chair, ECE Department; Vice Chair, IEEE/SEM-Computer Chapter; University of Detroit Mercy, Detroit, Michigan, USA*
- *Prof. Hamid R. Arabnia (World Congress Steering Committee); Professor, Computer Science; Editor-in-Chief, The Journal of Supercomputing (Springer); Elected Fellow, Int'l Society of Intelligent Biological Medicine (ISIBM); The University of Georgia, Department of Computer Science, USA*
- *Peyman Arebi; Assistant Professor, Department of Computer Engineering, Technical and Vocational University, Bushehr, Iran*

As Sponsors-at-large, partners, and/or organizers each of the followings (separated by semicolons) provided help for at least one track of the World Congress: Aldebaran Robotics Inc., USA (http://www.aldebaran-robotics.com); Altera Corporation, USA (http://www.altera.com/); Computer Science Research, Education, and Applications Press (CSREA); Impulse Accelerated Technologies, Inc., USA (http://www.impulseaccelerated.com/); NVIDIA Corporation, USA (http://www.nvidia.com/object/about-nvidia.html); Parallella Community, Supercomputing for Everyone, USA (http://forums.parallella.org/); Pico Computing, Inc., USA (http://picocomputing.com/); SemiWiki.com, The Semiconductor Wiki Project, USA (http://www.semiwiki.com/); Solarflare Communications, Inc., USA (http://www.solarflare.com/); Stream Computing, Performance Engineers, The Netherlands (http://streamcomputing.eu/); Taylor & Francis, UK (http://www.taylorandfrancis.com/); US Chapter of World Academy of Science (http://www.world-academy-of-science.org/) ; and WEBestSOL & Webest Solutions Ltd, UK (http://webestsol.com/). In addition, a number of university faculty members and their staff (names appear on the cover of the set of proceedings), several publishers of computer science and computer engineering books and journals, chapters and/or task forces of computer science associations/organizations from 5 countries, and developers of high-performance machines and systems provided significant help in organizing the conference as well as providing some resources. We are grateful to them all.

We express our gratitude to keynote, invited, and individual conference/tracks and tutorial speakers - the list of speakers appears on the conference web site. We would also like to thank the followings: UCMSS (Universal Conference Management Systems & Support, California, USA) for managing all aspects of the conference; Dr. Tim Field of APC for managing the printing of the proceedings; and the staff of the New Tropicana Hotel in Las Vegas for the professional service they provided. Last but not least, we would like to thank the Co-Editors and Associate Co-Editors of IKE'13: Prof. Hamid R. Arabnia, Prof. Leonidas Deligiannidis, Prof. Ray Hashemi, Prof. George Jandieri, Dr. Joan Lu, Ashu M. G. Solo, and Prof. Fernando G. Tinetti.

We present the proceedings of IKE'13.

***Steering Committee, 2013***
***http://www.world-academy-of-science.org/***

# Contents

## *SESSION:* KNOWLEDGE ENGINEERING AND MANAGEMENT + KNOWLEDGE ACQUISITION



## *SESSION:* DATABASES, INFORMATION RETRIEVAL AND SEARCH



## *SESSION:* DECISION SUPPORT SYSTEMS

## *SESSION:* MINING OF DATA RICH SOURCES



## *SESSION:* DATA AND INFORMATION MINING + FORECASTING METHODS



## *SESSION:* NOVEL METHODOLOGIES AND APPLICATIONS

## *SESSION:* POSTERS



## *SESSION:* LATE BREAKING PAPERS - INFORMATION RETRIEVAL, LEARNING METHODS, AND SOCIAL NETWORKS

## *SESSION:* DATA MINING, OPINION MANAGEMENT, SOFTWARE QUALITY ISSUES, BIOINFORMATICS, AND APPLICATIONS

# SESSION

# KNOWLEDGE ENGINEERING AND MANAGEMENT + KNOWLEDGE ACQUISITION

## Chair(s)

### TBA

# Knowledge Management in a Large Organization: a Practical Case Study

**Antonio Ballarin[1], Spartaco Coletta[1], Daniela Principi[4], Giulio Concas[2], Marco Di Francesco[3] and Katiuscia Mannaro[2]**
[1]Sogei Spa, v. M. Carucci n. 99, 00143 Roma, Italy
[2]Department of Electrics and Electronics Engineering, University of Cagliari, P.zza d'Armi Cagliari, Italy
[3]FlossLab Srl, v.le Elmas 142, Cagliari, Italy
[4]General Administration, Personnel and Services Department, Ministry of Economy and Finance, v. XX Settembre, 97, 00187 Roma, Italy

**Abstract**. *In this work we present an approach, based on a Knowledge Federation, for the management of the information regarding the life-cycle of Software Application ad IT services for organizations' operations. We need many information about software and IT to study the software product's life-cycle management, and to understand the life-cycle of information, which is based on four phases: introduction, growth, maturity, and decline. We need a knowledge base about the products and their costs to understand how to manage the single software products. We will focus our attention on mapping software applications, Cloud Infrastructure, application maintenance, cost tracking and management in a whole system. Our approach is based on dynamic, real-time extraction of data from existing repositories, and on its dynamic retrieval, depending on the needs to be addressed at strategic level. This level of knowledge can be used to support decision making.*

**Keywords:** Software life-cycle Management, PLM, Knowledge Management, Software Engineering, Cloud Computing, IaaS.

## 1 Introduction

Large organizations have to manage hundreds, often thousands, of different applications that are the key for the organization's operations. Such a management of them is a core issue for these organizations, and software applications assume the role of assets where the organization's knowledge is synthesized [21 - 23]. Product life-cycle Management (PLM) is generally defined as a strategic business approach for the effective management and use of corporate intellectual capital [31]. Software products differ from other products for many characteristic related to life-cycle [30]; a software have to be evolved with the organization and the new features, but it can be changed or updated relatively easy by using patches or released updates. The release frequency of a Software Product is very high; the evolution of the processes modifies the software. The maintenance phase is very large in the software's life-cycle. The custom applications have to be developed and maintained by the organization.

Sogei manages highly sophisticated services, projects, technology and project management consultancies on behalf of the Italian Ministry of Economy &Finance (MEF) and other central, local, health services Administrations. Its activities cover two main areas: Management and development of IT services for the MEF, through technical and project consultancies Implementation, on behalf of the MEF, of the Program for the Rationalization of Public Expenditure in Goods and Services through the use of information technologies and innovative purchasing tools. The Cloud Platform in Sogei is based on the paradigm [32] of Infrastructure as a Service (IaaS).

Infrastructure as a Service is a model that provides a full computer infrastructure, hardware, Middleware, OS and virtualization software. Moreover, these cloud deployment models are Private in Sogei. They can't use a Public or Hybrid Cloud because Sogei has security and privacy constraints for the managed data. In this private model, the company realizes a cloud computing environment that allows to store the data within their operational structure, with obvious advantages in terms of security and privacy. In this case, the cloud services are accessible only by authorized end-users. This model allows to enjoy the benefits of public model, especially in terms of costs and scalability, and at the same time to have the guaranteed standards of management and security, typical of the private models.

The management of these applications can be used at the tactical level where we consider the management of specific aspects of the application portfolio, such as functionalities dictionary, application maintenance, mapping between software and Cloud Infrastructure where the software resides, cost tracking and management, and the like. This portfolio contains a complex software [1-5] with subsystems or modules so that loads and features are strategically distributed, typically according to power-laws, among different parts of the software [6-9], [33]. We need to manage also other information to have comprehensive views of the general situation, the overall costs and functionalities, and their trends. This strategic information must be obtained also at the department level. Moreover, the definition of the strategic information is not static, but new needs must be addressed continuously, so the system able to get it must be highly dynamic and configurable. Typical examples are software systems organized as software networks, where software units are connected in a software graph, and software metrics are power-law distributed [12-13], [16-17], [19-20].

In this paper, we present an industrial application for a Software Application Management, based on Knowledge Federation, that we implemented for the Information Systems of the Italian Ministry of Economy and Finance. This application extracts the data from existing repositories and the data is manipulated based on the knowledge needs of the organization [21-26].

These studies resulted in a prototype system, called System Map Pilot, developed to demonstrate the feasibility of the approach, and which is currently in use in the organization.

## 2 The data sources

The study starts with the analysis of the available information in the organization.

There are many software applications used in the organization (almost one thousand in our case). All these applications are customized, i.e. the specific role of the organization here considered (the Ministry), does not easily allow to use and integrate standard software as they could be components off-the-shelf. There are also many information about the life-cycle of the applications.

The information about the applications are managed by various systems, under different perspectives:

1. Application maintenance and contractor activities monitoring (BIG): there is a ticketing system tracking and managing the applicative bug fixing and evolutionary maintenance requests.

2. Configuration management (CMS, CMA): the hardware farm is based on multi-core processors, with extensive use of virtualized environments; this systems tracks how applications are replicated and mapped to the hardware, to virtual systems, to databases and to the network.

3. Functionalities management (INFAP): the Organization keeps a list of all applications and of all their functionalities and size (in Function Points), together with their history. This repository has many uses, one of these concerns the size definition of an applications , i.e. its value.

4. Cost and project management (SIGI): the costs of the various applications and maintenance activities is tracked through an ERP system.

5. Contracts (DePF): the contracts made with the various suppliers are kept in a document management system (DMS), accessed through a dedicated portal.

6. Test factory (LINCE): the applications must be tested on their functionalities before releasing and this repository contains test plans defined during previous phases.

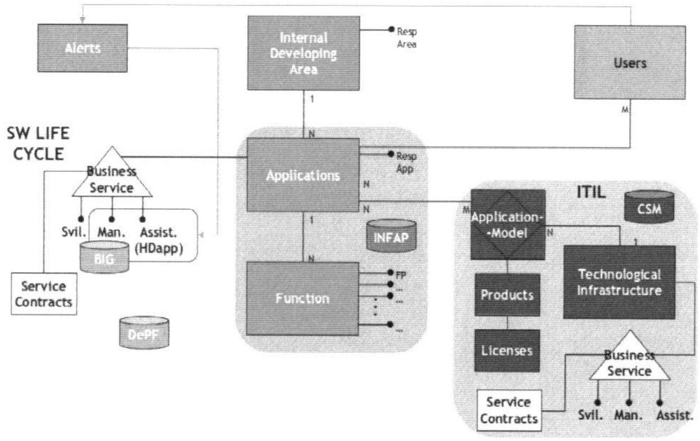


Figura 1 A schematic conceptual view of SMP.

Fig. 1 shows a schematic view of the existing relations between the various systems holding the above described data. These systems hold real data, subject to continuous updating and also to frequent schema modifications. From time to time, even new databases are introduced, to address new needs or to substitute existing ones. For instance, an inventory of functions and services (INVAPP system) will be added to the sources list, but it is not available yet. Two large classes of problem have to be addressed for such software management in general: refactoring [13-15] and software maintenance for fault detection, since bugs may largely affect more complex software [10-11]. Due to lack of space, we will not deal with them in this work. We will only consider these systems as the source of the information we used as a starting point for our work.

## 3 The information management

From a conceptual point of view, the information we need could be summarized with the architecture represented in Figure 2.

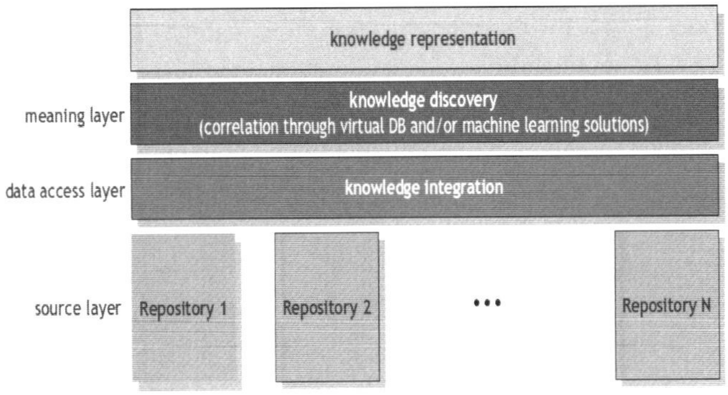


Figura 2 Knowledge federation architecture.

To define this knowledge we analyzed the original databases, chose the relevant data, and built macro-schema to reconcile the data. These data are tagged with meta-data carrying the relevant information about their meaning, so that they can be aggregated and analyzed dynamically. The data extracted from the various systems are linked through common identifiers, used throughout the systems.

The consolidate information make a very useful knowledge base of information about the applications and their evolutions, costs and infrastructure.

Fig. 3 shows the output produced by a query to System Map Pilot system and its information flow. Heterogeneous data sources, on the right side, cooperate to obtain the relevant business information of the left side.

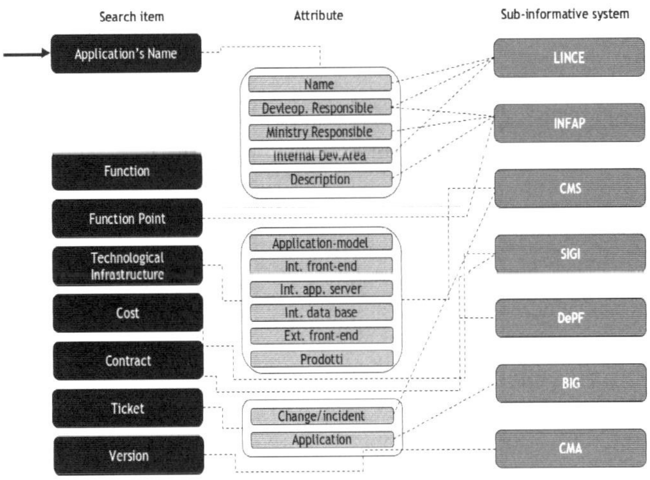


Figura 3 The output produced by a query to SMP.

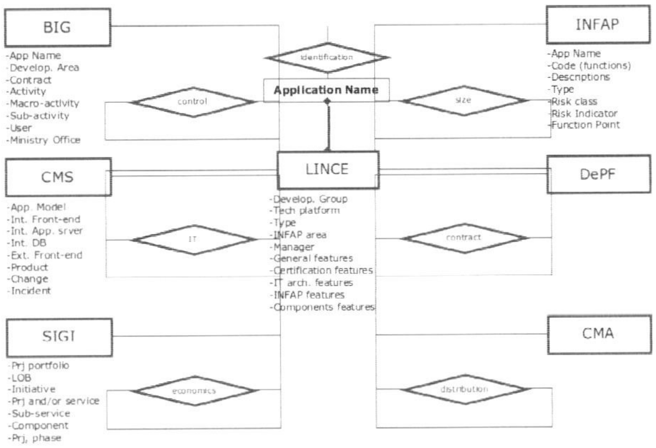


Figura 4 A schematic conceptual view of SMP.

Figure 4 shows a conceptual map of System Map Pilot and of its information flows. Each main block shares a list of metadata, allowing to link one block to any other block plugged into the system.

# 4 The Prototype of System Map Pilot

We implemented a prototype version of System Map Pilot, that is presently working and is used within the organization. It is a prototype because its user interface is still quite rough, and because the intervention of a programmer is still needed to build new query capabilities in it. The system is used mainly to aggregate data at department level, to manage departments' budget and to optimize maintenance at department level.

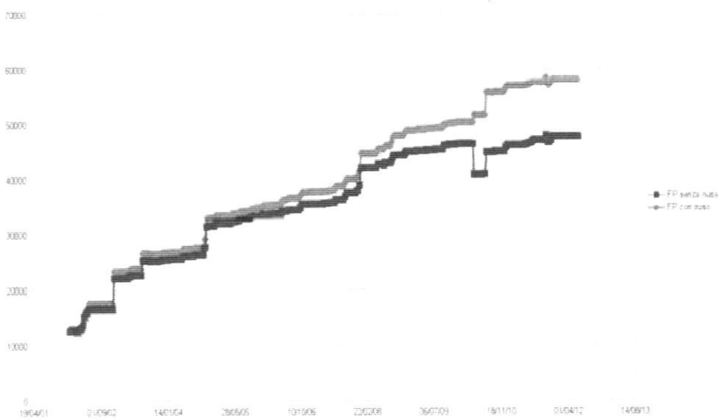

Figura 5 Total no. of Function Points developed for a Department, considering and not considering reuse.

Fig. 5 shows a specific query: the time trend of Function Points developed for a specific Department, with and without considering the reuse level. Note the restructuring performed in 2010, that reduced the deployed FPs, with no decrease in the total number of available Fps.

# 5 Conclusions

In this paper we described an Application Portfolio management system developed as a knowledge base to manage the information about hundreds, often thousands, of different applications that are the key for the organization's operations. We explored two main levels. We considered the management of specific aspects of the application portfolio, such as functionalities dictionary, application maintenance, mapping between software and hardware where the software resides, cost tracking and management. We considered also the comprehensive views of the general situation, the overall costs and functionalities, and their trends. This strategic information must be obtained also at the department level.

The System Map Pilot developed is based on the extraction of data from the existing repositories depending on the needs to be addressed at strategic level and the organization.

We showed how it is possible to tag data with meta-data carrying the relevant information about their meaning, so that they can be aggregated and analyzed dynamically, analyzing the original databases, choosing the relevant data, and building the view of the interesting knowledge.

We showed how the data extracted from the various systems are linked through common identifiers, used throughout the systems. While this emphasizes a real-time access to data, it is also endowed with a cache holding the most recently obtained data, that is periodically updated. In particular, we found how this approach reduced the deployed Function Points, with no decrease in the total number of available Function Points.

# 6 References


[1] M. Newman, "The Structure and Function of Complex Networks". Siam Review, vol. 45, pp. 167-256, 2003.

[2] S. Valverde, R. Ferrer-Cancho, and R. Sole´, "Scale-Free Networks from Optimal Design". Europhysics Letters, vol. 60, pp. 512-517, 2002.

[3] C. Myers, "Software Systems as Complex Networks: Structure, Function, and Evolvability of Software Collaboration Graphs". Physical Rev. E, vol. 68, 2003.

[4] R. Wheeldon and S. Counsell, "Power Law Distributions in Class Relationships", Proc. Third IEEE International Workshop Source Code Analysis and Manipulation, 2003.

[5] Tonelli, R., Concas, G., Locci, M., Three efficient algorithms for implementing the preferential attachment mechanism in Yule-Simon Stochastic Process, WSEAS Transactions on Information Science and Applications 7 (2), 2010, pp. 176-185.

[6] Locci, M., Concas, G., Tonelli, R., Turnu, I., Three algorithms for analyzing fractal software networks, WSEAS Transactions on Information Science and Applications 7 (3) , 2010, pp. 371- 380

[7] P. Louridas, D. Spinellis and V. Vlachos, "Power Laws in Software". ACM Trans. Software Eng. and Method., Vol. 18, No. 1, September 2008.

[8] D. Hyland-Wood, D. Carrington and S Kaplan, "Scale-Free Nature of Java Software Package, Class and Method Collaboration Graphs". Proc. 5th Int. Symp. on Empirical Software Eng., Rio de Janeiro, Brazil. September 21-22, 2005.

[9] I.Turnu, M. Marchesi, R. Tonelli, "Entropy of the degree distribution and object-oriented software quality" 3rd International Workshop on Emerging Trends in Software Metrics, WETSoM 2012 Proceedings, pp. 77-82

[10] H. Zhang, "On the Distribution of Software Faults", IEEE Trans. on Software Eng., 34(2), 2008.

[11] Concas, G., Marchesi, M., Murgia, A., Tonelli, R., Turnu, I., "On the distribution of bugs in the Eclipse system", IEEE Transactions on Software Engineering 2011, 37 (6) , art. no. 5928349 , pp. 872-877

[12] S. Chidamber, and . Kemerer, "A Metrics Suite for Object-Oriented Design", IEEE Trans. Software Eng., vol. 20, no. 6, pp. 476-493, June 1994.

[13] G. Concas, M. Marchesi, G. Destefanis, R. Tonelli " An empirical study of software metrics for assessing the phases of an agile project", International Journal of Software Engineering and Knowledge Engineering, Vol 22, 2012, pp. 525-548.

[14] A. Murgia, R. Tonelli, S. Counsell, G. Concas, M. Marchesi, "An empirical study of refactoring in the context of FanIn and FanOut coupling", Proceedings Working Conference on Reverse Engineering, WCRE, 2011, art. no. 6079863 pp. 372-376

[15] A. Murgia, R. Tonelli, M. Marchesi, G. Concas, S. Counsell, J. McFall, S. Swift, "Refactoring and its relationship with fan-in and fan-out:, an empirical study" Proceedings of the European Conference Software Maintenance and Reengineering, CSMR 2012, art. no. 6178854 , pp. 63-72

[16] V. Basili, L. Briand, and W. Melo, "A Validation of Object-Oriented Design Metrics as Quality Indicators", IEEE Trans. Software Eng., 22(10), pp. 751-761, 1996.

[17] G. Baxter, M. Frean, J. Noble, M. Rickerby, H. Smith, M. Visser, H. Melton, and E. Tempero, "Understanding the shape of Java software", Proc. of the 21st ACM SIGPLAN

conference Object-oriented programming languages, systems, and applications (OOPSLA).

[18] G. Destefanis, R. Tonelli, G. Concas, M. Marchesi, "An analysis of anti-micro-patterns effects on fault-proneness in large Java systems", Proceedings of the ACM Symposium on Applied Computing 2012, pp. 1251-1253

[19] M. Mitzenmacher, "Generative Models for Power Law and Lognormal Distributions", Internet Mathematics Vol. 1, No. 2: 226-251, 2004.

[20] M. Mitzenmacher, "Dynamic Models for File Sizes and Double Pareto Distributions", Internet Mathematics Vol. 1, No. 3: 305-333, 2004.

[21] Lunesu, M. I., Pani, F. E. and Concas, G., An approach to manage semantic informations from UGC, International Conference on Knowledge Engineering and Ontology Development, 2011.

[22] Lunesu, M. I., Pani, F. E. and Concas, G., Using a standards-based approach for a multimedia knowledge-base, International Conference on Knowledge Management and Information Sharing, 2011.

[23] Pani, F. E., Lunesu, M. I., and Concas, G., Optimization of Knowledge Availability in an Institutional Repository, International Conference on Knowledge Engineering and Ontology Development (KEOD), 2012.

[24] Pani, F. E., Lunesu, M. I., and Concas, G., Knowledge Formalization and Management in KMS, International Conference on Knowledge Management and Information Sharing (KMIS), 2012.

[25] G. Concas, F.E. Pani, M.I. Lunesu; Knowledge Management using Open Source Repository, Advance in Computer Science, Proceedings of the 6th WSEAS European Computing Conference, Prague, Czech Republic, September 24-26, 2012

[26] G. Concas, M.I. Lunesu; Multimedia Standard in UGC, Advance in Computer Science, 2nd International Conference on Environment, Economics, Energy, Devices, Systems, Communications, Computers, Mathematics (EDSCM '13) , Saint Malo & Mont Saint-Michel , France, April 2-4, 2012

[27] K. Smith: What is the Knowledge Economy? Knowledge Intensity and Distributed Knowledge Bases; INTECH Discussion Paper Series, 2002-6; United Nations University, Institute for New Technologies, Maastricht, NL, 2002.

[28] J. Mokyr: The Gifts of Athena – Historical Origins Of The Knowledge Economy; Princeton University Press, Princeton, NJ, 2002.

[29] A. Ballarin: La conoscenza e la sua gestione. Motivazioni economiche, modelli organizzativi e sistemi automatici; Quaderni Consip, 11, Roma, 2007

[30] Boehm, B.W. Software Engineering Economics. Prentice-Hall, Inc., Enwood Cliffs, N.J., 1981

[31] Amann K. Product life-cycle management: empowering the future of business: CIM Data, Inc.; 2002

[32] Raffaele Giordanelli, Carlo Mastroianni, The Cloud Computing Paradigm: Characteristic, Opportunities and Research Issues, RT-ICAR-CS Aprile 2010.

[33] Turnu, I., Concas, G., Marchesi, M., Tonelli, R., The fractal dimension of software networks as a global quality metric, 2013 Information Sciences, http://dx.doi.org/10.1016/j.ins.2013.05.014, (Article in Press)

# Kukulcan: Semantic Web Framework for Knowledge Management in the Domain of Digital Circuits

**F. Edgar Castillo-Barrera[1], R. Carolina Medina-Ramírez[2], J. Emilio Labra Gayo[3], and S. Masoud Sadjadi[4]**
[1]School of Engineering, Universidad Autónoma de San Luis Potosí, San Luis Potosí, México
[2]Department of Electrical Engineering, Universidad Autónoma Metropolitana, Distrito Federal, México
[3]Department of Computer Science, Universidad de Oviedo, España
[4]School of Computing and Information Sciences, Florida International University (FIU), Miami, USA

## Abstract

*In recent years Ontologies have boomed as artifacts to represent a domain and they are considered an important key to the success of the Semantic Web. Thus, Humans and Machines would be able to understand and share information on the Web which are also important in the context of Knowledge Management. Although the study of the relation between Ontologies and Knowledge Management is not new and this is applied in Knowledge Engineering, Semantic Web Techniques such as Reasoners and Ontology queries have been recently studied and applied. A Framework based on Semantic Web Techniques can give more options for sharing, increasing, reusing, and capitalizing the knowledge in organizations and companies. In digital circuits domain, a Semantic Web Framework can be employed for teaching logic gates (and, or, not, xor, etc.), and this approach has been deemed as an effective way for capturing and using the knowledge of the logic gates on assembling circuit systems. This knowledge can be reused by new developers gaining time and reducing circuits manufacturing costs. In addition, the correct assembling among logic gates and the right output of a circuit can be validated by using semantic techniques. In this paper, we describe a semantic web framework based on a core ontology, a Pellet reasoner and SPARQL queries for Knowledge Management based on the domain of digital circuits. We use an example and a prototype called Kukulcan to explain our approach.*

## 1 INTRODUCTION

New methods for verifying and validating logic circuits are neccesary during the design phase. These methods have to ensure the funcionality expected by the circuits designer before building it, and at the same time, simulating its behavior. This helps to prevent economic losses. Another important factor to consider is the circuit models reusability. The time for developing a complex circuit using a circuit repository decrease the cost of the project and reduce the learning curve of new people in the project. In this context, semantic technologies seem relevant. We can use Ontologies[41] in order to represent a logic circuit base on logic gates (and, or, not, etc.) and to verify a circuit design. Each connection of the circuit can be validated by means of ontology properties [41] and reasoners [40]. The new knowledge obtained for each part of the circuit assembled, can be stored in an ontology [32] by means of metadata, in this way the knowledge is capitalized [39][33]. This knowledge can be used by new developers or new members of the project to reduce manufacture time. In consequence, the company decreases costs. The circuits behavoir can be modelled by SPARQL queries. In fact, a complex circuit could be represented by one SPARQL query. The Ontology written in OWL-DL [36][26] (is stored as an XML file) can be exchanged among different systems and can be shared by all people in the company by means of the company intranet website.

The rest of the paper is structured as follows. In Section 2 we give the related work of ontologies based on logic circuits domain. In Section 3 we briefly explain concepts about Semantic Web, Ontologies, Core Ontologies, Reasoners, SPARQL queries and Semantic Web Techniques. Section 4 describes our approach for the Verification and Validation of logic circuits in a Semantic Factory Framework. In Section 5 we show the feasibility of our technique by describing an example and a prototype called Kukulcan. Finally, in Section 6 we conclude our work.

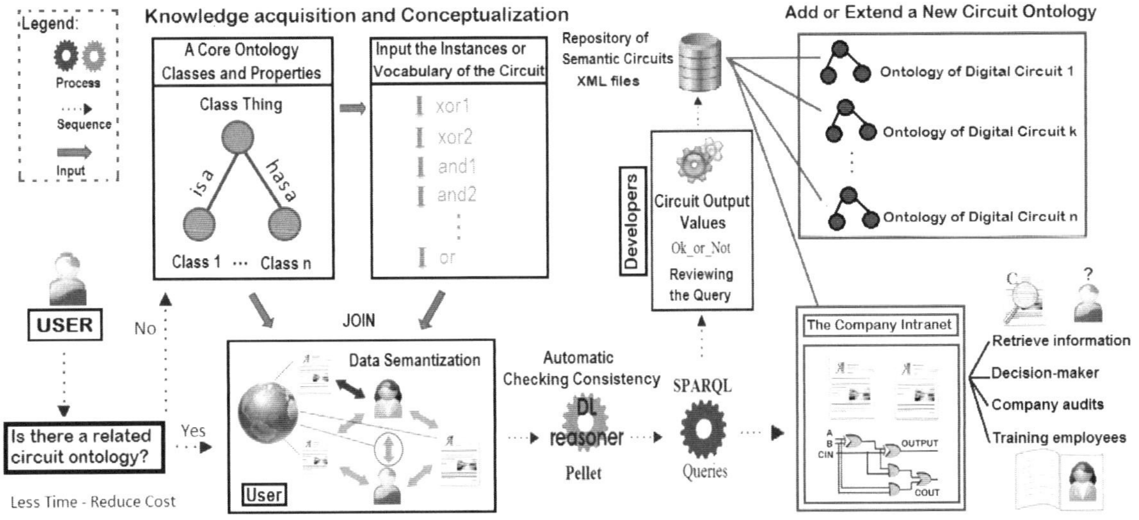


**Figure 1. Semantic Web Techniques for Knowledge Managment in the Domain of Logic Circuits**

## 2 RELATED WORK

There are several works about Ontologies and its relation with Knowledge Management and Knowledge Management Systems [1][6][34][15][31]. In the case of ontologies based on digital circuits for teaching is mostly represented by work of Robal et al.[38] who wrote an ontology-based intelligent learning object for teaching the basics of digital logic. Robal's ontology is oriented for teaching the basics of digital logic, our ontology can be used for teaching, validating and verifying logic circuits based on logic gates. An important method for verifying logic circuits is found in the work of J.N. Hooker and H. Yan [25]. The authors propose a new tautology checking algorithm for determining the correct boolean function in a circuit. This algorithm is non-numeric and equivalent to a numeric algorithm obtained by applying Benders descomposition. This proposal is similar to an integer programming problem, which requires calculations and computational resources. Although in our proposal the designer of the circuit does not apply formal verification methods, ontologies are based on formal logic (description logic [5][4]). In contrast to Banders descomposition method, our proposal is a semi-automatic verification method.

## 3 SEMANTIC WEB TECHNIQUES

The *Semantic Web* [12][11][37] is an extension of the World Wide created by the british scientist Tim Berners-Lee who defines it as *"a web of data that can be processed directly and indirectly by machines"* [9]. This is a collection of standards, a set of tools [14], and a community that shares data. *Semantic Technology* is a concept in computer science which goal is to give semantics to data[20]. Supported by semantic tools that provides semantic information about the meaning of words (RDF, SPARQL, OWL, and SKOS). The Web is a key focal. Semantic Web Techniques are methods and techniques based on semantic tools which allow us to manipulate information also. Semantic Web technologies enable people to create data stores on the Web, build vocabularies, and write rules for handling data [24].

### 3.1 Ontologies and Knowledge Management

Ontologies are the key for Semantic Web goals and they are an important block of the semantic web stack [9]. An Ontology [21][9][23][11][41] is defined by Gruber as *"a specification of a conceptualization"* [21]. An Ontology defines the basic terms used to describe and represent an area of knowledge, as well as the rules for combining terms and relations used to define extensions to the vocabulary. Thus, defines the vocabulary and the meaning of that vocabulary, are used by people and applications that need to share domain information. More specifically, an ontology is a formal representation of knowledge with semantic content which allows the companies and organizations to obtain information[17]. Such information can be retrieved by performing SPARQL queries or using a rule-based inference engine [42]. In our case, the logic circuits are the domain area. *Knowledge management* was defined by Alavi and Leidner [1] as "a systemic and organizationally specified process for acquiring, organizing and communicating both tacit and explicit knowledge of employees so that other em-

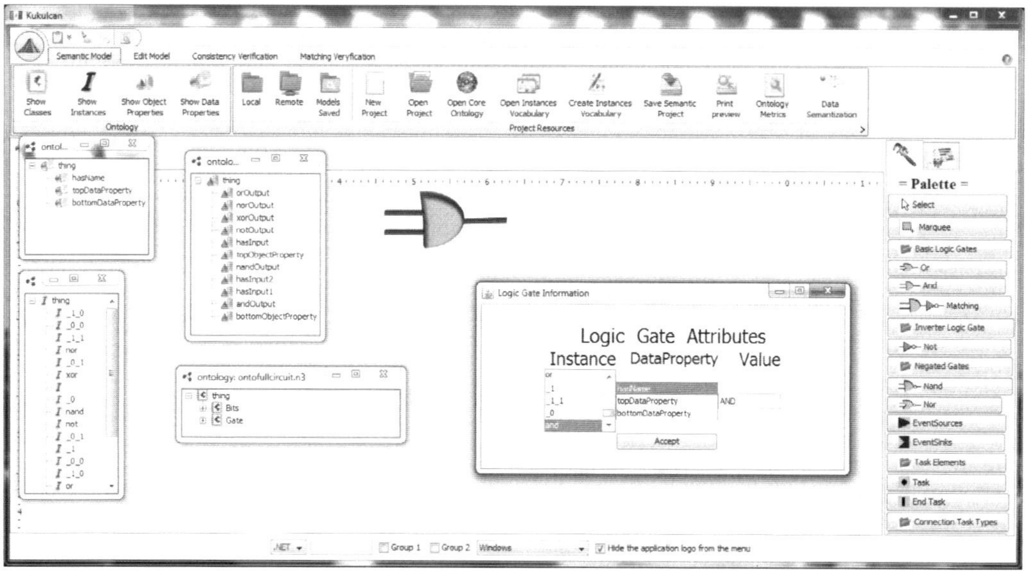


**Figure 2. Classes, Instances, Properties and Data Semantization screen**

ployees may make use of it to be more effective and productive in their work". A Semantic Web Framework can comply with the above definition. For that reason, we have selected this definition to support our approach in the field of Knowledge Management.

### 3.1.1 Core Ontologies

In philosophy, a **Core Ontology** [13] is a basic and minimal ontology consisting only of the minimal concepts required to understand the other concepts. It must be based on a core glossary that humans can understand. A **Core Ontology** is a complete and extensible ontology that expresses the basic concepts in a certain domain. In this work we have built a core ontology which consists of a logic gates glossary which developers of circuits understand well. We consider that these kind of ontologies can be reused. The ontology classes have been defined using **n3** notation. Ontologists of these kind of ontologies do not require a complex methodology [17] to do it, in fact, following the Ontology Development 101 [16] or An eXtreme method for developing lightweight ontologies [27] are enough.

## 3.2 SPARQL Query Language

SPARQL is a query language for the Resource Description Framework (RDF) which is a W3C Recommendation [43]. RDF Schema (RDFS) is extending RDF vocabulary for describing taxonomies of classes and properties. It also extends definitions for some of the elements of RDF, for example it sets the domain and range of properties and relates the RDF classes and properties into taxonomies using the RDFS vocabulary. We use Web Ontology Language OWL which extends RDF and RDFS. Its primary aim is to bring the expressive and reasoning power of description logic to the semantic web. Querying language is necessary to retrieve information [28] from input model (instances of the ontology and its relations). Unfortunately, not everything from RDF can be expressed in Description Logics (DL) [5][4]. For example, the classes of classes are not permitted, and some of the triplet expressions would make no sense in DL. To partially overcome this problem, and also to allow layering within OWL, three types of OWL are defined (FULL, Lite and DL). At this moment, we only have decided to explore semantic queries in SPARQL instead of applying another action such as: production rules [42].

## 3.3 Reasoners

A reasoner [40] is a program which its main task is checking the ontology consistency. It verifies if the ontology contains contradictory facts, axioms or wrong properties among concepts. Besides, new knowledge can be inferred after applyed it. The most popular reasoners are Cerebra, FACT++, KAON2, Pellet, Racer, Ontobroker, OWLIM. Pellet [40] is an open-source Java based OWL-DL reasoner. In our verification process we use Pellet for checking the consistency of the logic circuit ontology and classify the taxonomy. We select the Pellet reasoner, because it gives an explanation when an inconsistency was detected.

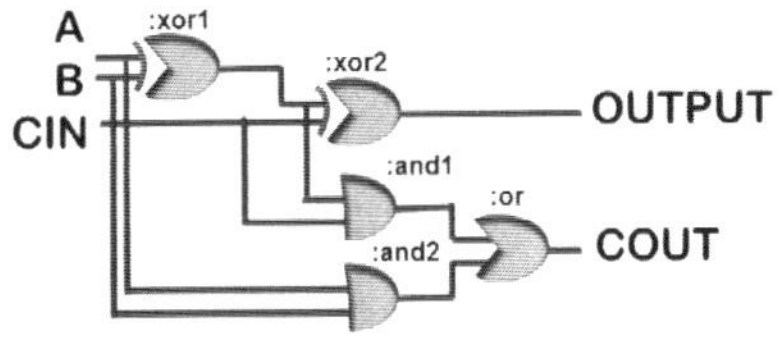


**Figure 3. 1-bit Full Adder**

# 4 A SEMANTIC WEB FRAMEWORK

Kukulcan is factory framework of semantic models which focuses on maximising the level of reuse in two dimensions: architecture design and logic circuits. One of the most important features of this framework is enabling knowledge reuse in logic circuits modelling using Semantic web techniques [19]. The aim of this framework is to allow to develop logic circuits using a friendly interface and a graphical arquitectural description language. Our main contributions are twofold. First, we define a framework that allows us to reusing logic circuit. Second, our approach supports the validation of the output values obtained from the logic circuit during the design phase. A prototype of the framework involves a visual editor. Figure 4. The tool makes use of the library Flamingo and the Ribbon component [29] implemented in Java. We have used Jena API [30][35] and Java language [18] for programming that and NetBeans IDE 7.0 [10]. The process of verification, within the Kukulcan framework, is done at very high level, using the ontologies information among logic gates and circuits to be assembled. Each logic gate is represented in a graphic way. That information, introduced in the ontology during the **Data Semantization process**, is evaluated and after that the reasoner verify if it is correct. In Addition, we capture the new knowledge in this new logic circuit, called "Capsule". In our framework, a Capsule has a graphical representation which is stored as a new logic circuit with its own characteristics. The process to verify the assembling among logic gates is easy for an user who building circuits. He introduce his model into the framework by means of a file or by the editor (the *option Create Instances Vocabulary*). Kukulcan transforms his vocabulary (logic gates that the user needs for building his circuit) from a text file into an ontology instances. Then, the user only has to establish its relations using the ontology properties (object and datatype) and he has to associate the logic gates instances created with classes defined in the logic circuit Ontology. This process is called **Data Semantization** See Figure 2.

## 4.1 A Core Ontology for Logic Circuits

We propose a core ontology called **OntoCircuit** which has the minimum concepts (logic gates) neccesary to represent the 1-bit Full Adder circuit. And, Or, Xor, Not, Nand, Nor and Xnor are universal gates and they do not require to be validate by experts. Besides, we only need 3 or 5 competency questions to validate the ontology [22]. These are adventages in this kind of ontologies which foment the reuse of them. Core Ontology is built by means of classes and relations among concepts. The Ontology is showed in Figure 2. A Logic Gates Ontology was created for capturing and verifying information about the input logic circuit models. This ontology consists of 3 classes (Circuit, Bits and Gate), 10 Object Properties (hasInput1, hasInput2, hasInput3, isTypeGate, andOutput, orOutput, notOutput, nandOutput, norOutput, xorOutput ), 1 Datatype Property ( hasName ) and 25 instances. The notation n3 is used by the ontology, because is a valid RDFS and OWL-DL notation. The Ontology use RDFS and OWL-DL language [2][36]. They are fundamentally based on descriptive logic languages. OWL-DL is a recommendation of the W3C [43]. The OWL-DL ontologies have the ability of: Automatic reasoning, Easy to be distributed through many systems, Compatibility with web standards for accessibility, Opening and extensibility.

## 4.2 Logic Circuits Verification: a Semantic Approach

Semantic verification and validation is the process which uses an Ontology and Semantic Technologies (SPARQL queries) to guarantee the correct construction of logic circuits with specific connections and outputs. The semantics of assembling the logic gates are described with object properties. An important aspect of the logic gates to consider during the assembling is the Input and Output connections. A logic gate has one output, but different number of input connections. The logic gate connections are based on the output of one of them using as input in the others.

# 5 BUILDING A 1-BIT FULL ADDER IN KUKULCAN FRAMEWORK

A 1-bit full adder is a logic circuit with 3 bit binary inputs (A, B, CIN) and two single bit binary outputs (OUTPUT, COUT). Having both carry in and carry out capabilities, the full adder is highly scalable and found in many cascaded circuit implementations. For that reason, we have chosen this circuit in this work. The truth table using the instance notation is showed in 4. This circuit is built with 5 logic gates (2 xor, 2 and, 1 or), as showed in Figure 3. The logic circuit model used for describe an 1-bit Full Adder circuit was made in Kukulcan Framework using its graphical interface of logic gates, and is shown in figure 4. The input model is created by the user who selects classes and relation among concepts and he creates the logic gates instances (:and1, :and2, :xor1, :xor2 and :or). In this case the input model only has 5 logic gates and we can create its instances and relations among them using the Kukulcan's menus (create instances vocabulary).

## 5.1 Assembling Verfication using The Pellet Reasoner

The Core Ontology written in OWL-DL, allow us to define restrictions which Pellet can verify during the consistency checking process. For instance, the following code establishes that the *and* gate has only 1 output, because a FunctionalProperty is defined for *:andOutput* Object Property.

```
:andOutput a owl:ObjectProperty ;
                 rdfs:domain   :Gate ;
                 rdfs:range    :Bits ;
    rdf:type  owl:FunctionalProperty .
```

An interesting property of the ontology used in this work is a blank node. It is a node in an RDF graph representing a resource without URI or literal. We used it as variable. If we put the same blank node, the result for this node has to be the same. In our example below, _:c1 and _:c2 are blank nodes (working as variables). The example shows how to *:xor1* and *:and2* gates are forced to have the same input (_:c2).

```
:xor1 :isTypeGate _:c1. # :xor1 is a member
                        #  of xor gates
_:c1  :hasInput2  _:c2. # :xor1 requires 2
                        #  input values
```

A difference with Logic Programming Paradigm, we can check our types using ontologies. In particular when we create a new logic gate, for example *:and2*, we do not have to introduce all input and output values. In this case, it is only neccesary to establish the property relation *:and2* **:isTypeGate** *:and* . Besides, the ontology allow us to see circuits and gates saving in the ontology at the same time because the *Gate* class is a subclass of *Circuit*.

```
:Circuit          a owl:Class .
:Gate rdfs:subClassOf :Circuit .
:isTypeGate a owl:ObjectProperty ;
            rdfs:domain   :Gate ;
            rdfs:range    :Gate .
```

The *disjointWith* property allow to verify restrictions in the input model. For example a logic gate is not a bit, these two classes are different. Defining disjoint classes is also possible [3].

```
 :Gate rdfs:subClassOf   :Thing ;
        owl:disjointWith :Bits .
```

All instances created, properties (object and datatype) established among instances, and blank nodes in the Ontology are checked by the reasoner Pellet during the consistency verification process.

## 5.2 Output Validation using a SPARQL Query

The second step after the reasoner have checked the ontology circuit consistency is to apply a SPARQL query for validating the correct output of 1-bit fadder circuit. In our case, we have defined a query which describes the circuit and obtain the output for given input values. Of course, all this process is transparent, for the user. He does not need to know nothing about ontologies, reasoners or SPARQL queries, only the manager of the ontology system has to know about that. We can think that SPARQL is the version of SQL for ontologies. Besides, we can use variables in the queries, constraints, filtering information, logic operators, if statements and more. Each triples (each line after) are linking by variables which begin with a question mark. In this code *?type1* and *?AB* are examples of variables. The same name of variable imply the same value to look for in the query. We can execute and edit queries in Kukulcan framework because the Jena API allowed us to use SPARQL queries in our framework programmed in Java language. The las step, when the logic circuit has been verified and validated, consists on storing the project independent of the ontology or include it in the core ontology. It is important to note that these challenges increase the reuse of this ontology and decrease the time in the development of future circuits. Benefiting the economy of companies (Knowledge Capitalization [33][39]). In our example, part of the code included in the core ontology was:

```
:fulladder :hasName "1-bit full
                adder"^^xsd:string .
:fulladder :hasInput3        :0_0_0 .
:fulladder :hasInput3        :0_0_1 .
:fulladder :hasInput3        :1_1_1 .
:0_0_0 :fullAdderOutput :0 .
:0_0_0 :fullAdderOutput :1 .
:1_1_0 :fullAdderOutput :0 .
                 :
```

In the code above, there are mainly three properties: *hasName*, *hasInput3* and *fullAdderOutput*. The meaning of the *hasName* property is an string with the name of the logic circuit. But the most interesting properties are *hasInput* and *fullAdderOutput*. The first is formed by a circuit instance (in this case called *fulladder*), second the name of the property *hasInput3* where the number 3 means that this gate receive 3 input values and finally with 3 bits values ending with a period. The second property begins with the 3 bits values following the *fullAdderOuput* property and finish with the bit output value with a period. The colon before each element and the ending period are only *n3* notation [7][8].

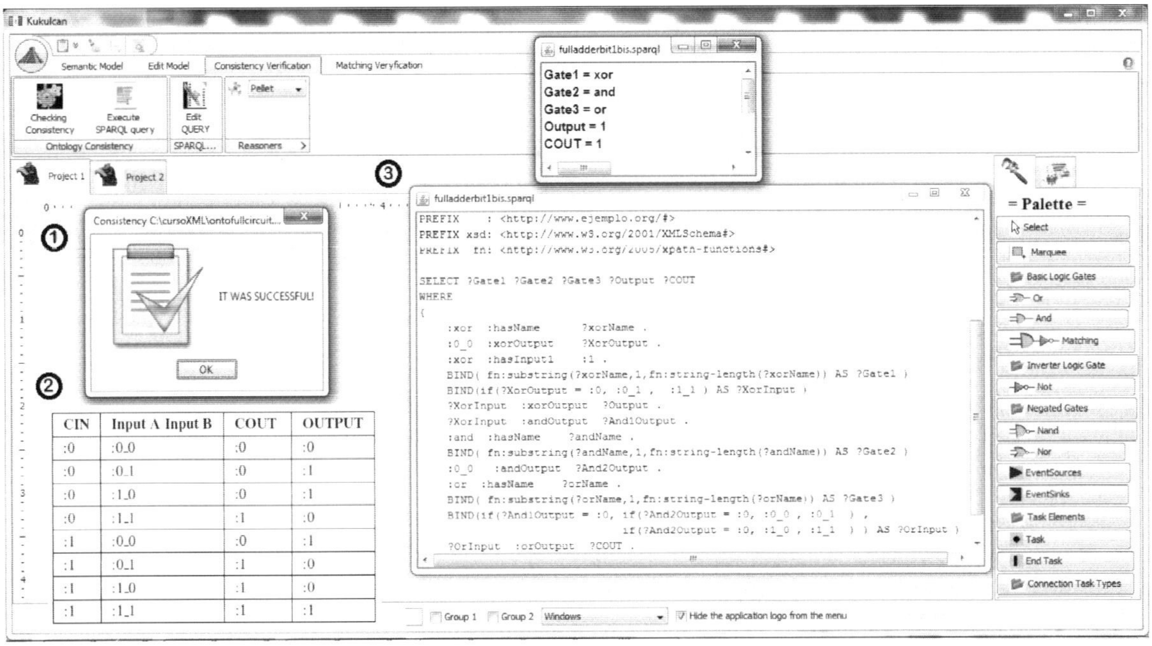


**Figure 4. Consistency checking (1), Full Adder Truth Table (2) and SPARQL query execution (3)**

## 6 CONCLUSIONS

Knowledge Management using Semantic Web Techniques, in organizations and companies based on Digital Circuits, is possible by means of core ontologies, reasoners, and SPARQL queries. Ontologies are usually expressed in a logic-based language (Description-Logic), enabling detailed, sound, meaningful distinctions to be made among the classes, properties and relations. Core Ontologies give more expressive meaning, maintains computability, do not require the validation of experts or apply a complex methodology for its construction. This core ontology for logic circuits increase the reuse of it and decrease the time in the development of future circuits. The use of an core ontology of logic circuits allowed us to validate the output of the 1-bit Full Adder and verify the correct assembling of its gates using the Pellet reasoner and a SPARQL query with semantics in comparison with a classic SQL query. The queries on the ontology are simple and easy to do for all users whereas a classic SQL query in a database requires computational knowledge. In this paper we have presented a Semantic Web framework called Kukulcan and described Semantic Web Techniques used for Knowledge Managment on the Digital Circuits domain.

## 7 Acknowledgments

This material is based upon work supported by the National Science Foundation under Grant No. OISE-0730065.

## References

[1] M. Alavi and D. Leider. Knowledge management systems: emerging views and practices from the field. In *System Sciences, 1999. HICSS-32. Proceedings of the 32nd Annual Hawaii International Conference on*, pages 8–pp. IEEE, 1999.

[2] D. Allemang and J. Hendler. *Semantic Web for the Working Ontologist: Effective Modeling in RDFS and OWL*. Morgan Kaufmann, 2011.

[3] F. E. Antoniou Grigoris and V. H. Frank. Introduction to semantic web ontology languages. 2005.

[4] F. Baader. *The description logic handbook: theory, implementation, and applications*. Cambridge Univ Pr, 2003.

[5] F. Baader, I. Horrocks, and U. Sattler. Description logics as ontology languages for the semantic web. *Mechanizing Mathematical Reasoning*, pages 228–248, 2005.

[6] R. Benjamins, D. Fensel, and A. Gómez-Pérez. Knowledge management through ontologies. CEUR Workshop Proceedings (CEUR-WS. org), 1998.

[7] T. Berners-Lee. N3 notation: http://www.w3.org/designissues/notation3.html.

[8] T. Berners-Lee, D. Connolly, and S. Hawke. Semantic web tutorial using n3. In *Twelfth International World Wide Web Conference*, 2003.

[9] T. Berners-Lee, J. Hendler, O. Lassila, and Others. The semantic web. *Scientific American*, 284(5):34–43, 2001.

[10] T. Boudreau. *NetBeans: the definitive guide*. O'Reilly Media, 2002.

[11] K. Breitman, M. A. Casanova, and W. Truszkowski. *Semantic Web: Concepts, Technologies and Applications (NASA Monographs in Systems and Software Engineering)*. Springer-Verlag London, 2006.

[12] W. P. Davies John, Stunder Rudi. Semantic web technologies trens and research in ontology-based systems. 2006.

[13] M. Doerr, J. Hunter, and C. Lagoze. Towards a core ontology for information integration. *Journal of Digital information*, 4(1), 2011.

[14] W. M. K. B. Duineveld A.J., Stoter R. and B. V.R. Wondertools? a comparative study of ontological engineering tools. 2000.

[15] D. Fensel, F. Van Harmelen, M. Klein, H. Akkermans, J. Broekstra, C. Fluit, J. van der Meer, H. Schnurr, R. Studer, J. Hughes, et al. On-to-knowledge: Ontology-based tools for knowledge management. In *Proceedings of the eBusiness and eWork*, pages 18–20, 2000.

[16] N. F.Noy and D. L.McGuinness. Ontology development 101:a guide to creating your first ontology. March 2006.

[17] A. Gómez-Pérez, M. Fernández-López, and O. Corcho. Ontological engineering with examples from the areas of knowledge management,e-commerce and the semantic web. 2003.

[18] J. Gosling, B. Joy, G. Steele, and G. Bracha. *Java (TM) Language Specification, The (Java (Addison-Wesley))*. Addison-Wesley Professional, 2005.

[19] J. Gracia, J. Liem, E. Lozano, O. Corcho, M. Trna, A. Gómez-Pérez, and B. Bredeweg. Semantic techniques for enabling knowledge reuse in conceptual modelling. *The Semantic Web–ISWC 2010*, pages 82–97, 2010.

[20] T. Gruber. Ontolingua: A mechanism to support portable ontologies. pages KSL 91–66. 1992.

[21] T. Gruber. Toward principles for the design of ontologies used for knowledge sharing. pages 907–928. 1995.

[22] M. Gruninger and M. S. Fox. The role of competency questions in enterprise engineering. In *Proceedings of the IFIP WG5.7 Workshop on Benchmarking - Theory and Practice*, 1994.

[23] N. Guarino. Formal ontology in information systems. pages 3–15. IOS-Press, June 1998.

[24] S. Heiner and V. H. Frank. Information sharing on the semantic web. 2005.

[25] J. Hooker and H. Yan. Logic circuit verification by benders decomposition. *Principles and Practice of Constraint Programming: The Newport Papers, MIT Press (Cambridge, MA, 1995)*, pages 267–288, 1995.

[26] M. Horridge, N. Drummond, J. Goodwin, A. Rector, R. Stevens, and H. Wang. The manchester owl syntax. *OWL: Experiences and Directions*, pages 10–11, 2006.

[27] M. Hristozova and L. Sterling. An extreme method for developing lightweight ontologies. In *In Workshop on Ontologies in Agent Systems, 1st International Joint Conference on Autonomous Agents and Multi-Agent Systems*, 2002.

[28] M. Hwang, H. Kong, and P. Kim. The design of the ontology retrieval system on the web. volume 3, pages 1815 –1818, feb. 2006.

[29] Java.net. Flamingo. http://java.net/projects/flamingo/, 2010.

[30] Jena. Jena a semantic web framework for java. 2000.

[31] I. Jurisica, J. Mylopoulos, and E. Yu. Using ontologies for knowledge management: An information systems perspective. In *Proceedings of the Annual Meeting-American Society For Information Science*, volume 36, pages 482–496. Information Today; 1998, 1999.

[32] S. L. and M. B. Ontology evolution within ontology editors. volume 62, pages 53–62. September 2002.

[33] F.-M. Lesaffre and V. Pelletier. A business case of the use of ontologies for knowledge capitalization and exploitation.

[34] A. Maedche, B. Motik, L. Stojanovic, R. Studer, and R. Volz. Ontologies for enterprise knowledge management. *Intelligent Systems, IEEE*, 18(2):26–33, 2003.

[35] B. McBride. Jena: Implementing the rdf model and syntax specification, 2001.

[36] D. McGuinness, F. Van Harmelen, et al. Owl web ontology language overview. *W3C recommendation*, 10:2004–03, 2004.

[37] K. T. S. Michael C. Daconta, Leo J. Obrst. *The Semantic Web: A guide to the future of XML, Web Services and Knowledge Management*. Wiley Computer Publishing, Inc., 111 River Street Hoboken, NJ, jun. 2003.

[38] T. Robal, T. Kann, and A. Kalja. An ontology-based intelligent learning object for teaching the basics of digital logic. In *Microelectronic Systems Education (MSE), 2011 IEEE International Conference on*, pages 106–107. IEEE, 2011.

[39] B. D. Rodriguez-Rocha, F. E. Castillo-Barrera, and H. Lopez-Padilla. Knowledge capitalization in the automotive industry using an ontology based on the iso/ts 16949 standard. volume 0, pages 100–106. IEEE Computer Society, Los Alamitos, CA, USA, sep. 2009.

[40] E. Sirin, B. Parsia, B. Grau, A. Kalyanpur, and Y. Katz. Pellet: A practical owl-dl reasoner. *Web Semantics: science, services and agents on the World Wide Web*, 5(2):51–53, 2007.

[41] S. H. Staab S., Studer R. and Y. Sure. Knowledge processes and ontologies. volume 16, pages 26–34. Jan-Feb 2001.

[42] SWRL. Swrl:a semantic web rule language.

[43] W3C. http://www.w3.org/consortium/. 1994.

# Extracting Human-readable Knowledge Rules in Complex Time-evolving Environments

**Pu Yang, and David L. Roberts**
Department of Computer Science, North Carolina State University, Raleigh, North Carolina, USA

**Abstract**—*A production rule system is a reasoning system that uses rules for knowledge representation. Manual rule acquisition requires a great amount of effort and time from humans. In this paper, we present a data-driven technique for autonomously extracting human-readable rules from complex, time-evolving environments that makes rule acquisition for production rule systems efficient. Complex, time-evolving environments are often highly dynamic and hard to predict. We represent these environments using sets of attributes, and transform those attributes to the frequency domain which enables analysis to extract important features. We extract human-readable knowledge rules from these features using rule-based classification techniques and translating the decision rules back to the time domain. We present an evaluation of our methodology on three environments: hurricane data, a real-time strategy game, and a currency exchange. Experiments show extracted rules are human-readable and achieve good prediction accuracy.*

**Keywords:** Knowledge Acquisition, Production Rule, Human-readable, Time Series Prediction

## 1. Introduction

A production rule system is one type of knowledge representation and reasoning system. It provides AI by a set of knowledge rules. These rules are a representation found useful in expert systems and automated planning. There are two ways to acquire the rules: manually and autonomously. Manual rule acquisition needs expertise and is tedious and inefficient, especially in a complex environment. This is called "the knowledge acquisition bottleneck" [1].

Directly extracting time domain rules can be problematic. Morchen [2] pointed out "A big problem when mining in time series data is the high dimensionality." Because looking at each point in time in isolation ignores valuable temporal information, sliding windows are used. However, by enlarging the window to capture more interesting patterns very high dimensional vectors result, introducing "the curse of dimensionality" [3] which is a major challenge for all rule-based classifiers. It seems feature selection can solve the problem. Unfortunately selecting features in the time domain introduces inaccuracies. Deng *et al.* [4] discussed how feature filtering and wrapper methods lead to low-quality feature subsets. Therefore, we avoid the aforementioned problem by selecting features in the frequency domain.

We present a method for autonomously extracting human-readable knowledge rules from time-evolving environments that leverages techniques from signal processing and machine learning. To make the time series easier to learn from, we transform the attribute values from the time domain to the frequency domain using wavelet transformations. The time domain is the traditional method of analysis in the AI or ML field for time series data. The time domain describes how a signal changes over time. On the other hand, the frequency domain describes how much of a signal lies within a given frequency range. The intuition behind transforming to the frequency domain is that transforming time series to the frequency domain keeps only the "clean" signals. Fugal [5] stated that the frequency transformation separates noise from the time series and keeps only the "clean" signals with more information. *Our insight is that using the frequency domain representation of these informative features, we can build rule-based classifiers to extract frequency domain knowledge rules more easily and accurately, and that those rules can be converted into easily human-interpretable knowledge rules.* To make these rules easily interpretable, we convert the frequency domain knowledge rules back to time domain knowledge rules which have a natural interpretation in terms of the original attributes. The intuition behind translating rules back to the time domain is that frequency coefficients, which keep a significant amount of the information in the original time series, can be translated back to the time domain in a manner that preserves the important information, but affords a more easily-understandable interpretation in terms of the original features.

To characterize the practicality and accuracy of our method, we tested it on three real-world time-series domains: the North Atlantic hurricane database; a corpus of action real-time strategy game replays; and financial exchange prices. These data sets were used both to train our model and to characterize its accuracy. A standard ML-style evaluation of the results verified that the extracted human-readable rules contained useful knowledge. Accordingly, our contributions are: (1) leveraging frequency domain features to create human-readable knowledge rules by translating the rules back to the time domain; (2) producing knowledge rules automatically, thereby dramatically reducing the effort required to extract human-readable knowledge from data.

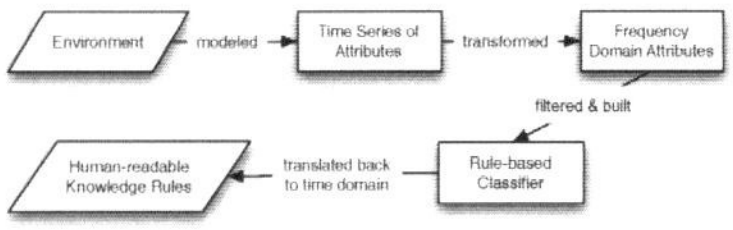


Fig. 1: Workflow: The environment is modeled as attribute time series that are transformed to the frequency domain. Rule-based classifiers that use features extracted from the frequency domain produce knowledge rules describing the important features of the time series. Finally, the knowledge rules are made human-readable by translating the output of the rule-based classifier back to the time domain.

## 2. Related Work

Manual knowledge acquisition is the process of transferring knowledge from a domain expert to an agent by encoding the acquired expertise in the agent's knowledge base. Sviokla *et al.* [6] and Turban *et al.* [7] indicated yearly productivity of a manual knowledge engineer is limited to hundreds of rules. To improve productivity, Wagner [8], [9] described a few end-user expert systems that do not rely on knowledge engineers, but (rightfully) acknowledged the difficulties in maintaining these systems. Wagner [1] also pioneered methods for breaking the knowledge acquisition bottleneck through the application of the principles of Bazaar-style, open-source development where knowledge is acquired in an open, bottom-up manner with broad testing before final adoption of the knowledge rules.

Autonomous knowledge acquisition is when agents build a knowledge base by learning from data, generally with little or no human involvement. Autonomous techniques have focused on a number of areas including developments in how knowledge rules are represented [10]. Kim *et al.* [11] used codified expressions for knowledge acquisition. Other techniques have focused on knowledge maintenance systems like the Knowledge Base Management Systems (KBMS) which is a development environment for knowledge-based systems [12]. In KBMS the expert does not need a knowledge engineer to encode rules because the KBMS automates much of the process of application building. Finally, there are techniques in autonomous knowledge acquisition which are process focused. For example, Dhar [13] extracted certain types of patterns from data or information stored at data repositories. The extracted knowledge led to interesting distributions of outcomes which are not directly observable in the data. This type of work is most similar to our approach. Our algorithm autonomously identifies knowledge rules which are easily interpretable by humans.

## 3. Methodology

Our basic process (shown in Figure 1) is:

1) The environment is represented using representative attributes, the values of which evolve over time. The values may, or may not, evolve at regular intervals.
2) Samples of the time series are made uniform in length by either up- or down-sampling and the values are normalized. Using signal processing techniques, the values are converted from the time domain to the frequency domain, which reduces the time series into a smaller, more manageable set of frequency domain attributes that capture important trends in the data.
3) A rule-based classifier is applied to the frequency domain attributes to output frequency domain rules.
4) The frequency domain rules are translated back into the time domain—the original variables and values—which retain the information in the frequency domain rules, but afford easier interpretation by humans.

### 3.1 Time Series Environments

Time series contain values of attributes that change over time, possibly at non-uniform intervals. Patterns in the ways these attributes evolve over time form the basis upon which we can draw conclusions. The challenge is to identify ways in which we can extract information about those patterns that enable humans to better understand what is happening in the environments. This is exactly what our technique addresses.

To enable these conclusions to be drawn, we first must identify and represent the important attributes of the environment. For example, a natural attribute representation for hurricanes may include wind speed, longitude, latitude, and air pressure samples taken at regular intervals during the hurricane's lifecycle. In a real-time strategy game, a representation may include the agility, damage, intelligence and strength of game characters—all attributes that relate to the abilities of the characters and the outcome of the game. Lastly, a natural choice for modeling a currency exchange environment is as multiple time series of prices.

### 3.2 Standardizing Time Series

We are not guaranteed that the environments we are modeling will result in time series that are all the same length. It depends on the phenomenon being modeled. Due to sampling variance, the amplitude of the observations may vary as well. For example, a time series representing the wind speed of hurricane KATRINA in Aug. 2005 has a range between 30 and 175 mph and length of 30 observations. A time series representing the wind speed of hurricane MARIA in Sep. 2005 has a range between 35 and 115 mph and length of 51 observations. To make the time series comparable between observational instances, we re-sample to make them uniform length and normalize the values.

To put all of time series into uniform length we compute the average length of all the time series we have access to for the environment we're working in. Then we down- or up-sample each of the time series to be that length. We assume that the important information in the time series is contained in the local maxima and minima values. When we down- or up-sample the time series, we always keep the local extremal values and interpolate or smooth the values in between. When up-sampling the time series, we interpolate additional values between the extremal values. When down-sampling the time series, we uniformly eliminate values between local extremal values to decrease its length to the average.

Once the time series are of uniform length, we have to normalize their values to account for uncertainty. We normalize the values to be between 0 and 1 by the formula:

$$n(x, S) = \frac{x - min_S}{max_S - min_S} \quad (1)$$

where $x$ is the original value of time series $S$, $max_S$ is the global maximal value of the time series, and $min_S$ is the global minimal value of the time series. $n(x, S)$ is then the normalized value of $x$. An example of a normalized time series is presented in Figure 2 in the top-most series.

## 3.3 Transforming to the Frequency Domain

Attribute time series are often noisy, reflecting small variances due to inaccuracies in measurements or the influence of spurious events that can safely be ignored when modeling important trends. This noise can also lead to spurious results in rule-based classifiers. Therefore, if we can eliminate noise and extract features that represent the important patterns contained in the data, we can likely get a more accurate description of any knowledge contained in the time series data. It can be challenging to filter noise in the time domain because noise and valuable pattern information are often conflated. Fortunately, the process of transforming time series to the frequency domain can effectively separate noise and important trends or patterns [2]. This process leverages the fact that noise is reflected in time series as high-frequency oscillations. In the frequency domain, these oscillations are reflected in the high frequency bands. In contrast, patterns or important trends produce low-frequency movements in values, and are therefore reflected in the low-frequency bands of the frequency domain. Due to these differences, noise and patterns can be separated clearly when converting from the time domain to the frequency domain.

Time-to-frequency analyses are a common tool used in the signal processing field. There are many existing techniques, including the discrete Fourier transform (DFT) [14], fast Fourier transform (FFT) [15], and discrete wavelet transform (DWT) [5]. Among them, DWT has an advantage because it can capture both frequency information and location (or temporal) information about trends. Because of this, we use the DWT to transform time series to the frequency domain, thereby eliminating (or greatly reducing) noise in our data and enabling us to extract informative knowledge rules.

DWT provides a compact time-frequency representation of the data while maintaining the information content present in the time series. To do so, the DWT separates a time series into high-frequency noise and a low-frequency approximation, both represented by a set of coefficients of

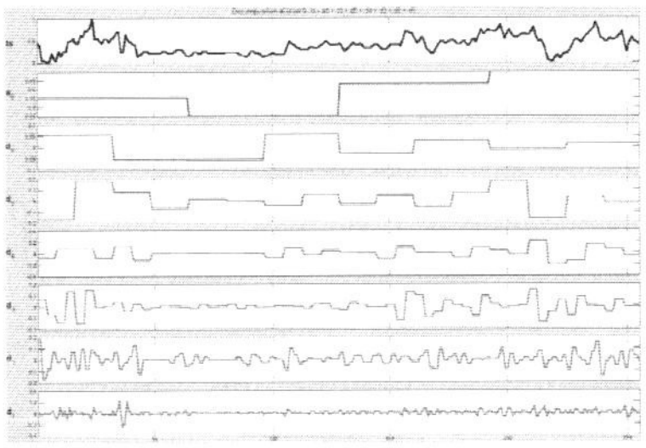

Fig. 2: A discrete wavelet transformation decomposition of a time series. The original time series is the top-most series. The low frequency part of the series is $a_6$ (second-from-top). The high frequency parts are $d_6, d_5, d_4, d_3, d_2,$ and $d_1$ (third-from-top to bottom respectively).

a "mother wavelet" function. There are lots of mother wavelet functions. Among them, Haar wavelets are good for capturing big jumps, or trends [5]. For example, in Figure 2, the top-most time series represents an original time series. Starting from the original time series, in level 1, the DWT process proceeds by computing two sets of coefficients: approximation coefficients and detail coefficients. Approximation coefficients represent the low-frequency part of the time series, which captures the global trends. Detail coefficients represent the high-frequency part of the time series, which capture the local oscillations (noise). To further filter the noise, the DWT can be recursively applied to the low-frequency approximation. Each recursive application of the DWT eliminates half of the coefficients to create successively more coarse approximations. In Figure 2, from the bottom of the figure going up are the six successive high-frequency detail series, and second-from-the-top is the approximation series. As can be seen in the figure, this approximation captures the global trends of the time series.

## 3.4 Extracting Frequency Domain Rules

After transforming time series to the frequency domain, we construct a rule-based classifier using the DWT coefficients as inputs. There are many rule-based classification algorithms including RIPPER [16], CN2 [17], RISE [18], and decision trees [19]. For the purposes of this work, we have chosen to use decision trees to extract these frequency domain rules, because, in a decision tree model, tracing a path from the root to the leaves enables us to extract rules much more easily than a more opaque method, like a support vector machine or artificial neural network.

Usually the decision tree algorithm outputs a tree with many nodes, and therefore has a lot of rules; however, some of the branches do not represent enough observational instances to be generalizable. So we have two criteria for rules: confidence and support. Confidence is the percentage of observational instances represented by the node in the decision tree that are associated with a target label. Support is the number of observational instances represented by the node in the tree. The higher the confidence, the more accurate the rule is. The higher the support, the more general the rule is. The combination of these two parameters allows knowledge engineers to make a tradeoff between the predictive power of the extracted rules and the number of rules extracted. Too few rules and important knowledge may be omitted. Too many, and spurious relationships may be reported in the rules. Further, the complexity of the rules can be controlled by the DWT level parameter. The more applications of the DWT, the shallower the rules will be.

### 3.5 Translating to the Time Domain

The rules generated from a rule-based classifier are in terms of the DWT coefficients in the frequency domain. In this form these rules aren't easily human-readable, and most likely aren't even in terms of the original environment attributes. To obtain human-readable rules, we need to translate frequency domain rules back to the time domain.

The rules read from the decision tree contain thresholds that an approximation coefficient for an attribute should be above or below. For example, a frequency domain rule $a_i(attri)[E] > \theta$ means the DWT approximation coefficient of attribute $attri$ in the $E$-th segment of the time series at the $i$-th DWT level is greater than a value $\theta$. The $E$-th segment of the time series is determined by dividing the time series into $N$ equal length segments where $N$ is the number of DWT coefficients at the $i$-th level. Note that because each successive application of the DWT results in half the number of coefficients, each coefficient represents the value trends of increasingly larger segments of the original time series as $i$ increases.

To convert any frequency domain rule to the time domain, we identify two sets of time series. Let $R_=$ be the set of time series with $a_i(attri)[E] = \theta$ and $R_{<>}$ be the set with $a_i(attri)[E] >$ or $< \theta$ (depending on the rule). If $R_=$ is $\emptyset$, in the spirit of "support vectors" for support vector machines we find the set with coefficient values closest to $\theta$. We then take the average time series value for $attri$ during segment $E$ for both $R_=$ and $R_{<>}$. The duration of each segment is determined by dividing the length of the original time series by the number of DWT approximation coefficients. Let $G_=$ be the set of instances $g$ which satisfy $R_=$. We define

$$v_=(attri)[E] = \frac{\sum_{j=1}^{N} AVG(g_j(attri)[E])}{|G_=|} \quad (2)$$

to be the time series value of attribute $attri$ in segment $E$ for observational instances in $G_=$. Here, $AVG(g_j(attri)[E])$ is the average of original values of attribute $attri$ in segment $E$ of the original time series for observational instance $g_j$ in $G_=$. We can compute $v_{<>}(attri)[E]$ similarly. If $v_=(attri)[E] < v_{<>}(attri)[E]$ then the corresponding time domain rule is $v(attri)[E] > v_=(attri)[E]$. Otherwise, it will be $v(attri)[E] < v_=(attri)[E]$.

## 4. Experiments

We tested our approach on data from three real-world domains: a corpus of data describing hurricanes in the Atlantic Ocean, a corpus of replay log files from professional gamers playing an action real-time strategy game, and historical data about currency exchange rates. Moreover, we did a ML-style evaluation of the rules to validate that the conversion process that yields human-readable rules also yields rules that capture useful information. The validation of the extracted rules with subject matter experts is left for future work; however, the ML-style evaluation indicates the extracted knowledge has predictive power. Further, the reader should be able to determine whether or not the extracted rules are human-readable.

For benchmarking, we also directly extracted rules from the time domain by using a sliding window to generate time series vectors, selecting relevant features and building a decision tree to create rules. We tried 3 different sliding windows (length 3, 4, and 5) and 5 different feature selection approaches (information gain, chi-square, hill climbing, correlation feature selection (CFS), and random forest with recursive feature elimination (RF-RFE)).

### 4.1 Hurricane Environment

The hurricane environment is a relatively smaller domain than the others we present results from in this paper. Further, the interpretation of the rules doesn't require advanced training in climatology, so this domain provides a reasonable first step for demonstrating the power of translating frequency domain rules back to the time domain.

We obtained data from the North Atlantic hurricane database (HURDAT) which is maintained by the National Hurricane Center. HURDAT contains records of all hurricanes in the Atlantic Ocean, Gulf of Mexico and Caribbean Sea from 1851 to 2010. According to the National Oceanic and Atmospheric Administration (NOAA), HURDAT "contains the 6-hourly (0000, 0600, 1200, 1800 UTC) center locations and intensity (maximum 1-minute surface wind speeds in knots) for all Tropical Storms and Hurricanes from 1851 through 2010." The data for each hurricane is represented as five attribute time series that correspond to the five attributes of the storms: latitude, longitude, wind speed in knots, direction of movement in degrees, and speed.

The average hurricane length was 12, 6-hour units, which is equivalent to three days. We up- or down-sampled all time series to be 12 samples long. We then recursively applied the DWT twice to obtain three approximation coefficients representing 1st one-third, 2nd one-third, and 3rd one-third of a hurricane lifetime. To use the data for a predication task, we labeled each of the time series with the binary label landfall or NOT-landfall which indicates whether or not the hurricane center reached the east coast of the United States. We used five attributes represented by three approximation coefficients each for a total of 15 approximation coefficients.

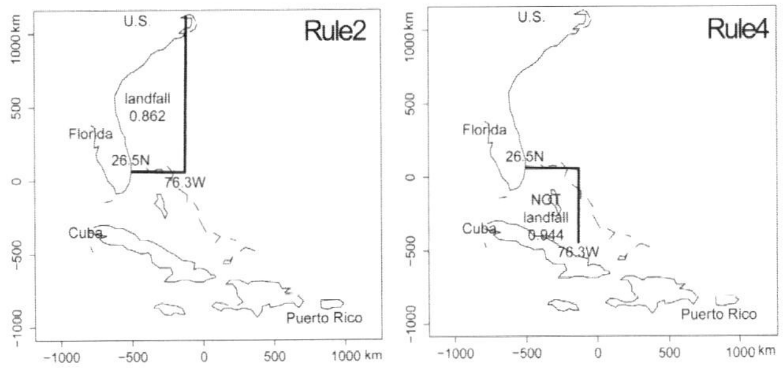


Fig. 3: Map illustration of Rule2 and Rule4 in Table 1. The horizontal line is latitude, vertical is longitude.

## 4.2 Hurricane Results

Table 1: Time domain rules for whether or not hurricanes in the North Atlantic Ocean make landfall on the east coast of the US. $H_{seg}(x)$ means attribute $x$ of the hurricane during the $seg$ one-third of the hurricane's lifetime. For instance, $H_{2nd}(lon)$ means the longitude of the hurricane during the 2nd one-third of the hurricane 's lifetime. Conf means confidence of the rule. LF means landfall.

| ID | Conf | Time Domain Hurricane Landfall Rules |
|---|---|---|
| 1 | 0.703 | $H_{2nd}(lon) > 75.2W$, LF |
| 2 | 0.862 | $H_{2nd}(lon) > 76.3W, H_{3rd}(lat) > 26.5N$, LF |
| 3 | 0.919 | $H_{3rd}(lon) > 77.0W, H_{3rd}(lat) > 26.4N$, LF |
| 4 | 0.944 | $H_{2nd}(lon) > 76.3W, H_{3rd}(lat) < 26.5N$, NOT LF |
| 5 | 0.867 | $H_{2nd}(lon) < 75.2W$, NOT LF |
| 6 | 0.950 | $H_{3rd}(lon) < 68.4W$, NOT LF |

To extract the rules, we set confidence above 70% and support above 100. There were 1,176 instances in the dataset. The most significant extracted rules are presented in Table 1. Interestingly, of the five attributes (latitude, longitude, wind speed in knots, direction of movement in degrees, and speed), only latitude and longitude are represented in our knowledge rules as predictive of hurricanes hitting the east coast of the US or not. From the perspective of time the 2nd one-third and 3rd one-third of hurricane lifetime are critical to whether or not the hurricane makes landfall.

Due to space constraints, we are unable to discuss all of rules in Table 1. The map illustrations of Rule2 and Rule4 are shown in Figure 3. In Rule2 and Rule4, latitude 26.5N is the critical value to distinguish landfall or not. When the longitude of a hurricane in the 2nd one-third of the hurricane's lifetime is to the west of 76.3W, the hurricane may curve north or south. When curving north above 26.5N during its 3rd one-third of the hurricane's lifetime, it is likely to hit the east coast of the US with probability 0.862. When curving to the south below 26.5N during the 3rd one-third of the hurricane's lifetime, it is not likely to make landfall with probability 0.944.

We performed 10-fold cross-validation to validate our rules for this binary classification problem. If landfall is a true positive (TP). If not-landfall is a true negative (TN). The overall accuracy is 0.87; the sensitivity is 0.85; the specificity is 0.89; the AUC is 0.87. The average length of rules is 2 conditions. With the same confidence and support threshold, the best of the 15 benchmarks is the use of a sliding window of length 4 and random forest with recursive feature elimination, which has accuracy 0.74, sensitivity 0.77, specificity 0.78, and AUC 0.88. The average length of rules is 10 conditions. It should be easier for humans to understand rules with fewer conditions.

## 4.3 Action Real-Time Strategy Games

For an action real-time strategy game environment, we collected a total of 2,863 replays from games played between 06/21/2010 and 02/14/2012 from GosuGamers. GosuGamers is an online community for Defense of the Ancients (a popular action real-time strategy game) players covering some of the largest international professional and amateur gaming events. It contains an online database with replays from professional tournaments. The replays contain the information needed to create time series.

The game has two teams; each has five representative attributes: Agility, Damage, Gold, Intelligence, and Strength. Because the game is played with two teams, we had two time series for each attribute for each game. To represent each game in terms of one time series for each attribute, we computed the difference between the individual team attributes at each sample point. Therefore, each game was represented as five time series comprised of the difference in the base attributes.

Table 2: Entries indicate the percentage of rules containing each attribute or game stage. The second through fifth columns refer to the $1st$ one-fourth, $2nd$ one-fourth, $3rd$ one-fourth, and $4th$ one-fourth of the game. The last five columns refer to agility ($agi$), damage ($dam$), gold ($gol$), intelligence ($int$), and strength ($str$). Conf is the confidence.

| Conf | $1st$ | $2nd$ | $3rd$ | $4th$ | $agi$ | $dam$ | $gol$ | $int$ | $str$ |
|---|---|---|---|---|---|---|---|---|---|
| 70% | 75 | 100 | 37.5 | 0 | 12.5 | 100 | 0 | 12.5 | 37.5 |
| 80% | 85.7 | 100 | 42.9 | 0 | 14.3 | 100 | 0 | 14.3 | 42.9 |
| 90% | 100 | 100 | 60 | 0 | 20 | 100 | 0 | 20 | 60 |

The average game length was 256 events. We up- or down-sampled the difference-team-capability time series to be 256 samples long using the procedure described above. We recursively applied the DWT six times to obtain four approximation coefficients representing 1st one-fourth, 2nd one-fourth, 3rd one-fourth, and 4th one-fourth of a game's lifetime. The four stages represented approximately 12 minutes of gameplay each. Then we used 20 approximation coefficients (five attribute time series represented as four approximation coefficients each) labeled with the winning team as input to the decision tree.

## 4.4 Real-Time Strategy Game Results

There were a total of 2,863 instances in the dataset. To obtain the rules from the decision tree, we used three confidence thresholds: 70%, 80%, and 90%. For each, we used 200 for the amount of support needed. At the 70% confidence level we identified eight rules, at the 80% level seven rules, and five rules at the 90% confidence level.

Due to space constraints, we choose the two rules with highest confidence values. $d_{attr[seg]}$ means the difference of capability **attr** between Team1 and Team2 in **seg** one-fourth of the game lifetime. $agi$, $dam$, $str$ means agility, damage, and strength. Rule1 (confidence 96%): "IF $d_{dam[2nd]} > 59.7$ THEN Team2 Lose" and Rule2 (confidence 97%): "IF $d_{dam[2nd]} > 59.7$, $d_{agi[3rd]} < -18.1$, and $d_{str[3rd]} < -27.7$ THEN Team2 Win". In Rule1, if the Team2 has a damage capability deficit greater than 59.7 during the 2nd one-fourth of the game lifetime, then the Team2 will lose with 96% chance. However, if the Team2 can achieve agility advantage greater than 18.1 and strength advantage greater than 27.7 during the 3rd one-fourth of the game lifetime, then the Team2 can win with 97% chance according to Rule2. Comparing Rule1 and Rule2, we can conclude advantage of agility and strength in 3rd one-fourth of the game lifetime can compensate for disadvantage of damage in 2nd one-fourth of the game lifetime.

Table 2 contains a high-level overview of the rules at each of the confidence levels. The entries indicate the percentage of the rules each attribute or game stage appeared in. Of particular interest is the importance of the damage attribute and the 2nd one-fourth of the game lifetime. At all confidence levels, every rule identified a test for the value of the damage attribute during the 2nd one-fourth of the game lifetime, indicating this value has the largest influence on the outcome of the game. Also, of particular interest is the lack of rules pertaining to the gold attribute. This indicates that while gold is useful for increasing capabilities, it must be used wisely or it won't help a team win. Similarly, while all rules contained statements about the 2nd one-fourth of the game lifetime and the majority contained statements about the 1st one-fourth of the game lifetime, fewer contained statements about the 3rd one-fourth of the game lifetime and none contained anything during the 4th one-fourth of the game lifetime. This indicates that advantages are gained before the end of the game.

Table 3: Evaluation metrics for game data. Classification accuracy (CA), Sensitivity (Sens), Specificity (Spec), and Area under the ROC curve (AUC).

| Metrics | 70% | 80% | 90% |
|---|---|---|---|
| CA | 0.7860 | 0.8213 | 0.8817 |
| Sens | 0.8227 | 0.7981 | 0.8902 |
| Spec | 0.7485 | 0.8449 | 0.873 |
| AUC | 0.7856 | 0.8303 | 0.8853 |

We performed three-fold cross validation to validate the accuracy of our model. The results are presented in Table 3. Because Defense of the Ancients is an adversarial game, this is a binary classification problem: one team wins or loses. If the team wins it is a true positive (TP). If the other team wins it is a true negative (TN). We used four metrics. Table 3 shows all values are above 0.74 for all confidence thresholds and partitions. The average accuracy is 0.83. The average length of rules is 3 conditions. The best of the 15 benchmarks is the use of a sliding window of length 5 and correlation feature selection, which has accuracy 0.712. The average length of rules is 15 conditions.

## 4.5 Currency Exchange Environment

We finally tested our method in a notoriously difficult to model and predict domain. The financial environment is a "challenge test" for our method. Additionally, we compared our method to the classification accuracy of various MA (moving average) techniques which are commonly applied to financial time series analysis.

We used currency and metal prices from the OANDA Corporation. Oanda reports price data using a 7-day daily average. We chose six currency or metal pairs: US Dollar to Euro (USDEUR), US Dollar to Canadian Dollar (USDCAD), US Dollar to Chinese Yuan (USDCNY), US Dollar to British Pound (USDGBP), US Dollar to Silver (USDXAG), and US Dollar to Gold (USDXAU). We collected these data from 01/01/1999 to 09/30/2012, a total 165 months. For each currency or metal pairs, there are 165 price time series labeled with "increase", "equal", or "decrease" that indicate whether the price on the first day of next month is greater than, the same, or less than the final day of the last month.

The average month is 30 days in length, so we up- or down-sampled time series to be 30 samples long. Since it is not obvious how many phases a monthly currency pair price has, we recursively applied the DWT once, twice, and three times to obtain 15-coefficient, 7-coefficient, and 3-coefficient approximations. Then we used 15 approximation coefficients labeled with increase, equal, or decrease as input features to a decision tree model. We repeated the process with 7 and 3 approximation coefficients. So, for each currency or metal pair, we have three sets of frequency domain rules according to 15, 7, and 3 approximation coefficients.

## 4.6 Currency Exchange Results

There were 165 instances in the dataset. We used 70% for the confidence level and 10 for the support level. Due to space constraints, we choose the two USDXAG rules with highest confidence values. $P_{[start,end]}$ means the average price of $start$-th to $end$-th of the current month. Rule1 (confidence 95%): "IF $P_{[1,5]} > 0.0879$ and $P_{[17,20]} > 0.09$ THEN decrease" and Rule2 (confidence 95%): "IF $P_{[1,5]} <= 0.0879$ and $P_{[24,30]} <= 0.073$ THEN increase". In Rule1, if the average price of first five days of the month is greater than 0.0879, the average price of 17th to 20th of the month is greater than 0.09, then the first day price of the next month will be lower than the price of last day in the current month with confidence 95%. In Rule2, if the average price of first five days of the month is not greater than 0.0879, the average price of 24th to 30th of the month is not greater than 0.073, then the first day price of the next month will be higher than the price of last day in the current month with confidence 95%.

Table 4: Accuracy summary of 10-fold cross-validation for each currency pairs. H-$x$ is the Haar mother wavelet at the $x$ DWT level. MAs (moving average series) include autoregressive integrated moving average, simple moving average, exponential moving average, weighted moving average, double-exponential moving average, and zero lag exponential moving average. The value in the MAs column is the highest prediction accuracy obtained using all of the MA techniques. Guess is random guess. BestBM is the best of the 15 benchmarks. The entries in bold face indicate the highest prediction accuracy.

| USD to | H-1 | H-2 | H-3 | MAs | Guess | BestBM |
|---|---|---|---|---|---|---|
| EUR | **58%** | **58%** | **58%** | 44% | 47% | 50% |
| CAD | **58%** | 57% | 57% | 47% | 45% | 57% |
| CNY | 52% | 59% | **62%** | 41% | 33% | 53% |
| GBP | **53%** | **53%** | **53%** | 49% | 34% | 48% |
| XAG | 55% | **91%** | 68% | 40% | 36% | 58% |
| XAU | **66%** | 49% | 49% | 44% | 40% | 48% |
| Average | 57% | 61% | 58% | 44% | 39% | 52% |

Table 4 shows 10-fold cross-validation accuracy for each currency pair using the three sets of rules our method identified (using the three DWT levels). For the baseline comparison, we have included various MA techniques and a random guess. This is a ternary classification problem: increase, equal, and decrease. The average accuracy of our method over the six currency pairs and three DWT levels is 58.7%. The average accuracy of traditional methods (various MAs) over the six currency pairs is 40.1%. The average accuracy of random guess over the six currency pairs is 39%. The average accuracy of the best of the 15 benchmarks over the six currency pairs is 52%. The entries in the table that correspond to the highest prediction accuracy on each data set are indicated in bold face. In all cases, those entires were for one of our knowledge rule sets. Perhaps more importantly, even our worst-performing sets of knowledge rules, in each case, resulted in a classification accuracy higher than the best performing MA method.

## 5. Conclusion and Future Work

In this paper, we have introduced a data-driven method for autonomously extracting human-readable knowledge rules from complex, time-evolving environments that makes rule acquisition much more efficient than manual knowledge acquisition. The only knowledge engineering in our method involves identifying and formatting the attributes for representation as a time series. This process doesn't require any value judgements or expert opinions. The extracted rules are both readable by humans and contain useful knowledge.

There are a number of exciting avenues for future research. First, to further improve the rules by help of a domain knowledge-driven approach such as a domain model or ontology to filter high-quality rules. Second, to cooperate with domain experts to further investigate the semantics of the rules. Third, our method has three free parameters: DWT level, confidence, and support threshold. In the future, we hope to develop a better understanding of how to set those free parameters. One approach is to use an optimization algorithm, such as a genetic algorithm [20] or randomized hill climbing [21], to determine the best values for these parameters. This way, we can ensure that there is a solid reasoning behind picking a specific threshold value or number of DWT coefficients.

## References

[1] C. Wagner, "Breaking the knowledge acquisition bottleneck through conversational knowledge management," *Information Resources Management Journal (IRMJ)*, 2006.

[2] F. Mörchen, "Time series feature extraction for data mining using dwt and dft," 2003.

[3] R. Bellman, *Dynamic Programming*. Dover Publications, Mar. 2003.

[4] H. Deng and G. C. Runger, "Feature selection via regularized trees," The 2012 International Joint Conference on Neural Networks (IJCNN), Brisbane, Australia, June 10-15, 2012, 2012, pp. 1–8.

[5] D. L. Fugal, *Conceptual Wavelets in Digital Signal Processing*. Space and Signals Technical Publishing, 2009.

[6] J. J. Sviokla, "An Examination of the Impact of Expert Systems on the Firm: The Case of XCON," *MIS Quarterly*, vol. 14, no. 2, pp. pp. 127–140, 1990.

[7] E. Turban, J. E. Aronson, and T.-P. Liang, *Decision support systems and intelligent systems*. Prentice Hall, 2005.

[8] C. Wagner, "End-users as expert system developers," *Journal of End User Computing*, 2000.

[9] Wagner, "Knowledge management through end user developed expert systems: potential and limitations," *Advanced topics in end user computing, Idea-Group Publishing*, 2003.

[10] S. Cauvin, "Dynamic application of action plans in the Alexip knowledge-based system," *Control Engineering Practice*, vol. 4, no. 1, pp. 99–104, 1996.

[11] G. Kim, D. Nute, H. Rauscher, and D. L. Loftis, "AppBuilder for DSSTools: an application development environment for developing decision support systems in Prolog," *Computers and Electronics in Agriculture*, vol. 27, pp. 107 – 125, 2000.

[12] R. C. Hicks, "Knowledge base management systems-tools for creating verified intelligent systems," *Knowledge-Based Systems*, vol. 16, no. 3, pp. 165–171, 2003.

[13] V. Dhar, "Data mining in finance: using counterfactuals to generate knowledge from organizational information systems," *Information Systems*, vol. 23, no. 7, 1998.

[14] Z. Wang, "Fast algorithms for the discrete W transform and for the discrete Fourier transform," *Acoustics, Speech and Signal Processing, IEEE Transactions on*, vol. 32, no. 4, pp. 803–816, 1984.

[15] R. W. Ramirez, *The FFT: Fundamentals and Concepts*. Prentice Hall PTR, Sept. 1984.

[16] W. W. Cohen, "Fast Effective Rule Induction," *Machine Learning: Proceedings of the Twelfth International Conference (ML95)*, 1995.

[17] P. Clark and R. Boswell, "Rule induction with CN2: Some recent improvements," *Machine learning—EWSL-91*, 1991.

[18] P. Domingos, "The RISE system: Conquering without separating," *Tools with Artificial Intelligence*, 1994.

[19] J. R. Quinlan, "C4.5: Programs for Machine Learning," Morgan Kaufmann Publishers, 1993.

[20] M. Mitchell, *An Introduction to Genetic Algorithms*. Cambridge, MA, USA: MIT Press, 1998.

[21] S. J. Russell and P. Norvig, *Artificial Intelligence: A Modern Approach*, 2nd ed. Pearson Education, 2003.

# Visualisation of Combinatorial Program Space and Related Metrics

**A.V. Husselmann and K.A. Hawick**
Computer Science, Massey University, North Shore 102-904, Auckland, New Zealand
email: { a.v.husselmann, k.a.hawick }@massey.ac.nz
Tel: +64 9 414 0800 Fax: +64 9 441 8181

**Abstract**—*Searching a large knowledge or information space for optimal regions demands sophisticated algorithms, and sometimes unusual hybrids or combined algorithms. Choosing the best algorithm often requires obtaining a good intuitive or visual understanding of its properties and progress through a space. Visualisation in combinatorial optimizers is more challenging than visualising parametric optimizers. Each problem in combinatorial optimisation is qualitative and has a very different objective, whereas parametric optimizers are quantitative and can be visualised almost trivially. We present a method for visualising abstract syntax trees in an interactive manner, as well as some certain enhancements for evolutionary algorithms. We also discuss the use of this in improving the convergence performance of a Geometric Particle Swarm Optimiser.*

**Keywords:** combinatorial information; knowledge engineering; visualisation, genetic programming, optimization.

## 1. Introduction

Combinatorial optimization[1] and the search methods associated with it remain important aspects of information and knowledge engineering. Obtaining a visual representation and hence an understanding of algorithms in combinatorial optimization remains a difficult challenge as the scale and complexity of the problems one wishes to tackle increases. A visual rendering of an algorithm can be an important means of assessing its suitability for a particular problem, particularly if the rendering can be formed in near interactive time and the human user is able to form an impression of an algorithm's progress – or lack of it from a recognizable visual pattern.

Much research has been dedicated towards furthering combinatorial optimizers, with classical problems such as the Traveling Salesman Problem (TSP) [2], [3], the Knapsack problem [4] and the Prisoner's Dilemma [5]. The primary focus of these problems is the search for a global optimum, analogous to that of parametric optimizers such as Kennedy and Eberhart's Particle Swarm Optimiser [6].

John Koza's pioneering work of 1994 [7], perhaps greatly inspired by earlier work of John Holland on the Genetic Algorithm [8] has seen the advent and widespread uptake and use of of Genetic Programming (GP) [9]. GP is a technique used to evolve programs to solve particular problems. Since the introduction of this algorithm, it has been used for solving many problems, such as evolving soccer Soft Bots [10], [11] for competitions, model induction [12], intrusion detection [13], modeling land change in Mexico [14], image enhancement [15] and many more.

Fig. 1
VISUAL REPRESENTATION OF A GENERATION OF AGENTS USING A TREE STRUCTURE.

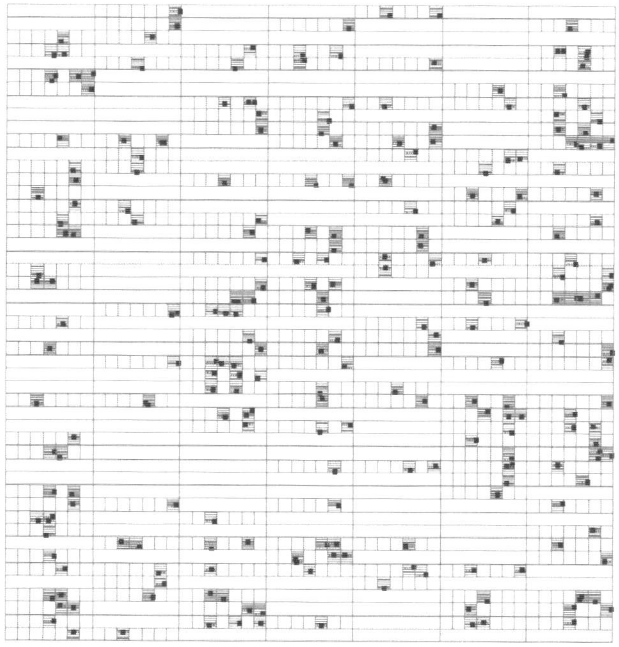

Many variations and improvements of the GP algorithm have been proposed in the past including Cartesian GP [16], distributed CUDA-based GP [17], a quantum-inspired linear GP [18], Strong GP [19] (a restrictive version of GP), as well as other GPU-based implementations [20], [21].

Visualisation of GP has typically been restricted to visualisation of the fitness function itself. In simulations such as soccer Softbots [10], [11], it is attractive to view the behaviour of the robots themselves, as it gives a good indication of the running efficacy of GP. Based on this information, one can sometimes infer modifications to parameters such as mutation and crossover rates.

In analysis of GP and its related variations, quantitative metrics typically take the place of visualisation. These also give valuable insights into the behaviour of the algorithm.

Techniques such as Landscape Analysis have long been an area of research, and was applied to GP in 1994 by Kinnear [22], the same year that GP was introduced by Koza [7]. In the article by Kinnear, the author also discussed comparing the difficulty of various fitness landscapes by plotting the cumulative probability of success (CPS) for each. Gustafson [23] presented a thorough analysis of diversity metrics in Genetic Programming which include unique programs, ancestral analysis, edit distances, and others.

Our efforts are focused on visualisation of the candidate programs as they are modified by genetic operators. We anticipated that this would assist in verifying the behaviour of each operator, as well as tuning it so as to maximise constructive recombination between candidates.

In Section 2, we describe the algorithms that we apply our visualisation and metrics to. This includes the Geometric Particle Swarm Optimiser using Karva for representation, as well as a Genetic Programming implementation also using Karva. In Section 3 we proceed to discuss our visualisation method, and related metrics, and following this we present and discuss some screen dumps of the visualisation. Finally, in Sections 5 and 6, we discuss our methods, and conclude with some possible future work.

## 2. Genetic Programming Background

We summarise the genetic programming algorithms of interest to us in this work and give some background and references on their main properties relevant to our test-bed system and visual rendering implementation.

Our test-bed algorithms include a data-parallel implementation of Genetic Programming using *Karva*[24] for representation of programs (which we shall denote K-GP) [25], as well as a data-parallel Geometric Particle Swarm Optimiser also using Karva (which we shall denote using K-GPSO) [26]. We present here a brief overview of these algorithms.

Karva is a program representation language developed by Ferreira in her Gene Expression Programming (GEP) algorithm [24]. GEP is attractive mainly for its representation, which has inherent support for introns in its representation; which brings it closer to the biological analogy of evolution. It is also attractive for its extremely simple and elegant crossover and mutation operators.

Since both K-GP and K-GPSO operate on the space of Karva programs (otherwise known as $K$-expressions), the main difference between these algorithms is in its recombination phase. K-GP relies on a tournament selection operator, followed by simple one-point crossover and point mutation. The K-GPSO operates using a multi-parent crossover with the global optimum (*gBest*) and a personal optimum (*lBest*), and a current position, analogous to the original PSO. A perturbation in solution space is accomplished using point mutation. The weighted multi-parent crossover operator we use is the one presented by Togelius in his paper introducing Particle Swarm Programming [27] from the concept of a Geometric Evolutionary Algorithm first presented by Moraglio in his thesis of 2007 [28]. The concept of a Geometric optimiser is essentially a method by which a parametric optimiser such as the PSO by Kennedy and Eberhart [6], [29] can be adapted for searching in an arbitrary space.

Part of our interest in developing visualisations and metrics for Evolutionary Algorithms (EAs) is the advent of the very recent concept of Geometric EAs. Poli and colleagues [30] have conceded that it is too early to assert the efficacy of Geometric EAs over traditional related algorithms; which has inspired interest in more metrics and visualisations, as well as new algorithms such as the K-GP and K-GPSO.

Both the K-GP and K-GPSO are implemented on Graphical Processing Units (GPUs) to improve wall-clock performance, but as we are only concerned with convergence performance, we omit a detailed discussion on this, and instead refer the reader to [25], [26], [31] for more detail.

The fitness function we use is a modified Santa Fe Ant Trail in 3D, where terminal symbols are: `Move`, `Right`, `Left`, `Up`, `Down`, and non-terminal symbols (functions) are: `IfFoodAhead` and `ProgN2`. The function `IfFoodAhead` executes its first argument if there is food directly ahead of the agent, and the second argument otherwise. `ProgN2` simply executes its arguments in order. The object of this simulation is to obtain an agent which is as effective as possible for picking up so-called "food" items scattered throughout the space. We omit a more thorough discussion of how this fitness function is implemented.

An example of a *Karva*-expression or $k$-expression which encodes a certain candidate program is as follows:

```
0123456789
PPIPMMRMML
```

This program is shown as a visual interpretation in Figure 2. It is a highly efficient program for solving this particular problem. The first line of the code above is simply an indexing convenience, whereas the second line is the program itself. The string of symbols is interpreted into a tree (as shown in Figure 2), and then executed in the normal fashion. The tree is constructed level by level, and filling arguments from the $k$-expression from left to right. This tree is often known as the phenotype for a particular candidate, whereas the string of symbols shown above is the genotype. It is important to note that the symbol at index 9 is not expressed in the phenotype, however, with an appropriate mutation, this symbol can easily be re-introduced into the phenotype.

Point mutation and one-point crossover is almost trivially easy on a representation like this. Point mutation is simply an exchange of one symbol with another uniform-randomly chosen symbol. One-point crossover involves choosing a random crossover site, and exchanging information between

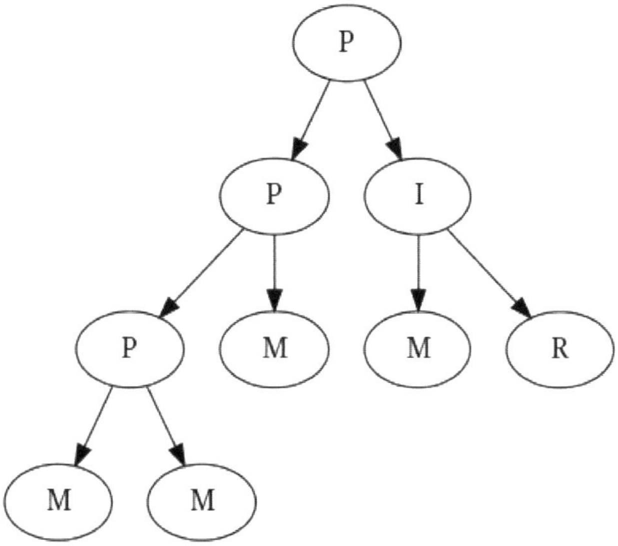


Fig. 2
A HIGHLY EFFECTIVE GENERATED AGENT. THE $k$-EXPRESSION FOR THIS IS *PPIPMMRMM*.

two candidates about this point.

It is important, however, to maintain a head and tail section in this expression, so that it is guaranteed that all functions in phenotype will have enough arguments supplied to them. Details of this is out of scope here, but it is important to note that, like other Genetic Programming approaches, Karva also has some idiosyncrasies.

## 3. Visualisation Method

Our method for visualising program space involves a successive subdivision of a 2D grid, where each subdivision represents the selection of a different codon or symbol. We have specifically engineered this method for *karva*-expressions, but it can easily extend to any other abstract syntax tree representation including pointer trees.

Figure 1 shows an example of what a randomly initialised population of candidate programs could look like. In this example, a dot represents a single program. The space is divided in a horizontal fashion, for selecting the first codon, then vertical for the second codon, and so forth, until all codons have been selected, at which point a dot is placed. It is worthwhile to note that in doing this, we are effectively viewing a combinatorial problem as a parametric one, where differences in programs are represented as spatial differences instead.

To further illustrate our method, we present Algorithms 1 and 2. Algorithm 1 shows the process by which we add an expression to the tree-based data-structure of the visualiser. Algorithm 2 is the method by which we actually draw the data-structure to the screen. We keeps Algorithms 1 and 2 separate in the implementation, so that interactive use of the program is more streamlined. The data-structure we use is similar in concept to k-D trees, where space is successively divided along each of the principal axes.

Also, to indicate candidate movement through this pseudo-space in successive generations, we draw a line from the previous candidate to the new candidate in each generation. This makes certain dynamics of EAs more clear, particularly the K-GPSO, which we discuss later.

In summary, for a new expression to be added to the program space visualisation, the space is first divided into $n$ sections vertically, where $n$ is the number of terminal and non-terminal symbols. Each section represents a symbol. The first symbol in the expression determines the section next divided. Suppose this is the third section from the top. This section is then divided into $n$ sections in a horizontal fashion. The next symbol in the expression determines which section will then be divided further, and so forth. Finally, when no symbols remain in the expression, a dot is drawn to indicate the location of the expression.

**Algorithm 1** Adding an expression to the data-structure.

```
with n candidate programs
with p as the top-level symbol drawable
set c = p
for i = 0 to n do
  with m symbols per program
  exp = programs[i]
  for j = 0 to m do
    nextindex = getCodonIndex(exp[i])
    if p.children.get(nextindex) is null then
      c = c.addChild(nextindex)
      c.setLabel(exp[i])
    else
      c = c.children.get(nextindex)
    end if
  end for
end for
```

The visualiser is perhaps best used interactively. Keystroke combinations allow the user to zoom in on specific locations within the program space, and move around to better understand how the algorithm under scrutiny works.

We have implemented our system using Java[32] and the Java Swing [33] two-dimensional graphical library. The operations we use to construct the tree visualisers could however be implemented with any modern graphical system. Java and Swing are convenient portable systems that can be easily attached to our framework and set up with simple graphical programmatic utilities.

## 4. Visualisation Results

We present a number of visual frames of various algorithms along with a commentary on what convergence

**Algorithm 2** Drawing the tree-based data-structure to the screen recursively.

```
with m symbols per program

render(top-level)

FUNCTION render(c)
for i = 0 to linecount do
  lines[i].paint()
end for
if children is not null then
  vector2d mystart = getMyStart();
  vector2d myend = getMyEnd();
  if orientation == Horizontal then
    drawDivisionsHorizontal(mystart,myend)
  else
    drawDivisionsVertical(mystart,myend)
  end if
  for j = 0 to childrencount do
    render(children[j])
  end for
else
  drawPoint(mycentre)
end if
END
```

actions that are visible. In particular, we now compare the characteristics of the K-GP and K-GPSO in terms of convergence. Figure 3 show successive generations of the K-GP. These figures show that the K-GP is very effective at maintaining diversity. This will become more clear when we discuss the K-GPSO.

Figure 4 shows the second frame of a sample generation in the K-GPSO optimiser. Immediate impressions that this image conveys is the clear use of a global optimum which is used in crossover. It also indicates that there may be an issue in population diversity. In [26], we discussed the parameters $\phi_p$, $\phi_g$ and $\omega$, and mentioned that they are best set to static empirically obtained values. This is as opposed to weighted values depending on the fitness values associated with the *gBest*, *lBest*, and current candidates. The problem with the latter is it is very common for the fitness distance between any candidate and the global best to be disproportionately high. This would cause the crossover point to be chosen so that it is simply the entire *gBest* candidate being replicated.

To make this more clear, we show a plot of the unique candidates by generation for the sample run in Figure 5. Having a good number of unique programs is important to ensure adequate diversity for future crossover operations. The difference in diversity by generation for the K-GP and K-GPSO algorithms is conclusive. We believe that an improvement upon diversity statistics in the K-GPSO would bring about a better convergence rate.

After observing the scores from the sample generation of the K-GPSO, a large number of the programs obtained a score of zero. Essentially, in the flow of the algorithm with score-weighted crossover, this would result in a replication of the global best. Ideally what is necessary, is a higher mutation rate.

Firstly, we adopted a much higher mutation rate of 0.3, (as opposed to 0.1), which did not improve the convergence of the algorithm. The standard deviation of the results was too high to be considered a reliable optimiser. Unique diversity in the population was not maintained, since 0.3 was still too low. The problem with increasing mutation probability further, is that the algorithm would fail to converge at all, as the better solutions would almost certainly be mutated to lower fitness values.

We then experimented with lowering the crossover rate. This was more fruitful, and resulted in a much lower standard deviation among average mean fitness values. A crossover probability of 0.1 seemed to improve the convergence rate. A crossover rate this low does not perform well for genetic algorithms, however. Figure 6 shows frame 2 of a sample generation with this modification. In comparison to Figure 4, what is clear is that most of the population remains stationary. The reason why this performs better, we believe, is due to the more paced movement of particles towards the global best. It is also possible that this K-GPSO algorithm is simply not well suited to this objective function, especially considering that there is some error associated with the function itself.

Figure 7 conveys a sense of how the visualiser might respond to interaction. The top-level program space is shown on the left (generation 100 of a sample run of K-GPSO), and successive zooming in on the area where the most candidate programs are quickly indicates the global best without a doubt. A subtle feature of this is that the lines indicate both a previous program, and a succeeding program. The previous program is represented by a grey dot, whereas the new program is a blue dot. This does add an indication of movement about the global optimum.

## 5. Discussion

A number of observations on algorithmic behaviours can be made from the visual renderings we obtained.

Most of the insights we obtained from the visualiser seems to give more and more credit to Poli and McPhee's concept of Homologous Crossover [34], where crossover preserves information already shared between candidates. The problem we observe with the K-GPSO is that the global best weighted score is often so great in comparison, that it is simply duplicated.

While the visualisation itself does assist in a qualitative manner, it is far more useful when used interactively. Zooming and movement across the program space is very useful,

Fig. 3
GENERATIONS 1-4 (TOP), 5, 10, AND 100 (BOTTOM) OF A SAMPLE RUN OF THE K-GP.

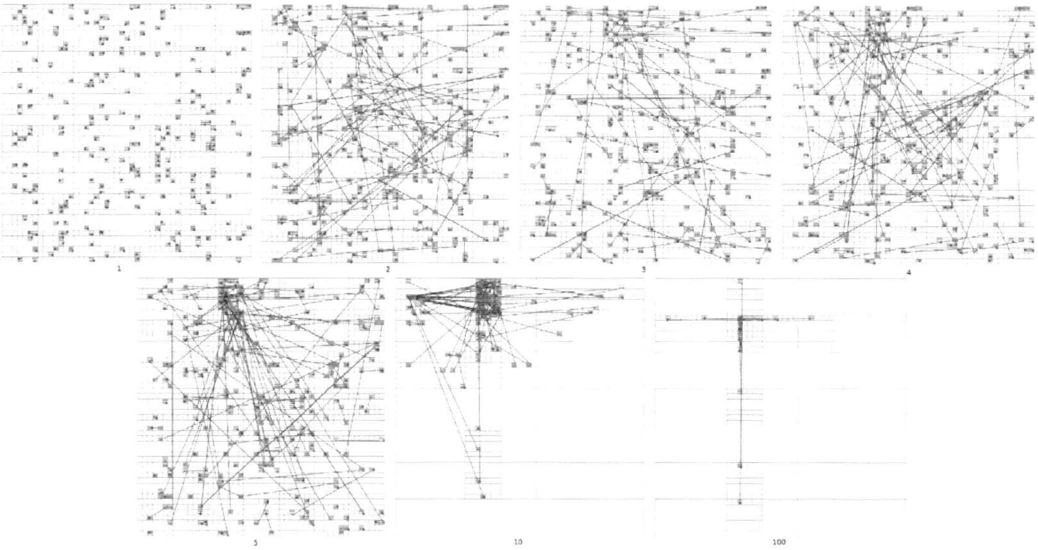


Fig. 4
A VISUALISATION OF AN EARLY FRAME OF A GENERATION IN THE K-GPSO OPTIMISER.

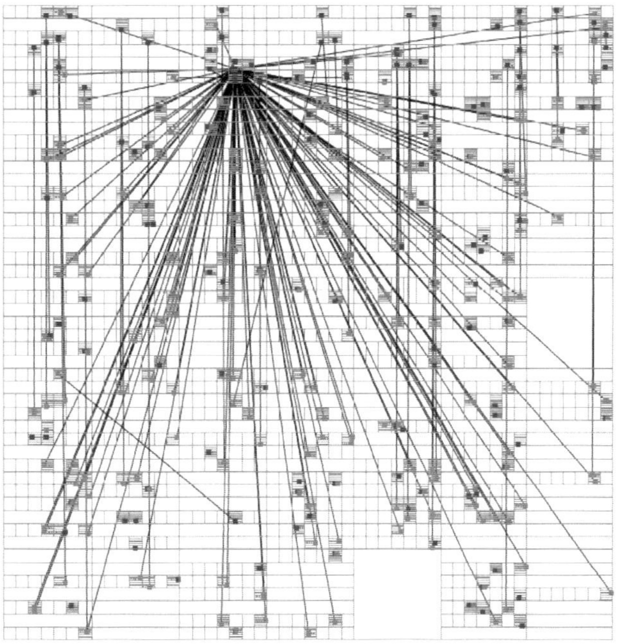

Fig. 5
DIVERSITY PLOT OF THE CUDA GP AND GPSO ALGORITHMS BOTH USING K-EXPRESSIONS.

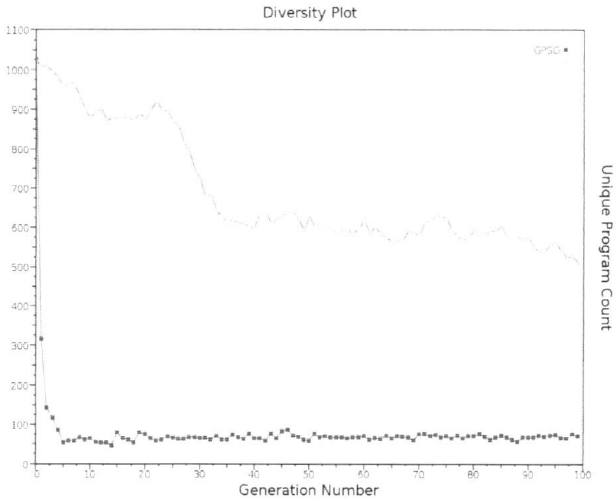


especially for gaining insight into how the algorithm behaves on a microscopic level.

Representing programs in this fashion has some drawbacks however. Spatial distance in the visualisation has no bearing over crossover and mutation operators in their ability to move candidate programs through space. These concepts do not share a similar concept of spatial distance to that of the visualiser. This can result in a more difficult to interpret visualisation at times, as crossover and mutation may translate a certain candidate very far away from the original, while the program may only differ in one symbol.

Indicating movement through this program space for the K-GP (Karva Genetic Programming) algorithm is less meaningful than for the K-GPSO (Karva Geometric Particle Swarm Optimiser) . The reason for this is in the implementation of tournament selection, where, depending on the outcome of the two tournaments, the candidates used in the end may be unrelated to the originals chosen.

Nevertheless, the use of this visualisation has led us to

Fig. 6
VISUALISATION OF FRAME 2 OF THE K-GPSO WITH MODIFIED PARAMETERS, AT THIS FRAME, 907 UNIQUE PROGRAMS ARE PRESENT.

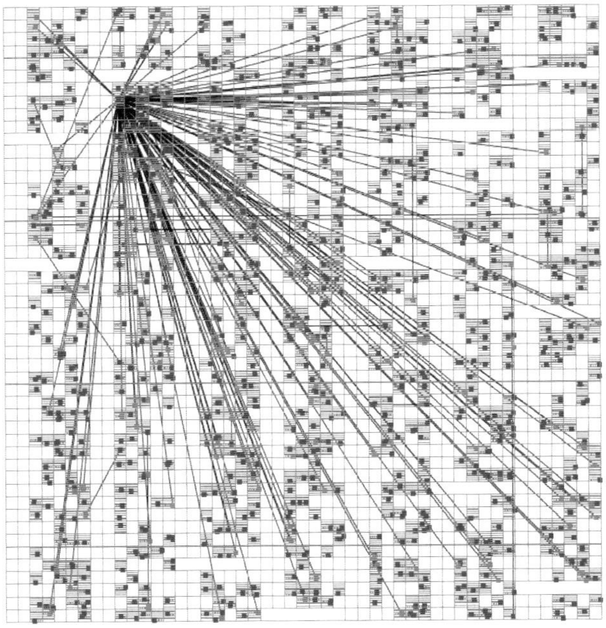

identify what we believe to be the main problem underlying the K-GPSO. The lack of program diversity in this algorithm, especially using weighted scores for multi-parent crossover, results in a great diversity deficiency. Our efforts to correct the K-GPSO saw limited success. From these observations, it seemed that using static values for the parameters in the K-GPSO is not conducive to avoiding local minima issues. Using weighted values according to scores does bring a limited improvement.

## 6. Conclusions and Future Work

In summary, we have presented an effective visualisation technique for Genetic Programming and its variants. We applied this to our K-GP (Karva Genetic Programming) and K-GPSO (Karva Geometric Particle Swarm Optimiser) algorithms and discussed the merits of this visualisation, and we also presented various modifications to these algorithms inspired from visual cues.

In the past, abstract syntax trees have mainly been analysed using quantitative methods. Visualisations were mostly restricted to the objective function itself, which does give limited information regarding the relative efficacy of candidate programs. We believe that a visualisation such as this gives effective visual cues that inspire improvements.

We have been able to make a number of qualitative observations concerning the algorithms under study by spotting emergent patterns and following visual cues that a interactive human user can readily make, but which would be hard to easily encode a supervisory pattern recognition program to identify. This emphasises the importance of a human-guided optimizer, implemented to work in near real-time.

We anticipate that future work could involve using Graphical Processing Units to further speed the process of rendering images, so that it can be used in real time. It could also be very beneficial to build in landscape analysis to this visualiser to perhaps produce a colour-coded image indicating higher fitness values, or even emit a 3D plot of the landscape itself. There is also scope for rendering trees in three dimensions. Generally 3D rendering is more expensive in terms of computational cost but potentially can pack more and more complex information onto a rendering for a human to spot patterns and changes.

## References


[1] William J. Cook, William H. Cunningham, and Alexander Schrijver. *Combinatorial Optimization*. Wiley, 1997. ISBN 0-471-55894-X.

[2] David L. Applegate, Robert E. Bixby, Vasek Chvatal, and William J. Cook. *The Traveling Salesman Problem: A Computational Study*. Applied Mathematics. Princeton, 2006. ISBN 978-0-691-12993-8.

[3] G. V. Wilson and G. S. Pawley. On the stability of the travelling salesman problem algorithm of Hopfield and Tank. *Biol. Cybern.*, 58:63–70, 1988.

[4] Michael R. Garey and David S. Johnson. *Computers and Intractability: A Guide to the Theory of NP-Completeness*. W.H. Freeman, 1979.

[5] Robert Axelrod. The emergence of cooperation among egoists. *The American Political Science Review*, 75:306–318, 1981.

[6] Kennedy and Eberhart. Particle swarm optimization. *Proc. IEEE Int. Conf. on Neural Networks*, 4:1942–1948, 1995.

[7] John R. Koza. Genetic programming as a means for programming computers by natural selection. *Statistics and Computing*, 4(2):87–112, June 1994.

[8] J. H. Holland. *Adaptation in natural and artificial systems*. Ann Arbor: University of Michigan Press, 1975.

[9] R. Poli, W.B. Langdon, and N.F. McPhee. *A field guide to genetic programming*. lulu.com, 2008.

[10] Sean Luke. Genetic programming produced competitive soccer softbot teams for robocup97. In J. R. Koza, W. Banzhaf, K. Chellapilla, D. Kumar, K. Deb, M. Dorigo, D.B. Fogel, M.H. Garzon, D.E. Goldberg, H. Iba, and R. Riolo, editors, *Genetic Programming 1998: Proceedings of the 3rd annual conference*, pages 214–222. Morgan Kaufmann, San Mateo, California, 1998.

[11] Sean Luke, Charles Hohn, Jonathan Farris, Gary Jackson, and James Hendler. Co-evolving soccer softbot team coordination with genetic programming. *Robocup-97: Robot soccer world cup I*, 1:398–411, 1998.

[12] Vladan Babovic and Maarten Keijzer. Genetic programming as a model induction engine. *Journal of Hydroinformatics*, 2(1):35–60, 2000.

[13] Mark Crosbie and Eugene H. Spafford. Applying genetic programming to intrusion detection. Technical report, Department of Computer Sciences, Purdue University, West Lafayette, 1995. AAAI Technical Report FS-95-01.

[14] Steven M. Manson. Agent-based modeling and genetic programming for modeling land change in the southern yucatán peninsular region of mexico. *Agriculture Ecosystems & Environment*, 111:47–62, 2005.

[15] Riccardo Poli and Stefano Cagnoni. Genetic programming with user-driven selection: Experiments on the evolution of algorithms for image enhancement. In *Genetic Programming 1997: Proceedings of the 2nd Annual Conference*, pages 269–277. Morgan Kaufmann, 1997.

[16] Julian F. Miller and Stephen L. Smith. Redundancy and computational efficiency in cartesian genetic programming. *IEEE Transactions on Evolutionary Computation*, 10(2):167–174, 2006.

[17] Simon L. Harding and Wolfgang Banzhaf. Distributed genetic programming on gpus using cuda. Submitted to Genetic Programming and Evolvable Machines, 2009.

Fig. 7

SUCCESSIVE ZOOMING TO THE GLOBAL OPTIMUM'S LOCATION.

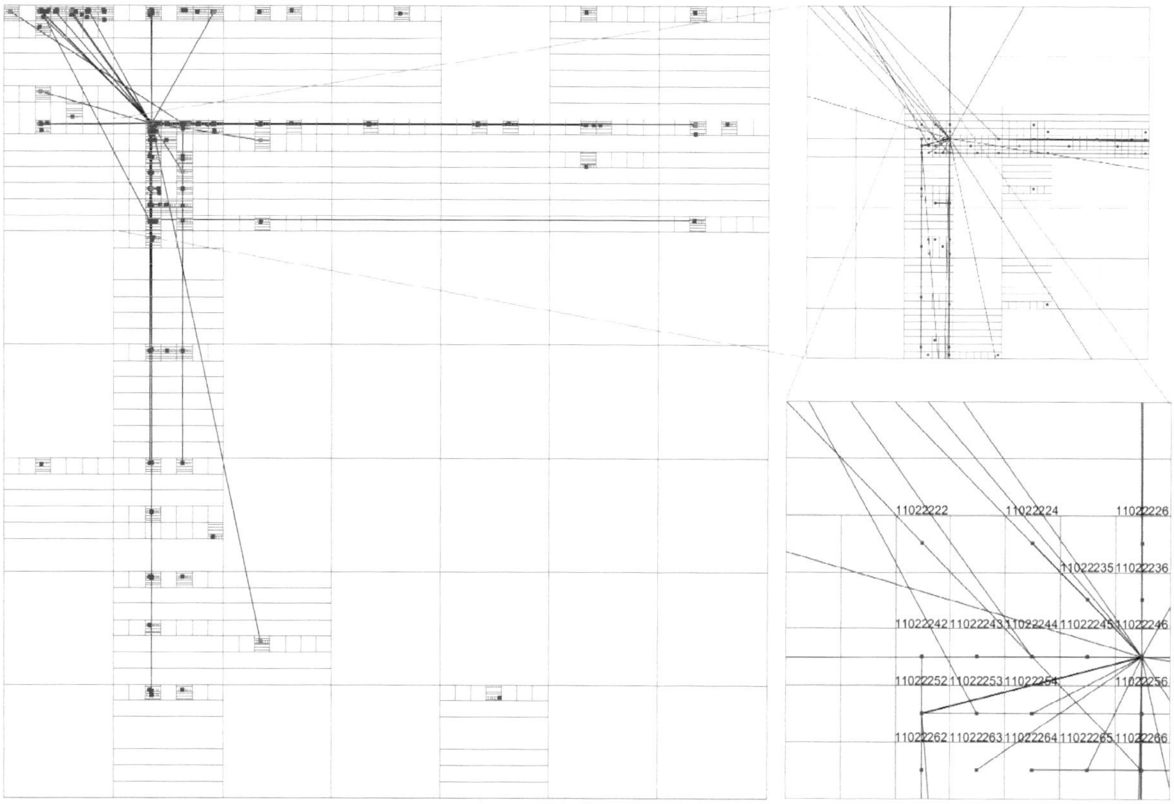



[18] Leandro Cupertino and Cristiana Bentes. Evolving cuda ptx programs by quantum inspired linear genetic programming. In *Proceedings of GECCO'11*, 2011.

[19] Tom Castle and Colin G. Johnson. Evolving high-level imperative program trees with strongly formed genetic programming. In *Proceedings of the 15th European Conference on Genetic Programming, EuroGP*, volume 7244, pages 1–12. Springer, April 2012.

[20] W. B. Langdon. A many-threaded cuda interpreter for genetic programming. In Ana Isabel Esparcia-Alcazar, Aniko Ekart, Sara Silva, Stephen Dignum, and A. Sima Uyar, editors, *Proceedings of the 13th European Conference on Genetic Programming, EuroGP*, pages 146–158. Springer, April 2010.

[21] W. B. Langdon and Wolfgang Banzhaf. A simd interpreter for genetic programming on gpu graphics cards. In M. O'Neill, L. Vanneschi, A.I. Esparcia, and S. Gustafson, editors, *Proceedings of the 11th European Conference on Genetic Programming, EuroGP*, March 2008.

[22] Kenneth E. Kinnear, Jr. Fitness landscapes and difficulty in genetic programming. In *Proceedings of the 1994 IEEE World Conference on Computational Intelligence*, volume 1, pages 142–147, Orlando, Florida, USA, 27-29 June 1994. IEEE Press.

[23] Steven M. Gustafson. *An Analysis of Diversity in Genetic Programming*. PhD thesis, School of Computer Science, University of Nottingham, England, 2004.

[24] Cândida Ferreira. Gene expression programming: A new adaptive algorithm for solving problems. *Complex Systems*, 13(2):87–129, 2001.

[25] Alwyn V. Husselmann and K. A. Hawick. Genetic programming using the karva gene expression language on graphical processing units. In *Proc. 10th International Conference on Genetic and Evolutionary Methods (GEM'13)*, number CSTN-171, page GEM2456. WorldComp, 22-25 July 2013.

[26] Alwyn V. Husselmann and K. A. Hawick. Geometric optimisation using karva for graphical processing units. In *Proc. 15th International Conference on Artificial Intelligence (ICAI'13)*, number CSTN-191, page ICA2335, Las Vegas, USA, 22-25 July 2013. WorldComp.

[27] Julian Togelius, Renzo De Nardi, and Alberto Moraglio. Geometric pso + gp = particle swarm programming. In *2008 IEEE Congress on Evolutionary computation (CEC 2008)*, 2008.

[28] A. Moraglio. *Towards a Geometric Unification of Evolutionary Algorithms*. PhD thesis, Computer Science and Electronic Engineering, University of Essex, 2007.

[29] Riccardo Poli, James Kennedy, and Tim Blackwell. Particle swarm optimization. *Swarm Intelligence*, 1:33–57, 2007.

[30] Riccardo Poli, Leonardo Vanneschi, William B. Langdon, and Nicholas Freitag McPhee. Theoretical results in genetic programming: the next ten years? *Genetic Programming and Evolvable Machines*, 11:285–320, 2010.

[31] Arno Leist, Daniel P. Playne, and K. A. Hawick. Exploiting Graphical Processing Units for Data-Parallel Scientific Applications. *Concurrency and Computation: Practice and Experience*, 21(18):2400–2437, 25 December 2009. CSTN-065.

[32] James Gosling, Bill Joy, and Guy Steele. *The Java Language Specification*. JavaSoft Series. Addison Wesley Longman, 1996. ISBN 0-201-63451-1.

[33] Marc Hoy, Dave Wood, Marc Loy, James Elliot, and Robert Eckstein. *Java Swing*. O'Reilly and Associates, 2002. ISBN:0596004087.

[34] Riccardo Poli and Nicholas F. McPhee. Exact schema theory for gp and variable-length gas with homologous crossover. In *Proceedings of the Genetic and Evolutionary Computation Conference (GECCO-2001)*, 2001.

# A Study on Information Connection Model using Rule-based Connection Platform

**Heeseok Choi , Jaesoo Kim**
NTIS Center, Korea Institute of Science and Technology Information, Daejeon, Korea

**Abstract** - *National Science & Technology Information Service (NTIS) collects national R&D information through the connection system in real time with specialized institutions under government ministries for R&D information service. However, because the information connection between the research management systems in each ministry (institution) and the NTIS is different, it is not easy to operate the connection system, and immediate data collection is thus not ensured. This study aims to propose an information connection model to be applied on the NTIS-like systems. To do this, we examine methods or styles of information connection and compare strength and weakness of connection methods. In this paper we also understand issues or characteristics of the methods through analyzing current information connection methods applied on the NTIS. Therefore, we design a rule-based information connection platform to minimize the information connection issues. Based on the platform, we also propose an information connection model.*

**Keywords:** Information Connection, Information Sharing, Rule-based Connection, NTIS

# 1 Introduction

National Science & Technology Information Service (NTIS) was developed for improving efficient research and development throughout the cycle from planning R&D to using the outcome thereof [1]. For this purpose, each representative institution under the government ministries and agencies comprehensively manages its R&D information for connection with the NTIS for the purpose of real-time collection of national R&D information (periodical update when collecting and changing the information at the time of project agreement). The NTIS has currently built a real-time connection system with representative institutions under government ministries and agencies [2].

However, since the connection criteria of each institution with external systems are different, the NTIS is connected with the research management system of each institution in various manners, to collect R&D information. Accordingly, immediate data collection is not ensured, and various manners of connection contribute to inefficient operation/maintenance.

This study aims to propose an information connection model to be applied on the NTIS-like systems. To do this, we examine methods or styles of information connection and compare strength and weakness of connection methods. In this paper we also understand issues or characteristics of the methods through analyzing current information connection methods applied on the NTIS. Therefore, we design a rule-based information connection platform to minimize the information connection issues. Based on the platform, we also propose an information connection model to be applied on the NTIS-like systems.

# 2 Related works

## 2.1 Technologies of information connection

For information connection between systems, P2P, EAI, ESB or combinations thereof are currently applied [3]. Features and characteristics of each method are described below.

① P2P: 1:1 connection between individual systems, and cannot be extended or reused. However, because connection between individual systems is simple, a connection system is easily built in conformity with features of each system.

② EAI: Individual applications are connected to the central hub by means of an adapter, and are connected to other applications through the central hub. This significantly improves typical complex connections. However, this method uses vender-dependent technology and adapter costs should be paid for each connected application.

③ ESB: This method was developed to avoid weakness of non-standard EAI (Hub & Spoke) and SPOF (Single Point Of Failure). However, because the current ESB solution market is controlled by the EAI solution providers, the tendency is that the previous EAI solutions are supplemented and developed. In general, this method is used for service connection.

Table 1 describes the strength and weakness of each technology in terms of complexity, extensibility, flexibility, and integration cost, etc.

**Table 1. Comparison of connection technologies**

| | Strength | Weakness |
|---|---|---|
| P2P | -Easy application to simple interworking between systems in a non-complex environment. | -As the number of systems to be connected increases, the cost for maintenance may sharply increase.<br>-Low extension capability and flexibility. |
| EAI | -Easy extension in introducing new applications.<br>-Increased productivity and convenience for development and maintenance. | -High cost of establishment and maintenance.<br>-Central hub failure affects the entire system. (Single Point of Failure) |
| ESB | -Reduced integration cost because standard technology is used and service units can be reused.<br>-Loose connection in a bus type contributes to high extension capability and flexibility. | -High cost of initial establishment. |

## 2.2 Styles of data provision (collection)

When systems of other organizations are connected, independency of system operation and system/data security of the organizations can be also an important issue. Therefore, the subject of data provision (collection) can be considered as an important factor in building and operatiing a connection system. Connection depending on the subject of data provision (collection) is divided into the push method and the polling method [4].

① Push method: an information source (information provider) who owns and manages original information pushes data into information targets (information consumers) in a given cycle according to the information provision policy. Therefore, information connection in this method is by a subject of information provision who leads information connection. This method is in favor of operation and security of data and institution systems for information providers, but does not ensure immediate information collection for information providers.

② Polling method: this is to access information providers (systems for information sources) when an information collector requires the information to bring required information. Therefore, this is a method of connection in which the subject of information collection leads information connection. This method ensures immediate information collection, but is not preferred by information providers in terms of operation independency and security of internal systems because information sources are directly accessed from external systems.

Table 2 describes the strength and weakness of provision styles in terms of security, maintenance, performance, and dependency, etc.

**Table 2. Comparison of data provision styles**

| | Strength | Weakness |
|---|---|---|
| Push | -High security in system connection between systems of institutions.<br>-Independent connection with external systems in system operation.<br>-Information providers lead connection. | -Because information providers lead information connection, integrated management of systems to be connected is not easy.<br>-Information connection varies with institution by institution, maintenance is not easy. |
| Polling | -Because information collectors lead information connection, integrated management is easily implemented according to information collection policies.<br>-Immediate data collection is ensured. | -Security is vulnerable in system connection.<br>-Because performance may be affected by connection with external systems in system operation, information providers do not like this method. |

# 3 Analysis of the NTIS connection system

We analyzed the case of NTIS. The NTIS established an information connection system with research management systems of representative institutions under government ministries and agencies in order to connect and collect national R&D information. In this case, the push method is applied as a connection method to enable each representative institution to have the right of providing data appropriate for the connection policy and system environment thereof with external systems, and to have the ownership of the data owned by each representative institution. That is, data are provided by means of DB connection according to a given cycle for data items defined in the national R&D information standard. However, the principle of providing data on a daily basis if data are created is not ensured by adding an approval procedure for data provision to the automatic connection process in actually operating the connection system. Also, although data are provided in the push method, the DB link method and the unidirectional EAI method are applied to each institution depending on each institution environment. More details are shown in Table 3 to show implemented connection systems in various types. The reason of application is because the method of data provision is determined and implemented in various types according to the preference of each institution (for tasks or system environment) when the push method is applied. This results in no assurance of immediate data provision, and also makes monitoring and operation of the connection system difficult.

**Table 3. Information connection styles in the NTIS**

| Method | Type | Description |
|---|---|---|
| DB Link | View | Direct connection to a DB in a connection server of an institution. The procedure Inquiry/Send is used. |
| | Snapshot | The copy of institution DB table refreshes the connection server DB in a given cycle. |
| | DB Trigger | Trigger is established to reflect relevant changes on the connection server DB in updating the institution DB. |
| | DB Trigger+ JDBC | Trigger is established to reflect relevant changes on the connection server DB in updating the institution DB (based on Java, etc.). |
| | DB Script | Uses script to send data from an institution DB to the connection server in a given cycle. |
| | Procedures | Transmits data from an institution to the connection server DB table by means of the procedure. |
| EAI | Program | Transmits data by means of the EAI program of each ministry (institution) (unidirectional). |

# 4 Design of an information connection model using rule-based connection platform

The current NTIS information connection system has been established in the P2P style through the DB link or the unidirectional EAI method as described in the chapter 3. However, it is necessary to improve the connection system in a standardized method for immediate provision, integrity, efficient connection system monitoring and operation of data connection. It is also important to design the method based on easily managable rules. In this study, parts which can be functionally standardized in information connection between the NTIS and specialized institutions under ministries and agencies are identified to design them as a major functional module of the connection platform. We design a rule-based information connection platform to be applied on the NTIS-like information connection systems. Based on the platform, we also propose an information connection model.

## 4.1 Rule-based connection platform

Rule-based connection platform should be basically designed on standardization for information connection among heterogeneous systems. The sections from which data are first acquired in connection with each institution are divided into variation areas for the purpose of information connection based on standardization, and the next phases are identified as standard functional areas. That is, as shown in Fig.1, the R&D information is first transferred to the connection DB from the institution's system DB. This section is defined as a variation area. Subsequent data processing in the connection DB and data transmission to the integration DB is defined as a major function of a common area which can be standardized.

**Figure 1. Basic steps of information connection**

Therefore, it is necessary to build the connection platform as a function to overcome variability of each institution in the variation areas and to process the functions in the common area. To this end, the connection platform includes functions of connection rule processing, mapping, connection error processing, and creation of update information and monitoring information. Fig.2 shows system architecture of a connection platform which includes the aforementioned functions.

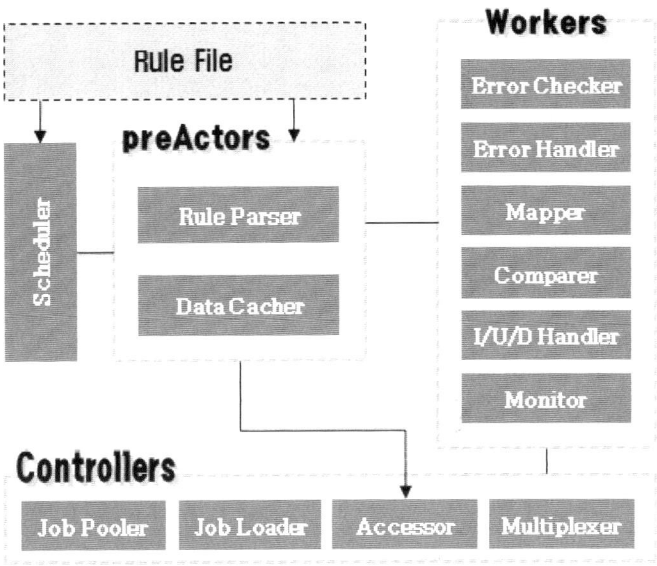


**Figure 2. Rule-based connection platform**

Fig. 2 shows the connection platform which is composed of rule processing (preActors), connection processing (Workers), and parallel task processing control (Controllers), and which performs connection of the common areas according to the rule predefined in the Rule File.

① Schema mapping (Mapper): this is carried out between an institution DB schema and the NTIS standard collection schema according to the schema mapping rule defined in the Rule File for the data transferred from the institution. Code mapping is also carried out from the code value in the institution DB to the code value in the NTIS integration DB according to the code mapping rule defined in the Rule File.

② Comparison of data (Comparer, I/U/D Handler): this is to compare the data transferred from an institution with the data transferred in the previous cycle to decide whether to update the data. On the basis of comparison result, the system in the connection institution system displays I(Insert), U(Update), or D(Delete) to indicate that the relevant data is new, updated or deleted data.

③ Connection error processing (Error Checker, Error Handler): this is to check errors in connection, for example, key errors, errors in essential connection items, code conversion errors, data conversion errors, data format errors, data length errors, etc. Details of the checked connection errors are created to be an error DB. Normal data are then stored as an OrgDB to be transmitted to the NTIS integration DB.

④ Connection monitoring information creation (Monitor): information is created about whether connection normally operates, for example, the number of connection data, details of updated data, execution of the connection module according to the schedule, or how much new data has been provided.

⑤ Rule Parser: this enhances data mapping through rule based processing. The Rule Parser interprets the Rule File which specifies schema mapping, code mapping and rules that should be observed when data are provided from an institution to the NTIS.

⑥ Scheduler: information connection is performed periodically or in real time depending on information type. Therefore, the function to control the information connection execution cycle is provided. Three types of execution scheduling is provided, including manual execution (immediate execution) by an operator, periodical execution and execution after standby for a given period of time in consideration of the features of NTIS connection.

⑦ Data Cacher: information frequently used, for example, schema information and code mapping tables, is internally cached to improve connection capability. Data are deleted after a given period of time.

⑧ Operation environment (Controllers): this controls listing tasks to be processed for optimized resource management and function processing by means of multi threads, and to carry out the tasks according to the processing sequence. Controllers also provide access to storages to store the connection result in the DB or a file.

The connection platform designed as such can improve data processing speed through internal data caching. It can enhance data mapping through rule-based data processing, and can operate and maintain the connection system by producing/changing rules. It sorts data sources from targets to manage data history, and systematically checks data errors. It can address difficulty in connection monitoring due to different connection methods between institutions, and processes data update information.

## 4.2 Information connection model using rule-based connection platform

On the basis of the rule-based connection platform designed in 4.1, information connections in the push method, and in the EAI method or the polling method by agents can be implemented. Therefore, two types of information connection models were designed and the two types of connection models were compared with respect to the important issues considered in information connection by the NTIS with the representative specialized institutions.

① P2P & Push method using the connection platform
For standardized information connection, the connection platform was defined, which processes the information connection rule, performs encryption, and creates connection error and monitoring information. The connection standard platform contributes to addressing limitations by different information connection methods of each institution. That is, although each institution provides data in a different method (entire relevant data or some of changed data), it is possible to identify details of data change, and to create consistent error and monitoring information. Consistent connection also contributes to easy management of information connection. This connection method, however, can provide data to a connection system at times desired by an institution. Fig.3 shows this method as described above.

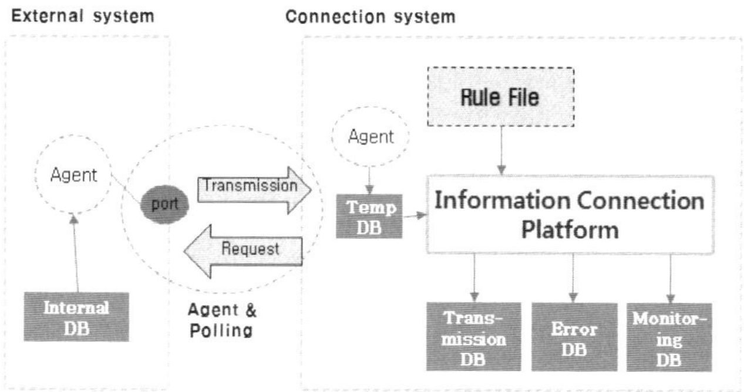


**Figure 3. Connection in P2P & Push method**

② Agent & Polling method using the connection platform
This is a method of connection to apply the Polling method which uses an agent to bring institution data while information connection is based on standardization. This method enhances the efficiency of using connection server resources, and ensures the initiative of data collection to ensure immediate data collection. Integrated connection system management can be also implemented. The system for jointly using administrative information employs this method. Fig.4 shows this method as described above.

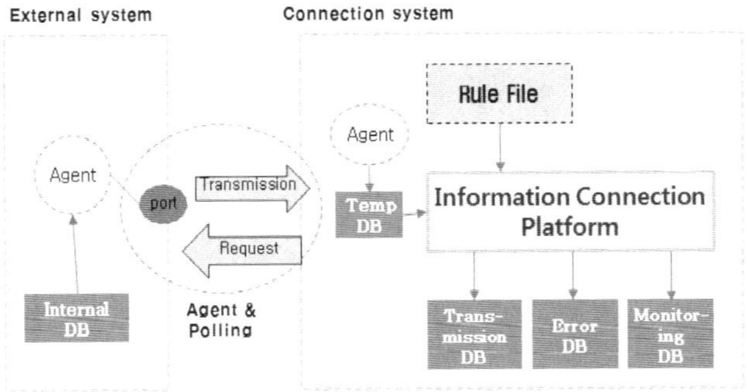


**Figure 4 Connection in Agent & Polling method**

Finally, Table 4 shows the strength and weakness of two connection methods in information connection. Of course, most external connection institutions prefer connection by the 'P2P & Push' methods because security is a key factor to determine their connection method. However, in consideration of the strength described in Table 4, it is necessary to employ a connection method which implements the aforementioned strength. Therefore, in this study, the method of 'Agent & Polling' using rule-based connection platform is suggested for future NTIS information connection. To this end, it is necessary to establish schemes for strengthening security, and to establish access supported by policies and strategies.

**Table 4. Comparison of the connection methods**

| | P2P & Push | Agent & Polling |
|---|---|---|
| Connection speed | Same | Same |
| Storage capacity | Great *Because each institution uses its own data provision method, data pre-processing is thus required. | Not great |
| Management efficiency | Because information providers are the subject of information connection, integrated management is not easy. | Because information collectors are the subject of information connection, integrated management is easy. |
| Immediate connection | Not ensured. | Ensured |
| Security | Relatively high (in terms of institution systems) | Relatively low (in terms of institution systems) |

# 5 Conclusions and future works

This study examined methods or styles of information connection and compare strength and weakness of connection methods. We also analyzed the current NTIS information connection system established with representative specialized institutions under government ministries and agencies. On the basis of this, the variation area and the common area were identified to design a connection platform for the functions of the common area. We also examined methods In this paper we also understand issues or characteristics of the methods through analyzing current information connection methods applied on the NTIS. Therefore, we designed a rule-based information connection platform to be applied on the NTIS-like information connection systems. Based on the platform, we also proposed an information connection model.

It is necessary to expand rule-based connection platform to establish a flexible and extensible connection system. In addition, it is necessary to develop a connection guideline for standardizing information connection.

# 6 References

[1] NTIS, "National Science and Technology Information Service", www.ntis.go.kr.

[2] Choi, H., etc, "Study on Real-time Integration System Extension of National R&D Information", Korea Computer Congress, 2010.

[3] Nah, Y., "ESB-based Data Service Connection" www.dator.co.kr, 2010.

[4] Choi, H. etc, "Technology Trends on Information Connection", Technical Reports, KISTI, 2012.

# Management of Knowledge on the Basis of Stochastic Mathematical Models

**James William Brooks**[1], **Dmitry Zhukov**[2], **Irina Samoylo**[3] **and Victoria Hodges**[4]
[1]Chancellor, Salem International University, Salem, West Virginia, USA
[2]Professor, Consultant, Department of Medical and Biological Physics,
I.M. Sechenov First Moscow State Medical University, Moscow, Russia
[3]Professor, Department of Medical and Biological Physics,
I.M. Sechenov First Moscow State Medical University, Moscow, Russia
[4]Consultant, Department of Medical and Biological Physics,
I.M. Sechenov First Moscow State Medical University, Moscow, Russia

**Abstract** - *This article discusses the questions of the use of stochastic models in the description of an educational process, which includes such parts as obtaining, loss (forgetting), and self-organization of educational information. The probability approach used by the authors led them to the deduction of differential equations of the second order of the type of the Kolmogorov equation. It also allowed the authors to formulate the boundary value problem of the management of the educational process. The solution to this boundary value problem allows to define the necessary volume of the educational information transferred to the object of training during one step of the educational process in order to make the process the most effective which means that the targeted educational level will be reached for the least number of steps. The solution of the boundary problem also permits creating necessary preconditions for the management of the educational process.*

**Keywords:** Modeling, mathematics, management, education, self-organization.

## Introduction

Paraphrasing Ian Stewart's expression about ruthless nonlinearity of the world surrounding us, it is possible to assert safely that each person, being a part of this world, is not less ruthlessly nonlinear and complicated. Therefore from the methodological point of view the use of the theory of complex systems and nonlinear dynamics for the solution to a wide range of social, medical, psychological, pedagogical and other problems is justified Haken, Stein, Chua, Mainzer [1-4].

Nonlinear modeling and the computing experiment contribute to finding effective levers of control for such an important process as an educational process is. This article studies the dynamics of the process of education and searches the ways of its efficient control.

Owing to the presence of the human factor which action has psychophysical nature, it is possible to classify training and management of training as stochastic processes [5, 6] which under certain conditions could be considered as semi-Markov processes.

## Formalization of the Model of Management of Educational Process

In order to create a model of the process which manages the formation of disciplinary thinking let us take some imaginary discipline in the frameworks of which an educational process or knowledge transfer will be performed. This imaginary discipline under study can be conditionally introduced as a set of interconnected elements and also conditionally divided into semantic test units.

The following operating factors define the condition of the object of the educational management process at each phase. Under the object of training, we understand either individual trainees or groups of trainees:

- Purposeful influence on the trainees, which leads to the increase of the volume of their knowledge (educational level). The volume of the educational information transferred during one step of training is individual for each object of training (a trainee) and depends on their abilities and background knowledge.
- Casual processes leading to loss of the educational information (forgetting) during each step of training. Loss of knowledge (forgetting) is also an individual characteristic parameter of a trainee.
- Information self-organization as a process of occurrence of the harmonious system of the trainee's knowledge, thanks to which the previously obtained knowledge becomes the source of new knowledge.

In order to evaluate the indicators of learning efficiency, it is necessary to study the information processes, which take place during the training and define their characteristics. In our opinion, the effective models of educational management can be received if the following assumptions are used:

1. It is necessary to consider any process of education as a step-by-step process, during each step of which, a trainee receives a certain individual portion of educational information.
2. Owing to specificity of human's memory, each person can forget certain quantity of the received information.
3. Knowledge self-organization takes place while allocating the basic ideas, skills, and discipline concepts [7].

4.The educational information organized in the mentioned above way can become by itself a source of new knowledge.

Let us consider some conditional trainee indicating them with the letter *i*. Let us also consider that this *i* - trainee is supposed to reach the educational level $L_i$ (where $L_i$ – is the sum of all semantic test units, or conditional points which the *i*-trainee should have (know) by the end of their training).

Let us enter the time of duration of one step of training equal to $\tau_0$. We consider that all trainees visit their classes with identical periodicity. However, they can receive different quantity of educational information during their classes and they forget it differently during the time of $\tau_0$. Thus, let us establish that the *i*-trainee, which has been educated during the period of time τ0, receives ε of educational units and forgets ξ of educational units (received during any of the previous steps of training).

After each step of education, the trainee passes into one of *k*-possible conditions, which are set by that quantity of the educational information, which the trainee possesses at present time (*k* can accept value from 0 to *L*). Let us introduce the concept of probability of the trainee's level of knowledge in some value.

Let after some number of steps of training *h*: $P_{x-\varepsilon,h}$ ,where *h* is the probability of the fact that an *i*-trainee possesses the level of knowledge equal to (*x* - ε) units; $P_{x,h}$ – is the level of knowledge equal to *x*-educational units and $P_{x+\xi,h}$ – is the level of knowledge equal to (*x* + ξ) educational units. At one step of training $\tau_0$, ε - units of the educational information can be received and ξ - educational units can be forgotten.

Thus, it is possible to enter the probability $P_{x,h+1}$ of the fact that at the following (*h*+1) step of training the trainee will know *x*-units of the educational information which will be equal to (see Fig. 1):

$$P_{x,h+1} = P_{x-\varepsilon,h} + P_{x+\xi,h} - P_{x,h} \qquad (1)$$

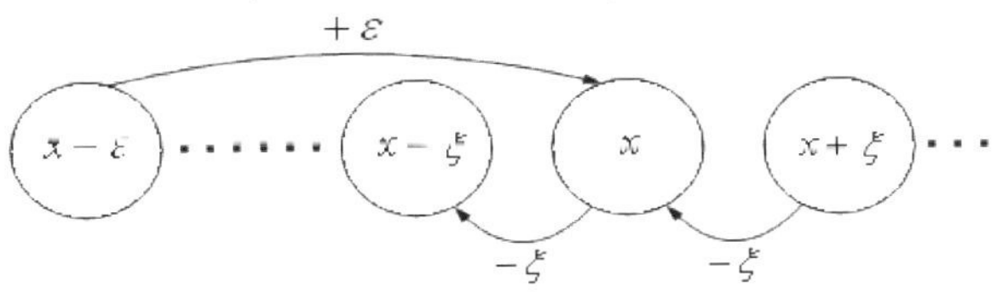


*Fig. 1 The scheme of possible transitions between educational conditions for i -trainee at h+1 step of training in nonlinear model*

Let us enter $t = h\tau_0$, where *t* – is the time of the process of training, h – is the number of the step, $\tau_0$ – is the duration of one step. Passing from *h* to *t*, we will spread out the equation (1) as a Taylor series and, considering in the right and left parts of the received equation no more than the second derivatives, we will receive:

$$\tau_0 \frac{\partial P(x,t)}{\partial t} + \frac{\tau_0^2}{2}\frac{\partial^2 P(x,t)}{\partial t^2} + \ldots = (\xi - \varepsilon)\frac{\partial P(x,t)}{\partial x} + \frac{\varepsilon^2+\xi^2}{2}\frac{\partial^2 P(x,t)}{\partial x^2} \qquad (2)$$

The member of the equation of the kind $\frac{\partial P(x,t)}{\partial t}$ – defines the general change of the condition of the educational level in some period of time. The member of the equation of the kind $\frac{\partial^2 P(x,t)}{\partial t^2}$ – describes the process at which the received knowledge is structured (self-organized knowledge) and it becomes itself the sources of additional knowledge for the trainee. The member of the equation of the kind $\frac{\partial^3 P(x,t)}{\partial t^3}$ – is insight, the member of the equation of the kind $\frac{\partial P(x,t)}{\partial x}$ – describes a structured transition either into the condition when knowledge increases ($\varepsilon > \xi$) or when it decreases ($\varepsilon < \xi$). The member of the equation of the kind $\frac{\partial^2 P(x,t)}{\partial x^2}$ – describes a casual change of the condition of the level of education ("washing out" of the received knowledge or the trainee's uncertainty in it).

**The Formulation of the Boundary problem in Knowledge Management Process**

Considering the function *P*(*x*,*t*) as continuous, we will pass from the probability of *P*(*x*,*t*) to the probability of density ρ (*x*,*t*) and we will formulate the boundary value problem, the solution of which will describe the training process.

At the condition of the educational level of the trainee where *x* = *L*, the educational process can be finished. The probability of finding out such condition will be distinct from 0. However, the density of probability defining the stream of the educational information in a condition when *x* = *L* is supposed to be equal 0 (we stop training, meaning we stop providing the stream of educational information), i.e.:

$$\rho(x,t)_{x=L} = 0 \qquad (3)$$

We will choose the second boundary condition proceeding from the following reasons: the condition of *x* = *0* defines the total absence of knowledge of the trainee. The probability of finding out such condition can be distinct from 0. However, the density of probability defining a stream of demands in the condition when *x* = 0 is supposed to be put equal to 0 (as we aspire to avoid this condition but even if it does not turn out this way, the volume of knowledge cannot be left in the area of negative values), i.e.:

$$\rho(x,t)_{x=0} = 0 \qquad (4)$$

Considering that ε and ξ do not depend on *x* and having entered the designation, when $a = \frac{\varepsilon^2+\xi^2}{2\tau_0}$, $b = \frac{\varepsilon-\xi}{\tau_0}$, and $c = \frac{\tau_0}{2}$ we will receive:

$$\frac{\partial \rho(x,t)}{\partial t} = a\frac{\partial^2 \rho(x,t)}{\partial x^2} - b\frac{\partial \rho(x,t)}{\partial x} - c\frac{\partial^2 \rho(x,t)}{\partial t^2} \qquad (5)$$

As at the moment of time *t* = 0 the condition of the *i*-trainee can be already equal to some value of $x_0$ (which is defined by the background knowledge of the trainee), then the entry condition can be set as:

$$\rho(x,t=0) = \delta(x-x_0) = \begin{cases} 1, x = x_0 \\ 0, x \neq x_0 \end{cases} \qquad (6)$$

As the entry condition contains the delta function, the solution for *ρ*(*x*,*t*) breaks into two areas:

( $\rho_1(x,t)$ at $x > x_0$ and $\rho_2(x,t)$ at $x \le x_0$ ). (7)

**The Solution of the Boundary Value Problem in Education Management Process**

At first, let us find the solution to the equation (5), without taking into account the possibility of the synergetic effects of knowledge self-organization.

Using the methods of operational calculation for the density of probability $\rho_1(x,t)$ and $\rho_2(x,t)$ of the detection of the educational level of the *i*-trainee in one of the values on a segment from *0* to *L*, we will receive the following solutions to the equation (5):

$$\rho_1(x,t) = \frac{2}{L} e^{-\frac{(x_0-x)+\frac{bt}{2}}{\frac{2a}{b}}} \sum_{n=1}^{M}(-1)^{n+1}\sin\left(\pi n\frac{x_0}{L}\right)\sin(\pi n\frac{L-x}{L})e^{-\frac{\pi^2 n^2 at}{L^2}} \quad \text{when } x > x_0 \qquad (8)$$

$$\rho_2(x,t) = \frac{2}{L} e^{-\frac{(x_0-x)+\frac{bt}{2}}{\frac{2a}{b}}} \sum_{n=1}^{M}(-1)^{n+1}\sin\left(\pi n\frac{x}{L}\right)\sin(\pi n\frac{L-x_0}{L})e^{-\frac{\pi^2 n^2 at}{L^2}} \quad \text{when } x \le x_0 \qquad (9)$$

Then we will receive the solution to the equation (5) for the case of knowledge self-organization. For the density of probability $\rho_1(x,t)$ and $\rho_2(x,t)$ it is possible to receive the equations (10, 11) in this case:

$$\rho_1(x,t) = \frac{2}{L} e^{-\frac{(x_0-x)}{\frac{2a}{b}}} e^{-\frac{t}{\tau_0}} \sum_{n=1}^{M}(-1)^{n+1}\sin\left(\pi n\frac{x_0}{L}\right)\sin\left(\pi n\frac{L-x}{L}\right)\times ch\left\{t\sqrt{\frac{1}{\tau_0^2}-\frac{b^2}{2a\tau_0}-2\frac{\pi^2 n^2 a}{\tau_0 L^2}}\right\} \quad \text{when } x > x_0 \qquad (10)$$

$$\rho_2(x,t) = \frac{2}{L} e^{-\frac{(x_0-x)}{\frac{2a}{b}}} e^{-\frac{t}{\tau_0}} \sum_{n=1}^{M}(-1)^{n+1}\sin\left(\pi n\frac{x}{L}\right)\sin\left(\pi n\frac{L-x_0}{L}\right)\times ch\left\{t\sqrt{\frac{1}{\tau_0^2}-\frac{b^2}{2a\tau_0}-2\frac{\pi^2 n^2 a}{\tau_0 L^2}}\right\} \quad \text{when } x \le x_0 \qquad (11)$$

**The Analysis and Discussion of the Received Models**

The equations (8-11) describe the behavior of the probability density while detecting the condition of the educational level (the volume of knowledge) of the *i*-trainee in one of the values on a segment from *0* to *L*.

If to calculate the integral *P(L,t)*:

$$P(L,t) = \int_0^{x_0}\rho_2(x,t)dx + \int_{x_0}^{L}\rho_1(x,t)dx \qquad (12)$$

then the function *P(L,t)* will set the probability of the fact that the condition of the educational level by the moment of time *t* will be on a segment from *0* to *L*, i.e. the threshold of the necessary educational level *L* will not be achieved.

Accordingly, the probability $Q_i\,(t)$ of the fact that the necessary threshold *L* will be reached by the moment of time *t* can be defined as follows:

$$Q_i(L,t) = 1 - P(L,t) \qquad (13)$$

*The Case when there is no knowledge self-organization.* Let us analyze the behavior of the probability of the achievement of the necessary threshold of the educational level $I(t)$ at $\varepsilon > \xi$. We take any values of $x_0$, $\varepsilon$ and $\xi$.

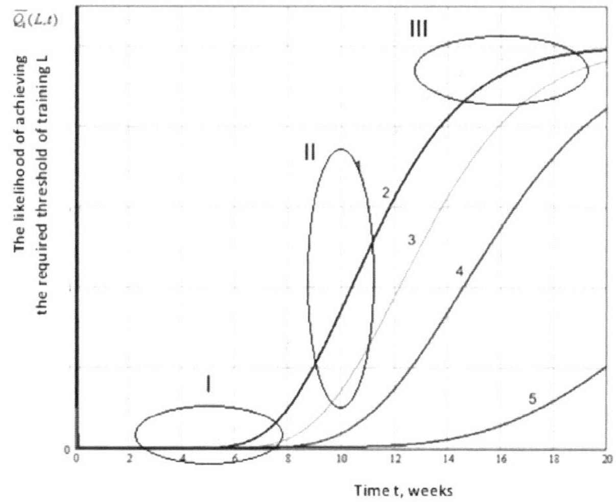


*Fig. 2 Dependence on time of the probability ($Q_i\,(t)$) of the achievement of the necessary educational level L (in the model without knowledge self-organization)*

In all cases, we receive the variants of the known S – shaped curve, which is characteristic for a logistical display (Fig. 2). The probabilities of the achievement of the necessary educational level (Curves 1-5) become distinct from *0* starting only at some moment of time and they move towards bigger values of time with the increase of value $\xi$ – which indicates the quantity of the lost educational information and thus, it is rather a logical result.

*The Case when knowledge self-organization is possible.* For the analysis of the model considering self-organization of knowledge in the educational process, let us take the following parameters: $x_0=50$, $\varepsilon=15$ and $\xi = 7$ ($\tau_0 = 1$ week) as an example. Fig. 3 illustrates the dependence on time of the probability $Q_i(t)$ of the fact that the educational level reaches the set threshold by the moment of time *t*. Curve 1 is for $L_1 = 75$, Curve 2 is for $L_2 = 80$, Curve 3 is for $L_3 = 85$, Curve 4 is for $L_4 = 90$ , and Curve 5 is for $L_5 = 100$.

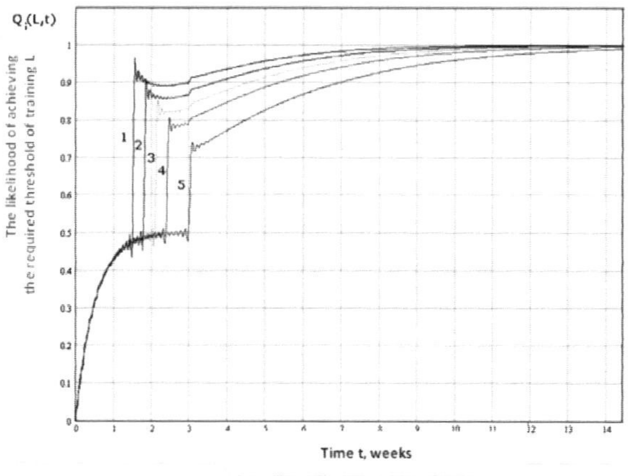


*Fig. 3 Dependence on time of the probability ($Q_i\,(t)$) of the achievement of the necessary educational level L*

The basic difference from the earlier received results is

the fact that in the case of knowledge self-organization the probability of the achievement of the set educational level becomes distinct from 0 immediately when the training begins.

The second essential difference is that the jump of the probability of the achievement of the set educational level, in which the condition when the lower the observed educational level L is, the earlier and more considerably the observed jump of the probability of the achievement of the necessary educational threshold occurs. Spasmodic growth of the probability of the achievement of the necessary educational level (the analogue of phase transition of the second order) testifies to the structural reorganization of thinking of the trainee. The formation of emergent property is considered disciplinary thinking, which will help the trainee operate effectively, based on the obtained by him/her knowledge.

The third important difference from the first model is that in case of knowledge self-organization, the received knowledge gets structured and it also becomes a source for new necessary knowledge. That in turn raises the probability of the achievement of the desired educational level for a shorter period.

Thus, the offered models expand the horizon of the trainee's possibilities as well as of the organizers of the educational process, and they allow choosing that model of training which in the best way corresponds to the problems of the current or projected educational process.

By the means of the methods of imitating modeling, the received results allow to define the necessary quantity of the educational information $\varepsilon$, which is transferred to the object of training (depending on their characteristics) during one step of training with the purpose of making the process more effective (the set educational level would be reached for the least possible number of steps).

Prognostic possibilities of the model demonstrate us that having evaluated a) the abilities of the trainee to synthesis of the studied material, and b) the trainee's initial level of knowledge and the quantity of the educational information received and lost during each step of training, it will make it possible to create for each trainee their individual graphs of the dependence on time of the probability of the achievement of the necessary educational level. The information received by the means of such graphs allows efficient management of the development of the educational process. It also allows to control the speed and the character of the growth of the educational level as well as to choose the strategy of the correction of the educational process.

The research of the model continues and if we follow Edgar Poe's statement that creativity submits to the accurate logic scheme, then it would be extremely interesting to receive the solution to the equation, which describes the moment of inspiration.

**Reference Literature**

1. Haken H. Synergetics in Nature/De Cruyter: New York (1995)

2. Stein D. l. (ed). Lectures in Sciences of Complexity. Santa Fe Institute Studies in the Sciences of Complexity. Vol 3 (1991)

3. Chua L. O. CNN: A Paradigm for Complexity. Wold Scientific: Singapore (1998)

4. Majntser K. Complexity Thinking - M: URSS, 2009. - p.464.

5. Cogan A.B. Biological Cybernetics - M, Visshaya Shkola, 1977.

6. Main X., Osaky S. Markov Processes of Decision-making. - M: "Science", 1977. – p. 175.

7. Kapitsa S. P., Kurdyumov S. P., Malinetsky G.G. Sinergetics and the Future Forecast - M: URSS, 2003. – p.203.

# SESSION

# DATABASES, INFORMATION RETRIEVAL AND SEARCH

## Chair(s)

**TBA**

# A Method for Search Result Accuracy and Indexing Efficiency on Author Name Search

**Heejun Han, Heeseok Choi, Jaesoo Kim**
NTIS Management Team, NTIS Center, Korea Institute of Science and Technology Information, 245 Daehak-ro, Yuseong-gu, Daejeon, Korea

**Abstract** - *Most academic information has its creator, that is, a subject who has created the information. The subject can be an individual, a group, or an institution, and can be a nation depending on the nature of the relevant information. Most web data is composed of a title, an author, and contents. A paper which is under the academic information category has metadata including a title, an author, keyword, abstract, data about publication, place of publication, ISSN, and the like. A patent has metadata including the title, an applicant, an inventor, an attorney, IPC, number of application, and claims of the invention. Most web-based academic information services enable users to search the information by processing the meta-information. An important element is to search information by using the author field which corresponds to a personal name. This study suggests a method of efficient indexing and using the adjacent operation result ranking algorithm to which phrase search-based boosting elements are applied, and thus improving the accuracy of the search results of author name. This method can be effectively applied to providing accurate search results in the academic information services.*

**Keywords:** Author name search, Information Retrieval, Indexing, Search Algorithm, Boosting

## 1 Introduction

Personal names on the web are an important element which accounts for 30% of all search engine queries, and search by means of personal names is an important function in web applications [1][2].

All current information is produced by a creator, who is referred to as an author for a paper, an applicant, an inventor, and an attorney for a patent, a research participant for research reports, an inspector and an analyzer for trend analysis data, in terms of academic information. The creator of information referred to as such various names can be an individual, an institution, a group, a nation, or a computer system, for example, a crawler [2].

The creator of academic information is mostly a personal name. For example, in more than approximately 95% of all data, the creator field, including authors, applicants, and research participants, is described by personal names, the format of which is shown in Table 1, as can be found in papers, patents, theses, research reports, industrial standards, science and technology work forces, trend analysis information, and factual information for the National Discovery for Science Leaders service provided by the KISTI (Korea Institute of Science and Technology Information).

Table 1. Exemplary metadata for personal name in academic information

| Category | Classification | Format |
|---|---|---|
| Korean paper | author | Park, Sung-Joon ; Kim, Ju-Youn ; Kim, Young-Kuk |
| Overseas paper | author | Zhou, Fushan ; Yang, Deng-Ke ; Molitor, R.J. |
| Patent | inventor | Sakurada, Masahiro ; Yamanaka, Hideki ; Ohta, Tomohiko |
| Research report | reporter | Ryu, Beom-Jong ; Kim, Jin-Sook ; Jin, Doo-Seok |
| Trend analysis | analyzer | Rohak Park ; James Lee |

The academic information search service on the web undergoes the process of indexing data required for search. Person names are data which cannot be decided with compound words and postpositional words, so most academic information search services carry out delimiting white spaces or separation in delimiters in indexing the author name field. Also the process of indexing data in English undergoes stemming, singular and plural number processing, etc. However, for personal names in English, indexes are extracted by tokenizing data in white spaces or delimiters. Web of Science, Scopus, the NDSL science and technology information integration service, and most academic information services enable information to be searched through the author name field for paper search. In particular, Scopus or the NDSL provides an independent function for finding author names through Find Author after building and indexing an author name DB [3].

This study describes an efficient method of indexing for searching author names focusing on the NDSL or NTIS service, and refining the process of search. Section 2 describes related studies; Section 3 describes issues associated with searching author names; Section 4 describes a method suggested in this study; and Section 5 gives a conclusion.

# 2 Related studies

While searching personal names is considered increasingly important in all web document searches, including academic information services, news, and other knowledge information, an issue involved is that indexing and searching technology based on simple strings and tokenizing by white space can provide information including inaccurate personal names. If data is provided for identifying the author name included within the academic information, and a given personal name notation is provided, accurate search results can be achieved. However, a prerequisite is the record linkage method for connecting different records that show the same personal name, and a process of author identification for forming a group of entities represented from identification properties, for example, language analysis, paper titles, e-mail addresses, journal names, and institutions to which authors belong [4][5][6]. Various personal name notations should also be standardized. However, there is currently no system for building and using author identification data for searching personal names, or for extending personal name queries into various notation formats for searching.

The Web of Science, Scopus, the NDSL site, and other exemplary academic information service providers provide the function of personal name or author search, which is included in the basic search field in addition to title, contents, and source fields. All white spaces included in a user query are processed with the AND operator, and include inaccurate search results if the relevant query is a personal name. In the NDSL and Scopus, the double quotation marks can be used in order to process phrase search for personal name queries. However, this method still results in inaccurate information in the author field in which a plurality of person names is written.

# 3 Issues involved in author name search

## 3.1 Inaccurate search result

In the paper, author and co-author names are listed with delimiters as shown in Table 1. Indexing the author name field is carried out by tokenizing white spaces and possible special delimiters ( ; - , . ) to produce indexes. Table 2 shows an exemplary indexing result for an author name field.

Table 2. Result of indexing author name

| | |
|---|---|
| Original data 1 | Park, Sung-Joon ; Kim, Young Kuk. ; Song, Byung-Soo |
| Indexes 1 | park sung joon kim young kuk song byung soo |
| Original data 2 | Aron Culotta ; Pallika Kanani ; Robert Hall ; Michael Wick ; Andrew McCallum |
| Indexes 2 | aron culotta pallika kanani robert hall michael wick andrew mccallum |

All search systems convert application user's queries to those that can be processed by a search engine. Most search applications in the NDSL or NTIS translate a white space of user query to AND operation for search engine. If personal names in Korean are used as a query, search accuracy does not matter because the white space is not included at person name in Korea, but unwanted search results are obtained if a query is in English. The words 'park', 'sung', and 'joon' are unwanted search results because they exist regardless of the order and the position of the author field of the relevant paper if the query is 'Park Sung Joon', as shown in Table 3.

Table 3. Exemplary inaccurate search result

| | |
|---|---|
| User query | Park Sung Joon |
| Search engine query in NDSL or NTIS service | (AU:Park) and (AU:Sung) and (AU:Joon) where 'AU' is author name search field |
| Wanted search result | Park, Sung-Joon ; Kim, Ju-Youn ; Kim, Young Kuk |
| Unwanted search result | Park, Dong In ; Kim Sung-Joon ; Oh, Seung Wan |
| | Park, Sung-Chul ; Lee, Young-Joon ; Choi, Min-Ki |
| | Kim, Sung-Hae ; Lee Joon ; Park, Myoung-Soo |

The phrase search may be applied at this case in order to exclude the unwanted search results shown in Table 3, but search results not wanted by users still exist. For example, if a user intends to search papers by a person called 'Kanni Robert', papers with an author list are presented as a search result if the query words are adjacent with a delimiter(,) as shown below, and it is obviously a result not wanted by the user.

ex) Pallika Kanani, Robert Hall, Michael Wick, Andrew McCallum

## 3.2 Inefficient indexing in NDSL service

The NDSL includes 'Find Author' function which is one of the paper search functions. 'Find Author' contributes to searching author names in all author lists of about 56 million papers. This is subject to the following pre-processes:

① Extract metadata from a paper

② Check redundant author name at the character level

③ Create an author name for sorting

④ Extract the first character for searching an initial sound (the alphabet in case of English)

⑤ Load author information onto the Oracle DB table

⑥ Index the author information and then provide searching function

The number of author records of which the redundancy was extracted from 56 million paper records in the NDSL and then removed by string processing is approximately 22 million. Approximately 50,000 pieces of paper information are acquired weekly, which means that independent author information continues to be created at the rate of 40%. It is a waste in terms of indexing and management to additionally index author names which already exist in the paper index information in order to implement Find Author. This has a negative impact on search speed and disk load in hardware.

# 4 Proposed Method

## 4.1 Improving accuracy of search result

Searching an author name is required within units of semicolons (;) which are used to divide listed personal names in order to exclude unwanted search results. A limiter is specified to enable the search operator to operate only in the relevant delimiter. That is, the delimiter (separator) property is specified with a semicolon for all metadata fields described as personal names in all academic information, such as papers, patents, research report, and analysis trend information for indexing. In this case, phrase search brings search results only when there are successive indexes matching the sequence in the semicolon as shown in Table 4.

Table 4. Accuracy of result through index property change and phrase search

| | |
|---|---|
| user query | Won-Jae Lee |
| search engine query | (AU:"Won-Jae Lee", mode="PHRASE") |
| result of suggested phrase search | Sung-Jae Chung ; Won-Jae Lee ; Keun-Shik Lee ; Moon-Sun Chang |

The same personal name can always be written the same way in Korean, but the notation thereof in Roman characters is not always the same. In many cases, the order of the surname and the first name, characters of the names and detailed alphabets do not always match. For writing the name of 'Michael Wick' and '김철수', although there is a rule of notation in Roman characters for writing personal names, it may be different depending on personal tastes or the requirements of writing paper as shown in Table 5.

Table 5. Many expressions on person name or Romanize Korean

| | |
|---|---|
| Michael Wick | M. Wick ; M., Wick ; ML Wick ; M Wick |
| 김철수 | Kim Chul Soo ; Kim, Chul-Soo ; Chul-Soo Kim ; Chul Soo Kim ; Kim, C. S. ; Kim, Chulsoo ; Kim Chul Su ; Chul-Su Kim ; Kim, Chulsu ; Kim. Choel-Soo |

The context is the name of a person is not unique in that about 100 million people share 90,000 personal names [1][2]. It is impossible to get a search result of 'M. Wick' or 'ML Wick' with a search word of 'Michael Wick' without extending the characters and type of personal name, measuring and matching string and phonetic similarity in order to supplement different notations for the same personal name in terms of the search system while the step of author identification is not carried out. That is, when a user uses one of the above notations as a query to find all papers by 'Michael Wick', the issue of author identification should be involved in order to find all results of different notations. However, this study does not handle the issue of author identification. This study intends to suggest author names in different notations only with the metadata not analyzed and processed, and with a search method, and to suggest the result of notations of which the query string is the same but in a different sequence.

If a delimiter is specified in an index property and phrase searching is carried out, this process ensures an accurate search result shown in Table 4. However, if the sequence of notations in Roman characters for the last name and the first name of personal names in Korean or an abbreviation is used for last name in Roman expression, even the same personal name is not included in the search result. To address this issue, the near search is combined among the operators supported by most search engines with the phrase search, and the boosting factor is applied to improve the search method.

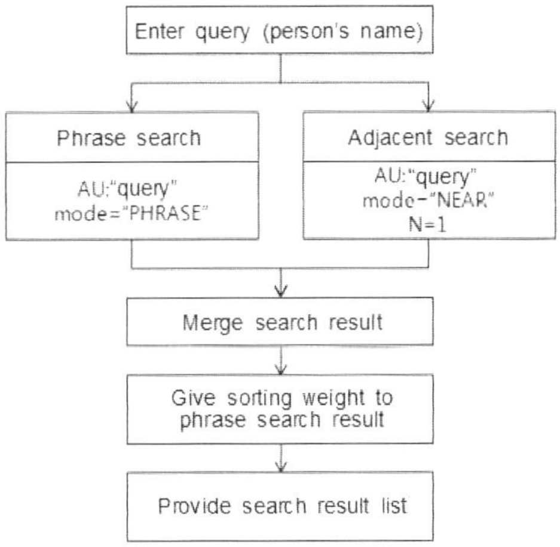


Figure 1. Algorithm for improving search results

Using the search algorithm in Figure 1 results will include a search for 'Chul-Soo Kim' if the query is written as 'Kim, Chul-Soo'. Because the phrase search depends on the sequence of writing query words, the phrase search result in which the user query was used is combined with the search result for adjacent operation which operates in a delimiter, and the ranking algorithm is then applied. Because the user wanted a matching result with 'Kim Chul-Soo' which is correct for the sequence of the words, the phrase search result is boosted to the higher layer through ranking.

First, the paper list including the author name exactly matching the personal name query by the suggested algorithm is suggested. The papers including the author name in which the sequence of notations for the surname and the first name changes according to the notations in Roman characters is also suggested. The search algorithm in the search engine FAST of the NDSL system is written as shown in equation 1.

$$\begin{aligned} &XRANK(OR(AU:query, mode=PHRASE),\\ &(AU:query, mode=NEAR, N=1)),\\ &(AU:query, mode=PHRASE), boostall=yes) \end{aligned} \quad (1)$$

If the sequence of notations for the surname and the first name changes but they indicate the same personal name in writing personal names of Koreans or foreigners, a result suggesting the relevant papers is significantly more efficient for users. An experiment was carried out in the following condition in order to prove usability of paper search results to which this result improvement algorithm was applied. In our testing, search 1 is an existing method of searching author names in which the white spaces are processed with AND. Search 2 is a method of carrying out the phrase search only in the delimiter described in Table 4. Search 3 is a method of search based on the suggested algorithm described in Figure 1.

- search target : 56,752,186 papers provided by the NDSL service.
- 50,000 personal name (written in English) query test sets.
- search 1 : processes white spaces with AND.
- search 2 : phrase search in a delimiter.
- search 3 : combines phrase search with near search in a delimiter.

Table 6. Exemplary experiment data for improving search results

| User Query | Number of results | | | (A)-(C) | (C)-(B) |
|---|---|---|---|---|---|
| | Search 1 (A) | Search 2 (B) | Search 3 (C) | | |
| Lee, Won-Jae | 4,863 | 321 | 332 | 4,531 | 11 |
| Hwang, Woo-Suk | 174 | 57 | 59 | 115 | 2 |
| Kim, Young-Jin | 13,545 | 682 | 712 | 12,833 | 30 |
| Choi, Jin Young | 4,628 | 291 | 299 | 4,329 | 8 |
| Lee, Jong Ho | 5,475 | 491 | 507 | 4,968 | 16 |
| Ahn, Kang-Min | 375 | 27 | 28 | 347 | 1 |
| Eun-Hee Kim | 3,756 | 0 | 199 | 3,557 | 199 |
| Kim, Dae-Jung | 2,102 | 107 | 115 | 1,987 | 8 |
| Choi, Jung | 13,597 | 1,226 | 1,238 | 12,359 | 12 |
| Choi, J. H. | 34,678 | 3,032 | 3,153 | 31,525 | 121 |
| Park Jae Hyun | 3,459 | 205 | 288 | 3,171 | 83 |
| Oh, Jae-Eung | 126 | 90 | 91 | 34 | 1 |
| Tom P | 1,930 | 262 | 267 | 1,663 | 5 |
| Alex, S. | 1,547 | 354 | 361 | 1,186 | 7 |
| James K | 13,828 | 3,193 | 3,201 | 10,627 | 8 |

Table 6 shows the number of paper search results by each search method. If the query is 'Lee, Won-Jae', 4,863 paper results with all of 'lee', 'won' and 'jae' are obtained regardless of the sequence and position thereof, according to the algorithm of search 1. According to the result of search 2, there are 321 results in which 'lee won jae' is positioned in sequence within semicolons in the author field among 4,863 papers. This is regarded as an accurate result for the user query. However, search 3 corresponding to the suggested algorithm provides 11 more paper results which include 'Won-Jae Lee'. This cannot ensure the identified real same personal name, but is considered as a very useful search result in consideration of the method of writing personal name strings. (A)-(C) in Table 5 are search results not related to the user query. (C)-(B) are the paper results with the author name the same for the personal name in which the characters used in writing the personal name are the same but the sequence of the surname and the first name is changed.

Table 7 shows the average of paper search results for 50,000 queries for personal names. The number in ((A)-(C))/(A) means that the existing paper search by using the author field results in about 86% inaccuracy, and provides search results not wanted by the user. The suggested algorithm does not include inaccurate search results in paper search by means of personal names, and even includes different notations for the same personal name which are approximately 9% shown by the number in ((C)-(B))/(C) in the search results.

Table 7. Improved performance for search results

| Average results | | | ((A)-(C)) / (A) | ((C)-(B)) / (C) |
|---|---|---|---|---|
| search1 (A) | search2 (B) | search3 (C) | ((A)-(C)) / (A) | ((C)-(B)) / (C) |
| 7,433 | 884 | 975 | 0.868 | 0.093 |

## 4.2 Efficient indexing

Author names are first searched in the author field included in the paper information without searching an independent author list. The personal name grouping information is then created from the paper result set to list the papers which have more authors in sequence. Table 8 shows the result of searching personal names. This method does not need a process of indexing 22 million author names extracted from 56 million papers only for finding authors. Therefore, this method reduces approximately 28% of the volume of indexing, and improves approximately 10% of disk storage efficiency for storing index binaries.

- (1) Sum of paper and author information indexes : approx. 78 million indexes

- (2) Indexes of papers : approx. 56 million indexes
- Index volume improvement : ((1)-(2))/(1) = 0.282
- (3) Capacity for storing paper and author information indexes : 840GB
- (4) Capacity for storing paper indexes : 750GB
- Disk capacity improvement : ((3)-(4))/(3) = 0.107

Table 8. Exemplary personal name search results
(A Korean character '김철수' is expressed 'Kim Chul Soo' in English)

| | |
|---|---|
| User query | Kim Chul Soo |
| Author field of paper search result (7 papers) | 김철수 ; 김주연 ; **Kim, Chul-Soo** ; Kim, Ju-Youn |
| | 김철수 ; 박명수 ; **Chul-Soo Kim** ; Myoung-Soo Park |
| | 김성해 ; 김철수 ; Kim, Sung-Hae ; **Kim, Chul-Soo** |
| | **Kim, Chul-Soo** ; Kim, Sung-Hae |
| | Lee, Joon ; **Kim, Chul-Soo** ; Han, Hee-Jun |
| | **Chul-Soo Kim** ; Ki-Won Lee |
| | **Chul-Soo Kim** ; Jong-Suk Lee ; Ki-Won Lee |
| Author name search results through grouping information | **Kim, Chul-Soo (4)**<br>**Chul-Soo Kim (3)**<br>**김철수 (3)**<br>Ki-Won Lee (2)<br>Kim, Sung-Hae (2)<br>김성해 (1)<br>Lee, Joon (1)<br>Han, Hee-Jun (1)<br>Kim, Ju-Youn (1)<br>김주연 (1)<br>Myoung-Soo Park (1)<br>박명수 (1)<br>Jong-Suk Lee (1) |

## 5 Conclusions

All information has creator data in the form of author names (authors for academic information, inventors, researchers, applicants, or analyzers). Searching personal names is one of the important functions in search services through the web. Most academic information systems for metadata of personal names cannot often provide accurate search results because of the same indexing and searching as other information, for example, titles, abstract, etc.

This study described a method of searching information and improving the accuracy of search in consideration of various personal name notations and properties in order to refine searching personal names in the academic information services. An efficient index design was also described for finding personal names, which was proved to reduce approximately 28% of index capacity and 10% of disk capacity in the NDSL science and technology information integration service. A method of effectively providing users with useful information, for example, co-authors and involved researcher lists in searching personal names was described. Figure 2 shows our paper search system based on our proposed personal name search method.

Figure 2. Paper Search based on proposed method

It is necessary to further study a method of analyzing metadata including personal names, e-mail addresses, and institutions for which the relevant person works to combine a plurality of properties and to apply the concept of author identification, in order to provide academic information related to the relevant person identified in the real world. More useful academic information services can be implemented by combining accurate metadata search by using a search engine with the result of author identification.

## 6 References

[1] Guha, R. V., & Garg, A., "Disambiguating People in Search," In Proceedings of the 13th World Wide Web Conference, ACM Press, 2004.

[2] Christen, P., "A comparison of personal name matching: Techniques and practical issues," In Data Mining Workshops, ICDM Workshops, Sixth IEEE International Conference on IEEE, 290-294, 2006.

[3] http://www.ndsl.kr

[4] W. Winkler, "Overview of record linkage and current research directions," Research Report Series #2006-2, Statistical Research Division, U.S. Census Bureau, 2006.

[5] A. Culotta, P. Kanani, R. Hall, M. Wick, and A. McCallum, "Author disambiguation using error-driven machine learning with a ranking loss function," IIWeb-2007, 2007.

[6] Kanani, P., McCallum, A., & Pal, C., "Improving author coreference by resource-bounded information gathering from the Web," IJCAI-2007, 2007.

[7] Vu, Q. M., Masada, T., Takasu, A., & Adachi, J., "Disambiguation of people in web search using a knowledge base," In Research, Innovation and Vision for the Future, 2007 IEEE International Conference on IEEE, 185-191, 2007.

[8] Artiles, J., Gonzalo, J., & Verdejo, F., "A testbed for people searching stategies in the www," In Proc. of SIGIR'05, 569-570, 2005.

# A Novel G-tree for Accelerating the Time-consuming Skyline Query

**Y. C. Chen, H. C. Liao, and C. Lee**
Department of Computer Science and Information Engineering, National Cheng Kung University, Tainan, Taiwan, R.O.C.

**Abstract** - *The skyline query problem has become an important issue in the database area. Given a set of data points in a multidimensional data space, the skyline query returns the points that are not "dominated" (detailed in the paper) by any other point. A common approach for this type of query is to construct an R-tree for the database and find the skyline points by using this tree. However, the nature of R-tree may increase the I/O cost in some circumstances. In this paper, a novel tree, named the G-tree, is devised to upgrade the performance of a skyline query. This tree is designed based on the Gaussian function and able to overcome the difficulties that R-tree has in the skyline problem. A set of simulations in the end of this paper demonstrates the efficiency of utilizing the G-tree in the skyline problem.*

**Keywords:** Database, Skyline, Tree Structure

## 1 Introduction

In recent years, skyline algorithms [1] have been widely applied in database searches. These algorithms allow users to select their prefer objects. For example, if a user were planning a seaside holiday, he/she could search a hotel database. It is assumed that this database would provide hotel prices and the distance from each hotel to the beach, as shown in Table I. Figure 1 shows the results of mapping the hotel data to biaxial coordinates where the $x$ axis is price and the $y$ axis is distance from the beach. The figure shows that Hotel F is better than Hotel L in both price and distance to the beach (i.e., F *dominates* L). Users will therefore select Hotel F rather than Hotel L. Compared to Hotel F, Hotel B is closer to the beach but has higher prices. The two hotels therefore cannot be compared (i.e., *incomparable*). Skyline algorithms operate by identifying all non-dominated data points. In this case study, the skyline data points are B, F and G, as these hotels are not dominated by any other hotels.

Skyline algorithms can be divided into two types, which are non-index-based algorithms and index-based algorithms. Non-index-based algorithms were developed first and the Block Nested Loops Algorithm (BNL) [1] and Divide and Conquer Algorithm (DAC) [1] are two of the more well-known algorithms. However these algorithms often have excessive I/O costs [5] because they require all data to be scanned in order to obtain the skyline answer. Researchers then began using index-based algorithms to reduce the I/O costs of skyline algorithms. Rather than reading all data, this type of algorithm only reads those data points that may potentially become skyline data, thereby reducing I/O costs. Index-based algorithms include the Nearest Neighbor (NN) algorithm [4] and Branch and Bound Skyline (BBS) algorithm [5]. The BBS algorithm is currently the most widely used skyline algorithm.

TABLE I. THE HOTEL DATASET

| Hotel | Price | Distance | Hotel | Price | Distance |
|---|---|---|---|---|---|
| A | 10 | 5 | I | 9 | 9 |
| B | 7 | 2.5 | J | 9 | 3 |
| C | 9 | 4 | K | 6.5 | 7 |
| D | 6 | 8.5 | L | 6 | 3.5 |
| E | 4.5 | 9 | M | 10 | 10 |
| F | 4 | 2.8 | N | 5 | 8 |
| G | 1 | 7.5 | R | 2 | 8.7 |
| H | 7 | 8 | S | 4.4 | 7.4 |

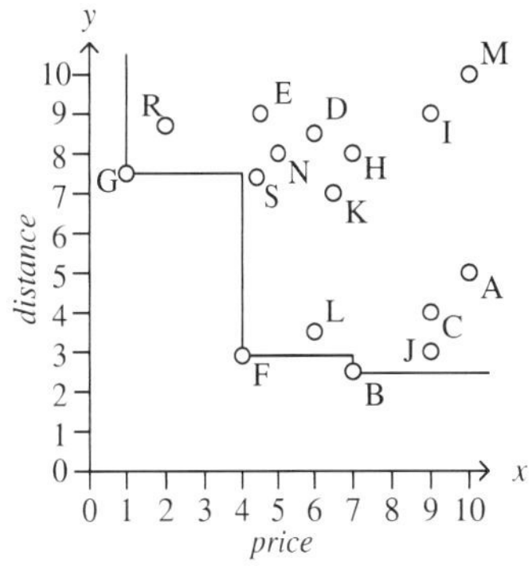


Fig. 1. The hotel dataset.

The BBS algorithm utilizes an R-tree index [3]. Figure 2 presents an R-tree constructed from Fig. 1. The figure shows that in the R-tree similar data points are bundled into the same node. These nodes generally have the minimum area during construction and are termed the minimum bounding rectangle (MBR). With the assistance of the R-tree, the BBS algorithm needs only to read the MBR data points that intersect with the skyline when conducting a search, as shown by the grey-highlighted region in Fig. 3. As illustrated, the BBS algorithm is only required to read B, D, F, G, J, L, N, R, and S in $e_3$, $e_4$, $e_6$, and $e_9$ to conduct its search. Naturally, this reduces I/O costs.

However, the R-tree is not the most suitable index for the BBS algorithm because it has two disadvantages which

This work was supported by NSC under the Grant NSC 100-2221-E-006-249-MY3.

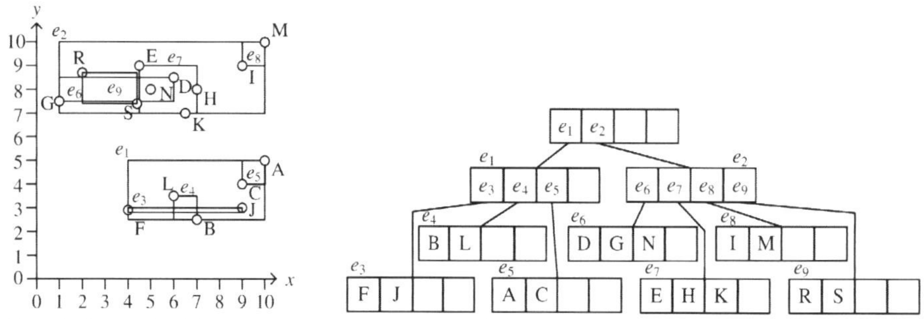


(a) An index result of the R-tree (b) The tree structure of the R-tree.

Figure 2 An example of R-tree.

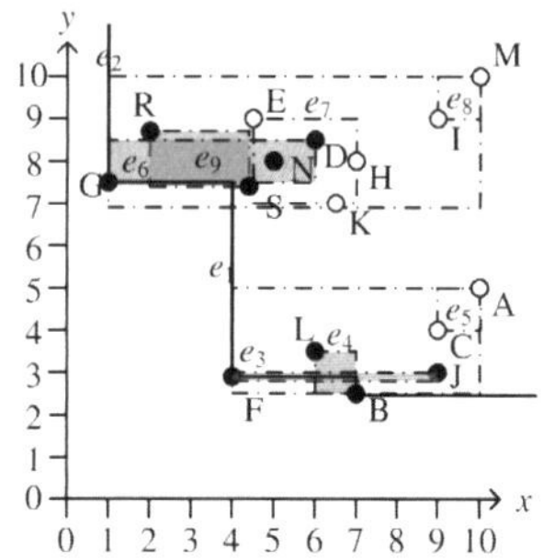

Fig. 3. The loaded MBRs and points in the BBS algorithm.

raise I/O cost. They are (1) repetition in the MBR increases the frequency with which data must be extracted and processed. As shown by Fig. 2(a), when we need to use Node N, because N falls into two overlapping MBRs ($e_6$, $e_7$), we must load $e_6$ and $e_7$ before we can ascertain that N is positioned in $e_6$. Rather than directly reading $e_6$, the need to read additional data from $e_7$ unnecessarily increases I/O cost [6]. (2) Correlation between data points within the same node is low. This is because the R-tree constructs the MBR based solely on area and does not consider the correlations among node data. As shown in Fig. 2(a), the MBR $e_5$ formed by A and C and the MBR $e_3$ formed by F and J both have an area of 1. However, F and J have almost no correlation to speak of. This is to say that when the skyline algorithm reads an MBR, it may also simultaneously read many non-correlated data points, thereby increasing I/O cost. The above discussion shows that using the R-tree in the BBS algorithm may unnecessarily increase I/O costs. The following sections outline our development of an entirely new data structure to replace R-tree and improve the efficiency of skyline queries.

This study developed a Gaussian function-based data structure called the Gaussian-tree (G-tree) to process skyline queries. Compared to the R-tree which is based on node area, the G-tree is constructed in accordance with the Gaussian function. In the G-tree, the node where each data point is located is clearly shown and data within the same node is strongly correlated. Consequently, applying the G-tree to the BBS algorithm can reduce costs. The remainder of this paper is organized as follow: Section 2 defines skyline and describes several previous skyline processing methods. Section 3 outlines the design of the G-tree, while Section 4 explains the methods and advantages of applying the G-tree to the BBS algorithm. Section 5 provides experimental results and lastly Section 6 presents the conclusions of this study.

# 2 Definitions and related works

## 2.1 Definitions

Definitions of skyline are as follows:

**Definition 1**. ***p dominates q.*** *A point p =(p[1],p[2], ...,p[d]) is said to dominate q=( q[1],q[2], ...,q[d]) if and only if p[i]≤q[i] for 1≤ i ≤ d and there exists at least one dimension j such that p[j]<q[j].* ■

**Definition 2**. ***Skyline.*** *A point p is a skyline of S if and only if there does not exist a point q (q ∈S) that q dominates p.* ■

## 2.2 Related work

There are two approaches to solving the skyline problem, which are non-index-based algorithms and index-based algorithms. Unlike non-index-based algorithms, index-based algorithms use an index structure such as the R-tree to improve performance. The following section discusses some of the most well-known algorithms in these two categories.

The first non-index-based algorithms were the block nested loop (BNL) algorithm and divide-and-conquer (DAC) algorithm [1]. These two algorithms did not perform well due to overly high I/O cost. Scholars next proposed bitmap algorithms [2] which mapped all data points to a bitmap and utilized bit-wise operation to enhance efficiency. The greatest problem with this type of algorithm is that all data must be converted to binary format before processing, which is a difficulty also faced by all non-index-based algorithms. All data points must be read and this generates extremely high I/O cost, prompting the development of index-based algorithms as a solution. Data is first processed by an index structure and categorized to negate the need to scan all data during the operation of a skyline algorithm. The most well-known index-based algorithm is the branch-and-bound (BBS) algorithm [5]. The BBS algorithm uses the R-tree to categorize data which eliminates the need to read all data and reduces I/O cost. The BBS algorithm is described in detail in Section 4, in order to identify the respective advantages and disadvantages of using the R-tree and the G-tree in the BBS algorithm.

# 3 G-tree algorithm

This Section is divided into two parts. The first part describes the structure of the proposed G-tree while the second part introduces the G-tree algorithm.

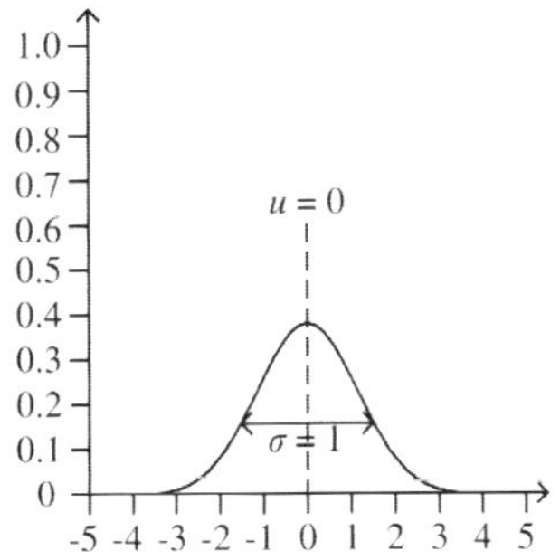


Fig. 4. An example of the Gaussian function.

## 3.1 G-tree structure

Because the G-tree is based on the Gaussian function, before introducing the G-tree we will outline the Gaussian function. The Gaussian function is a normally distributed density function, as shown in (1),

$$f(x) = \frac{1}{\sigma\sqrt{2\pi}} e^{-(x-u)^2/2\sigma^2} \quad (1)$$

Figure 4 illustrates the Gaussian function using axis coordinates, where $u$ is the mean of the function that determines the location of the bell-shaped curve and $\sigma$ is the standard deviation of the function that determines the width of the bell curve. The structure of the G-tree is described in the following.

Figure 5(a) shows the G-tree results built on the scenario in Fig. 1. Figure 5(b) illustrates the corresponding node relationship. Note that for ease of explanation, this study only used two-dimensional examples. Three-dimensional or high-dimensional structures and operational methods can be inferred from the two-dimensional scenarios. The G-tree includes two types of nodes: internal nodes and leaf nodes. As shown in Fig. 5(b), $e_1$ is an example of an internal node and includes other internal nodes such as $e_3$, $e_4$, and $e_5$; $e_5$ is an example of a leaf node and incudes data points such as A, C, and J. In addition, Fig. 5(a) shows that neighbouring nodes are included in the same oval, which in this study is termed the Minimum Bounding Gaussian function (MBG). Figure 5(c) shows that MBG comprises two Gaussian functions $f(x)$ and $f(y)$. The mean and standard deviation of $f(x)$ are $u_x$ and $\sigma_x$, respectively, and the mean and standard deviation of $f(y)$ are $u_y$ and $\sigma_y$, respectively. The MBG comprises three different parameters and one function, being mean $(u_x,u_y)$, standard deviation $(\sigma_x,\sigma_y)$, boundary $\alpha$ and the correlation equation between this node and any data point. The boundary of MBG is shown by the dotted line in the figure. The correlation between this node and any point on this line equals $\alpha$. The correlation between any point in the database and this MBG can be calculated using (2),

$$\mathbf{P}_q = \frac{1}{2\pi\sigma_x\sigma_y}\left(e^{-(\sigma_y{}^2(q_x-u_x)^2+\sigma_x{}^2(q_y-u_y))^2)/2\sigma_x{}^2\sigma_y{}^2}\right) \quad (2)$$

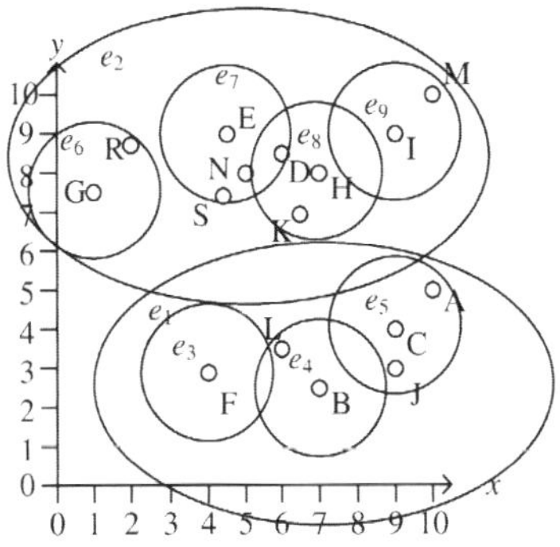


(a) An index result of the G-tree.

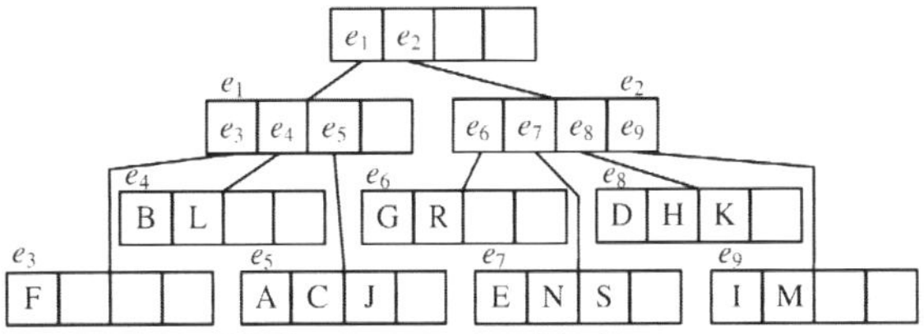


(b) The tree structure of the G-tree.

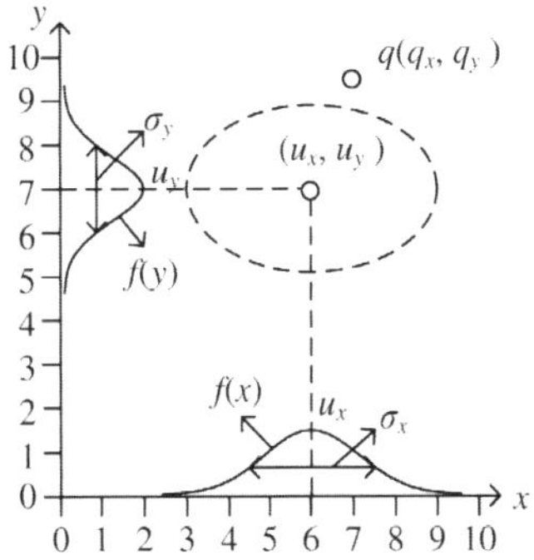


(c) An example of MBG

Fig. 5. An example of the G-tree.

However, because the cost of (2) is very high, it should ideally be excluded from subsequent algorithms. After observing (2), we found that if point $q(q_x,q_y)$ and the mean of an MBG $(u_x,u_y)$ are beyond three standard deviations, then the relationship $P_q$ between $q$ and this MBG would approach 0 and would not fall within this MBG. We therefore eliminated the use of (2) to calculate the probability of $q$ falling within this MBG.

## 3.2 G-tree algorithm

The G-tree comprises three sub-algorithms which are the search algorithm, insert algorithm, and delete algorithm. These are outlined in the following.

### 3.2.1 G-tree search algorithm

A flow chart of the G-tree search algorithm is presented in Fig. 6 and is divided into three parts. Assuming that the search point is $Q$ $(q_x,q_y)$, the first step is to identify the node that $Q$ falls within three standard deviations. These nodes are indicated by **R**. The second step is to calculate the real possibility $Pqr$ $(r \in \mathbf{R})$ that $Q$ falls within the **R** nodes. The

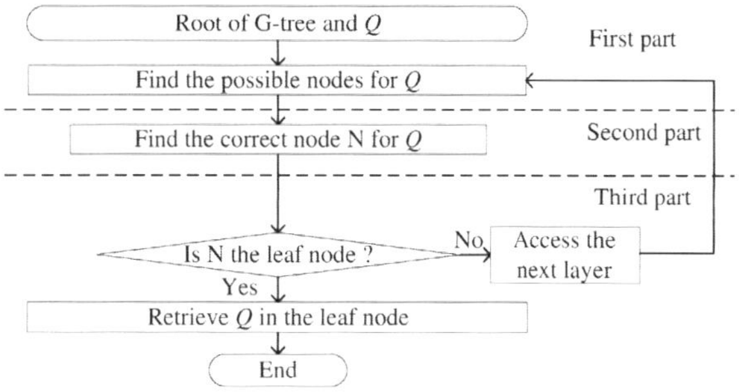


Fig. 6. The flow chat of the G-tree search algorithm.

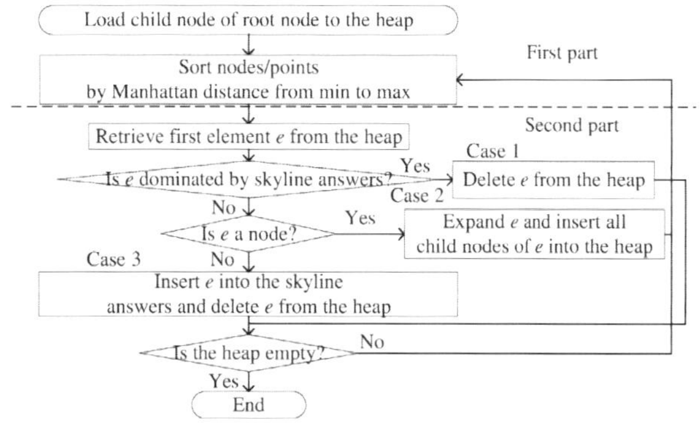


Fig. 8. The flow chat of the BBS algorithm.

node with the highest P*qr* is the node that includes *Q*. The third phase is to determine whether the node is a leaf node. If so, the leaf node is accessed to find *Q* and the search algorithm is completed. If not, we return to step 1 to continue searching for the sub-nodes of this internal node.

Next, we use Figs. 5(a) and 5(b) as examples to further explain the search algorithm. If point D is to be searched, we first insert D and the uppermost layer node of the G-tree into the algorithm, in which this node includes $e_1$, $e_2$. Next we consider the possibility that D falls within $e_1$, $e_2$. Because the distance between D and $e_1$ on *x*, *y* exceeds three standard deviations, D cannot fall within $e_1$. The *x*, *y* dimensionality of D and $e_2$ is less than three standard deviations, so D may fall within $e_2$. Because $e_2$ is the only node that D has any possibility of being included, $e_2$ is determined to be the node that includes D. Lastly, because $e_2$ is not a leaf node, we must recalculate to determine the MBGs into which $e_2$ D might fall. $e_2$ comprises four nodes, $e_6$, $e_7$, $e_8$, and $e_9$. We first consider whether D falls within three standard deviations of $e_6$, $e_7$, $e_8$, or $e_9$, and the results show that D could only be included in nodes $e_7$ and $e_8$. Next, we separately calculate the real possibility that D falls within $e_7$ and $e_8$. $P_D e_7$ is less than $P_D e_8$, which indicates that D must fall within $e_8$. Finally, as $e_8$ is a leaf node, the search function is ended.

### 3.2.2 G-tree insertion

The insertion algorithm for the G-tree is shown in Fig. 7. The insertion point is specified as *I*. We first apply the search algorithm to find a suitable insertion node. Assuming that this node is *N*, there are three possible cases for *N*.

**Case 1: *N* does not exist.** In this case, the algorithm will construct a new *I*-centered MBG and identify the internal

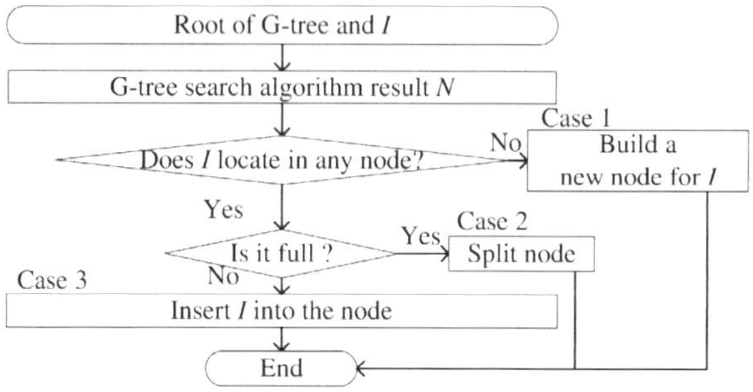


Fig. 7. The flow chat of the G-tree insert algorithm.

nodes that this node can be inserted into. If the distance between *I* and all the MBGs exceeds three standard deviations, then *I* cannot be inserted into any node, in which case we construct a new *I*-centred MBG *e*. After *e* is constructed, the algorithm searches the parent node of *e*. Lastly, the algorithm is used to check the MBGs surrounding *e* and the data points therein are re-allocated in accordance with (2) to nodes with the strongest correlation.

**Case 2: *N* does exist but *N* has already reached maximum capacity.** In this situation, *I* is inserted into *N* and then *N* is split into $N_1$ and $N_2$, where the centre of *N* is the central point of $N_1$ and the furthest point of *N* is the center of $N_2$. Next, the data points surrounding *N* are re-allocated (2) to the nodes to which they are most strongly correlated.

**Case 3: *N* exists and has not yet reached maximum capacity**. In this case, *I* is directly inserted into *N*.

### 3.2.3 G-tree deletion

Assuming that the point of deletion is *D*, the deletion algorithm must first find the node where *D* is located and then determine whether *D* is the center of this node. If not, the algorithm directly deletes *D* from this node. Otherwise, the algorithm first marks the node center as virtual and then deletes *D*.

The section above outlines the basic operation of the Gaussian function-based G-tree. The next section describes the application of G-tree to the skyline algorithm.

# 4 Applying G-tree to the skyline search algorithm

In this Section, we discuss how the G-tree and R-tree are respectively used to complete the BBS algorithm and compare the advantages and disadvantages of each.

## 4.1 R-tree and BBS algorithm

The process of applying the R-tree to the BBS algorithm [5] is shown in Fig.8. The algorithm comprises three data structure, which are the R-tree, a heap, and a list. The heap is used to store temporary data in the algorithm and may include points or MBRs. For ease of explanation, we will refer to these as elements. The list is used to store skyline answer data. All the skyline sets indicated by S and any point in the set is

TABLE II. BBS ALGORITHM: EXAMPLE FOR R-TREE

| Step | Heap | Action | Skyline (S) |
|---|---|---|---|
| 1 | ∅ | Access root | ∅ |
| 2 | <$e_1$, 6.5> <$e_2$, 8> | Expand $e_1$ | ∅ |
| 3 | <$e_3$, 6.8> <$e_2$, 8> <$e_4$, 8.5> <$e_5$, 13> | Expand $e_3$ | ∅ |
| 4 | **<F, 6.8>** <$e_2$, 8> <$e_4$, 8.5> <J, 12> <$e_5$, 13> | Move F to **S** | {F} |
| 5 | <$e_2$, 8> <$e_4$, 8.5> <J, 12> <$e_5$, 13> | Expand $e_2$ | {F} |
| 6 | <$e_4$, 8.5> <$e_6$, 8.5> <$e_9$, 9.4> <$e_7$, 11.5> <J, 12> <$e_5$, 13> <$e_8$, 18> | Expand $e_4$ | {F} |
| 7 | <$e_6$, 8.5> <$e_9$, 9.4> <B, 9.5> <L, 9.5> <$e_7$, 11.5> <J, 12> <$e_5$, 13> <$e_8$, 18> | Expand $e_6$ | {F} |
| 8 | <G, 8.5> <$e_9$, 9.4> <B, 9.5> <L, 9.5> <$e_7$, 11.5> <J, 12> <N, 13> <$e_5$, 13> <D, 14.5> <$e_8$, 18> | Move G to **S** | {F, G} |
| 9 | <$e_9$, 9.4> <B, 9.5> <L, 9.5> <$e_7$, 11.5> <J, 12> <N, 13> <$e_5$, 13> <D, 14.5> <$e_8$, 18> | Expand $e_9$ | {F, G} |
| 10 | <B, 9.5> <L, 9.5> <R, 10.7> <$e_7$, 11.5> <S, 11.8> <J, 12> <N, 13> <$e_5$, 13> <D, 14.5> <$e_8$, 18> | Move B to **S** | {F, G, B} |
| 11 | ~~<L, 9.5>~~ <R, 10.7> <$e_7$, 11.5> <S, 11.8> <J, 12> <N, 13> <$e_5$, 13> <D, 14.5> <$e_8$, 18> | Delete L from Heap | {F, G, B} |
| 12 | ~~<R, 10.7>~~ <$e_7$, 11.5> <S, 11.8> <J, 12> <N, 13> <$e_5$, 13> <D, 14.5> <$e_8$, 18> | Delete R from Heap | {F, G, B} |
| 13 | ~~<$e_7$, 11.5>~~ <S, 11.8> <J, 12> <N, 13> <$e_5$, 13> <D, 14.5> <$e_8$, 18> | Delete $e_7$ from Heap | {F, G, B} |
| 14 | ~~<S, 11.8>~~ <J, 12> <N, 13> <$e_5$, 13> <D, 14.5> <$e_8$, 18> | Delete S from Heap | {F, G, B} |
| 15 | ~~<J, 12>~~ <N, 13> <$e_5$, 13> <D, 14.5> <$e_8$, 18> | Delete J from Heap | {F, G, B} |
| 16 | ~~<N, 13>~~ <$e_5$, 13> <D, 14.5> <$e_8$, 18> | Delete N from Heap | {F, G, B} |
| 17 | ~~<$e_5$, 13>~~ <D, 14.5> <$e_8$, 18> | Delete $e_5$ from Heap | {F, G, B} |
| 18 | ~~<D, 14.5>~~ <$e_8$, 18> | Delete D from Heap | {F, G, B} |
| 19 | ~~<$e_8$, 18>~~ | Delete $e_8$ from Heap | {F, G, B} |
| 20 | ∅ | End | {F, G, B} |

expressed as *s* (*s*∈ S). The algorithm is divided into two parts; in the first part, the algorithm inputs internal nodes under the root node into the heap. Note that the elements in the heap are arranged in ascending order according to their Manhattan distance [5]. In the second phase, the uppermost element *e* of the heap is extracted and checked for domination with each point in **S**. This will produce one of three types of results:

**Case 1:** If the *e* is dominated by the existing skyline answer *s*, then the algorithm deletes *e* from the heap.

**Case 2:** If *e* cannot be dominated by the existing skyline answers and is an MBR, then the algorithm expands *e* and places its internal nodes or data points into the heap. Next, the algorithm repeats part 1.

**Case 3:** If *e* cannot be dominated by the existing skyline answers and is a data point, then the algorithm will input e into S and delete it from the heap.

The BBS algorithm is completed when all the elements in the heap have been checked (i.e., the heap is empty). At this point, **S** is the final skyline answer.

Table II is extended from Fig. 2 as an example of applying the R-tree to the BBS algorithm. In Step 1, the algorithm extracts the root node of the R-tree and adds $e_1$ and $e_2$ to the heap according to their Manhattan distance. In Step 2 the first element $e_1$ is extracted from the heap. Because **S** is ∅, $e_1$ cannot be dominated by the existing skyline, which matches the scenario in Case 2. Consequently, $e_1$ is expanded into $e_3$, $e_4$, and $e_5$. These MBRs are inserted into the heap based on their Manhattan distance. Step 3 - Step 20 repeats the above-described processes. As Steps 4, 11, and 20 are a further interpretation of Cases 1 and 3, these steps are further discussed below.

In Step 4 the first element F is extracted from the heap. However, **S** is empty; therefore, F cannot be considered as dominated by the existing skyline, which matches Case 3. Therefore, F is the skyline answer and we input F into **S**. In Step 7, the first element in the heap is L, and from Fig. 2(a) we can derive that L will be dominated by F as described in Case 1. Consequently, L is eliminated from the heap. In Step 20, if the heap is empty then the skyline algorithm comes to an end. The final skyline answer is **S**={F, G, B}.

## 4.2 G-tree and BBS algorithm

This section explains how to use the G-tree in the BBS algorithm. Firstly, because MBG is an oval, the BBS algorithm cannot be directly inputted as in the rectangular MBR. Before applying the G-tree to the BBS algorithm, we must first record the minimum dimensional values of each MBG.

An extension of Fig. 5(a), Table III is an example of using the G-tree to complete the BBS algorithm. The methodology of this table is largely similar to that of Table 2. Due to space limitations this study does not expound further on this example. The paragraphs below use Tables 2 and 3 to compare the advantages and disadvantages of the G-tree and the R-tree.

Step 3 of Fig. 2(a) shows that both F (which is correlated with the skyline) and J (which is not correlated with the skyline) are read when $e_3$ is expanded. However, in Step 3 in Fig. 5(b) and Table III, only F is read when $e_3$ is

TABLE III. BBS ALGORITHM: EXAMPLE FOR G-TREE

| Step | Heap | Action | Skyline (**S**) |
|---|---|---|---|
| 1 | ∅ | Access root | ∅ |
| 2 | <$e_1$, 6.5> <$e_2$, 8> | Expand $e_1$ | ∅ |
| 3 | <$e_3$, 6.8> <$e_2$, 8> <$e_4$, 8.5> <$e_5$, 12> | Expand $e_3$ | ∅ |
| 4 | **<F, 6.8>** <$e_2$, 8> <$e_4$, 8.5> <$e_5$, 12> | Move F to **S** | {F} |
| 5 | <$e_2$, 8> <$e_4$, 8.5> <$e_5$, 12> | Expand $e_2$ | {F} |
| 6 | <$e_4$, 8.5> <$e_6$, 8.5> <$e_7$, 11.8> <$e_5$, 12> <$e_8$, 13> <$e_9$, 18> | Expand $e_4$ | {F} |
| 7 | <$e_6$, 8.5> <B, 9.5> <L, 9.5> <$e_7$, 11.8> <$e_5$, 12> <$e_8$, 13> <$e_9$, 18> | Expand $e_6$ | {F} |
| 8 | <G, 8.5> <B, 9.5> <L, 9.5> <$e_7$, 11.8> <$e_5$, 12> <$e_8$, 13> <$e_9$, 18> | Move G to **S** | {F, G} |
| 9 | <B, 9.5> <L, 9.5> <R, 10.7> <$e_7$, 11.8> <$e_5$, 12> <$e_8$, 13> <$e_9$, 18> | Move B to **S** | {F, G, B} |
| 10 | ~~<L, 9.5>~~ <R, 10.7> <$e_7$, 11.8> <$e_5$, 12> <$e_8$, 13> <$e_9$, 18> | Delete L from Heap | {F, G, B} |
| 11 | ~~<R, 10.7>~~ <$e_7$, 11.8> <$e_5$, 12> <$e_8$, 13> <$e_9$, 18> | Delete R from Heap | {F, G, B} |
| 12 | ~~<$e_7$, 11.8>~~ <$e_5$, 12> <$e_8$, 13> <$e_9$, 18> | Delete $e_7$ from Heap | {F, G, B} |
| 13 | ~~<$e_5$, 12>~~ <$e_8$, 13> <$e_9$, 18> | Delete $e_5$ from Heap | {F, G, B} |
| 14 | ~~<$e_8$, 13>~~ <$e_9$, 18> | Delete $e_8$ from Heap | {F, G, B} |
| 15 | ~~<$e_9$, 18>~~ | Delete $e_9$ from Heap | {F, G, B} |
| 16 | ∅ | End | {F, G, B} |

TABLE IV. A SUMMARY OF EXPERIMENT PARAMETERS

| Parameter | Range of value |
|---|---|
| Dimensionality (*d*) | **2**、3、4、5、6 |
| Data size (*s*) | **100k**、100m |
| Node size (*n*) | **50**、100、150、200 |

expanded. This indicates that by using the G-tree we can avoid loading data points that are not correlated with the skyline in the BBS Algorithm.

In Steps 7 and 9 of Fig. 2(a) and Table II, it is evident that because the nodes of the R-tree are highly repetitious, the skyline may have multiple intersecting MBRs. For example, the skyline between G and F will intersect with MBRs $e_6$ and $e_9$. Therefore in Steps 7 and 9 $e_6$ and $e_9$ must be expanded. However in Step 3 of Fig. 5(b) and Table III, the same stretch of skyline only intersects with a single MBG. For example, the skyline between G and F will only intersect with $e_6$, which means that only $e_6$ must be expanded. Combining the G-tree rather than the R-tree with the BBS algorithm reduces I/O cost because the repetition between MBGs is avoided.

# 5 Performance

This section describes a number of experiments conducted to verify the effectiveness of the G-tree, using three types of data distribution [2] [5] that are frequently employed for skyline purposes. These are the independent dataset, the anti-correlated dataset, and the correlated dataset. Generally, the anti-correlated dataset is the worst case for the skyline problem, as it produces the highest number of skyline results. The correlated dataset is the best case because it produces the fewest skyline results. The independent dataset is considered a general case [2] [5]. Our first experiment dealt with the time relationship between data size and skyline searching. The second dealt with the time relationship between node size and skyline searching. We did not test for cardinality in this simulation because skyline search time shows linear growth in accordance with cardinality.

The parameter range is presented in Table IV, with the default parameters marked in bold. All of our experiments were conducted using Intel Core i5-750 2.6GHz,4GB main memory, windows 7 64bit. The C compiler was used for all of our programs.

We first analyze the time relationship between dimensionality and skyline searching. Figures 9(a), 9(b), and 9(c) show the time costs of using the independent dataset, anti-correlated dataset, and correlated dataset, respectively. Four phenomena are observed in these figures. First regardless of data form, the time required to compute the BBS algorithm was shorter when using G-tree compared to R-tree. The data points in the R-tree MBRs are not usually strongly correlated, and as a result, when each MBR is expanded, the BBS algorithm must process many non-correlated data points. In contrast, the data points in the G-tree MBGs are usually highly correlated which saves the BBS algorithm from having to process non-correlated data. It is more effective to compute the BBS algorithm using the G-tree as compared to using R-tree. Next, after observing the experimental results of the three dataset types, we found that regardless of whether we used the G-tree or R-tree, the skyline search times were as follows: anti-correlated dataset > independent dataset > correlated dataset. The anti-correlated dataset is the most time consuming because it has the most skyline answers and so must read more nodes and search more frequently for dominated data points. The correlated dataset requires less time because it has the least skyline answers, which means that the I/O cost required to complete the search is reduced. Third, in most cases, the time cost of both the G-tree and the R-tree grows exponentially with dimension, because the I/O cost required for the dataset skylines also grows exponentially [2][5]. However, in the R-tree of the anti-correlated dataset, although time cost also increases with dimension, it converges to a fixed value. This is because in a high-dimension anti-correlated dataset, almost all the nodes must be inserted. In these circumstances, the I/O cost of using the

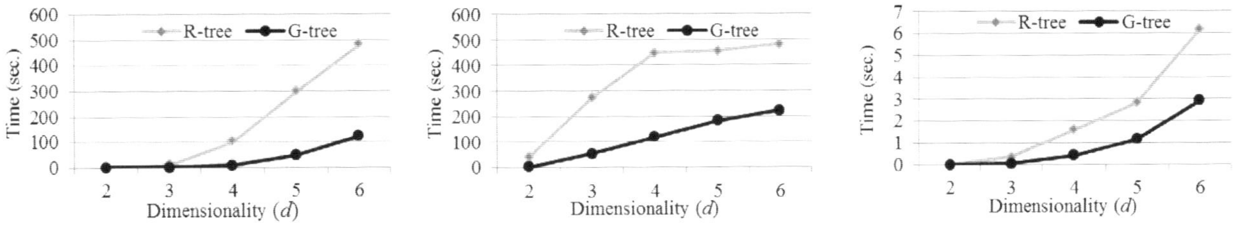


(a) Independent dataset. (b) Anti-correlated dataset. (c) Correlated dataset.

Fig. 9. Time relationship between dimensionality and skyline searching.

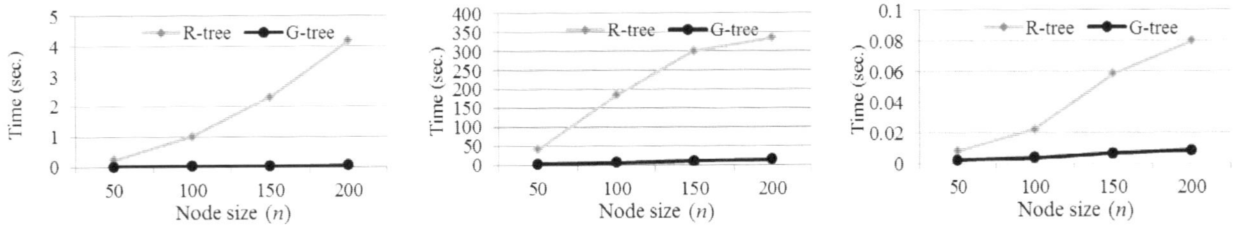


(a) Independent dataset. (b) Anti-correlated dataset. (c) Correlated dataset.

Fig. 10. Time relationship between node size and skyline searching.

R-tree for the BBS algorithm does not differ significantly, which is why time cost converges.

Next we discuss the time relationship between node size and skyline searching. Figures 10(a), 10(b), and 10(c) show the time costs of using the independent dataset, anti-correlated dataset, and correlated dataset, respectively. As demonstrated, regardless of node size, the G-tree was far more time-efficient than the R-tree, and this difference became more pronounced as node size increased. This phenomenon can be attributed to two reasons. First, Unlike the R-tree, the G-tree does not need to process multiple data points which are not correlated with the skyline. Second, Nodes in the R-tree are repetitious and become even more so as node size increases. This results in a high volume of intersection among MBRs, which means that more MBRs must be expanded, which in turn raises I/O costs and time cost. In the G-tree however, nodes are not distinctly repetitious even when node size increases. This means that fewer MBGs intersect with the skyline and translates into lower I/O cost and time cost.

# 6 Conclusions

This paper introduced a novel index structure G-tree to upgrade the performance of a skyline query. The disadvantages of using the R-tree in the skyline algorithm were explored in the paper. The structure and algorithms of G-tree were introduced. Some analyses were given to explain the merits of using the G-tree in the skyline algorithm. Finally, the performance study confirmed the efficiency of using the G-tree in the skyline algorithm. In our next step, we plan to apply the G-tree in other type of skyline query and demonstrate that G-tree is more suitable for all types of skyline queries than R-tree.

# 7 References

[1] S. Borzsonyi, D. Kossmann, and K. Stocker, "The skyline operator," *proceeding on ICDE*, pp. 235-254, 2001.

[2] K. L. Tan, P. K. Eng, B. C. Ooi, "Efficient progressive skyline computation," *proceeding on VLDB*, pp. 301-310, 2001.

[3] A. Guttman, "R-trees: A dynamic index structure for spatial searching," *SIGMOD Record*, vol. 14, no. 2, pp. 47-57, 1984.

[4] D. Kossmann, F. Ramsak, and S. Rost, "Shooting stars in the sky: an online algorithm for skyline queries," *proceeding on VLDB*, 2002.

[5] D. Papadias, Y. Tao, G. Fu, and B. Seeger, "An optimal and progressive algorithm for skyline queries," *proceeding in SIGMOD*, 2003.

[6] N. Beckmann, H. P. Kriegel, R. Schneider, and B. Seeger, "The R*-tree: an efficient and robust access method for points and rectangles," *proceeding on SIGMOD*, 1990.

# Relevance Feedback for Collaborative Retrieval Based on Semantic Annotations

Fatiha NAOUAR*, Lobna HLAOUA*, Mohamed Nazih OMRI*

*MARS Unit of Research, Department of computer sciences

Faculty of sciences of Monastir, University of Monastir

Monastir, 5000, Tunisia

**Abstract** - *A collaborative retrieval, based on the concept of sharing between users, is increasingly used to facilitate the research and to satisfy the needs. In this context, we suggest to improve the performance of collaborative research, taking account of the annotations as a new source of information describing the documents. In our contribution, we suggest to apply the relevance feedback to expand the user query. We also suggest a new approach based on co-occurrence to extract the relevant terms from annotations in the semi-structured documents returned by the collaborative retrieval systems. Experiments have shown their interest especially for the top ten documents returned by the system that have exceeded a value of 70% as the improvement rate.*

**Keywords:** Collaborative retrieval system, co-occurrence, annotation, relevance feedback.

## 1 Introduction

Information retrieval has been one of the main human activities for a long time. Learn quickly and effectively find information in its environment has always been a necessity. To achieve this result, a development of the mode of work is done from autonomy to cooperation. This evolution has been shown to improve the performance of the research, particularly as regarding the number of found relevant information and the time taken to perform the search. Working in collaboration allows the sharing of historical research and the formulation of collaborative applications. This can be done in several ways including annotations that involve assigning a set of keywords. Despite this collaborative environment, the user still has many problems to express his needs by the bad choice of terms for his modest knowledge. It is in this context that we suggest to improve the performance of collaborative research using the relevance feedback to expand the original query. This technique consists of extracting terms from documents considered relevant and considers a new query extended. It has already been applied in classical IR [16] and semi-structured Information Retrieval [6] and has shown its interest. In our research work we consider annotations as a new source of information because it allows us to describe the document with judgments of the users. However, the works of searches that are based on the annotations can give results relatively preferment, since the annotations can be performed by experts or non-specialist users.

Thus the relevance feedback, using annotations in a collaborative framework, brings us to solve two main problems, namely the choice of annotations that are carriers of data to consider and the extraction of relevant terms as they may be reinjected to extend the query?

Several researches have been interested in the validation annotations. We have focused in this work on the extraction of relevant terms used in the valid annotations. To do this, we suggest an approach based on co-occurrence of words annotations.

The next section presents a literature on the methods developed for a better collaborative research. We then describe our approach to extract information in section 3. In Section 4 we describe the experiments performed and results obtained. Finally, in Section 5, we discuss the perspectives of our work.

## 2 Related Works

The development of the work mode from autonomy to cooperation has shown an improvement in search performance of the users in several researches works [3] [4], regarding the number of relevant information found and the time needed to perform the search. Collaborative search can reduce the search time to share histories with others.

Indeed, the collaborative work can be done in a synchronous manner through instant messages or in an asynchronous manner through email and annotations. Collaborative search can reduce the search time by users of the same profile, to formulate collaborative queries through dialogue and mutual consultation of queries sent and the search results received by everyone. It also allows sharing search histories by displaying search results in order of relevance. Several techniques are used in this context: among the most popular tools for sharing results and personal judgment are the annotations.

According to several studies, the annotation can be performed by the contents of the document or from an external source to the document [7] [10]. Despite the importance of annotations for its link binding to the document, annotations can be carried out by specialist users or non-specialists. In this context, several research projects were conducted to determine whether the annotations are considered "correct" or not setting a platform for social validation and judgment of 173 participants [2].

To improve the performance of the collaborative research, we find that the main approaches are based on historical research or on support systems or suggested the profiles of the users [11] [15].

We note that the problem is always a problem of data mining, which has been developed in several works. We can mention the work of Omri [13] which is based on the flexible systems of knowledge extraction and are capable of to facing the vagueness and uncertainty of the extraction process. Other works have been trying to develop systems for extracting knowledge from the Web [5] or more precisely from Wikipedia [1]: These methods are based on the grammatical analysis of words for a specific language.

In our work, to extract the relevant terms of valid annotations for relevance feedback, we made use of the concept of semantic terms. We are interested in exploiting an approach based on the co-occurrence of terms and the calculation of relevance will be performed according to a possibilistic model.

## 3 An approach based on co-occurrence for Information extraction

### 3.1 Motivation

Our objective is to enrich the initial query composed of simple user's keywords by relevance feedback in order to find relevant information. In view of the importance of the annotations in Collaborative Research, we have considered them a new source of information that can really describe the document. Since the relevance of a term is not certain: we talk about a degree of relevance which expresses a preference of the user. We use the theory of possibility which translates the uncertainty, then the notion of possibility. Our model is based on a possibilistic network to present the various dependency relationships. This approach will be detailed in the next section.

While examining the annotations, we distinguished the appearance of the original query's terms in the latter.

It is in this context that we thought of distinguishing the two types of appearance: the terms that appear just before or after a term of the query and the terms that appear from a distance of $d > 1$ from term of the query. Thus, we calculate the relevance of a term of the annotation.

## 3.2 Architecture of the model

We suggest a model based on a possibilistic network (Figure 1) which nodes represent documents D composed of several annotations $A_i$. Each annotation can be made of a set of terms $T_i$. The query Q is an original user query which also consists of a few terms as $N_j$. Arcs represent the dependency relationships.

The nodes $A_i$ represent elements "Annotation". Each node $A_i$ is a binary random variable taking the values in the set $dom(A_i) = \{a_i, \neg a_i\}$. The instantiation $A_i = a_i$ means that the $A_i$ is relevant to the document D. The instantiation $A_i = \neg a_i$ means that the $A_i$ is irrelevant for the document D. The instantiation $W_i = \neg w_i$ means that the word $W_i$ is not representative of $M_i$ parent node to which is connected. Each variable $A_i$ depends directly on parent node is the root node D in possibilistic network. Thus, each variable $W_i$, $W_i \in W = \{W_1, W_2, \dots W_n\}$ depends only on the parent node is an annotation. We consider that W(A) is the set of words constituting the annotation A and W (Q) is the set of words constituting the query Q.

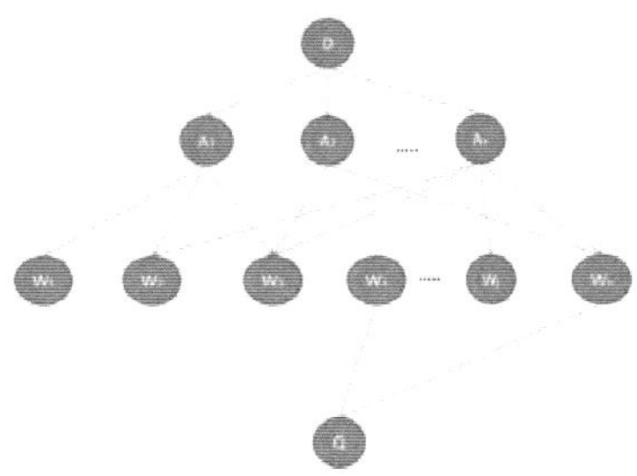

Figure 1. The model based on possibilistic network

## 3.3 Calculation of relevance according to the possibilistic model

The relevance of a term is based on the following two definitions: ***Definition 1***: A term of the annotation is considered necessarily relevant if it is juxtaposed to a term which appears in the query. ***Definition 2:*** A term of the annotation is considered potentially relevant if it is in co-occurrence with a term constituting the query.

The relevance in our case is defined by the co-occurrence and proximity of the term of the annotation in relation to the term constituting the initial query. The concept of co-occurrence refers to the general phenomenon by which words may be used in the same context [9]. So the co-occurrence reflects that the presence of a word constituting the query gives an indication of the presence of another word of the annotation. While the proximity translates that a word is juxtaposed with the word of annotation which appears in the query.

To evaluate the relevance of a term by co-occurrence we calculated the index of co-occurrence of two terms: a term of the query and a term belonging to a valid annotation. The index of co-occurrence measures the relationship between the words, more this index is higher, more the terms are semantically related. Specifically, more the index is higher, more the term annotation is seen necessary to be added to the original query. In our work, this index is expressed in the distance. In this case more the terms are related, more the distance is weak. In general, the co-occurrence index ignores the order of words. In the framework of our model the co-occurrence frequency C of a term $t_i$ of the query Q is represented by a vector $C(t_i) = (c_{i1}, c_{i2}, \dots, c_{i|A|})$. Each component $c_{ij}$ is the frequency of co-occurrence of the term $t_i$ if the query Q with a term $a_j$ of the annotation [14]. We have built in this case a data matrix in which each row of the vector represents the different terms ($t_1$,

$t_2,\ldots, t_m$) constituting the query Q, and each column of the vector represents the different words ($a_1$, $a_2$, …, $a_n$) constituting a valid annotation. For each term in the query of co-occurrence a value is calculated with every word of the annotation. The figure 2 represents the matrix found.

| | $a_1$ | $a_2$ | $a_3$ | …. | $a_n$ |
|---|---|---|---|---|---|
| $t_1$ | $c_{11}$ | $c_{12}$ | $c_{13}$ | …. | $c_{1n}$ |
| $t_2$ | $c_{21}$ | $c_{22}$ | $c_{23}$ | …. | $c_{2n}$ |
| …. | …. | …. | …. | …. | …. |
| $t_m$ | $c_{m1}$ | $c_{m2}$ | $c_{m3}$ | …. | $c_{mn}$ |

Figure 2 : Example of co-occurrence matrix

## 3.4 Association of Terms

Our objective is to improve the performance of collaborative retrieval systems using valid annotations of documents returned by a search system. Our work consists mainly of selecting the correct annotations of documents resulting from a user query to extract the relevant terms according to our model, reformulate and compare. These documents can be text, image or video. Once the terms are extracted, we calculate values $C_{ij}$. The values $C_{ij}$ are evaluated using the following formula:

$$C_{1i} = fp(t_1, a_i|A) \qquad (1)$$

To give a representative sense of a word of a valid annotation for a relevant document, we used the factor fp ie frequency of appearance of the pairs of words. It is from this value that we can measure the association of co-occurrence.

Calculating the frequency of occurrence of pairs of terms is calculated using the following formula:

$$fp(t_1, a_i|A) = \frac{\sum_{i=1..n} Occ(t_1, a_i)}{size(A)} \qquad (2)$$

With size(A) is the size of annotations valid and $Occ(t_1, a_i)$ is the number of occurrences at a distance d from the term $t_1$ of query and the terms $a_i$ constituting a valid annotation A. It is defined by the following formula:

$$Occ(t_1, a_1) = \sum_{k=1..n} 1/d_k \qquad (3)$$

To give an importance to the position of appearance of a term a1 of an annotation A with respect to a term $t_1$ of the initial query, we considered in our work the distance d. The distance is determined by the number of words between $t_1$ and $a_1$ given by the formula:

$$d_k(t_1, a_1) = Nb(M_i \in [t_1, a_1]) \;\; With\; i = 1..n \qquad (4)$$

For a query term $t_1$ and a word of a valid annotation $a_1$, we can calculate their presence and their absence. These data are presented in the following possibility table:

Table I: Possibility table for calculating the degree of association between t1 and a1

| | $a_1$ present | $a_1$ absent |
|---|---|---|
| $t_1$ present | Val1 | Val2 |
| $t_1$ absent | Val3 | Val4 |

The calculation of the degree of association is based on the data in Table 1 which contains the frequency of appearance of a pair of words: a term in the query and a word from a valid annotation. The value **Val1** represents the number of times the term $t_1$ and the word $a_1$ appear together, the value **Val2** represents the number of times the term $t_1$ appear without the word $a_1$, the value **Val3** represents the number of times the word $a_1$ appears without the term $t_1$ and the value **Val4** represents the number of times any of the two words appear.

We have defined in this framework that the context must include a term in the query and a word of a valid annotation to consider that they appear together. The co-occurrence in this context is seen as the tendency of a term in the query and a word that appears in a valid annotation.

To estimate the semantic dependency between a query term $\mathbf{t_1}$ and a word $\mathbf{a_1}$ from a valid annotation, we used the possibility defined as follows:

- The possibility that the term $\mathbf{t_1}$ and the word $\mathbf{a_1}$ both:

$$E_{11} = Poss1 \cdot Poss2 \cdot N \qquad (5)$$

Witch, **Poss1** is the possibility that the term **t1** appears, and **Poss2** is the possibility that the word **a1** appears, defined as follows:

$$Poss1 = (\mathbf{Val1} + \mathbf{Val2}) / N \qquad (6)$$

$$Poss2 = (\mathbf{Val1} + \mathbf{Val3}) / N \qquad (7)$$

With **Val1**, **Val2** and **Val3** are the values represented in Table 1. In our work, **Val1** is calculated by the formula (2), N is the total number of valid annotations, **Val3** is equal to zero while **Val2** is calculated by the formula (3).

# 4 Experiments and results

Our objective in this section is to measure the contribution of the relevance feedback based on annotations.

## 4.1 Evaluation framework

To do so, we have considered the environment of the following evaluation:

- A collaborative retrieval system: We chose the « YouTube » which is a popular and social system and which can offer a collaborative service of annotation of Multimedia resources.

- A collection of document: It will be built by the documents returned by the system itself and which will be saved for the extraction of different parts already described in the previous sections.

We started with 9 queries in different areas and the judgment was made by students and researchers.

To evaluate our approach, we used the precision rate for the 5, 10 and 20 first documents using relevance feedback residual. The use of residual diagram is able to show the actual impact of relevance feedback (instead of freezing method). In the residual evaluation, the documents which are used for the re-injection are removed from the collection. For each query, the number of judged documents is marked until the first relevant document is judged. In the following, the results based on the test correspond to the residual value.

To evaluate the efficiency of our approach, we calculated the rate of improvement TA for different queries as follows:

$$TA = \frac{new\,precision - old\,precision}{old\,precision} \qquad (8)$$

With TA (5) the rate of improvement is to show the importance of relevance feedback of the top five documents and TA (10) and TA (20) to show the performance of respectively the top 10 and the top 20 documents found. The new precision and the old precision are respectively the results of the research after relevance feedback and basic results, in the same residual collection.

## 4.2 The impact of co-occurrence for the extraction of relevant terms

In this section, we study the impact of co-occurrence criterion to extract the relevant terms of the annotation judged "correct". For each term of each query, we calculate the frequency of appearance of pairs of annotation terms. To reformulate a query, we added the term with the highest score without taking into account the terms already included in the original query. Table 2 contains the results compared with basic execution.

According to Table 2, we note that the precision is improved compared to the original query particularly in the top 10 returned documents. It reaches an

| | 5 Docs | 10 Docs | 20 Docs |
|---|---|---|---|
| Average initial precision | 0.2 | 0.19 | 0.18 |
| Average precision Reformulation | 0.23 | 0.29 | 0.30 |

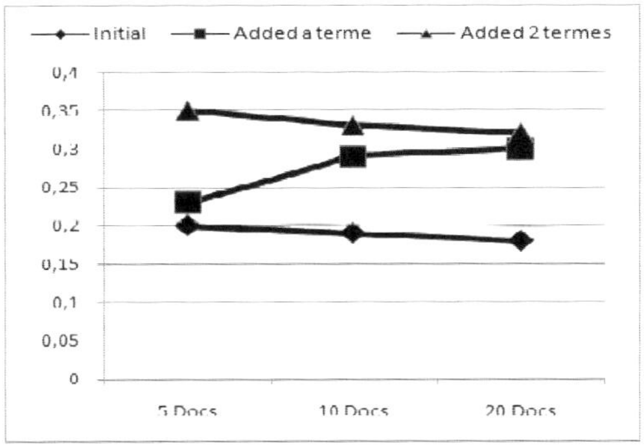


| | 5 Docs | 10 Docs | 20 Docs |
|---|---|---|---|
| Precision Initial | 0.2 | 0.19 | 0.18 |
| Precision after Reformulation | 0.35 | 0.33 | 0.32 |

| | TA (5) | TA (10) | TA (20) |
|---|---|---|---|
| Added a term | 15% | 53% | 67% |
| Added 2 terms | 75% | 74% | 78% |

broadening our test database and checking the stability of these results.

# 6 References

[1] S. Auer, C. Bizer, G. kobilarov, J. Lehmann, R. Cyganiak and Z. Ives. "DBpedia: A Nucleus for a Web of Open Data". In *Proc. of ISWC 2007 (Busan, Korea)*. November 2007.

[2] G. Cabanac. "Annotation collective dans le contexte RI : définition d'une plate-forme pour expérimenter la validation sociale". In *Conférence en Recherche d'Information et Applications, CORIA 2008*. p.385-392. 2008.

[3] E.T. Diamadis and G.C. Polyzos. "Efficient cooperative searching on the Web: system design and evaluation", In *International Journal of Human-Computer Studies*, 61, 699-724, 2004.

[4] J. Dinet. "Deux têtes cherchent mieux qu'une ? " In *Medialog*, 63. 2007.

[5] G. Grefenstette. "Conquering language: Using NLP on a massive scale to build high dimensional language models from the web". *In Proceedings of the 8th International Conference on Computational Linguistics and Intelligent Text Processing*, pages 35. 2007.

[6] L. Hlaoua. "Reformulation de requêtes par structure en RI dans les documents XML", *CORIA 2006, Lyon*. 2006.

[7] K. Khelif, R. Dieng-Kuntz and P. Barbry, "An ontology-based approach to support text mining and information retrieval in the biological domain", *Special Issue on Ontologies and their Applications of the Journal of Universal Computer Science (JUCS)*, Vol. 13, No. 12, pp. 1881-1907, 2007.

[8] C. Lioma M.F. Moens and L. Azzopardi. "Collaborative annotation for pseudo relevance feedback", *ECIR workshop on exploiting semantic annotation in information retrieval (ESAIR 2008)*. 2008.

[9] N. Manning and H. Schütze. "Foundations of Statistical Natural Language Processing". *MIT Press, Cambridge, United States,* May 1999.

[10] N. Mokhtari et R. Dieng-Kuntz. "Extraction et exploitation des annotations contextuelles", *Extraction et gestion des connaissances (EGC'2008)*. 2008.

[11] H. Naderi, B. Rumpler and J.M. Pinon. "An Efficient Collaborative Information Retrieval System by Incorporating the User Profile". *Adaptive Multimedia Retrieval: User, Context, and Feedback Lecture Notes in Computer Science*. 2007.

[12] W. Njmogue, D. Fontaine et P. Fontaine, "Identification des thèmes d'un document relativement à un référentiel métier", *In Proceedings of MAJECSTIC'04*, Calais, France, 2004.

[13] M.-N. Omri. "Pertinent Knowledge Extraction from a Semantic Network: Application of Fuzzy Sets Theory". In *International Journal on Artificial Intelligence Tools (IJAIT)*. Vol. 13, No. 3, p. 705-719. 2004.

[14] M. Rajman and T A. Bonne. "Corpora-base linguistics: new tools for natural language processing". In *1st Annual Conference of the Association for Global Strategic Information, Bad Kreuznach,* Germany. 1992.

[15] T. Razan. "Soutien Personnalisé pour la Recherche d'Information Collaborative". In *2ème Congrès MAJECSTIC 2004. Manifestation de JEunes Chercheurs Sciences et Technologies de l'Information et de la Communication*, Calais, France. 2004.

[16] J. Rocchio. "Relevance feedback in information retrieval", *The SMART retrieval system-experiments in automatic document processing*, Prentice Hall Inc, p. 313,323. 1971.

[17] R. Vivian et J. Dinet. "La recherche collaborative d'information ; vers un système centre utilisateur". *Les cahiers du numérique*. 2008a.

# A System for Keyword Search on Probability XML Data

**Weidong Yang[1], Hao Zhu[1], Zheng Zheng[1], Huirong Chen[2], Lei Wang[2]**
[1]Computer School, Fudan University, Shanghai, China
[2]Commercial Aircraft Corporation of China, Ltd, Shanghai, China

**Abstract**— *Many probabilistic XML data models have been proposed to store XML data with uncertainty information, and based on them the issues such as structured querying are extensively studied. As an alternative to structured querying, keyword search in probabilistic XML data needs to be concerned. In this paper we addressed the issue of keyword search on probabilistic XML data. The probabilistic XML data is viewed as a labeled tree, and a concept of Minimum Meaningful Fragment (MMF) is defined as the searching result. A MMF is a minimum subtree of the probabilistic XML data which has a positive probability of containing all keywords. To sort the MMFs a novel scoring function mainly considering the degree of uncertainty information is presented. We propose a system to compute top-k searching results efficiently based on the scoring function. The experiments shows the efficiency for our system.*

**Keywords:** Probabilistic XML Data, Keyword Search

## 1. Introduction

Recently, there is a growing interest in researching XML data with uncertainty. In the last few years, a plethora of probabilistic XML data models have been proposed [4], [7], [1], [2], [5], [3], and most of them are modeled in trees. B. Kimelfeld et al. performed an elaborate survey of them in [6]. They also presented a flexible model called *p-documents* in [5], trying to cover all existing ones. To the best of our knowledge, there is no research about keyword search in probabilistic XML data before this. However, it is very natural to employ keyword search over probabilistic XML data. As a typical scenario, integrating heterogeneous XML data not only generates a mass of uncertainty in the result, but also lets the schemas go out of control. As an effective information discovery technique keyword search is very suitable to such a case [9].

On the other hand, many effective approaches have been proposed to do keyword search on XML data, and the most popular ones of them are the SLCA (Smallest Lowest Common Ancestor) method [8]. In SLCA method the XML document is viewed as a rooted, labeled, unordered tree and a searching result is defined as a subtree of it that: (1) the labels of whose nodes contain all the keywords, (2) none of its subtree satisfies the first condition except itself. The root of such a subtree is called a SLCA node. Similarly, ELCA method is trying to find a set of ELCA nodes which is a superset of all SLCA nodes. There is a naive way to find all ELCA nodes, and this will help us to understand the concept of an ELCA node: first, retrieve all SLCA nodes and remove all the subtrees rooted in them from the tree; second, repeat the first step until there is no SLCA node can be found.

To evaluate queries on probabilistic data, a well known model adopted is the *possible world* model in which each possible world of the original data is a piece of deterministic data with its existence probability. The query will be executed upon each possible world and some deterministic results can be obtained. Afterwards all the same results are clustered into one with their corresponding possible world's probabilities being summed up. At last, a group of separate results are obtained and each is attached with a value to indicate its probability of existence. The same model is adopted by us. The searching object is defined as a *Probabilistic XML Tree* which is a family from *p-documents* (denoted as $\mathsf{PrXML}^{\{ind,mux\}}$ in [5]). In a naive way, we generate all the possible pieces of the tree and calculate the probabilities, then evaluate the keyword search on them and retrieve the ELCA nodes. Each ELCA node is considered as a searching result, and the probabilities of the same result are added up. Since the number of possible worlds is exponentially large, we provide another efficient approach to retrieve all the ELCA nodes and get their probabilities. Also, we prove the correctness of the approach.

The remainder of this paper is organized as follows. Section 2 gives some preliminary definitions. Section 3 presents some basic formulas for calculating the uncertainty information. In Section 4, we propose the ranking model for results Afterwards, the algorithms of finding top-$k$ results and system are given in Section 5. Experimental results are exhibited in Section 6.

## 2. Preliminaries

We define the searching object as a tree structure called *Probabilistic XML Tree*. The formal definition of a probabilistic XML tree is as follows.

*Definition 1. (Probabilistic XML Tree)* A probabilistic XML tree (PXT) $p$ is an 8-tuple $p = (O, D, E, root, L, \lambda, \sigma, \omega)$, in which:

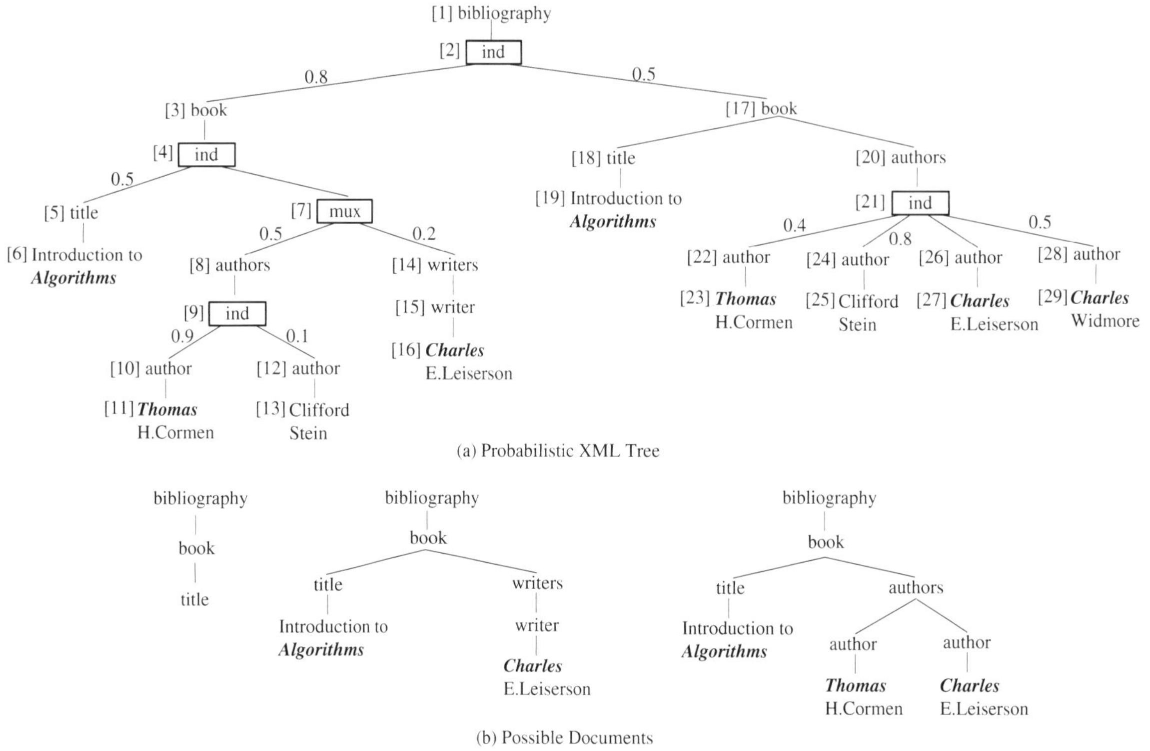


Fig. 1: Example of Probabilistic XML Tree and Possible Documents

- $O$ is a finite set of ordinary nodes;
- $D$ is a finite set of distributional nodes;
- $E \subseteq (O \cup D) \times (O \cup D)$ is an edge set constructing a tree structure along with all nodes in $O \cup D$;
- $root \in O$ is the root node of the tree;
- $L$ is a finite set of labels;
- $\lambda : O \to L$ is a surjective function that returns the label of an ordinary node;
- $\sigma$ is a function that returns a real number in (0, 1] for any node as its occurrence probability on the premise of its parent being present;
- $\omega : D \to \{ind, mux\}$ is a function that retrieves the distribution type of any distributional node;
- $\forall d_i \in D$: (1) $d_i$ has at least one child node, (2) suppose $\omega(d_i) = mux$ and $children(d_i)$ is the set of $d_i$'s child-nodes, then $\sum_{v \in children(d_i)} \sigma(v) \leq 1$.

An example of a PXT is illustrated in Figure 1 (a). For those edges without numbers attached, the corresponding nodes all have a default probability as 1. Now we define the concept of a PXT's possible worlds which are called the possible documents of it.

*Definition 2. (Possible Document of Probabilistic XML Tree)* For a PXT $p = (O, D, E, root, L, \lambda, \sigma, \omega)$, $m$ is a subtree which satisfies: (1) the root node of $m$ is $root$; (2) for any distributional node $d$ in $m$ that $\omega(d) = mux$ $d$ can have at most one child node in $m$. A corresponding possible world can be easily built by removing all the distributional nodes in $m$ and connecting the ordinary nodes directly.

Figure 1 (b) illustrates three of the possible document of the PXT in Figure 1 (a). The calculation for each distributional node is described as follows.

Given a distributional node $d_i$, $C$ is the set of its child nodes. Suppose we choose a subset from $C$ as $C'$ and $\overline{C'}$ is the set of $d_i$'s children that are not in $C'$. If $\omega(d_i) = ind$, then apparently the probability of choosing the subset $C'$ is $\prod_{v \in C'} \sigma(v) \prod_{v \in \overline{C'}} (1 - \sigma(v))$. Otherwise if $\omega(d_i) = mux$, there are only two cases to choose child nodes. Case one is to choose any child, and the second case is choosing none. If choose $c_i$ from $C$, then the probability is simply $\sigma(c_i)$ itself. And when choose none of the children, the probability will be $1 - \sum_{v \in C} \sigma(v)$.

Let $pw(p)$ be the set of all the possible documents of $p$ and $g$ is any one in it. We use $Pr(g)$ to denote the probability of $g$, then it can be easily proved that $\sum_{g \in pw(p)} Pr(g) = 1$.

*Definition 3. (Minimum Meaningful Fragment)* A minimum meaningful fragment (MMF) of searching $W$ in $p$ is a subtree $m = (O, D, E, root, L, \lambda, \sigma, \omega)$ of $p$ which satisfies: (1) the labels of nodes in $K \subseteq D$ contain all keywords in $W$. (2) $\forall n_i, n_j \in K, lca(n_i, n_j) \in O$ or $lca(n_i, n_j) \in D, \omega(lca(n_i, n_j)) = ind$. (3) no subtree of $m$ is also a MMF except $m$ itself.

We use MMF as searching results. It is for two reasons: First, we do believe the structure is the most important property of XML keyword searching results needs to be kept intact. Second, an integrated result is much more preferred than a number of random documents generated by possible-worlds model.

## 3. Calculating the Uncertainty

In this section we present the scoring function for results and indicate how to calculate each score. For a certain PXT and any two different nodes $n_i$ and $n_j$ in it, we classify the relations between them in three cases: (1) ancestor-descendant (denoted as $n_i \prec n_j$ if $n_i$ is an ancestor node of $n_j$), (2) parent-child, which is actually a special case of the first relation, and (3) otherwise ($n_i \nprec n_j$ and $n_j \nprec n_i$). If $n_i$ is the parent node of $n_j$, in the light of the semantics of local and global probabilities we have $\sigma(n_j) = Pr(n_j|n_i)$, and then $\sigma(n_j) = Pr(n_i|n_j) \times Pr(n_j)/Pr(n_i)$ through the *Bayes' Theorem*. Since $n_j$ only exists when $n_i$ surely does, $Pr(n_i|n_j) = 1$. Hence, $Pr(n_j) = \sigma(n_j) \times Pr(n_i)$. Furthermore, in terms of this formula we can calculate the global probability of any node by multiplying the local probabilities of all nodes on the path from the node to the PXT's root. For instance, in Figure 1 it's easy to find that $Pr(n_{11}) = 0.9 \times 0.5 \times 0.8 = 0.36$ and $Pr(n_{23}) = 0.4 \times 0.5 = 0.2$.

*Definition 4. (Probability Dependency Tree and Set)* For a certain PXT $p = (O, D, E, root, L, \lambda, \sigma, \omega)$ and any node set $N \subseteq O$ and $N \neq \emptyset$, another PXT $p' = (O', D', E', root', L', \lambda', \sigma', \omega')$ can be formed from $p$ by keeping the original root (let $root' = root$) and using all nodes from $descendants(N)$ as leaf-nodes. The function $descendants(N)$ returns a node set $N' \subseteq N$, and $N'$ contains all the nodes which don't have any descendant node in $N$. $p'$ is called the *Probability Dependency Tree* of $N$ in $p$, and $O' \cup D'$ is called the *Probability Dependency Set* of $N$ in $p$. Moreover, they are denoted as $pdt(N)$ and $pds(N)$ respectively. For example, in Figure 1 $pdt(\{n_3, n_5, n_6, n_8, n_{11}, n_{13}\})$ is a part of the original PXT which still keeps the root $n_1$ and uses nodes in $\{n_6, n_{11}, n_{13}\}$ as leaves. Then, $pds(\{n_3, n_5, n_6, n_8, n_{11}, n_{13}\})$ is the set of sequential nodes from $n_1$ to $n_{13}$.

Given any node set $N$, to compute $Pr(\bigcap_{n_i \in N} n_i)$ and $Pr(\bigcup_{n_i \in N} n_i)$ we conclude the possibilities of the distributions between nodes into three cases. First, $\forall n_i, n_j \in N$, $n_i \nprec n_j$ and $n_j \nprec n_i$: $lca(\{n_i, n_j\})$ is a *mux* distributional node. Second, $\forall n_i, n_j \in N$, $n_i \nprec n_j$ and $n_j \nprec n_i$: $lca(\{n_i, n_j\})$ is an ordinary node or an *ind* distributional node. Third, other situations. In other words, for all nodes in $pdt(N)$, either only *mux* distributions exist between siblings, or only *ind* distributions do, or some distributions are *mux* ones while some are *ind* ones. Two integrated formulas are introduced as follows. For a node set $N$ with $n$ random nodes in a PXT, we have:

$$Pr(\bigcap_{n_i \in N} n_i) = \begin{cases} \prod_{n_i \in pds(N)} \sigma(n_i) & \text{only } ind \\ 0 & \text{otherwise} \end{cases} \quad (1)$$

and

$$Pr(\bigcup_{n_i \in N} n_i) = \begin{cases} \sum_{n_i \in N} \big( \prod_{n_j \in pds(n_i)} \sigma(n_j) \big) & \text{only } mux \\ F & \text{otherwise} \end{cases} \quad (2)$$

in which

$$F = \sum_{k=1}^{n} ((-1)^{k-1} \sum_{I \subset \{1,\ldots,n\}, |I|=k} Pr(\bigcap_{j \in I} n_j))$$

is a formula of the *Inclusion-Exclusion Principle*.

## 4. Ranking

In this section, we investigate the extra factor needed to be considered when ranking the results of searching probabilistic XML data comparing to the ranking models in conventional XML keyword search approaches.

Before discussing how to score a MMF, let us review the ranking models in conventional XML keyword search researches. For convenience, we name a node whose label contains some keyword as a *keyword node*. When searching results are regarded as XML fragments with various kinds of structures, most of the former researches employed simple approaches considering intuitive factors of these structures. Commonly accepted factors are: result size (amount of all nodes), number of keyword nodes, number of distinct keywords, and the compactness (number of keyword nodes divided by result size). When applying keyword search techniques to retrieve meaningful information from probabilistic XML data, an extra factor needs to be imposed on the scoring function to reflect the uncertainty degree in results. Since the factor is proposed from a totally different aspect, the conventional ranking factors are orthogonal to it.

For a MMF $r$ not all its random documents are meaningful to users. We define a concept of *Meaningful Random Document* as follows.

*Definition 5. (Meaningful Random Document)* For a PXT $p$ and a keyword set $W$, one of $p$'s MMF is $r$. Then, a random document of $r$ can be generated in two steps. First, for any distributional node $d_i$ in $r$ whose ancestor nodes are all ordinary ones, either remove $d_i$ and all its descendant nodes from $r$, or (1) choose any number of $d_i$'s children and connect the subtrees rooted in them to $d_i$'s parent if $\omega(d_i) = ind$, (2) choose exact one child and connect the subtree rooted in it to $d_i$'s parent if $\omega(d_i) = mux$. Second, implement the first step repeatedly until there is no distributional node. Finally, a random document of MMF is called a meaningful random document (MRD) if the labels of nodes contains all keywords in $W$.

We use $mrd(r)$ to denote the set of meaningful random documents of $r$. For any $rd \in mrd(r)$, suppose the probability of $rd$ is $RP(rd, r)$ and $D$ is the set of distributional nodes in $r$ considered when generating $rd$. Then, apparently

$$RP(rd, r) = \prod_{d_i \in D} P(d_i, rd) \ ,$$

in which: if $\omega(d_i) = ind$ and none of $d_i$'s child is chosen,

$$P(d_i, rd) = \prod_{n_j \in children(d_i)} (1 - \sigma(n_j)) \ ;$$

else if $\omega(d_i) = ind$ and nodes in $C \subseteq children(d_i)$ are chosen,

$$P(d_i, rd) = \prod_{n_j \in C} \sigma(n_j) \times \prod_{n_k \in children(d_i), n_k \notin C} (1 - \sigma(n_k)) \ ;$$

else if $\omega(d_i) = mux$ and none of $d_i$'s child is chosen,

$$P(d_i, rd) = 1 - \sum_{n_j \in children(d_i)} \sigma(n_j) \ ;$$

else if $\omega(d_i) = mux$ and $d_i$'s child $c_j$ are chosen,

$$P(d_i, rd) = \sigma(c_j) \ .$$

Formally, for a MMF $r$ in which $rt$ is the root, we define the degree of uncertainty in $r$ as the *Uncertainty Score* of $r$ denoted as $US(r)$, and

$$US(r) = Pr(rt) \times \sum_{rd \in mrd(r)} RP(rd, r) \qquad (3)$$

This is actually the extra factor reflecting the uncertainty degree of searching results, and $Pr(rt)$ is taken into account because the existence of $rt$ is the precondition of calculating the uncertainty information of $r$. As mentioned the scoring functions of other intuitive factors are orthogonal to $US(r)$, thus we define a compositive function for other factors as $OS(r)$. Finally, we have the ultimate scoring function $score(r)$ of a MMF $r$ as follows.

$$score(r) = US(r)^{\alpha} \times OS(r)^{\beta} \qquad (4)$$

# 5. Retrieving Top-k Results

## 5.1 Indistinguishable Set and Score Bounds

As mentioned in Section 2, our ultimate purpose is: given a PXT $p$, a keyword set $W$, and a positive integer $k$ given by users, finding $k$ MMFs with the largest ranking scores. When calculating the ranking score for a MMF $r$ ($US(r) \times OS(r)$), $OS(r)$ (the number of keywords in $r$) is quite easy to obtain while $US(r)$ is not. Actually, to figure out the uncertainty score for each MMF is a nontrivial task. Therefore, the key problem here is: how to obtain top-$k$ results with computing as less uncertainty scores as possible. We propose a simple yet effective ranking algorithm as follows: when retrieving a MMF, lower and upper bounds of its score are calculated, which costs negligible time; at the same time an *Indistinguishable Set* of MMFs is maintained; after the results-finding process the top-$k$ results are affirmatively in the set, then the real scores of the MMFs in this set are calculated and top-$k$ results are obtained through any popular sorting algorithm.

*Definition 6. (Indistinguishable Set)* For any MMF $r$, suppose $ub(r)$ and $lb(r)$ are the upper-bound and lower-bound functions of $r$ respectively (which means $lb(r) \leq score(r) \leq ub(r)$). Given a certain positive integer $k$ and a MMF set $R$ which satisfies $|R| > k$, we can sort the MMFs in $R$ by the upper bounds in descending order and get a list $ubl(R)$, also we can sort them by the lower bounds in descending order and get a list $lbl(R)$, then $R$ is called a $k$-indistinguishable-set ($k$-i-set) if: the upper bound of the last MMF in $ubl(R)$ is greater than or equal to the lower bound of the $k$th MMF in $lbl(R)$. This kind of set is called an indistinguishable set because in a top-$k$ search results cannot be distinguished from it yet. The detail of the procedure is presented in Section 5.2.

*Definition 7. (Tightest Meaningful Tree)* Let $K$ be the set of all keyword nodes in the MMF $r$, then a PXT is called the *Tightest Meaningful Tree* generated from $r$ if it uses $lca(K)$ as root and the nodes in $descendants(K)$ as leaves. The tightest meaningful tree of $r$ is denoted as $tmt(r)$.

*Upper Bound 1.* Suppose $rt'$ is the root of $tmt(r)$, then $Pr(rt')$ is an upper bound of $US(r)$. Since $rt'$ is an ancestor of any keyword node (or itself could be one), $US(r) = Pr(E) = Pr(E|r') \times Pr(r') \leq Pr(r')$.

*Upper Bound 2.* $Pr(\bigcup_{n_i \in children(rt')} n_i)$ is used as the second upper bound, in which $children(rt')$ is the child-node set of $rt'$ in $tmt(r)$.

*Upper Bound 3.* Using the same proof from upper bound 2, a smaller upper bound can be deduced. We use a function $ancestors(K)$ to get a keyword-node set $K' \subseteq K$, and $K'$ contains all the nodes in $K$ which don't have any ancestors in $K$. Obviously the nodes in $ancestors(K)$ separates all the keyword nodes below (only $rt$ could be an exception). Consequently, we can have the upper bound 3 as the middle one of following inequation:

$$US(r) \leq Pr(\bigcup_{n_i \in ancestors(K) n_i}) \leq Pr(\bigcup_{n_i \in children(rt')} n_i) \qquad (5)$$

Next three lower bounds of $US(r)$ are introduced. As we will see the lower bounds are set more casually.

*Lower Bound 1.* Suppose a random set $R \subseteq K$, $R$ contains all keywords and $|R| = t$ as the number of keywords. Thus, we have $Pr(\bigcap_{n_i \in R} n_i) \leq US(r)$.

*Lower Bound 2.* For any keyword in the $R$ of lower bound 1, apparently a higher place of it in the tree often brings a higher probability. So, for each keyword-node set

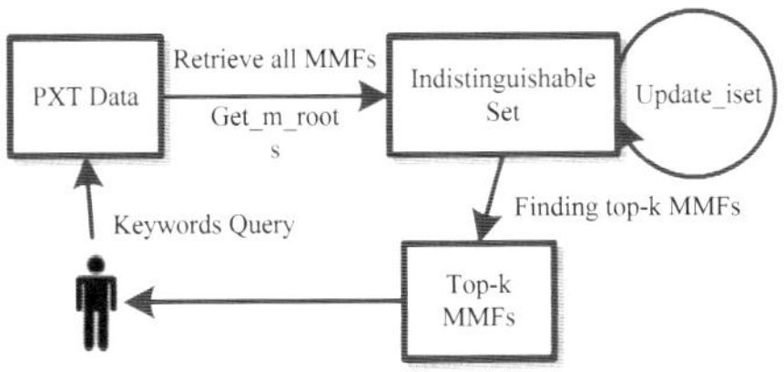


Fig. 2: System overview

of a keyword we choose the one which has a shortest path to the root. Therefore a set $R'$ is obtained, and we have $Pr(\bigcap_{n_i \in R'} n_i) \leq US(r)$.

*Lower Bound 3.* Actually we can get a lower bound more casually. If $E(N)$ is used as the DNF logic formula which denotes "the probability $N$ containing all keywords". Then, obviously for any $N \subseteq K$ we have $Pr(E(N)) \leq US(r)$, and based on $N$ a subpart of the MMF can be generated and afterwards a new uncertainty score can be figured out. Apparently, it is significant to choose a small number of $N$ and get a close value to $US(r)$, however there is one thing should be noticed that whatever a keyword-node set is chosen, it must contain all the keywords.

### 5.2 System Overview

Here, we proposed the overview architecture for our algorithms.

The system gets the keyword query from users, and perform query algorithm on the target PXT.

Firstly, the system retrieved all MMFs satisfying the query. As a keyword searching result MMF is defined as a subtree of the PXT, to retrieve a MMF is equal to finding its root. Hence, For the target PXT, we use the procedure *get_m_roots* to denote finding the roots of all MMFs that satisfying the query.

Then, for these candidate MMFs, we are filtering out some candidates which are definitely not in the top-k results using Score Bounds introduced in the previous section. The system use the procedure *update_iset* in the indistinguishable set and eliminate these candidates from the set.

Finally, the system calculates the actual ranking scores for candidates in the indistinguishable set and output the top-k results to the users.

These procedures are illustrated in details in the following section.

### 5.3 System in details

The procedure $update\_iset(r, R)$ illustrates the process of updating and maintaining the indistinguishable set.

To implement the results-finding algorithm, for a PXT $p$ as the searching object we code all the nodes in it with *Dewey Code* and build an inverted list for all terms in the labels of all the ordinary nodes. For any term (input keyword), we can find a list storing the Dewey codes as the occurrence positions in the tree in pre-order. For any node $n_i$ in $p$, a function $pre(n_i)$ is defined to get the sequence number of $n_i$ in pre-order. Thus $pre(n_i) < pre(n_j)$ means $n_i$ is at a position top-left to $n_j$ in the tree. Furthermore, two mapping tables are also built to store the types of a distributional nodes and the local probabilities.

procedure $update\_iset(r, R)$

Input: $k$, i-set $R$, $ubl(R)$, $lbl(R)$, MMF $r$
Output: $\varnothing$

**if** $|R| < k$
  insert $r$ into $R$;
  insert $r$ into $ubl(R)$, $lbl(R)$ at the right places;
**else**
  $l_k$ = the $k$th item in $lbl(R)$;
  **if** $ub(r) \geq lb(l_k)$
    insert $r$ into $R$;
    insert $r$ into $ubl(R)$, $lbl(R)$ at the right places;
    $l_k$ = the $k$th item in $lbl(R)$;
    **for** each $r'$ in $ubl(R)$ (from tail to head)
      **if** $ub(r') < lb(l_k)$
        remove $r'$ from $R$, $ubl(R)$, and $lbl(R)$;
      **else**
        **break**;

As a keyword searching result MMF is defined as a subtree of the PXT, to retrieve a MMF is equal to finding its root. For a PXT $p$ and a set of keywords $W = \{w_1, w_2, \ldots, w_t\}$, $K_i$ is the set of keyword nodes whose labels contain $w_i$ in $p$. We use $m\_roots(K_1, K_2, \ldots, K_t)$ to denote the procedure of finding the roots of all MMFs of searching all the keywords in $p$, and if only the keywords $\{w_1, w_2, \ldots, w_{t-1}\}$ are considered then the corresponding roots are $m\_roots(K_1, K_2, \ldots, K_{t-1})$. We use $K'$ to denote the list of the roots, and the nodes in $K'$ are regarded as keyword nodes whose labels contain a new keyword $w'$. Then the MMF roots of searching $\{w', w_t\}$ in $p$ are $m\_roots(K', K_t)$. It can be easily proved that:

$$m\_roots(K_1, K_2, \ldots, K_t) = m\_roots(K', K_t)$$

Apparently, through conducting the formula recursively we can turn the problem into finding the MMF roots for two keywords $m\_roots(K_i, K_j)$. Suppose $n_i$ is a certain node in $K_i$, $\forall n_j \in K_j$, $pre(n_j) < pre(n_i)$, and $\omega(lca(\{n_i, n_j\})) \neq mux$, we call the one with the largest $pre(n_j)$ as the *left neighbor* of $n_i$ in $K_j$. Similarly, $\forall n_j \in K_j$, $pre(n_j) > pre(n_i)$, and $\omega(lca(\{n_i, n_j\})) \neq mux$, we call the one with the smallest $pre(n_j)$ as the *right neighbor* of $n_i$ in $K_j$. Moreover, the left and right neighbors of $n_i$ in $K_j$ are denoted as $ln(n_i, K_j)$ and $rn(n_i, K_j)$ respectively. Then, the procedure of getting the MMF roots for two keywords $w_i$ and $w_j$ is as follows.

The approach of finding all MMFs is similar to the algorithm proposed in [8]. The only difference is the definition of two neighbor nodes. Finally, the algorithm of finding top-$k$ MMFs is given.

procedure $get\_m\_roots(K_i, K_j)$

Input: $K_i$, $K_j$, and $R = \emptyset$

Output: $R$

$mr$ = the root of the PXT;
**for** each node $n_i$ in $K_i$
  **if** $lca(\{n_i, ln(n_i, K_i)\}) \prec lca(\{n_i, rn(n_i, K_i)\})$
    $l = lca(\{n_i, rn(n_i, K_i)\})$;
  **else**
    $l = lca(\{n_i, ln(n_i, K_i)\})$;
  **if** $pre(mr) \leq pre(l)$
    **if** $mr \npreceq l$
      add $mr$ in $R$;
    $mr = l$;
**return** $R \cup \{mr\}$

**Algorithm** Finding top-$k$ MMFs

Input: the PXT $p$, keyword set $W = \{w_1, w_2, \ldots, w_t\}$

Output: top-$k$ MMFs with the largest scores

$R = \emptyset$; // i-set
when considering the last two keyword sets;
**for** each MMF $r$ retrieved
  $update\_iset(r, R)$;
compute the ranking sore for each MMF in $R$;
sort $R$ according to scores;
**return** top-$k$ MMFs in $R$ with largest scores;

# 6. Experiments

The main purposes of our experiments include: (1) to show the efficiency of calculating the scores (2) to estimate the efficiency of the algorithm retrieving top-$k$ MMFs provided in Section 5. The hardware environment of the experiments is a laptop with a 2.1GHZ Duo-CPU and 2G RAM running Windows XP. All programs are developed in Java 6.0. We added the uncertainty information into the encrypted TreeBank data set (document size 82M, containing 2437667 nodes, max-depth 36, and average-depth 7.9) to build a PXT as the searching object. A certain amount of distributional nodes with random types are inserted into the original XML tree, afterwards any child node of them are given a random real number in (0, 1]. We call the generated PXT as the $P$-$TreeBank$ data set, and a vocabulary containing frequent terms is built upon it. To get more exact results, some keywords are randomly chosen from the vocabulary and then utilized to search the $P$-$TreeBank$. For a certain number of keywords, the process is conducted for many times, and then average values are figured out as the final experimental results.

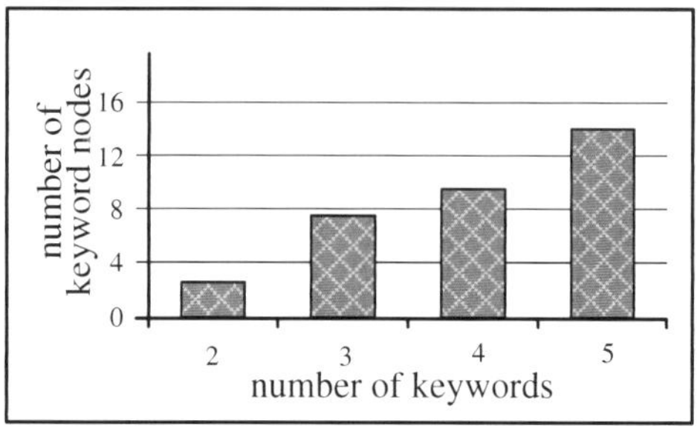


Fig. 3: Average number of keyword nodes in a MMF

## 6.1 Calculating ranking scores

As we can see, when computing the ranking score for any MMF it is set to be conducted automatically each time a new MMF is generated or a MMF is modified. It means at any time we are considering a tightest meaningful tree. Figure 3 illustrates the average number of keyword nodes in MMF for each certain number of keywords. For a MMF $r$, suppose $K$ is the set of keyword nodes in $r$, then apparently in the worst case calculating $US(r)$ will cost $O(|K| \times 2^{|K|})$. Although the computation complexity could fall to $O(|K|)$ through employing the strategies, we cannot calculate the score with the brute approach when $|K|$ is really large. Actually it is found that the time cost becomes unbearable when $|K| > 27$. From the semantics of a MMF, we can see that such condition is really hard to fulfill except some extreme cases. For example all the keyword nodes are siblings and share an *ind* distribution. Figure 4 shows that the time cost of calculating the uncertainty score will rise when there are more keyword nodes and more distributional nodes in the MMF. The cost doesn't grow in geometric progression as in a first thought, because many ancestor-descendant relations exist between the distributional nodes, and in this case much less random documents are generated.

## 6.2 Retrieving top-$k$ MMFs

To estimate the efficiency of the top-$k$ results finding algorithm, 5 integers are selected as $k$ (10, 20, 30, 40, and 50), and for each $k$ the size of indistinguishable set is counted. Due to the difficulty of calculating ranking scores, the smaller the i-set size is, the higher efficiency we will get. Figure 5 shows the results when different bounds are used. "u-bound 2 & l-bound 2" means utilizing the upper bound 2 and lower bound 2 defined in Section 5, "u-bound 3 & l-bound 3" indicates using upper bound 3 and lower bound 3. The average amount of all the MMFs is 12834, thus we

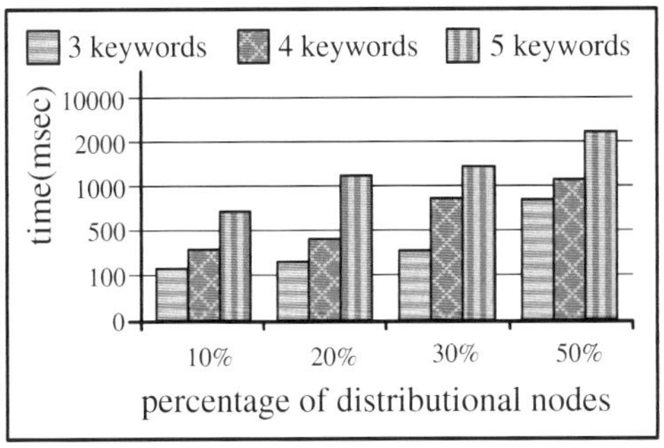


Fig. 4: Calculating scores with different amount of distributional nodes

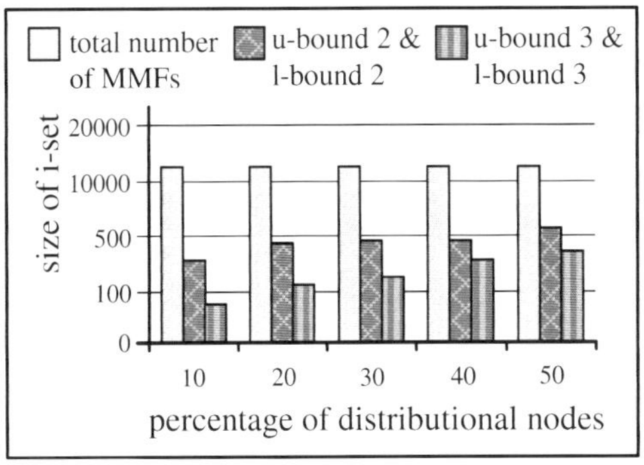


Fig. 5: Size of Indistinguishable Sets

can see the dramatic abatements of the MMFs needs to be considered to retrieve top-$k$ results when upper bound 3 and lower bound 3. Also, from their definitions it's easy to find that these four bounds all have negligible costs.

### 6.3 Acknowledgments

This work is supported by Airplane Research Project(MJ-Y-2011-39), Shanghai High-Tech Project(11-43), Chinese Polar Project(CHINARE2012-04 07).

## References

[1] S. Abiteboul and P. Senellart, "Querying and updating probabilistic information in xml," in *Proc. 2006 International Conference on Extended Data Base Technology (EDBT'06)*, 2006, pp. 1059-1068.

[2] S. Cohen, B. Kimelfeld, and Y. Sagiv, "Incorporating constraints in probabilistic xml," in *Proceedings of the 27th ACM SIGMOD-SIGACT-SIGART symposium on Principles of database systems (PODS'08)*, 2008, pp. 109-118.

[3] S. Cohen, B. Kimelfeld, and Y. Sagiv, "Running tree automata on probabilistic xml," in *Proceedings of the 28th ACM SIGMOD-SIGACT-SIGART symposium on Principles of database systems (PODS'09)*, 2009, pp. 227-236.

[4] E. Hung, L. Getoor, and V. S. Subrahmanian, "Probabilistic interval xml," in *ICDT*, 2003, pages 358-374.

[5] B. Kimelfeld, Y. Kosharovsky, and Y. Sagiv, "Query efficiency in probabilistic xml models," in *Proceedings of the 2008 ACM SIGMOD international conference on Management of data (SIGMOD'08)*, 2008, pp. 701-714.

[6] B. Kimelfeld and Y. Sagiv, "Modeling and querying probabilistic xml data," *SIGMOD Record*, vol. 37(4), pp. 69-77, 2008.

[7] W. A. M. van Keulen, A. de Keijzer, "A probabilistic xml approach to data integration," in *Proc. International Conference on Data Engineering (ICDE'05)*, 2005, pp. 459-470.

[8] Y. Xu and Y. Papakonstantinou, "Efficient keyword search for smallest lcas in xml databases," in *Proceedings of the 2005 ACM SIGMOD international conference on Management of data (SIGMOD'05)*, 2005, pp. 537-538.

[9] W. Yang and H. Zhu, "Semantic-distance based clustering for xml keyword search," in *The 14th Pacific-Asia Conference on Knowledge Discovery and Data Mining (PAKDD 2010)*, 2010, pp. 369-381.

# SESSION

# DECISION SUPPORT SYSTEMS

## Chair(s)

**TBA**

# A Fuzzy Multiple Objective Decision Making Methodology for Electricity Generation Planning

**Mehtap Dursun, E. Ertugrul Karsak, and Zeynep Sener**
Industrial Engineering Department, Galatasaray University, Istanbul, Turkey

**Abstract** - *Although conventional energy resources are widely used for electricity generation globally as well as in Turkey, the renewable energy resources that do not deteriorate environmental quality and economic efficiency are increasingly favored to meet the energy demands in a sustainable way. Alternatively, limitations on land availability and high initial investment costs impede the development of renewable energy resources. This paper proposes a decision model based on fuzzy multiple objective programming for electricity generation planning in Turkey. Conflicting objectives with their corresponding importance degrees are taken into account to improve the quality of decision making process. Linguistic variables are employed to represent the qualitative data concerning energy alternatives and the importance degree of each objective. The proposed methodology enables to illustrate the trade-off between economic, environmental, social, and political factors in energy planning.*

**Keywords:** Decision analysis; Decision support system; Energy alternatives; Fuzzy data; Fuzzy multiple objective programming.

## 1 Introduction

The worldwide energy consumption has been increasing rapidly due to the rise in population, industrialization, and technological development. The consumption of electricity and the economic development maintain a direct relationship. Indeed, considering the rise of the income per capita and the demographic growth, the demand for electricity will reach very high levels in developing countries.

Satisfying the world's electric power requirements, we strongly depend on the systems based on the fossil fuels, which represent nearly 81% of total world consumption. U.S. Energy Information Administration estimates that about 19% of world electricity generation is from renewable energy, i.e. resources constantly replenished, like the sun, the wind and the hydro power, with a projection of nearly 23% in 2035.

The production and the consumption of electricity in Turkey have increased rapidly during the past 20 years. The needs for the energy sources used for the electricity production, where the production cannot satisfy the demands, are provided via imports. Turkey is a country where the local resources of energy are limited. The Ministry of Energy and Natural Resources (MENR) estimates that the ratio of imported energy will be 68% in 2015 and 70% in 2020. Thus, we have to re-examine our energy policy carefully to prevent the energy crisis which can occur in the future.

For this reason, this paper focuses on the detailed evaluation of diverse energy resources for electricity to identify the most suitable planning for Turkey. Energy planning decisions are complex due to the fact that various criteria that are in conflict must be considered in decision making process. As energy planning decisions require considering multiple conflicting criteria incorporating vagueness and imprecision with the involvement of a group of experts, energy resource planning is an important multi-criteria group decision making problem. Recently, the focus on global environmental protection has resulted in the use of multi-criteria decision making (MCDM) methods in energy systems [1, 2].

In the literature, there are few papers that evaluate different energy alternatives for Turkey. Gungor and Arikan [3] employed a fuzzy preference model for energy policy planning of Turkey. Topcu and Ulengin [4] used the PROMETHEE method in order to select a suitable electricity generation alternative for Turkey. Erdogmus et al. [5] employed analytic network process (ANP) for evaluating fuel alternatives. Kaya and Kahraman [6] determined the most appropriate renewable energy alternative for Istanbul using an integrated VIKOR-analytic hierarchy process (AHP) methodology. Talinli et al. [7] used fuzzy AHP and conducted a comparative analysis of three different energy production process scenarios for Turkey. Lately, Erol and Kilkis [8] applied AHP for energy resource planning for the district of Aydin in Turkey. These studies provide a ranking of alternatives by employing different decision making tools. As an improvement over earlier studies that identify a rank-order of the alternatives, in here we determine the most appropriate electricity generation planning for Turkey through a multiple objective programming framework that yields the utilization rates for the energy alternatives.

Generally the energy policy consists of an institutional structure, in which the decisions are based on capital and operating costs, $CO_2$, $SO_2$ and $NO_x$ emissions, safety and reliability, sustainability, suitability, and foreign dependency of energy resources. Capital costs include expenses for tangible goods such as the purchase of plants and machinery, as well as expenses for intangibles assets such as trademarks and software development. Operating costs are the expenses which are related to the operation of a business, or to the operation of a device, component, equipment or facility. Renewable technologies have high capital expenditure, and low operating expenditures. These characteristics make them more attractive in the long-term, though less attractive in a competitive setting when cost minimization is aimed.

Albeit the new legislation has not resulted in substantial changes in the environmental policy strategy, it has caused a significant progress. The total internalization of the environmental cost is conditioned by an exhaustive evaluation of the social cost of the damage and the natural resources exploitation. The external cost is imposed on the company and the environment, but not represented by the energy producers and the consumers, thus it is not included in the market price. The criteria regarding external cost are taken into account with $CO_2$, $SO_2$ and $NO_X$ emissions [9].

The needs of the developing countries must be translated in terms of energy sustainability as well as considering its economic, social and environmental dimensions. Indeed, it is possible to estimate the relative sustainability of the energy technologies on the basis of their resource consumption.

The safety of the energy resources can be defined as the possibility to have energy in sufficient amounts, in various forms and for reasonable prices for the consumer. The reduction of the supply breaks in imported energy is considered only as an aspect of the energy safety. The reliability of the electricity provisioning has a significant priority. In the industrialized countries, the consumers demand 100% reliability, whereas those of the developing countries often suffer frequent breaks.

It is necessary to consider suitability in energy cooperation. The use of energy strictly depends on the government policy. The use of the energy resources must be compatible with political, legislative and administrative structure. As for Turkey with heavy dependence on energy imports, some energy resources like natural gas and oil possess uncertainty since the political instability among countries are likely to affect the imports [9].

The rest of the paper is organized as follows. Section 2 provides a brief presentation of the conventional and renewable energy resource alternatives. Section 3 introduces a fuzzy multiple objective programming framework. Section 4 presents the application of the proposed methodology for electricity generation planning in Turkey. The concluding remarks are given in the final section.

# 2 Energy sources used for electricity production

Turkey has become one of the fastest growing energy markets in the world parallel to its high economic growth realized in the last decade. The Turkish Electricity Transmission Company estimates that Turkey's demand for electricity will increase at an annual rate of six percent between 2009 and 2023. The growing energy demand in Turkey is one of the significant factors along with market liberalization and the country's potential role as an energy terminal in its region. Turkey's ambitious vision of 2023 envisages elaborate targets for the energy sector in Turkey. These targets include increasing installed capacity from 54,423 MW in 2010 to 125,000 MW and increasing share of renewables to 30 percent [10].

In this research, the potentially viable electricity resources considered for Turkey are coal, oil, natural gas, nuclear, wind, solar power, biomass, hydropower, and geothermal. These energy resources can be classified into two major categories as renewable and non-renewable. Renewable energy resources are constantly replenished, unlike coal, oil or gas, which have finite reserves. Renewable energy can therefore be consumed in a sustainable way. Solid fossil fuels (coal), oil, natural gas and nuclear power are non-renewable. These are all conventional energy resources [5]. Imported fossil fuels currently play an important role in Turkey's electricity generation [11].

Coal is a highly efficient and cheap energy resource for Turkey, and as of today there are 12.4 billion tons of coal reserves, but only 3.9 billion tons can be used. Although fossil fuels are highly efficient and cheap, fossil fuel extraction and conversion has several environmental impacts. Fossil fuels can be seen as one of the major contributors to global warming, greenhouse gases and a cause of acid rain; thus, expensive air pollution controls are required [5].

The main oil company in Turkey is Turkish State Society of Oil, which roughly accounts for 80% of Turkey's oil production. Since the beginning of the last century, the petroleum has become the most important energy source. However, as a result of several energy crises and the dramatic increase in the price of oil, other sources of energy have gained importance [12].

The natural gas is a fossil source of energy, which has been in a strong progress since the seventies. Due to its economic and ecological advantages, the natural gas has become more attractive for a number of countries, and also it has been one of the most important energy sources [13]. Although natural gas is generally accepted as a fossil fuel, it is generally examined separately from coal, lignite and oil since its related $CO_2$ emissions and contribution to global warming figures are much lower than fossil resources [5]. Turkey has plans to increase natural gas use for electricity production.

The nuclear energy does not generate greenhouse gases such as $CO_2$, $SO_2$, $NO_x$. On the other hand, it generates radioactive waste. The nuclear fuel is inexpensive and easy to transport. Although there is no emission of gas, it carries health risks both for the human kind and the environment. The storage of nuclear waste is a major problem. First-aid organizations and systems of storage are necessary but their costs are very high [14]. For the continuity of electricity generation, nuclear power plants are safer and have higher availability compared to thermal power plants. It is targeted that nuclear power plants will have a minimum of 5% share in electricity production in Turkey by 2020. In May 2010, an intergovernmental agreement was signed between Turkey and Russia regarding the construction of a nuclear power plant in Mersin-Akkuyu.

The wind causes no emission, and it is free and available. A windy site with no or a low level of turbulence, with wind predominantly blowing from one direction, or directions at 180° to one another, is a perfect site for a wind turbine. It works well in coastal areas and on high ridges. The site must be far away from the dwellings and the bird's migration routes. It is noisy to generate the power by the wind and the equipment is expensive to maintain. It also requires expensive means for the storage of energy like large batteries [5]. Turkey has a considerable potential for the electricity production from wind. With Turkey Wind Energy Potential Atlas (REPA), which was realized in 2007, it is calculated that Turkey has a minimum wind energy potential of 5,000 MW in regions with annual wind speed of 8.5 m/s and higher, and 48,000 MW with wind speed higher than 7.0 m/s. Turkey's installed wind energy capacity reached the level of 802.8 MW as of the end of 2009. After the inurement of the renewable energy law, licenses were granted to 93 new wind projects which deliver a total installed capacity of 3,363 MW. Out of these projects, powers plants which correspond to an installed capacity of 1,100 MW are now under construction.

Hydropower is a technology widely used for the electricity generation. It is capable of delivering strong power. It is entirely renewable and does not cause any $CO_2$ emission. Once a hydroelectric plant or a hydroelectric dam is built, the operation cost is very little. On the other hand, the plant can affect the landscape and it can damage the fish [5]. The geographic position of Turkey is favorable for the hydroelectric energy generation. Turkey has approximately 1% of the total world's hydroelectric potential. Turkey's technically feasible hydroelectric potential is 140 GWh/year.

It is also possible to use photovoltaic (PV) modules as a resource of electricity production. PV modules produce electricity directly from light without emissions, noise, or vibration. The sunlight is free but the cost of power generation is exceptionally high. Solar energy has a low energy density, which requires a large surface for the generation of small amount of energy [4]. Having a high potential for solar energy due to its geographical position, Turkey's average annual total sunshine duration is calculated as 2,640 hours (daily total is 7.2 hours), and average total radiation pressure as 1,311 kWh/m²-year (daily total is 3.6 kWh/m²). On the other hand, there are several disadvantages of PV modules, high cost being the primary disadvantage. However, in the near future, it will be cheaper especially in the Mediterranean region due to more direct sunlight [5].With the decrease in the cost of using PV modules and increase in their efficiency, PV dependent energy generation is expected to increase in Turkey.

Biomass is a principal energy source in Turkey. It is used to meet different energy needs, including electricity and heating system for the industrial plants. The biomass energy includes fuel wood, agricultural residues, livestock wastes, charcoal and other fuels drawn from biological sources [15].

Geothermal energy is the heat energy obtained from hot water, steam and dry steam and hot dry rocks, which is formed when heat accumulated in deep subterranean rocks is carried by fluids and stored in reservoirs. Geothermal resources mainly form around active fault systems, and volcanic and magmatic units. Modern geothermal power plants based on geothermal energy are also regarded as a clean source of energy since emission of $CO_2$, $NO_x$ and $SO_x$ gases are considerably low. As Turkey is located on the Alpine-Himalayan belt, it holds a substantially high geothermal potential. Turkey ranks the seventh in the world and the third in Europe concerning geothermal energy potential [10]. Geothermal potential of Turkey is about 31,500 MW. While 1,500 MW of Turkey's geothermal energy potential is assessed to be suitable for electricity generation, as of the end of 2009, Turkey's installed power of geothermal energy reached around 77.2 MW.

## 3 Fuzzy multiple objective decision making procedure

In this section, a fuzzy multiple objective decision making framework that incorporates imprecise and subjective information inherent in the energy planning process is presented.

Define $X$ as the set of energy alternatives to be considered and $Y$ as the set of objectives employed to determine the level of utilization of the energy alternatives. There exist objectives to be maximized denoted by $Z_k$ and the ones to be minimized represented by $W_s$. Employing these definitions, the model formulation is as follows:

$$\text{Max } \tilde{Z}(\mathbf{x}) = (\tilde{\mathbf{y}}_1\mathbf{x}, \tilde{\mathbf{y}}_2\mathbf{x}, \ldots, \tilde{\mathbf{y}}_1\mathbf{x})$$

$$\text{Min } \tilde{W}(\mathbf{x}) = (\tilde{\mathbf{y}}'_1\mathbf{x}, \tilde{\mathbf{y}}'_2\mathbf{x}, \ldots, \tilde{\mathbf{y}}'_{\mathbf{r}}\mathbf{x})$$

subject to (1)

$$\mathbf{x} \in X = \left\{ \mathbf{x} \geq \mathbf{0} \middle| \tilde{\mathbf{A}}\mathbf{x} * \tilde{\mathbf{b}} \right\}$$

where $l$ is the number of objectives to be maximized, $r$ is the number of objectives to be minimized, $\tilde{\mathbf{y}}_{\mathbf{k}}$ $(k = 1,....,l)$, $\tilde{\mathbf{y}}'_{\mathbf{s}}$ $(s = 1,....,r)$ are $n$-dimensional vectors, $\tilde{\mathbf{b}}$ is an $m$-dimensional vector, $\tilde{\mathbf{A}}$ is an $m$ x $n$ matrix, $\tilde{\mathbf{y}}_{\mathbf{k}}, \tilde{\mathbf{y}}'_{\mathbf{s}}, \tilde{\mathbf{A}}, \tilde{\mathbf{b}}$ 's elements are fuzzy numbers, and "*" indicates "$\le$", "$\ge$" and "$=$" operators. The formulation given above is a fuzzy multiple objective linear programming model. Here, the coefficients of the constraints and the objective functions are fuzzy numbers. Triangular fuzzy numbers are useful means for quantifying the uncertainty in decision making due to their intuitive appeal and computational-efficient representation [16, 17]. In this paper, we assume that all of the fuzzy coefficients in the model are triangular fuzzy numbers represented by $\tilde{Q} = (q_1, q_2, q_3)$ with the membership function as follows:

$$\mu_{\tilde{Q}}(x) = \begin{cases} (x-q_1)/(q_2-q_1) & , \quad q_1 \le x \le q_2 \\ (q_3-x)/(q_3-q_2) & , \quad q_2 \le x \le q_3 \\ 0 & , \quad otherwise \end{cases} \tag{2}$$

If $(\tilde{Q})^L_\alpha$ and $(\tilde{Q})^U_\alpha$ are defined as the lower bound and the upper bound of the $\alpha$-cut of $\tilde{Q}$, respectively, then the $\alpha$-cut of $\tilde{Q}$ can be expressed as

$$\begin{aligned} (\tilde{Q})_\alpha &= \left[ \left(\tilde{Q}\right)^L_\alpha, \left(\tilde{Q}\right)^U_\alpha \right] \\ &= \left[ q_1 + (q_2 - q_1)\alpha, q_3 - (q_3 - q_2)\alpha \right] \end{aligned} \tag{3}$$

The importance degree of each objective can be incorporated into the formulation using fuzzy priorities [18]. The general representation for the membership function corresponding to the importance degrees can be given as

$$\mu_I(x) = \begin{cases} 0 & , \quad x < i_1 \\ (x-i_1)/(i_2-i_1) & , i_1 \le x \le i_2 \\ 1 & , \quad x > i_2 \end{cases} \tag{4}$$

For a given value of $\alpha$, using the maxmin approach, the formulation that incorporates fuzzy priorities of the objectives is stated as a deterministic linear problem with multiple objectives as

$$\text{Max } \beta$$

subject to (5)

$$\beta \le \mu_I \circ \mu_k^\alpha (Z_k)$$
$$\beta \le \mu_I \circ \mu_s^\alpha (W_s)$$
$$x \in X_\alpha$$
$$\beta \in [0,1]$$
$$x_j \ge 0, \; j = 1,...,n$$

where "$\circ$" is the composition operator, $\beta$ is the grade of compromise to which the solution satisfies all of the fuzzy objectives while the coefficients are at a feasible level $\alpha$, and $X_\alpha$ denotes the set of system constraints. Employing the $\alpha$-cuts of the constraints and the objectives, and the fuzzy priorities of the objectives, the model can be stated as

$$\text{Max } \beta$$

subject to (6)

$$\beta \le \frac{\left[ \sum_{j=1}^{n} \left[ y_{kj3} - (y_{kj3} - y_{kj2})\alpha \right] x_j - (\tilde{Z}_k)^-_\alpha - i_{k1}((\tilde{Z}_k)^*_\alpha - (\tilde{Z}_k)^-_\alpha) \right]}{\left[ ((\tilde{Z}_k)^*_\alpha - (\tilde{Z}_k)^-_\alpha)(i_{k2} - i_{k1}) \right]} \quad ,k = 1,...,l$$

$$\beta \le \frac{\left[ (\tilde{W}_s)^-_\alpha - \sum_{j=1}^{n} \left[ y'_{sj1} + \left( y'_{sj2} - y'_{sj1} \right)\alpha \right] x_j - i_{s1}\left( (\tilde{W}_s)^-_\alpha - (\tilde{W}_s)^*_\alpha \right) \right]}{\left[ \left( (\tilde{W}_s)^-_\alpha - (\tilde{W}_s)^*_\alpha \right)(i_{s2} - i_{s1}) \right]} \quad , s = 1,...,r$$

$$x \in X_\alpha$$
$$\beta \in [0,1]$$
$$x_j \ge 0, \; j = 1,..., n$$

where $(\tilde{Z}_k)^*_\alpha$, $(\tilde{W}_s)^*_\alpha$ and $(\tilde{Z}_k)^-_\alpha$, $(\tilde{W}_s)^-_\alpha$ are the ideal and anti-ideal solutions respectively, which can be obtained by solving the model for each objective separately subject to the constraints.

The "min" operator is non-compensatory, and thus, the results obtained by the "min" operator indicate the worst situation and cannot be compensated by other members that may be very good. A dominated solution can be obtained due to the non-compensatory nature of the "min" operator. A compensatory operator such as the arithmetic mean operator would be more desirable; however, the solution obtained using the arithmetic mean operator might be unbalanced. This problem can be overcome by applying a two-phase approach employing the arithmetic mean operator in the second phase to assure an undominated solution [19].

Lee and Li [20] proposed a two-phase approach, where in the first phase they solve the problem parametrically for a given value of $\alpha$, and in the second phase, they obtain an undominated solution using the value of $\alpha$ determined in phase I. In this paper, a modified version of the algorithm proposed by Lee and Li [20] is employed as follows:

**Phase I.**

*Step 1.* Define $\lambda$ = step length, $\tau$ = accuracy of tolerance, $k$ = multiple of step length, $c$ = iteration counter. Set $k := 0$, $c := 0$.

*Step 2.* Set $\alpha_c := 1 - k\lambda$.

*Step 3.* Solve the problem for $\alpha_c$ to obtain $\beta_c$ and $x_c$.

*Step 4a.* If $\alpha_c - \beta_c > \tau$ then $c := c + 1$, $k := k + 1$, go to step 2.

*Step 4b.* If $\alpha_c - \beta_c < -\tau$ then $\lambda := \lambda/2$, $k := 2k - 1$, go to step 2.

*Step 4c.* If $|\alpha_c - \beta_c| \le \tau$ then go to step 5.

*Step 5.* Output $\alpha_c$, $\beta_c$, and $x_c$.

**Phase II.** After obtaining the values of $\alpha$ and $\beta$ according to the procedure given above, we can solve the following problem in order to obtain an undominated solution for the situation where the solution is not unique.

$$\text{Max } \frac{1}{l+r}\left(\sum_{k=1}^{l}\beta_k + \sum_{s=1}^{r}\beta'_s\right)$$

subject to (7)

$$\beta \le \beta_k, k = 1,\dots,l$$

$$\beta_k \le \frac{\left[\sum_{j=1}^{n}\left[y_{kj3} - (y_{kj3} - y_{kj2})\alpha\right]x_j - (\tilde{Z}_k)^-_\alpha - i_{k1}((\tilde{Z}_k)^*_\alpha - (\tilde{Z}_k)^-_\alpha)\right]}{\left[((\tilde{Z}_k)^*_\alpha - (\tilde{Z}_k)^-_\alpha)(i_{k2} - i_{k1})\right]}, k = 1,\dots,l$$

$$\beta \le \beta'_s, s = 1,\dots,r$$

$$\beta'_s \le \frac{\left[(\tilde{W}_s)^-_\alpha - \sum_{j=1}^{n}\left[y'_{sj1} + \left(y'_{sj2} - y'_{sj1}\right)\alpha\right]x_j - i_{s1}\left((\tilde{W}_s)^-_\alpha - (\tilde{W}_s)^*_\alpha\right)\right]}{\left[\left((\tilde{W}_s)^-_\alpha - (\tilde{W}_s)^*_\alpha\right)(i_{s2} - i_{s1})\right]}, s = 1,\dots,r$$

$$x \in X_\alpha$$

$$\beta_k, \beta'_s \in [0,1],\ k = 1, \dots, l;\ s = 1, \dots, r$$

$$x_j \ge 0,\ j = 1,\dots,n$$

# 4 Electricity generation planning in Turkey

Nine alternatives including fossil fuels, nuclear power and renewables, namely coal ($x_1$), oil ($x_2$), natural gas ($x_3$), nuclear ($x_4$), wind ($x_5$), photovoltaic ($x_6$), biomass ($x_7$), hydro ($x_8$) and geothermal ($x_9$) are considered for electricity generation planning in Turkey.

Sustainability ($Z_1$), safety and reliability ($Z_2$) and suitability ($Z_3$) are the objectives to be maximized, whereas capital cost ($W_1$), operating cost ($W_2$), $CO_2$ emission ($W_3$), $SO_2$ emission ($W_4$), $NO_x$ emission ($W_5$) and foreign dependency ($W_6$) are the objectives to be minimized.

An effective way to express sustainability, safety and reliability, suitability and foreign dependency of the energy alternatives, and importance degrees of the objectives, which are difficult to assess by crisp values or random processes, is using linguistic variables. A linguistic variable can be defined as a variable whose values are not numbers, but words or sentences in natural or artificial language. The concept of a linguistic variable appears as a useful means for providing approximate characterization of phenomena that are too complex or ill-defined to be described in conventional quantitative terms [21]. The value of a linguistic variable can be quantified and extended to mathematical operations using the fuzzy set theory. In this paper, foreign dependency, sustainability, safety and reliability, and suitability are expressed using linguistic variables "very low (VL)", "low (L)", "medium (M)", "high (H)" and "very high (VH)". These linguistic variables can be represented by triangular fuzzy numbers as depicted in Fig. 1.

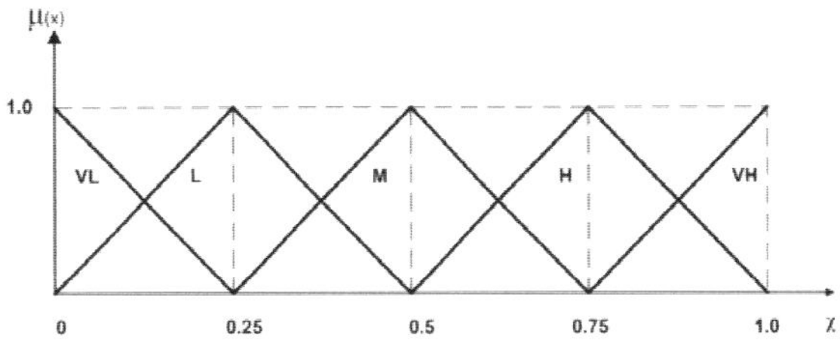


**Fig 1.** A linguistic term set where VL :(0, 0, 0.25), L :(0, 0.25, 0.5), M :(0.25, 0.5, 0.75), H :(0.5, 0.75, 1), VH :(0.75, 1, 1)

The evaluation of the energy alternatives with respect to qualitative factors is conducted by a committee of three experts. Using expert opinion, upper bounds ($u_j$) for potential use of the considered energy alternatives in year 2017 are determined as 0.30, 0.10, 0.50, 0.03, 0.10, 0.03, 0.10, 0.25 and 0.03, respectively.

After rearranging formulation (6), the following mathematical programming model is obtained:

$$\text{Max } \beta$$

subject to (8)

$$\beta \le \frac{\left[\sum_{j=1}^{9}\left[y_{kj3} - (y_{kj3} - y_{kj2})\alpha\right]x_j - (\tilde{Z}_k)^-_\alpha - i_{k1}((\tilde{Z}_k)^*_\alpha - (\tilde{Z}_k)^-_\alpha)\right]}{\left[((\tilde{Z}_k)^*_\alpha - (\tilde{Z}_k)^-_\alpha)(i_{k2} - i_{k1})\right]}, k = 1,2,3$$

$$\beta \le \frac{\left[(\tilde{W}_s)^-_\alpha - \sum_{j=1}^{9}\left[y'_{sj1} + \left(y'_{sj2} - y'_{sj1}\right)\alpha\right]x_j - i_{s1}\left((\tilde{W}_s)^-_\alpha - (\tilde{W}_s)^*_\alpha\right)\right]}{\left[\left((\tilde{W}_s)^-_\alpha - (\tilde{W}_s)^*_\alpha\right)(i_{s2} - i_{s1})\right]}, s = 1,\dots,6$$

$$x_j \le u_j,\ j = 1,\dots,9$$

$$\sum_{j=1}^{9} x_j = 1$$
$$0 \le \beta \le 1$$
$$x_j \ge 0,\ j = 1,...,9$$

After introducing the importance degrees of the objectives given in Table 1, we employ formulation (8). The step length ($\lambda$) and the accuracy of tolerance ($\tau$) are set to be 0.05 and 0.005, respectively. The algorithm delineated in the previous section yields the results given in Table 2.

**Table 1.** Importance degrees of the objectives

| Objective | Type | Importance degree | Membership function |
|---|---|---|---|
| Capital cost | Min | Medium | (0.2, 0.5, 0.5) |
| Operating cost | Min | High | (0.5, 0.7, 0.7) |
| $CO_2$ emission | Min | Very high | (0.7, 1, 1) |
| $SO_2$ emission | Min | High | (0.5, 0.7, 0.7) |
| $NO_x$ emission | Min | High | (0.5, 0.7, 0.7) |
| Foreign dependency | Min | Medium | (0.2, 0.5, 0.5) |
| Sustainability | Max | High | (0.5, 0.7, 0.7) |
| Safety & reliability | Max | High | (0.5, 0.7, 0.7) |
| Suitability | Max | Medium | (0.2, 0.5, 0.5) |

According to the results given in Table 2, the most suitable value of the $\alpha$ parameter is 0.8375, for which $\beta$ is equal to 0.842371. Here, $\alpha$ indicates the level of possibility at which all fuzzy coefficients are feasible, and $\beta$ is the compromise solution among the objectives. In case of a unit increase in $\alpha$, the limitations on the coefficients become stronger. The algorithm reaches a compromise solution by maximizing $\beta$ while keeping the coefficients at the highest possible feasibility level. The compromise solution is obtained when $\alpha$ and $\beta$ are close enough within the limits of the accuracy of tolerance, i.e. $|\alpha - \beta| \le \tau$.

In order to ensure an undominated solution, the model is solved using the $\alpha$ value determined at the end of Phase I and the arithmetic mean operator by employing formulation (7). Undominated solution for the electricity generation planning is given in Table 3. The results of Phase II indicate that six out of nine objectives are fully satisfied $(\beta_1 = \beta_2 = \beta_3 = \beta_1^{'} = \beta_4^{'} = \beta_5^{'} = 1)$, and the degree of compromise obtained using the arithmetic mean operator is equal to 0.947456.

The results given in Table 3 favor renewable energy alternatives and indicate the use of wind, hydro and geothermal at their potential upper bounds. On the other hand, environmental challenges, sustainability, safety and health considerations degrade the popularity of fossil fuels to meet the energy requirements.

# 5 Conclusions

As the global energy consumption increases rapidly, decision support tools to arrive at better solutions in energy planning have gained outmost importance through time. In this paper, a fuzzy multiple objective programming framework that considers economic, environmental, social and political factors is employed for electricity generation planning in Turkey.

The proposed approach enables to incorporate conflicting objectives with imprecise data into the decision framework, and thus improves the quality of decision process for electricity generation planning. Another contribution of the proposed approach is that one can distinguish between the importance of each objective for evaluating energy alternatives by integrating the objective's membership function and the membership function corresponding to its importance degree employing the composition operator.

It is also worth noting that the fuzzy multiple objective programming framework presented in here possesses advantages compared to decision making approaches using fuzzy number ranking methods. First, the proposed approach avoids the troublesome fuzzy number ranking process, which may yield inconsistent results for different ranking methods. Moreover, fuzzy multiple objective programming approach enables system constraints such as upper bounds for potential use of

**Table 2.** Results of the phase I of the decision algorithm

| $\alpha_c$ | $\beta_c$ | $\alpha_c$ - $\beta_c$ | $x_1$ | $x_2$ | $x_3$ | $x_4$ | $x_5$ | $x_6$ | $x_7$ | $x_8$ | $x_9$ |
|---|---|---|---|---|---|---|---|---|---|---|---|
| 1 | 0.708135 | 0.291865 | 0.104481 | 0.00 | 0.460269 | 0.03 | 0.10 | 0.025250 | 0.00 | 0.25 | 0.03 |
| 0.95 | 0.738252 | 0.211748 | 0.097549 | 0.00 | 0.465861 | 0.03 | 0.10 | 0.026589 | 0.00 | 0.25 | 0.03 |
| 0.9 | 0.792557 | 0.107443 | 0.082727 | 0.00 | 0.480549 | 0.03 | 0.10 | 0.026724 | 0.00 | 0.25 | 0.03 |
| 0.85 | 0.832580 | 0.017420 | 0.072484 | 0.00 | 0.490026 | 0.03 | 0.10 | 0.027490 | 0.00 | 0.25 | 0.03 |
| 0.8 | 0.871259 | -0.071259 | 0.062632 | 0.00 | 0.499089 | 0.03 | 0.10 | 0.028279 | 0.00 | 0.25 | 0.03 |
| 0.825 | 0.852237 | -0.027237 | 0.067459 | 0.00 | 0.494667 | 0.03 | 0.10 | 0.027874 | 0.00 | 0.25 | 0.03 |
| 0.8375 | 0.842371 | -0.004871 | 0.069985 | 0.00 | 0.492329 | 0.03 | 0.10 | 0.027685 | 0.00 | 0.25 | 0.03 |

**Table 3.** Undominated solution for the electricity generation planning

| $\alpha$ | $\beta$ | $\lvert\alpha - \beta\rvert$ | $x_1^*$ | $x_2^*$ | $x_3^*$ | $x_4^*$ | $x_5^*$ | $x_6^*$ | $x_7^*$ | $x_8^*$ | $x_9^*$ | $\bar{\beta}$ |
|---|---|---|---|---|---|---|---|---|---|---|---|---|
| 0.8375 | 0.842371 | 0.004871 | 0.069985 | 0.00 | 0.492329 | 0.03 | 0.10 | 0.027685 | 0.00 | 0.25 | 0.03 | 0.947456 |

energy alternatives to be incorporated into the decision process, which is a key aspect lacking in decision aids using fuzzy number ranking methods.

## 6 References

[1] S. D. Pohekar , M. Ramachandran. "Application of multi-criteria decision making to sustainable energy planning - A review", Renewable and Sustainable Energy Reviews, Vol. 8, 365-381, 2004.

[2] J. J. Wang, Y. Y. Jing, C. F. Zhang, J. H. Zhao. "Review on multi-criteria decision analysis aid in sustainable energy decision-making", Renewable and Sustainable Energy Reviews, Vol. 13, 2263-2278, 2009.

[3] Z. Gungor, F. Arikan. "A fuzzy outranking method in energy policy planning", Fuzzy Sets and Systems, Vol. 114, 115-122, 2000.

[4] Y. I. Topcu, F. Ulengin. "Energy for the future: An integrated decision aid for the case of Turkey", Energy, Vol. 29, 137–154, 2004.

[5] S. Erdogmus, H. Aras, E. Koc. "Evaluation of alternative fuels for residential heating in Turkey using analytic network process (ANP) with group decision-making", Renewable and Sustainable Energy Reviews, Vol. 10, 269-279, 2006.

[6] T. Kaya, C. Kahraman. "Multicriteria renewable energy planning using an integrated fuzzy VIKOR & AHP methodology: The case of Istanbul", Energy, Vol. 35, 2517-2527, 2010.

[7] I. Talinli, E. Topuz, M. U. Akbay. "Comparative analysis for energy production processes (EPPs): Sustainable energy futures for Turkey", Energy Policy, Vol. 38, 4479-4488, 2010.

[8] O. Erol, B. Kilkis. "An energy source policy assessment using analytical hierarchy process", Energy Conversion and Management, Vol. 63, 245–252, 2012.

[9] F. H. Benjamin, P. Meier. "Energy decision and the environment", Kluwer Academic Publishers, 2000.

[10] The Republic of Turkey Prime Ministry Investment Support and Promotion Agency, 2013. www.invest.gov.tr/en-US/sectors/Pages/Energy.aspx

[11] Z. B. Erdem. "The contribution of renewable resources in meeting Turkey's energy-related challenges", Renewable and Sustainable Energy Reviews, Vol. 14, 2710-2722, 2010.

[12] Petrol, 2005. http://r0.unctad.org/infocomm/francais/petrole/marche.htm

[13] K. Kaygusuz, A. Kaygusuz. "Renewable energy and sustainable development in Turkey", Renewable Energy, Vol. 25, 431 453, 2002.

[14] O. K. Kadiroglu, C. N. Sokmen. "Electricity production using nuclear energy (in Turkish)", 1994. http://www.nukle.hun.edu.tr

[15] I. Thiaw. "Le sommet mondial pour le développement durable... Et après?", Bulletin d'information du Bureau régional de l'UICN pour l'Afrique de l'Ouest, 2003.

[16] A. Perego, A. Rangone. "A reference framework for the application of MADM fuzzy techniques to selecting AMTS", International Journal of Production Research, Vol. 36, 437-458, 1998.

[17] E. E. Karsak, E. Tolga. "Fuzzy multi-criteria decision-making procedure for evaluating advanced manufacturing system investments", International Journal of Production Economics, Vol. 69, 49-64, 2001.

[18] R. Narasimhan. "On fuzzy goal programming - some comments", Decision Sciences, Vol. 12, 532-537, 1981.

[19] E. E. Karsak. "Fuzzy multiple objective programming framework to prioritize design requirements in quality function deployment", Computers and Industrial Engineering, Vol. 47, 149–163, 2004.

[20] E. S. Lee, R. J. Li. "Fuzzy multiple objective programming and compromise programming with Pareto optimum", Fuzzy Sets and Systems, Vol. 53, 275-288, 1993.

[21] L. A. Zadeh. "The concept of a linguistic variable and its application to approximate reasoning-I", Information Sciences, Vol. 8, 199-249, 1975.

## Acknowledgement

This research has been financially supported by Galatasaray University Research Fund.

# Relationship between DSS categories and different methodologies

Marjan Abdyazdan[1], Mohammad Ganji[2], Mohammad Heidari Reyhani [3], Sheida Shirazi[4]
[1]Department of Computer Engineering, Mahshahr branch, Islamic Azad University, Mahshahr, Iran.
E-mail: m.abdeyazdan@mahshahriau.ac.ir , abdeyazdan87@yahoo.com
[2]Department of Computer Engineering, Tarbiat modares University, Tehran, Iran.
E-mail: m_ganji2011@yahoo.com
[3]Department of Computer Engineering, Mahshahr branch, Islamic Azad University, Mahshahr, Iran.
E-mail: mohammad.hr2010@gmail.com
[4]Department of Computer Engineering, Mahshahr branch, Islamic Azad University, Mahshahr, Iran.
e-mail: shirazi85@gmail.com

**Abstract**

Decision support systems are information system that developed by utilization models, data, information, and collected knowledge for help the manager in solve the not made and simulated problems. Define a specific methodology for each project is needed. In this research by evaluation the decision support system and introduce well developed framework for category decision support system. We want to make a connection between these methodologies and classifications of this system.

Keywords: decision support system, developed framework, decision support methodologies.

## 1-introduction:

Decision support system are systems that developed by tools and technique to support high level management decisions. Among the most important advantages of decision support system can refer to quick and easy access to the information, quick calculation, simple use, simple user interface, further communication with manager, ability to offer complex reports, and save a lot of information.

The researcher of decision support methodologies believe that development process of these types of systems is with certain features and activities, that distinguishes them from trading systems development process. So development method of decision support system is with special consideration efforts and researches to define appropriate methodologies in area of decision support system. Although there have been ups and down, but been the subject of research in recent years. Researcher had conducted that related to analytically comparison and study and apply to identify strengths and weaknesses. The main methodologies were designed from 1978 to 1991. Within a few years of hiatus, in the years from 1996 to 2005 some other methodologies defined based on previous methodologies. Although more than 30 methodologies about development decision support systems had represented so for, however lack of a unified and standard methodology is beheld. The major problem of all existence special methodologies of development decision support system is project ably and it is eligible to apply for various scale system development during the past few years. Terms like used for business intelligence, data mining and etc. for the notification and supporter of decision makers Decision backup system is not a new consideration, but its complex and developed.

A good frame work shows some part of issue and also the relationship between them. In this article tries to introduce some frames for charting DSS like DSS data oriented , model oriented, knowledge oriented, communication oriented, inner organization, outer organization, based on web and its features. Frame use an organized theory and idea to show how ideas are related. The big deal is to design some titles to help ordering individuals and also data. Decision system is not a new topic. But it is complicated and also in changing process. A good frame work shows some part of issue and also the relationship between them.

In other word, today's developments process of decision support systems for a multinational organization is different from that for a small organization. So every organization needs its own methodology for its projects and must define that.

This study continues as this way: in the second section we review the development decision support systems methodologies. In the third section we review the needs developed frame work. In fourth we introduce the developed framework. In part sixth we examine the relationship between this framework and methodologies. In seventh part we check the related works and at the end we conclude.

## 2. A review of development decision support systems methodologies.

Various methodologies defined for decision support systems. In general there are three categories about decision support methodologies.

**First group – based decision methodologies:**

This kind of methodologies is old and deals with issues of management decisions. In this kind of methodologies general steps defined for decision. So the major weakness for these methodologies is in attention to engineering consideration about design and construction a decision support system. The most famous methodologies of this group [7] functional mapping, [8] decision graph [9] decision oriented DSS development process can be noted.

**Second group – based on systems engineering methodologies:** These kinds of methodologies in the course of building a decision support system also helped by engineering software and other tools to define a specific process to develop the decision support system. So it has a bit of distance of general based decision methodologies. Nevertheless the methodologies of this group also remain we within the definition of life cycle, and abstracts away the details and phases of the intermediate steps. These methodologies: [10, 11] end user development, [12, 14] prototyping system development life cycle, are the most famous methodologies of this group.

**Third group – accumulated methodologies:** the methodologies of this group are combined with methodologies from 1, 2 group. These methodologies are combination of consideration relating to decision support and consideration of engineering software , and activities defined in their process are complete than two previous groups. Although this group of methodologies are more interested to the audience of this area nevertheless except some methodologies, yet these methodologies have a general description about their various phases and don't attention to details and this matter make use them difficult [2].This group of methodologies are more famous for their more mature, more coverage the aspects of decision support systems, their effectiveness on decision support methodologies. General description of this group of methodologies is in table 1.

## 3- Reasons for requirement to developed framework

DSS is tries to give speed and improve the processes between persons who decide or related to decision – makers. For managers and designers of DSS it is necessary to be aware about the classification of decision support systems, so they can improve communication for development systems for awareness and support the decisions. There are large volume frameworks for categorizing decision support systems. More than 20 years ago Strive Alter introduced one of the frameworks. It seems need to more general frameworks compared to alter framework. Because, decision support systems from present his study and framework have become more widespread and diverse. In 1980, Strive Alter presented his categorization about decision support systems.

Seven categories that they are still up for debate some of DSS, but not necessary for all of them. It is how that decision support systems can classify according to general operation that performers, apart from the issue, functional area, and shape decision. Seven classes that he presented from the DSS are including: file receiver systems, data analysis systems, information analysis systems, accounting and financial models, descriptive models, optimization models, suggested models. For keep the number of categories in a controllable framework can and should be merging. Alters' typology led into three board types of backup systems. Years that three primary types of alters DSS had named data-oriented and next three types named model-oriented. Alter also suggested a type of DSS that named smart DSS or knowledge – oriented. The aim of present DSS developed framework is to help persons to collect, evaluate, and choose for support and inform to decision – makers.

## 4- Representing developed framing:

If someone classify decision support systems that used more than other, has a good help to category a large number of software packages and systems.

Framework focus on a main dimension with five types of DSS and 3 laterals demonstrate. Primary dimension is the completing the dominant technology or decision support system stimulant. Next dimensions included of: target user, special purpose system, initials developed technology. Some DSS classified as combine-oriented system with more than a DSS part.

**5- Classification decision support system:**

**First group – data –oriented DSS:** The data – oriented DSS are the first kind of overall decision support systems. These systems are consists of file receiver and management reporting system , storage and data analysis systems, executive managers information systems ,and the systems that support the distance systems. Business intelligence systems are sample of data-oriented DSS. Data –oriented DSS emphasis on access and change ability in structured large data base, specially use in time series of data within the company and often extend data.

Data warehouse systems that let to changing data by computer tools, or create and deploy for perform a specific task, or provide more efficient by general tools and other factors.

**Second group- model oriented DSS:** It's consists of systems that use accounting and finance models descriptive models and optimization models. The model oriented DSS emphasis on achieve to model, create and change it. Base levels of performance are possible by simple statistical and analytical tools. Model-oriented DSS utilize data and factors that provided by the decision makers to help them in analysis of the situation, but sometimes the data are not concentrated. The large database usually not to need model oriented DSS.

**Third group-knowledge oriented DSS:** Finding new terms for this group is still ongoing. The best term for this case is knowledge oriented. Sometimes it seems be more appropriate and even better to use the Alters' term ''management expert system''. The knowledge oriented DSS can suggest or command do some tasks.

This DSS are individual computer systems that have expertise in solving specific problems. The term ''expert'' contain have knowledge in a field, ability to understand the problem in that and have skill to solve problem such as these. Data mining concept, applies in this case. This relationship refers to analytical applications that search the hidden patterns in database. Data mining is a process that produce data of piles of data that their content are relate. The used tools for create knowledge oriented DSS, sometimes called <<intelligent support decision methods >>. Its can be use up of data meaning tools that have main data and knowledge components fourth group – document oriented DSS: Recently, a new kind of DSS, as document oriented DSS or knowledge management system created to help the managers in marketing, document management, and unstructured web pages. A document oriented DSS integrate variety of storage and processing technologies preparation a perfect, retrieved, and analyzed document. Web provided access to huge volumes of database (database are combining of text documents, pictures, sounds and mores). Procedures and policies, catalogue of production features, historic documents of company, are samples of documents that available by document oriented DSS, and also contain of minutes of meeting, the company notes and important agreements. A search engine is powerful auxiliary tool for decision making, and in communication with document oriented DSS.

Fifth group – group and communication oriented DSS:

Group decision support systems (GDSS), have been discussed long ago but this time can be define board categories communication – oriented DSS or groupware. Fifth of total of decision support systems, is include of communications and this is techniques for decision support and assistance and there is not in Alters' classification. So it's necessary to introduce these systems as a specific DSS. Group DSS, is a type of mixture decision support system that emphasis on use communication and decision – making models. Group decision support system is interactive system based on computer that tries to make it easy to solve the problem of decision makers that works together. Groupware support the electronic communications, timing, share documents, and other activities that associated with group productivity and decision support.

A large number of capabilities and technologies as group DSS, e-mail, billboards, and video conferencing, are in this category of framework.

**Sixth group – within and outside the organization DSS:** Customers and suppliers are the almost new aims for DSS users that cause of new technology and rapid growth of internet. This type of DSS that targeted for user outside the organization we called it within organization DSS. Internet has created connection like for many variety of within organization that also consists of DSS. Within the organization DSS provides the access to the internal network of organization, and also provides the advantages and authority to use a special DSS. Companies can create a data oriented DSS to access suppliers or model oriented DSS for access to customer to design or select a product.

They are the most outside organization DSS that are for personal use in a organization, as independent DSS, or for group of managers in company as group DSS, or designed for widely use in commercial. The prefix ''outside'' means that DSS is used in a particular organization, and the prefix ''within'' means DSS is widely used.

**Seventh group –DSS with special performance or public purpose:** most DSS are designed for support specific business function or use in variety of marketing industries. These decision support systems called special performance DSS or particular industry DSS. A special performance DSS as a budgeting system may purchase from a vendor or ordered for use in general purpose. The seller develops DSS for functional area of business like marketing and finance.

Some DSS designed to assume the task of deciding in specific industries like scheduling crew in an airline. a DSS with a specific task has important role in solving daily problems or repetitive decisions . the DSS with specific function or task can classify and understand based on components of prevailing DSS as a model oriented DSS , data oriented , suggested DSS. A DSS with specific function or task keep up and guide knowledge relevant to a decision about tasks that organization offers (for example: production task or marketing) these DSS classify base on the goal. Specific performance DSS helps to group or person that does specific decision.

DSS software with general goal , support tasks like project management , decision analysis , or business planning most decision support with general goal , sometimes know as generator DSS.

The generator DSS designed based on the way that can be used in the creation or product in the faster utilizations, they are not complete utilization and not have a specific language, but contained in a mixture of language, user interface, reporting abilities, graphics comforts, and facilities like them and they can give them to users, to whenever its needed in order to build a new DSS [15]

**Eight group-based on web DSS:** eventually, development of this technology may be in range of central computer, a local network, or web-based structure. All a general DSS that discussed can extend by web technologies, these system called web-oriented DSS. A web-oriented DSS is a computer system that shows the information of decision support or provides decision support tools for managers.

The marketing analyzers used web explorer as Mozilla or internet explorer. The server computer that is host of DSS programs connect with user's computer. In most companies, web-oriented DSS has same meaning with internal network or extensive trade DSS. Internal network support altar number of manager who use the explorers in network space. managers are accessing to databases , and analyzing tools increase used for create within the organization DSS that support customer and distributers decision . web or internet technologies are guidelines for create DSS , but some outside organization DSS create with elementary programming language, like enabling technology for central computers. When target users are customers and other external users. it seems that the term " within organization" is suitable for this DSS when all users have internal DSS for company , the term of "outside organization " is appropriate describer .As noted , the decision support systems can category base on DSS gal . Most of DSS have more limited, more focused, and more special dual than general goal.

It is can be use of DSS components dominant, targeted users, goal, and developed technology for classify a special system. For example can create a model oriented DSS, within the organization, product design based on web.

**6- Relationship between DSS categories and methodologies:**

According to the definition model oriented DSS and regard to three group methodologies, this type of DSS it is among the first batch of classification of decision support system.

The first methodology just help to decide and indeed deals with general issues that is correspond with the data oriented DSS. Model oriented DSS used models for furtherance goal, so take place in second category of methodologies because have been established based on model. Because the knowledge-based DSS are advanced and expert, and help to decide and also command they belong to third category of methodologies.

Third category of methodologies are combined with two other categories , so it's more complete and with model and analysis that perform by software engineering tools works better in suggest to managers.

Document oriented DSS must helped by software engineering to help the managers , because use of this DSS storage and document management , and process needed to software analysis that software engineering tools are related to second category of methodologies.

- Group DSS and communication oriented are the third category of methodologies. Because they are the combination of communications.
- Inside and outside organization DSS used both of model oriented and data oriented, use internet and communications too, by conclusion these can be image that belongs to third category.
- DSS with special performance or public goal regard to these DSS use in project management and decision support analysis and programming belongs to third category. Since needs to both of design model and software engineering.
- Web-based DSS, because this DSS used in network, and network built up according to models and communications are belongs to third category that are complete category of methodology.

**7-related works:**

Data oriented DSS, document oriented, and knowledge oriented needed technical data base. Model oriented DSS may use a simple data base, but model elements are so important. Even data oriented is running the designer have to notice to users interests in using DSS at new and unpredictable situation. Although important difference creates because of special tasks and extent DSS, but all of the decision support system have technical elements and mutual goal that support decide. Database of data oriented DSS is a collection of historical and current structured data from different sources that organized for easy achievement to analysis.

Data elements can be developed in such a way that unstructured documents be in document oriented DSS, and also knowledge in a form of rules and templates be in knowledge oriented DSS.

To create understanding of structured data or document in database use of decision support management tools that are computer tools. Statistical and analytical models are the main elements in model oriented DSS.

Each model oriented DSS following special goal and for this reason different models must be use, select the appropriate models is one of the important issues in design. Also the program that used for create specific models must organize required data and users relationships.

Information derived from models also sometimes analyzes and evaluate by decision makers. knowledge oriented DSS use special models for processing roles or defining relationship in data DSS architecture and elements of network design specify how organize hardware , how software data distributed on system . And how the system elements integrated and connected together. Now, the important issue is that how can access DSS on web explorers, in internet inside companies, and also on internet.

Networking is a key pivot of communication oriented DSS.

| Name of methodology | Strengths | weakenesses |
|---|---|---|
| Gochet | • According to third category of methodologies defined a methodology based on architecture and covered short comings in term of architecture.<br>• By definition on concepts creates container , containerized and core of architecture that support separation of policy from mechanism nicely , and provides independence of the life cycles because by this order container and containerized development performs as independent<br>• Architecture oriented : development is based on system architecture .container architecture (data sources), containerized (decision support system), and core (interface between the container and containerized )<br>• This to create a strong relationship between the issues related to DSS and software engineering issues. | • Is not based of activity, and to define the architecture not well define activates.<br>• Don't define required rules and products to methodology activities.<br>• Don't notice some important aspects of decision support development like consideration related data sources. |
| Design cycle | • Based on supplementary prototyping.<br>• Rockon as grandfather of other decision support methodologies, and while is old but it is very implemented. | • Its activities and levels are not fully defined –<br>• Don't define roles and necessary products for methodologies activity<br>• Don't notice some important aspects of decision support development, like consideration related to data sources. |
| Romc | • Based on supplementary prototyping<br>• Frequent feedback and interaction between individuals, during the development process to solve shortcomings. | • Activities and levels are not fully defined.<br>• Do not define roles and necessary products for methodologies activity.<br>• Do not notice some important aspects of decision support development, like consideration related to data sources. |
| Dse | • Based on supplementary prototyping ,<br>• Based on interaction between decision maker and computer creator.<br>• Frequent feedback and interaction between individuals, during the development process to solve shortcomings. | • Do not define roles and necessary product for methodology activities.<br>• Do not notice some important aspects of decision support development, like consideration related to data sources. |
| BIR | • Architecture oriented<br>• Supplementary prototyping<br>• Review meeting at the end of release version.<br>• Due the legacy system to operation of the reusable assets.<br>• Define essential roles and activities in the way of development. | • Weakness can't be found. it seems BIR is complete methodology in area of decision support system development. |
| DSS-Unified process | • strength : defined base on RUP methodology<br>• Based on supplementary prototyping. | • Weaknesses cannot be found. |

Table 1. Aggregation methodologies of decision support system development

**Conclusion**

For perform each project, definition of methodology is needed .this matter is applies about decision support system development. In this study by review decision support methodology and provide a framework for category these system, we have established good relationship between these two categories. Nevertheless mythologies of decision support system development have not reached puberty and mainly remain in the defining the life cycle.

The area of decision support system suffering of widespread use of DSS word in different ways. Apprise and communication use same definitions. each decision support system not similar , and both of researchers and managers needs to a framework of concept to support the decision makers by information technology this article provided a framework for name and category system that support deision makers. A special decision support system most discuss and explain based of four descriptors. Factor or factors of dominant technology, targeted user, specific goal of system, and developed primary technology.

# References

[1] R.R.Veronica, Decision Support Systems Developmentavailable at:http://steconomice.uoradea.ro/anale/volume/2007/v2-statistics-and- economic-informatics/36.pdf.

[2]A.Gachet,P.Haettenschwiler,Development Processes of Intelligent Decision-making Support Systems: Review and Perspective.

[3] B.Arinze,A contingency model of DSS development methodology. Journal of Management Information Systems 8(1): 149-166,1991.

[4] DR.Arnott, A framework for understanding decision support systems evolution. 9th Australasian Conference on Information Systems, Sydney, Australia: University of New South Wales, 1998.

[5] G.M.Marakas, Decision support systems in the 21st century. Upper Saddle River, NJ, Prentice Hall, 2003.

[6] A.Gachet , R.Sprague, A context-based approach to the development of decision support systems, International workshop on Context Modeling and Decision Support, Paris, France, 2005..

[7] T.Moss.Larissa, Atre Shaku, Business Intelligence Roadmap: The Complete Project Lifecycle for Decision-Support Applications, Addison Wesley, 2003.

[8] R.R.Veronica, Decision Support Systems Development.

[9] RW.Blanning, The functions of a decision support system, Information and Management 2, Page 71-96, 1979.

[10] Martin MP, Determining information requirements for DSS, Journal of Systems Management, Page14-21, 1982.

[11] CB. Stabell, A Decision-Oriented Approach to Building DSS. Building Decision Support Systems. J. L. Bennett. Reading, MA, Addison-Wesley, Page 221-260,1983.

[12] Sage AP (1991) Decision support systems engineering. New York, Wiley.

[13] JC.Courbon, J.Drageof, J.Tomasi, L'approche évolutive, Informatique et Gestion,1979.

[14] JC.Courbon, J.Grajew , J.Tolovi, Design and Implementation of Decision Supporting Systems by an Evolutive Approach, Unpublished working paper, 1980.

[15] M.Alavi, IR.Weiss, Managing the risks Associated with end-user computing, Journal of Management Information Systems 2(3), Page 5-20, 1985.

[16] S. W. Ambler, Process Patterns: Building Large-Scale System Using Object Technology, Cambridge University Press, 1998.

[17] J. O. Coplien, A Generative Development Process Pattern Language, In Pattern Languages of Program Design, ACM Press/Addison-Wesley, 1995, pp. 187-196.

[18] J.O.Coplien, A Development Process Generative Pattern Language. In Proceedings of the First Annual Conference on Pattern Languages of Programming (PLoP), 1994.

[19] Harmsen, A. F., Situational Method Engineering, Moret Ernst & Young, 1997.

Conference (CSICC'08), Kish Island, Persian Gulf, Iran, March 2008.

[20] S.Tasharofi, R.Ramsin, "Process patterns for Agile methodologies", In Situational Method Engineering: Fundamentals and Experiences, J. Ralyté, S. Brinkkemper, B. Henderson-Sellers (Eds.), Springer, 2007, pp. 222-237.

[21] E.Kouroshfar, H.Yaghoubi Shahir, R.Ramsin, "Process patterns for component-based software development", In Proceedings of the $12^{th}$ International Symposium on Component-Based Software Engineering (CBSE'09), 2009, pp. 54-68.

[22] D. F. D'Souza, A. C. Wills, Objects, Components and Framewroks with UML: The Catalysis Approach,Addison-Wesley, 1998.

[23] L.T. Moss, S.Atre, Business Intelligence Roadmap: The Complete Project Lifecycle for Decision-Support Applications, Addison Wesley, 2003.

[24] E.Turban,Decision Support Systems And Intelligent Systems, Seventh Edition,Printic-Hell, 2006.

[25] Solomon, Ensuring a successful data warehouse initiative, information systems management, Vol. 22 Iss. 1, p26, 2005.

[26] R.Weir, T.Peng, J.M. Kerridge, Best Practice for Implementing a Data Warehouse: A Review for Strategic Alignment, Proceedings of the 5th Intl. Workshop DMDW'2003, Berlin, Germany, September 8, 2003.

# SESSION

# MINING OF DATA RICH SOURCES

## Chair(s)

### Prof. Ray Hashemi

# Visualization Tools for Results of Entity Resolution

**Cheng Chen**[1], **Mahmood Mohammed**[1], **and John R. Talburt**[1]
[1] Information Science Department, University of Arkansas at Little Rock, Little Rock, AR, USA

**Abstract** - *This paper introduces methods for visualizing the results of Entity Resolution processes. They allow users to visualize the results from any resolution process. These tools will also help users to compare results from different rules-set in the process of Entity Resolution in Entity Identity Information Management. This will facilitate finding false positive and false negative errors. These methods have been applied to the results produced by OYSTER, an open source entity resolution system.*

**Keywords:** Entity Resolution, Entity Identity Information Management, Visualization Tools, Information Visualization

## 1 Background

Entity Identity Information Management (EIIM) is a component of entity identity management (EIM) that utilizes data structures, data integration, and entity resolution (ER) methods and algorithms. EIIM aims at maintain entity identity integrity. Entity identity integrity requires that each entity in the domain should have one and only one representation in the system, which is called an identity. [1] Figure 1 shows a high-level view of EIIM components and processes.

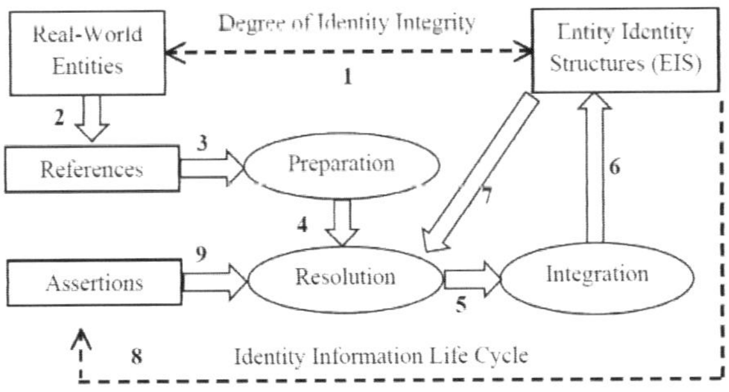


Figure 1: EIIM Components and Interactions.

Figure 1 makes it clear that steps 4, 5, 7, and 9 are related to the resolution process. It is apparent that ER is the core process for EIIM. Entity resolution is the process of determining whether two records in an information system are referring to the same object or to different objects. The term entity describes the real-world object, a person, place, thing, etc. A reference is a collection of attribute values for a specific entity. According to the requirements of entity identity integrity in EIIM, the fundamental law of ER is that two entity references should be linked if and only if they are equivalent [2].

## 2 Problem Statement

In EIIM, the primary goal is to achieve and maintain entity identity integrity. Entity identity integrity is essential a one-to-one correspondence between the entity identity structures (EIS) in the information system and the real-world entities in the domain of interest. In practical applications, EIIM managers are responsible for evaluating the degree of entity identity integrity existing between EIS and real-world entities. For large amounts of data, it is hard for EIIM managers to perform this task by simply browsing and evaluating EIS at random.

In addition, for certain EIIM tools such as OYSTER, the EIS are written to storage as XML documents that can be accessed and updated in a future runs [2]. This requires an EIIM manager to understand XML in order look through and evaluate the EIS. Programming skills may also be needed in order to measure the degree of identity integrity. Even for the managers who have a solid foundation and experience in programming and data analysis, it is difficult to find the false negative errors if the references for a single identity are spread across several EIS.

Moreover, EIIM is a cyclical process not a one-time process. Consequently, EIS are not produced once, but are constantly improved based on better understandings of the data and the matching logic that compares the references. The matching logic is usually implemented as one or more matching rules [3]. Matching rules are the primary determinate in maintaining entity identity integrity in the ER process. Another problem occurs when EIIM managers change results in an attempt to improve the level of entity identity integrity. Isolating and observing the differences in the results produced by two different rule sets can be difficult.

There are numerous techniques that can solve part of the above two problems, but few use information visualization. Information visualization directly addresses the requirements of human perception to help users analyze complex relationships. Humans have the ability to recognize the spatial configuration of elements in a picture and notice the relationships between elements quickly. This highly developed visual ability allows people to grasp the content of a picture much faster than they can scan and understand text [4]. Information visualization methods could save EIIM manager's time, and help them to make quick and accurate decisions, thus saving money for corporations or organizations. Moreover, even for people who do not know programming at all, information visualization tools provide them with the tools for information and data analysis in EIIM.

# 3 Information Visualization Methods

There are two information visualization methods to completely address the above two problems respectively: Treemap and Graph. Treemap methods solve the problem of visualizing EIS. EIIM managers can elucidate differences between EIS from different cycles of EIIM through Graph methods.

## 3.1 Treemap Methods

Treemapping is a visualization method for presenting hierarchical data by using nested rectangles. It maps hierarchical information to a rectangular 2-D display in a space-filling manner [5, 6], which is shown in Figure 2.

Figure 2: A treemap

Treemaps have three significant features:

1) Each box on the chart may be contained in another box, hence the hierarchical view.
2) The size is usually determined by the relative size of a parameter in comparison to the full size of the chart (i.e. the 'bigger' the value of X, the bigger it is on the chart).
3) The color shows another dimension in the parameters, like a movement in time [7].

Even though EIS do not have a strong hierarchical relationship, the second and third features of treemaps show huge advantages for visualization of EIS. In EIIM, combining two references or EIS that are not equivalent is a false positive error. In contrast, failing to combine two references or EIS that are equivalent is a false negative error [1]. It is easy to infer that the EIS with bigger size are prone to have false positive errors while the EIS with smaller size are comparatively easy to get false negative errors. So it is a very important feature of treemaps that they can show the size of EIS by drawing a collection of rectangular bounding boxes whose sizes are entirely dependent on the number of references of EIS.

In addition to rectangle sizes, the color of each rectangle in treemaps can represent other features of EIS. For example, cohesion of EIS can be represented by the color of each rectangle in treemaps. In computer programming, cohesion refers to the degree to which the elements of a module belong together [8]. Similarly, the cohesion of EIS represents the degree to which the references comprising one EIS have similar values. Colors are set to vary due to the cohesion of each EIS, so EIIM managers can see the EIS with low cohesion and high cohesion immediately from color.

## 3.2 Graph

Graph visualization is based on the mathematical theory of networks and graph theory. A graph consists of vertices, also called nodes, and of edges (the connecting lines between the nodes). Directed graph is a graph, or set of nodes connected by edges, where the edges have a direction associated with them [9].

Due to the direction edges, directed graph is suitable to illustrate differences between EIS produced by ER processes with different rule sets. For example, two EIS A and B are produced in first EIIM cycle and then in second EIIM cycle EIS A and B are resolved as equivalent. Therefore, they integrated into a single EIS C. This difference can be revealed as a directed graph in Figure 3(a). The other case where EIS A in first EIIM cycle is resolved to two EIS, B and C, in second EIIM cycle is shown in Figure 3(b). For cases where EIS do not have any changes within several EIIM cycles, those changeless EIS are ignored most of the time because EIIM managers often focus more on differences than agreements.

The graph methods can also be used to compare ER results with a truth set. In Figure 3(a), if EIS C is the truth, the EIS A and B shows that the ER process made a false negative error. In Figure 3(b), if EIS B and C are the truth, EIS A illustrates a false positive error in this ER process.

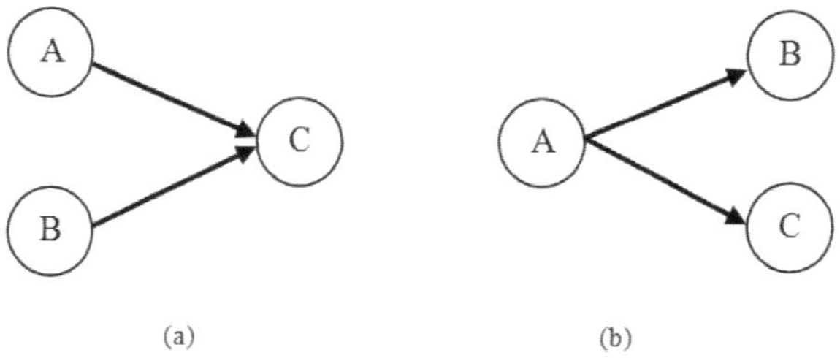


Figure 3: Directed graph

# 4 Implementation with OYSTER

OYSTER (Open sYSTem Entity Resolution) is an ER system developed by the Center for Advanced Research in Entity Resolution and Information Quality (ERIQ) at the University of Arkansas at Little Rock. OYSTER provides access to a variety of entity resolution algorithms as well as support for EIIM and persistent entity identifiers [10].

Two information visualization methods, Treemap and Graph, have been applied to the EIS produced by OYSTER. In OYSTER, EIS are written to storage as XML documents, and each EIS is enclosed in an <Identity> element of an XML document <root>. OYSTER assigns each EIS a unique 16-character identifier known as an OYSTER ID [10].

## 4.1 Treemap Identity Viewer Prototype

The interface of Treemap Identity Viewer Prototype is shown in Figure 4. This prototype demo can be found online at https://sourceforge.net/p/treemapidentity/. This prototype implements treemap methods from JTreeMap API [7].

In this prototype, treemaps of EIS with OYSTER ID inside rectangles accordingly is shown in the upper part of the interface. When a user clicks a certain EIS rectangle in treemaps, a window showing the raw data from references of this EIS will pop up. The colors inside the treemap are determined by the cohesion of EIS. The bigger cohesion in EIS, the lighter the treemaps, and the darker rectangles show the smaller cohesion. The cohesion of EIS in the prototype is calculated by the formula

$$cohesion = \sum_{i \in \Gamma} c(A_i) \quad (1)$$

Where $\Gamma$ is attribute domain, $A_i$ represents certain attribute, and

$$c(A_i) = \frac{pairs \quad of \quad equal \quad records}{total \quad pairs} \quad (2)$$

Pairs here refer to pairs of records independent of order.

For example, one EIS has two attributes, first name and last name, and four records. The first names of four records are "Jim", "Jim", "Jim", and "James", so

$$c(A_1) = \frac{pairs \quad of \quad equal \quad records}{total \quad pairs} = \frac{3}{6} = 0.5$$

The last names of the records are "Jones" "Jones" "Jolson" "Jove", so

$$c(A2) = \frac{pairs \quad of \quad equal \quad records}{total \quad pairs} = \frac{1}{6} = 0.17$$

Therefore, the cohesion of this EIS is 0.5+0.17=0.67.

Additionally, the search field and the slider for the size filter are both located in the middle of the panel. The search

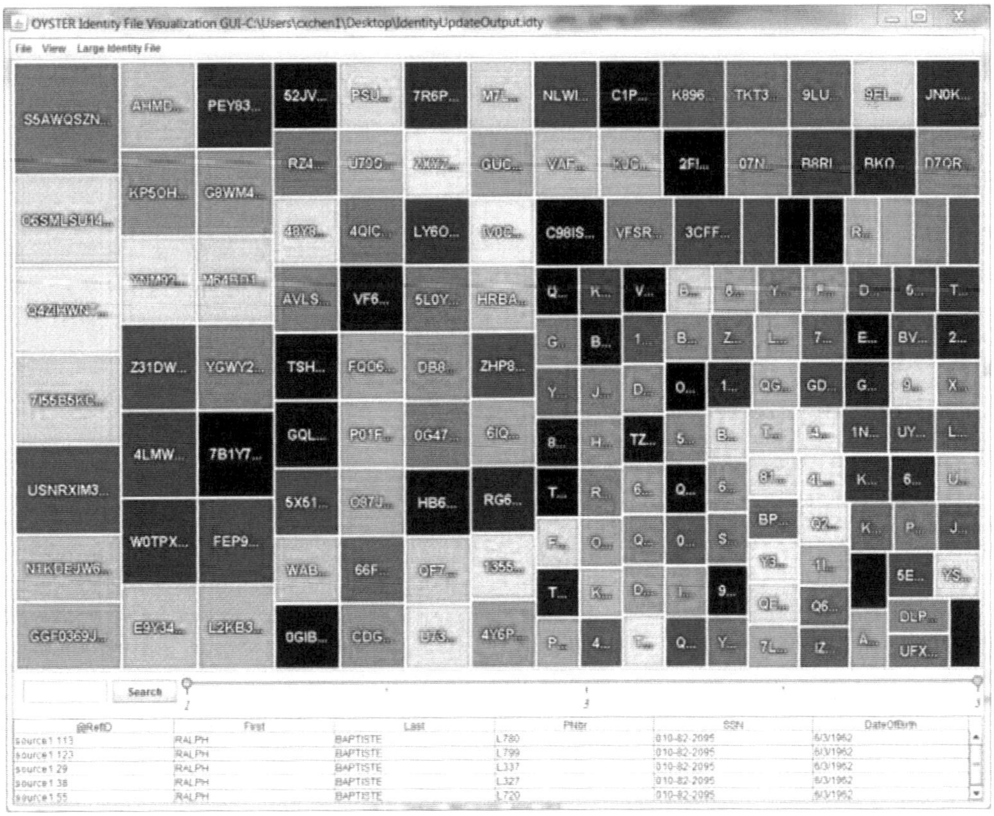

Figure 4: Treemap Identity Viewer Display

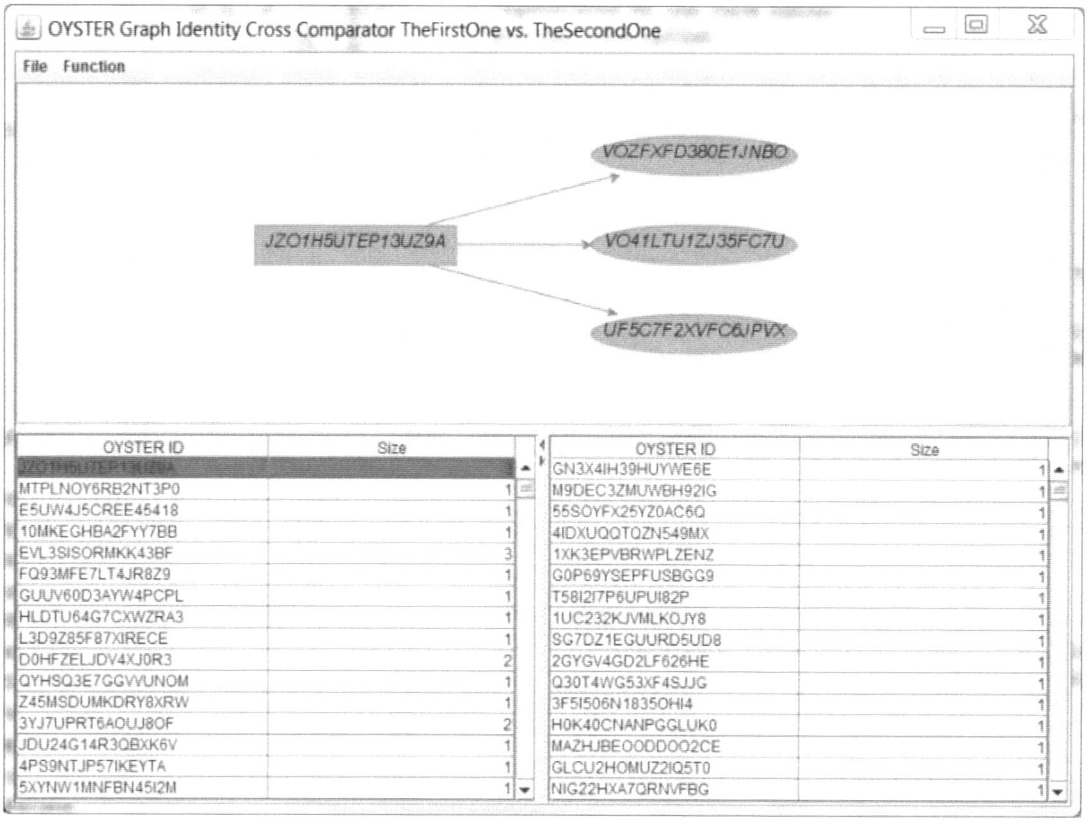


Figure 5: Graph Identity Cross Comparator Display

function employs Apache Lucene 4.1.0 [11] to: scan all references from the input XML file to build indices. This allows the user to find EIS whose references contain the query words. Furthermore, users can limit the size of EIS using the size filter. The treemaps view will adjust according to the size setting.

## 4.2 Identity Cross Comparator Prototype

Figure 5 shows the interface of the Graph Identity Cross Comparator Prototype. The demo can be downloaded from the link http://sourceforge.net/p/graphicc/. The technology implementation of the graph in this prototype is JGraphX Version 1.11.0.0 [12].

The prototype's interface is divided into two parts: graph and table. The table part located on the lower half of interface shows OYSTER ID and size of respective EIS from two ER processes. When the user clicks any OYSTER ID from the left table, that row will be selected and changed to green in color. At the same time, the graph part in the upper half of interface will show the graph of this EIS as green in color and one or more EIS which share the same references with the selected EIS from the other ER processes as orange in color. The selection from the right table also works in the same way as the left table.

There is the "Function" menu item in the menu bar of the interface. There are two functions under this menu item. The first function can hide the equal EIS from both left and right tables. This function was added because changes are the main point for this analysis. The equal EIS here refers to the EIS which are constant in two ER processes. The equal EIS not only occupies table space, but will waste the users' time when analyzing. This hidden function helps with users' analysis. The other function is calculating Talburt-Wang Similarity Index (TWI). The TWI of similarity is defined as

$$TWI = \frac{\sqrt{|A| \times |B|}}{|V|} \quad (3)$$

Where A and B are two partitions of a set S and V is the set of overlaps between A and B [2].

# 5 Conclusion

This paper discusses using information visualization methods to help EIIM manager to evaluate entity identity integrity. The treemap and graph information visualization methods are presented to help to solve the following questions.

- ✧ How to visualize the results from Entity Resolution through raw data of output from ER?
- ✧ How to compare results from different rules-set in the process of ER in EIIM to find the false positive and false negative errors?

Application of these two methods to the results produced by OYSTER shows that information visualization methods do make sense on analyzing the ER results, and improving entity identity integrity in EIIM. And the visualization methods display huge potential to provide convenience for EIIM manages after being tested by few researchers in University of Arkansas at Little Rock.

## 6 Future Work

For the two information visualization methods, Treemap and Graph, there are prototyped demos now. More trials and testing with humans will be executed in the future to determine the effectiveness of these tools.

On the other hand, more functions will be added to make the tools more robust. For example, the formula to calculate the cohesion needs to be studied in more depth for Treemap Identity Viewer, as well as additional calculation functions for calculating the similarity of EIS from different EIIM cycles. Additionally, zoom-in and zoom-out functions will be added to Treemap view to make the program more user-friendly. Moreover, compatibility to different systems, devices and the big data is another challenge for the tools.

## 7 Acknowledgment

The research discussed in this paper was funded in part by a grant from the University of Arkansas for Medical Sciences and Arkansas Department of Education.

## 8 References

[1] Y. Zhou and J. R. Talburt, "Entity Identity Information Management (EIIM)," in Proceedings of the 16th International Conference on Information Quality, 2011.

[2] J. R. Talburt, Entity Resolution and Information Quality, San Francisco: Morgan Kaufmann, 2010.

[3] S. E. Whang and H. Garcia-Molina, "Entity Resolution with Evolving Rules," in Proceedings of the VLDB Endowment, Singapore, 2010.

[4] T. Kamada and S. Kawai, "A general framework for visualizing abstract objects and relations," ACM Transactions on Graphics (TOG), vol. 10, no. 1, pp. 1-39, 1991.

[5] B. Johnson and B. Shneiderman, "Treemaps: a space-filling approach to the visualization of hierarchical information structures," in VIS '91 Proceedings of the 2nd conference on Visualization '91, 1991.

[6] B. Shneiderman, "Tree visualization with tree-maps: 2-d space-filling approach," ACM Transactions on Graphics (TOG), vol. 11, no. 1, pp. 92-99, 1992.

[7] "JTreeMap API," L. Dutheil and ObjectLab Financial Ltd, 2005. [Online]. Available: http://jtreemap.sourceforge.net/.

[8] E. Yourdon and L. L. Constantine, Structured Design: Fundamentals of a Discipline of Computer Program and Systems Design, Prentice Hall, 1979.

[9] R. Diestel, Graph Theory, Springer-Verlag, 2010.

[10] Y. Zhou and R. J. Talburt, "OYSTER: An Open Source Entity Resolution System Supporting Identity Information Management," in ID360 - The Global Forum on Identity, Austin, 2012.

[11] "Apache Lucene," The Apache Software Foundation, 2011. Available: http://lucene.apache.org/core/.

[12] "JGraphX Version 1.11.0.0," JGraph Ltd, 2004. Available: http://www.jgraph.com/jgraph.html.

# Evaluation of Entity Resolution Results through Benchmarking and Truth set Development

**Huzaifa Syed, Fan Liu, Daniel Pullen, Pei Wang and John Talburt**
Information Science Department, University of Arkansas at Little Rock, Little Rock, Arkansas, USA

**Abstract** -*This paper describes methodology for creating a truth set for the evaluation of entity resolution (ER) results. The methodology combines the techniques of benchmarking and truth set development into an iterative, easy to use process. The paper also describes how the truth set developed by the methodology can be applied to calculate five key measures of ER outcome.*

**Keywords**: Entity Resolution Rules, Benchmarking in Entity Resolution, Refining rules in Entity Resolution, OYSTER, Truth Set Development.

## 1 Introduction

Entity Resolution (ER) is the process of determining whether the two references to real world objects in an information system are referring to the same object or two different objects [1]. References referring to the same real-world entity are said to be equivalent. An ER process tries to infer which references are equivalence by apply matching rules that compare the similarity between the values of certain attributes in the records.

The fundamental law of ER is that an ER process acting on a set of records (entity references) should link two records if and only if the two records are equivalent. Most ER systems represent these inferred decisions by appending special values, called link identifiers, to the records. All records that share the same link identifier value are those that the ER process has inferred to be equivalent.

Even though the goal of ER is to link equivalent references, there is almost always some degree of error. There are two types of ER process errors. The first is linking records that are not equivalent, called a *false positive* error [2]. The second is failing to link records that are equivalent, called a *false negative* error. Because most records pairs are not linked in a typical ER process, false negative errors are usually the most difficult to find and count.

Many measurements have been proposed to assess the accuracy of ER results. These include False Positive Rates, False Negative Rate, Precision, Recall, F-measure, Accuracy, Talburt-Wang Similarity Index, Pairwise Comparison, Cluster Comparison and others [3]. The computation of these measures is driven by certain statistics and counts that describe the ER results. The values are not always obvious or easy to obtain. The purpose of this paper is to describe a methodology that combines two common ER analysis techniques in order to obtain these values. The two analysis techniques are benchmarking and truth set development.

## 2 Evaluation by Benchmarking

Benchmarking is when an ER process outcome is compared against a previously established ER outcome that is regarded as reliable. Benchmarking is commonly undertaken when an organization is considering changing its approach to ER. For example, a business that has its own internally developed ER process that has been in use for some time is considering changing to a commercial or open source ER system [4]. Typically evaluating the new system is done by selecting a test file and processing it through the existing system. Then the same file is processed by the new system, and the differences are analyzed.

In this scenario, the results from the existing system serve as a benchmark to measure the new system. Benchmarking has two primary characteristics, it is a relative measure, and it is a population measure. Benchmarking is a relative measure in that even though the existing system may be providing acceptable results, it typically not 100% accurate. Many times the reason for considering a new system is the recognition that there are problems with the existing system that need to be addressed. In this case there is an expectation that the new system will provide different results, and that the differences will be better.

Another important feature of benchmarking is that it can be used to measure an entire population of entity references. The new system can be evaluated against the existing system over all of the same data configurations that actually occur in the system. The negative aspect is that for a large dataset, the number of differences can also be very large making it impractical to manually inspect each difference. In general, the approach to benchmarking evaluation is that the places where the existing and new systems agree represent good results. The analysis is focused on the differences, in particular, to verify whether each difference is a correction or an error made by the new system. If the overall analysis of differences shows that the new system makes more corrections than errors, then the outcomes produced by the new system are judged to be better than the outcomes from the existing system.

However, there are two problems with this type of measurement. The first is that even though benchmarking can be applied to a large population, when there are a large number of differences, sampling is still required in order to reduce the number of differences that must be analyzed to a reasonable number. The second problem is that just because the existing and new systems agree to link or not link a pair of references, it does not mean that the decision is correct. The linking decision can still be a false positive or false negative error made by both systems.

## 3 Evaluation by Truth Set

Truth set evaluation, sometimes called certified record or golden record evaluation, is an alternative to benchmarking evaluation. It reverses benchmarking in that the first step is the manual verification of equivalence among a set of records. The result is a set of records (the truth set) for which each pair of records has been verified to be equivalent or not equivalent. The records are manually linked into clusters known to be referencing the same entity. Truth set evaluation has two primary characteristics, it is an absolute measure, and is necessarily a sample measure.

The big advantage of truth set evaluation is that it is an absolute measure against the truth rather than relative to another ER outcome. The obvious problem with truth set development is that the records must be manually verified. The verification dictates that a truth set can only be developed for a sample of the records in the entire population. Just as in statistical sampling in general, for the truth set to be helpful it must somehow represent all the data configurations that might occur in the general population.

However truth set sampling is different than general statistical sampling. In statistical sampling, the focus is on values in each individual record, but for ER sampling the focus is on the relationship between records. For example, if a small random sample were taken from a large dataset with a relatively low match rate, all of the pairs in the sample are likely to be true negative pairs. The probability of selecting a set that includes true positive, false positive, or false negative pairs is very low.

In the case of truth set sampling, the real goal is to sample entities rather than the references. The desired characteristic of an ER truth set is that includes all of the references for the same entity for some sample of the entities in the population. This is where benchmarking and truth set development are complementary. The following section describes how these can be used together.

# 4 Benchmarking in Truth Set Construction

The following description assumes the context of benchmarking evaluation where there are two ER processes in place. One is an existing system (System A) considered to have somewhat reliable results and a new ER system (System B) that gives different and presumably better results. Another assumption is that there is at least one large dataset (Base Dataset) of entity references that refer to the population of entities being managed.

## 4.1 Initial Seeding of the Truth Set

The first step in the construction of truth set is to process the Base Dataset with System A. The links applied by System A will be called A-links. Next the Base Dataset is processed with System B to apply B-links. This should be done in such a way that both links are preserved in the references, i.e. each reference record has both an A-link and a B-link.

Next sort the base dataset in order by A-link. After the base dataset is sorted by A-link, extract a sample of the records using the method of systematic sampling where every N-th record is extracted for a fixed value of N. The value N will depend upon how many records are desired in the initial sample. Because the truth set will have to be manually inspected, it is better to be conservative and select a small number of records for the initial sampling of no more than 100 records. If a larger truth set is desired, the same process can be repeated to increase the size of the truth set.

## 4.2 Union of A and B Clusters

The next step is to add to the truth set all of the records that are linked to each of the initial seed records by either A-links or B-links. Since each seed record has both an A-link and a B-link, it is an easy matter to locate and bring into the set all of the records in the Base Dataset that share those same links. If both the A and B systems have similar recall, then most of the records retrieved in the process will be the same. However, there will likely be cases in which the seed record is linked to another record that has a different B-link or vice versa. After this process is completed, the truth set should comprise the union of the A-link clusters and the B-link clusters that contain the initial seed records.

## 4.3 Inspection for False Positives and Addition of True Links

Next each union cluster should be inspected to determine if any of the links made by either System A or B represents a false positive link with respect to the initial seed record of the cluster. This assumes that the person or persons performing the inspection possess enough direct knowledge about the entities to make a correct decision or at least have ready access to other experts that have this knowledge. For example, in the case of student records, this might be teachers or administrators who personally know the students. Simply making the decision based on matching similarity without direct knowledge is not sufficient.

Once all of the false positive records have been identified, they should be removed from the truth set and the remaining records in each cluster should be assigned a third link. This third link, called the True-link is manually created and assigned in such a way that each record in the cluster has the same True-link value, and records in different clusters have different True-link values. Again the True-link should be separate from, and in addition to, the A-link and B-link values in the record. Figure 1 describes the process so far:

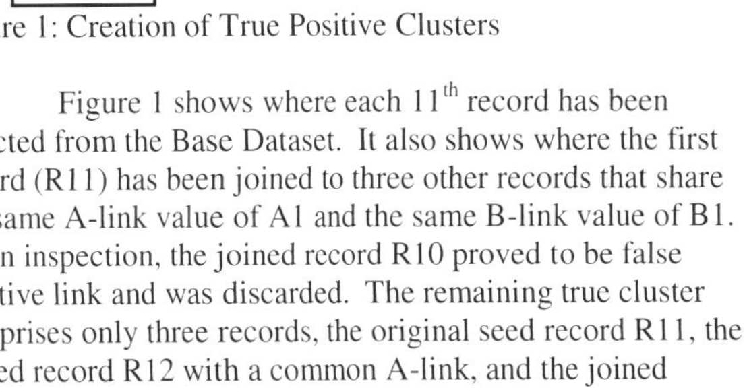


Figure 1: Creation of True Positive Clusters

Figure 1 shows where each $11^{th}$ record has been selected from the Base Dataset. It also shows where the first record (R11) has been joined to three other records that share the same A-link value of A1 and the same B-link value of B1. Upon inspection, the joined record R10 proved to be false positive link and was discarded. The remaining true cluster comprises only three records, the original seed record R11, the joined record R12 with a common A-link, and the joined record R35 with a common B-link. These records are all assigned the True-link value of T1.

## 4.4 Search for False Negatives

The process should assure that the truth set has only clusters of true positive records. However, it is likely that there still some true positive links that neither System A or B were able to find. The next step is to mount a search for these false negative records and add them to the true clusters.

One systematic approach is to relax the matching rules in System A or System B and inspect any new records that are linked to the seed records that are not already in the union cluster from the previous step. Rules can be relaxed by introducing approximate match or by omitting certain attributes. For example suppose than one of the standard rules for System A is an exact match on first name and exact match on last name. Changing from exact match to an approximate match such as the Levenshtein Edit distance or Soundex would likely bring in more matching records. Although many may be false positives, it may also uncover some number of false negatives that were cause by misspelling or other data quality issues.

Alternatively, this single rule might be replaced with two rules, one that matches only on first name and another that only matches on last name. This change would bring together all of the records with either the same first name or the same last name. Although it would create more false positives than the previous approach, thus creating more work in inspecting the records, it may also be more effective in finding false positives than simply relaxing the match on either first or last name. This method also has the advantage that it finds matches among all of the records, not just particular records.

Searching for false positive records for a particular seed record is best done using done by loading the Base Dataset into a relational database and running queries based on data values in the seed record. This can be particularly effective, especially those that include "wild card" or "like" functionality. Whenever a false negative record is found that is not already in the TruthTable, then the records should be added to the TruthTable and labeled with the appropriate TrueLink value.

# 5 ER Measures Based on Truth Set

Table 1 shows an example intersection matrix that compares the clusters of an ER process (Process B) to the Truth Set over a set of 22 records. The matrix shows that the Truth Set has 4 true clusters that comprise the rows of Table 1 and are labeled T1 to T4. Process B has produced 5 clusters that comprise the columns Table 1 and are labeled B1 to B5.

Table 1: Partition Intersection Matrix

| Process B vs. Truth Set | B1 | B2 | B3 | B4 | B5 | |
|---|---|---|---|---|---|---|
| T1 | 2 | 1 | 0 | 0 | 1 | 4 |
| T2 | 0 | 3 | 2 | 0 | 2 | 7 |
| T3 | 0 | 0 | 4 | 2 | 0 | 6 |
| T4 | 0 | 2 | 0 | 2 | 1 | 5 |
| | 2 | 6 | 6 | 4 | 4 | 22 |

The cell at the intersection of each row and column contains the number of records in the intersection of the clusters. The non-empty intersections are called the overlaps between the two partitions generated by Process B and by the Truth Set. For example the first cell of the table contains the value 2 which means there are 2 overlaps between T1 and B1.

If C(n, k) represents the combinations of n things taken k at a time, then for 22 records there are C(22, 2)=231 possible record pairs that can be linked together by an ER process. In addition the number of overlaps (11 in Table 1), the intersection matrix also provides four key counts of record pairs. These are

- TP, the number of true positive pairs – pairs linked by the process that are true links
  $$TP=\sum_{i=1}^{n}\left(\sum_{j=1}^{m}C(s_{i,j},2)\right)$$ , where $s_{i,j}$ is the count in row i and column j
- FN, the number of false negative pairs – pairs not linked by the process that are true links
  $$FN=\left(\sum_{i=1}^{n}C(t_i,2)\right)-TP$$, where $t_i$ is the size of cluster Ti
- FP, the number of false positive pairs – pairs linked by the process that are not true links
  $$FP=\left(\sum_{i=1}^{n}C(b_i,2)\right)-TP$$, where $b_i$ is the size of cluster Bi
- TN, the number of true negative pairs – pairs not linked by the process that are not true links
  TN=C(R,2)-TP-FP-FN, where R is the total number of records

From Table 1 these values are TP=15, FN=37, FP=28, TN=151. These factors drive several measures of ER outcome. Some of these are listed below [2].

$$Accuracy=\frac{TP+TN}{TP+FP+TN+FN}$$, for Table 1 the value is 0.72

$$Precision=\frac{TP}{TP+FP}$$, for Table 1 the value is 0.35

$$Recall=\frac{TP}{TP+FN}$$, for Table 1 the value is 0.29

$$Specificity=\frac{TN}{TN+FP}$$, for Table 1 the value is 0.84

The Talburt-Wang Index (TWi) [1] also measures the similarity between two partitions. However, the TWi is based only on the number of overlaps (V) and does not use the TP, FP, FN, and TN counts. The TWi takes on values from 0 to 1. If A and B are two partitions of a set S, the TWi similarity between A and B is defined as

$$TWi=\frac{\sqrt{|A|\cdot|B|}}{|V|}$$, for Table 1 the value is 0.41

# 6 Conclusion

The ability to evaluate ER outcomes is essential in any continuous improvement cycle such as the TDQM define-measure-analyze-improve cycle [5]. The process described for truth set development is a practical and effective way to generate a truth set that can underpin these evaluations. In a recent education study, this process was used to create a truth set of more than 3,800 records. The truth set was used to evaluate the results of entity resolution performed on student data.

# 7 Acknowledgement

Funding for the research in this paper was provided through research grants by the Arkansas Department of Education.

# 8 References

[1] Talburt, J. R., *Entity Resolution and Information Quality*, Burlington, MA: Morgan Kaufmann Publishers, 2011.

[2] Fellegi, I.,Sunter, A., A Theory for Record Linkage, Journal of the American Statistical Association, Vol. 64 No. 328, 1183-1210, 1969

[3] Christen, P, *Data Matching: Concepts and Techniques for Record Linkage, Entity Resolution and Duplicate Detection*, New York, NY: Springer, 2012

[4] Syed, H. F., Talburt, J. T., Liu, F., Pullen, D., Wu, N., Developing and Refining Matching Rules for Entity Resolution, *Proceedings of the Information Knowledge Engineering*, 2012

[5] Lee, Y.W., Pipino, L.L., Funk, J.D., & Wang, R.Y. (2006). Journey to Data Quality. Cambridge, MA: MIT Press.

# Mitigating Data Quality Impairment on Entity Resolution Errors in Student Enrollment Data

**Daniel Pullen, Pei Wang, John Talburt, and Ningning Wu**
Information Science Department, University of Arkansas at Little Rock, Little Rock, AR, USA

**Abstract-***Entity resolution and record linking processes are often required to process input records of poor data quality. The matching errors caused by poor quality data can often be overcome by categorizing the quality problems, then applying a cyclic process that continuously refines the match rules to overcome these problems. This paper presents a case study of this process for student enrollment data which describes the unique data quality issues that were identified throughout this cyclic process and how different similarity functions were used to mitigate these issues.*

**Keywords:** Student Enrollment Data, Boolean matching rules, entity resolution, OYSTER, Data Quality (DQ)

## 1 Background

An entity refers to a unique real world object that is described through its characteristics which are referred to as attributes. Entity Resolution (ER) is the process of determining whether two references to real world objects in an information system are referring to the same object or two different objects [1]. A reference corresponds to a tuple or row in a relational database composed of a set of attribute values belonging to a particular entity.

The ER processes discussed and undertaken throughout this paper are based on the Fellegi-Sunter model [5]. This model allows for two records to be judged as three different outcomes. Only two of these are pertinent to this discussion: "link" pairs which have been labeled as belonging to the same real world entity or "non-link" pairs which have been labeled as belonging to two different and unique real world entities. To come to these judgments, Boolean match rules are utilized [6]. A result of one of these rules produces a yes or no result. These Boolean rules are based on the Fellegi-Sunter model. On this basis, the yes corresponds to a "link" pair, and the no corresponds to a "non-link" pair.

The rule structure used throughout this process is based in Fellegi-Sunter. This structure consists of five components: attribute, comparator, term, rule, and rule set. The relation and implications of each of these components has been clearly summarized in recent research [7]. The output of this rule structure will produce the previously described outcomes. Each of the rules are linked together through OR logic, If any one of the rules produces a yes based on the attributes selected the two records will be considered a "link" pair.

Throughout the ER process, the results of the matches are analyzed and categorized into four outcomes. True positives (TP) are correctly labeled "link" pairs. True negatives (TN) are correctly labeled "non-link" pairs. In contrast to these true or correct results, there are two types of incorrect resolution results. False positives (FP) are pairs of records that have been identified as matches or "link" pairs by the ER algorithm or process but refer to two different real world entities. False negatives (FN) are pairs of records that have been identified as non-matches or "non-link" pairs by an ER algorithm or process but refer to the same real world entity [8]. An effective and well implemented ER process should strive to produce the lowest FPs and FNs obtainable.

To perform the ER processes throughout this research, the Open System for Entity Resolution (OYSTER) will be utilized. This is an open source ER system developed by the Entity Resolution and Information Quality (ERIQ) center at the University of Arkansas at Little Rock that includes features covering the ER process to the life cycle management of the entities and their identity information established during that process [9]. For this research, the focus will be on the ER results and not the life cycle management components.

The testing focuses on using the identity capture run mode of OYSTER. This mode is used to build a set of identities from the input references that are processed [10]. OYSTER offers several other features and run modes that are out of the scope of this research.

## 2 Similarity Functions

Similarity functions are used to calculate the similarity of two attribute values. Such a similarity function can be defined as [8]:

$$s = \mathrm{sim}(a_i, a_j) \quad (1)$$

This is where $a_i$ and $a_j$ are two attribute values belonging to two different references. Utilization of these functions is necessary to measure the degree of similarity between the attribute values contained in different references. There are many different approaches to comparing the similarity of two attribute values. Several of these algorithms will be discussed later in the context of overcoming data quality through the usage of such similarity functions. These similarity functions play the role of the comparator in the Fellegi-Sunter model.

## 3 ER Impact of Data Quality Issues

The data set used throughout this testing is a collection of student enrollment data spanning two academic years. Only the student identity information was used. Any results discussed in this paper have been made anonymous to allow the sharing and description of the unique cases identified. In the data available, a few strong identifying attributes are of particular interest. These are first name, middle name, last name, date of birth, and student identifier. Examples of some data quality (DQ) issues identified with these attributes and their rates are summarized below in Tables 1 and 2.

**Table 1 Data Quality Issues in Set A**

| Data Quality Issue | Data Set A | % |
|---|---|---|
| Number in First Name | 121 | 0.003741 |
| Number in Middle Name | 165 | 0.005102 |
| Number in Last Name | 35 | 0.001082 |
| Virgule in First Name | 24 | 0.000742 |
| Asterisk in First Name | 93 | 0.002875 |
| Total Problems | 438 | 0.013542 |
| Total Records | 3,234,292 | |

**Table 2 Data Quality Issues in Set B**

| Data Quality Issue | Data Set B | % |
|---|---|---|
| Number in First Name | 135 | 0.004147 |
| Number in Middle Name | 136 | 0.004178 |
| Number in Last Name | 31 | 0.000952 |
| Virgule in First Name | 27 | 0.000829 |
| Asterisk in First Name | 66 | 0.002027 |
| Total Problems | 395 | 0.012133 |
| Total Records | 3,255,513 | |

These tables point out some of the obvious and easily quantifiable data quality issues present in these two data sets. There are several other cases that occur over these different attributes. The student name fields have some particularly interesting and challenging problems. They occur frequently enough throughout the data set to increase the amount of errors made by the ER process.

The first name field has many records where the field is treated not only as the student's first name but also as nickname. This creates examples that look like "Joseph (Joey)" or "Joseph Joey." Other records contain a nickname instead of the student's given first name. An example is "Joey" instead of "Joseph." The middle name field is the least populated of these selected attributes. Many cases have only the middle initial instead of the full middle name. The worst example of DQ issues in this field involves the placement of some last names in the middle name field. Many Hispanic students have a hyphenated name where one comes from the father and the other comes from the mother. Upon data entry, the first of the two names may be placed in the middle name field. This has a detrimental impact on matching using the middle and last name fields. In addition to these issues, there is the presence of numbers or special characters in all three of the name fields as summarized in the previous table.

The DQ problems do not end with the name fields. The student identifier has a plethora of issues. Often, a student identifier may be erroneous and completely different from the value given on other records for the same student. In other cases, there is a simple typing error resulting in the transposition of two or more characters in the field. An example would be "123456789" for one record and "132456789" in another record belonging to the same student. Not all schools use the same student identifier criteria. This prevents, or at a minimum makes difficult, to use data quality rules to detect erroneous identifiers in the data. The largest cause of errors with a match rule containing the student identifier is students that share the same student identifier on at least one record. This typically creates an FP judgment. Most commonly, this occurs when two siblings, or even twins, have their student identifiers swapped during a transfer to a new school district. Manual data entry, or reentry in the case of student transfers, is the root cause of many of these problems.

In addition to problems specific to certain attributes, there are issues that affect multiple attributes. Some of these unique cases can be summarized briefly. There are cases where one attribute has been placed in the incorrect field. Cases involving the phone number, student identifier, and address field have been identified; these values are actually in one of the student name fields. The data also shows a trend in naming twins. Parents will often name twins with very similar names such as “Terrell” and “Jerrell.” These names are difficult to differentiate when using a similarity function like normalized Levenshtein edit distance (LED). In other cases, this similarity in naming is even extended to middle name fields. With the date of birth and last name fields already identical, differentiating twins in the match rules is problematic. Some cases mix this with an erroneous student identifier causing the consolidation of the entity identity structures that correspond to each unique student.

## 4 Mitigating Data Quality Impact

How can entity identity management managers overcome data quality problems when performing ER? As mentioned above, there are many problems in the name field such as special characters or nickname provided instead of given name. Some appropriate similarity functions and comparator functions can make a drastic improvement and overcome these issues.

**Scan**–Scan is a multipurpose similarity function developed for use in OYSTER [11]. It performs transformations on the input strings based on the parameters passed to the function. Once the transformations are completed, an exact comparison is performed between the two strings. Scan can be used to overcome a variety of data quality problems. It includes the capability to filter all special characters and only include letters or alphanumerical characters. For example, value1 = "JAMES\\" and value2 = "JAMES" can be found similar. Also, scan can reorder strings or even read them from right to left as opposed to left to right and perform transformations regarding the casing of alphabetical characters. It can force all characters to be lower case, upper case, or the original case present in the string. For example "Eric" can be generated as "ERIC" after using scan.

**QTR**–The Q-Gram Tetrahedral ratio uses all q-gram subsequences for string comparison [4] allowing a match though two string may be distinctly different. This can overcome the issues with both nickname and given name in first name field. For example, value 1 = "Jacob (Jake)" and value2 = "Jacob". With these it is possible to set the QTR threshold to 0.25 and judge them similar.

**LED**–The Normalized Levenshtein Edit Distance helps solve typographical errors. It counts the number of edits that are made to make the strings similar and then divides the value by the length of the longer string. For example, value1 = "Mariah" and value2 = "Miriah". If the LED threshold is set to 0.83, it will judge them similar.

**Soundex**–Soundex can be used to find the values which have similar pronunciation but different spelling. This function is typically used to fix misspelled and even transposed characters. For example value1 = "Damieva" and value2 = "Dameiva." These two values will produce the same Soundex hash value, creating a match.

**Nickname**–For cases where a nickname is provided instead of given first name in the first name field, a nickname comparator can be utilized. This comparator uses a lookup table to find nicknames that are considered to be synonymous to a given name or other nickname [11]. For example, value1 ="William" and value2 = "Bill". Nickname can overcome this and create a match between the two records.

Sometimes, these similarity functions will cause FP and FN errors. For example, suppose there are two different rules used to produce two different ER results from the same data set. The first rule uses student first name, student last name and date of birth with an exact match for each of them. The second rule is student first name QTR with a threshold of 0.2, last name and date of birth with an exact match. Split analysis is a methodology used to analyze splits in the clusters between two different link identifiers. How this process works has been discussed in detail in recent research [7]. After performing this comparison between the two results, the FPs and FNs created by the second rule can be identified and their rates can be calculated. The calculation for approximate FP percentage rate and approximate FN percentage rate are shown in equation 2 and 3. The results are shown in table 3 [2]. Since these FNs and FPs were identified using split analysis, these are considered to be worst case FP and FN rates.

$$FP\% = \frac{FP\ Count}{Linked\ Count}(100) \quad (2)$$

$$FN\% = \frac{FN\ Count}{Linked\ Count}(100) \quad (3)$$

**Table 3 Results of false positive and false negative**

| | False Positive | False Negative |
|---|---|---|
| Number of | 18 | 14 |
| Rate of | 0.54% | 0.42% |
| Total number of | 3333 | 3333 |

From the table, it is apparent that the second rule creates more FPs than FNs. This was caused by the low value specified to QTR which matched similar records. Therefore, if the user decides to use a function that handles a numeric value of similarity as an input, it is imperative to pay close attention to the value specified.

It is requisite to understand that the rate of the FPs and FNs indicate how well the rules are performing.

# 5 Conclusion

Data quality problems often present a formidable obstacle to obtaining an accurate and effective ER result. The approaches to overcome data quality issues in the student enrollment data during ER described in this paper have been successfully implemented in OYSTER. The success of any ER process is often directly related to the time spent profiling the data and identifying these types of data quality problems. Effectively identifying and categorizing these types of problems directly affect the quality of the ER results at the end of such processes.

These approaches above include similarity functions such as LED and QTR that can overcome issues including both nickname and given name contained together in one field, transposed characters, and other typographical errors. Additionally, other similarity functions such as Nickname and Soundex can overcome the issues such as special characters, numbers, misspellings and nickname provided instead of given name. While these approaches contribute greatly to improving the ER results, there is a limit to which these approaches can aid in reducing FP and FN rates. ER is a deeply synergistic process. A point will be reached when modifying rules to reduce FPs or FNs will have a detrimental effect on the ER results. The point, at which this occurs, is tied to the context of the application. Thus, some data sets may reach limitations in their error rate reduction quicker and require more stringent management of the entity identity information knowledge base and regular application of asserted linking. This is a technique discussed in contemporary literature and applied in ER systems today [1].

# 6 Future Work

Depending on the type and impact of data quality issues, there may be a limit to how much these similarity functions can help. Cross-attribute comparison and data preparation functions can assist users in overcoming some issues. In the future, OYSTER will implement different types of data preparation functions that can be performed before the ER comparison.

Data Preparation functions would provide the ability to clean data. Currently in OYSTER this can be done using the scan function to remove the special characters and numbers before performing Entity Resolution using exact match criteria. This functionality could be improved and expanded upon. A particular case where this would be applicable is in student enrollment data where some records use the number 0 instead of letter "O" and put special characters and nickname together in one field. For example "MO0REA" and "MOOREA", "Nan*//" and "Anna". Additionally, the ability to perform tokenization of input strings based on certain criteria will be implemented. This will also help with cases where multiple names are placed in the same attribute field.

Cross-attribute comparison can compare the values in different attributes [3]. Some records in student enrollment data have student middle name into the first name field and have student first name in middle name field. For example, several records that indicate one student but have flipped the first name and middle name are displayed below in Table 4. With this example, none of these similarity functions can overcome this problem.

**Table 4 First name and Middle name flipped**

| | First Name | Middle Name |
|---|---|---|
| 1 | DYLAN | GOVERNOR |
| 2 | G. | DYLAN |
| 3 | GOVERNOR | DYLAN |

In order to indicate which matches by the rules may be FPs or FNs, the uniqueness of each cluster needs to be calculated. This is assuming that the cluster with high value of uniqueness for different attributes will indicate a FP. This uniqueness in combination with a cluster level entropy score can help users adjust their match rules or apply a clerical review process.

# 7 Acknowledgment

The research described in this paper has been supported in part through grants from the Arkansas Department of Education.

# 8 References

[1] John Talburt. "Entity Resolution and Information Quality". Morgan Kaufmann, 2010.

[2] Melody Penning and John Talburt. "Information Quality Assessment and Improvement of Student Information in the University Environment". *Information and Knowledge Engineering,* 2012, pp. 351-357.

[3] Yinle Zhou, John Talburt, Fumiko Kobayashi and Eric D. Nelson. "Implementing Boolean Matching Rules in an Entity Resolution System using XML Scripts". *Information and Knowledge Engineering*, 2012, pp. 332-337

[4] Holland, G. &Talburt, J. (2010) q-Gram Tetrahedral Ratio (aTR) for approximate pattern matching. *2010 Conference on Applied Research in Information Technology,* University of Central Arkansas, Conway, AR.

[5] Iven Fellegi and Alan Sunter. "A Theory for Record Linkage"; *Journal of the American Statistical Association,* Vol. 64 No. 328, 1183-1210, 1969

[6] Steven Whang and Hector Garcia-Molina. "Entity Resolution with Evolving Rules"; *Proceedings of the VLDB Endowment,* Vol. 3 Issue 1-2, 1326-1337, September 2010

[7] Huzaifa Syed, Fan Lui, Daniel Pullen, Ningning Wu, John Talburt. "Developing and Refining Matching Rules for Entity Resolution"; *Information and Knowledge Engineering,* 2012, pp. 345-350

[8] Peter Christen. *Data Matching*, Springer, 2012.

[9] Zhou, Y. and Talburt, J. (2011). Entity Identity Information Management (EIIM). *International Conference on Information Quality (ICIQ-11),* Adelaide, Australia, November 18-20, 2011, pp. 327-341

[10] Zhou, Y. and Talburt, J. (2011). The Role of Asserted Resolution in Entity Identity Management. The 2011 International Conference on Information and Knowledge Engineering (IKE'11), Las Vegas, Nevada, July 18-20, 2011, pp. 291-296

[11] Fumiko Kobayashi. (May 30, 2013). OYSTER v3.3 Reference Guide. In SourceForge. Retrieved May 24, 2013, http://sourceforge.net/projects/oysterer/files/OYSTER_3.3/Documentation/OYSTER_v3.3_Reference_Guide.pdf.

# Probabilistic Scoring Methods to Assist Entity Resolution Systems Using Boolean Rules

**Fumiko Kobayashi, John R. Talburt**
Department of Information Science
University of Arkansas at Little Rock
2801 South University Ave. EIT 550
Little Rock, AR, USA

**Abstract-** *This paper describes methods to provide clerical review indicators for Entity Resolution (ER) systems that use Boolean match rules. These clerical review indicators are generated by the use of a supplemental probabilistic scoring algorithm. Four scoring methods that generate a probabilistic match score are discussed. When this match score is combined with a predefined threshold, an ER system can suggest possible near matches for clerical review. This allows the user a method to more effectively address false negative resolutions made by the system.*

**Keywords-** Scoring Rules; Attribute Weights; Clerical Review; OYSTER; Boolean Rules

## 1 Introduction

Entity Resolution (ER) is the process of determining whether two references to real-world objects in an information system are referring to the same object, or to different objects [5]. Real-world objects are identified by their attribute similarity and relationships with other entities. Some examples of attributes are First Name, Last Name, and Social Security Number (SSN) for references about people or Latitude, Longitude, Description, Name for references to places. ER has also been studied under other names including but not limited to record linkage [1], deduplication [3], reference reconciliation [6], and object identification [4].

ER systems take entity references and make matching decisions based upon the degree to which two references have similar attribute values. However, there are two families of entity resolution rules that can be used to make these matching decisions. The first and most commonly used type of rules employee Boolean rules [12, 13] to perform "matching" to make match/no-match decisions for reference pairs. Boolean rules are used most often due to the fact that the attributes and match functions are clearly spelled out which allows the user to easily understand them and provide more configuration control to the user or system administrator. Many ER systems follow the Fellegi-Sunter Model for record linking [11] in which record pairs are judged to be "link" or "non-link" pairs depending upon which attribute values agree or disagree. In addition to the "link" and "non-link" decisions, the Fellegi-Sunter Model also introduces the concept of a "possible link". These three states are determined by setting a LOWER and UPPER threshold and determining the state of the link as:

- If R > UPPER, then denote pair as a "link".
- If LOWER <= R <= UPPER, then denote pair as a "possible link".
- If R < LOWER, then denote pair as a "non-link".

Where R is the probability of a match between a record pair. It is this "possible link" state that is discussed in this paper and the probability associated to the record pair in this "possible link" state is referred to as the clerical review indicator.

Since most ER systems use Boolean match rules, there is no inherent ability to identify the clerical review indicator and only function by identifying the "link" and "non-link" pairs. For example, the pattern that two student enrollment records agree on first name values, last name values, and date-of-birth values but disagree on school identifier values might be designated a link rule, i.e. the decision is that the records refer to the same real-world entity (student). These decision making methods that give a yes or no (match/no-match) decision are called Boolean matching rules.

The second family of ER rule uses mathematical models to compute a probabilistic numerical match score which represents the distance between a record pair. Probabilistic scoring methods are becoming more common but are not as easy to understand by users and provide them less control of the configuration since probabilistic methods are mostly predefined algorithms that only accept some form of threshold value to make match decisions.

Although there are a variety of algorithms for implementing ER processes, at a basic level they all involve making decisions about the similarity of the references. ER systems make the match/no-match decisions and assert their decisions by appending an identifier value, called a "link" to each record representing a reference. Equivalent records are assigned the same links. This paper suggests a hybrid ER system that will allow probabilistic scoring methods to supplement standard Boolean match rules by identifying a list of "near matches" that require a level of clerical review.

# 2 Problem Definition

Boolean rules are used in most ER systems because they are easy to understand, however, one weakness is that they do not inform users of "near matches". Being strictly match/no-match decisions the Boolean rules do not inherently contain the mechanisms required to identify these "near matches". Boolean ER systems have the capability to resolve a set of input references against themselves or an entity repository and generate a resulting repository of entity clusters through linking. Although this knowledge is useful to the requestor, it may also be prudent for the system to provide a list of the most closely related potential matches as well as the matches determined by the Boolean matching rules. This can be done in the form of a list containing the reference identifier, a link, and the probabilistic score value between the source reference and the reference in the link. These potential matches can be beneficial for various reasons; one such reason is that if the source reference does not contain the correct combination of attribute values, it is possible that none of the Boolean match rules will have the ability to link the reference to any entity cluster in the repository. However, with the correct algorithm, potential matches can still be identified which may allow the user to manually assert a link that the ER system could not do automatically without user intervention.

These potential matches can be found through the use of a probabilistic scoring algorithm that can calculate a normalized score, such that 0 <= score <=1, for a reference pair. By incorporating these scoring methods into an existing ER system that uses Boolean rules, the concept of review indicators can be introduced to the system. These review indicators are the scores which provide a list of "near match" candidates which could not be identified by the Boolean Rules. These review indicators can be used for clerical reviews that allow the user to apply assertion techniques [5] to resolve the false negative errors made by the ER system.

This paper discusses two (2) variations of a probabilistic scoring algorithm that can, with a high degree of accuracy, provide review indicators for a list of potential matches to be reviewed.

# 3 Probabilistic Scoring

Scoring is the process of assigning a numerical value (normalized between 0 and 1) that predicts the probability that a reference in the entity repository matches the source reference. The score can be run on all of the references that are specified as possible matches by the index, but do not fully match based on the specified Boolean match rules. After scores are calculated, any scores that meet the predefined threshold could then be returned, as the review indicator, in a review list to the requestor along with the record identifier and the link to which it is a likely match. This type of probabilistic score can help requestors find possible matches beyond what can be identified by Boolean matching rules.

## 3.1 Scoring Prerequisites

In ER, one of the first things that must be done is profiling of data to verify the data quality. This allows for a knowledge expert to cleanse the data prior to building the initial entity repository. One of the profiling statistics that is generated by most profiling tools is the population frequency of each attribute that compose the entity references. This population frequency is calculated for each attribute (n) as:

$$PF_n = \frac{FC_n}{RC} \qquad (1)$$

In this formula, $FC_n$ represents the non-null/non-blank field count for a given attribute and RC represents the total record count in the entity reference population (a count of all references that make up all the entity clusters).

The population frequency of each attribute is significant in the proposed probabilistic score methods in that it is used as a modifier that assigns a significance to each attribute. This is based on the idea that a more heavily populated attribute will provide more value to the resulting score value than a sparsely populated attribute and thus should carry a higher significance.

This population frequency is calculated based on the references located in the entity repository in which the input references are compared against if one is available otherwise it must be calculated by preprocessing the set of source references. This value can be calculated and held in memory along with the entity repository when the entity repository is initially loaded. This allows the population frequency to be readily available when each score is calculated.

The second value that is required for the proposed probabilistic score methods is an attribute flag. This attribute flag ($AF_n$) is calculated for each reference that is processed the system. The attribute flag stores a simple Boolean value (1 or 0) and is calculated for each attribute as:

$$AF_n = \begin{cases} 1 \; if \; n \neq \emptyset \\ 0 \; if \; n = \emptyset \end{cases} \qquad (2)$$

The last value that is required is not actually used in calculating the score values but is used in selecting which scores are considered strong enough to represent a likely match and are strong review indicators for the review list that is returned. This is a threshold value that should be provided to the ER system by a knowledge expert and must be tuned based on the data the score is being generated for.

Both the population frequency and the attribute flag values are used in each of the following proposed scoring methods to generate the score values.

## 3.2 Population Frequency Weight

This method of scoring uses the population frequency (PF) of each attribute in conjunction with the attribute flag (AF) and a Normalized LED [9] function to calculate a score value that relates an entity reference in the entity repository to the input reference in terms of a numerical score value

This method works by defining a set of attributes to be used in the scoring algorithm by setting a use ($U_n$) value which is associated to each attribute. This value is a Boolean (1 or 0) value which in turn is used as a multiplier in the scoring algorithm to signify "Use (1), or Don't Use (0)".

A Population Frequency Weight score is calculated through the following algorithm:

1. Retrieve the $PF_n$ value for each attribute.
2. Calculate the $AF_n$ value for each attribute.
3. Calculate the $LED_n$ value for each corresponding attribute pair for the reference pair
   a. i.e. $LED_n = LED(IR_n, CR_n)$
4. Set the $U_n$ value for each attribute.
5. Perform the following calculation for the pair of reference:

$$Score(\mathrm{IR}, \mathrm{CR}) = \frac{\sum_{i=1}^{n} LED(IR_i, CR_i) * PF_i * AF_i * U_i}{\sum_{i=1}^{n} PF_i * AF_i * U_i} \quad (3)$$

Where $IR_i$ is the input reference attribute and $CR_i$ is the comparing reference attribute.

This algorithm can be implemented as three different methods:

**All-Attribute Scoring** – uses every reference attribute that exists in the input reference except unique ID fields. This method sets the $U_n$ value of every attribute to 1 and provides an all-encompassing score value that considers all possible attribute values in its final decision.

**Rule-Attribute Scoring** – uses every reference attribute that exists in the input reference except unique ID field and are used in any of the Boolean match rules specified for the ER system. As stated previously, an ER system uses a set of Boolean match rules to make match/non-match decisions for reference pairs. This sub-method works on the assumption that if the knowledge expert included an attribute in any of the defined Boolean match rules, that the attribute must be an identifying attribute for the references in the dataset. An identifying attribute is defined as any attribute that contributes some personal information that can be used to resolve the reference to a unique entity. This method sets the $U_n$ value of each attribute that is used in any of the defined Boolean match rules to 1 and all others to 0. Used as a method to calculate reliable scores for data that contains a lot of non-identifying attributes.

**Selected-Attribute Scoring** - uses only the attributes that are specified by a knowledge expert when configuring the ER system or in some systems configurations by the requestor and are present in the input reference. This method sets the $U_n$ value of each attribute that is specified to be used to 1 and all others to 0. Provides a score that allows the knowledge expert to configure exactly which fields they want to be used when generating score values for reference pairs

## 3.3 Probabilistic Weight

This scoring method is similar to the All-Attribute Scoring application of the Population Frequency Weight scoring method in that the process of generating a score is based on all reference attributes that exist in the source reference that are not unique ID fields (unique keys). This type of scoring works on the assumption that some attributes may identify a probable match more efficiently than other attributes and should have a larger impact on the final score generated for the reference. It also allows for adjustments to be made to the score for attributes that have a low PF but are important indicators of matching. (i.e. the School Assigned Identifier (SAI) only has 32% populated but when present, has 10 times more likelihood to indicate a match than a Middle Name field that is 99% populated).

For this Probabilistic Weight scoring algorithm a weight algorithm was selected that generates both an agreement and a disagreement weight [10]. The weights ($w_n$) are calculated as:

$$w_n = \begin{cases} \log_2\left(\dfrac{m_n}{u_n}\right) \; if\ agreement\ in\ attribute\ n & (4) \\ \log_2\left(\dfrac{(1-m_n)}{(1-u_n)}\right) \; if\ disagreement\ in\ attribute\ n \end{cases}$$

Where:

$$m_n = prob(a_n\ agree \mid ref\ pair\ match) \quad (5)$$
$$u_n = prob(a_n\ agree \mid ref\ pair\ do\ not\ match) \quad (6)$$

These weight calculations require a truth set so for this method, an ER system must already have an entity repository which can be considered the truth set for the already resolved entities clusters. Given this entity repository, $m_n$ and $u_n$ can be calculated as follows:

1. For each attribute in the entity reference, define the following:
   a. $A_n$ - Agree count – count of record pairs that the attribute being considered matches and both records in the pair are in the same entity cluster.

   b. $D_n$ - Disagree count - count of record pairs that the attribute being considered matches and the records in the pair are in different entity clusters.
2. For each record pair (RxR) do the following:
   a. Increment $A_n$ - If attribute n match between the records in the record pair and the references belong to the same entity cluster.
   b. Increment $D_n$ - If attribute n match between the records in the record pair and the references do not belong to the same entity cluster.
   c. Increment M - If both references belong to the same entity cluster
   d. Increment U - If the references belong to different entity clusters.
3. The formulas for $m_n$ and $u_n$ can now be re-written as follows:

$$m_n = \left({}^{A_n}/_{M}\right) \quad (7)$$

$$u_n = \left({}^{D_n}/_{U}\right) \quad (8)$$

For this algorithm, the weight is split into agreement ($a_n$) and disagreement ($d_n$) and the formulas now become:

$$a_n = \log_2\left(\frac{{}^{A_n}/_{M}}{{}^{D_n}/_{U}}\right) \quad (9)$$

$$d_n = \log_2\left(\frac{\left(1 - {}^{A_n}/_{M}\right)}{\left(1 - {}^{D_n}/_{U}\right)}\right) \quad (10)$$

For the purposes of the Probabilistic Weight scoring method proposed in this paper, the weight must be normalized such that $0 <= w_n <= 1$. To do this the agreement and disagreement weights of each attribute must be updated as follows once the above formulas are used to get the initial weights.

$$NA_n = \frac{(|\min(d_1 \dots d_n)| + a_n)}{(|\min(d_1 \dots d_n)| + |\max(a_1 \dots a_n)|)} \quad (11)$$

$$ND_n = \frac{(|\min(d_1 \dots d_n)| + d_n)}{(|\min(d_1 \dots d_n)| + |\max(a_1 \dots a_n)|)} \quad (12)$$

Where $NA_n$ is the normalized agreement weight and $ND_n$ is the normalized disagreement weight. The absolute value of the minimum value of the set of disagreement weights is used since the disagreement weights are always negative.

Once the weights are calculated and normalized, a Probabilistic Weight score is calculated through the following steps:

1. Retrieve the $PF_n$ value for each attribute.
2. Calculate the $AF_n$ value for each attribute.
3. Calculate the $LED_n$ value for each corresponding attribute pair for the reference pair
   a. i.e. $LED_n = LED(IR_n, CR_n)$
4. Retrieve the weight of each attribute where:

$$w_n = \begin{cases} NA_n & if\ LED_n \geq threshold \\ ND_n & if\ LED_n \leq threshold \end{cases} \quad (13)$$

5. Perform the following calculation for the pair of reference:

$$Score(\text{IR}, \text{CR}) = \frac{\sum_{i=1}^{n} LED(IR_i, CR_i) * PF_i * AF_i * w_i}{\sum_{i=1}^{n} PF_i * AF_i * w_i} \quad (14)$$

Where $IR_i$ is the input reference attribute and $CR_i$ is the comparing reference attribute.

This probabilistic score method provides the weight to skew the impact of each attribute based on knowledge of resolutions that have already occurred between reference pairs.

# 4 Experiments

To test the various scoring methods discussed in the previous section, two (2) different sets of data were used. In addition to the data sets, two (2) tools were used to test the effectiveness of the various scoring methods. These tools consisted of the OYSTER system, and a custom built scoring system designed around the four proposed scoring methods.

## 4.1 OYSTER

OYSTER (Open sYSTem Entity Resolution) is an open source project sponsored by Center for Advance Research in Entity Resolution and Information Quality (ERIQ) and the University of Arkansas at Little Rock [5]. OYSTER was originally designed to support instruction and research in ER by allowing users to configure its entire operation through XML scripts executed at run-time. The resolution engine of the current version (3.3) supports probabilistic direct matching, transitive linking, and asserted linking [2, 7]. OYSTER builds and maintains an in-memory repository of attribute values to identities that allows it to manage identities quickly and efficiently. Because OYSTER has an identity management system, it also supports persistent identity identifiers.

OYSTER is driven by multiple XML scripts that tell the system where to locate the input repository, how the input source files are structured, and what match rules should be used to determine matches. OYSTER can be configured, through these XML files, to handle:

- Record Linking
- Identity Resolution
- Identity Capture/Update
- Five types of Assertions

When configured for assertions, OYSTER provides a method for users to override decisions made by the Boolean Resolution Engine. These assertions are the mechanisms which allow false negative matches identified during clerical review to be fixed in the entity repository.

One of the most noticeable features of OYSTER is its ability to handle an Identity Update architecture which effectively allows OYSTER to combine Identity Capture and Identity Resolution into a single run. This allows for a repository of identities to be defined and maintained.

OYSTERs Resolution engine functions through the use of Boolean match rules and supports various matching algorithms such as: Normalized LED [9], SOUNDEX [14], q-Gram Tetrahedral Ratio [15], and many others.

OYSTER source code and documentation are freely available at http://sourceforge.net/projects/oysterer/.

## 4.2 Test Data

The first set of test data is comprised of synthetic data that was created as the input for a class project for an Entity Resolution course. Quality issues were deliberately introduced to this synthetic dataset to view the effects of lower quality data on the discussed scoring methods. The second set of data is a set of real world data that was provided by the state's Department of Education. This data cannot be disclosed in detail but the results of the experimentation are provided later in this paper.

### 4.2.1 Synthetic Data

The synthetic dataset consists of records that are created to mimic student person records. A random sample of 4,300 records was selected from the dataset. The references consist of the following attributes: RefID, Fname, Mname, Lname, Suffix, SAI, DOB, and Phone #.

The first step is to generate a set of match rules to be used in an OYSTER run to generate a truth set. The rules consist of 4 rules:

- Rule 1
  - SAI – Exact match
  - Lname – Exact_ignore_case
- Rule 2
  - Fname - Soundex
  - Lname - Exact_ignore_case
  - DOB - Exact_ignore_case
- Rule 3
  - Fname - Soundex
  - Lname - Exact_ignore_case
  - Mname - Exact_ignore_case
- Rule 4
  - Fname - NICKNAME
  - Lname - Exact_ignore_case
  - Mname - Exact_ignore_case

After the OYSTER run completed it was found the 4,300 references resolved into 1,550 entity clusters. From the link index that was produced by the OYSTER run a count of matches for each of the 4,300 references was calculated by counting the number or references that were clustered with each reference.

Next, Rule 3 was removed and OYSTER was run against the same dataset. It was found that 47 references out of the 4,300 were no longer linked and were placed into individual entity clusters. These 47 represent false negative results for this run. These 47 references were extracted into a new dataset and used as a list of source references to be run through the scoring tool against the original 4,300 references and their match count generated by the scoring tool was compared against the match count generated for these records by the first OYSTER run.

The scoring tool generated the information shown in Table 1 about the 4,300 references in the entity repository.

Table 1: Synthetic data PF and Weights

| Attribute | PF | Agreement Weight | Disagreement Weight |
|---|---|---|---|
| Fname | 0.9333 | 0.386308 | 0.024562 |
| Mname | 0.7404 | 0.22573 | 0.016748 |
| Lname | 1 | 0.47589 | 0 |
| Suffix | 0.0016 | 0.599105 | 0.041901 |
| SAI | 0.9537 | 1 | 0.010654 |
| DOB | 0.3828 | 0.34999 | 0.039992 |
| Phone | 1 | 0.739681 | 0.039913 |

The OYSTER run identified that the 47 references contained a total of 150 matches in the 4,300 reference population. The scoring tool identified the match counts shown in Table 2 for each of the four scoring methods.

Table 2: Synthetic Data Result Comparisons

| Count Source | Threshold | Count | Percentage identified |
|---|---|---|---|
| OYSTER | N/A | 150 | 100% |
| All-Attribute Score | 0.7 | 131 | 87.33% |
| Selected-Attribute Score | 0.7 | 130 | 86.66% |
| Rule-Attribute Score | 0.7 | 144 | 96% |
| Probabilistic Weight Score | 0.95 | 122 | 81.33% |

It was found that due to the quality of the data, the threshold had to be lowered to find the best amount of matches. All the matches represented in the counts above were verified to be accurate. The Percentage Identified represent the probability for which the corresponding score algorithm would return a list of review indicators to the user.

### 4.2.2 Student Data

The data is comprised of student enrollment records. There are 3,234,292 student references with each containing 40 attributes (inclusive of the ID field).

Twelve rules were created for the OYSTER run and OYSTER generated 526,012 entity clusters. The PF and the agreement and disagreement weights of each attribute calculated by the scoring tool cannot be shared in this paper. Next, one rule was removed and OYSTER was run again against the full population. This rule provided 332 references that no longer clustered and a random sample of 100 records was selected from these 332 references to be used as input for the scoring tool. These 100 records were run against the 3,234,292 references and the counts in Table 3 were generated for the 100 input references.

Table 3: ADE Data Result Comparisons

| Count Source | Threshold | Count | Percentage identified |
|---|---|---|---|
| OYSTER | N/A | 688 | 100% |
| All-Attribute Score | 0.8 | 629 | 91.4% |
| Selected-Attribute Score | 0.8 | 632 | 91.8% |
| Rule-Attribute Score | 0.8 | 632 | 91.8% |
| Probabilistic Weight Score | 0.955 | 625 | 90.8% |

The data quality of the references in the student dataset is very good so the thresholds did not need to be set as low as they were for the synthetic data. These thresholds should be determined by a knowledge expert so that the algorithms return the most probable matches. All the matches represented in the counts in Table 3 were verified by hand to be accurate. This verification was the reason a small (100 references) random sample was selected.

### 4.2.3 Further Analysis

During testing of the various algorithms many runs were performed on both the synthetic and student datasets in the attempt to find the optimal threshold to be used for the scoring method on the dataset. After each run was complete, the output was analyzed looking for the point in which the scoring algorithm stopped producing false positive results. Because a probabilistic scoring algorithm inherently will score some non matches with relatively high scores, the objective is to find the point where the false matches stop while there is still a high level of true matches returned as review indicators for the user. The charts in Figure 1 and Figure 2 depict the various thresholds tested for each of the proposed methods.

- Chart a = All-Attribute Score
- Chart b = Selected-Attribute Score
- Chart c = Rule-Attribute Score
- Chart d = Probabilistic Weight Score

Multiple runs were performed and show the optimal threshold. It would have been entirely acceptable to select a lower threshold and simply return the possible matches but the attempt was made to depict the accuracy of the algorithms at which all the matches returned are true matches.

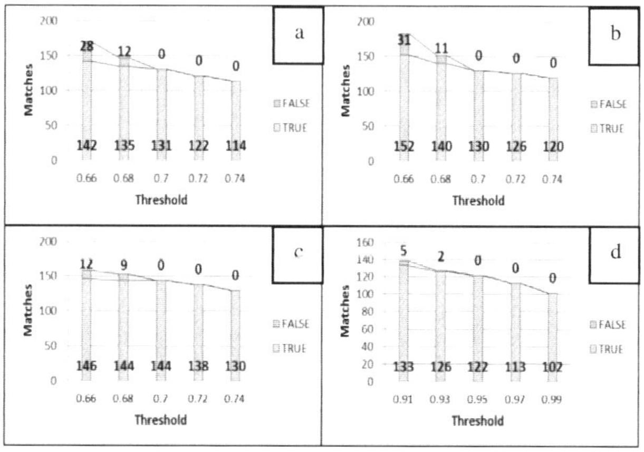


Figure 1: Synthetic Data True/False Matches

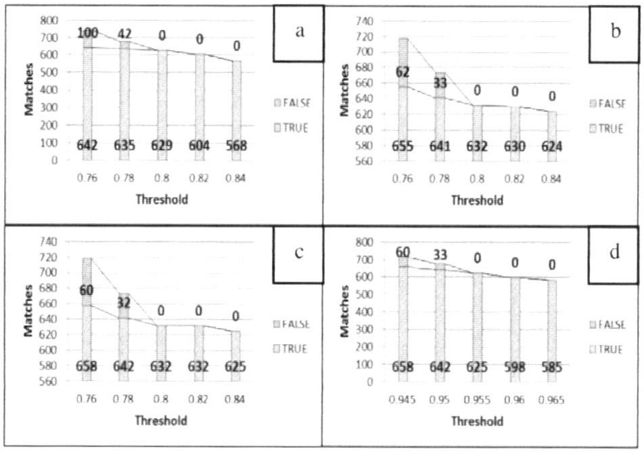


Figure 2: Student Data True/False Matches

Another finding is that by using the Probabilistic Weight score, the resulting scores shift strongly towards 1 for matching references and the majority of non-matching references had a score that dropped quickly into the 80 percentile range or lower. The Probabilistic Weight score could provide more confident results in the upper bounds of the normalized score range. It does however provide less of a range of control for the values since even a 0.5% shift in the threshold can cause a dramatic increase in the false matches in the real-world data.

# 5 Conclusion

It was found that the all-attribute score is a very robust and straight forward scoring method that can be applied to a wide range of data sets with nearly any level of data quality. This method is most useful for systems in which there is no knowledge expert that can confidently identify specific identifying attributes or in situations where it is decided that all the data has some significance to the reference. For both the synthetic and student data, the all-attribute score was able to correctly identify close to 90% of the correct match results and assign them an appropriate score.

The selected-attribute score also performed well in that it actually provided slightly better results than the all-attribute score method in each test. This is a viable alternative to the all-attribute score when there is a knowledge expert that can provide enough certainty about the attributes to disable the use of some of them in the scoring algorithm.

The rule-attribute score produced good results on the test data by using only attributes that are present in the rules used in the OYSTER runs. This method produces some of the best results but could be of limited use in an interactive system in which there are no constraints as to which attribute values the requestor must populate in their request.

Lastly, the probabilistic weight score did not outperform the other methods but it showed potential in the way it skewed the match scores. The true match scores were skewed almost entirely into the upper 90 percentile and false matches were skewed down into the 80 percentile or lower.

Although Entity Resolution (ER) systems are designed specifically to resolve entities into entity clusters, there is a gap in their capabilities since the systems that use Boolean rules cannot provide a list of “near matches” based on their clerical review indicator. It was found that all of the proposed methods in this paper are viable options for supplying the system with this flexibility. Each of the different probabilistic scoring methods has its own strengths and can be applied in different situations to closely meet the needs of the underlying data. These probabilistic scoring algorithms can be used not only as review indicators but could also be used as part of the Boolean match rules as one of the comparators. i.e. FirstName = exact, LastName = exact, and Score > 0.8. This type of rule could be used to make deterministic decisions in any ER system.

## 6 Future Work

The next step is to explore alternative similarity distance measures (nLED in the above methods) that automatically take into consideration the most common types of discrepancies found in the student data. For example, the transpositions of characters and nicknames. If the attribute values in the attribute pairs are found to fall into either of these categories then the similarity measure should be 1. e.g. nLED(sam,asm) = 0.333 but since it is a transposition, this should return a 1.0 in the context of generating a score for the reference pairs.

## Acknowledgment

The research described in this paper has been supported in part by funding from the Arkansas Department of Education.

## References

[1] HB Newcombe, JM Kennedy, SJ Axford, and AP James. Automatic linkage of vital records. *Science*, 130:954–9, 1959.

[2] Nelson, E., & Talburt, J. (2011). Entity Resolution for Longitudinal Studies in Education using OYSTER. *The 2011 International Conference on Information and Knowledge Engineering (IKE'11).* Las Vegas, Nevada: (accepted for publication).

[3] S. Sarawagi and A. Bhamidipaty. Interactive deduplication using active learning. In *Proceedings of the eighth ACM SIGKDD international conference on Knowledge discovery and data mining*, pages 269–278. ACM New York, NY, USA, 2002.

[4] S. Tejada, C.A. Knoblock, and S. Minton. Learning object identification rules for information integration. Information Systems, 26(8):607–633, 2001.

[5] Talburt, J. R. (2011). *Entity Resolution and Information Quality.* Burlington, MA: Morgan Kaufmann.

[6] X. Dong, A. Halevy, and J. Madhavan. Reference reconciliation in complex information spaces. In *Proceedings of the 2005 ACM SIGMOD international conference on Management of data*, pages 85–96. ACM New York, NY, USA, 2005.

[7] Zhou, Y., & Talburt, J. (2011). The Role of Asserted Resolution in Entity Identity Management. *In Proceedings of the 2011 Iinternational Conference on Information and Knowledge Engineering (IKE'11) (pp.291-296). Las Vegas, Nevada.*

[8] Zhou, Y., Talburt, J., and Nelson, E. The Interaction of Data, Data Structures, and Software in Entity Resolution Systems. *Software Quality Professional:* Vol. 13 No. 4, pp. 32-41, 2011.

[9] M. Jaro, “Advances in record-linkage methodology as applied to matching the 1985 census of Tampa, Florida,” *Journal of the American Statistical Association*, Vol.84, Issue 406, pp. 414-420, 1989.

[10] T.M Herzog, F.J. Scheuren, and W.E. Winkler. (2007). *Data Quality and Record Linkage Techniques.* New York, NY: Springer Science.

[11] Iven Fellegi and Alan Sunter. “A Theory for Record Linkage”; Journal of the American Statistical Association, Vol. 64 No. 328, 1183-1210, 1969

[12] Steven Whang and Hector Garcia-Molina. “Entity Resolution with Evolving Rules”; Proceedings of the VLDB Endowment, Vol. 3 Issue 1-2, 1326-1337, September 2010

[13] Zhou, Y., Talburt, J., Kobayashi, F., Nelson, E., (2012) Implementing Boolean Matching Rules in an Entity Resolution System using XML Scripts. *The 2011 International Conference on Information and Knowledge Engineering (IKE'12).* Las Vegas, Nevada: (accepted for publication).

[14] Odell, M. and Russell, R. (1918). U.S. patent number 1,261,167, Washington, D.C. U.S. Patent Office

[15] G. Holland and J. Talburt, “q-Gram tetrahedral ratio (qTR) for approximate string matching,” in *Proc. 2010 Ann. Acxiom Laboratory for Applied Research Conf. (ALAR-10)*, 2010

# Intelligent Mobile App for Identifying Skin Pigments

**Mark Smith**
Central Arkansas
Conway, Arkansas USA

**Ray Hashemi**
Armstrong Atlantic State
Savannah, Georgia USA

**Azita Bahrami**
IT Consultation
Savannah, Georgia USA

**Abstract** - *The foundation is a cosmetic makeup applied to the face before other makeup is applied. In this research effort, a novel algorithm used to assist the selection of the optimal cosmetic foundation makeup color is presented. The algorithm is implemented as a mobile application on iPhone's iOS platform. The selection process is done by: (1) Intelligent segmenting of a pre-selected facial image into different skin regions, (2) Selecting (done by user) one of the facial region (or regions), (3) Merging regions based on their size and adjacency, if applicable, (4) Clustering the regions into 16 different colors using the k-means algorithm, (5) Selecting and averaging the top 4 clusters, (6) Mapping the average on a standard industry color table of cosmetic foundations, (7) Applying the identified color to the facial image. Results are shown for numerous samples from standard videos and images taken from the cameras used on the iPad.*

## 1. Introduction

The interest in mobile devices has exploded in recent years, especially the usage of the Apple's iPhone and iPad [3]. These devices allow users to capture pictures and live video in instantaneously while processing these images in real-time by an App. The App described in this paper is applied to the Cosmetic Chemistry make-up substance known as Foundation. Foundation make-up is applied to the user's face initially before any other make-up products are applied. The challenge many users have in applying Foundation is selecting the best color that matches their facial skin. Often a trial and error process is utilized where several different colors are experimented with before a color is chosen. But the process is far from optimal and mistakes are often made when selecting and applying foundation colors. The purpose of this app is to eliminate most of the uncertainty involved when selecting the best foundation color. A novel algorithm implemented for this app consists of the following steps:

1. Automatic segmentation of facial regions into objects.
2. Quantize colors of largest facial region to 16 clusters.
3. Color matching is performed between dominant facial region and other facial regions
4. Adjacent facial regions are merged based on the color matching.
5. The four dominant colors are selected from all color regions

The dominant colors are matched with a table of possible foundation colors provided by a major cosmetic manufacturer.

## 2. Image Segmentation

There are several image segmentation algorithms available in the literature, thus providing many different possibilities for this step in our system as in [1,7,8,9,10,11,12,13]. The image segmentation process used in this system is fully described in an earlier work of the authors [4,14] and is applied to each image when detecting facial regions. Examples of the image segmentation applied to standard test images are shown below in Figure 1. The images shown in Figure 1 are extracted from the standard MPEG-4 videos *Susie*, *The Foreman*, and *Miss America*. These videos are very commonly used for research as well as the images extracted from them. These same images – *Susie*, *The Foreman*, and *Miss America*, are stored in the Cameral Roll of the iPad and subsequently tested by the algorithm described in this paper. The algorithm's results for these images are displayed in Table 1 of Section 7. Note the different facial regions considered, along with many other different objects such as clothes, hair, and background features. This image segmentation algorithm does a superior job in fully dividing the pictures into real-world objects.

# 3. Color Quantization and Matching

The next step in the process is to quantize the facial regions colors to a manageable number and then match the colors to a set of pre-defined colors as set by the manufacturer. There are tens of thousands of unique colors in a given image and perhaps millions of unique colors across several frames of a video sequence. The quantization of all possible colors to only a few levels is an important simplification step, since the comparison so many different color possibilities prove difficult when identifying the optimal foundation color to be applied to a facial region.

Fig 1: Segmentation Results for Test images

The largest facial region undergoes a standard k-means clustering algorithm [7] and 16 quantized colors are extracted from this initial object. The motivation behind using 16 colors is because it has been found that most realistic facial regions can be represented by this many discrete labels - thus shading, textured regions, etc can be modeled most accurately this way. Before clustering, the original RGB pixel colors are converted to the CIE- L*a*b* color space which has been shown to be perceptually uniform and therefore preserve more accurate distances than the RGB color space, thus providing superior results [1]. The clustering results on the CIE-L*a*b* colors are then converted back to the RGB colors. The color feature utilized in this measurement consists of all quantized RGB colors.

The quantized colors in the largest facial region are then compared with the actual colors in the other facial regions. The colors will be classified in one of two ways:

1. An existing color found in the largest facial region
2. A new color not found in the facial region

In the following discussion, the symbol pcn will be used to represent the actual color in an additional facial region whereas pcp represents the corresponding matching color in the largest facial region. A new color is identified in the additional facial regions by (1) given by

$$\| \mu\text{-}pcn\| > \max\|\mu\text{-}pci\| + \alpha\sigma \qquad (1)$$

where μ is the mean of the cluster that pcp belongs to, pci is the ith color belonging to this cluster with i =1, 2,….N, and N is the total number of colors grouped with the cluster. σ is the standard deviation of the distances computed between μ and the colors in its cluster and is given by (2) as:

$$\sigma = \sqrt{\frac{\sum_{i}^{N}\|\mu - pci\|}{(N-1)}} \qquad (2)$$

and α is a scaling factor. We have found that α equal to 2 works well for the application considered in this work. This color-matching step is illustrated in Figure 2.

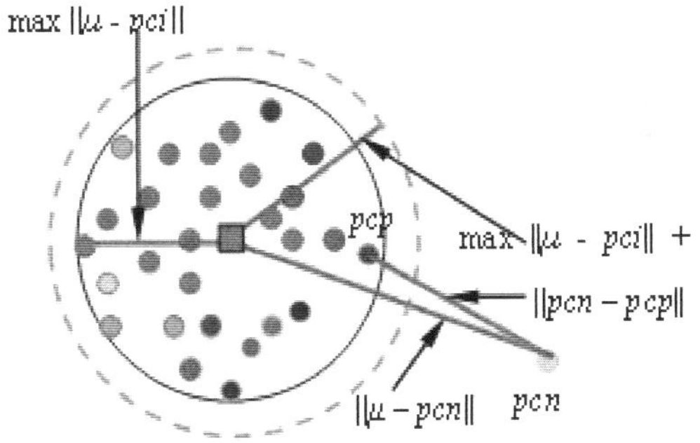


Fig. 2: Illustration of Color Matching Algorithm

In the example shown in Figure 2, pcn is classified as a new color.

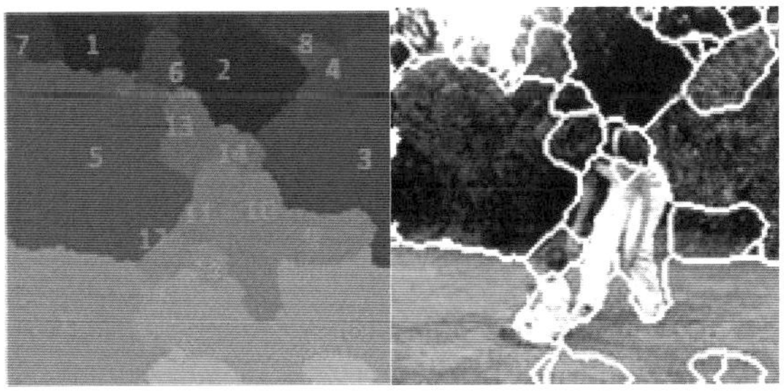

Fig. 3: Original Region Labels from Segmentation

# 4. Region Merging Algorithm

A step that merges smaller facial regions with the larger, adjacent region is needed to provide optimal facial segmentation. The region merging algorithm introduced in this section demonstrates that small color samples extracted near the boundaries of adjacent facial regions provide an excellent criteria for merging the areas. The algorithm utilized in this system relies on the dominant (quantized) colors when comparing adjacent regions. Therefore, the adjacent facial regions are merged based on how similar their colors are to the largest facial region. The example shown below is for a standard image. The algorithm is summarized as:

1. The regions created by the image segmentation are extracted. The regions (and their corresponding labels) as well as their contours overlaid onto the original color frame are shown in Figure 3.

2. All neighboring segments for each region are determined and only those neighboring segments that are larger are considered as merging candidates. The main concept is that smaller regions are only merged with larger, bordering regions. For example, region 12 has larger neighboring segments 5,11,16 and 17, whereas region 17 has larger adjacent segment region *5*.
3. Each region's quantized colors are then compared with the quantized colors of each of its larger, neighboring segments. The smaller region will be merged with the larger one if their quantized colors are sufficiently close [5]. The steps utilized in this process are outlined as follows:
   a. A windowed area running the length of the adjacent boundary between neighboring objects is selected for each region. Each area provides a representative sample of the quantized colors for the object. Colors selected at their adjacent boundary provide the best measurement on whether the objects should be merged, thus minimizing the effects from outlying colors. The sampled regions usually have a maximum width of 5 pixels and are parallel to the entire length of the boundary. Additional points are selected when the sampled regions consist of 25 pixels or less. Examples of these sampled regions are shown in Figure 4 for selected neighboring objects.

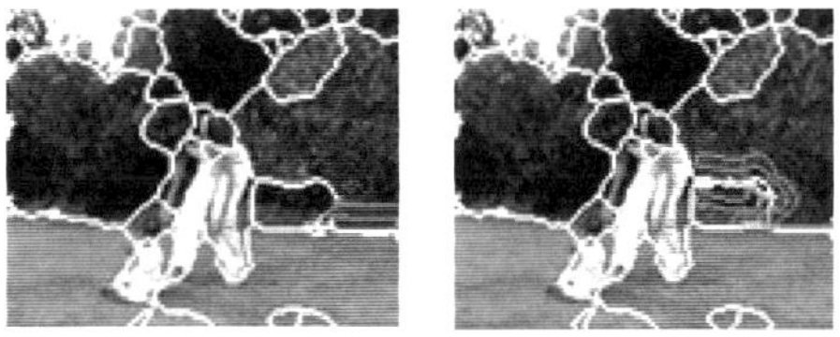

Fig. 4. Selected Regions

   b. Each quantized color (i.e., discrete label) and its corresponding concentration (measured in percentage) are extracted from each sampled area within each region. Only those quantized colors with a concentration greater than 5% are considered.
   c. If the majority of the quantized colors of the smaller region match those of the larger region, the larger region is then selected as a candidate for merging with the smaller one.
4. Step 3 is repeated for all larger neighboring objects and all candidates for merging with the smaller objects are maintained [2].
5. The candidate which best matches the smaller object's quantized color concentration is then selected as the best matching region for merging. The smaller region is then marked for merging with the larger region – but the actual object merging is not done at this time.
6. Steps 1 – 5 are repeated for all remaining objects.
7. All smaller objects previously marked for merging are then merged with their best matching neighboring objects.

The results of this algorithm as applied to the original segmentation, Figure 3, is shown in Figure 5.

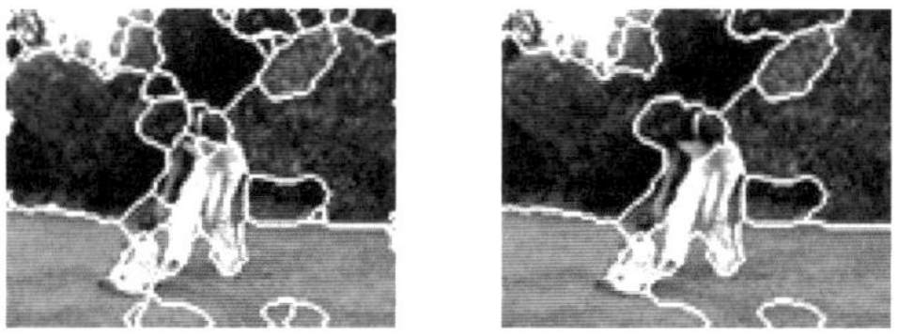

Fig. 5: Region Merging Results

# 5. Dominant Color Selection

The color feature utilized in this measurement consists of all quantized RGB colors having a concentration greater than 5% extracted from a given object. These colors are also referred to as the dominant colors of the object. The Dominant Colors is one of the standard MPEG-7 features [6] and provides one of the simplest but effective attributes for matching similar colors.. The previous sections demonstrate the algorithm that quantizes/matches the color regions of the facial regions. The color processing to detect those colors with 5% or more concentration is illustrated below in Figure 6. The threshold of 5% is chosen by the MPEG-7 and is shown to provide the best results for matching image regions that are comprised of similar colors.

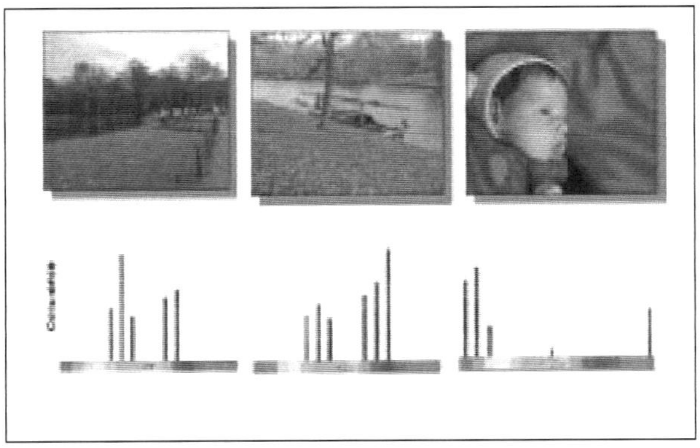

Fig. 6: Detection of Dominant Colors

## 6. Foundation Color Matching

The dominant colors extracted from the merged facial regions are next matched with a foundation color chart. The foundation color chart consists of the all possible colors available for the foundation make-up. An example of a color chart is shown below in Figure 7.

The dominant colors extracted from all merged facial regions must undergo a processing step before the matching can be performed. The steps required for the matching is summarized using the following steps:

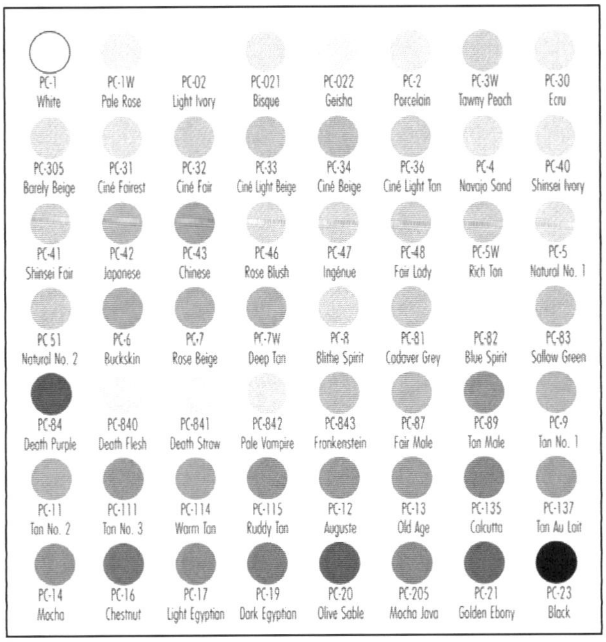


Fig. 7: Color Chart for Foundation

1. The CIE-Lab color space for all dominant colors is detected.
2. Each Foundation color from the color chart in Figure7 is also converted to CIE-Lab color space. Each color is considered a set of dominant colors.
3. A similarity measurement between the average dominant colors and Foundation colors are computed as below in (3):

$$CC_i = 1 - \frac{T_{ci \cap pi}}{T_{ci}} \tag{3}$$

where Tci is the set of dominant colors in the merged regions, while Tpi is the set of dominant colors in the color chart. The Color Chart's color that maximizes the Common Color measurement (CCi) is selected as the best matching color from the foundation color chart.

## 7. Testing and Results

The algorithm has been implemented in the form of an iPhone/iPad App. The initial display of the application referred to as the *Home* display is shown in Figure 8

Fig. 8: Startup View for iPad App

Note the content tab. The user can take a new picture via the iPad camera using the Camera tab. An example for this screen is shown below in Figure 9:

Fig. 9: Picture Taken Using App

Fig. 10: Picture and Foundation Color Chart

Once the picture has been taken, the user can process the picture by pressing the *Process Picture* button as shown below in Figure 10:

The color chart is shown below the picture. The user is given the option to select the color and test on automatically segmented facial regions, or the user can choose the completely automated mode where the best matching foundation is color is chosen by the app.

The following table computes the results for the three standard images which were tested by this algorithm. These images were selected from the standard MPEG-4 video database and have been tested previously by the author's image segmentation algorithm given in [4].

In *Table 1*, the *#Objects* column refers to the total number of regions automatically segmented in the image – facial, clothing, hair, etc. The *Facial* column refers to the number of objects pertaining to only facial regions of the subject. The *Correct* column compares the automatically selected foundation color with the appropriate one chosen manually for each facial region. The results in the table below are computed only for the facial regions – the other regions such as hair, clothing, eyes, lips, etc. are not considered in the table shown below.

**Table 1: Results**

| Image | #Objects | Facial | Correct | Percent Correct |
|---|---|---|---|---|
| Ms America | 12 | 9 | 8 | 97.1% |
| Foreman | 23 | 12 | 10 | 91.3% |
| Susie | 9 | 6 | 5 | 90.9% |

The algorithm applied the correct foundation color over 90% of the time for the 3 cases tested. Some regions were misclassified due to imperfections in the image segmentations algorithm for the facial regions. For instance, some facial regions included portions of other regions such as hair, clothing, etc.

# 8. Conclusion and Future Research

This proposed algorithm automatically selects the best matching cosmetic foundation color for a given facial region which has been automatically segmented. The results are very promising and illustrate that the algorithm is properly choosing the best foundation color over 90% of the time.

One challenge the algorithm has is properly classifying the facial region from non-facial regions. This unfortunately is currently being done in a manual fashion rather than automated at this time. A future research plan is to enhance the algorithm so facial regions are automatically identified based on standard features. The standard features would be extracted from the MPEG-7 facial attributes and integrated with our current algorithm for properly classifying the automatically segmented regions as facial/non facial.

Once the facial regions have been properly identified, the next algorithm enhancement would be to merge all facial regions in to one object. – the face. This one object would provide much more appealing results and would provide a more pleasing experience for the users of our app. An incremental step would be to allow the user to manually select the facial regions presented to her and allow these to be merged into one large object.

Additional testing needs to be done concerning the usage of the Dominant Color feature as the primary means for matching skin pigments. Additional color features as described by the MPEG-7 standards [8] as color histograms [9] and color layout [10] are available and should be tested as well. These additional attributes could also be combined with the current dominant color feature in a type of voting algorithm as well.

The foundation chart shown in Fig. 7 is taken from L'Oreal Corporation and pertains only to the foundation colors used by their company. More robust testing in the future should involve additional foundation color charts from other manufactures such as Cover Girl, Revlon, etc.

A more extensive set of test images should also be used in future testing. Many standard images exist in the MPEG-4 video database and these images could be used as well as the three illustrated in this work. A complete database consisting of at least 10 such images should be utilized to provide a thorough set of results and data.

# 9. References

[1] Y. Deng and B. S. Manjunath, "Unsupervised segmentation of color-texture regions in images and video," *IEEE Trans. on Pattern Analysis and Machine Intelligence*, vol. 22, no. 6, pp. 939-954, 2001.

[2] T. Aach, A Kaup, and R. Mester, "Statistical model-based change detection in moving video," *IEEE Trans. on Signal Processing*, vol. 31, no 2, pp. 165-180, March 1993.

[3] A. Nagasak and Y. Tanka, "Automatic video indexing and full video search for object appearances," in *Visual Database System II*, Elsevier, 1992, pp. 113-127.

[4] M. Smith and A. Khotanzad, "Unsupervised object-based video segmentation using color and texture features," *IEEE Southwest Symposium on Image Analysis*, March, 2006.

[5] J. Goldberger and H. Greenspan," Context-based segmentation of image sequences," *IEEE Transactions On Pattern Analysis And Machine Intelligence*, vol. 28, no. 3, pp. 463-468, March 2006.

[6] H. Tao, "Object tracking with Bayesian estimation of dynamic layer representations," *IEEE Trans. On Pattern Anal. And Mach Intelli.*, vol. 24, no. 1, pp. 75- 89, January 2002.

[7] F. Porikli, "Real-time video object segmentation for MPEG encoded video sequences,"*TR-2004-011*, pp. 178-189, March 2004.

[8] J. Goldberger and H. Greenspan,", A probabilistic framework for spatio-temporal video representation and indexing," in *European Conference on Computer Vision*, vol. 4, pp. 461, 2002.

[9] H. Greenspan, "Probabilistic space-time video modeling via piecewise GMM," *IEEE Transactions On Pattern Analysis And Machine Intelligence*, vol. 26, no. 3, pp. 384-396, March 2004.

[10] L. Atzori, D. D. Giusto, and C. Perra, "A novel block-based video segmentation algorithm," *2001 IEEE International Conference on Multimedia and Expo*, pp. 653-656, 2001.

[11] F. Marques and J. Llach, "Tracking of generic objects for video object generation," in International Conference on Image Processing, ICP 98, Chicago, IL, USA, pp. 124-128, October 4-7, 1998.

[12] C. Carson, S. Belongie, and J. Malik, "Blobworld: image segmentation using Expectation-Maximization and its application to image querying," *IEEE Transactions On Pattern Analysis And Machine Intelligence*, vol. 24, no. 8, pp. 1026-1038, August 2002.

[13] P. Williams, T. Reed, and M. Kurt, "Image sequence coding by split and merge," *IEEE Transaction on Communications*, vol. 39, pp. 1845-1855, December 1991.

[14]. M. Smith, R. Hashemi, and L. Sears, "Identification of Human Skin Regions Using Color and Texture," Proc. of the IEEE 2011 International Conference on Information Technology, New Generation (ITNG'11), July, 2011.

# Tackling Financial and Economic Crime through Strategic Intelligence: The EMPRISES Framework

Simon Andrews, Simon Polovina, Simeon Yates, Babak Akhgar
C3RI, Sheffield Hallam University, UK
{S.Andrews, S.Polovina, S.Yates, B.Akhgar} @shu.ac.uk

P. Saskia Bayerl
Rotterdam School of Management, Erasmus University, Burgemeester Oudlaan 50, 3062 PA Rotterdam, the Netherlands, pbayerl@rsm.nl

*Abstract*—**For the successful monitoring and combatting of Serious Organised Economic Crime (SOEC) and fraud, further integration of Member States systems across Europe is needed. This paper describes a system for strategic intelligence management providing a more coherent and coordinated approach for detecting and deterring SOEC and fraud. The EMPRISES framework increases the effectiveness of communication between Member States by developing an agreed common language (taxonomy) of SOEC and fraud with automated multi-lingual support. By appropriating and applying existing business tools and analysis techniques to the illegitimate businesses of SOEC and fraud, this new system can support Member States to better target these crimes and the criminals involved.**

*Index Terms*—**strategic intelligence management, serious organised economic crime, fraud, business techniques, illegitimate businesses**

## I. Introduction

Serious Organised Economic Crime (SOEC) and the associated activity of fraud are growing multinational businesses without respect of national borders. In the European Union (EU) alone these criminal activities cost member states billions of Euros annually. The ability to discover and develop sophisticated new weapons to detect and fight these crimes is thus an imperative. At present, however, each European police force and Financial Intelligence Unit (FIU) has its own Financial SOEC and fraud monitoring system. This severely hampers effective detection and deterrence of these crimes. To be effective at the multinational level requires a collaborative strategy across national systems based on the comprehensive integration of national systems into one multilingual pan-European system. Such a system would federate the large volume of SOEC and fraud information into a single shared inventory of SOEC and fraud. This inventory would employ a pan-European taxonomy of SOEC and fraud capturing even low-level and low intensity activities, hence, providing member states with a comprehensive, common language. It is with this objective in mind that we propose the *Economic criMe PReventIon for a Strengthened European Society* (EMPRISES) framework as a key strategic intelligence asset for law enforcement agencies in combating financial and economic crime.

## II. Developing an Enterprise Architecture of SOEC and Fraud

SOEC and fraud can be described in the framework of Enterprise Architectures (EA). SOEC consists of 'business' enterprises just like any other legitimate enterprise, with the difference, however, that the transactions it engages in are inherently unbalanced in their favour. Put simply, SOEC enterprises consider breaking the law as a normal cost of their 'business operations'. Fraudsters follow the same semantics. Victims to these transactions can be individuals, businesses, organisations or societies as a whole. It is this economic risk and its adverse effects on others that distinguish the structure of SOEC and fraud from other forms of economic activity. Yet, this feature not only serves to differentiate SEOC and fraud from other business activities, it can also be used as a first step to identify and stop their activities.

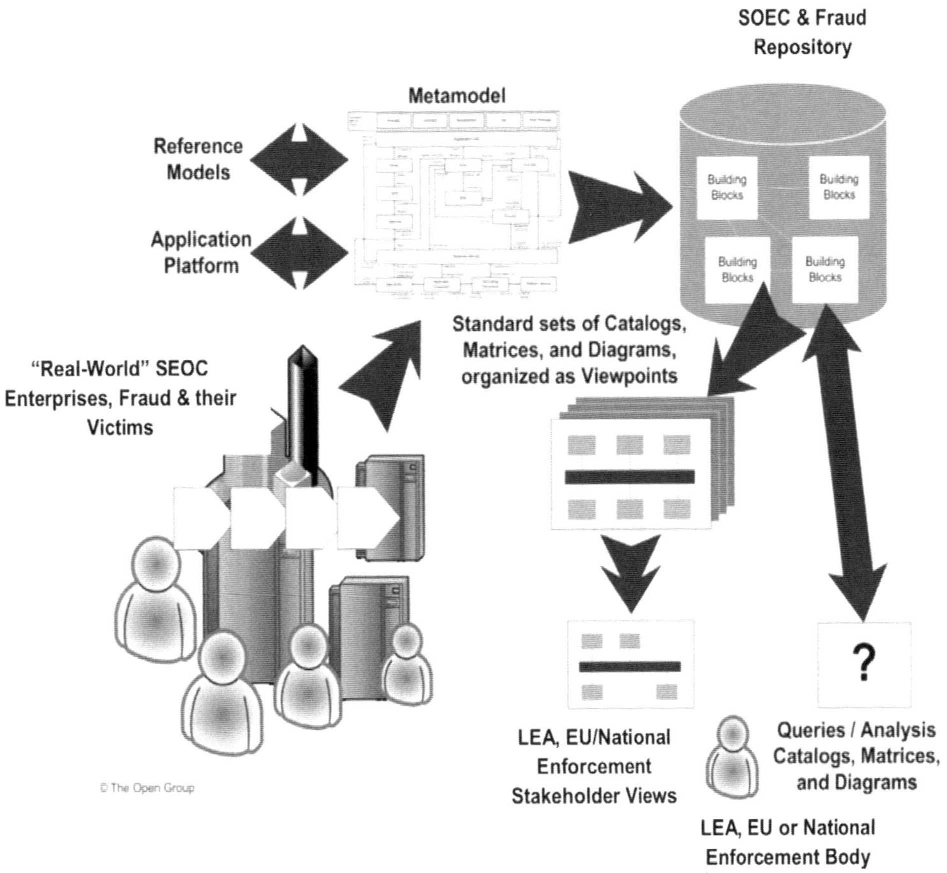


The EMPRISES framework employs state of the art knowledge of EA to obtain a clearer understanding of SEOC and fraudulent transactions. With this the EMPRISES framework provides a solid basis for the application of EA procedures to SOEC and fraud by revealing their fundamental enterprise anatomy. Subsequently, their supply and consumer chains can be identified and trapped, and/or potential victim(s) alerted. The general framework is based on best practices from the Open Group Enterprise Architecture Framework (TOGAF) [1]. The diagram above is an adaption from TOGAF to 1llustrate the general structure of SEOC and fraud systems including their protagonists (i.e., the criminal enterprises), their involuntary agents (i.e. the victims) as well as the Local Enforcement Agencies (LEAs) and EU-wide and National Enforcement Bodies aiming to combat these activities..

## III. The SOEC and Fraud Transaction Concept in the EMPRISES Framework

The conceptualisation of SOEC and fraud transactions in EMPRISES is based on the Transaction Concept that is based on the Resource-Events-Agents (REA) framework [2]. The *Transaction Concept* (TC) identifies the 'real-world' agents in enterprise transactions including *how* they transact (the economic events) and *what* they transact (the economic resources) [3, 4, 5]. The TC highlights the value and costs of each transaction as well as its effect on the local, national or international ecosystem. This approach captures the adverse effects on EU economies for each economic resource in a SOEC or fraud transaction, however large or small (e.g., overall social and political impact in the wider ecosystem or loss of state revenues). In the EMPRISES framework an *economic event* thus details the victim(s) (individual, corporate or jurisdiction) as well as the effects of illegal exchanges of resources for each type of victim. The model differentiates agents according to their location as either inside or outside agents. The *inside agent* is the illicit propagator of the SOEC or fraud, the *outside agent* refers to the victim. Adding these semantics distinguishes the 'good' from the 'bad' according to the consequences of the transaction.

The Transaction Concept also captures the pragmatics as well as semantics of SOEC, thus minimising the impact of 'cat-and-mouse' games as the SOEC enterprises or fraudsters try to beat the detection system [6, 7]. To capture and represent this complex information, EMPRISES will make use of *Conceptual Graphs* (CGs) [8]. CGs offer conceptual structures. They align the creativity of humans with the productivity of computers, providing knowledge capture and reasoning at this semantic level. Additional rigour is provided at the mathematical level by including a further Conceptual Structure in form of *Formal Concept Analysis* (FCA) [8].

To understand the direct and indirect economic impacts of SOEC and fraud, the Transaction Concept will be combined with *Computable General Equilibrium* (CGE) *analysis*. CGE is well respected in many fields and used, for instance, in fiscal studies [9, 10, 11]. CGE analysis has demonstrated its capacity to capture the intrinsic mechanisms of the economy to translate inefficiencies through all the productive structures and institutional sectors. Introducing previously identified economic distortions and computing their chained effects in the whole economic system will thus allow a more accurate estimation of the full impact of SEOC and fraud on states [12]. In the context of EMPRISES, a pilot system in form of a *Pan-EU Monitoring System* (PEUMS) will be realised. In a first step, the EMPRISES PEUMS (E-PEUMS) aims at the integration of existing LEA systems in five Member States, namely Finland, Poland, Spain, Turkey, and UK.

## IV. The EMPRISES Pan-EU Monitoring System (E-PEUMS)

EMPRISES will be implemented based on the E-PEUMS architecture taking advantage of existing solutions, particularly FIU.NET and SIENA. FIU.NET for Europe together with the Egmont Group works on coordinating and facilitating information exchange between Financial Investigation Units (FIU) on a national and international level. Most EU member states are currently members of FIU.NET. FIU.NET allows members to exchange information on economic crimes using their bespoke MA3tch system. This system allows FIUs to share data in an anonymous way among all members or between specific members by converting data into uniform information. Representatives from member states on FIU.NET range from the Serious Organised Crime Agency (SOCA; a law enforcement but not police agency) in the UK to SEPBLAC in Spain (coordinated by Bank of Spain) to the National Intelligence Unit of the Finnish Police Service.

EUROPOL's SIENA system provides a similar platform for the exchange of operational information between EUROPOL and its partners in the form of structured data. This system aims to coordinate and assist all member states to maximise collective data sharing and analysis and thus to allow a more detailed and comprehensive picture of available information and intelligence. SIENA uses Analytical Work Files (AWF) to process and analyse data/intelligence it receives from its members. Using this data it supports and helps to coordinate member states on a high strategic level to help tackle serious cross-border criminality.

At present both systems work independently. Still, both organizations acknowledge the need for closer cooperation given the high level of finances associated with serious organised crime.

## V. The Added Value of the EMPRISES System

The objective of EMPRISES is to provide an integrative interface to existing databases such as FIU.NET and SIENA. The EMPRISES end-user monitoring systems will allow access, for instance, through the Finish National Police Results Data System (PolStat), the Police Information System (Patja), the West Yorkshire Police intelligence analysis system in the UK, or the Central Intelligence Analysis Unit in Spain.

For this several steps need to be taken to reach beyond existing infrastructures. A known difficulty of traditional RDBMS systems is to represent complex relationships, transactions, actions and events. EMPRISES will employ state-of-the-art RDF triple-store ontology to tackle this issue [14, 15]. This ontology will hold the SOEC and fraud inventory and taxonomy, referred to as the *EMPRISES SOEC and Fraud Knowledge Repository*. Thanks to its knowledge-based architecture, this semantic-web technology is far better suited to express the relational complexity and conceptual, human-based nature of the problem domain [16]. As both RDF and UMF are XML dialects, a simple RDF/UMF conversion will take place as part of data transfer.

EMPRISES will also provide an easy frontend for querying the integrated databases. The RDF query language SPARQL is a powerful tool to exploit the expressivity of ontology, yet normally requires considerable user expertise. EMPRISES will develop simple, intuitive SPARQL Wizards and APIs for all of its SPARQL Endpoint tools to facilitate highly complex queries also for less experienced users. This frontend will build on existing approaches used in FP7 projects such as

CUBIST [16]. For the economic evaluation of SEOC and fraud, EMPRISES will create a set of financial functions (macros) using the recently added SPARQL aggregation functions [15]. EMPRISES will further exploit the popularity and ease of use of existing spread-sheet software, such as Microsoft Excel, by building SPARQL plug-ins for data visualisations such as charts, plots and graphs. By using a simple, ontology-based visualisation of the SOEC and fraud repository, end-users will have a clear view of the underlying data structure and relationships therein. New FCA-based visual analytics will allow extended inventory queries of the underlying SOEC and fraud ontology, allowing semantic, relational, hierarchical, recursive and propagating queries well beyond the current state of the art in traditional data base systems.

## VI. CONCLUDING REMARKS

Sharing data and collaborating in the development of pan-European tools and techniques is vital to effectively combat SOEC and fraud. Yet, although basic data exchange is taking place in the EU, there is currently no central repository of SOEC and fraud for EU member states. EMPRISES will support new forms of cooperative analyses by creating a suite of new tools, technologies and techniques to provide new methods of monitoring, detection, evaluation and deterrence of SOEC and fraud. Functionalities include, amongst others, the investigation of effective interventions in SOEC and fraud (e.g., to inform new guidelines and methods of combating and deterring such crimes), the reporting of SEOC and fraud trends, the identification of differences in EU/Country based legislation and tax law, the identification of common modus operandi, situation assessments, economic evaluations of damaged markets, alerts about newly organised investment fraud schemes, predictions of new types of crime by extrapolation of trends and new crime methods, visualizations of the management structure of known groups and gangs as well as early warnings about new SOEC and fraud by matching SOEC's components in several member states. Global and EU businesses, governments and markets can add the EMPRISES architecture to their current sophisticated models, tools and techniques to better detect trends and predict opportunities. This combined approach can thus provide LEAs with better insights and understanding of the crimes and criminal groups that they are investigating and a more powerful way of detecting and deterring such crimes.

## REFERENCES


[1] TOGAF, "Content Metamodel," 2011. [Online]. Available: http://pubs.opengroup.org/architecture/togaf9-doc/arch/chap34.html. [Accessed 22 11 2012].

[2] D. Vymětal and C. V. Scheller, "MAREA: Multi-Agent REA-Based Business Process Simulation Framework," in *ICT for Competitiveness 2012*, Karviná, Czech republic, 2012.

[3] S. Polovina, "The Transaction Concept in Enterprise Systems," in *Proceedings of the 2nd CUBIST workshop, The 10th International Conference on Formal Concept Analysis (ICFCA 2012)*, Leuven, Belgium, 2012.

[4] I. Launders, The Transaction Graph: Requirements Capture in Semantic Enterprise Architectures, Saarbrücken, Germany: Lambert Academic Publishing, 2012.

[5] S. Polovina and S. Andrews, "A Transaction-Oriented Architecture for Structuring Unstructured Information in Enterprise Applications," in *Intelligent, Adaptive and Reasoning Technologies: New Developments and Applications*, Hershey, PA, USA, IGI-Global, 2011, pp. 285-299.

[6] R. Stamper, "Signs, Norms, and Information Systems," in *Signs at Work*, Berlin, Germany, Walter de Gruyter, 1996, pp. 349-397.

[7] T. Mifflin, C. Boner, G. Godfrey and J. Skokan, "A random graph model for terrorist transactions," in *Aerospace Conference*, 2004.

[8] S. Polovina, "An Introduction to Conceptual Graphs," in *Conceptual Structures: Knowledge Architectures for Smart Applications*, Berlin - Heidelberg, Springer Lecture Notes in Artificial Intelligence, 2007, pp. 1-15.

[9] S. Andrews and S. Polovina, "A Mapping from Conceptual Graphs to Formal Concept Analysis," in *Conceptual Structures for Discovering Knowledge (The 19th International Conference on Conceptual Structures, ICCS 2011)*, Derby, UK, 2011.

[10] S. C. Turner, "Essays on Crime and Tax Evasion, Paper 64," 18 8 2010. [Online]. Available: http://digitalarchive.gsu.edu/econ_diss/64.

[11] E. B. Sennoga, "Essays on Tax Evasion," Georgia State University, 2006.

[12] A. Sandmo, "The Theory of Tax Evasion: A Retrospective View," *National Tax Journal,* vol. 58, no. 4, pp. 643-663., 2005.

[13] R. Meersman, T. Dillon and P. Herrero, On the Move to Meaningful Internet Systems: Confederated International Conferences: CoopIS, IS, DOA and ODBASE, Hersonissos, Crete, Greece, October 25-29, 1010, Proceedings, Berlin - Heidelberg: Springer Lecture Notes in Computer

Science, 2010.

[14] PR-OWL, "A Bayesian Framework for Probabilistic Ontologies," 2012. [Online]. Available: http://www.pr-owl.org/.

[15] F. Dau, "Towards Scalingless Generation of Formal Contexts from an Ontology in a Triple Store," in *Proceedings of the second CUBIST workshop 2012*, Leuven, 2012.

[16] J. P. Carvalho and J. A. Tomè, "Rule Based Fuzzy Cognitive Maps-Fuzzy Causal Relations," in *Computational Intelligence for Modelling, Control and Automation*, 1999.

[17] CUBIST, "CUBIST - Combining and Uniting Business Intelligence with Semantic Technologies," 14 11 2012. [Online]. Available: http://www.cubist-project.eu/. [Accessed 22 11 2012].

# Discovery of Predictive Neighborly Rules from Neighborhood Systems

**Ray Hashemi[1], Azita Bahrami[2], Mark Smith[3], Nicholas R. Tyler[4], Matthew Antonelli[1], and Sean Clapp[1]**

[1]Department of Computer Science
[4]Department of Biology
Armstrong Atlantic State University
Savannah, GA, USA

[2]IT Consultation
Savannah, GA, USA

[3]Department of Computer Science
University of Central Arkansas
Conway, AR, USA

***Abstract*** *- The use of "data closeness" for clustering, concept generalization, and imprecise query processing has been frequently reported in the literature. In this paper, however, we introduce the use of "data closeness" for building a prediction tool. To do so, we: (1) Generate the workable neighborhood system for every record, $R_i$, of a training set, (2) build and expand the "record tree" for $R_i$ using its workable neighborhood system, (3) Extract a neighborly rule from each expanded record tree, and (4) Use the rules for prediction. The empirical results revealed that the predictive power of the neighborly rules is comparable with that of ID3and Rough Sets.*

***Keywords:*** *Machine Learning, Neighborhood System, Workable Neighborhood System, Record Tree, Expanded Record Tree, and Neighborly Rules.*

## 1. Introduction

During a machine learning process the patterns of interest in a dataset are learned by observing similarity, dissimilarity, or the closeness of data [1]. For example, if two specific values belong to two different attributes are frequently observed together within the dataset, the two values may be identified as a pattern of interest. In this research effort, we are interested in learning from the closeness of data. To explain it further, frequently observing a group of close values of one attribute in a given dataset with a group of close values of another attribute in the same dataset may also represent a pattern of interest. The learning methodologies overwhelmingly ignore the closeness observations within a dataset simply because of its inherent low level of certainty. Nevertheless, these patterns are worthy of investigation if one can compensate for the low level of certainty.

Generally speaking, the closeness of data is primarily used as a generalization tool and not as a prediction tool. The goal of this paper is to (1) expand the *neighborhood system* as a methodology that discovers the patterns of interest based on the closeness of data, (2) expresses the patterns in form of *neighborly* rules, and (3) use the rules as a prediction tool.

The rest of the paper is organized as follow: The previous works is provided in Section 2, the methodology is covered in Section 3, the empirical results are discussed in Section 4, and the conclusion and future research are the subject of Section 5.

## 2. Previous Works

The closeness of data, neighborhood, plays a major role in clustering techniques [2, 3, 4], processing of imprecise queries [5], and generalization of the concepts [6, 7, 8].

In clustering techniques, all the records of a dataset that are close to a seed in terms of values collectively make a cluster. One may look at members of a cluster as generalization of the seed.

Motro sued the closeness of data to implement the imprecise queries (goal queries.) For example, implementing the query of "Get the list of Chinese restaurant in a town is easily done by using a data language to issue a query against a given restaurant database. However, finding the list of gourmet restaurants close to the Armstrong campus is not easy to find because we assume that (a) the gourmet restaurant type is not included in the database and (b) the physical distance of the restaurant to the Armstrong campus cannot explicitly be found in the database. The only way that this imprecise query can be answered is through finding restaurants that their food is close to be considered as a gourmet food and their distances from Armstrong campus are within a neighborhood radius.

The concept of *sophomore students* may include a set of student records that their number of passed courses is within an interval. The half of the interval makes the neighborhood radius [9].

The closeness of data also used in conjunction with the Rough Sets [10, 11, 12] to make the upper approximation space produced by the Rough Sets more useful. That is, Rough Sets approach delivers better *local possible* rule.

In short, closeness of data is used frequently for generalization and to the best of our knowledge it has not been used as prediction tool.

# 3. Methodology

Neighborhood system, learning from a neighborhood system, and generation of neighborly rules are presented in the following three sub-sections.

## 3.1. Neighborhood System

Let us start with some formal definitions for better understanding of the *neighborhood system* concept.

*Definition 1:* Let U be universe of objects. For $x \in U$, the neighborhood of x is $n(x) = \{y \mid y \in U \text{ and } dist(x, y) \leq t\}$, Where dist(x, y) is a distance function and t is a threshold value.

*Definition 2:* Let T be the set of all the possible values for the distance threshold of t, the $k=|T|$ neighborhoods of x collectively make the neighborhood system of x and denoted as NS(x).

If i and j are two possible values of distance threshold t such that $t_i < t_j$ then $n_i(x)$ is closer to x than $[n_j(x)-n_i(x)]$ and it is denoted as $n_i(x) \Diamond [n_j(x)-n_i(x)]$

*Definition 3:* Let NS(x) and NS(z) be two neighborhood systems generated for k possible values of distance threshold of t,

a) $NS(x) \cap NS(z) = \{n_i(x) \cap n_i(z)\}$ $\forall i$
Where $n_i(x) \in NS(x)$ and $n_i(z) \in NS(z)$

b) $NS(x) \cup NS(z) = \{n_i(x) \cup n_i(z)\}$ $\forall i$
Where $n_i(x) \in NS(x)$ and $n_i(z) \in NS(z)$

$|NS(\bullet)|$ may be too large to have a practical use. As a result, we need to trim $NS(\bullet)$ to have a workable neighborhood system.

*Definition 4:* NS(x) is a workable neighborhood system if NS(x) includes only three neighborhoods of $n_{closest}(x)$, $n_{closer}(x)$, and $n_{close}(x)$ for which the threshold values are t, $t \pm \epsilon$ and $t \pm 2\epsilon$, where $t \neq 0$ and $\epsilon$ value depends on x. If x is a discretized value, then $\epsilon$ is an integer; otherwise, it is a real value.

Let S be an information system, as defined by Pawlak [13], Table1.

Table 1: An Information System

| Records | A1 | A2 | A3 | A4 | A5 | Decision |
|---|---|---|---|---|---|---|
| $R_1$ | 1 | 2 | 1 | 3 | 4 | 1 |
| $R_2$ | 1 | 1 | 2 | 2 | 2 | 1 |
| $R_3$ | 2 | 2 | 3 | 1 | 2 | 2 |
| $R_4$ | 1 | 2 | 1 | 3 | 2 | 1 |
| $R_5$ | 3 | 3 | 2 | 2 | 3 | 2 |
| $R_6$ | 3 | 1 | 3 | 1 | 2 | 3 |
| $R_7$ | 2 | 1 | 1 | 2 | 1 | 3 |
| $R_8$ | 3 | 2 | 2 | 3 | 3 | 3 |

The attribute $A_j$ has the value of $v_{ji}$ for the record $R_i$ of S. The workable neighborhood system for $R_i$ considering only $A_j$ is denoted as $NS_{Aj}(R_i) = \{r_p | v_{jp} \in NS_{Aj}(v_{ji})$ and $NS_{Aj}(v_{ji})$ is a workable neighborhood system of $v_{ji}$. The neighborhood system for $R_i$ considering all q attributes of $A_1, \ldots, A_q$ is: $NS_{A1, \ldots, Aq}(R_i) = \cap NS_{Aj}(R_i)$ for j =1 to q. The record $R_i$ is referred to as the *seed* and the closest, closer, and close neighbors of record $R_i$ are referred to as *granules* of the seed. (Note: If t = 0 be used then $n_{closest}(x)$ includes records that are duplicates of $R_i$. We assume that there are either no duplicate records in S or duplicate records have been replaced by only one copy. )

As an example let us determine the workable neighborhood for the seed $R_1$: $NS_{A1...A5}(R_1)$. We find neighborhood R1 in reference to each of its attribute values and then get their intersections that represents the neighborhood system of R1. We start with attribute A1:

$$NS_{A1}(R_1) = \{r_p | v_{A1p} \in NS_{A1}(1)\}$$

We use t = 0.1, t =1.1, and t = 2.1 (the $\epsilon$ value is = 1) to identify the workable neighborhoods of closest, closer and close values to $R_1$ in reference to $v_{11}$=1.

All the records in S for which their A1 value is in the range of [0-1.1] make the closest neighborhood of $R_1$, $\{R_1, R_2, R_4\}$. All the records in S for which their A1 value is in the range of [0-2.1] make the closer neighborhood of $R_1$, $\{R_1, R_2, R_3, R_4, R_7\}$. All the records in S for which their A1 value is in the range of [0-3.1] make the close neighborhood of $R_1$, $\{R_1, R_2, R_3, R_4, R_5, R_6, R_7, R_8\}$. Following the same process one can build the workable neighborhood systems for all attribute values of record R1.

$n_{closest}(R_1) = \cap\, n_{closest}(A_i) = \{\}$ (for i = 1 to 5)

$n_{closer}(R_1) = \cap\, n_{closer}(A_i) = \{\}$ (for i = 1 to 5)

$n_{close}(R_1) = \cap\, n_{close}(A_i) = \{R_2, R_3, R_4, R_5, R_6, R_8\}$ (for i = 1 to 5)

Therefore, $NS(R_1) = \{n_{closest}(R1), n_{closer}(R1), n_{close}(R1)\} = \{\{\}, \{\}, \{R_2, R_3, R_4, R_5, R_6, R_8\}\}$.

## 3.2. Learning from the Neighborhood Systems

The following two-step pre-processing is applied on a given dataset D:

- Only one copy of the duplicated records in D are kept.
- Conflicting records are removed from D (Two records are conflicting if they are exactly the same except for their decision values.)

The dataset D, then split into a pair of training and test sets. The test set includes the same percentage of the records for each decision value in D and the records are chosen randomly. After removing the records of the test set from D, the records for the training set are chosen such that for each decision value the same number of records exist in the training set to support an unbiased training process.

For each record of the training set, the workable neighborhood system is generated. If the number of records in the training set is M, then there are M Closest, Closer, and Close neighborhoods (one per record). For each record, R, a certainty factor, CF, is calculated for its Closest(R), Closer(R), and Close(R). Formula 1 shows the calculation of the CF for the Closer(R) neighborhood.

$$CF_{Closer(R)} = \frac{G}{|Closer(R)|} \quad (1)$$

Where, G is the number of records in the Closer(R) that have the same decision as R.

The following algorithms can be applied on any of the three M neighborhoods of the workable neighborhood system of the training set. These algorithms are used to build a tree for each record, *record tree*, of the training set. However, if the record tree for record $R_i$ of the training set includes records Rj, and Rk, for example, then $R_j$ and $R_k$ will not have their own trees.

Let us consider only the M Closer neighborhoods of the training set records. The record tree for the record Ri is built as follows:

a. The record Ri is the root of its tree
b. All the records in Closer(Ri) make its children.
c. Each child may serve as root of a new sub-tree—if it is qualified.
d. This process continues until the record tree cannot be expanded further.

The qualification for expansion of a child is determined based on the records of the Closer(Child) neighborhood. We use two different sets of qualifications. As a result, we introduce two algorithms (TREE-ONE and TREE-TWO) that they may produce two different record trees for a given record. The qualifications used in the algorithm TREE-TWO are more restricted. The record trees are the basis for generating neighborly rules.

**Algorithm TREE-ONE**

*Given:* A training set with M records and M Closer neighborhoods (one per record). Each Closer neighborhood has its own certainty factor, CF. N is a set of M Closer neighborhoods and $E_d$ is a threshold value.

*Objective:* Building record trees for each record of the training set.

1. Repeat steps 1-7 while N is not empty
2. Identify a record, R, in N such that its Closer(R) has the highest CF value; If there is a tie, then pick the one that its Closer neighborhood has the highest cardinality. If the tie has not been resolved yet, then select R randomly from the records that are tie.
3. Build the *record tree* of R in which:
   /*R is the root, All the records in Closer(R) make the children of the root*/
   $CF_{Tree} = CF_{Closer(R)}$;
   Create average record, AR, such that the value for attribute Ai of AR is the average of the attribute

values of $A_i$ of all the records in the record tree of R;
4. Repeat steps 5-6 while the record tree can be expanded
5. Repeat step 6 while a child of the same tree level has not been processed/*Breadth first expansion*/;
6. Process a new node, r, of the tree by:
   (i) Expand node r /*records in the Closer(r) make the children of r.*/
   (ii) Remove those children of r that have already appeared as a node somewhere in the tree;
   (iii) If the Euclidean distance of a child record of r from AR record is greater than the threshold value of, $E_d$, then remove the child;
7. Update AR and its $CF_{Tree}$ ;
8. N = N- (all the Closer neighbors of those records that are in the record tree of R);
End;

The algorithm TREE-TWO is the same as the algorithm TREE-ONE with one extra sub-step in Step 6. As a result, we show only the Step 6 for the Algorithm Tree-TWO

6. Process a new node r of the tree by:
   (i) Expand node r /*records in the Closer(r) make the children of r.*/
   (ii) Remove those children of r that have already appeared as a node somewhere in the tree;
   (iii) If the CF for the remaining children of the sub-tree in which r is the root is ≤ 0.67 then undo the expansion of r;
   (iv) If the Euclidean distance of a child record of r from AR record is greater than the threshold value of, $E_d$, then remove the child;

The threshold of 0.67 is the minimum acceptable value because it says that the decision for at least 2/3 of the remaining records in the Closer(r) agrees with the decision of r.

## 2.3. Generation of Neighborly Rules

Use of both algorithms generates a set of AR records. Each AR record has the same number of attributes as any of the records in the training set. The attribute Ai of an AR record is the average of all Ai attribute values of the records participating in the underlying record tree.

Let us assume that every AR has n attributes of $A_1 \ldots A_n$. In addition, let us assume that for one particular AR, the attribute values are $(a_1, \ldots, a_n)$, the root of the underlying record tree is $R_i$, the decision for $R_i$ is $d_j$, and $CF_{Tree} = \alpha$. The AR may be converted into a *neighborly rule* as follow:

$$(A_1 = a_1 \ \& \ldots \& \ A_n = a_n) \rightarrow d_j \ (CF = \alpha)$$

Conversion of AR records produced by the two algorithms delivers two different sets of neighborly rules. All the rules with the CF ≤ 0.67 will be removed from the sets. The reason behind such action is that the effects of the rules with lower CF are almost as good as flipping a coin to predict an outcome.

The nature of the neighborly rules is different from those rules that one can extract directly from the records of a training set. The difference lies on the fact that the neighborly rules are extracted from the neighborhood of the records and not the records themselves. As a result, these rules are applied differently. To explain it further, let us assume that decision for a test record, R', needs to be predicted using a set of k neighborly rules. The total distance of each rule from R' is calculated using formula 2.

$$\text{Total Distance} = \Sigma(|Ai\text{-}A'i|)\ \forall i \qquad (2)$$

The winner rule is the one with the smallest total distance. The predicting decision for R' is the decision associated with the winner rule and the certainty prediction of the decision is equal to the certainty factor associated with winner decision.

# 4. Empirical Results

Two datasets are used to examine the prediction power of neighborly rules generated by the neighborhood system. The first dataset is a small one and it is a collection of data regarding blue color workers of an aluminum factory. The dataset has 134 records and fourteen attributes. The dataset was cleaned by removing:

a. The extra copies of a duplicated record,
b. The records with missing data, and
c. The conflicting records (i.e. records that only differ in their decision.)

The dataset has been reduced to 53 records after cleaning.

The second dataset is a set of 1018 chemical agents and their properties. The number of properties for each record is 240 plus a decision. Whether the agent produces liver cancer in human or not serves as the decision for the agent record.

Each dataset has been split into pairs of training and test sets using the following process. Fifteen percent of the records for each decision value are randomly selected to serve as a test set. From the remaining records in the dataset equal number of records from each decision is selected randomly to serve as a training set. This process is repeated to generate all possible training and test sets that satisfy one major restriction. The restriction is that none of the records of dataset can serve in more than one test set. The creation of the training and test pairs stops when a test set cannot be generated without violating the restriction. Since the test set of every pair is different from the next pair, then so the training set.

Table2: The prediction results for both datasets using cross validation

| Cross Validation Approach | | Using Rules Generated by TREE-ONE | Using Rules Generated by TREE-TWO |
|---|---|---|---|
| Dataset #1 | Average % of Correct Classifications | 76.4 | 82 |
| | Average % of Incorrect Classifications | 24 | 18 |
| | Average % of not predictable | 0 | 0 |
| | Average % of False Positives | 17 | 10 |
| | Average % of False Negatives | 7 | 8 |
| Dataset # 2 | Average % of Correct Classifications | 73 | 81 |
| | Average % of Incorrect Classifications | 25 | 18 |
| | Average % of not predictable | 2 | 1 |
| | Average % of False Positives | 6 | 6 |
| | Average % of False Negatives | 4 | 5.5 |

The two different sets of neighborly rules generated by applying algorithms TREE-ONE and TREE-TWO on every training sets. The resulting rules from each training set were used to predict the decision for the records of the corresponding test set. The average of the correct classifications for all test sets was used to represent the prediction power of the proposed methodology. Results for both datasets are shown in Table 2. In addition the average number of false positives and false negatives were calculated that are also shown in Table 2.

Since the number of the records in the first dataset is small, cross validation produces small test sets that may be objectionable. However, we also used both the *re-sampling* and k-1 testing approaches that are more proper for small datasets. The re-sampling approach is done as follow: A training set is randomly generated from the cleaned dataset. There is equal number of records for each decision in the training set. The training set serves as a new dataset. After the rules are generated from the new set, different test sets are built out of the new dataset as follow. Each test set is generated by re-sampling the new dataset. The number of the records in the test set is the same as the number of records in the new dataset. The results of the proposed methodology performance using re-sampling are shown in Table3.

The k-1testing approach is done as follow: One record at a time from the cleaned dataset is set aside as a test set and a training set is generated from the remaining of the records in the dataset. The results are also shown in Table 3.

Table3: The prediction results for only the first dataset using re-sampling and K-1 testing approaches.

| | | Using Rules Generated by TREE-ONE | Using Rules Generated by TREE-TWO |
|---|---|---|---|
| Re-Sampling | Average % of Correct Classifications | 72 | 81 |
| | Average % of Incorrect Classifications | 28 | 17 |
| | Average % of not predictable | 0 | 0 |
| | Average % of False Positives | 22 | 5 |
| | Average % of False Negatives | 6 | 12 |
| K-1 | Average % of Correct Classifications | 72 | 77 |
| | Average % of Incorrect Classifications | 27 | 22 |
| | Average % of not predictable | 0 | 0 |
| | Average % of False Positives | 11 | 10 |
| | Average % of False Negatives | 16 | 12 |

To establish the predictive power of the proposed methodology, its performance was compared to that of Rough Sets [12, 13] and ID3 [14]. The results of applying Rough Sets, ID3, and the algorithm TREE-TWO on both datasets, are shown in Table 4. Reader needs to be reminded that the results shown for the algorithm TREE-TWO in reference to dataset 1 and dataset 2 are produced by the cross validation approach and K-1 testing approach respectively. Therefore, the results for ID3 and Rough Sets are reported for the same testing approaches in Table 4.

Table4: The prediction results for ID3, Rough sets, and the algorithm TREE-TWO: (a) Results for Dataset 1and (b) Results for dataset 2.

| **(a) Results for Dataset 1** | | | |
|---|---|---|---|
| | ID3 | Rough Sets | TREE-TWO |
| Average % of Correct Classifications | 79 | 72 | 82 |
| Average % of Incorrect Classifications | 14 | 18 | 18 |
| Average % of not predictable | 7 | 9 | 0 |
| Average % of False Positives | 4 | 9 | 10 |
| Average % of False Negatives | 10 | 8 | 8 |
| **(b) Results for Dataset 2** | | | |
| | ID3 | Rough Sets | TREE-TWO |
| Average % of Correct Classifications | 77 | 68 | 84 |
| Average % of Incorrect Classifications | 10 | 20 | 16 |
| Average % of not predictable | 13 | 12 | 0 |
| Average % of False Positives | 7 | 12 | 9 |
| Average% of False Negatives | 3 | 8 | 6 |

# 5. Conclusion and Future Research

Closeness of data that is the backbone of the Neighborhood systems has been used almost exclusively to generalize concepts, clustering techniques and processing of imprecise queries. However, we tried to use the neighborhood systems as a prediction tool that produces neighborly rules. The application of rules that were obtained from two different algorithms (algorithms TREE-ONE and TREE-TWO) reveals that: (a) the rules obtained from expanded record trees generated by algorithm TREE-TWO have a better performance than the rules obtained from the product of the algorithm TREE-ONE, (b) neighborhood systems have a high potential to be used as a prediction tool, and (c) The predictive power of the proposed system is comparable b the predictive power of ID3 and the Rough sets approach.

As future research, development of a new algorithm is in progress that expands the record trees using the depth first expansion—in contrast with the breadth first expansion reported in this paper.

# 6. References

[1] J. Han and M. Kamber, “Data Mining: Concepts and Techniques”, Morgan Kauf- mann Publishers, 2006.

[2] M., Marina. "Comparing Clusterings by the Variation of Information". *Learning Theory and Kernel Machines*, B. Schölkopf and M. K. Warmuth (Eds.), Springer Lecture Notes in Computer Science, Volume 2777, 2003, pp. 173–187.

[3] V. Estivill-Castro, "Why so many clustering algorithms". *ACM SIGKDD Explorations Newsletter, Volume 4, Issue 1, 2002*, pp. 65-75.

[4] T. Zhang, R. Ramakrishnan, M. Livny, "An Efficient Data Clustering Method for Very Large Databases", The ACM SIGMOD International Conference on Management of Data, 1996, pp. 103–114.

[5] A. Motro, “Extending the Relational Database Model to Support Goal Queries”, The First International Conference on Expert Database Systems, L. Kerschberg (Ed.), 1986, pp. 129-150.

[6] Y. Yao, Information Tables with Neighborhood Semantics, *Data Mining and Knowledge Discovery: Theory, Tools, and Technology II*, Published by the international society for optics and photonics, Volume 4057, 2000, pp. 108-116.

[7] R. Hashemi, J. Danley, A. Tyler, W. Slikker, and M. Paule, "Quality of Information Granulation: Kohonen Self-organizing Map vs. Neighborhood System", Proceedings of the *Fourth International Joint Conference on Information Sciences*, G. Georgiou, C. Janikow, and Y. Yao (Eds), Research Triangle Park, NC, Oct. 1998, pp 294-297.

[8] X. Yang, TY Lin, Knowledge Operations in Neighborhood System, 2010 IEEE International Conference on Granular Computing (GrC), Aug 2010, pp. 822-825.

[9] R. Hashemi, S. D. Agustino, and B. Westgeest, "Data Granulation and Formal Concept Analysis", Proceedings of the 2004 International Conference of North American Fuzzy Information Processing Society (NAFIPS'04), S. Dick, L.Kurgan, P. Musilek, W. Pedrycz and M. Reformat (Eds.), Sponsored by IEEE, Banff, Alberta, Canada, June, 2004, pp. 79 - 83.

[10] T. Y. Lin, "Rough Sets, Neighborhood Systems and Approximation," *Fifth International Symposium on Methodologies of Intelligent Systems, Selected Papers*, Oct. 1990.

[11] T. Y. Lin., and Y. Yao, "Mining Soft Rules Using Rough Sets and Neighborhoods," *Symposium on Modeling, Analysis and Simulation*, CESA'96 IMACS Multiconference (Computational Engineering in Systems Applications), Lille, France, July 9-12, 1996, Vol. 2 of 2,pp.1095-1100.

[12] R. Hashemi, A. Tyler, A. Bahrami, "Use of Rough Sets as a Data Mining Tool for Experimental Bio-Data", A book chapter in: "*Computational Intelligence in Biomedicine and Bioinformatics: Current Trends and Applicationjs*", Tomasz G. Smolinski, Mariofanna G. Milanova, and Aboul Ella Hassanien, Editors, Springer-Verlag Publisher, June 2008, pp. 69-91.

[13] Z. Pawlak Z, "Rough Classification", Journal of Man-Machine Studies 1984, 20: 469-83.

[14] J.R. Quinlan, "Induction of Decision Trees", Machine Learning 1, 1 , 1986, 81-106.

# SESSION

# DATA AND INFORMATION MINING + FORECASTING METHODS

## Chair(s)

### TBA

# An approach for Mining Complex Spatial Dataset

Grace L. Samson[1], Joan Lu[1], Lizhen Wang[2], Dave Wilson[1]

[1]Informatics, School of Computing and Engineering, University of Huddersfield; Huddersfield, UK
[2] School of Information Science and Engineering, Yunnan University, China PRC

***Abstract**: Spatial data mining organizes by location what is interesting as such, specific features of spatial data mining (including observations that are not independent and spatial autocorrelation among the features) that preclude the use of general purpose data mining algorithms poses a serious challenge in the task of mining meaningful patterns from spatial systems. This creates the complexity that characterises complex spatial systems. Thus, the major challenge for a spatial data miner in trying to build a general complex spatial model would be; to be able to integrate the elements of these complex systems in a way that is optimally effective in any particular case. We have examined ways of creating explicit spatial model that represents an application of mining techniques capable of analysing data from a complex spatial system and then producing information that would be useful in various disciplines where spatial data form the basis of general interest.*

**Keywords**: Spatial data; Complex systems; Patterns mining; Spatial models; Spatial database

## 1 Introduction

Spatial data mining is the quantitative study of phenomena that is located in space. This means that there is an explicit consideration of the location and spatial arrangement of the object to be analysed [9].We have focused on the unique features that distinguish spatial data mining from classical data Mining, and present major accomplishments of spatial data mining research, especially regarding predictive modelling, spatial outlier detection, spatial co-location rule mining, and spatial clustering. Spatial data mining organizes by location what is interesting therefore, the main purpose of spatial data mining is to search for interesting, valuable, and unexpected spatial patterns; which can be useful in so many application domains. Most often than not the pattern discovered always provide a new understanding of the real world as such, the search must be a non-trivial one and should be as automated as possible with a large search space of plausible hypothesis. Attention to location, spatial interaction, spatial structure and spatial processes lies at the heart of activities in several disciplines today and as such demands the urgent development of tools capable of analysing and managing such data which typically can only be represented by means of geometric features, for instance, consider the examples of spatial data described by [23] as (a) Percentage cover of woody plants along a line division; (b) Land cover from some rangeland types within a specified area of a coastal region; these include some special cases of spatial data. Finding implicit regularities, rules or patterns hidden in spatial databases is an important task for example in geo-marketing, traffic control or environmental studies [6]. The ultimate goal of spatial data mining is to integrate and further extend methods of traditional data mining in various fields for the analysis and management of large and complex spatial data. The underlying concept is based on the fact that spatial data types (e.g *points, lines, polygons and regions*) are not supported by the *conventional database management system*. Studying spatial data management helps us to discover the relationship between spatial and non-spatial data and to be able to build and query a spatial knowledgebase.

### 1.1 Related research

Geospatial data is the data or information that identifies the geographic location of features and boundaries on earth (such as natural or constructed features), oceans etc. Spatial data are usually stored as *co-ordinates* and *topology* that can be mapped. They are often accessed, manipulated and analysed through geographic information system. Spatial data mining and geographic knowledge discovery has emerged as an active research area focusing on the development of theory, methodology, and practice for the extraction of useful information and knowledge from massive and complex spatial databases, Therefore, there is an urgent need for effective and efficient methods to extract unknown and unexpected information from spatial data sets of unprecedentedly large size, high dimensionality, and complexity [18]. According to [13] geographic information systems contain high level spatial operators that are uncommon in conventional database management system (DMS). This has led to an increased development of research issues that focus on technologies, techniques and trends that identifies properties that a spatial data model, dedicated to support spatial data for cartography, topography, cadastral and relevant applications, should satisfy. These properties concern the data types, data structures and spatial operations of the model [22]. In their work, [15] asserted that for every spatial data object, the attribute data are referenced to a specific location; which means that they are highly dependent on location and also influenced by neighbouring object (which has given rise to the mining of collocation pattern between spatial objects). Existing DBMS do not support complex spatial relations that exist between spatial objects thus to achieve this, the functionalities of the DBMS should be extended to incorporate the facilities of these complex spatial relations into their query language by providing for the DBMS a model of how to process and optimize queries over spatial relations [4]. Spatial database management refers to the extraction of implicit knowledge, spatial relations or other patterns not explicitly stored in spatial databases. Traditional data organisation and retrieval tools can only handle the storage and retrieval of explicitly stored data [15]. The importance of handling a spatial database derives from the need to deal with geometric, geographic or spatial data (i.e data related to space). According to [22] one remarkable feature of a spatial database is based on the fact that the management of geographic data is split into two distinct types of processing, one for the spatial data and another for the attributes of conventional data and their association with spatial data. In other words, according to [12], spatial database systems deals with the fundamental database technology for geographic information systems and other applications and querying this database is to connect the operations of a spatial algebra (including predicates to express spatial relationships) to the facilities of a DBMS query language.

# 2 Methods of mining spatial patterns

The major activities involved in mining spatial patterns include:

1. Dataset Preparation

2. Initial Data Exploration

3. Predicting Process And Mining Predictions

In this work, we looked at modelling (PREDICTIVE), querying and implementing a spatial database for event prediction using basic spatial data mining algorithm.
The term spatial database system is associated with a view of a database as containing sets of objects in space rather than images or pictures of a space. Consequently, mining spatial patterns from a complex spatial system would basically involve the description of the two categories of data obtainable in all geographic data (i.e spatial data and attribute data). In doing this, some of the major issues to consider include: data description, data manipulation and data representation.

## 2.1 Data description

### 2.1.1 Describing spatial data

- Properties of location in a map are often *"autocorrelated" (patterns exist)*

- Spatial data types are *complex (e.g points, lines and polygons)*

  Spatial data *denotes continuous feature*

- *Spatial operators include (overlay, re-class, distance etc.)*

### 2.1.2 Describing non-spatial data

- Data deals with simple domains e.g *numbers and symbols*

- Data *describe discrete object*

  Data *are independent* of each other

These descriptions identify properties that a spatial data model, dedicated to support spatial data for cartography, topography, cadastral and relevant applications, should satisfy. These properties concern the *data types, data structures and spatial operations* of the model as listed below:

- *Spatial operations (spatial query, layering/overlaying, buffering)*

- *Spatial data* which describes location (where)

- *Attribute data* which specifies characteristics at that location (what, how much, and when)

## 2.2 Spatial Data Representation

Representing spatial data in the form that the computer would understand requires grouping the data into layers according to the individual components with similar features (example layer could be waterlines, elevation, temperature, topography e.t.c).
In general, two distinct data structures are considered when representing spatial data digitally these include; (i) raster data structure (ii) vector data structure.

### 2.2.1 Raster data structure

According to [21], raster cell is usually a square, but could theoretically be another regular polygon that is able to fully cover an image area without leaving holes in the covered region, e.g. a triangle, hexagon or rectangle. Raster data structure according to [11], is similar to placing a regular grid over a study region and representing the geographical feature found in each grid cell numerically: for example, 1 for loamy, 2 for clay and so on. A raster consists of a matrix of cells (or pixels) organized into rows and columns (or a grid) where each cell contains a value representing information, such as temperature (as you can see in the figure below)

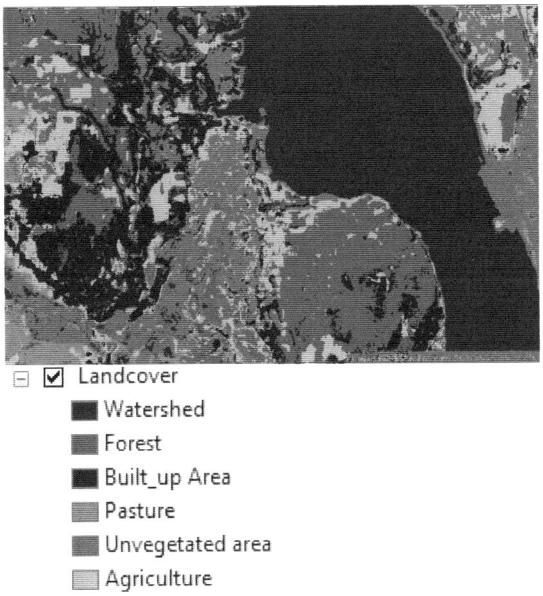


Figure 1: example of a raster data representation

#### 2.2.1 Vector data structure

Vector data structure represents geographic objects with the basic elements *points*, *lines* and *areas*, also called polygons. From the description given by [11], vector data is based on recording point locations (zero dimensions) using *x and y coordinates, stored within two columns of a database*. By assigning each feature a unique ID, a relational database can be used to link location to an attribute table describing what is found there.

### 2.3 Spatial Data Types

[25] Observed that in trying to discover pattern in real world data, the different models in which real world data is organised and the pattern discovery technique to be applied to this models must be considered. Data types of a spatial set are the major element of a spatial database as we have described by the examples below.

*Continuous data types:* elevation, rainfall, ocean salinity

*Areas data types:*

- *unbounded:* land-use, market areas, soils, rock type
- *bounded:* city/county/state boundaries, ownership parcels, zoning
- *Moving:* air masses, animal herds, schools of fish

*Networks data types:* roads, transmission lines, streams

*Points data types:*

- *fixed:* wells, street lamps, addresses
- *moving:* cars, fish, deer

### 2.4 Data manipulation

The main application driving research in spatial database systems are GIS. Hence we consider some modelling needs in this area which are typical also for other applications. Examples are given for two dimensional *space (length and breadth)*, but almost everywhere, extension to the three - or more-dimensional case is possible. There are two important alternative views of what needs to be represented:

- *Objects in space*: in this case, we are interested in distinct entities arranged in space each of which has its own geometric description allows us to model, for example, *cities, forests, or rivers*

- *Space*: here, we wish to describe space itself that is describing every point in space. Models thematic maps describing e.g. *land use/cover* or the partition of a *country into districts.*

## 3 Knowledge discovery task in spatial data mining

The essence of data mining is to demonstrate the possible contribution of general KDD methods that are not specifically designed for spatially referenced data. Knowledge discovery in a *spatial database* involves finding *implicit regularities*, *rules* or *patterns* hidden in spatial databases. These are grouped under several basic categories in terms of the kind of knowledge to be discovered. Spatial data mining encompasses various tasks and, for each task, a number of different methods are often available, which could be *computational*, *statistical*, *visual*, or some combination of them. Some common spatial data mining task includes:

- *Spatial classification/prediction*
- *Spatial association rule mining*
- *Spatial cluster analysis*
- *Geo-visualization e.t.c*

These tasks can generally be classified into two categories:

- Modelling and
- Querying of a given spatial database

In general, the major tasks a spatial data miner may face would include of these (as shown in table 1):

Table 1: Example tasks in spatial pattern mining

| |
|---|
| *Location Prediction*<br>Predict that is trying to identify where a phenomenon will occur.<br>➢ predicting location of protein sub cellular [5]<br>➢ Predicting location of a mobile cellular networks user [1] |
| *Spatial Interactions*<br>The researcher is trying to find out which subsets of spatial phenomena interact?<br>➢ Application of spatial information to mobile computing [8]<br>➢ Applying spatial interactions to the analysis of crime incidents [14] |
| *Hot spot* -Finding which locations are unusual or share commonalities through spatial clustering<br>➢ Detecting spatial hot spots in landscape ecology [19]<br>➢ *Spatial* Organization of DNA in the Nucleus May Determine Positions of Recombination Hot Spots [25]<br>➢ Applying clustering techniques to crime hot-spot analysis [7]<br>➢ Other application areas include earthquake analysis, vehicle crashes, agricultural situations ….. |
| *Spatial outliers' detection*<br>Trying to identify abnormal patterns (outliers) from large data sets<br>➢ *Detecting Outliers* in Gamma Distribution [20]<br>➢ *Bearing Based Selection* in Mobile Spatial Interaction [27] |

# 4 Results and Discussion

[2] Has established that the data inputs of spatial data mining are more complex than the inputs of classical data mining because they include extended objects such as points, lines, and polygons. The data inputs of spatial data mining have two distinct types of attributes: non-spatial attribute and spatial attribute. Non-spatial attributes are used to characterize non-spatial features of objects, such as name, population, and unemployment rate for a city. They are the same as the attributes used in the data inputs of classical Data Mining. Spatial attributes are used to define the spatial location and extent of spatial objects The spatial attributes of a spatial object most often include information related to spatial locations, e.g., longitude, latitude and elevation, as well as shape.

One feasible way to deal with implicit spatial relationships is to materialize the relationships into traditional data input columns and then apply classical data mining techniques - although the materialization may result in loss of information.

However, in [26], it was also established that spatial context such as *autocorrelation* is the key challenge in spatial data mining especially in the area of spatial classification. And then we saw the most obvious challenge of spatial data mining (which is a general problem in field on data mining) in [28] as missing data. [28] acknowledged that since data mining process deals greatly with the development of association rule, patter recognition, classification, estimation and prediction, it will be very pertinent to have serious concern on the accuracy of the database to be modelled and on the sample data chosen for building a training set, in other words, the issue of *missing data* must be addressed since ignoring this problem can lead to a partial judgement of the models being evaluated and then finally lead to inaccurate data mining conclusions.

## 4.1 Data selection

- Measuring per cent occurrence of objects from digital images can save time and expense relative to conventional field measurements [3]
- Ecological assessments incorporating ground-cover measurements (as shown in figure 2) have relied on point sampling using point frames [16]; [17]

## 4.2 Data preparation

In addition to the DM process, which actually extracts knowledge from data, KDD process includes several pre-processing (*data preparation*) and post-processing (*knowledge refinement*) phases [10].

## 4.3 Points sampling

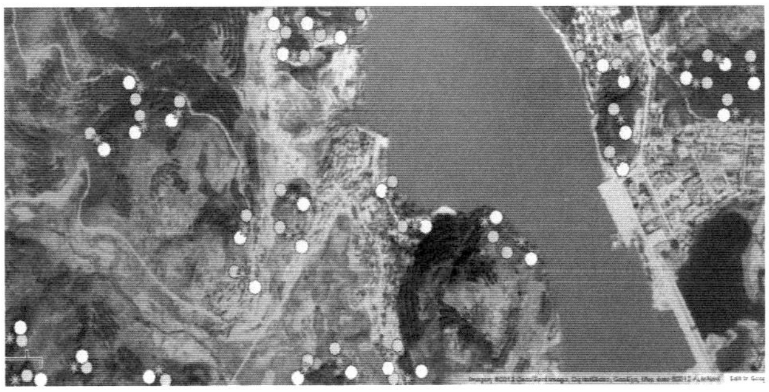

Figure 2: showing locations where sample point where selected on our base-map

### 4.3.1 Sampling methods

"The main aim of the analysis of mapped point data is to detect patterns (i.e., to draw inference regarding the distribution of an observed set of locations)" [29]. We have adopted the *sampling* method of data collection, because we are dealing with data that change across a surface over a period of time e.g temperature, precipitation, and so on. According to [3], measuring per cent occurrences of objects from digital images can save time and expense relative to conventional field measurements. Also, [30] established that ecological assessments incorporating ground-cover (the area, usually expressed as a percentage, of ground covered by the vertical projection of vegetation, litter, and rock) measurements have relied transect methods.

The measurement of ground cover from images has several potential advantages, including acceleration of field work, increased flexibility, repeatability, and convenience in the time and place actual measurements are made.

# 5 Conclusion

Spatial data mining is a branch of data mining where space and location of object is an important factor. In work, we have carried out an extensive research on the field of data mining and we have developed a framework for spatial data mining which is suitable for further expansion and research. We looked at the various branches and tools for data mining and we had a detailed study of spatial data mining; tools techniques, methods, and tasks. We also looked at the various application areas of spatial data mining and the nature of specific pattern that could exist in a given spatial dataset.

# References:

[1]. Anagnostopoulos, T., Anagnostopoulos, C. and Hadjiefthymiades, S. (2012) "Efficient Location Prediction in Mobile Cellular Networks",

International Journal of Wireless Information Networks. 19 (2), pp. 97-111.

[2]. Bolstad, P. (2002). GIS Foundamentals: A Fisrt Text on GIS. Eider Press.

[3]. Booth, D. T., Cox S. E., and Berryman, R. D. (2006) "Point Sampling Digital Imagery with 'Samplepoint'" Environmental Monitoring and Assessment Springer. 123, pp. 97–108

[4]. Clementini, E., Sharma, J., and Egenhofer M. J. (1994) "Modelling Topological Spatial Relations: Strategies for query processing" Computer and graphics. 18 (6), pp.815 – 822.

[5]. Chou, K. and Shen, H. (2007) "Recent progress in protein subcellular location prediction", Analytical Biochemistry, 370 (1), pp. 1-16

[6]. Esther, M., Kriegel, H. and Sander, J. (2001) "Algorithm and Application for Spatial Data Miming" Geographic data Information and Knowledge Discovery Research Monograph in GIS.

[7]. Estivill-Castro, V. and Lee, I. (2002) "Multi-level clustering and its visualization for exploratory spatial analysis" GeoInformatica, 6 (2002), pp. 123–152

[8]. Fröhlich, P., Simon, R., Baillie, L., Roberts, J. and Murray-Smith, R. (2007) "Mobile spatial interaction", ACM. pp. 2841

[9]. Gatrell, A.C. and Bailey, T.C. (1995) Interactive spatial data analysis, Harlow: .Longman Scientific &Technical.

[10]. Ghosh, A. and Freitas, A., A. (2003) "Guest editorial data mining and knowledge discovery with evolutionary algorithms", IEEE Transactions On Evolutionary Computation. 7 (6), pp. 517 - 518.

[11]. Gregory, D., Johnston, R. and Pratt, G. Eds. (2009) Dictionary of Human Geography. 5th ed. Hoboken, NJ, USA: Wiley-Blackwell. [Online] Available at :http://site.ebrary.com/lib/uoh/Doc?id=1030820 8&ppg=816 [Accessed 18 August 2012]

[12]. Güting, R., H. (1994) "An introduction to spatial database systems" The International Journal on Very Large Data Bases. 3 (4), pp. 357 – 399

[13]. Gunther, O. and Buchmann, A. (1990) "Research Issues in Spatial Database" SIGMOD RECORD. 19 (4), pp.61-68

[14]. Kakamu, K., Polasek, W. and Wago, H. (2008) "Spatial interaction of crime incidents in Japan", Mathematics and Computers in Simulation. 78 (2), pp. 276-282.

[15]. Koperski, K. and Han, J. (1995) Discovery of spatial association rules in geographic information databases. In Proceeding of the 4th Int'l Symposium on Large Spatial Databases (SSD'95): Portland, Maine, Aug. pp 47-66.

[16]. Levy, E. B. (1927) "Grasslands of New Zealand", New Zealand Journal of Agriculture 34, 143–164.

[17]. Levy, E. B. and Madden, E. A. (1933) "The point method of pasture analysis", New Zealand Journal of Agriculture. 46, pp. 267–269.

[18]. Mennis, J. and Guo, D. (2009) "Spatial data mining and geographic knowledge discovery—An introduction",Computers, Environment and Urban Systems. 33 (6), pp. 403-408

[19]. Nelson, T.A. and Boots, B. (2008) "Detecting Spatial Hot Spots in Landscape Ecology", Ecography, 31 (5), pp. 556-566

[20]. Nooghabi, M. J, Nooghabi, H. J. and Nasiri, P. (2010) "**Detecting Outliers** in Gamma Distribution" Communications in Statistics - Theory and Methods. 39 (4), pp. 698 - 706

[21]. Neuman, A., Freimark, H. and Wehrle, A. (2010) "Geodata Structures and Data Models" [online] Available at: https://geodata.ethz.ch/geovite/ -Version September 2010. [Accessed 12th August 2012]

[22]. Papadopoulos, A.N., Manolopoulos, Y. and Vassilakopoulos, M.G. (2004) Spatial databases: technologies, techniques and trend. US: Idea Group

[23]. Perry, J. N., Liebhold, A. M., Rosenberg, M. S., Dungan, J., Miriti, M., Jakomulska A., and Citron-Pousty S. (2002). "Illustrations and guidelines for selecting statistical methods for quantifying spatial pattern in ecological data" ECOGRAPHY. 25, pp. 578–600

[24]. Pudi, R. and Krishna, P. R. (2009) *Data Mining*. India: Oxford University Press

[25]. Razin, S.V. and Larovaia, O.V. (2005) "Spatial Organization of DNA in the Nucleus May Determine Positions of Recombination Hot Spots", Molecular Biology. 39 (4), pp. 543-548.

[26]. Shekhar, S., Schrater, P.R., Vatsavai, R.R., Weili Wu and Chawla, S. (2002) "Spatial contextual classification and prediction models for mining geospatial data". pp. 174.

[27]. Strachan, S. and Murray-Smith, R. (2009) "Bearing-based selection in mobile spatial interaction", Personal and Ubiquitous Computing. 13 (4), pp. 265-280.

[28]. Wang, J. eds. (2003) Data Mining: Opportunities and Challenges. US: IGI Global

[29]. Waller, L. A. and Gotway, C. A. (2004) *Applied Spatial Statistics for Public Health Data.* New York: Wiley

[30]. Interagency Technical Team (ITT): 1996, Sampling Vegetation Attributes, Interagency Technical Reference, Report No. BLM/RS/ST-96/002+1730. Denver, CO: U.S. Department of the Interior, Bureau of Land Management – National Applied Resources Science Centre. [Online] Available at:http://www.blm.gov/nstc/library/pdf/samplveg.pdf. [Accessed 22 Sept. 2012]

# Wavelet Based Exchange Rate Forecasting with Improved Instance Based Learning

**Pushpalatha M P**[1], **and Nalini N** [2],
[1]Department of CSc and Eng,Sri Jayachamarajendra College of Engineering, Mysore ,Karnataka, INDIA
[2]Department of ISc and Eng, Nitte Meenakshi Institute of Technology, Bangalore, Karnataka, INDIA

**Abstract**— *In this paper we present a novel wavelet based exchange rate forecast model integrating wavelet filters for denoising and Improved Instance Based Learning(IIBL) approach. The proposed model implements a novel technique that extends the nearest neighbor algorithm to include the concept of pattern matching so as to identify similar instances thus implementing a nonparametric regression approach.The work demonstrates the feasibility of integrating with suitable non-redundant orthogonal wavelet filters at the preprocessing stage to achieve accurate forecasting. The multi-scaling property of the wavelet transform enhances the prediction with high accuracy for volatile time series. The impact of using Discrete Wavelet Transform (DWT) has been systematically illustrated in the preprocessing stage on the accuracy of forecasting. The analysis of simulations demonstrate that the proposed wavelet based IIBL model results in accurate predictions and encouraging results for exchange rate series when compared with the conventional neural network, wavelet and wavelet denoising methods.*

**Keywords:** Instance based learning, Wavelet transforms, Exchange rate forecast.

## 1. Introduction

Time series forecasting is a challenging task due to its high volatility and noisy environment. Classically, the time series data are assumed to be stationary: their characterising quantities behave homogeneously over time. Multi-step ahead time series forecasting has become an important activity in various fields of science and technology due to its usefulness in future events management. In the context of time series, the long-term or multi-step prediction problem is an interesting problem since it obtains predictions several steps ahead into the future starting from information at current instant [?], [4], [5], [7], [8]. Nearest Neighbour(NN) method is widely known for its computational simplicity. The Single Nearest Neighbour (SNN) method involves computing the proximity of the current value with all the data in the training period. It uses Euclidean distance to compute the proximity of current value with all the data in the estimation period. The K-Nearest Neighbour (KNN) method extends the SNN method, chooses k neighbours that have the k highest proximity values and involves computing the proximity of the current value with all the data in the training period. The KNN method uses a simple averaging technique to predict multi-steps ahead which usually does not result in an accurate forecast. A novel wavelet based prediction model integrating wavelet filters for denoising and Improved Instance Based Learning approach developed has been presented.The proposed model implements a novel technique that extends the nearest neighbour algorithm to include the concept of pattern matching so as to identify similar instances thus implementing a non-parametric regression approach. A hybrid distance measure combining correlation and Euclidean distance to select similar instances has been proposed. Hence modification in the standard nearest neighbour method results in improved forecasting accuracy without affecting the simplicity of the nearest neighbour method. Daubechies wavelets is applied at the preprocessing stage mainly to supress the noise in the signals, to result in better prediction values in terms of performance indices used [29].

## 2. Multi-step Prediction

In many time series applications, one-step prediction schemes are used to predict the next sample of data x(k+1), based on previous samples. The disadvantage of one-step prediction is that, it may not provide enough information especially in situations where a broader knowledge of the time series behaviour is desirable to anticipate the behaviour of the time series process. Hence the long-term or multi-step prediction model is used as it obtains predictions several steps ahead into the future i.e., x(k+1), x(k+2), x(k+3), starting from information at current instant k as in [4],[9],[11],[2],[19],[22].

Many techniques exist for the approximation of the underlying process of a time series, linear methods such as Auto Regressive external input (ARX), Auto Regressive Moving Average (ARMA) model etc., and nonlinear ones such as Artificial Neural Networks (ANN). In general, these methods try to build a model of the process. The model is then used on the last values of the series to predict the future values. The common difficulty of all the methods is the determination of sufficient and necessary information for an accurate prediction as stated in [11],[18].

Accuracy of multi-step ahead forecasting using nearest neighbour depends upon the quality of the search for the best matched pattern. Hence, it is very important to search for the most similar pattern from the stored patterns. Euclidean distance based search used in the standard nearest neighbour method minimizes the distance between the reference pattern and the patterns stored in the database without considering the similarity of the shape of the patterns [11],[12]. Further, model based multi-step ahead forecasting fails in many cases because the model cannot learn the dynamics of the system completely. And most of the existing methods are useful for single-step ahead time series forecasting and their accuracy degrades in the case of multi-step ahead forecasting.

Hence the proposed work incorporates a hybrid distance measure combining correlation and Euclidean distance to select similar instances from the stored patterns. It has been motivated by the effective preprocessing capability of wavelet filters and the predictive power of improved instance based learning system, to represent a hybrid prediction system [10],[23].

## 3. Wavelet Theory

Let $L^2(\mathbb{R})$ denote the space of all square integrable functions in R. Let $\psi(t) \in L^2(\mathbb{R})$ be a fixed function. The function $\psi(t)$ is said to be a *wavelet* if and only if its Fourier Transform (**FT**) $\hat{\psi}(\omega)$ satisfies

$$C_\psi = \int_0^\infty \frac{|\hat{\psi}(w)|^2}{|w|} dw < \infty \tag{1}$$

The equation (1) is called the *admissibility condition*[29], [**?**], which implies that the wavelet must have a zero average

$$\int_\infty^\infty \psi(t)dt = \hat{\psi}(0) = 0 \tag{2}$$

and therefore must be oscillatory.
Let us define the function $\psi_{a,b}$ by

$$\psi_{a,b}(t) = \frac{1}{\sqrt{a}}\psi(\frac{t-b}{a}) \tag{3}$$

where $b \subset \mathbb{R}$ is a translation parameter, whereas $a \in \mathbb{R}^+ (a \neq 0)$ is a dilation or scale parameter. The factor $a^{-\frac{1}{2}}$ is a normalization constant such that $\psi_{a,b}$ has the same energy for all scales $a$. It is observable that the scale parameter $a$ in equation (3) rules the dilations of the spatial variable $(t-b)$. In the same way, factor $a^{-\frac{1}{2}}$ rules the dilation in the values taken by $\psi$.
With equation (3), it is able to decompose a square integrable function $f(t)$ in terms of dilated-translated wavelets.
We define the continuous wavelet transform (CWT) of $f(t) \in L^2(\mathbb{R})$ by

$$\begin{aligned} T_\psi[f](a,b) &= \langle f, \psi_{a,b}\rangle = \int_{-\infty}^{+\infty} f(t)\overline{\psi}_{a,b}(t)dt \\ &= \tfrac{1}{\sqrt{a}} \int_{-\infty}^{+\infty} f(t)\overline{\psi}(\tfrac{t-b}{a})dt, \end{aligned} \tag{4}$$

where $\langle , \rangle$ is the scalar product in $L^2(\mathbb{R})$ defined as

$$\langle f, g\rangle := \int f(t)\overline{g}(t)dt,$$

and the symbol bar denotes complex conjugation. The CWT (4) measures the variation of $f$ in a neighborhood of point $b$, whose size is proportional to $a$.
Reconstructing $f$ from its wavelet transform, the reconstruction formula given by [**?**]

$$f(t) = \frac{1}{C_\psi}\int_0^{+\infty}\int_{-\infty}^{+\infty} T_\psi[f](a,b)\psi_{a,b}(t)\frac{dadb}{a^2} \tag{5}$$

the above equation implies the need of equation (1).
However, some data are represented by finite number of values hence it is important to consider a discrete version of CWT of equation(4). In our proposed work the orthogonal (Discrete) wavelet bases are employed. This method associates the wavelet with orthonormal bases of $L^2(\mathbb{R})$. The expansion of a arbitrary signal $x(t)$ on an orthonormal wavelet basis takes the form

$$x(t) = \Sigma_m \Sigma_n x_n^m \psi_{m,n}(t) \tag{6}$$

$$x_n^m = \int_{-\infty}^{+\infty} x(t)\psi_{m,n}(t)dt \tag{7}$$

where the orthonormal wavelet basis functions are related according to

$$\psi_{m,n}(t) = 2^{\frac{m}{2}}\psi(2^m t - n) \tag{8}$$

with both $m$ and $n$ as the dilation and translation indices, respectively. The family of equation (8) can be obtained from equation (3), setting the parameters $a = 2^{-m}$ and $b = \frac{n}{2^m}$. The contribution of the signal at a particular wavelet level $m$ is given by

$$x_m(t) = \Sigma_n x_n^m \psi_{m,n}(t) \tag{9}$$

Equation (9) gives us information of the time behaviour of the signal within different scale bands, and gives their contribution to the total signal energy.

## 4. Wavelet Denoising

The main advantage of modelling with wavelets lies in the fact that is possible to represent the transitory characteristics of the time series in more efficient way. This advantage derives from the fact that wavelets are limited duration functions, moreover the shape of the wavelets used for modelling can be chosen according to the characteristics and behaviour of the time series to be modelled. A filter based on wavelet transform can be implemented to obtain a more accurate signal of the process under interest as in [23][25].

Multiscale analysis varying from one to several levels of decompositions have been performed and the improvement in accuracy is seen at higher level of decompositions as described in[27],[28],[29],[10],[13],[17]. One way to model a time series is to consider it as a deterministic function with noise incorporated. When the noise element in a time series is carefully minimized by a process called denoising, a better model can be obtained for that series.

Many denoising methods have been compared in the literatures of [30], [26], [3], [12], [14]. A good denoising approach consists in setting the smallest coefficients to zero and shrinking the remaining ones above a certain threshold as in [24].

Hence, the idea behind wavelet denoising is to threshold the wavelet coefficients at every multiresolution level so that the amounts of noise present in the detail coefficients are removed. Of the wide choice of wavelet filters, orthogonal wavelets have been considered such as Haar and Daubechies at the preprocessing stage mainly to suppress the noise in the signals, which results in better prediction values in terms of performance indices used [27],[21].

The denoising objective is to suppress the noise part of the signals and to recover function *f*. It is reported that soft thresholding is more effective than hard thresholding approach, hence soft thresholding has been employed as in [13],[24].

## 5. PROPOSED ALGORITHM

Instance Based Learning is a frame work and methodology that can be applied to generate time series prediction using specific instances [4]. The data preprocessing method adopting wavelet filters facilitates to the process of data representation and is able to deal with the non-stationary involved in most of the real time series [1]. The de-noising objective is to suppress the noise part of the signals and to recover function $f$. The denoising procedure is adapted considering appropriate wavelet filters [?], [?]. The proposed approach extends the nearest neighbor algorithm to include the concept of pattern matching to identify similar instances. Pattern matching in the context of time-series forecasting refers to the process of matching current state of the time series with its past states. The specific instances chosen by the proposed approach are combined using non-linear regression to generate multi-step ahead predictions. We extend IIBL with a significant test to distinguish noisy instances by cascading with wavelet filters. Given a time series data set the instance based classification aims at locating similar pieces of information independently of their location in time. While locating the most similar neighbors the method tries to eliminate outliers present in the time series data. In our approach the time series data set is partitioned into training period set and test period set. The training period is then subpartitioned into 'N' instances termed as 'windows' each of specific number of observations 'L' and referred as sliding window size. The number of nearest neighbors 'H' refer to the best instances out of 'N' instances required for the process of forecasting. The optimal values of 'H' and 'L' are determined by conducting several trials so as to obtain optimal results in terms of RMSE and MAPE. The instance that lies just before the time value to be predicted is chosen as the critical instance (reference pattern) against which the similarity of other instances (candidate patterns) is to be estimated. Euclidean correlation is used as the similarity metric to choose similar instances. Once the similar instances (patterns in this case) are chosen they are combined using nonlinear regression method to predict future forecast pattern. The forecasted instance is then added to the training set, now treated as the new reference pattern, against which the similarity of other candidate patterns is estimated. This process is continued till the required number of forecast value is generated.

The proposed learning algorithm is given below.

1) Opt suitable train_ period (TR) and test period (TS) from total data set size.
2) Initialise L and H to suitable values.
3) Select Ref_ pattern = $X_{cur}$.
4) Set Candidate_ patterns = $X_i$ where $i = 1, 2, 3 \dots n-1$
5) for j=1:L
   if corr[t]$> 0$
   $$Euclid\_corr[t] = \sqrt{\Sigma(x_{j,cur} - x_{j,i=1,2,3,\dots})^2}$$
   $j = 1, 2, 3, \dots$ for t=1,2,3 $\dots$ (size/L) where size is the total number of observations in the training set.
6) Choose H lowest values from Corr[i]
   for $j = 1, \dots (size/L)$
   Low[i] = min(Corr[j]); where i = 1:H
7) for i=1:L
   for j=1:H
   $X_{i,cur+1} = \alpha + \beta X_{i,j}$
8) Add $X_{cur+1}$ to train _ period and set $X_{cur}$to $X_{cur+1}$
9) Set Candidate_ patterns = $X_i$ where $i = 1, 2, 3 \dots n$
10) Repeat steps 5 to 9 until all values in test_ period (TS) are generated.

## 6. Experimentation and Results

The importance of real exchange rate time series is characterized with high volatility while Mackey-Glass(MG) time series changes direction slowly. And MG series volatility curve has same regular patterns whereas the exchange rate volatility curve does not have any regular pattern. Hence MG time series prediction tasks cannot fully reflect the forecasting ability and not predominantly used as benchmark problem in the fields of economics and finance.There are a large number of publications reported in [14],[15] dealing

Table 1: Notations used in the proposed algorithm

| Term | Meaning |
|---|---|
| TR | size of the training data set |
| TS | size of the test data set |
| L | sliding window size |
| H | number of windows for the best instances |
| Corr[] | vector containing correlation values |
| Euclid_ dist | vector of Euclidean distance values |
| $X_{cur+1}$ | Next pattern to be predicted |
| $X_{cur}$ | Current pattern to be predicted |
| $X_i$ | Candidate patterns |
| Size | Number of observations in the data set |
| $X_{i,j}$ | $i^{th}$ observation in the $j^{th}$ pattern |
| $\alpha, \beta$ | Regression coefficients |
| Low[] | vector of 'H' lowest Eucledian distances. |

with issue of exchange rate forecasting. However, different publications use different data sets and experimental set-ups. To make the comparison with reported works, we have carried out experiments on Japanese yen, Canadian and Australian dollar exchange rate series as defined in Chong Tan [15] to evaluate the robustness of the proposed method.

Table 2: Performance Results for Japanese Yen, Canadian and Australian Dollar rate series

| Filter | Steps L | Training | Forecasted | MSE | RMSE | MAPE |
|---|---|---|---|---|---|---|
| Japanese Yen Series 252 | | | | | | |
| none | 6 | 100 | 100 | 0.4933 | 0.07146 | 0.0049 |
| none | 1 | 100 | 100 | 0.3891 | 0.6238 | 0.0044 |
| **db3** | 1 | 100 | 100 | 0.0443 | 0.2104 | 0.0015 |
| **db3** | 6 | 126 | 126 | 0.0194 | 0.1392 | 0.00085 |
| **db1** | 6 | 126 | 126 | 0.2760 | 0.5254 | 0.0025 |
| Canadian Dollar Series 2000 | | | | | | |
| none | 1 | 100 | 100 | 0.000031 | 0.0056 | 0.0030 |
| none | 6 | 100 | 100 | 0.000044 | 0.0066 | 0.0035 |
| **db3** | 1 | 100 | 100 | 0.00000496 | 0.0022 | 0.0012 |
| **db3** | 6 | 1000 | 1000 | 0.0000038 | 0.0020 | 0.0010 |
| Australian Dollar Series 2000 | | | | | | |
| none | 6 | 100 | 100 | 0.000021 | 0.0047 | 0.0055 |
| **db3** | 6 | 100 | 100 | 0.0000011 | 0.0011 | 0.0012 |
| **db3** | 6 | 1000 | 1000 | 0.0000033 | 0.0018 | 0.0015 |
| **db3** | 1 | 1000 | 1000 | 0.0000053 | 0.0023 | 0.0022 |

Figures 1 and 2 show the forecast responses for Japanese yen rate series without filter and with db3 filter for L=1 step ahead prediction considering 100 for training and 100 points for forecasting respectively. It is evident from the table 2 and figures 1 and 2 that prediction with db3 filter results in good performance with MAPE of 0.0015, whereas without filter a MAPE of 0.0044.

Figures 3 and 4 show the forecast responses with filter db3 and L=6 and for db1 and L= 6 considering 126 points each for training and forecasting respectively. For this rate series, db3 wavelet filter shows better prediction with

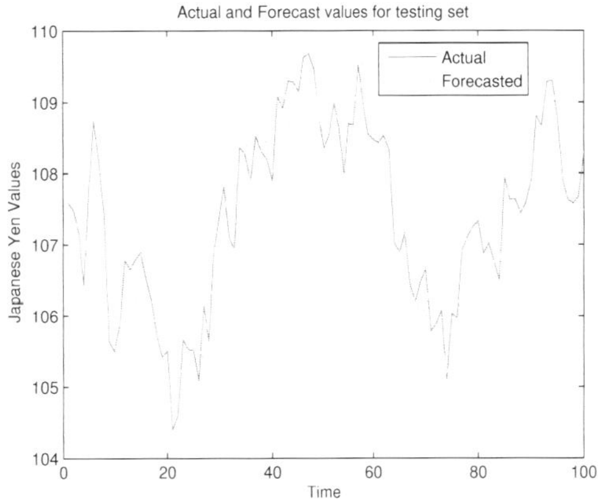


Figure 1: Japanese Yen Without filter L=1

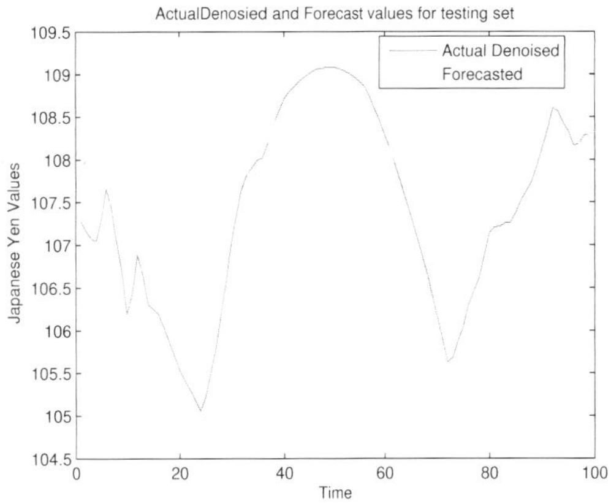


Figure 2: Japanese Yen with db3, L=1

MAPE value of 0.00085 than db1 filter with MAPE of 0.0025.

Forecasting for Japanese Yen rate series was done considering various compositions of data points and adopting different wavelet filters in the preprocessing stage. We have achieved considerably good forecasting performance for Japanese Yen rate series with and without filters and better performance with adopting filters.

Figures 5 and 6 show the forecast responses for Canadian dollar rate series without filter for L=1 and L=6 steps, considering 100 points each for training and forecasting respectively. It is observed from the table 2 and figures 5 and 6 that there is no significant improvement in prediction performance and also with MAPE values tabulated. The difference in MAPE for L=1 and 6 steps are negligible.

Figure 7 shows the forecast response with filter db3 and

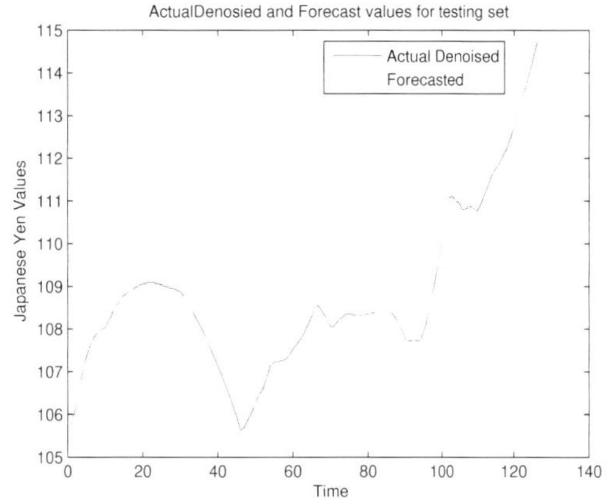


Figure 3: Japanese Yen with db3 ,L=6

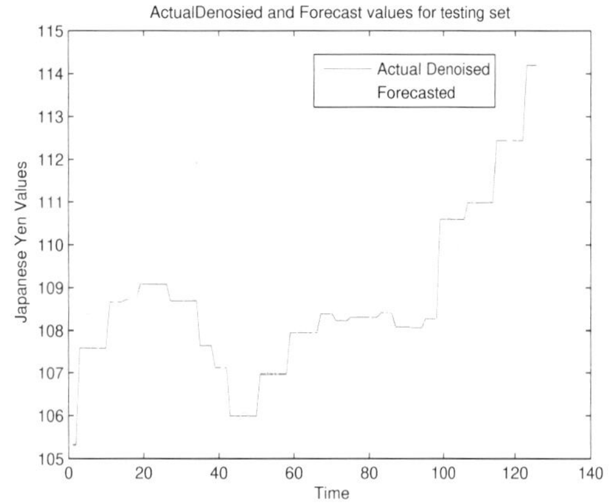


Figure 4: Japanese Yen with db1, L=6

L=1 considering 100 data points for training and forecasting respectively. Figure 8 shows the forecast response with filter db3 and L=6 considering 1000 points each for training and forecasting. Observations based on the responses obtained for this rate series indicate good forecasting performance for various compositions of data points. The results obtained on experiments are tabulated in table 2.

Figures 9 and 10 show the forecast responses for Australian dollar rate series without and with db3 filter for L=6 steps ahead prediction considering 100 points for training and forecasting respectively. It is evident from the table 2 and figures 9 and 10 that prediction with db3 filter results in good performance with MAPE being 0.0012, whereas without filter MAPE being 0.0055.

Figures 11 and 12 show the forecast responses with db3 filter and L=6 and L=1, considering 1000 points each for training and forecasting respectively. For this dollar rate

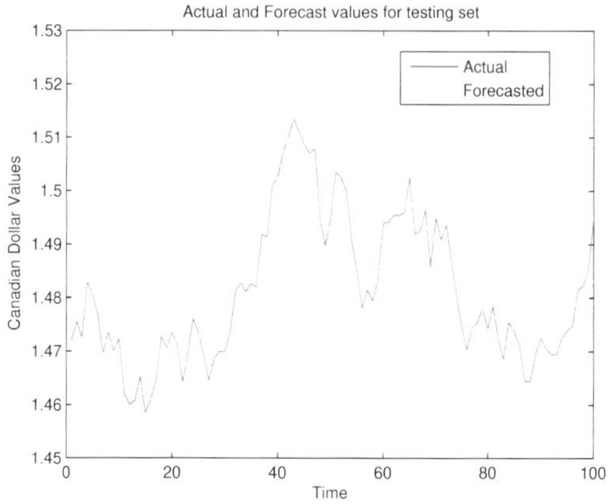


Figure 5: Canadian Dollar Without filter, L=1

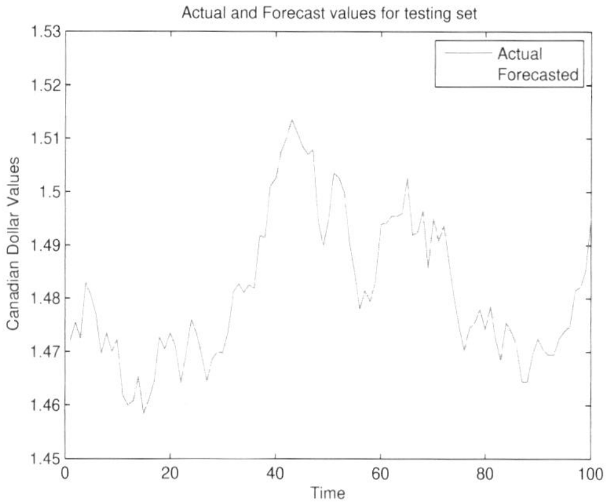


Figure 6: Canadian Dollar Without filter, L=6

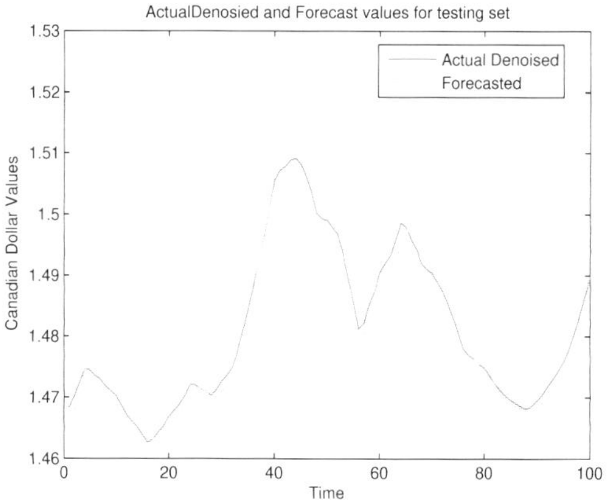


Figure 7: Canadian Dollar with db3, L=1

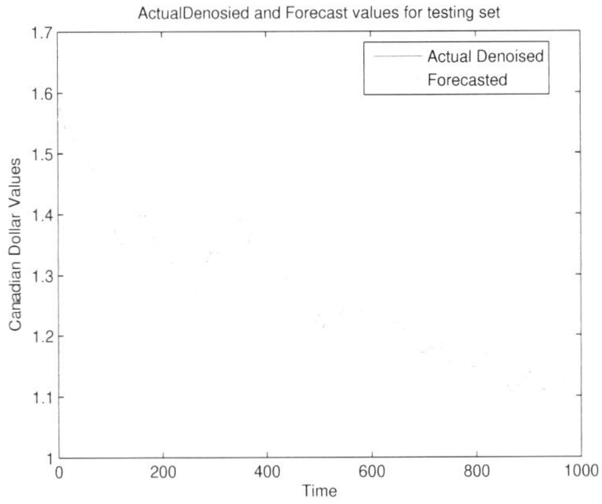


Figure 8: Canadian Dollar with db3, L=6

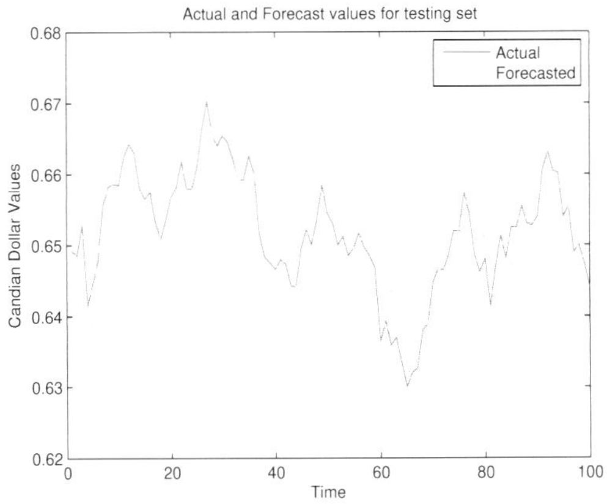


Figure 9: Australian Dollar Without filter, L=6

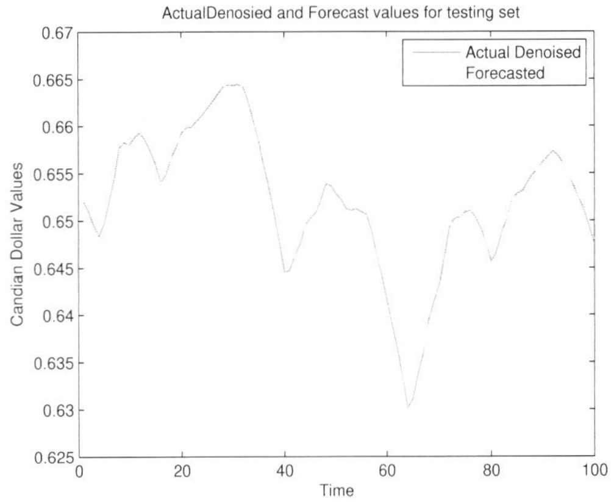


Figure 10: Australian Dollar with db3, L=6

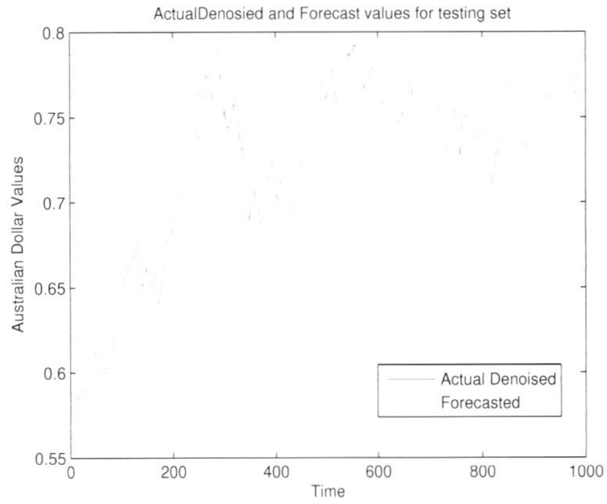


Figure 11: Australian Dollar with db3, L=6

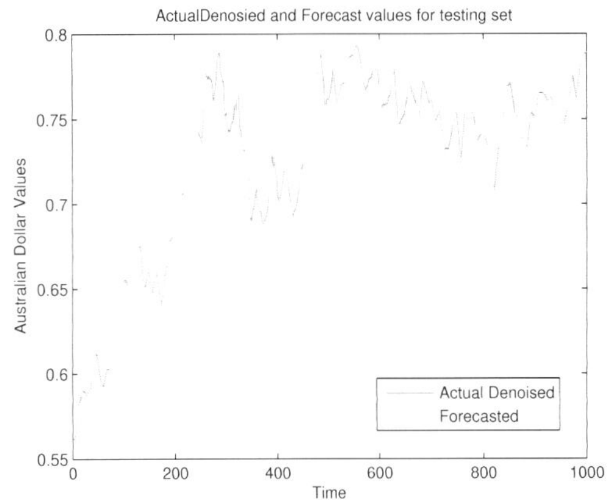


Figure 12: Australian Dollar with db3, L=1

series, from results in table 2 it is observed that with db3 wavelet filter for L=6-steps shows better prediction with MAPE of 0.0015 than for L=1 with MAPE of 0.0022.

Forecasting for Australian dollar rate series was done considering various compositions of data points and adopting db3 wavelet filters in the preprocessing stage and achieved considerably good forecasting performance.

Table 3 shows the comparative prediction performance results for Japanese Yen, Canadian and Australian dollar rate series obtained for the proposed method with and without filters with the approaches from [15].

From observations of results on comparative performance, the proposed hybrid model provides far more accurate forecasts than the approaches reported in [15] and this method with and without filters adaptation has also resulted in lesser Root mean square error(RMSE).

Table 3: Comparative Predicition performance

| Method | RMSE Japan | Canada | Australian |
|---|---|---|---|
| NN+Wavelet Denoising* | 3.3492 | 0.0114 | 0.0104 |
| NN+Wavelet Packet Denoising * | 4.3423 | 0.0089 | 0.0058 |
| New Method(DWT) * | 0.5182 | 0.0080 | 0.0021 |
| without Statistical Feature* | 1.1507 | - | 0.0072 |
| New Method(SWT) * | 0.9967 | 0.0137 | 0.0052 |
| **Proposed IIBL** | 0.07146 | 0.0056 | 0.0047 |
| **Proposed WIIBL with db3** | 0.1392 | 0.0020 | 0.0011 |
| * values are taken from [15] | | | |

## 7. Conclusions

Integrated multi-step prediction systems for predicting the exchange rate time series has been proposed.The work demonstrates the feasibility of integrating with daubechies wavelet filters at the preprocessing stage to achieve accurate forecasting.The proposed work incorporates a hybrid distance measure combining correlation and Euclidean distance to select similar instances from the stored patterns. WIIBL has been motivated by the effective preprocessing capability of wavelet filters and the predictive power of improved instance based learning system, to represent a hybrid prediction system. The multiscaling property of the wavelet transform enhances the prediction with high accuracy for volatile time series. To observe the impact of size of dataset used and also to analyse the learning characteristics of the proposed model, experiments were conducted considering various partition size of data set for training and testing input sample values. The most important conclusion of this study is that the propososed WIIBL is a useful tool for forecasting exchange rate series behaviour, with use of appropriate filters during preprocessing for accurate predictions.

## References


[1] ByGuy P.Nanson and Rainer von Sachs,*"Wavelets in time series analysis "*,Phil.Trans R.S,London,vol 357,no 1760,pp 2511–2526,September,1999.

[2] Sanjeev Kumar Aggarwal and Lalit Mohan Saini and Ashwani Kumar, *" Electricity Price Forecasting in Ontario Electricity market Using Wavelet Transform in Artificial Neural Network Based Model"*,"International Journal of Control, Automation and Systems ", no 5,vol 6,pp 639–650, October ,2008.

[3] Yuehui Chen and Bo Yang and Jiwen Dong , *" Time series prediction using a local linear wavelet neural network "* Neurocomputing ,no. 5,Vol 69, pp 449–465, October,2006.

[4] David W. Aha and Dennis Kibler and Marc k Albert , Instance Based Learning Algorithms ,*" Machine Learning "*, vol "6", "pp.37-66 ","1999".

[5] Pei-Chann Chang and Chin-Yuan Fan ,*" A hybrid system Integrating a Wavelet and TSK Fuzzy Rules for Stock Price Forecasting "*," IEEE Transactions on Systems, Man, and Cybernetics-Part C: Applications and Reviews ",no."6",vol 38, "pp. 639-650", November,"2008".

[6] Guy P. Naosn and Rainer Von Sachs,*"Wavelets in time series analysis"*, " Department of Mathematics, University of Bristol UK",1999.

[7] Sameer Singh and Jonathan Fieldsend ,*"Financial time series forecasts using fuzzy and long memory pattern recognition systems"*," PANN Research,Department of Computer Science, University of EXETER, UK","1999".

[8] Sameer Singh and P McAtackney,*Dynamic Time-Series Forecasting using Local Approximation*, 10th IEEE Interantionsl Confernce on Tools with AI,Taiwan,1998,pp 392-399.

[9] Haibin Cheng and Pang-Ning and Jing Gao and Jerry Scripps , *"Multistep-ahead Time Series Prediction"*, "Michigan State University".

[10] Andrej Dobnikar, *" Matrix Formualation of the Multilayered Perceptron with a Denoising Unit "*, " Electrotechnical Review ", "April ", "2003".

[11] Syed Rahat Abbas and Muhammad Arif , " Modified Nearest Neighbor Method for Multistep Ahead Time Series Prediction ", *" International Journal of Pattern Recognition and Artificial Intelligence "*, No "3",Vol "21", "pp. 463-481"," October ", "2007".

[12] Sushmita Mitra and Sankar K.Pal and Pabitra Mitra, *" Data Mining in Soft Computing Framework: A Survey "*, "IEEE Transactions on Neural Networks ",No 1,Vol 13,"pp. 639–650,January,2002.

[13] S. Blanco and A.figliola and R. Quian Quiroga and O.A. Rosso and E. Serrano , *"Time-frequency analysis of electroencephalogram series, Wavelet Packets and information cost function "*, "Physical Review ",No 1,Vol 57,pp. 639-650,January, "1998".

[14] Hu Tao , *"A Wavelet Neural Network model for Forecasting Exchange Rate Integrated with Genetic Algorithm"*," IJCNS International Journal of Computer Science and Network Security ",No. 8A,Vol 6,August,"2006".

[15] Chong Tan,*Financial Time Series Forecasting Using Improved Wavelet Neural Network* ,No. "20034244",May, 2009.

[16] Yevgeniy Bodyanskiy and Iryna Pliss and Olena Vynokurova, *" Adaptive wavelet neuro fuzzy network in the Forecasting and Emulation tasks "*, " International Journal on Information Theories and Applications ",Vol 15,pp. 639-650,"2008".

[17] G Nunnari , *" Modelling air pollution time-series by using wavelet functions and genetic algorithms"* ," Soft Computing ",Vol "8",pp.173-178,October"2004".

[18] Wen Wang, Pieter H. A, J. M. Van Gelder and J.K. Vrijling, *Some Issues About the Generalization of Neural Networks for Time Series Prediction*, ,Proceedings of the ICANN 2005-LNCS 3697,pp 559-564,2005.

[19] Achilleas Zapranis Stratos Livanis , Forecasting the Day-Ahead Electricity Price in Nord Pool with Neural Networks: some Preliminary Results , *""Value Invest Magazine "*.

[20] Yeo- Howo Lim and Leonard M. Lye , " Wavelet Analysis of Tide-affected Low Streamflows Series ", *"Journal of Data Science "*, Vol 2,"pp. 149-163"," October ","2004".

[21] Abdurazzag A Aburas and Nural Fariza Zulkurnain, Investigation of the Time series Medical data based on Wavelets and K-means Clustering , *"Transactions on Engineering, Computing and Technology "*, No 3, vol 3, pp 112–122 , " September ", " 2007".

[22] R.Keith oswald and Dr.william T.scherer and Dr.Brian L.smith,*Traffic flow forecasting using Approximate Nearest Neighbour Non parametric Regression*, University of Hong Kong,December,2001.

[23] Michael W. Frazier,*An Introduction to wavelets through Linear algebra*

[24] D.L. Donoho and I.M. Johnstone,*Adapting to unknown smoothness via wavelet shrinkage* , Journal of the American Statistical Association,No.90(432),pp.1200–1224, October,1995.

[25] I.Daubechies,*The wavelet transform, time-frequency localization and signal analysis*, IEEE Transforms on Inforamtion Theory,Vol 36,pp 961–1005,1990.

[26] G.Strang and T. Nguyen, Wellesley, MA ,*Wavelets and Filter Banks* , Wellesley-Cambridge Press , 1995.

[27] Stephane G. Mallat,*A Theory for Multiresolution Signal Decomposition: The Wavelet Representation*,IEEE Transactions on Pattern Analysis and Machine Intelligence ,No.7,Vol 11,pp 674–693,July,1989.

[28] Bjorn Jawerth and Wim Sweldens,*An Overview of Wavelet based Multiresolution Analyses*, pp 1–40, University of South Carolina, February,1993.

[29] I. Daubechies ,*Ten lectures on wavelets*,CBMS-NSF Regional Conference Series in Applied Mathematics ,Vol 61,Society for Industrial and Applied Mathematics, Philadelphia, PA,1992.

[30] S. Sitharama Iyengar E.C. Cho Vir V.Phoha ,*Foundations of Wavelet Networks and Applications* , A CRC Press Company, Newyork, Washington, D.C., 2002.

# Mining Mixed-drove Co-occurrence Patterns For Large Spatio-temporal Data Sets: A Summary of Results

**Xiangxiang Cong, Zhanquan Wang(Corresponding Author),Man Kong, Chunhua Gu**
Computer Science&Engineer Department, East China University of Science and Technology,Shanghai,China

**Abstract** - *Discovering mixed-drove spatiotemporal co-occurrence patterns (MDCOPs) is an important field with many applications such as identifying tactics in battlefields, crime detection, etc. In practical applications, it is difficult to mine MDCOPs from large spatio-temporal data sets. Firstly, mining MDCOPs is computationally very expensive because the set of candidate co-occurrence instances is exponential in the number of object-types. Secondly, the spatio-temporal data sets are large and can't be managed in memory. In order to reduce the number of candidate co-occurrence instances, we present a novel and computationally efficient MDCOP Graph Miner algorithm by using Time Aggregated Graph. The LDMDCOP Graph Miner algorithm is presented, which can deal with large data sets by means of file index. The correctness, completeness and efficiency of the proposed methods are analyzed. Experimental results show that the proposed MDCOP Graph Miner is computationally more efficient than the fast MDCOP-Miner and the LDMDCOP Graph Miner can effectively deal with the large spatiotemporal data sets.*

**Keywords:** Mixed-drove Spatiotemporal Co-occurrence pattern; Large Spatiotemporal Data Set; Time Aggregated Graph (TAG); File Index

## 1 Introduction

As the volume of spatiotemporal data continues to increase significantly due to both the growth of database archives and the increasing number of spatiotemporal sensors, automatic and semi-automatic pattern analysis becomes more essential. It is meaningful and challenging for us to extract interesting patterns from these large spatiotemporal data sets.

Given a large spatiotemporal database, a neighbor relationship and mixed-drove interest measure thresholds, our aim is to discover mixed-drove spatiotemporal co-occurrence patterns (MDCOPs). To mine co-occurrence patterns, Celik et al. proposed MDCOP-Miner and fast MDCOP-Miner [4]. The two methods are based on the join-based collocation algorithm proposed by Huang et al. [9]. The basic co-occurrence pattern mining procedure involves four steps. First, candidate co-occurrence instances are gathered from the spatiotemporal data set. Prevalent co-occurrence pattern sets satisfying the given prevalence thresholds are filtered. Finally, co-occurrence patterns satisfy the given prevalence thresholds are generated. Most of the computational time of co-occurrence pattern mining is devoted to finding co-occurrence instances. The approach is Apriori like, which is costly as it enumerates all possible co-occurrence instances over all time instances. Thus, we propose adding a step for materializing the neighbor relationships to increase the efficiency of co-occurrence mining.

While the volume of the spatiotemporal data set is large, we can't manage to discover the MDCOPs by existed methods. Since the existed methods are based on memory, we can't get enough memory space. For example, we have 300 MB vehicle data. As movements of vehicle change over time, their co-occurrences also move in the same way. We can know the military strategy from the co-occurrences. So mining those patterns is really meaningful. As another example, China's Zhejiang province public security bureau has more than 2GB of crime data. We can discover a lot of useful information from the large data set, such as the co-occurrence of crime type. For example, gamble and larceny usually occur together and they are co-occurrence. Mining these patterns is very useful for the police to analyze the movement of criminals. But the volume of crime data is too large for us to discover the patterns by using existed methods. As a result, the issue related to mining correct and complete patterns from large spatiotemporal data sets is a difficult problem. In order to solve the problem, new efficient storage method for MDCOPs must be proposed.

The rest of this paper is organized as follows: Section 2 reviews related work. Section 3 presents basic concepts to provide a formal model of MDCOP Graph and the problem statement of mining MDCOPs. In Section 4, we present our proposed MDCOP mining algorithms. Analysis of the algorithms is given in Section 5. Section 6 presents the experimental evaluation, and Section 7 presents conclusions and future work.

## 2 Related Work

The MDCOPs problem differs from the co-location pattern. Previous approaches of MDCOP mining can use a spatial co-location mining algorithm for each time slot to find spatial prevalent co-locations, and then apply a post-processing step to discover MDCOPs by check their time prevalence. To mine co-locations, Huang et al. proposed a join-based approach [1] [2]. Celik et al. [4] formalizes the problem, propose a new monotonic mixed-drove interest measure to discover and mine MDCOPs, and also propose an efficient algorithm (MDCOP-Miner).

MDCOPs represent object types co-located over space and time forming a spatial network (edges between objects in the network indicate existence of a neighborhood relationship) that dynamically changes over time. A common and naïve approach to model such a network is to use time expanded graph, as described by Köhler et al. [5] where in the network is replicated across discrete time instants. A more efficient method of modeling temporal spatial networks was proposed by George et al. [6] by incorporating the properties of nodes and edges in the graph as a time series. This paper also proposed efficient algorithms for computing the shortest path and connectivity in time dependent networks modeled using time aggregated graphs. The problem of mining MDCOPs with high spatial and time prevalence is described by Celik et al. [4], However the approach is Apriori like and involves candidate generation, which is costly as it enumerates all possible cliques over all time instances.

Although experts obtained many achievements in MDCOP mining, we still have no correct and efficient approach dealing with large spatiotemporal datasets. In this paper, we materialize the neighbor relationships for efficient co-occurrence pattern mining. We solve the problem of efficient storage of MDCOPs by using the Time Aggregated Graph model [6] and create our own storage model MDCOP Graph for mining MDCOPs. Finally, we provide a correct and efficient co-occurrence pattern mining algorithm to deal with large spatiotemporal datasets.

# 3 Co-occurrence Pattern Mining

In this section, we present basic concepts to provide a formal model of MDCOP Graph and the problem statement of mining MDCOPs.

## 3.1 Basic Concepts

### 3.1.1 Mixed-drove Prevalence Measure

The focus of this study is to mine MDCOPs with multiple prevalence measures from large spatiotemporal data sets. The basic MDCOP algorithm [4] defines two interest measures namely spatial prevalence θ p and a time prevalence measure θ time. Hence, a pattern is defined as an MDCOP if it has the property [4]

$$Prob_{t_m \in TF}[s\_prev(P_i, time\_slot \quad t_m) \geq \theta_p] \geq \theta_{time} \qquad (1)$$

Where, Prob (.) is the probability of overall prevalence time slots, s_prev stands for spatial prevalence. There are more details in [6]

### 3.1.2 Time Aggregated Graph (TAG)

We propose a graph based data structure to capture the information required to mine MDCOPs from the data set. This data structure is motivated by Time Aggregated Graphs (TAG) which models time varying road conditions as time series on the edges of a road network. Defines the time aggregated graph as follows.

$$TAG = (N, E, TF, f_1 ... f_k, g_1 ... g_m, w_1 ... w_p \mid f_i : N \rightarrow R^{TF}; g_i : E \rightarrow R^{TF}; w_i : E \rightarrow R^{TF}) \quad (2)$$

Where $N$ is the set of nodes, $E$ is the set of edges, $TF$ is the length of the entire time interval, $f_1 ... f_k$ are the mappings from nodes to nodes, $g_1 ... g_m$ are mapping from edges to edges, and $w_1 ... w_p$ indicate the dependent weights (eg.travel times) on the edges.

Each edge has an attribute, called an edge time series that represents the time instants for which the edge is present. This enables TAG to model the topological changes of the network with time. . There are more details in [6].

## 3.2 Modeling MDCOP Graph

Given a set of spatiotemporal mixed object-types E, a neighborhood relation R, a set of time slots TF, a threshold pair (θ p, θ time), MDCOP Graph can be represented as a neighbor graph in which a node is an object type and edge between two nodes represents the neighbor relationship over all time slots. We use MDCOP Graph to materialize neighbor relationships. As we know that most of the computational time of co-occurrence pattern mining is devoted to finding co-occurrence instances. By means of MDCOP Graph, we don't need to generate all possible candidate co-occurrence instances. We just generate real co-occurrence instances through visiting the MDCOP Graph. Thus, we can increase the efficiency of co-occurrence mining.

***Definition 3.1*** Given a set of co-occurrence instances CI, instance type level graph (*IG*) is used to captures the existence of co-location instances between two instance types over time. We define instance type level graph as follows.

$$IG = (I, CI, TF, f_0 ... f_{k-1}, e_0 ... e_{n-1}, | f_i : I \rightarrow R^{TF}; e_i : CI \rightarrow R^{TF}) \quad (3)$$

Where $I$ is the set of instances of all object-types, $CI$ is the set of co-location instances, $TF$ is the length of the entire time interval, such that $TF = [T_0, ..., T_{n-1}]$, $f_0 ... f_{k-1}$ are the mappings from object-types to object-types , $e_0 ... e_{n-1}$ indicate the existence of co-occurrence instances between two instance types over time on the edges.

For example, we generate instance type level graph (Figure.1) using the data set given [6]. In Figure.1, we use time-series [1 1 1 0] to show that A1 and C1 are co-located at time slot 0, time slot 1, time slot 2 and disappear at time slot 3. Therefore we can easily capture the existence of co-occurrence instances over time by traversing instance type level graph.

*Definition 3.2* Given a set of candidate co-occurrence patterns (*CP*), object type level graph (*OG*) is used to indicate the participation count of particular object-types contributing to particular co-occurrence patterns. We define object type level graph as follows.

$$OG=\left(E,CP,TF,f_0\cdots f_{k-1},p_0\cdots p_{n-1} \mid f_i : E\in CP^{TF}; p_i : E\in CP^{TF}\right) \quad (4)$$

Where E is the set of spatiotemporal mixed object-types, CP is the set of co-occurrence patterns, TF is the length of the entire time interval, f0…fk-1 are the mappings from particular object-types to the particular co-occurrence patterns , p0…pn-1 indicate the participation count of particular object-types contributing to particular co-occurrence patterns over time on the edges.

For example, we generate object type level graph (Figure.2) using the data set given in[7]. The co-occurrence pattern AC has co-occurrence instances sets {{A1, C1}, {A3, C2}} at time slot 0, time slot 1 and time slot 2. At time slot 3, AC has no co-location instances. In Figure.2, since A1 and A3 are different instances of A, we use time-series [2 2 2 0] to show the participation count of object-type A contributing to co-location pattern AC. By using object type level graph, we can get the spatial prevalence index values and time prevalence index values.

*Definition 3.3* Given instance type level graph and object type level graph, MDCOP Graph is composed of two parts: instance type level graph and object type graph. The instance type level and object type graphs are connected through links. We define MDCOP Graph as follows.

$$MDCOP\ Gragh = \left(IG,OG,TF,E,I,l_0..l_{k-1} \mid l_i : I \rightarrow E^{TF}\right) \quad (5)$$

Where *IG* is instance type level graph, *OG* is object type level graph. *TF* is the length of the entire time interval, *E* is the set of spatiotemporal mixed object-types, *I* is the set of instances of all object types. $l_0 \dots l_{k-1}$ are the mappings from object-types to their own instances.

For example, we generate MDCOP graph (Figure.3) using the data set given in[4]. In Figure.3, both the instance type level and object type graphs are connected through links for easy traversal.

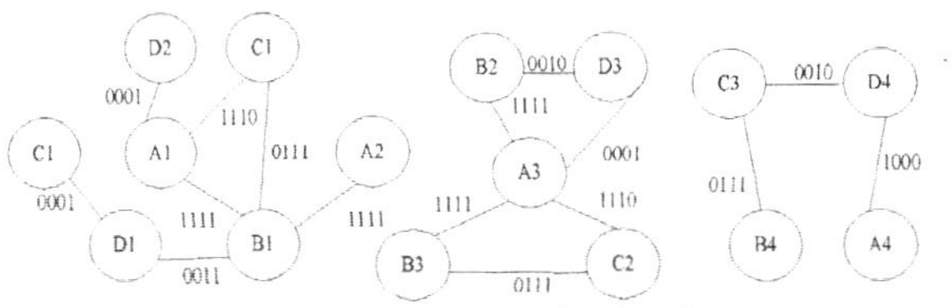

Figure. 1. Instance type level graph

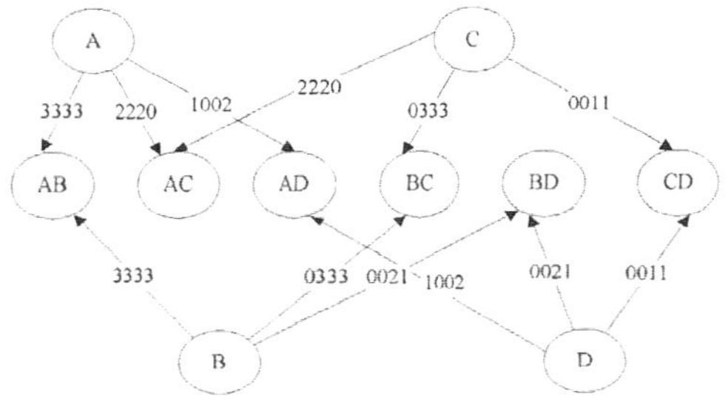

Figure. 2. Object type level graph

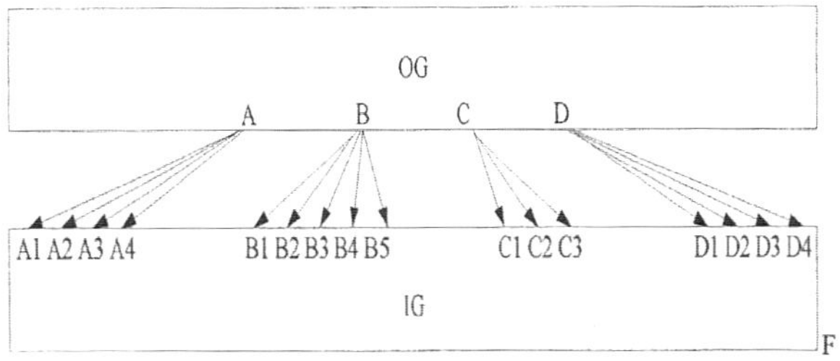

Figure. 3. Object type level graph

# 4 Mining MDCOPS

In this section, we discuss fastMDCOP-Miner and then propose two novel MDCOP mining algorithms: MDCOP Graph Miner and LDMDCOP Graph Miner to mine MDCOPs. We also give the execution trace of these algorithms.

## 4.1 FastMDCOP-Miner

FastMDCOP-Miner [8] uses a spatial co-location mining algorithm for each time slots to find spatial prevalent co-locations and prune time non-prevalent patterns as early as possible between the time slots to discover MDCOPs. To mine co-locations, Huang et al. proposed a join-based approach, Yoo et al. proposed a partial join-based approach and a join-less approach [3], [9], [10], this approach is based on the join-based collocation algorithm proposed by Huang et al., but it is also possible to use other approaches. FastMDCOP-Miner [8] will first discover all size k spatial prevalent MDCOPs and prune time non-prevalent patterns as early as possible between the time slots to discover MDCOPs. Then the algorithm will generate size $k+1$ candidate MDCOPs using size $k$ MDCOPs until there are no more candidates. However, this approach is Apriori like and involves candidate generation which is costly as it enumerates all possible cliques over all time instants.

## 4.2 MDCOP Graph Miner

To eliminate the drawbacks of fastMDCOP-Miner, we propose a MDCOP mining algorithm (MDCOP Graph Miner) to discover MDCOPs by storing all the MDCOPs in the MDCOP Graph. This data structure is motivated by Time Aggregated Graphs (TAG) [7], which models time varying road conditions as time series on the edges of a road network.

In our case, we use two different types of series over the edges. One of the series captures the existence of co-occurrence patterns between two instances over time. Based on the existence time series of co-occurrence patterns between pairs of instances, we aggregate the information to object types. At the object type graph, each time series contains the participation count of a particular object contributing to a particular co-location pattern. Both the instance type level and object type graphs are connected through links for easy traversal.

We give the pseudo code of the algorithm and provide an execution trace of it using the data set in [7]. Algorithm1 give the pseudo code of the MDCOP Graph Miner algorithm. This pseudo code is used to explain two algorithms: MDCOP Graph Miner and LDMDCOP Graph Miner which will be discussed in the next section. The choice of the algorithm is provided by the user. In the algorithm, steps 1-14 create the MDCOP Graph. Steps 15-21 give an iterative process to mine MDCOPs, steps 15-21 continue until there is no candidate MDCOP to be generated. Step 22 gives a union of the results. The execution trace of MDCOP Graph Miner are explained below.

*Algorithm 1* pseudo code for the MDCOP Graph Miner

```
    Inputs:
    E: a set of spatial object types
    ST: a spatiotemporal data set < object_type, object_id, x, y, timeslot >
    R: spatial neighborhood relationship
    TF: a time slot frame {t0, ..., tn-1}
    θ p:a spatial prevalence threshold
    0 time: a time prevalence threshold
    Output: MDCOPs whose spatial prevalence indices, i.e., participation
indices, are no less than θ p, for time prevalence indices are no less than θ
time.
    Variables:
    t : time slots(t0, ... ,tn-1)
    k:co-occurrences size
    Tk: set of instances of size k co-occurrences
    SPk: set of spatial prevalent size k co-occurrences
    TPk: set of time prevalent size k co-occurrences
    Ck: set of candidate size k co-occurrences
    MDPk: set of mixed-drove size k co-occurrences
    MDG: graph stores all the MDCOPs
    Address: address for storing time series to the file
    Method:
1.  k = 2
2.  Ck (0) = gen_candidate_co_occ(E)
3.  for each time slot t in TF
4.     Tk (t) = gen_co_occ_inst(Ck (t),ST, R)
5.     set timeSeries [t] =1 for Tk (t)
6.     SPk (t) = find_spatial_prev_co_occ(Tk (t), θ p)
7.     TPk (t) = find_time_index(SPk (t))
8.     MDPk(t) = find_time_prev_co_occ(TPk (t), θ time)
9.     Ck (t) = MDPk (t)
10.    if(alg_choice == "LDMDCOP Graph Miner")
11.       Address = gen_co_occ_address (Tk (t) )
12.       access the MDG file by the addresses
13.       set timeSeries [t] =1 for Tk (t) if required
14.    if(alg_choice == "MDCOP Graph Miner")
15.       MDG = gen_MDCOP_Graph(MDPk)
16.  while (not empty MDPk)
17.     Ck+1 = gen _candidate_co_occ ( MDPk)
18.     Tk+1= gen _instancesTree (Ck+1,MDG)
19.     SPk+1 = find_spatial_prev_co_occ(Tk+1, θ p)
20.     TPk+1 = find_time_index(SPk+1 )
21.     MDPk+1 = find_time_prev_co_occ(TPk+1, θ time)
22.     k = k+1
23. return union( MDP2 , ... , MDPk)
```

*The execution trace of the MDCOP Graph Miner* is given in Figure.4. This data set in[7]. contains four object-types A, B, C, and D and their instances in four time slots (i.e., A has four instances). The instances of each object-type have a unique identifier, such as A1. To discover MDCOPs, we use a monotonic composite interest measure which is a composition of the spatial prevalence and time prevalence measure. The spatial prevalence measure shows the strength of the spatial co-location when the index is greater than or equal to a given threshold [8], [9]. The time prevalence measure shows the frequency of the pattern over time.

In step1, by dividing each entry in Figure.4a with the corresponding number of instances for an object, we get the participation ratio of an object type in co-location. For example, the participation index of collocation AB is [3/5 3/5 3/5 3/5], which is the minimum participation ratio of type A and B in all time slots. We prune time non-prevalent patterns whose participation indices are less than a given threshold as early as possible. For example, there are four time slots and the time prevalence threshold is 0.5. In this case, a size k pattern should be present for at least two time slots to satisfy the threshold. If the time prevalence index of a pattern is 0 for the first (or any) three time slots, there is no need to generate it and check its prevalence for the rest of the time slots even if it is time persistent for the remaining time slots. Spatial prevalent patterns AB, AC, and BC are selected as MDCOPs since they are time prevalent (their time prevalence indices satisfy the given time prevalence threshold 0.5). In contrast, spatial prevalent patterns AD, BD and CD are pruned since they are time non-prevalent.

In step2, three sub-graphs on the bottom of Figure 4b are created. It also creates links from the instance types to the object type, for example, Link between A3 and A if A3 is part of at least one co-occurrence. The links between the object and the instance type help in traversing the data set efficiently to calculate the spatial prevalence index values. Connections between the object type graph and the instance type graph are missing in order to reduce clutter and the series in the object graph has not been represented for the same reason. After the algorithm has been executed, the series on edge A and AB would be [3/4 3/4 3/4 3/4] because of co-locations A1B1, A2B1, A3B2 andA3B3. Note that A3 is counted only once at each time interval though it appears in two co-locations at every time instant.

In step3, the candidate MDCOP ABC is generated through AB, AC and BC. Generally, the number of candidate patterns is large. Then if we generate temporal time prevalence index for every candidate pattern, candidate pattern whose temporal time prevalence index is less than a given threshold can be pruned. For example, ABC is a candidate pattern, the temporal time series of ABC is [0 1 1 0] equals to time series of AB [1 1 1 1] & AC [1 1 1 0] & BC [0 1 1 1], the time prevalence index is 0.5 which is no less than the given threshold. So we generate instances of candidate pattern ABC. By building instances-trees for candidate patterns, instances of candidate pattern ABC could be generated.

In step4, the participation indices of pattern ABC are 2/5 in time slots 1 and 2 and its time prevalence index 0.5 equals to the threshold. Since there are not enough subsets to generate the next superset patterns, the algorithm stops at this stage and outputs the union of all size MDCOPs, i.e., A B, AC, BC, and ABC.

*Step1: Generate size 2 co-occurrence patterns.*

| Object Type | Candidate MDCOP | Paticipation Count | Paticipation Ratios | Paticipation Index | Time Series | Time Prevalence index |
|---|---|---|---|---|---|---|
| A | AB | 3 3 3 3 | 3/4 3/4 3/4 3/4 | 3/5 3/5 3/5 3/5 | 1 1 1 1 | 4/4 |
| B | AB | 3 3 3 3 | 3/5 3/5 3/5 3/5 | | | |
| A | AC | 2 2 2 0 | 2/4 2/4 2/4 0 | 2/4 2/4 2/4 0 | 1 1 1 0 | 3/4 |
| C | AC | 2 2 2 0 | 2/3 2/3 2/3 0 | | | |
| A | AD | 1 0 0 2 | 1/4 0 0 2/4 | 1/4 0 0 2/4 | 0 0 0 1 | 1/4(prune) |
| D | AD | 1 0 0 2 | 1/4 0 0 2/4 | | | |
| B | BC | 0 3 3 3 | 0 3/5 3/5 3/5 | 0 3/5 3/5 3/5 | 0 1 1 1 | 3/4 |
| C | BC | 0 3 3 3 | 0 3/3 3/3 3/3 | | | |
| B | BD | 0 0 2 1 | 0 0 2/5 1/5 | 0 0 2/5 1/5 | 0 0 1 0 | 1/4(prune) |
| D | BD | 0 0 2 1 | 0 0 2/4 1/4 | | | |
| C | CD | 0 0 1 - | 0 0 1/3 - | 0 0 1/4 - | 0 0 0 - | (prune) |
| D | CD | 0 0 1 - | 0 0 1/4 - | | | |

(a)

*Step2: Generate MDCOP Graph.*

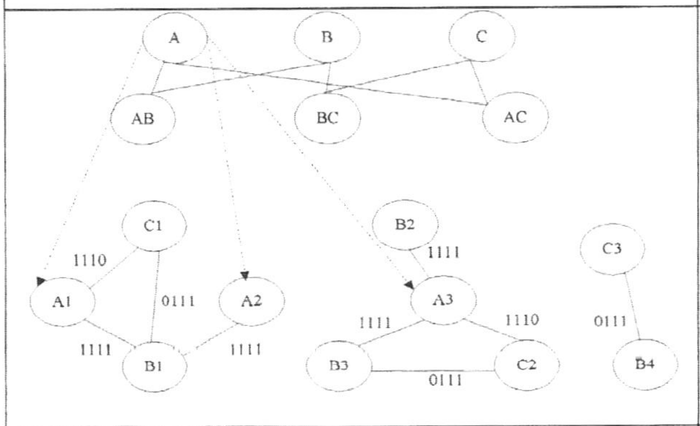


(b)

*Step3: Generate candidate co-occurrence patterns and generate instances-tree.*

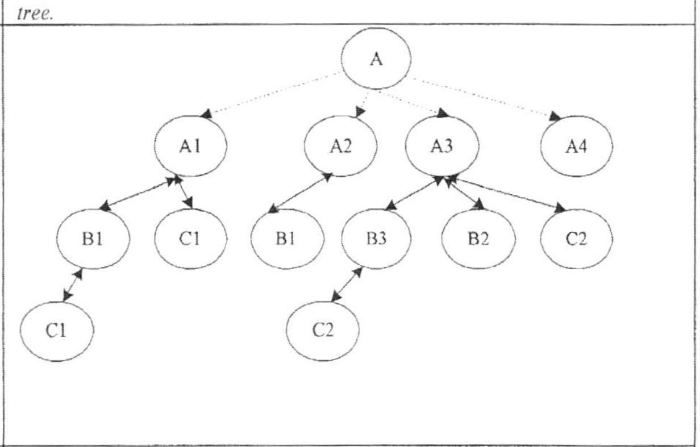


(c)

*Step 4: Generate size 3 co-occurrence patterns*

| Object Type | Candidate MDCOP | Paticipation Count | Paticipation Ratios | Paticipation Index | Time Series | Time Prevalence index |
|---|---|---|---|---|---|---|
| A | ABC | 0 2 2 0 | 0 2/4 2/4 0 | 0 2/5 2/5 0 | 0 1 1 0 | 2/4 |
| B | ABC | 0 2 2 0 | 0 2/5 2/5 0 | | | |
| C | ABC | 0 2 2 0 | 0 2/3 2/3 0 | | | |

Figure. 4. Execution trace of the MDCOP Graph Miner algorithm. (a) Step 1. (b) Steps 2. (c) Steps 3. (d) Steps 4

## 4.3 LDMDCOP Graph Miner

In this section, we propose a new algorithm, called LDMDCOP Graph Miner, which can deal with large date sets by using file index. MDCOP Graph is an efficient storage method to capture the information required to mine MDCOPs from the data sets. When the data set is quite large, we possibly need plenty of space to store MDCOP Graph. Since the capacity of memory is limited, there is no enough space to store large data set or big MDCOP Graph. As a result, we use file to store big MDCOP Graph. This approach brings us two problems. One is how to store the big MDCOP Graph in the file, the other is how to capture the information required to mine MDCOPs from the MDCOP Graph in the file. In order to solve these problems, we use adjacency matrix to store the MDCOP Graph. The largest convenience of adjacency matrix is the ability to determine the existence of a particular edge in constant time, and access the storage media only once. According to this method, we can calculate the address for a particular edge to store its time series in the file and also access the time series by the same address, there is no need to store the address of the time-series, we calculate the address according to the same expression which used to calculate the address for storing. The expression is as follows.

$$address(R_i, C_j) = ((R_i \times N + C_j - E(R_i, C_j)) \times S) \quad (6)$$

Where $R_i$ is the row number, $C_j$ is the column number, $N$ is the total number of instance, $E(R_i, C_j)$ is the number of patterns whose instances are of the same type. $S$ is the size of time series.

The pseudo code of the LDMDCOP Graph Miner is given in Algorithm 1. When the LDMDCOP Graph Miner is chosen, the algorithm will activate steps 10, 11, 12 and deactivate steps 13 and 14. We use adjacency matrix to store the MDCOP Graph. At the same time, the addresses for storing time series of co-occurrence instances could be calculated and the addresses also are used to access the file for getting the information required to mine MDCOPs.

# 5 Experiment Results

We use Real Data Sets and Synthetic to evaluate the proposed algorithm. The real data includes 15 time snapshots and 21 distinct vehicle types and their instances. The minimum instance number is 2, the maximum instance number is 78, and the average number of instances is 19. To evaluate the performance of the algorithms, spatiotemporal data sets were generated based on the spatial data generator proposed by Huang et al. [8]. Synthetic data sets were generated for spatial frame size $D \times D$. For simplicity, the data sets were divided into regular grids whose side lengths had neighborhood relationship R.

## 5.1 Experiment Results for Real Data Sets

### 5.1.1 Effect of Number of Time Slots

We evaluated the effect of the number of time slots on the execution time of the MDCOP algorithms using the real data set. The participation index, time prevalence index, and distance were set at 0.2, 0.8, and 100 m, respectively. Experiments were run for a minimum of 1 time slot and a maximum of 14 time slots. Results show that the MDCOP Graph Miner requires less execution time than the fastMDCOP-Miner (Figure. 5a). As the number of time slots increases, the ratio of the increase in execution time is smaller for MDCOP Graph Miner than for the fastMDCOP-Miner.

### 5.1.2 Effect of Number of Object-Types

The participation index, time prevalence index, number of time slots, and distance were set at 0.2, 0.8,15, and 100 m, respectively. Results show that the MDCOP Graph Miner outperforms the fastMDCOP-Miner when the number of object-types increases (Figure. 5b). It is observed that the increase in execution time for the fastMDCOP-Miner is bigger than that of the MDCOP Graph Miner as the number of object-types increases for the real data set.

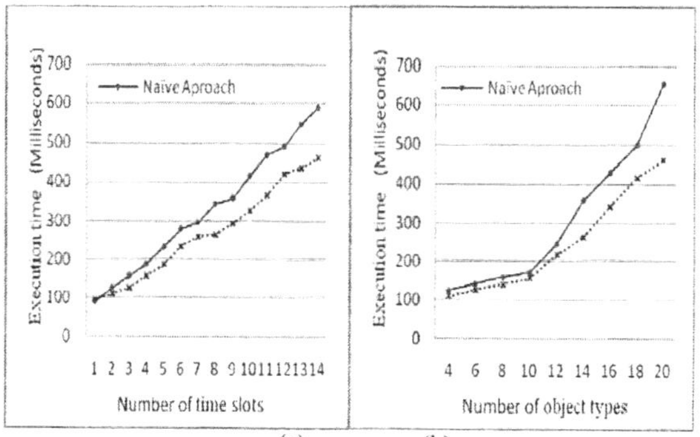


(a) (b)

Figure. 5. (a) Effect of number of time slots using real data set. (b) Effect of number of object types using real data set

## 5.2 Experiment Results for Synthetic Datasets

We evaluated the effect of the spatial prevalence threshold on the execution times of MDCOP mining algorithms. The fixed parameters were participation index, distance, and number of time slots, and their values were 0.4, 20 m, and 100, respectively. Experimental results show that the MDCOP Graph Miner is more computationally efficient than the fastMDCOP-Miner (Figure. 6a). The execution time of the MDCOP Graph Miner decreases as the time prevalence threshold increases.

We also evaluated the effect of the time prevalence threshold on the execution time of the LDMDCOP Graph Miner using synthetic data sets. The participation index, distance and number of time slots, were set at 0.5, 20 m, 200, respectively. The results showed that the execution time of the LDMDCOP Graph Miner decreases as the time prevalence threshold increases (Figure. 6b).

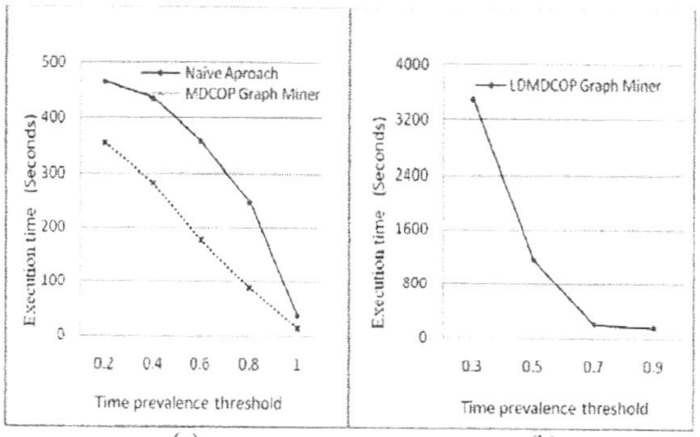


(a) (b)

Figure.6. (a), (b) Effect of the time prevalence threshold using synthetic data sets

## 6 Conclusions and Future Work

We presented a novel and computationally efficient algorithm (the MDCOP Graph Miner) for mining MDCOPs. We also presented an improved MDCOP Graph Miner algorithm (the LDMDCOP Graph Miner) which can deal with large spatiotemporal data sets. We compared the MDCOP Graph Miner with fastMDCOP-Miner, which isApriori like and involves candidate generation, which is costly as it enumerates all possible co-occurrence instances over all time instants. We proved that the proposed algorithms are correct, complete and effective in finding mixed-drove prevalent (i.e., spatial prevalent and time prevalent) MDCOPs. Our experimental results using real and synthetic data sets provide further evidence of the viability of our approaches.

Further, we would like to extend the MDCOP graph and the subsequent mining algorithm for insertions of object types at arbitrary time interval. Also we would like to extend the current methodology to address zonal co-location problems where the spatial prevalence changes according to the local patterns observed. Finally, we hope to investigate the idea of multi-scale relationship for different pattern families.

## 7 References


[1] Shashi Shekhar, Yan Huang. Discovering Spatial Co-location Patterns. A Summary of Results. SSTD 2001: 236-256

[2] Yan Huang, Shashi Shekhar, Hui Xiong. Discovering Co-location Patterns from Spatial Data Sets: A General Approach. IEEE Trans. Knowl. Data Eng. 16(12): 1472-1485 (2004)

[3] S. Banerjee, B.P. Carlin, and A.E. Gelfrand, Hierarchical Modeling and Analysis for Spatial Data. CRC Press, 2003.

[4] Mete Celik, Shashi Shekhar, James P. Rogers, James A. Shine, Jin Soung Yoo. Mixed-Drove Spatio-Temporal Co-occurence Pattern Mining: A Summary of Results. ICDM 2006: 119-128.

[5] Ekkehard Köhler, Katharina Langkau, Martin Skutella. Time-Expanded Graphs for Flow-Dependent Transit Times. ESA 2002: 599-611.

[6] Betsy George, Shashi Shekhar. Time-Aggregated Graphs for Modeling Spatiotemporal Networks. ER (Workshops) 2006: 85-99

[7] Mete Celik, Shashi Shekhar, James P. Rogers, James A. Shine. Mixed-Drove Spatio-Temporal Co-Occurence Pattern Mining. IEEE Trans. Knowledge and Data Eng., vol. 20, no. 10, Oct. 2008.

# SESSION

# NOVEL METHODOLOGIES AND APPLICATIONS

## Chair(s)

**TBA**

# Face Recognition for the Visually Impaired

**Rabia Jafri[1], Syed Abid Ali[2], and Hamid R. Arabnia[3]**
[1]Department of Information Technology, King Saud University, Riyadh, Saudi Arabia
[2]ISM-TEC LLC, Wilmington, Delaware, U.S.A
[3]Department of Computer Science, University of Georgia, Athens, GA, U.S.A.

**Abstract:** *The inability to recognize known individuals in the absence of audio or haptic cues severely limits the visually impaired in their social interactions and puts them at risk from a security perspective. In recent years, several prototype systems have been developed to aid this population with the face recognition task. This paper aims to provide an overview of the state of the art in this domain, highlighting the strengths and weaknesses of different solutions and discusses some of the issues that need to be addressed and resolved to expedite the practical deployment and widespread acceptance of such systems.*

**Keywords:** Visually impaired, assistive technologies, face recognition, computer vision, survey, review

## 1. Introduction

Visual impairment afflicts approximately 285 million people worldwide according to recent estimates by the World Health Organization (WHO) [1] and, without additional interventions, these numbers are predicted to increase significantly [2]. One of the many challenges faced by this population is their inability to recognize the faces of known individuals when they encounter them in their daily lives. One consequence of this is that whenever a visually impaired individual arrives in a social setting (e.g., in a conference room or at a dinner party), the conversation has to be interrupted to announce which people are already present on the scene which may result in some social awkwardness. The importance of being able to view faces in social interactions is also confirmed by several studies which indicate that most of our communication takes place not through words but via non-verbal means, the majority of which consist of facial expressions [3]. Furthermore, the ability to determine if an approaching person is a friend or a stranger is essential from a security perspective and also contributes to a person's general awareness of his context and surroundings.

The exponential increase in computing power per volume coupled with the decreasing size of computing elements and sensors in recent years has opened up the possibility of running computationally demanding applications on wearable electronic devices. These advances, in conjunction with the needs specified above, have fueled research into developing wearable face recognition aids for the visually impaired in the past few years. This area of research is still in its infancy with only a few prototype systems being implemented for this purpose so far. These solutions are characterized by their emphasis on portability, convenience, intuitiveness, and cost-effectiveness. The objective of this paper is to provide an overview of the state of the art in this domain, highlighting the strengths and weaknesses of different solutions, to discuss some of the issues that need to be addressed and resolved to expedite the practical deployment and widespread acceptance of such systems, and to facilitate and inspire further research in this realm.

The rest of this paper is organized as follows: Section 2 briefly discusses previous work done on face recognition and describes other technologies that are currently being utilized to assist the visually impaired. Section 3 provides an overview of the various solutions that have been developed in recent years to aid the visually impaired in the face recognition task. Section 4 highlights several issues and challenges faced by these systems and identifies some directions for future research. Section 5 concludes the paper.

## 2. Related work

Automated face recognition has been the focus of extensive research for the past four decades (see [4] for a detailed survey). The approaches for this task can be broadly divided into two categories: 1) Feature-based methods [5, 6], which first process the input image to extract distinctive facial features, such as the eyes, mouth, nose, etc., as well as other fiducial marks and then compute the geometric relationships among those facial points, thus, reducing the input facial image to a vector of geometric features. Standard statistical pattern recognition techniques are then employed for matching faces using these measurements. 2) Appearance-based (or holistic) methods [7-9], which attempt to identify faces using global representations, i.e., descriptions based on the entire image rather than on local features of the face. Though face recognition methods traditionally operate on static intensity images, in recent years, much effort has also been directed towards identifying faces from video [10] as well as from other modalities such as 3-D [11] and infra-red [12].

Several computer vision-based solutions have been developed lately to assist the visually impaired in their daily activities (see [13] for a detailed survey). Most of these systems focus on navigation and obstacle detection: e.g., vision based simultaneous localization and mapping (SLAM) has been recently proposed to support blind mobility [14-16]. Extensive research has also been conducted on printed information and web access mainly by harnessing the power of OCR [17-20]. Relatively less attention has been directed towards application areas such as generic object recognition [21, 22] and face recognition but research in these domains has started gaining momentum in the past few years.

It should be noted that several alternate sensing technologies such as RFID [23], infrared [24]and sonar [25] have also been used either on their own or in conjunction with computer vision to aid the visually impaired. However, these technologies suffer from some limitations, e.g., they all require special sensing equipment while infrared and RFID require specific tags; also, sonar and infrared are not very effective in indoors environments since such surroundings tend to be cluttered and the obstacles present therein may cause the reflected echoes to become distorted resulting in unreliable information being conveyed to the user.

# 3. Overview of face recognition systems for the visually impaired

We will now present an overview of some of the most innovative solutions that have been developed in recent years to assist the visually impaired in recognizing faces. A summary and comparison of these approaches is provided in Table 1 at the end of this section.

## 3.1 iCare Interaction Assistant

Krishna et al. [3] have developed the iCare Interaction Assistant, an assistive system that acquires video from a pinhole aperture analog CCD camera embedded in a pair of eyeglasses, digitizes it and then transmits it over a USB cable to a tablet PC. The video is analyzed to detect faces using adaptive boosting [26] which are passed to a face recognition module that utilizes the Principal Components Analysis (PCA) [27] and Linear Discriminant Analysis (LDA) [28] algorithms. If a face is recognized in 5 consecutive frames, the name of the identified individual is converted from text to speech and transmitted to the user via head phones. One main concern expressed by Krishna et al. is that even though some publicly available face databases contain images captured under a range of poses and illumination angles, however, none of them use a precisely calibrated mechanism for acquiring these images, nor is each image explicitly annotated with this information. Krishna et al. have therefore, put together their own database called FacePix [29] which contains face images of 30 people with pose angles and illumination angles between -90 and +90 degrees annotated in 1-degree increments (Figure 2). An empirical evaluation of four of the most widely used face recognition algorithms – PCA [27], LDA [28], BIC (Bayesian Interpersonal Classifier) [30] and HMM (Hidden Markov Model) [31] – on this database showed the two subspace methods (i.e., PCA and LDA) to be the best performing ones with respect to both pose and illumination angle variance. These two methods were, therefore, selected for the face recognition module of the system. The system was tested with 10 known individuals and PCA's performance was found to be better than (or similar to) LDA. Since PCA's computational complexity is also lower than that of LDA, hence it is the preferred algorithm for future development work on this device.

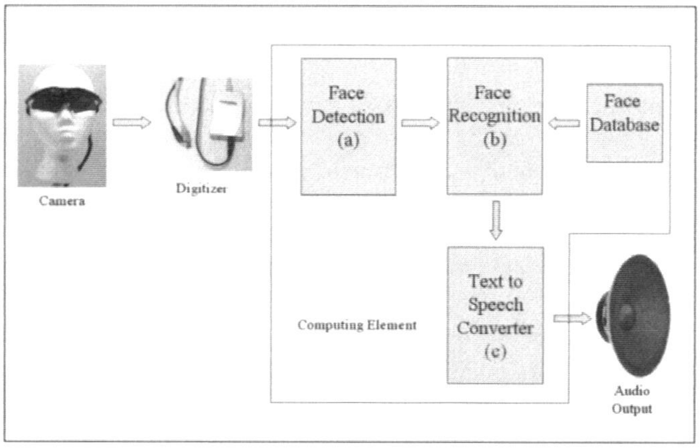


**Figure 1. Block diagram of the wearable face recognition system [3] (©2005 ACM).**

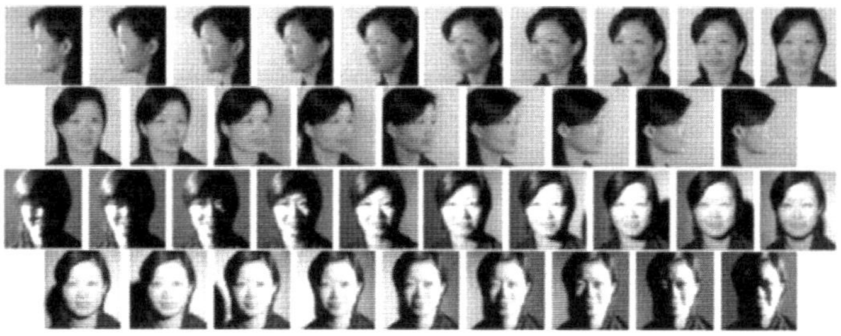

**Figure 2. A subset of one face set taken from the FacePix(30)database, with pose and illumination angles ranging from +90 degrees to –90 degrees, in steps of 10 degrees [3] (©2005 ACM).**

## 3.2 Balduzzi et al.'s approach

Balduzzi et al. [32] have developed a prototype for a compact PC that acquires a video stream from a small form video camera and analyzes it to detect human faces in the scene (by detecting skin-colored regions and finding faces among them using a cascade of Support Vector Machine (SVM) classifiers [33]; eye and nose detection is then applied to the face regions to select the faces in which these features are unoccluded). The face recognition module, which is based on Local Binary Patterns (LBP) [34], attempts to recognize the detected faces. To avoid audio spamming, this module aggregates the results over $N$ consecutive frames and provides feedback only if the last $N$ frames have provided some concrete results. If the person is identified or an unknown person is detected, in either case, an audio feedback is provided to the user via a speaker set. LBP descriptions were selected based on some initial tests that demonstrated their superiority over Local Ternary Patterns [35] and Histogram of Gradient [36]. The system was found to be robust to viewpoint changes of up to 30 degrees. Interviews conducted with prospective users of this prototype revealed that though most people were satisfied with the face detection and feedback speeds, however, the I/O interface and the face recognition capabilities need to be substantially improved to meet the users' expectations.

## 3.3 Kramer et al.'s approach

Kramer et al. [37] have implemented a client application for a smartphone that acquires images using the phone's built-in camera, wirelessly transmits them to a remote server for identification, receives the recognition results and then transmits them to the user via the phone's speech interface. The server application utilizes VeriLook [38], a commercially available face recognition package, with the ability to detect and recognize multiple faces per frame. To determine the robustness of the VeriLook technology to changes in viewpoint, images of 10 subjects were taken from 15 different positions with different head orientations. To make the test more realistic, images of 78 additional people were also downloaded from the CalTech and GeorgiaTech face databases and added to the database of known faces. Experiments showed that VeriLook could tolerate up to $40^o$ and $20^o$ changes in viewpoint and head tilt angles, respectively. The system has been reported to have high recognition accuracy based on initial tests conducted with 10 known users.

## 3.4 Blind Assistant

Blind Assistant [39] is a software platform that integrates many different functionalities for the visually impaired, namely, face recognition, text recognition (restricted to labels and short sentences), place recognition, e-mail (reading and dictating), color recognition and barcode reading. We will focus our discussion on the face recognition module of this system. This solution utilizes the *Nanodesktop*, a freely available, open-source software aimed at developing computer vision applications on embedded systems [40]. The system consists of a handheld console equipped with a pair of RISC microprocessors, a video accelerator, a wireless connection, a USB port and a slot for flash memory cards. A webcam connected to the console is used to acquire images of the scene in front of the user. The images are normalized with respect to luminosity, the faces within them are detected using the Viola-Jones algorithm [41] and recognition is performed based on the PCA algorithm. If a person is recognized, a spoken message relays his identity and average position to the user. The system was tested with 15 visually impaired users and though the PCA algorithm featured an accuracy of only around 80%, but the face recognition part was still rated as reliable and interesting by most users. The most attractive aspect of their system is that it is an open source platform running on widely available hardware and is, thus, accessible to the largest community of users and developers.

## 3.5 Project F.A.C.E.

Astler et al. [42] have proposed to develop a device that will communicate the names of familiar conversation partners, as well as their expression states, differentiated as six universal macroexpressions (i.e. happiness, sadness, disgust, surprise, fear, and anger) to facilitate social interaction for the visually impaired. A pair of stereovision cameras mounted either on the forehead or embedded in sunglasses, to better emulate human vision, would be used to acquire image data which will then be transmitted to a Microsoft Windows capable laptop computer (which the user can carry in a backpack) via a USB connection. Face recognition based on the PCA-SIFT algorithm [43] and expression analysis based on a parametric flow model [44] will be performed and the results will be conveyed to the user via a voice recognition and an audio feedback system with text-to-speech capabilities as well as a haptic feedback belt. The user interface will be built upon the framework already developed by Caperna et al. [45]. Astler et al. plan to conduct interviews with visually impaired users individually as well as in focus groups and intend to incorporate their feedback into the product design. They also plan to survey a group of sighted subjects in order to better understand how society may view users of their technology. The system will first be tested for accuracy and efficiency with facial images from the Cohn-Kanade Database [46] using a method similar to Krishna et al. [3] before being tested with the target population.

# 4. Issues and challenges

Though all the systems described in the previous section are still proof-of-concept, however, preliminary research conducted for developing these solutions has provided some valuable insights into the kind of capabilities that users expect from such a device and the minimum set of requirements that such a system should fulfill. Some of the requisites indicated by these prototypes are discussed below:

- The system should be portable allowing the user to carry it to different venues. This entails that it should be small both in terms of size and weight.
- It should be wearable. This enables constant interaction between the user and the system and also frees the user's hands allowing him to multi-task.
- It should be able to operate in real-time so that the feedback given to the user would be of immediate use to him. For instance, if a person's identity is revealed to the user 40 seconds after the person is first encountered, that information will not be of much use to him in either a social or a security scenario.
- It should be as inconspicuous as possible, preferably

**Table 1. Summary of face recognition solutions for the visually impaired.**

| Approach | Face recognition technology/ algorithm | Input device | Output device | Number of test subjects | Number of gallery subjects | Recognition accuracy |
|---|---|---|---|---|---|---|
| iCare Interaction Assistant [3] | LDA [28] and PCA [27] | Glasses fitted with an analog CCD video camera | Speech output from tablet PC via headphones | 10 | 10 | PCA: 96.3% to 98.6% LDA: 96.3% to 97.8% *values estimated from the bar graph provided in the paper |
| Balduzzi et al. [32] | LBP representations [34] (similarity measured by histogram intersection) | A compact video camera (not specified if camera is held or worn) | Speaker set | 10 known subjects + an unspecified number of unknown subjects | 10 | - |
| Kramer et al.[37] | Verilook [38] | Smartphone camera | Smartphone radio | 10 | 88 | 96% |
| Blind Assistant [39] | PCA [27] | Webcam connected to handheld console | Speech output from console via headphones | 15 | 10 (at the most) | Close to 80% |
| Project F.A.C.E. [42] | PCA-SIFT [43] | A pair of stereovision cameras mounted either on the forehead or embedded in sunglasses | Speech output and haptic feedback belt | - | - | - |

hidden unobtrusively in the user's clothing since multiple studies have now indicated that the visually impaired are not eager to use devices that advertise their disability and that they rate the cosmetic acceptability of a device as more important than the actual functionality that it provides [47].

- It should be cost-effective. Since 90% of the visually impaired live in developing countries while 65% are aged 50 years or older [48], most commercial assistive devices are beyond the financial reach of this population. Hence, appropriate measures must be taken to ensure that when the system reaches the mass production stage, it will be affordable for most of its intended users. Most of the systems described in this paper seem to have taken the cost factor into account by opting to use consumer components that are widely available.
- It should be easy and intuitive to use and should require minimum technical skills and knowledge.
- It should be able to operate under a wide variety of conditions including changes in illumination, pose, and scale which constantly occur especially in group social interactions. Some of the above systems, such as the iCare Interaction Assistant [3], have explicitly taken pose and illumination angles into account and all of them implicitly or explicitly plan to improve their solutions to be better able to handle variations in these conditions.
- It should provide limited and meaningful output to the user avoiding spamming. All the above systems provide audio output to the user while Astler et al. [42] also plan to offer haptic feedback. Since visually impaired users heavily rely on their senses of hearing and touch to discern environmental cues, it is essential not to overwhelm these senses with continuous feedback from the face recognition system any time a person is spotted but rather, to alert the user only when a person has been within range for a certain number of frames and his identity is established with some degree of confidence. This also suggests that some options for customizing the output would be desirable, e.g., the user may or may not

choose to be informed every time an unknown person is encountered.

Some additional considerations pointed out by the developers of the above systems are as follows:

- The features utilized by these assistive devices may be different from those used by face recognition systems developed for security applications: e.g., algorithms for security purposes assume that the face may be disguised and thus, try to minimize the effect of glasses, facial hair, makeup, etc. when recognizing faces. However, in a social scenario, facial paraphernalia and features such as these may be a distinctive part of the person's appearance and may actually aid in recognition [3].
- On the same note, the number of individuals that need to be recognized by such an assistive device is much smaller than that for a security application. A visually impaired person needs to recognize only a handful of family members, caregivers and acquaintances in his daily life and so the face recognition algorithm does not need to match an unknown face against a database of thousands of known individuals as may be the case with a general purpose security application in a public place. This consideration can significantly impact the choice of the face recognition algorithm utilized and its complexity. As can be seen from Table 1, all the prototype systems have been tested with only 10 to 15 known persons.
- The development of face recognition aids in a work environment may be facilitated by the fact that face databases are already available in many organizations for security purposes. Moreover, an option can be provided in such systems allowing willing colleagues to self-enroll themselves by emailing their facial images with their names on the subject line [37].
- Feedback from the target population has revealed that users would prefer such a system to be able to identify individuals whom they may not have personally met but who may be of interest to them as a community, e.g., care operators at a rehabilitation facility [39].

## 5. Conclusion

The inability to recognize known individuals in the absence of audio or haptic cues severely limits the visually impaired in their social interactions and puts them at risk from a security perspective. An overview of several systems being developed to aid this population in the face recognition task was presented in this paper. Though all these systems are still in the prototype stage, however, the initial research, development and testing of these solutions has demonstrated their feasibility and has provided several valuable insights into requirements for assistive devices for this task. Nevertheless, several issues and challenges (which have been highlighted in the previous section) still need to be addressed and resolved to expedite the practical deployment and widespread acceptance of such systems.

## Acknowledgements

The authors extend their appreciation to the Deanship of Scientific Research at King Saud University for partially funding the work through the research group project number RGP-VPP-157.

## References

[1] D. Pascolini and S. P. Mariotti, "Global estimates of visual impairment: 2010," *British Journal Ophthalmology,* 2011.

[2] "Elimination of Avoidable Blindness Report by the Secretariat," World Health Organisation, Fifty-sixth World Health Assembly2003.

[3] S. Krishna, G. Little, J. Black, and S. Panchanathan, "A wearable face recognition system for individuals with visual impairments," in *Proceedings of the 7th international ACM SIGACCESS conference on Computers and accessibility*, Baltimore, MD, USA, 2005, pp. 106-113.

[4] R. Jafri and H. R. Arabnia, "A Survey of Face Recognition Techniques," *Journal of Information Processing Systems,* vol. 5, pp. 41-68, 2009.

[5] I. J. Cox, J. Ghosn, and P. N. Yianilos, "Feature-based face recognition using mixture-distance," presented at the Proceedings of IEEE Conference on Computer Vision and Pattern Recognition, 1996.

[6] L. Wiskott, J.-M. Fellous, N. Krüger, and C. von der Malsburg, "Face Recognition by Elastic Bunch Graph Matching," *IEEE Transactions on Pattern Analysis and Machine Intelligence,* vol. 19, pp. 775-779, July 1997.

[7] M. Turk and A. Pentland, "Eigenfaces For Recognition," *Journal Of Cognitive Neuroscience,* vol. 3, pp. 71-86, Winter 1991.

[8] P. N. Belhumeur, J. P. Hespanha, and D. J. Kriegman, "Eigenfaces vs. Fisherfaces: Recognition using class specific linear projection," *IEEE Transactions on Pattern Analysis and Machine Intelligence,* vol. 19, pp. 711-720, July 1997.

[9] R. Jafri and H. R. Arabnia, "PCA-Based Methods for Face Recognition," in *The 2007 International Conference on Security and Management (SAM'07)*, Las Vegas, USA, 2007, pp. 534-541.

[10] S. Zhou and R. Chellappa, "Beyond a single still image: Face recognition from multiple still images and videos," in *Face Processing: Advanced Modeling and Methods*, ed: Academic Press, 2005.

[11] K. W. Bowyer, K. Chang, and P. J. Flynn, "A survey of approaches and challenges in 3D and multi-modal 3D+2D face recognition," *Computer Vision And Image Understanding,* vol. 101, pp. 1-15, 2006.

[12] S. G. Kong, J. Heo, B. R. Abidi, J. Paik, and M. A. Abidi, "Recent advances in visual and infrared face recognition - a review," *Computer Vision And Image Understanding,* vol. 97, pp. 103-135, Jan 2005.

[13] R. Manduchi and J. Coughlan, "(Computer) vision without sight," *Commun. ACM,* vol. 55, pp. 96-104, 2012.
[14] V. Pradeep, G. Medioni, and J. Weiland, "Robot vision for the visually impaired," in *Proc. Workshop on Applications of Computer Vision for the Visually Impaired*, San Francisco, CA, 2010, pp. 15-22.
[15] J. Saez and F. Escolano, "Stereo-based aerial obstacle detection for the visually impaired," in *Proc. Workshop on Computer Vision Applications for the Visually Impaired*, 2008.
[16] J. Wilson, B. N. Walker, J. Lindsay, C. Cambias, and F. Dellaert, "SWAN: System for Wearable Audio Navigation," in *Proceedings of the 11th IEEE International Symposium on Wearable Computers*, 2007, pp. 1-8.
[17] B. Leporini, P. Andronico, and M. Buzzi, "Designing search engine user interfaces for the visually impaired," in *Proceedings of the 2004 international cross-disciplinary workshop on Web accessibility (W4A)*, New York City, New York, 2004, pp. 57-66.
[18] S. Liu, W. Ma, D. Schalow, and K. Spruill, "Improving Web access for visually impaired users," *IT Professional,* vol. 6, pp. 28-33 2004.
[19] M. Tanaka and H. Goto, "Text-Tracking Wearable Camera System for Visually-Impaired People," in *International Conference on Pattern Recognition (ICPR 2008)*, Tampa, FL, 2008, pp. 1-4.
[20] T. Dumitras, M. Lee, P. Quinones, A. Smailagic, D. Siewiorek, and P. Narasimhan, "Eye of the Beholder: Phone-Based Text-Recognition for the Visually-Impaired," in *10th IEEE International Symposium on Wearable Computers*, Montreaux, 2006, pp. 145-146.
[21] J. Sudol, O. Dialameh, C. Blanchard, and T. Dorcey, "Looktel—A comprehensive platform for computer-aided visual assistance," in *IEEE Computer Society Conference on Computer Vision and Pattern Recognition Workshops (CVPRW)*, San Francisco, CA, 2010, pp. 73-80.
[22] T. Winlock, E. Christiansen, and S. Belongie, "Toward real-time grocery detection for the visually impaired," in *Computer Vision Applications for the Visually Impaired (CVAVI)*, San Francisco, CA, 2010.
[23] M. Murad, A. Rehman, A. A. Shah, S. Ullah, M. Fahad, and K. M. Yahya, "RFAIDE – An RFID Based Navigation and Object Recognition Assistant for Visually Impaired People," in *7th International Conference on Emerging Technologies (ICET)*, Islamabad, Pakistan, 2011, pp. 1-4.
[24] W. Crandall, J. Brabyn, B. L. Bentzen, and L. Myers, "Remote Infrared Signage Evaluation for Transit Stations and Intersections," *Journal of Rehabilitation Research & Development,* vol. 36, pp. 341-355, 1999.
[25] "Bay Advanced Technologies Ltd. (http://www.batforblind.co.nz/).".
[26] P. Viola and M. Jones, "Robust Real-time Object Detection," in *Second International Workshop on Statistical and Computational Theories of Vision – Modeling, Learning, Computing, and Sampling*, Vancouver, Canada, 2001.
[27] M. Turk and A. Pentland, "Face recognition using Eigenfaces," in *Proc. of IEEE Conference on Computer Vision and Pattern Recognition*, 1991, pp. 586–591.
[28] K. Etemad and R. Chellappa, "Discriminant Analysis for Recognition of Human Face Images (Invited Paper)," in *Proceedings of the First International Conference on Audio- and Video-Based Biometric Person Authentication*, 1997, pp. 127-142.
[29] J. Black, M. Gargesha, K. Kahol, P. Kuchi, and S. Panchanathan, "A framework for performance evaluation of face recognition algorithms," in *ITCOM, Internet Multimedia Systems II*, 2002.
[30] B. Moghaddam and A. Pentland, "Probabilistic Visual Learning for Object Representation," *IEEE Trans. Pattern Anal. Mach. Intell.,* vol. 19, pp. 696-710, 1997.
[31] A. Nefian and M. H. H. III, "Hidden markov models for face detection and recognition," in *IEEE International Conference on Image Processing*, 1998, pp. 141–145.
[32] L. Balduzzi, G. Fusco, F. Odone, S. Dini, M. Mesiti, A. Destrero, and A. Lovato, "Low-cost face biometry for visually impaired users," in *Biometric Measurements and Systems for Security and Medical Applications (BIOMS), 2010 IEEE Workshop on*, 2010, pp. 45-52.
[33] V. N. Vapnik, *Statistical Learning Theory*: Wiley, 1998.
[34] T. Ahonen, A. Hadid, and M. Pietikainen, "Face Description with Local Binary Patterns: Application to Face Recognition," *IEEE Trans. Pattern Anal. Mach. Intell.,* vol. 28, pp. 2037-2041, 2006.
[35] X. Tan and B. Triggs, "Enhanced local texture feature sets for face recognition under difficult lighting conditions," in *Proceedings of the 3rd international conference on Analysis and modeling of faces and gestures*, Rio de Janeiro, Brazil, 2007, pp. 168-182.
[36] N. Dalal and B. Triggs, "Histograms of Oriented Gradients for Human Detection," in *Proceedings of the 2005 IEEE Computer Society Conference on Computer Vision and Pattern Recognition (CVPR'05) - Volume 1 - Volume 01*, 2005, pp. 886-893.
[37] K. M. Kramer, D. S. Hedin, and D. J. Rolkosky, "Smartphone based face recognition tool for the blind," in *Engineering in Medicine and Biology Society (EMBC), 2010 Annual International Conference of the IEEE*, 2010, pp. 4538-4541.
[38] "VeriLook SDK. http://www.neurotechnology.com/verilook.html."
[39] F. Battaglia and G. Iannizzotto, "An open architecture to develop a handheld device for helping visually impaired people," *Consumer Electronics, IEEE Transactions on,* vol. 58, pp. 1086-1093, 2012.

[40] F. Battaglia, G. Iannizzotto, and F. L. Rosa, "An open and portable software development kit for handheld devices with proprietary operating systems," *IEEE Trans. on Consum. Electron.,* vol. 55, pp. 2436-2444, 2009.
[41] P. Viola and M. Jones, "Rapid object detection using a boosted cascade of simple features," in *IEEE Computer Society Conference on Computer Vision and Pattern Recognition*, 2001, pp. 511-518.
[42] D. Astler, H. Chau, K. Hsu, A. Hua, A. Kannan, L. Lei, M. Nathanson, E. Paryavi, K. Ripple, M. Rosen, H. Unno, C. Wang, K. Zaidi, and X. Zhang, "A Portable Computer Vision Device for Improving Social Interactions of the Visually Impaired," University of Maryland2010.
[43] Y. Ke and R. Sukthankar, "PCA-SIFT: a more distinctive representation for local image descriptors," in *Proceedings of the 2004 IEEE computer society conference on Computer vision and pattern recognition*, Washington, D.C., USA, 2004, pp. 506-513.
[44] M. J. Black and Y. Yacoob, "Recognizing Facial Expressions in Image Sequences Using Local Parameterized Models of Image Motion," *Int. J. Comput. Vision,* vol. 25, pp. 23-48, 1997.
[45] S. Caperna, C. Cheng, J. Cho, V. Fan, A. Luthra, and B. O'Leary, "A navigation and object location device for the blind," University of Maryland, Gemstone Team Research2009.
[46] T. Kanade, Y. Tian, and J. F. Cohn, "Comprehensive Database for Facial Expression Analysis," in *Proceedings of the Fourth IEEE International Conference on Automatic Face and Gesture Recognition*, 2000, p. 46.
[47] R. Golledge, R. Klatzky, J. Loomis, and J. Marston, "Stated preferences for components of a personal guidance system for nonvisual navigation," *Journal of Visual Impairment & Blindness,* vol. 98, pp. 135-147, 2004.
[48] "Visual impairment and blindness: Fact sheet number 282. http://www.who.int/mediacentre/factsheets/fs282/en/," ed: WHO media center, 2012.

# Face recognition system based on Doubly truncated multivariate Gaussian Mixture Model

**D.Haritha[1], K. Srinivasa Rao[2], B. Kiran Kumar[3], Ch. Satyanarayana[4]**
[1]Department of Computer Science and Engineering, University College of Engineering, JNTU, Kakinada. Andhra Pradesh, INDIA.
[2]Department of Statistics, Andhra University, Visakhapatnam. Andhra Pradesh, INDIA.
[3]APTRANSCO, Kakinada. Andhra Pradesh, INDIA.
[4]Department of Computer Science and Engineering, University College of Engineering, JNTU, Kakinada. Andhra Pradesh, INDIA.

**Abstract:** *A face recognition algorithm based on doubly truncated multivariate Gaussian mixture model with DCT is introduced. The truncation on the feature vector with a significant influence on improving the recognition rate of the system using EM algorithm with K-means or hierarchical clustering is implemented. The characteristic model parameters are estimated. The EM algorithm containing the updated equations of the model parameters derived for the doubly truncated multivariate Gaussian mixture model. A face recognition system is developed under Bayesian frame using maximum likelihood conditions. The efficiency of the developed face recognition system is analyzed by conducting experimentation with two face image databases, via, of Jawaharlal Nehru Technological University Kakinada (JNTUK) and Yale. The performance of these algorithms are evaluated by computing the recognition rates, false acceptance rate, false rejection rate, true positive rate and half error rate. From the ROC curves, it is observed the developed models perform better. A comparative study of the present face recognition systems with that of the face recognition systems based on Gaussian mixture models reveal that the proposed algorithms perform better.*

**Keywords:** Face recognition system, EM algorithm, Doubly truncated multivariate Gaussian mixture model, DCT coefficients under logarithm domain.

## 1 Introduction

Face recognition means identifying the person from a pool of N persons by using the visible physical structure of an individual's face. Face recognition is an important task and it is adopted in many real time systems. It is useful in a wide range of applications including security, surveillance, criminal identification, gateway controls, Biometric authentication, mobile personal devices, document securities, etc,. Face recognition is a complex task due to the complexity involved in the face images. A single change in the face can alter total look of the face. To have an efficient recognition of faces there is a need to automation of this process. ( Chellappa et al., (1995), Zhao w. et al., (2003), Satyanarayana et al., (2008)). Although the concept of recognizing someone from facial features is intuitive, facial recognition, as a biometric, makes human recognition a more automated, computerized process. Compared to the biometrics, the face recognition is efficiently used for surveillance purposes. For example, the wanted criminals are easily identified. (muhamad et al., (2008)).

Face recognition systems are generally divided into two groups, namely, verification or identification. In face verification, we check the similarity between two images and found that there is a match or mis-match. In case of an identification, the similarity between a given face image is checked with the face images present in the database. The one which is giving highest score is considered as the identity of the subject.

Face recognition is a pre-requisite for many authentication systems. It is highly difficult to model the facial features in detail with physio-physical and neuro-physiological changes in the face. In many of the complex situations, the face recognition is done through automation. The basic difficulty in developing the face recognition systems arise because of change in facial expressions, aging, illumination conditions and the efficiency of the device used to capture the image. To have an efficient face recognition system one has to consider several factors.

Generally, the constituent processes of the face recognition systems are feature vector extraction and classification. The feature vector extraction is done by different methods known as Principal Component Analysis, eigen-matrices, Independent Component Analysis, different types of Discrete Cosine Transformations, Wavelet transformations, histograms, Fourier transformations, vector normalization, etc,. The classification can be done by two approaches, namely, hierarchical methods and modeling methods(Ziad M. Hafed et al., (2001), Kresimin et al., (2008),

Govinda raju et al., (1990), Ahmed et al., (1974) and (Ziad et al., (2001)).

In hierarchical methods the classification is done based on different approaches like distance measures, similarity measures, Graph-cut theory, decision rules, association rules, histogram matching, etc. In model based classification, the feature vector is modeled by probability distributions, Hidden Markov Models, neural networks, membership functions, etc. Among these methods, the face recognition systems based on probability distribution gained lot of importance due to their ready applicability in several practical situations (Cardinaux et al.,(2003), Conrad Sanderson et al., (2003), Cardinaux et al., (2004) and Conrad Sanderson et al., (2005)).

.

Recently, much emphasis is given for developing and analyzing face recognition systems based on Gaussian Mixture Models. However, there are some drawbacks with the face recognition systems based on Gaussian Mixture Models and their accuracy rate is around $90 \pm 2$. This shows that the face recognition systems based on Gaussian Mixture Model are to be modified or generalized in order to have efficient and accurate recognition of the systems with less error rate. Hence, in this thesis an attempt is made to develop and analyze, some face recognition systems based on generalized / modified Gaussian Mixture Model with different types of feature vectors.

No serious work has been reported in literature regarding face recognition with doubly truncated multivariate GMM. So, we propose a generric model for face recognition based on doubly truncated multivariate GMM. This model also includes GMM as a limiting case when the truncation points tend to infinite. The doubly truncated multivariate Gaussian mixture model is capable of portraying several probability distributions like asymmetric / symmetric / platy-kurtic / lepto-kurtic distributions (Norman Johnson et al., (1994), Sailaja et al., (2010)].

In mixture models the number of components has significant influence on the performance of face recognition system. The number of components are determined by K-means algorithms. The model parameters are estimated by E.M. algorithm. The face recognition system is developed based on maximum likelihood functions of the face image. The efficiency of the proposed system is studied by conducting experimentation with the face data bases namely, Yale database and Jawaharlal Nehru Technological University Kakinada (JNTUK) database. The performance measures like false acceptance rate false rejection rate and percentage of correct recognition rate, etc., are computed. A comparative study of the developed algorithm with that of GMM is also carried. The effect of the number of DCT coefficients in the feature vector extraction is also studied.

The paper is structured as follows. Section 2 summarizes feature extraction using DCT coefficients, Section 3 summarizes doubly truncated multivariate Gaussian mixture face recognition model, Section 4 summarizes the estimation of the model parameters, Section 5 summarizes initialization of model parameters and Section 6 summarizes the face recognition algorithm, experimental results are given in Section 7 and finally conclusions are presented in Section 8.

# 2 Feature vector extraction using DCT coefficients

For developing the face recognition model, the important consideration is deriving the features of each individual face image. Several techniques are adopted to extract the feature vector associated with each individual face (Conrad Sanderson et al., (2003)). Among the transformations used for feature vector extraction, the 2D DCT is used as it is simple and more efficient in characterizing the face of the individual. This method has been recognized as a worldwide standard [JPEG] technique for image compression (Annadurai et al., (2004)). In transform coding systems, the mean square reconstruction error of DCT is relatively less with respect to other compression methods. Even though it is a lossy compression technique, it has good compression ratio, information packing ability and reconstruction capability. Compared to other input independent transforms it has advantages of packing the most useful information into the fewest coefficients and minimizing the block appearance called blocking artifice that results when boundaries between sub images become visible.

The reason for preferring DCT over KLT, which is known to be the optimal transform in terms of compactness of representation, is mainly because of its data independent bases. For data representation, one has to align training face images properly; otherwise the basis images can have noisy appearance. Although alignment can be done for the entire face with respect to some facial landmarks such as the centers of the eyes, it is almost impossible to align local parts of the face as successful as the entire face image. Suitable landmarks for each part of the face cannot be easily found. Hence, noisy basis images from the KLT on a training set of local parts are inevitable. Moreover, since DCT closely approximates KLT in the sense of information packing, it is a very suitable alternative for compact data representation. DCT is a well-known signal analysis tool used in compression standards due to its compact representation power. Although KLT is known to be the optimal transform in terms of information packing, its data dependent nature makes it unfeasible for use in some practical tasks. Furthermore DCT closely approximates the compact representation ability of the KLT, which makes it a very useful tool for signal representation both in terms of information packing and in terms of computational complexity due to its data independent nature (Hazim Kemal Ekenel et al., (2005)).

These specific characteristics of DCT coefficients attracted the attention of researchers in proposing them as feature vector for face recognition system. The DCT is an orthogonal transform and consist of phase shifted cosine functions. The DCT can be used to transform an image from spatial domain to frequency domain. For obtaining the feature vector associated with each individual face, it is assumed to be consisting of ( $N_P$ x $N_P$ ) blocks. In each block the 2D DCT coefficients are computed using the method given by Conrad Sanderson et al., (2003). These coefficients are ordered according to a zig-zag pattern (consisting of 15 coefficients) reflecting the amount of stored information (Gonzales and Woods et al., (1992)). From the DCT coefficients, we get the feature vector of the each individual face as $\vec{x_i} = [\ c_1\ c_2 \ldots c_K\ ]^T$ consisting of $N_P$ x 15 coefficients.

.

# 3 Doubly truncated multivariate Gaussian Mixture face recognition model

In this section, we briefly discuss the probability distribution (model) used for characterizing the feature vector of the face recognition system. After extracting the feature vector of each individual face, it is modeled by a suitable probability distribution, such that the characteristics of the feature vector should match the statistical characteristics of the distribution. Since, each face is a collection of several components like mouth, eyes, nose, etc, the feature vector characterizing the face is to follow a M-component mixture distribution. In each component, the feature vector is having finite range such that it can be assumed to follow a doubly truncated Gaussian distribution. This in turn, implies that the feature vector of each individual face can be characterized by a M-component doubly truncated multivariate Gaussian mixture model. The probability density function of the feature vector associated with each individual face is

$$h((\vec{x}|\lambda)) = \sum_{i=1}^{M} \alpha_i\, d_i\,(\vec{x}) \qquad (1)$$

where, $d_i(\vec{x})$ is the probability density function of the ith component feature vector which is of the form doubly truncated Gaussian distribution (sailaja et al., (2010)).

$$d_i(\vec{x}) = \left(\frac{1}{(B-A)(2\pi)^{\frac{D}{2}}|\Sigma_i|^{\frac{1}{2}}}\right) * exp\left\{-\frac{1}{2}(\vec{x_i} - \vec{\mu_i})'\ \Sigma_i^{-1}\ (\vec{x_i} - \vec{\mu_i})\right\} \qquad (2)$$

where, $\vec{x}$ is a D dimensional random vector $(\vec{x_t} = (x_1\ x_2 \ldots x_t))$ is the feature vector, $\vec{\mu_i}$ is the i[th] component feature mean vector, $\Sigma_i$ is the i[th] component of co-variance matrix,

$$A = \int_{-\infty}^{x_L} \ldots \int_{-\infty}^{x_L} d_i\,(\vec{x_t})\vec{d}x_t$$

and

$$B = \int_{-\infty}^{x_M} \ldots \int_{-\infty}^{x_M} d_i\,(\vec{x_t})\vec{d}x_t\,.$$

where, $x_L$ , $x_M$ are the lower and upper truncated points of the feature vectors. $d_i(\vec{x}), i = 1 \ldots . M$ are the component densities and $\alpha_i(\vec{x}), i = 1 \ldots . M$ are the mixture weights, with mean vector. The mixture weights satisfy the constraints $\sum_{i=1}^{M} \alpha_i = 1$

The DTGMM is parameterized by the mean vector, Co-variance matrix and mixture weights from all components densities. The parameters are collectively represented by the parameter. Set $\lambda_i = \{\alpha_i\ ,\ \mu_i\ ,\ \Sigma_i\ \}\ i = 1,2, \ldots M$. For face recognition each image is represented by its model parameters. This simplifies the computational complexities. The doubly truncated multivariate Gaussian mixture model includes the GMM model as a particular case when the truncation points tend to infinite.

# 4 Estimation of the model parameters

For developing the face recognition model, it is needed to estimate the parameters of the face model. For estimating the parameters in the model, the EM algorithm which maximizes the likelihood function of the model for a sequence of i training vectors $(\vec{x_t} = (x_1\ x_2 \ldots x_t))$ is considered.

The likelihood function of the sample observations is

$$L(\vec{x}\ ;\ \lambda_j) = \prod_{i=1}^{T} h(\vec{x}\ ;\ \lambda_j) \qquad (3)$$

where, $h(\vec{x}\ ;\ \lambda_j)$ is given in equation (1).

The likelihood function contains the number of components M which can be determined from the K-means algorithm or Hierarchical clustering algorithm. The K-means algorithm or Hierarchical clustering algorithm requires the initial number of components which can be taken by plotting the histogram of the face image using MATLAB code and counting the number of peaks. Once M-is assigned the EM algorithm can be applied for refining the parameters. The updated equations of the parameters of the model are:

$$\alpha_k^{\ l+1} = \frac{1}{T} \sum_{i=1}^{T} h(i|\vec{x_t}\ ,\lambda_j) \qquad (4)$$

$$\mu_k^{\ l+1} = \frac{\sum_{i=1}^{T} \vec{x_t}\, h(i|\vec{x_t},\lambda_j) + \sum_{i=1}^{T} \frac{f(\vec{x_M}) - f(\vec{x_L})}{B-A}\ \sigma_k^{\ 2}\ h(i|\vec{x_t},\lambda_j)}{\sum_{i=1}^{T} h(i|\vec{x_t},\lambda_j)} \qquad (5)$$

$$\sigma_k^{\ l+1} = \frac{\sum_{i=1}^{T} h(i|\vec{x_t},\lambda_j)(\vec{x_t} - \mu_i^{\ l+1})}{c\ \sum_{i=1}^{T} h(i|\vec{x_t},\lambda_j)} \qquad (6)$$

where,

$$c = \frac{1}{B-A}(1 + \mu_k^{\ l+1})\left[\left(f(\vec{x_M}) - f(\vec{x_L})\right) + \left(x_M f(\vec{x_M}) - x_L f(\vec{x_L})\right)\right],$$

$$f(x_M) = \int_{-\infty}^{x_M} d_i\,(\vec{x_t})\vec{d}x_t\ ,$$

$$f(x_L) = \int_{-\infty}^{x_L} d_i\,(\vec{x_t})\vec{d}x_t \quad \text{and}$$

$$h(i|\vec{x_t}\ ,\lambda_j) = \frac{\alpha_i\, d_i(\vec{x_t})}{\sum_{i=1}^{k} \alpha_i\, d_i(\vec{x_t})} \qquad (7)$$

# 5 Initialization of model parameters

To utilize the EM algorithm we have to initialize the parameters $\{\alpha_i\ ,\ \mu_i\ ,\ \sigma_i\ \}, i = \{1 \ldots . M\}$. $X_M$ and $X_L$ are estimated with the maximum and the minimum values of each feature respectively. The initial values of $\alpha_i$ can be taken as

$\alpha_i = \frac{1}{M}$ . The initial estimates of $\alpha_i$ , $\mu_i$ and $\sigma_i$ of the i$^{th}$ component are obtained by using the method given by A.C.Cohen(1950).

# 6 Face recognition system

Face Recognition means recognizing the person from a group of H persons. The Figure 1 describes the flow chart for the proposed face recognition algorithm.

Let us considered our face recognition system has to detect the correct face with our existing database. Here, we are given with a face image and a claim that this face belongs to a particular person C to classify the face a set of feature vectors $X = \{x_i\}_{i=1}^{T}$ is extracted using the computational methodology of feature vector extraction is discussed in section 2.

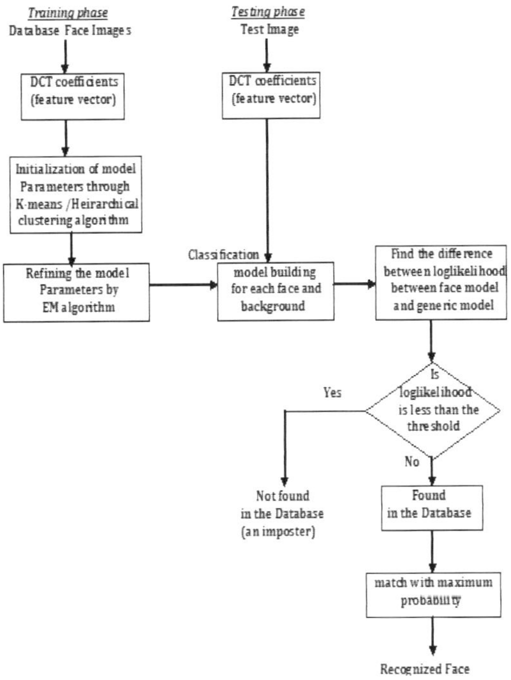


FIGURE 1: FLOW CHART FOR FACE RECOGNITION ALGORITHM USING DCT COEFFICIENTS

The universal background model is used to find the likelihood of the face belonging to an imposter. $L(X|\lambda_{generic})$ is the likelihood function of the claimant computed based on the parameter set $\lambda_{generic}$. The $\lambda_{generic}$ is computed by considering all faces in the dataset and obtaining the average values of the parameters.

The decision on the face belonging to the person C is found using

$$O(X) = \left| \log L(X|\lambda_C) - \log L(X|\lambda_{generic}) \right|.$$

The final decision for the recognition of a given face is as follows. Given a threshold t for O(X) the face is classified as belonging to person C, when $O(X)$ is greater than or equal to t. It is classified as belonging to an imposter, when $O(X)$ is less than t.

For a given set of training vector $\lambda_C$ for all faces in the data bases and $\lambda_{generic}$ are computed by using the updated equations for the model parameters discussed in section 4 and using the initial estimates of the model parameters obtained by using either K-means algorithm or hierarchical clustering algorithm.

# 7 Experimental results

The performance of the developed algorithm is evaluated using two types of databases namely Jawaharlal Nehru Technological University Kakinada (JNTUK) and Yale face databases (Satyanarrayana et al., (2009) and Qian et al., (2007)). The JNTUK face database consisting of 120 face database and Yale database consists of 120 faces. Sample of 20 persons images from JNTUK database is shown in Figure.2.

**Figure.2: Sample Images from JNTUK database**

Using the method discussed in section 2, the feature vectors consisting of DCT coefficients under logarithm domain for each face image for both the databases are computed. For each image, the sample of feature vectors are divided into K groups representing the different face features like neck, nose, ears, eyes, etc.

For initialization of the model parameters with K-means algorithm or Hierarchical clustering algorithm, a sample histogram of the face image is drawn and counted the number of peaks. After diving the observations into three categories by both the methods and assuming that the feature vector of the whole face image, follows a three component finite doubly truncated multivariate Gaussian mixture model. The initial estimates of the model parameters $\alpha_i$ , $\vec{\mu_i}$ , $\vec{\Sigma_i}$ are obtained by using the method discussed in section 5 with K-means algorithm or Hierarchical clustering algorithm.

With these initial estimates the refined estimates of the model parameters are obtained by using the updated equations of the EM algorithm and MATLAB code discussed in section 4. Substituting these estimates, the joint probability density function of each face image is obtained for all faces in the database. By considering all the feature vectors of all faces in the database the generic model for any face is also obtained by using the initial estimates and the EM algorithm discussed in section 4 and 5, respectively. The parameters of the generic model are stored under the parametric set $\lambda_{generic}$. The individual face image model parameters are stored with the parametric set $\lambda_i$ , i= 1,2,...N, where N is the number of face images in the database.

Using the face recognition system discussed in section 6, the recognition rates of each database is computed for different threshold values of t in (0, 1). The false rejection rate, false acceptance rate and half total error rate for each threshold are computed using the formula's given by (Conrad Sanderson et al. (2005)). The Half Total Error Rate (HTER) is a special case of Decision Cost function and is often known as equal error rate when the system is adjusted.

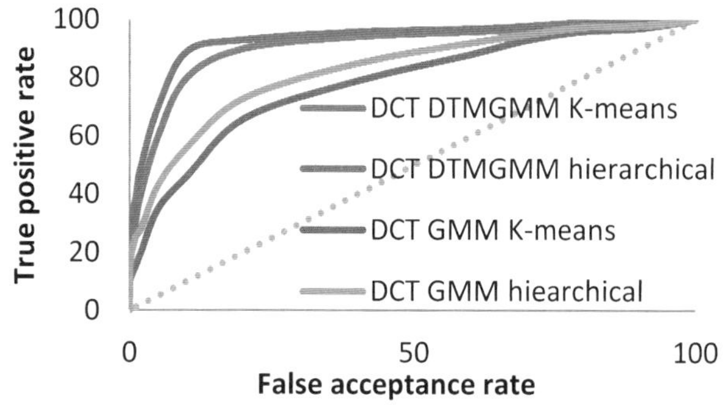


**Figure 3: ROC curve for DTMGMM and GMM for JNTUK**

Plotting the FAR and FRR for different threshold values, the ROC curves for both the databases are obtained are shown in Figures 3 and 4. From this ROC, the optimal threshold value 't' for each database is obtained. These threshold values are used for effective implementations of the face recognition system.

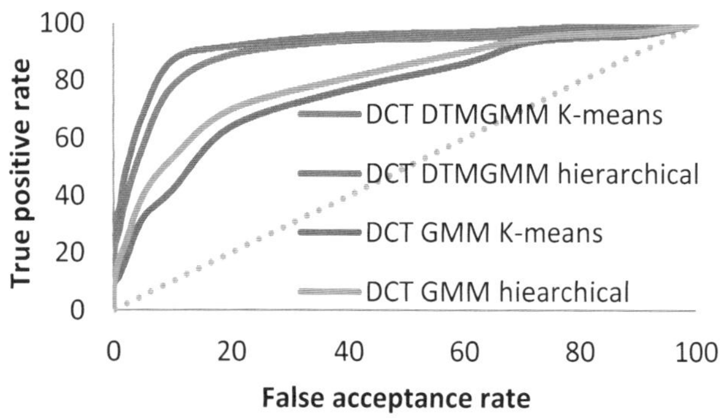


**Figure 4: ROC curve for DTMGMM and GMM for Yale**

Table 1 shown the values of HTER and recognition rates of both face recognition systems.

**Table 1: face recognition rates**

| Database | Recognition system | HTER | Recognition rate |
|---|---|---|---|
| JNTUK | GMM with K-means | 5.5834 | 88.33±1.5 |
| | GMM with hierarchical | 4.75 | 90±1.3 |
| | DTMGMM with K-means | 3.7484 | 96.7±1.3 |
| | DTMGMM with hierarchical | 3.3333 | 97.5±0.9 |
| Yale | GMM with K-means | 6 | 87.5 ±2.1 |
| | GMM with hierarchical | 5.1667 | 89.17±1.8 |
| | DTMGMM with K-means | 4.1667 | 95.83±1.2 |
| | DTMGMM with hierarchical | 3.749 | 96.93±0.8 |

From the above discussions, it is observed that the face recognition system with doubly truncated multivariate Gaussian mixture model and hierarchical clustering algorithm is more efficient compared to that of the systems based on doubly truncated multivariate Gaussian mixture model and GMM and with K-means algorithm.

# 8 Conclusions

A face recognition system based on doubly truncated multivariate Gaussian mixture model with DCT coefficients is developed and analyzed. The feature vector extraction is done by computing the DCT coefficients of the face image of each individual face. The feature vector of the DCT coefficients of the face image data is assumed to follow a doubly truncated multivariate Gaussian distribution. Expectation Maximization algorithm (EM algorithm) is used for estimating the model parameters. The initialization of the model parameters is done through K-means or hierarchical clustering and moment's method of estimation. A face recognition algorithm with maximum likelihood under Bayesian frame using threshold for the difference between the estimated likelihoods of claimants and imposters is developed and analyzed.

The efficiency of the presently developed face recognition system is studied by conducting experimentation with two face image databases, via, JNTUK and Yale. The performance of the developed algorithm is studied by computing the recognition rates, false acceptance rate, false rejection rate, true positive rate and half total error rate. Plotting the ROC curves with different values of the threshold, it is observed that the developed systems have good recognition. Among the developed systems, the systems developed with hierarchical clustering algorithm giving better performance compared to the systems developed with K-means algorithm.Page numbering

# 9 References

[1] Ahmed N., Natarajan T., and Rao K. "Discrete cosine transform", IEEE Trans. on Computers. 23(1), 90–93 (1974).

[2] Annadurai S. and Saradha A. "Discrete Cosine Transform based face recognition using Linear Discriminant

Analysis", Proceedings of International Conference on Intelligent Knowledge Systems (IKS-2004). 16-20 (2004).

[3] Cardinaux F., Sanderson C., and Marcel S. "Comparison of MLP and GMM classifiers for face verification on XM2VTS", 4th International Conference on Audio- and Video-Based Biometric Person Recognition (AVBPA). 911–920 (2003).

[4] Cardinaux F., Sanderson C., Bengio S. "Face Verification using Adaptive Generative Models", Proc. of 6th IEEE Int. Conf. on Automatic Face and Gesture Recognition (AFGR). 825-830 (2004).

[5] Chellappa R., Wilson C., and Sirohey S. "Human and machine recognition of faces: A survey", Proc. of IEEE. 83(5), 705-740 (1995).

[6] Conrad Sanderson, Kuldip K. Paliwal, "Fast features for face Recognition under illumination direction changes", Pattern Recognition Letters. 24(14), 2409-2419 (2003).

[7] Conrad Sanderson, Fabien Cardinaux and Samy Bengio. "On Accuracy/Robustness/ Complexity Trade-Offs in Face Verification", Proceedings of the Third International Conference on Information Technology and Applications (ICITA'05). 638-645 (2005).

[8] Douglas A. Reynolds, and Richard C. Rose, "Robust Text Independent speaker identification using Gaussian Mixture Speaker Model", IEEE Tran. Speech and Audio Processing. 3, 72-83 (1995).

[9] Gonzalez R. and Woods R. "Digital Image Processing", New Jersey: Prentice Hall 1992.

[10] Govindaraju V., Srihari S., and Sher D. "A Computational model for face location", Proc. 3rd Int. Conf. on ComputerVision. 718–721 (1990).

[11] Haritha D. and Satyanarayana Ch. "Performance evaluation of face Recognition using DCT approach", International Conferrence on statistics, probability, operations, Research, Computer Science & allied Areas in conjunction with IISA & ISPS. 86 (2010).

[12] Haritha D., Srinivasa Rao K., and Satyanarayana Ch. "Face recognition algorithm based on doubly truncated Gaussian mixture model using DCT coefficients", International journal of Computer Applications, vol no 39, Issue No. 9, pp.23-28, 2012.

[13] Haritha D., Srinivasa Rao K. and Satyanarayana Ch. "Face recognition algorithm based on doubly truncated Gaussian mixture model using hierarchical clustering algorithm coefficients", International journal of Computer science issues. 9(2), 388-395 (2012).

[14] Hazim Kemal Ekenel and Rainer Stiefelhagen. "Local appearance based face recognition using discrete cosine transform", European Signal Processing Conference. 3-6 (2005).

[15] Kresimin Delac, Mislav Grgic and Marian Stewart Bartlett. "Image Compression in Face Recognition -a Literature Survey", I-Tech, Vienna, Austria: (2008).

[16] Muhammad Almas Anjum. "Improved Face Recognition using Image Resolution Reduction and Optimization of Feature Vector", Ph.D. thesis, National University of Sciences and Technology (NUST) Rawalpindi Pakistan, 2008.

[17] Norman L. Johnson Samuel kotz, N. Balakrishnan. "UNivariate Distributions", volume 1, second edition, New York: wiley student edition 1995.

[18] Qian Tao and Raymond Veldhuis. "Illumination normalization based on simplified local binary patterns for a face verification system", IEEE international Symposium on Biometrics. 1-6 (2007).

[19] Satyanarayana Ch., Haritha D., Sammulal P. and Pratap Reddy L. "Incremental training method for face Recognition using PCA", Proceeding of the international journal of Information processing. 3(1), 13-23 (2009).

[20] Satyanarayana Ch., Haritha D., Sammulal P. and Pratap Reddy L. "updation of face space for face recognition using PCA", Proceedings of the international conference on RF & signal processing system (RSPS-08). 1, 195-20 (2008).

[21] Satyanarayana Ch., Potukuchi D. M. and Pratap Reddy L. "Performance Incremental training method for face Recognition using PCA", Springer, proceeding of the international journal of real image processing. 1(4), 311-327 (2007).

[22] Ch. Satyanarayana, D. Haritha, D. Neelima and B. Kiran kumar, "Dimensionality Reduction of Covariance matrix in PCA for Face Recognition", Proceesings of the International conference on Advances in Mathematics: Historical Developments and Engineering Applications (ICAM 2007). 400-412 (2007).

[23] Ch. Satyanarayana, D. Haritha, P. Sammulal and L. Pratap Reddy, "updation of face space for face recognition using PCA", Proceedings of the international conference on RF & signal processing system (RSPS-08). 1, 195-202 (2008).

[24] Sailaja V., Srinivasa Rao K. and Reddy K.V.V.S. "Text independent Speaker Identification with Doubly Truncated Gaussian Mixture Model", International Journal of Information Technology and Knowledge Management. 2(2), 475-48 (2010).

[25] Zhao W., Chellappa R., and Rosenfeld A. "Face Recognition: A literature survey", ACM Computing surveys, vol.35, pp.399-458, (2003).

[26] M. Ziad M. Hafed and Martin D. Levine. "Face Recognition using Discrete Cosine Transform", Proc. International Journal of Computer Vision. 43(3), 167–188 (2001).

# Towards a Framework for Modelling and Reusing Medical Knowledge in South Africa

[1]Muhandji Kikunga and [2]Obeten Ekabua
Department of Computer Science, North-West University, Mmabatho, Mafikeng, South Africa
{[1]24088935, [2]obeten.ekabua}@nwu.ac.za

**Abstract -** *In today's medical world, there is large amount of information and knowledge that need professionally This information includes patient's medical history, diseases, diagnosis and treatment methods. However, the problem of making this medical knowledge and data sharable over applications and reusable for several purposes is a serious challenge. Though different computer technologies have emerged as leverage in the medical industries, most health institutions are yet to effectively utilize them to manage patients' information and medical knowledge for fast decision making. In South Africa (SA) , there is a rapid development of medical institutions and services , which require effective exchange of patient's medical histories and information. But information exchange among medical information systems is difficult and it can sometimes go against medical ethics of privacy and confidentiality. This poses a great challenge to health-care practitioners as they have to identify a common ground where relevant medical information can be utilized effectively at the right time. Thus, using uniform standards for medical information is indispensable. This paper, proposes a framework based on the possibility theory, including knowledge representation (KR) and the building of a medical knowledge base to be used by the physicians in making diagnostic decisions.*

**Keywords:** Framework, medical, reuse, knowledge, diagnosis, physicians, health-care, information

## 1 Introduction

In today's medical society, the discipline of medicine is known to incorporate massive amounts of existing and ever-increasing medical knowledge and information about patients. This information includes patients' medical history, diseases, diagnostics and treatment methods. As a result, medicine is directly or indirectly becoming more increasingly a science saturated with information and managing this medical knowledge and information is positing serious challenges for health-care practitioners. The major challenge health-care providers or practitioners face is finding and using the relevant information at the right time [1]. Accordingly, knowledge representation (KR) is another area that is used to solve important problems in today's science world especially where the knowledge has to be reasoned out effectively as part of a decision support system. KR which is described within the abundance of existing expert knowledge plays a key role in the medical domain as practically each of its specializations has a constantly growing and interacting number of relevant guidelines. Basically, the long term goal of KR, is the representation of this knowledge in a format that can be used by systems in support of medical decision making. An approach of this undertaking is needed to facilitate systematic representation of different types of medical knowledge that can be used for various types of reasoning [2].

In the medical world today, there are several healthcare systems, and managing a patient in a share-care context is referred to as a knowledge intensive activity. With the knowledge embedded in the systems, health-care providers are able to apply their medical knowledge for making various clinical decisions, such as prognosis, diagnosis, therapeutic related problem solving and prediction treatment effects [3 ,5]. The complex nature of the medical of medical field has resulted in medical knowledge growing continuously and exponentially, which in turn adds to the complexity of existing medical problem solving. Dilemmas are becoming increasingly challenging and failure-prone even for specialists in a highly specialized domain [4]. For instance, conventional medical diagnosis in clinical examinations relies heavily upon physicians' experience and these physicians have to intuitively apply the knowledge based on the symptoms that were found in previous patients.

In everyday practice, medical knowledge grows steadily. Such that, it becomes increasingly difficult for physicians to keep up with essential information gained from the practice. Thus, for physicians to be able to be quick and accurately diagnose a patient there is a critical need for computer technologies [6, 11, 12]. Computer technologies have become important tools in assisting firstly inexperienced physicians in making medical diagnosis and secondly experienced physicians in supporting complex decisions, retrieving medical information as well as making decisions to overcome medical complications that are prevalent in today's world [1, 7]. An example of this technology is the Medical Diagnostic System.

In South Africa, the development of medical services, scaling up, grouping of medical institutions, the exchange of patients' medical histories and information is increasingly gaining momentum. In particular, the area of patients' medical histories and information is facing a huge challenge due to the fact that, the existing medical information systems are heterogeneous in development, architecture and suppliers. Consequently, information exchange among medical information systems is difficult (i.e the manual method of exchange of patients' information). This also goes against medical practices of privacy and confidentiality [8]. This means that managing the medical knowledge and information is a serious challenge for the health-care practitioners in SA. The underlying problem is to identify a common ground, where relevant medical information can be utilized at the right time and effectively. Hence, applying uniform standards for medical information in SA is crucial.

In this paper, our objective is to provide a solution to the existing problems in SA medical services, particularly, effective management of patients' medical information and medical knowledge for the practitioners. Our intent is to connect both privately and publicly held relevant information such as patients' personal data, medical reference books, websites, research information and statistical report to a general medical information system in order to effectively assist health-care providers to make consistent and reliable decisions. This research, therefore intends to develop a generic framework and its associated system to enhance the modelling and reuse of medical knowledge for medical diagnosis in SA. The rest of the paper is organized as follows: section 1 gives the introduction, 2 is the literature survey, 3 outlines the research problem statement, and 4 describes the proposed solution. Accordingly, sections 5 and 6 are the research work in progress and conclusions respectively.

## 2 Literature Survey

Various kinds of research have been done in the field of medical knowledge and different approaches have been used in order to solve the problems that the health-care practitioners are facing today and these are discussed as follows:

Uzoka et. al [9] designed a framework for the development of low cost cell phone based application that employs an inference mechanism based on Fuzzy logic and analytic hierarchy process (AHP), in the diagnosis of common tropical diseases such as typhoid fever, diarrheal diseases, pneumonia, Tuberculosis, malaria and amebiais. The system offered patients the ability to just enter their symptoms on the cell phone and receive immediate advice on a preliminary diagnosis of the system. The advice that the patients would get from the system would be either to buy non-prescription drugs from the pharmacy, to visit a physician's to undergo an examination or to do nothing and report the progress of the symptoms within a particular time frame.

Shujun et. al [10] developed a Medical Diagnosis System for the health- care to be available at any time and any place. They designed a context-awareness framework and introduced UPPAAL as a new tool for modeling, simulating and verifying a real-time system in the medical diagnosis system. This system was using a context Aware Database that was responsible for storing information of doctors, nurses, patients and diseases, completing context information processing. The Database was able to store patients' information; Doctors' information; nurses' information; relations between doctors and patients, and between nurses and patients; the trust- worthiness of patient to the doctors and nurses, and disease diagnosis. They stated that their model of Medical Diagnosis System was still simple and that it had to be improved and extended in future.

Another researcher in this field is B. Iantovics [11, 16, 17] who developed a Blackboard –Based Medical Diagnosis System (BMDS) for solving medical diagnosis problems that were based on combination of illness. The system allowed physicians with a medical specialization plan treatment, to cure illnesses that were in advanced stages. However, the system had some limitation because the treatment to cure illnesses in the less advanced stages was not included in the system. BMDS system is composed of medical expert system agents and different classes of assistant agents. The system showed that medical expert agents can be used successfully as members of diagnosis multi-agent system. It also stated that Medical expert agents required future improvement in order to increase their autonomy and flexibility in problem solving.

In another research, he proposed a CMDS (Contract Net Based Medical Diagnosis System) that can solve medical problems randomly. The system allowed medical expert system agents and physicians to be capable of elaborating medical diagnosis. It composed of physicians, medical expert system agents and assistant agents. The physicians and artificial medical agents are limited in diagnostic knowledge. The advantage that CMDS has over BMDS is in its autonomy and flexibility in handling medical diagnosis problems.

Therefore, based on the existing knowledge and information, our aim is to take advantage of the existing knowledge and develop a generic framework and its associated system to enhance the modelling and reuse of medical knowledge for medical diagnosis in SA.

# 3 Problem Statement

In the face of rapid development of medical services, scaling up and grouping of medical institutions in SA is becoming increasingly obvious. As a result, between hospitals, hospitals and medical insurance organizations frequently require to exchange patient's medical histories and information. But because most medical information systems are developed independently by different software vendors, the heterogeneity in platform layer, system and data layer frequently leads to the challenge of information exchange among medical information systems even in the same hospitals. In a worst case scenario, a patient's medical information may be spread out over a number of different medical institutes which do not interoperate against the backdrop of privacy and confidentiality. This usually leads to most SA medical institutes or organizations to exchange patient's information through manual methods which are insufficient, unsafe and operate against the rule of medical practice of privacy and confidentiality [8]. Therefore, managing the medical knowledge and information becomes an increasing challenge for the health-care practitioners. Medicine as a science that incorporates an enormous amount of existing and ever-increasing medical knowledge and information about patient's medical history, diseases, diagnostic, and treatment methods is necessarily becoming a science of information [1, 8]. Therefore, using uniform standardized methods for medical information in SA is imperative [8].

The real problem faced by the patients and health care providers is to identify a common ground where relevant medical information can be accessed and utilized at the right time [12]. The main goal is to connect the privately held patient personal data, such as medical record, diagnosis, treatment plan and the outcome of treatment to a general public medical information system, medical reference books, websites, research information and statistics report so as to make consistent and reliable decisions [1, 12, 18]. This research therefore intends to advance this knowledge in the context of the South African medical environment by developing a generic framework and its associated system to enhance the modelling and the reuse of medical knowledge for medical diagnosis in SA.

# 4 Proposed Solution

Heath-care is a special commodity in developing economies, in both economically and socially terms. SA is not an exception to this claim. For many developing and under-developed countries, health care is a problem on a priority scale dominated by poverty, a growing population and rural to urban migration. Most of the SA population lives in rural areas where they receive insufficient health services, because most health services are concentrated in the urban areas [13]. For this reason, it becomes a challenge for health care practitioners to share medical information among different hospitals, prompting exchange to be carried out manually. In order to discontinue the practice that goes against patient's privacy and confidentiality, we propose to build a generic framework that will be used for the modeling and reusing of medical knowledge and a medical diagnosis system that will offer physicians or health care practitioners all the required information to get adequate medical diagnosis.

The proposed medical diagnosis system will assist the physicians in the following ways:

- It will consist of a central database/server for keeping the medical record of the patients and the diagnosis records. The medical record of the patients will consist of the patient's information such as name, address, identity number, marital status and unique health care medical care that allows the physicians to have access to the patient's information in the system and the diagnosis record will consist of the information that will allow the doctors/physicians to make diagnostic decisions.

- The system will improve in poor medical record keeping for keeping patient's information manually is very difficult to manage. As patients files can be misplaced or get lost. This can lead to the patients' information being exposed to any person and this goes against the medical practices of privacy and confidentiality. Therefore designing this system will make it easy to manage patient's information Since this information will be kept in digital format which makes it difficult or impossible to be misplaced or get lost and eliminates exposure to anyone else except authorized people (physicians/doctors) who will have access to patient information through a login account to log onto the system.

- The system will improve the existing disease management and imprecision of medical diagnosis. It will assist physicians to manage, control, and understand the condition of the disease, make a precise disease diagnosis, provide prevention, provide better treatment of the disease and finally improve the quality of health care.
- The physicians/ doctors will be able to access and share information stores in the database to make a precise medical diagnosis decision. The information in the system and can be reused anytime and anywhere which then improves knowledge sharing among physicians.
- With the designed system, it will be easy to make statistical reports on the prevalent common diseases that people suffer in a particular province of SA. It will also be easy to monitor the patients and to know how many patients are improving in terms of recovery. The system will also be able to give information on how many patients complied with the consecution appointments with the doctor or not.

# 5 Work in Progress

This part consists of the design of the system and how the system is going to function. This is designed as follows:

## 5.1 Data Collection

The collection of the data is the first phase in designing the system as it helps in the building of the proposed medical diagnosis system. This phase involves interaction with medical practitioners in order to obtain experimental knowledge on the diagnosis of the diseases. This is done through structured interviews and questionnaire. A major aspect of data collection is the process of establishing the significance of specific symptoms of the diseases. Usually, a combinatorial analysis of symptoms determines possible diseases and is obtained through the physicians' experience in the diagnosis of diseases. At this stage, we have to interview many different experienced physicians from different hospitals to get a better understanding of the diseases and their symptoms, how they can be prevented and treated and also getting some information of the history of each disease.

## 5.2 Framework and Medical Diagnosis System Design

The medical diagnosis system is designed as a web application with 3 tier architecture that is shown below:

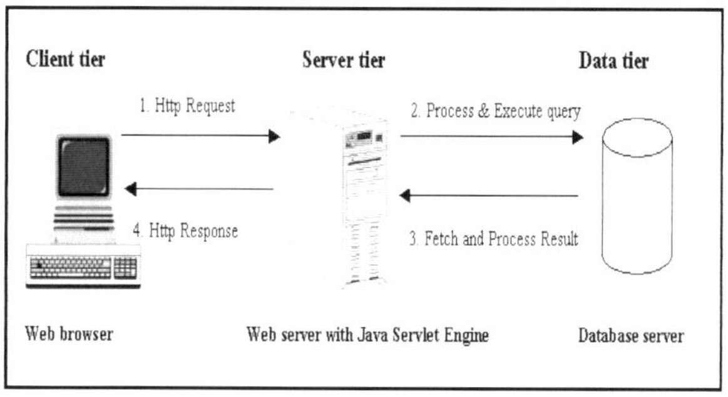


**Fig. 1:** The 3-tier Architecture

The 3 tier Architecture consists of:

*1) The client tier:* this one consists of a web browser as user interface. It receives input from the users and sends a request to the server tier.
*2) The Server tier:* receives and processes the request, passing it to the database tier (MySQL server)
*3) The database Server:* retrieves the data and sends the data back to the server tier. Finally the server tier receives the data, executes the MySQL –query and passes the results to the client tier. The design of the framework/medical diagnosis system is shown below:

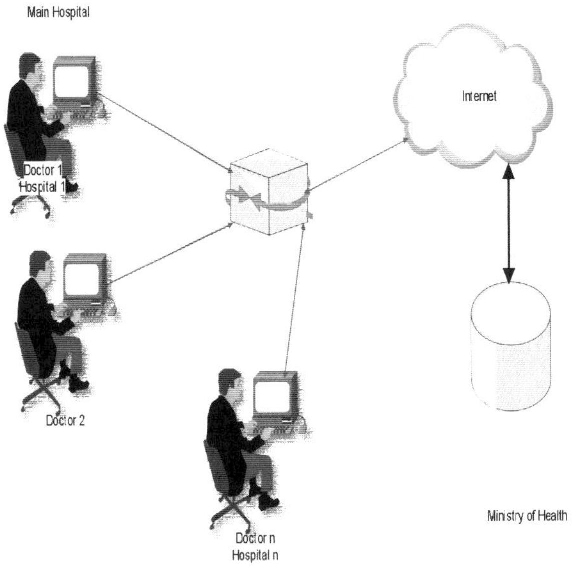


**Fig. 2:** The Architecture of the Framework

The structure of the proposed framework consists of four main components:

*1) The Doctor's Interface:* The Desktop/laptop computer serves as the doctor's interface to send and receive information from the central database. In this system there are three different hospitals with each doctor sending and receiving data from the database through the internet. In order for each doctor to send data from their desktop/laptop computer into the central database, the data need to pass through the gateway, which in turn is sent via the network (internet) onto the database. By the same token, if the physicians/doctors need to retrieve any information from the central database, that information needs to pass through the internet via the gateway to the doctor's interface which the doctor can then use for consultation purposes.

*2) The Gateway:* The gateway is a node that allows physicians to gain entrance into a network on the Internet. The gateway serves as the bridge between the Internet and the doctor's interface (computer). In order for the computer to receive information from the central database through the internet, there should be a gateway or an entrance. Furthermore, in order for the information to be sent to the database through the internet, the gateway is also there to link the computer to the internet. Even though the gateway gives the doctors access into the network, it is not every person who is authorized to enter into the network; only authorized people are authorized into the network. Therefore, the gateway is also being used as a firewall to prevent any unauthorized persons to have access into the network since the integrity, confidentiality, and privacy of medical records is highly required to protect the patient's information.

*3) The Internet:* The internet is a global network that connects millions of computers. This system shows that there are three different computers in three different hospitals that are connected to the internet in order to exchange data in the database. Here the internet plays a crucial role because no computer can send or receive any information from the database or vise versa. Therefore we can say that the internet connects each computer to the central database or the central database to the computers and vice visa. The type of internet browser that will be used in each hospital is the Microsoft Internet Explorer. It is only through this, that doctors/physicians will be able to send or receive information in the database.

*4) The Central database Server:* The database server is located in the South African Health Ministry or any government agency responsible for keeping medical records. The Health Ministry ensures integrity, confidentiality and privacy of medical records. The central database will store both the hospitals information (patient's information, doctors' information, the administrator's information) and the medical diagnosis system. The patients' information will consist of patient's personal details (name, surname, id number and unique heath care number) and the patient's medical diagnosis details (disease diagnosed by the doctor). The doctors' information will be such as full name, surname, identity number and field of specialisation. The administrator will be responsible for registering both patients and doctors in the hospital and also create unique health care number for patients that will allow the doctors to retrieve their information for consultation and create accounts for doctors that will consist of username and password for them to able to log into the system to retrieve both the patient's information through their unique health care numbers and retrieve the medical diagnosis information to make a diagnosis decision. The medical diagnosis system will consist of information of particular diseases (Tuberculosis, HIV/AIDS, cancer, Malaria, etc...), disease symptoms (headache, fever, weight loss, night sweat, etc…), prevention of the disease (advice from doctors to the patient such as health alimentation, exercise, no drinking/smoking) and treatment/ prescription for medication. The administrator will only be able to view, update, modify or delete the patient's personal details but he is not allowed to access/view the patient's medical diagnosis information in order to safeguard confidentiality and privacy such as only doctors will be allowed to have access to all the patients' information.

## 6 Conclusion

The effective management of medical knowledge and information has become a serious challenge for health-care providers especially when it comes to finding and using the relevant information at the right time in which SA is not an exception. In this paper, we have proposed a framework for building a medical knowledge-based system to be used by physicians in order to make fast diagnostic decisions. SA is faced with rapid development of medical services and institutions which goes with effective exchange of patient's medical histories and information. However, the exchange of information between medical information systems is always difficult if not impossible and sometimes goes against medical practices of privacy and confidentiality. The proposed framework is designed to solve the ugly situation faced by health-care practitioners and tends to introduce uniform standard for medical information handling. With the implementation of the proposed system, medical knowledge will be utilized for effective diagnostic decisions and patient's medical information accessed and shared across medical institutions while preserving the privacy and confidentiality principles.

## 7 References

[1] L. Aleksovska-stojkovska, S. Loskovska, "Clinical Decision Support System Medical Knowledge Acquisition and Representation Methods, "in electro/Information Technology (EIT), IEEE International Conference on Digital Object identifier, 2010, pp. 1-6.

[2] A. Jovic, M. Prcela, D.Gamberger, "Ontologies in Medical Knowledge Representation, " in Information Technology Interface, 29th International Conference on Digital Object Identifier, 2007, pp. 535-540.

[3] A. Aguilera, A. Subero, "A multi-agent architecture and system for dynamic medical knowledge acquisition, "in Computational Intelligence for Modeling Control & Automation, International Conference on Digital object identifier , 2008, pp.1165-1170.

[4] A Kabakcioglu, "Artificial intelligence for medical knowledge representation/reasoning/ acquisition," Processing of International Biomedical Engineering days, 1992, pp. 186-191.

[5] G. Lanzola, S. Falasconi and M. Steffanelli, M "Cooperative Software Agents for Patient Management", Artificial Intelligent medicine, 5th Conference on Artificial Intelligence in Medicine in Europe, 1995, vol. 934.

[6] P. Meesad, GG.Yen "Combined Numerical and Linguistic Knowledge Representation and its Application to medical Diagnosis", Systems, Man and Cybernetics, Part A, Humans, IEEE Transaction on Digital object identifier, 2003, pp. 206-222.

[7] E. Coiera, "Guide to Health Informatics", Arnold, London, October 2003, (2nd Edition), Chapter 25.

[8] C. caiping, W. Huijing "A Framework for Medical Information Integration Based on ontology and web services," Information Engineering and Computer Science (ICIECS), 2nd International Conference, 2010, pp.1-4.

[9] F.M.E. Uzoka,J Osuji, F.O Alaji, O.U Obot, " A Framework for Cell Phone Diagnosis and Management of Priority Tropical Diseases, " IST-Africa Conference Proceedings, 2011, pp. 1-13.

[10] Z. Shujun, W.Kaiyu, Y.Zongyuan, " Modelling and Verifying of Medical Diagnosis system Based on Context-awareness Framework," in Frontier of Computer Science and Technology (FCST), Fifth International Conference on Digital Object Identifier, 2010, pp. 299-304.

[11] B. Iantovic "The CMDS Medical Diagnosis System" symbolic and Numeric Algorithms for scientific Computing, SYNASC 9th International Symposium, 2007, pp. 246- 253.

[12] H. Lieberman, C. Mason Media Laboratory, MIT, Cambridge, MA, USA, University of California, Berkeley, CA, USA, "Intelligent-Agent Software for Medicine" Stud HealthTechno, 2002, pp. 80:99- 109.

[13] Michael O. Kachienga, "Challenges of Managing Telehealth Technology in South Africa",IEMC Conference, Europe, 2008, pp. 1

[14] L.P.Seka et al. "Computer assisted medical diagnosis using the web" Int. J. Med. inform, vol. 47, no 1-2, pp. 51-56, 1997.

[15] G.P.K Economou, et al. "A new concept toward Computer-aided medical diagnosis- a prototype implementation addressing pulmonary diseases", IEEE Trans. Inform. Technol.Biomed, , vol. 5, pp.55-66, March 2001.

[16] B. Iantovics "A novel diagnosis system specialized in difficult medical diagnosis problem solving", Processing of

the emergent Properties in Naturals and Artificial Dynamical Systems, A workshop within European Conference on Complex Systems. Aziz-Alaoui, M.A Bertelle, C. (Eds), Le Havre University Press, Paris, 2005, pp. 107-112.

[17] B. Iantovics "A novel diagnosis system specialized in difficult medical diagnosis problem solving", Processing of the emergent Properties in Naturals and Artificial Dynamical Systems, A workshop within European Conference on Complex Systems. Aziz-Alaoui, M.A Bertelle, C. (Eds), Le Havre University Press, Paris, 2005, pp. 107-112.

[18] D. Gamberger et al. "Medical Knowledge representation within Heartfaid platform" In Proc. of Biostec, International Joint Conference on Biomedical Engineering Systems and Technologies, 2008, pp.205-217.

# OEEM Taxonomy- A Novel Layered-Based Energy Efficiency Taxonomy for ICT Organizations

***Girish Bekaroo*†*, Chandradeo Bokhoree*‡ *& Colin Pattinson*‡‡**

† School of Science and Technology,
Middlesex University (Mauritius Branch Campus)

‡ School of Sustainable Development and Tourism,
University of Technology, Mauritius

‡‡ Faculty of Arts, Environment & Technology,
Leeds Metropolitan University, UK

## ABSTRACT

*The global climate change effects being faced around the world plus the effects of global recession and rising energy costs is compelling organizations to save costs. One of the effective ways which is beneficial to both organizations and the natural environment is towards going green. In the process of going green, it is important to be able to effectively manage energy use within ICT organizations. However, due to the complex nature of an organization, managing energy efficiency can only be simplified by categorizing energy efficiency via the adoption of an appropriate taxonomy. This paper formulates a taxonomy for energy efficiency management within ICT organizations, referred to as OEEM Taxonomy, using the layered approach, and is based on the main areas of energy consumption within such organizations. This paper also elaborates on the method and preliminary experimentation conducted within one ICT organization and also discusses on the results and feedback obtained on the proposed six-layer energy efficiency taxonomy.*

## KEYWORDS

OEEM Taxonomy, Energy Efficiency, Energy Consumption Analysis, Layered Approach, ICT Organisations.

## INTRODUCTION

The rising energy expenses along with the adverse effects of energy production and the increase in climate change impacts have been compelling businesses and organizations to go green (Citrix, 2008). Even though many studies have been done during recent years towards going green, the work concentrated more on power management, optimisation and the formulation of energy efficiency metrics. Today, many energy efficiency metrics and measurement techniques are available and research in these areas are continuously being conducted by researchers and organisations including Green Grid. However, management of energy efficiency of an organisation is a complex process due to the various contributing factors which can affect the energy efficiency within an organisation (Bekaroo, Bokhoree & Pattinson, 2013). Similarly, the management of energy efficiency metrics is a complex process due to the existence of linked and duplicate metrics. There is no standardized way for representing and summarizing the metrics within organizations (Wang & Khan, 2011). As a simplification process for the management of the energy efficiency within organisations, a taxonomy for energy efficiency management is deemed important (Wang & Khan, 2011).

Taxonomies, which are basically classification systems for the identification of content types and the relationships between these content, are important as guide especially when conducting and synthesizing research. They help to facilitate the evaluation of newly proposed constructs (Corno, et al., 2002). Also, as stated by Bailey (1994), "*Classification is arguably one of the most central and generic of all our conceptual exercises...without classification, there could be no advanced conceptualization, reasoning, language, data analysis, or for that matter, social science research*". A taxonomy acts as a reference point for further analysis given that an organization is a large entity in itself and there are many items (e.g. computers, building, staff, etc) within which energy efficiency management is important (Corno, et al., 2002). Individually managing the energy efficiency of each item can greatly simplify the energy efficiency management within organization and also better lead to energy consumption reduction within the same organization. As such, this paper attempts to develop an energy efficiency taxonomy for ICT organisations based on the main areas of energy consumption within such organisations before describing the methods and results of the preliminary experimentation conducted.

## Review of Existing Energy Efficiency Taxonomies

Different studies have been conducted in the past to simplify energy efficiency management in the form of taxonomies. One such work is by Beloglazov et al. (2011) for classifying power/energy within computing systems into static power management and dynamic power management (see Fig. 1). Static power management contains optimization methods applied at design time to circuit, logic, architectural and system levels where as dynamic power management include methods and strategies for run-time system behavior adaptation according to hardware or software resource requirements or system states. However, the problem with this taxonomy is that the focus is on power management and that many other areas (including building, business processes and employees) are missing for its adaptation with ICT organisations.

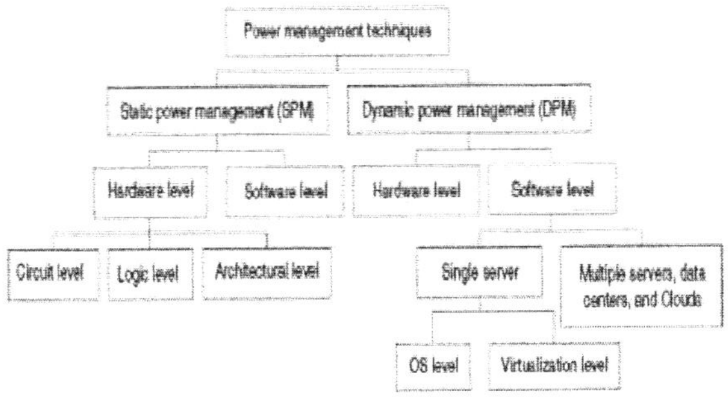


Fig. 1. Taxonomy by Beloglazov et al (2011)

Similarly, Wang & Khan (2011) attempted to categorise green computing performance metrics within data centres into basic metrics and extended performance metrics. The basic metrics included green house gas, humidity, thermal metrics and power/energy metrics where as the extended performance metrics included multiple data centre indicators and total cost of ownership as shown in Fig. 2.

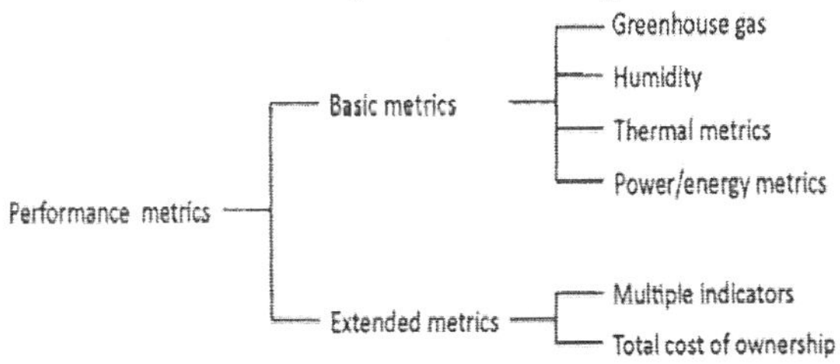


Fig. 2. Taxonomy by Wang & Khan (2011)

Furthermore, different green maturity models adopt energy efficiency taxonomies for energy efficiency management. For instance, the green maturity model proposed by Accenture manages energy efficiency in 5 different levels namely end user working practices, office environment equipment, office infrastructure/data centre, procurement and corporate citizenship (Nunn, 2008). Similarly, the Green IT maturity model proposed by Infosys manages energy efficiency in terms of company's data centre and facilities, end user computing, asset lifecycle, IT service management and people practices (Desai & Bhatia, 2011).

## Energy Consumption Within ICT Organizations

The existing taxonomies showed limitations in terms of the classification areas for energy efficiency management. A novel approach towards energy efficiency management adopted in this study, is the consideration of the main areas of energy consumption within ICT organisations. Micro-level analysis of energy consumption within ICT organisations showed that energy is consumed in the following main areas (Curtis 2008; Bekaroo, Bokhoree & Pattinson, 2013):

1. *Power utilising devices*

There is a close relationship between power and energy where power is the system with which energy is harnessed. Several electrical and electronic devices are present within ICT organisations that consume electricity. This category can be further broken down into critical computational systems, cooling, power conversion and hostelling (Curtis, 2008). Critical computational systems involve power consumption from computer systems, servers, networks and storage devices where as cooling systems involve the removal of waste heat generated by the use of the different electrical and electronic devices. Power conversion involves energy consumption from uninterrupted power supplies and power distribution units; and hostelling is about energy consumption from everything else not included in the above main categories - examples include lighting and building overheads.

2. *The building*

Buildings provide shelter to organisations and is an important source of energy consumption (Bekaroo, Bokhoree & Pattinson, 2013). Different factors including placement, design, and construction materials used can affect its energy efficiency.

3. *Business Processes*

Energy is consumed in doing work during business processes, which are referred to as the collection of tasks designed in order to produce a specific output (Bekaroo, Bokhoree & Pattinson, 2013). Examples of business processes include accountability process, procurement process and marketing process.

4. *Business Products and Services*

Business products and services are the basis of profit-making for organisations and during the product creation or maintenance process, work is done and hence energy is consumed (Bekaroo, Bokhoree & Pattinson, 2013).

5. *The employees*

By doing work during working days within the ICT organization, energy is consumed by all the employees and the amount of energy consumed depends on the amount of work done by individual employees (Bekaroo, Bokhoree & Pattinson, 2013).

Having identified the different main sources of energy consumption within ICT organisations, the next step was to formulate the taxonomy.

## A Six Layer Taxonomy for Improved Energy Efficiency Management

### Taxonomy Requirements

As a starting point to create the energy efficiency taxonomy, gathering the taxonomy requirements was of utmost importance. These requirements help to better define the criteria to which the proposed taxonomy should adhere to. As such, the identified requirements for the proposed taxonomy are:

*1. Completeness*

The taxonomy should not miss out important components in the measurement process which would cause inaccurate energy consumption values. In other words, the metrics set should be scientifically accurate and used precisely.

*2. Easy to manage*

The taxonomy should be easy to manage in the sense that it should not be having too few or too many areas. A taxonomy with a small number of areas means that the energy consumption factors are not split enough and will cause measurement to be difficult. Having too many areas in turn will be difficult to manage. Therefore, the number of energy efficiency areas should be reasonable.

*3. Independent Layers*

The areas in the taxonomy should be independent, meaning that each area should only be responsible in the management of related issues to that area only. Following this taxonomy, the total energy consumed within an ICT organization should ideally be the sum of the energy consumed at the different levels of the taxonomy.

*4. Adaptability*

The taxonomy being used should be adaptable to varying types of ICT organizations and should be independent of organizational factors including geographic location, size, years of existence, and sub-field.

### Layered Model Approach

To better suit the above defined requirements, a layered model was adopted. The layered model approach uses a hierarchy of subcategories where the top levels are normally broad and become more specific when going down. This type of taxonomy is also based on the 'divide and conquer' analogy where a large or complex task is better handled through splitting it into smaller subtasks. It has a rigid and strict structure and each layer worries only about the layer directly above it or the one directly below it. This type of taxonomy is particularly useful when wanting to allow information sources to be chosen from specific categories. However, the main problems of its adoption is that the entire taxonomy has to be created and this is time consuming especially when data has to be mapped to another type of taxonomy. The OSI 7-layer reference model is one of the most common examples of the adoption of the layered approach and is still used as a framework to teach networking (Aune, 2004). In this approach, the output of one layer provides the input to the second layer which models interaction between the different layers and ideally, changes in one layer should not require changes to other layers.

### The Proposed Six-Layer Taxonomy

The proposed energy efficiency taxonomy, called OEEM Taxonomy, is based on the different main areas of energy consumption as discussed earlier. As such, using the layered approach, each pillar of energy consumption within an organisation is turned into an independent layer within the taxonomy. These different layers include ICT layer, Office Environment Layer, Product/Service Layer, Business Process Layer, Business Process Layer and Building Layer. A pictorial representation of the taxonomy is depicted in Fig. 3 where the different taxonomy layers are connected based on the requirements defined earlier.

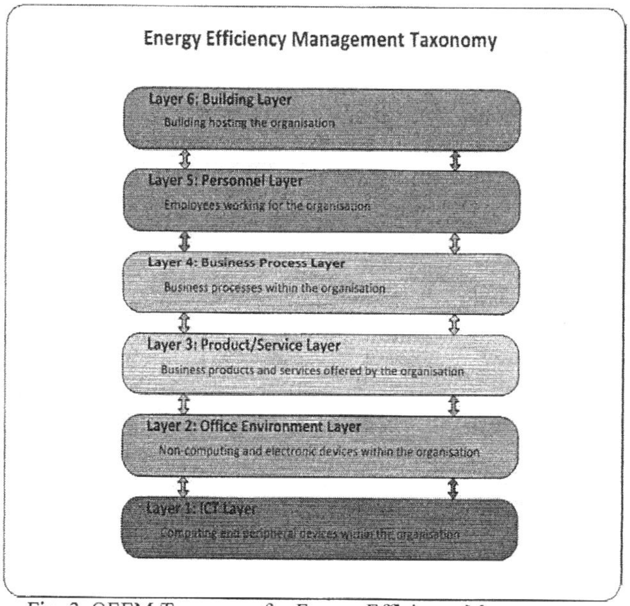


Fig. 3. OEEM Taxonomy for Energy Efficiency Management

In Fig. 3, as per the layered approach, the lowest layer is Layer 1 and specifically manages energy efficiency of ICT equipments and resources. Moving up the layers makes energy efficiency broader until the building layer. The taxonomy layers are further described in the next sections.

*Layer 1: ICT Layer*

The ICT Layer is the first layer of the OEEM Taxonomy and encompasses energy efficiency of computers and its associated components or peripheral devices used for the purpose of computing and data transmission. In more specific terms, the different energy efficiency components for which the ICT layer is responsible for is better depicted in Fig. 4.

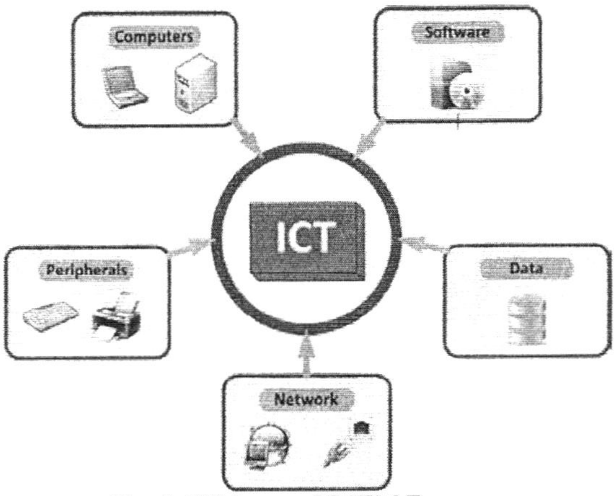


Fig. 4. ICT Layer of OEEM Taxonomy

The components represented by the ICT layer include:

*1. Computer*

This component is about the energy efficiency of the different computers present in the organisation or in its data centres within the same building. Four types of computers are commonly used within organisations include microcomputers, minicomputers, mainframes and supercomputers. Microcomputers are the most common types of computers used in the form of desktop computers, laptops, tablets and personal digital assistants within organisations (O'Leary, 2009). Minicomputers are more powerful than microcomputers and are used as servers for email, file-sharing or web-hosting. Mainframes are mostly used in banks or large ICT companies and have higher processing power and storage space as compared to micro and mini computers. Supercomputers are the most powerful type of computers and is used in very large organisations or for research purposes.

*2. Peripherals*

In addition to computers, the energy efficiency of associated hardware and peripheral devices is also important. Typical peripheral devices include input and output devices, in the form of keyboards, pointing devices, printers, scanners, web cameras, monitors, etc, along with the energy efficiency of the storage and memory capabilities of the computer system via hard disks and optical disks.

*3. Network*

Furthermore, the ICT layer is also responsible for the energy efficiency management for networking and data transmission. It deals with the energy efficiency of transmission media in the form of wired based twisted-pairs, coaxial cables and optical fibre; and wireless based transmission in the form of radio waves, micro waves and infra-red. In terms of networking, the ICT Layer manages the energy efficiency of networking devices which permit interconnection of computers and devices for communication and sharing. Examples of such networking devices include hubs, bridges, switches, modems, firewalls, and routers, among others.

*4. Software*

The next component of the ICT Layer is about the energy efficiency of software and instructions being operated by the computer system. Software is defined as a set of instructions or procedures that are meant to perform different tasks on a computer system and while being in front of computers, users spend most of their time utilising software. In general, computer software systems can be purchased off the shelf as ready-made software or can also be designed and developed by software development companies and free-lance software engineers as tailor made software. Software used in computer systems can also be classified into two main types where the energy efficiency of both types is important. These two types of software include system software and application software. System software helps to abstract hardware features of a system. It can be in the form of operating systems (e.g. Windows Vista, Windows 7 and Linux), device drivers, and disk formatting tools, among others. Application software are referred to as computer programs. This type of software is commonly used by users in order to perform different functions or tasks including web browsing, word processing, etc.

*5. Data*

This category within the ICT Layer is about energy efficiency of data or information. Unlike software, which is a set of instructions, data is the remaining part of software which is not considered as program code. The energy efficiency of data is important within the ICT layer since much redundant data leads to increased energy consumption and proper data management can improve the energy efficiency of an organisation (Brocade, 2007).

*Layer 2: Office Environment Layer*

The second layer of the OEEM Taxonomy is about energy efficiency of non-computing and electronic devices present within the organisation. These devices serve for the main purpose of lighting, cooling, heating, storage, among others. Devices within this layer do not form part of the four types of computer, or associated peripheral devices, as discussed in the first layer. Main examples of office environment electrical and electronic devices include air conditioners, lamps, heaters, etc. Among these devices, cooling or heating devices are the largest power consumers (Nuventix, 2008). Cooling is not only used in server rooms but also to regularise working temperature within buildings in countries with average temperatures higher than room temperature.

Similarly, in cold countries, heating facilities are provided within working environments which is again an energy guzzling monster.

Other devices forming part in this layer include embedded systems including microwave, televisions, kettles, alarm systems, etc, which are now very common within organisation and are made available to staffs for daily use. These devices do not consume big amount of energy as air conditioners but if regarded for a longer period of time, energy efficiency of such devices do have a significant importance. Also, in case an organisation has special machinery or electronic non-computing equipment (e.g. for a gym in the company premises), energy efficiency of all these equipments are categorised in the Office Environment Layer as well.

***Layer 3: Product/Service Layer***

The aim of most businesses is to produce and sell for a profit, goods, products, solutions, and services in order to fulfil the needs, wants or desires of a society. The Product/Service Layer is the third layer of the OEEM Taxonomy and is concerned with energy efficiency management of the product or service offered by the organisation. Both a business product and service lifecycle have got their life-cycle and throughout their lifecycle, energy efficiency management is of utmost importance.

For a product, the lifecycle goes through several phases starting from its conception, through design and fabrication, to service and disposal, as shown in Fig. 5. The management of the life-cycle of a product is also known as the product lifecycle management.

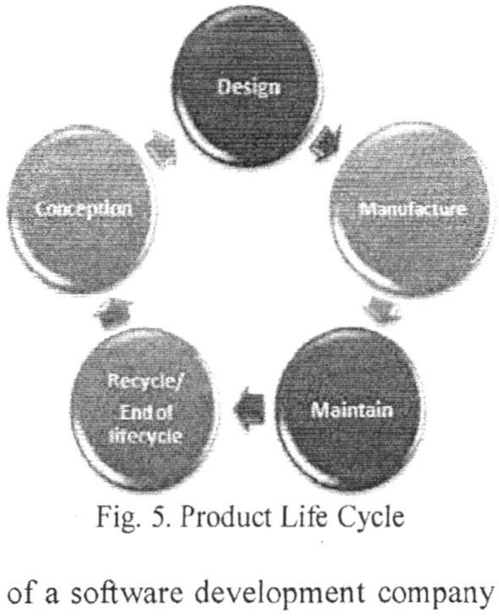


Fig. 5. Product Life Cycle

In the case of a software development company specialised in software solutions, the product lifecycle is in the form of the adopted software lifecycle for the business products of the company. A typical software lifecycle starts with the requirements engineering phase followed by the design and architecture phase, development and testing phase to maintenance and support. An example of a software lifecycle is shown in Fig. 6. Several software development process models do exist today in order to better represent the different stages in the lifecycle of a software and the Product/Service Layer of the taxonomy manages the energy efficiency of all the different stages through the lifecycle of the product, in the form of software in this case.

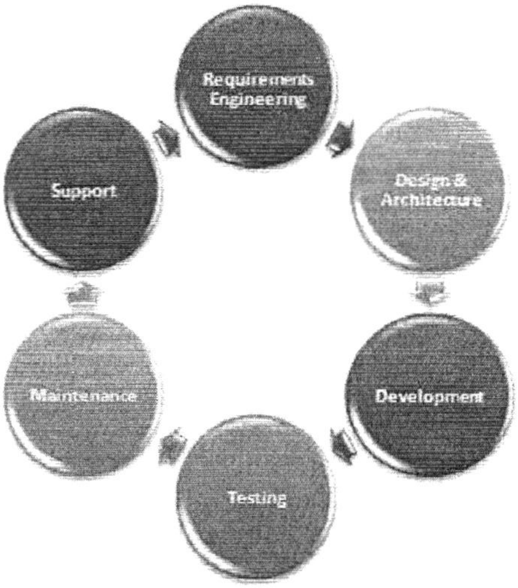


Fig. 6. Example of Software Lifecycle

Similar to business products of a company, the services being offered also have a life cycle throughout which energy efficiency is an important factor. A typical service lifecycle has got the plan, deliver, operate and manage phase and is depicted in Fig. 7. For example, an ICT company offering disaster recovery services to another organization has to start with the plan phase where the service is planned and optimized in order to support the goals and objectives of the organization. Then, the service is effectively developed, deployed in the delivery phase before actually the operation of the service, during which necessary support and maintenance is also provided in order to meet the client's business needs and expectations. Finally, the service has to be managed in terms of operating procedures and best practices in order to make sure that ICT investment delivers the expected business value at an acceptable level of risk where risk, compliance, change and configurations are identified.

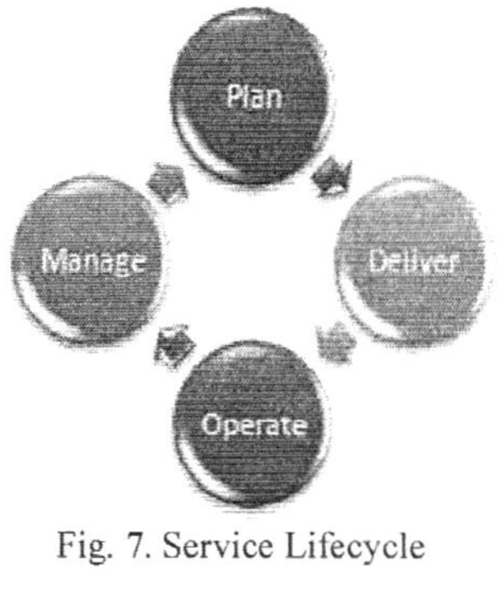


Fig. 7. Service Lifecycle

***Layer 4: Business Process Layer***

The Business Process Layer is all about energy efficiency management of the way work is done during business processes in an organisation. A business process, also called a business method, is a set of interconnected, structured activities or tasks performed in order to produce a specific service or product. Each process normally includes one or multiple required inputs where inputs and outputs can be received from or sent to other business processes, other organisational units, or internal and external stakeholders. In general, common examples of business processes include the ordering of goods from a supplier, processing insurance claim or creating a marketing plan amongst others. Within ICT organisations, the three main types of business process include management process, operational process and supporting process and the Business Process Layer deals with their energy efficiency. These types of business processes are better described as follows:

1. *Management processes*

These include processes that govern management of the organisation. Examples include corporate governance, strategic management, etc.

2. *Operational processes*

These include processes that constitute the core business and create the primary value stream. Purchasing, manufacturing, advertising and marketing, sales, among others, form part of operational processes.

3. *Supporting processes*

These are processes that support the core processes of organisations. Common examples include accounting, procurement, recruitment, and technical support, among others.

***Layer 5: Personnel Layer***

The Personnel Layer accounts for the energy efficiency of the personnel within an organisation. People are the most important part of an organisation and or information system and as discussed in the second chapter, energy is consumed while employees are working. Within organisations, two main groups of employees are present based on computer usage capabilities. These include:

• *ICT users*

This category of users utilise computers during most part of a normal working day. Such profiles in organisations include staffs from the software engineering team, support team, accounting team, management team and administration team, among others.

• *Non-ICT Users*

This category of staffs do not utilise computers during most part of a normal working day. Profiles include drivers, messengers, cleaners, etc, who also form an important part of an organisation.

Both the ICT and the non-ICT personnel consume energy while working and as such, the Personnel Layer manages energy efficiency of both the ICT users and Non-ICT Users. Employees behaviour can make a big difference to energy efficiency of the whole organisation since employees are the driving force of the whole organisation and are responsible for management of the building, business products and services, business processes, electronic and computing devices and even other personnel. For this reason, in case energy efficiency of the whole organisation is to be improved, one starting point is the energy efficiency of its employees.

***Layer 6: Building Layer***

Buildings are very important to businesses as they serve a shelter to the employees to weather conditions and also provide a living space with privacy and comfort whereby also providing a store for belongings. As described earlier, buildings are an important source of energy consumption depending on the design and construction factors taken into consideration during the building process. Businesses can have their own building(s) or can share the building(s) with other companies or businesses within the same tower.

The Building Layer of the proposed six-layer taxonomy deals with energy efficiency of the building in which the organisation is placed or hosted. It is the top most layer in the taxonomy, and is responsible for the energy efficiency of the physical infrastructure, thermal flow, operation and maintenance of the building (or part of) owned by the organisation. Also, in case the building is shared with other businesses or companies, then the company has to manage the energy efficiency of the offices or floors being shared and not the whole building. Furthermore, if an organisation has more than one building in which it operates, then the energy efficiency of the different buildings have to be separately taken into consideration for the organisation to move towards energy efficiency.

## PRE-EXPERIMENTATION RESULTS & DISCUSSION

For the evaluation of the OEEM Taxonomy, preliminary experimentation was conducted within an ICT organisation. The experimentation method and results are discussed as follows:

### Method

The proposed taxonomy was preliminarily applied within an ICT organisation to verify whether the taxonomy is effective, meets its requirements and that the taxonomy layers are adequate. The participating organisation is specialised in providing ICT solutions in the form of software and services to local and international clients and the main branch of the organisation has 62 employees. The participants of the experiment were employees of the organisation involved at management level and who have spent at least two years in this same organisation. These criteria were selected since the participants of this experiment needed a good understanding of the organization and its resources at different levels. The preliminary experimentation involved6 getting feedback from 8 participants from different departments within the organisation during an interview session.

**Preliminary Results & Discussion**

The overall preliminary feedback on the OEEM Taxonomy was positive where the participants claimed that all the different energy efficiency areas were actually covered. The participants were also asked to suggest other energy efficiency areas which could be integrated within the model in addition to the six areas, but unfortunately no suggestion was obtained. In terms of its requirements, the participants found that the layers were on overall well split which and that the number of layers were adequate and manageable. However, two participants suggested about the merging of the ICT Layer and Office Environment Layer into a single layer. Also, the participants found that most taxonomy layers were quite independent except the Business Process Layer which can involve employees from different departments in order to manage the energy efficiency of this layer. The adaptability of the taxonomy in turn can only be verified after conducting repeated experiments in different ICT organisations, similar to the completeness of the taxonomy which involves the adoption of energy efficiency and measurement techniques. As such, further experimentations are required and accordingly the planned criteria are discussed in the next section.

**Future Work**

The OEEM Taxonomy needs to be further evaluated in selected organisations with varying parameters such as size, location and business aims. In order to better test the taxonomy, energy efficiency metrics and measurement techniques have to be studied and adopted. For each layer within the proposed taxonomy, appropriate energy efficiency metrics and measurement techniques have to be applied, following which the experimentation process can be compared, based on data obtained, in order to deduce the effectiveness and efficiency of the proposed taxonomy. During the process, feedback can be collected from the participants via interviews or questionnaires.

## CONCLUSION

In this paper, a six-layer taxonomy, called OEEM Taxonomy, was presented for improved energy efficiency management within ICT organisations. The taxonomy is based on the main areas of energy consumption within ICT organisations to include the ICT Layer, Office Environment Layer, Product/Service Layer, Business Process Layer, Personnel Layer and Building Layer, all interlinked using the layered model approach. Preliminary experimentation conducted was quite positive but more case studies involving the use of energy efficiency metrics and measurement techniques have to be adopted in order to confirm whether the proposed taxonomy meets all its requirements.

## REFERENCES

Aune, F. (2004). *Cross-Layer Design Tutorial.* Norway: Creative Commons License.

Bailey, K. D. (1994). *Typologies and taxonomies: An introduction to classification techniques.* Thousand Oaks, CA: Sage Publishing.

Bekaroo, G.; Bokhoree, C.S.; Pattinson, C. (2013). *Towards Green IT Organisations: A Framework for Energy Consumption and Reduction.* The International Journal of Technology, Knowledge and Society, Volume 8, Issue 3, pp.23-36.

Beloglazov, A.; Buyya, R.; Lee, Y.; & Zomaya, A. (2011). *A Taxonomy and Survey of Energy-Efficient Data Centers and Cloud Computing Systems.* Advances in Computers, vol. 82 , 48-111.

Brocade (2007*). Going "Green" with Brocade.* SAN White Paper. Brocade Communications Systems

Citrix (2008). *Green IT: Reducing your Carbon Footprint with Citrix.* Citrix Systems Inc. White paper.

Corno, L.; Cronbach, L.; Kupermintz, H; Lohman, D.; Mandinach, E.; Porteus, A.; et al. (2002). *Remaking the concept of aptitude: Extending the legacy of Richard E. Snow.* Lawrence Erlbaum Associates.

Curtis, L. (2008). Environmentally Sustainable Infrastructure Journal. The Architecture Journal, 2-8.

Desai, M.; & Bhatia, V. (2011). *Green IT Maturity Model: How does your Organisation Stack up?* Infosys Research. SETLabs Briefings, Vol 9-No 1.

Nunn, S. (2008). *Green IT: beyond the data center. How IT can contribute to the environmental agenda across and beyond the business.* Accenture.

Nuventix (2008). *SynJet: Low-Power "Green" Cooling.* Nuventix, Inc

O'Leary, T.J. (2009). *Computing Essentials.* McGraw Hill International Edition

Wang, L.; & Khan, S. (2011). *Review of Performance Metrics for Green Data Centers: A Taxonomy Study.* The Journal of Supercomputing.

# An adaptive navigation support based on a new technology

Rim Zghal Rebaî, Corinne Amel Zayani and Ikram Amous
MIRACL
ISIMS, El Ons City, Sfax University, Tunis Road Km 10, Sakiet Ezzit 3021 Sfax, Tunisia
rim_zghal@yahoo.fr, zayani@irit.fr, ikram.amous@isecs.rnu.tn

*Abstract*— **In the current information systems and especially in the case of a large amount of data, the user can be easily disoriented and cannot get the required information. Several methods are proposed to support the user along his navigation. All these methods are applied only on simple links by taking into account a set of parameters related to the user, the context, etc. In this paper we propose an adaptive navigation method which allows (i) to identify the best navigation path between semi-structured result documents by taking into account the user's history, needs and device's characteristics, (ii) to apply on both simple and extended links the adaptive navigation technologies and (iii) to reduce the navigation space by using a new adaptive navigation technology "Extended XLINK technology" which is based on the basic idea of the XLINK extended links.**

***Keywords—navigation path, user profile, adaptive navigation technology, XLINK extended links***

## I. INTRODUCTION

Nowadays, data sources have become heterogeneous and distributed all over the world. As a result, the data volume grows and the users can lose their time in order to find the pertinent data or can be lost in the huge number of links. That is why navigation adaptation becomes a necessity because it helps the user to easily find the pertinent information and reduces the disorientation problem. Several adaptive navigation methods [18, 5, 4] and adaptive navigation technologies [2, 3] have been proposed. It adapts the navigation by (i) guiding the user from a document to another [4], (ii) providing the user by a set of links leading to the pertinent documents [10] and (iii) applying on simple links the suitable adaptive navigation technologies [15, 1].

So, in order to adapt the navigation we propose a method that allows to: (1) Provide the best navigation path between semi-structured result documents. This path is able to reduce the required number of steps to locate the pertinent information. (2) Apply on simple and extended links the suitable adaptive navigation technologies. (3) Reduce the number of simple links based on a new adaptive navigation technology called "Extended link technology". This technology reduces the number of links in semi-structured documents by using the idea of XLINK extended links (W3C[1]). In our method we take into account several adaptive parameters. These latter are related not only to the user but also to the used device and the visited documents.

Two algorithms are proposed. The first one allows to identify the best navigation path. The second one applies on documents, before being displayed to the user, the adaptive navigation technologies. To evaluate our proposal, we implement a prototype which allows the user to lunch query and search documents from the INEX collection. A series of experiments are performed and proved the user's satisfactions

This paper is organized as follows. Section 2 presents a state of the art in some works dealing with navigation adaptation. In section 3, we explain the proposed navigation adaptation method and the new technology. The efficiency and precision of our method and technology are illustrated by an exhaustive experimental evaluation in section 5. Finally, a conclusion and ongoing works are presented in section 6.

## II. SATE OF THE ART

Several works studying navigation problems have been proposed to provide the user with an adaptive navigation support. We propose to classify the works that we will study in this state of the art into three categories. The first category mainly adapts the navigation by adapting the presentation of links according to the user's preferences, knowledge, history, etc., by means of the adaptive navigation support technologies. The AHA! tool [12], for example, applies the link hiding technology [2] to irrelevant links and the link annotation technology [2] to the remaining links by using different colors depending on the user's model. Web Watcher [1] and ELM-ART [15] are the most popular adaptive hypermedia systems that use the direct guidance technology [2] to suggest a link to the "next best" page or document for the user to visit according to his goals, knowledge, etc. Hypadapter [8] is the first system that introduced the link ordering technology. The idea is to put the links in order of relevance according to the user's model. WebIC [18], ELM-ART [15] are among the systems that use the link generation technology [2]. This technology provides new links to documents deemed relevant to the user's profile.

The second category aims to provide one or more links to the best nodes (document, page). These latter are identified by means of different methods that vary from one system to another depending on the objectives and the application areas. The adaptive system proposed by Verma et al.[13] calculates and rank the weight of each web page in the priority of descending order according to click-count, hyperlink weight and most frequent visits to the webpage. Then, it proposes a direct link to the first page. Wanga et al. [16] analyze navigation paths of website visitors to identify the frequent surfing paths and provides the user with a set of links that leads to the next visited web pages. Seo et al. [10] propose two methods to navigation adaptation. The first one suggests the

[1] http://www.w3.org/TR/xlink11/

next link to be followed by the user and the second one generates quick links as additional entry points into Websites.

The third category suggests the best navigation path allowing the user to reach relevant information with fewer clicks. The identification of this path varies from one system to another. The system proposed by Chiou et al. [4] provides the best navigation path between u-learning objects according to the student's personal and environmental situation. This path is determined by using a meta-heuristic or a heuristic based algorithm. These algorithms take as input a set of ubiquitous environment specific parameters that are related to the learner, the environment and the learning objects. In [5] the authors propose a system that analyses Web logs to identify the best navigation path by skipping irrelevant nodes and providing shortcuts to popular nodes. The system proposed in [18] extracts the links and the key words from the already visited pages in order to propose a set of links that lead to the relevant pages.

We notice that all the detailed adaptation studies adapt homogenous and known in advance data. Moreover, the used navigation adaptation technologies and the proposed methods are applied only on simple links.

In this paper, we propose an adaptive navigation method that identifies the best navigation path between semi-structured results (documents) not designed to be adapted. We propose as well a new adaptive navigation technology called "Extended link technology" based on the idea of the XLINK extended links. The adaptation process is based on several parameters related to the user history, the visited documents and the used device. So, a user profile and a meta-document [20] that describes the visited documents are proposed.

## III. PROPOSED ADAPTIVE NAVGATION METHOD

In our earlier work, we proposed a distributed architecture [17] for adaptive access to heterogeneous semi-structured data. This architecture contains a component that allows adapting the navigation called "Navigation Adaptation Engine" (NAE). This component adapts the navigation based on the proposed method in this paper by taking into account several parameters.

```
<PROFIL>
 </USER_IDENTITIE>
 <CONTENT>
  </PREFERENCE>
 </CONTENT>
 <NAVIGATION_HISTORY>
  <SESSION_PARAM>
   <NB_SESSION>2</NB_SESSION>
   <DURATION>20</DURATION>
 </SESSION_PARAM>
  <USER_PARAM>
  <THEMES>
   <THEME>
    <ID_THEME>20</ID_THEME>
    <INTITULE_THEME>
    Computer sciences
    </INTITULE_THEME>
    <NB_VISIT>3<NB_VISIT>
    <VISITED_DOCUMENTS>
     <DOC>
      <ID_DOC>19.XML<ID_DOC>
      <NB_ACCESS>1<NB_ACCESS>
      <SPENT_TIME>5</SPENT_TIME>
     <VISITED_LINKS>
      <LINK>
       <ID_LINK>4<ID_LINK>
       <NB_CLICK>1<NB_CLICK>
      </LINK>
     </VISITED_LINKS>
     </DOC>
    </VISITED_DOCUMENTS>
   </THEME>
  </THEMES>
  <USER_PARAM>
 <NAVIGATION_HISTORY>
 </PROFIL>
```

Fig. 1. XML proposed user profile

These latter are related to: (i) the user's navigation history which are stored in a user profile (cf figure 1), (ii) the visited documents which are stored in meta-documents (cf. figure 2) and (iii) the used device which are detected online on each session and limited to the operating system and the memory size. The use of these parameters in our proposed navigation method will be detailed below.

```
<META_DOCUMENT>
 <DOC>
  <URL>http://...../20.XML
  <CONFIGURATION>
   <OS>XP</OS>
   <RAM>1024</RAM>
 </CONFIGURATION>
  <SPECIFIC_THEMES>
   <THEME>
    <ID_THEME>20</ID_THEME>
    <BENEFIT>0.7</BENEFIT>
   </THEME>
  </SPECIFIC_THEMES
 </DOC>
</META_DOCUMENT>
```

Fig. 2. XML Proposed meta-document

Generally, information systems provide the result documents in random order. So, to adapt the navigation we propose a method that identifies the best navigation path between the result documents and before displaying documents to the user, it applies the suitable adaptive navigation technologies and a new proposed technology called "Extended link technology" which is based on the XLINK extended links.

### A. *Identification of the navigation path*

The best navigation path is the path which allows to reduce the required number of steps to locate the pertinent information. It is identified by taking into account the user's query and the already cited parameters.

To identify this path we proposed in [17] an algorithm called "Identify the navigation path". It takes as input the user's navigation history and the list of the result documents. For each document, it calculates its score by using equations 1, 2 and 3.

$$Doc\_Score(di) = \frac{benefit(di) + freq(di) + tm(di)}{Cp} \quad (1)$$

*Benefit*, *freq* and *tm* denote respectively the access benefit of the document, the frequency of the access to the document and the spent average time on the visit of the document. The benefit [17] it is a value ranged from 0 to 1. It is extracted from meta-document and generally identified by the document's author based on the relevance of the document's content to a theme.

*Cp* is a constant that assumes 1 as a value when the user's device manages to display the document, otherwise, it assumes any value greater than 1; in our proposal we take 10 as value. This value is resulted from a comparison between the configuration of the used device and the required device configuration to display the document which is specified in meta-document (cf figure 2).

$$doc\_freq(di) = \frac{nb\_acces(di)}{nb\_total\_doc} \quad (2)$$

*Nb_access* represents the access number to the document, $nb\_total\_doc$ is the total number of the accessed documents during all sessions.

$$tm(di) = \frac{\sum t(di)}{\sum_{k=1}^{nb\_session} tk} \quad (3)$$

$t_m(di)$ corresponds to the ratio of the total time of visiting the document $d_i$ and the total time of all sessions.

Based on the obtained scores, the algorithm sorts the result documents to identify the best navigation path between them.

### B. The "Extended link technology"

To reduce the number of links in the document and enables the user to have an idea about the related theme of each link, we propose a new technology based on the XLINK extended links. W3C[2] "An extended link is a link that associates an arbitrary number of resources. The participating resources may be any combination of remote and local". We will apply this technology with the well-known technologies [2] on document online without modifying the original version.

The basic idea of "Extended link technology" is to regroup several simple links that belong to the same theme into a single extended link. The founded extended links in document will be generated and take the theme's name as a title. Then, the resources of each extended link are subsequently reordered by using the "ordering link technology" [2] and annotated by the "annotation link technology" [2]. Figure 3 illustrates an example of an extended link.

```
<ExtendedLink xlink:type="extended">
<loc xlink:type="locator" xlink:href="..." xlink:label="source" xlink:title="s1" />
<loc xlink:type="locator" xlink:href="..." xlink:label="target" xlink:title="t1" />
<loc xlink:type="locator" xlink:href="..." xlink:label="target" xlink:title="t2" />
<action xlink:type="arc" xlink:from="source" xlink:to="target">
</ExtendedLink>
```

Fig. 3. Example of an extended link

To apply the suitable adaptive navigation technologies (the well-known technologies and "extended link technology"), we proposed in [21] an algorithm called "Apply Navigation Technologies". This algorithm is based on two functions. The first function, called "Calculate Link Score" which calculates the scores of links. These scores allow differentiating links (more relevant and less relevant). The second function, called which allows applying the "extended link technology".

Algorithm "Apply Navigation Technologies" precedes as follows: for each link related to theme other than the requested by the user, it applies the hiding technology. Then, for each link in the remaining links, it determines the target documents, the benefit of these documents, calculates their scores by using equation 1, and calculates the link's score by means of the function "Calculate Link Score". This function takes as input the score of the target documents, the user history and the link. Firstly, it extracts, from the user's history, the number of clicks on the link and the total number of clicks. Secondly, it calculates, by means of equation 5 the average frequency of clicking on the link. Finally, it uses equation 4 to calculate the link's score. The obtained scores allow distinguishing links and choosing the suitable adaptive navigation technologies to be applied. They are provided with links to the "Extended Link Technology" function. This function extracts, if exist, extended links from the remaining simple links (after applying the hiding technology) in order to be generated in the document before being displayed to the user. The basic idea is to regroup all simple links that belong to the same theme into a single extended link. Then, the resources of each extended link are reordered and annotated according to their scores by the annotation link technology.

$$Link\_Score(li) = \frac{\sum Doc\_Score(target\_doc)}{nb\_target\_doc} + link\_freqm(li) \quad (4)$$

*Doc_Score* is the score of the link target document. It is calculated by using equation 1. In the case of an extended link (having more than one target documents), we proceed to sum the scores of all target documents, then divide it by the total number of the target documents *nb_target_doc*. *link_freqm(li)* is the average frequency of clicking on the link during all sessions and it is calculated by equation 5.

$$link\_freqm(li) = \frac{\sum \frac{nb\_click(li)}{nb\_total\_click}}{nb\_total\_session} \quad (5)$$

*nb_click(li)* is the number of clicks on the link in one session, *nb_total_click* is the total number of the visited links, $\sum \frac{nb\_click(li)}{nb\_total\_click}$ is the sum of the average frequencies of clicks on the link in each single session and *nb_session* is the total number of sessions.

## IV. IMPLEMENTATION AND EVALUATION OF THE PROPOSED METHOD

In order to exploit and test our proposed navigation method, we implemented a prototype based on this method. This prototype allows the user to launch a query and navigate between result documents. These latter are documents of INEX 2007 corpus, which is part of the collection WIKIPEDIA XML. In this corpus documents are related to one or more themes and containing XLINK simple links.

After being authenticated, the user sends his query through the interface shown in figure 4. This interface allows searching for documents based on their themes and the value of their benefit.

[2] http://www.w3.org/TR/xlink11/

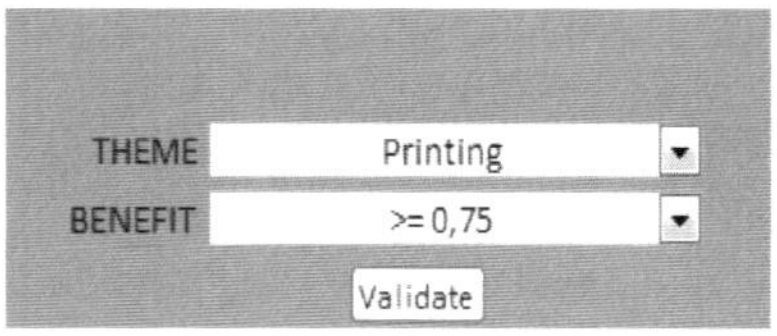


Fig. 4. Query interface

After specifying the elements of the query and validating it by the user, the prototype identifies the user's profile and searches the result documents. Then, it executes our proposed method and displays the adapted result documents to the user.

We take the example of the proposed query in figure 4 consists on "Searching for documents that belong to the printing theme with a benefit more than 0.75". This query is proposed by two users "User1 and User2" having two different profiles. Knowing that, the device's memory of the user1 is able to display only 4 images at the same time.

The prototype provides 5 documents as result to this query. These documents are illustrated in table 1.

TABLE 1. RESULT DOCUMENTS

| ID_doc (INEX) | 26498 | 45621 | 3975 | 22016 | 34458 |
|---|---|---|---|---|---|
| **Title** | Postscript | Letter | writing | Printing | Typoraphy |
| **Benefit** | 0.77 | 0.77 | 0.8 | 0.82 | 0.82 |
| **Content** | Text | Text | Text 1image | Text 3 images | Text 5 images |

In this table, each document is identified by its identifier in INEX corpus and its title. The element "Content" in this table represents the content type in document. Based on this result, we carried out two series of experiments: (i) we present the variety of the obtained navigation paths, and (ii) we evaluate the use of the already existing technologies and "extended link technology".

## A. *The obtained navigation paths*

The navigation path identification is based on the obtained scores of the result documents. These scores are calculated by using equation1 based on: the benefit, the frequency, the average time and the constant Cp. All these parameters for the two users are illustrated in table 2.

TABLE 2. PARAMETERS AND SCORES OF RESULT DOCUMENTS

| ID_doc | Frequency | Tm | Cp | Score | |
|---|---|---|---|---|---|
| 3975 | 0.27273 | 0.2 | 1 | 1.27 | USER1 |
| 22016 | 0 | 0 | 1 | 0.82 | |
| 34458 | 0.36364 | 0.35 | 10 | 0.1532 | |
| 26498 | 0 | 0 | 1 | 0.77 | |
| 45621 | 0.09091 | 0.05 | 1 | 0.91 | |
| 3975 | 0 | 0 | 1 | 0.8 | USER2 |
| 22016 | 0.25 | 0.3333 | 1 | 1.4033 | |
| 34458 | 0 | 0 | 1 | 0.82 | |
| 26498 | 0 | 0 | 1 | 0.77 | |
| 45621 | 0.25 | 0.26667 | 1 | 1.2866 | |

As we can see in the obtained results in table 2, the scores of documents change with the user's history (frequency and Tm) and Cp (constant related to the used device). In fact, the score of document 34458 is 0.1532 for user 1 and 0.82 for user 2 despite it is frequently visited by the first user. We explain this by the limited capacities of the used device (only 4 images at the same time and the document contains 5 images; Cp=10).

Thus, based on these scores we obtain two different paths one for each user (cf. figure 5). For example, document 3975 is the first document to be displayed for user 1 but it is the fourth one for user 2. This is simply because this document is frequently visited by user 1 and never visited by user 2.

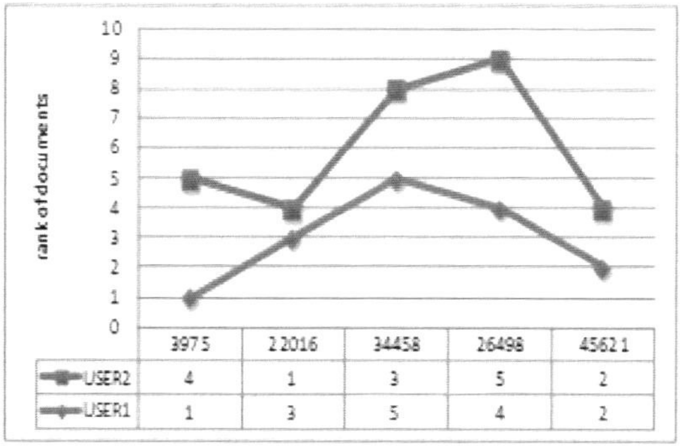


Fig. 5. Obtained navigation paths

The different displayed interfaces to each user are presented in figure 6 and figure 7.

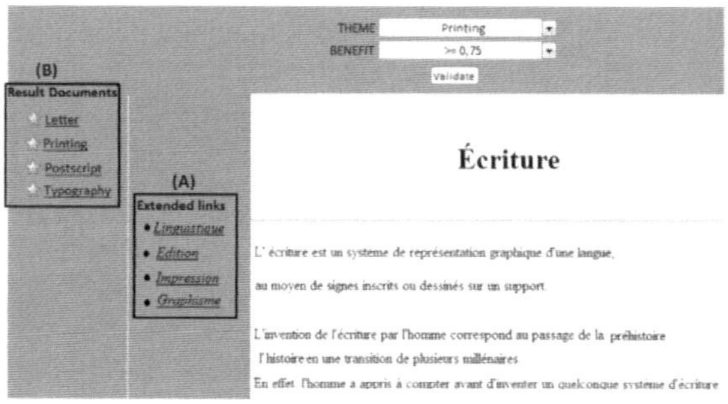


Fig. 6. Displayed interface to user 1

For user 1, the first document "Writing" is displayed, 4 extended links figure 6/(A) and the remaining result documents are sorted by their scores and presented in figure 6/(B).

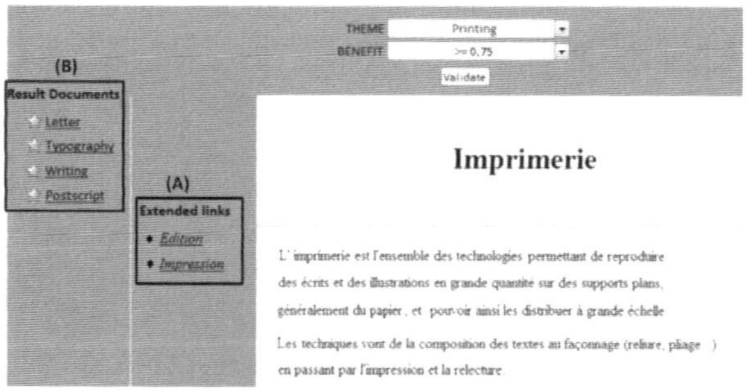


Fig. 7. Displayed interface to user 2

As we can see in figure 7, the first document "Printing" is displayed to user 2, 2 extended links figure 7/(A) and the remaining result documents are sorted by their scores and presented in figure 7/(B).

*B. Evaluation of the adaptive navigation technologies*

To evaluate the use of the navigation technologies and especially "extended link technology" in navigation adaptation, we propose to compute the obtained links number in each document result. For this, we calculate the number of links: (1) without navigation adaptation and (2) with our proposal by combining the "hiding link technology" with the "extended link technology". Figure 8 depicts the obtained links number.

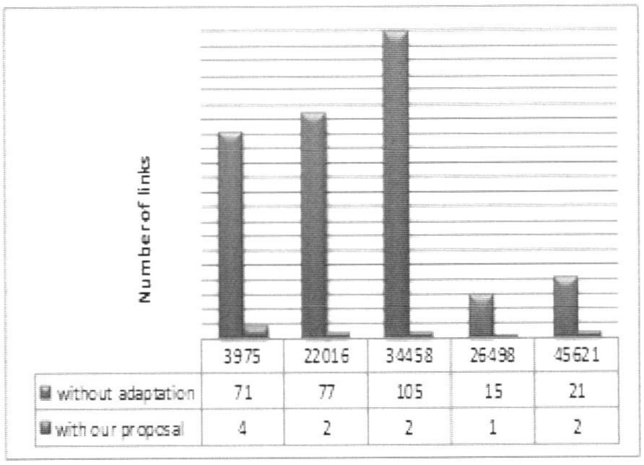


Fig. 8. Evaluation of the links number

As we can see in figure 8, the number of pertinent links is reduced in each document. For example, in document 22016 the initial number of links is 77. After the application our proposal this number is reduced to 2. In all result documents the number decreases from 289 to 11.

To make sure about the usefulness of our proposal, we evaluate the users' satisfactions. For this, we propose to each user two document versions: a version without adaptation and an adapted version with our proposal. Then each user, after comparing the two versions, indicates the number of the eliminated relevant links and the number of the persistent irrelevant links. The obtained result is shown in table 3.

TABLE 3. NUMBER OF IRRELEVANT LINKS

| **ID_doc** | 3975 | 22016 | 34458 | 26498 | 45621 |
|---|---|---|---|---|---|
| **Initial number** | 71 | 77 | 105 | 15 | 21 |
| **User1** | 9 | 14 | 20 | 3 | 3 |
| **User2** | 13 | 10 | 25 | 3 | 5 |

Based on the obtained result in table 3, we calculate the precision of links and we obtain figure 9. The obtained precision rates confirm the satisfaction of both users.

## V. CONCLUSION

In this paper, we proposed an adaptive navigation method for semi-structured documents not designed to be adapted. On the one hand, our method provides the user with the best navigation path by taking into account the user navigation history and the device capacities. On the other hand, our method uses a new adaptive navigation technology called "extended link technology" based on the idea of the XLINK extended links. This method is evaluated by a series of experiments and shows the users satisfactions.

In the continuation of our work, we aim to evaluate our method by a group of users. Then, we plan to propose and implement a learning method which automatically removes irrelevant user profile elements after several updating operations.

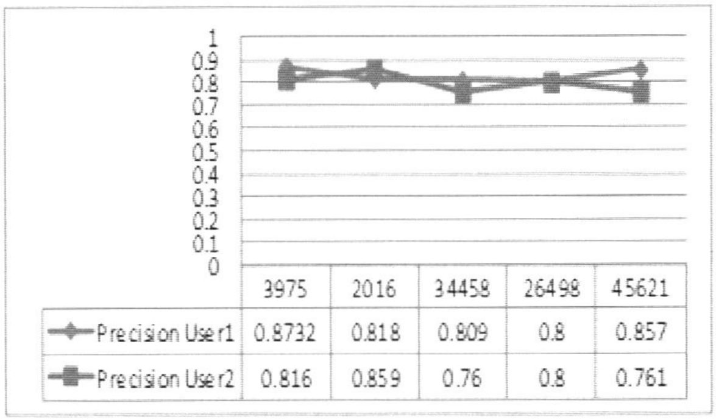


Fig. 9. Precision rates of our proposal

## REFERENCES

[1] R. Armstrong, D. Freitag, T. Joachims, T. Mitchell, "WebWatcher: A learning apprentice for the World Wide Web," Knoblock, C., Levy, A. (eds.) Proc. Of AAAI Spring Symposium on Information Gathering from Distributed, Heterogeneous Environments, AAAI Press, 1995, pp 6-12.

[2] P. Brusilovsky, "Methods and techniques of adaptive hypermedia," User Modeling and User-Adapted Interaction 6, 2-3, 1996, pp 87-129.

[3] P. Brusilovsky, "Adaptive hypermedia," User Modeling and User Adapted Interaction 11, 1/2, 2001, pp 87-110.

[4] Ch. Chuang-Kai, C.R. Judy, H. Gwo-Jen, H. Shelly, "An adaptive navigation support system for conducting context-aware ubiquitous learning in museums," Journal: Computers & Education, 2010, pp 834-845

[5] Ch. Doerr, D. Dincklage and A. Diwan, "Simplifying Web Traversals By Recognizing Behavior Patterns," Hypertext and Hypermedia, 2007, pp 105-114.

[6] D. Brickley and L. Miller, "Foaf vocabulary specification," Technical report, FOAF project, Published online on May 24th, 2007.

[7] G. Klyne, F. Reynolds, Ch. Woodrow, H. Ohto, J. Hjelm, M H. Butler, and L. Tran, "Composite capability/preference profiles (cc/pp) :Structure and vocabularies 1.0," Technical report, World Wide Web Consortium (W3C), W3C Recommendation, 2003.

[8] H. Hohl, H. D., Böcker, R. Gunzenhäuser, "Hypadapter: An adaptive hypertext system for exploratory learning and programming," User Modeling and User-Adapted Interaction, 1996, pp 131-156.

[9] 1I. Amous, A. Jedidi, F. Sedes, "A Contribution to Multimedia Document Modeling and Organizing," Object-Oriented Information Systems, 2002, pp 434-444.

[10] J. Seo, F. Diaz, E. Gabrilovich, V. Josifovski, B. Pang, "Generalized Link Suggestions via Web Site Clustering," World Wide Web, 2011, pp 77-86.

[11] J. Kay, "The um toolkit for cooperating user modeling," User Modeling and User-Adapted Interaction, 1995, pp 149-196.

[12] P. De Bra, A. Aerts, B. Berden, B. De Lange, B. Rousseau, T. Santic, D. Smits, N. Stash, "AHA! The Adaptive Hypermedia Architecture," Hypertext and Hypermedia , 2003, pp 81-84.

[13] S. Verma, S. Patel, A. Abhari, "Adaptive web navigation," Spring Simulation Multiconference, 2009, Article No. 126.

[14] S. Buchholz, T. Hamann, and G. Hübsch, "Comprehensive Structured Context Profiles (CSCP): Design and Experiences," In PerCom Workshops, 2004, pp 43-47.

[15] G. Weber, P. Brusilovsky, "ELM-ART: An adaptive versatile system for Webbased instruction," International Journal of Artificial Intelligence in Education 12, 4 , 2001, pp 351-384.

[16] Y. Wanga, A.J.T. Lee, "Mining Web navigation patterns with a path traversal graph," Expert Systems with Applications, Vol. 38, 2011, pp 7112-7122.

[17] R. Zghal, C. Zayani, I. Amous, "MEDI-ADAPT: A distributed architecture for personalized access to heterogeneous semi-structured data," Web Information Systems and Technologies, 2012, pp 259-263.

[18] R. Zghal, C. Zayani, I. Amous, "An adaptive navigation method for semi-structured data," Advances in DataBases and Information Systems, 2012, pp. 207-215.

[19] T. Zhu , R. Greiner, G. Haeubl, 2003, "Learning a model of a web user's interests", The 9th International Conference on User Modeling, Lecture Notes in Computer Science, Vol. 2702, 2003, pp 65-75.

[20] I. Amous, A. Jedidi, F. Sedes, "A Contribution to Multimedia Document Modeling and Querying," Multimedia Tools Applications, 25(3), 2005, pp 391-404.

[21] R. Zghal, C. Zayani, I. Amous, "A new technology to adapt the navigation," 2013, in press.

# Bayesian Structural Learning with Minimum Spanning Tree Algorithm

Safiye Sencer
Sakarya University
Sakarya, Turkey

Orhan Torkul
Sakarya University
Sakarya, Turkey

Harun Taskin
Sakarya University
Sakarya, Turkey

Ercan Oztemel
Marmara University
Istanbul, Turkey

Cemalettin Kubat
Sakarya University
Sakarya, Turkey

Gultekin Yildiz
Sakarya University
Sakarya, Turkey

Email: safiyesencer@yahoo.com, {sencer, torkul, taskin, kubat, yildizg@sakarya.edu.tr}, eoztemel@marmara.edu.tr

***Abstract*** **- Bayesian Belief Network (BBN) is a kind of graphical model which provides a compact and main representation of probabilistic data. It represents the relationships among several variables and includes conditional probability distributions that make probabilistic statements about the variables. The probabilistic form of database's learning and classification in Bayesian Network structure is complex problem and still one of the most exciting challenges in machine learning. It is widely used heuristics search for the optimal graphs locally by defining a score metric and employs a search strategy to identify the network structure having the maximum or minimum score. In this paper, we focus on Bayesian classification and learning which is derived from minimum spanning tree based algorithm (Sollin's algorithm) model alternative for network structure learning.**

**Keywords:** Bayesian Network, Structural Learning, Minimum Spanning Tree Algorithm, Score

## I. Introduction

Bayesian network is important part of artificial intelligence due to their ability to support probabilistic reasoning from data with uncertainty. Also, it is part of the machine learning for prediction of unknown situations. Bayesian network is a Directed Acyclic Graph (DAG), where the nodes are random variables and where the arcs specify the independence assumptions between these variables. During the past few years, several algorithms have been developed for learning the structure of BN from a database which is the score metric based methods and structure based methods [1]. The score metric-based methods based on the quantity metric measures to quality of the network structures or the conditional dependence among variables with maximization of the metric over the structure space in the database. In network approach, probabilistic inference can be conducted to predict the values of some variables based on the observed values of other variables. For this reason Bayesian networks are widely used in many areas, such as decision support systems [2] and [3], diagnostic and classification systems [4], [5] and [6], information retrieval [7], troubleshooting, data mining [8], [9], and learning algorithm [10], [11], [12].

Bayesian network learning includes the parameters and structure learning arrangement. Also it covers incomplete databases, which contains the missing values or hidden variables in the records. The evaluation and optimization process covers the several algorithms such as Gibbs sampling [13], [14], and Bound-and-Collapse method [15], [16]. Structure learning can be classified into two main categories [12], the dependency analysis approach [17] and the score-and-search approach [14], [18]. The results of dependency tests are employed to construct a Bayesian network conforming to the findings. Scoring metric is used to evaluate candidate networks while a search method employed to find a network structure with the best score. At the same time, concerning the score evaluation for structure learning, some researchers proposed calculating the expected values of the statistics to approximate the score of candidate networks.

The suggested new algorithm uses score tests to restrict the available scope of candidate arcs, reduce the space of candidate solutions, and induce network arc trees to avoid many unnecessary searches effectively. And then, by combining the global score increase of a solution with the local mutual information between nodes, a new heuristic function with better heuristic ability is given to induct the process of stochastic searches. We also apply the suggested method to alarm data set and compare the performance on several other learning algorithms in the Bayesian networks. Our suggested model is better than the several other learning algorithms by the induced the computing score values and processing time.

The paper is organized as follows. In Section 2, we present the background of Bayesian networks and the basic idea with the minimum spanning tree algorithm. In Section 3, we describe the Bayesian structure learning with minimum spanning tree algorithm and the next section represents the application. Finally, we conclude the paper in Section 5.

## II. Bayesian Network Structure Learning

In this section, firstly, Bayesian networks literature reviewed, after structure learning and Bayesian network structure learning subjects discussed with together.

### *A. Bayesian Networks*

A Bayesian network (BN) is a graphical model that combines elements of graph theory and probability theory. It describes a set of causal relationships among a set of variables of interest, a set of conditional independence assumptions, and their related joint probabilities. BN can be denoted as a triple group <X, A, Θ>, where <X,A> defines a directed acyclic graph (DAG) structure $G$, X is the set of nodes; $X_i \in X$ represents a random variable in a special domain. A is a set of directed arcs, $a_{ij} \in A$ describes a direct probabilistic dependency between $X_i$ and $X_j$, $X_i \leftarrow X_j$; and $\Theta = \{\theta_i\}$ is a set of parameters. $\theta_i = p(X_i|\Pi(X_i))$ is the conditional probability distribution of $X_i$ which is given the parent set of the variable $X_i$. A directed acyclic graph (DAG) describe the causal relationships among the variables, or nodes, and represents both dependent (i.e., related) nodes and independent (i.e., unrelated) nodes (in Fig.1). Each node represents a variable that has an associated conditional probability distribution [19]. As the graph structure, $G$ qualitatively characterizes the independence relationship among random variables, and the conditional probability distribution quantifies the strength of dependencies between a node and its parent nodes. Therefore Bayesian network <X, A, Θ> uses a graph structure and a set of parameters to encode uniquely the joint probability distribution of the domain variables $X = \{X_1, X_2, \cdots, X_n\}$:

$$p(X_1, X_2, \ldots, X_n) = \prod_{i=1}^{n} p(X_i|\Pi(X_n)) \quad (1).$$

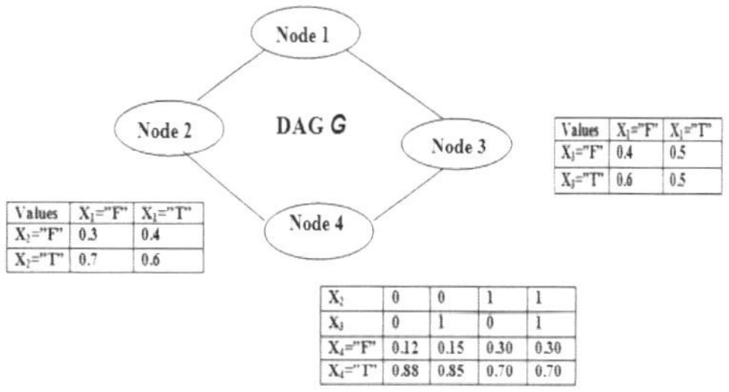


Fig. 1. Bayesian network example

### *B. Bayesian Network Structure Learning*

Bayesian network structure learning categorized in two parts, which are score-and search based approach and constrained based approach. The score-search based approach refers to the greedy learning approach from an initial structure and move to the neighbors with the best score on the structure space with determinately or stochastically until to obtain a local maximum of the selected criteria is reached [20]. The constraint-based approach considers the statistical significance of the pairs of variables conditioning on other variables to test and induce conditional independence [21], [17]. The pairs of variables pass some threshold, which are considered as directly connected in the Bayesian networks. The other variables which uncover the threshold value, that are eliminated by the algorithm. The complete Bayesian network structure is constructed from the taking conditional independence and dependence information.

In Bayesian network structure learning, the score and search based approach consists of the structure space, the search strategy and the model selection criteria. The structure space in score and search refers to the all the possible structures of directed acyclic graphs (DAGs) that are given the number of variables in the domain. Also it refers from search methods from artificial intelligence, such as depth-first, width-first, best first or simulated annealing, greedy search. During the making of a graph model, structure learning is used to deal with information and inference throughout description of the knowledge from large experimental samples [22].

According to Bayesian rules, posterior probability of Bayesian network is:

$$P(G^h|D) = \frac{P(G^h|D)P(G^h)}{\Sigma_{S^{\cdot}} P(D|G^{h^{\cdot}})P(G^{h^{\cdot}})} \quad (2).$$

Where $P(D|G^h)$ is marginal likelihood and it is:

$$P(D|G^h) = \Sigma\, P(D|G^h, \theta)P(\theta|G^h)d\theta \quad (3)$$

where $p(D)$ is a normalization constant which does not depend on the Bayesian network structure $G$. $P(G^{h})$ is prior probability, $\theta$ is parameter of model is often used for model selection [23] and D represents the experimental sample set.

The comparing score is

$$Score(S,D) = \sum Score(v_i, Pa(v_i), D(v_i, pa(v_i))) \quad (4).$$

Scoring function calculates the how well a given network G matches the data $D$. The best one is obtained maximizes by the scoring function in Bayesian structure learning.

Constraint-based methods in Bayesian network structure train many dependencies and (conditional) independencies of the underlying model. The algorithms of this approach try to discover the dependencies and conditional independencies from the data, and then use these dependencies and conditional independencies to infer the Bayesian network structure. The conditional independence tests are used in practice are statistical tests on the data set for use the results to reconstruct the structure, several assumptions have to be made with causal sufficiency assumption, causal Markov assumption, and faithfulness assumption.

Briefly, score and scope based structural learning is very important for the evaluation of the Bayesian networks for the next prediction processes.

## III. Bayesian Network Structural Learning Algorithm with Minimum Spanning Tree

Minimum spanning tree algorithm (MSTA), proposed by Boruvka in 1926, which is a kind of meta-heuristic algorithm [24]. It is often used to solve combinatorial optimization problems. In minimum spanning tree, $T$ of $G$ is a connected acyclic sub graph that spans all the nodes. Every spanning tree of $G$ has n-1 arcs. Given an undirected graph $G$= (N, A) with n=|N| nodes and m=|A| arcs and with a length or cost $c_{ij}$ associated with each arc (i,j) $\in$ A, we wish to find a spanning tree, called a minimum spanning tree. It has the smallest total cost (or length, failure rate) of its constituent arcs, measured as the sum of costs of the arcs in the spanning tree. Also, in Bayesian network, between nodes i and node j, any conditional status affects final decision a certain probability $p_{ij}$. If we represent the nodes status in resulting $G$, we would like to identify a spanning tree $T$ that minimizes the probability of failure given by expression $\{1 - \Pi_{(i,j)\in T}(1 - p_{ij})\}$.

For every non-tree arc (k,l) of G, $p_{ij} \leq p_{kl}$ for every arc(i,j0 contained in the path in $T^*$ connecting nodes k and l.

Given an $n$ th-order probability distribution $P(x_1, x_2, \ldots x_n)$, $x_i$ is being discrete, we want to find a distribution of tree dependence $P_T(x_1, x_2, \ldots, x_n)$ such that $I(P, P_T) \leq I(P, P_t)$ for all $t \in T$, where $T_n$, is the set of all possible first-order dependence trees. The solution $\tau$ is called the optimal first-order dependence tree. Also, Sollin's algorithm repeatedly performs the nearest-neighbor process and mutual information as a basic operation.

Nearest-neighbor consists of the ($N_k$, $i_k$, $j_k$) variables. This operation takes as an input a tree spanning the nodes $N_k$ and determines an arc ($i_k$, $j_k$) with the minimum cost among all arcs emanating from $N_k$[i.e.,$c_{i_kj_k}=\min\{c_{ij}(i,j)\in A, i\in N_k$ and $j\notin N_k\}$]. In Bayesian network maximum probabilty degree reflects to the minimum cost in suggested study. To perform this operation we need to scan all the arcs in the adjacency lists of nodes in $N_k$, and find a minimum cost arc among those arcs that have one endpoint not belonging to $N_k$. The merge($i_k$,$j_k$) operation takes as an input two nodes $i_k$ and $j_k$, and if the two nodes belong to two different trees, then merges these two trees into a single tree [24], [25].

The mutual information $I(x_i, x_{i(i)})$ between two variables $x_i$ and $x_j$ is given by

$$I(x_i, x_j) = \sum_{x_i, x_j} P(x_i, x_j) \log\left(\frac{P(x_i, x_j)}{P(x_i)P(x_j)}\right) \quad (5).$$

It is well known that $I(x_i, x_j)$ is non-negative. In the graphical representation of dependence relations, we assign a branch weight $I(x_i, x_{j(i)})$ to every branch of the dependence tree. Given a dependence tree $t$, the sum of all branch weights is a useful quantity. Since there are $n^{n-2}$ trees with n vertices, the number of dependence trees in $T_n$, for any moderate value of n is so enormous as to exclude any approach of exhaustive search. To describe our solution in this optimization problem, we can give the following definition.

A maximum-weight dependence tree is a dependence tree t such that for all t' in $T_n$

$$\sum_{i=1}^{n} I(x_i, x_{j(i)}) \geq \sum_{i=1}^{n} I(x_i, x_{j'(i)}) \quad (6).$$

The first result stated as follows. A probability distribution of tree dependence P(x) is an optimum approximation to P(x) if and only if its dependence tree t has maximum weight.

$$I(P, P_t) = -\sum_x P(x)\sum_{i=1}^{n} \log P(x_i|x_{i(i)}) + \sum_n P(x)\log P(x)$$
$$= -\sum_x P(x) \sum_{\substack{i=1 \\ j(i)\neq 0}}^{n} \log \frac{P(x_i, x_{j(i)})}{P(x_i)P(x_{j(i)})} - \sum_x P(x)\sum_{i=1}^{n} \log P(x_i)$$
$$+ \sum_x P(x)\sum_{i=1}^{n} \log P(x_i) \quad (7).$$

Since $P(x_i)$ and $P(x_{i(i)})$ are components of $P(x)$,

$$-\sum_x P(x)\log P(x_i) = -\sum_{x_i} P(x)\log P(x_i) \quad (8)$$

which is denoted by $H(x_i)$ and

$$\sum_x P(x)\log\frac{P(x_i, x_{j(i)})}{P(x_i)P(x_{j(i)})} = \sum_{x_i, x_{j(i)}} P(x_i, x_{j(i)})\log\frac{P(x_i, x_{j(i)})}{P(x_i)P(x_{j(i)})}$$
$$= I(x_i, x_{j(i)}) \quad (9)$$

Thus, (4) becomes

$$I(P, P_i) = -\sum_{i=1}^{n} I(x_i, x_{j(i)}) + \sum_{i=1}^{n} N(x_i) - N(x) \quad (10)$$

Since N(x) and N($x_i$) for all *i* are independent of the dependence tree and *I(P, $P_t$)* is non-negative, minimizing the closeness measure *I(P, $P_t$)* is equivalent to maximizing the total branch weight [26].

TABLE 1 MSTBSL Algorithm

Algorithm: Minimum Spanning Tree Based Bayesian Structural Learning (Based on Sollin's algorithm)-MSTBSL

**Input** : Distributed data and node ordering N sites
**Output** : Minimum Spanning Tree based BN structure

1. Construct the new network ***G*** with nodes C, $X_1$, ...,$X_n$, with joint distribution of class
2. Insert the links C→$X_i$, i=1,...,n ∈ ***G***
3. Estimate the network density for C, and conditional network density for each $X_i$, i=1,...,n given its parents in ***G***

**begin**
  **for** each i∈X **do** $X_i$:={i};
    $T^*$:=∅;
    **while** |$T^*$| < (x-1) **do**
      **begin**
        **for** each tree $X_k$ **do** nearest_neighbor
        **for** each tree $X_k$ **do**
        **if** nodes $i_k$ and $T_k$ belong to different trees **then** merge($i_k$,$j_k$) and update $T^*$:= $T^*$∪{($i_k$, $j_k$)}; run the validation algorithm of the structure to check whether it violates the Bayesian network standards. If cycles are not generated by inserting new edges into the ***G***, then add the edges into the ***G***, then add the edges. If it creates cycles, then delete the edges or skip the generation.
        **end**;
    **end;**

**4.** Let P be the set of estimated densities.
**5.** Let Bayesian Network learning be a Bayesian network with structure G and distributions P.

In Minimum Spanning Tree Based Bayesian Structural Learning (Based on Sollin's algorithm)-MSTBSL algorithm is divided into two steps. The first step is creating with global network analysis for structure learning, and the second step is update with minimum spanning tree based probability estimation (Table 1).

The suggested algorithm applied to alarm dataset and compared with the other Bayesian algorithms such as Bayesian Network, Greedy, and Greedy DAG in next section.

## IV. Experimental Evaluation

In this section we illustrated the effectiveness of the minimum spanning tree algorithm based Bayesian network structure learning. So we compared the results of minimum spanning tree algorithm based DAG search algorithm with Bayesian Network, Greedy and Greedy DAG algorithms. The Alarm network is used which related to the medical domain for potential anesthesia diagnosis in the operating room with 37 nodes and 46 directed edges (Fig.2). The random variables in the alarm network are discrete in nature. The number of discrete states depends on the node [28].

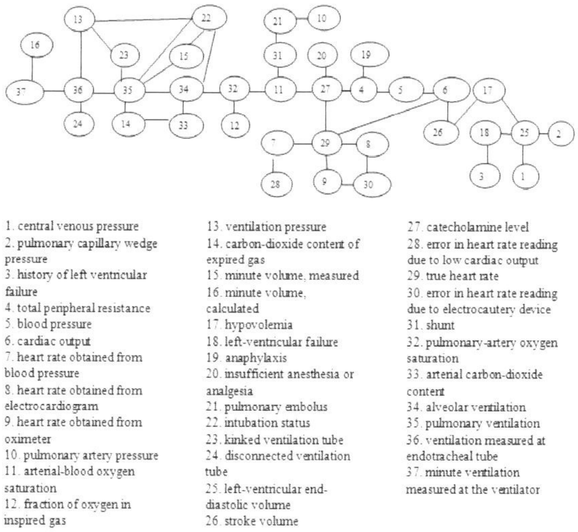


Figure 2. Example of a Minimum Spanning Tree for Alarm B

The performance of the minimum spanning tree based structure learning algorithm is tested on alarm data set, which generated from known network structures using probabilistic logic sampling. Data sets are generated from the well-known benchmarks of Bayesian network including the Alarm data set. It used in application section and depicted in Table 1. For data set network with the size 100, 200, 500, 1000, 5000, 10000 are sampled. Table 2 and Table 3 give a summary of the data sets used in our experiments.

Bayesian Network has 37 nodes and 46 edges. The sample set was randomly generated using the structure and conditional probability distribution. We used Kevin Murphy's BN toolbox executed in Matlab [27] for both the data generation and the experiments.

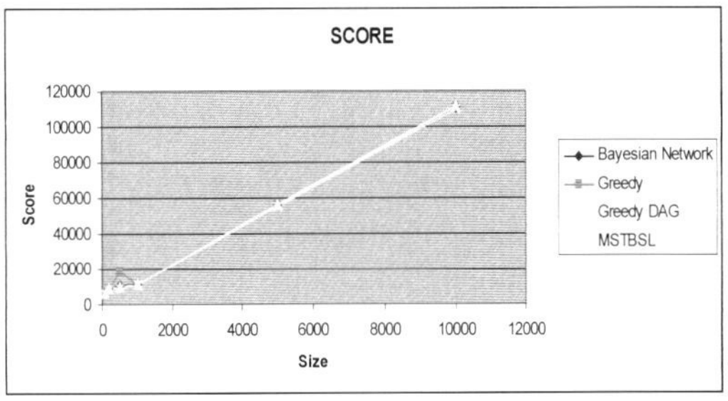


Fig.3. Comparing of the Bayesian Structural

TABLE 2 Score values on alarm data set

| Size | Bayesian Network | Greedy | Greedy DAG | MSTBSL |
|---|---|---|---|---|
| 100 | 6893 | 6232 | 6343 | 6152 |
| 200 | 9155 | 8543 | 9543 | 8233 |
| 500 | 10655 | 18399 | 9957 | 9563 |
| 1000 | 11759 | 11814 | 11837 | 11253 |
| 5000 | 56079 | 56296 | 56073 | 55056 |
| 10000 | 111091 | 111281 | 111181 | 110299 |

From the Fig 3 and Table 2, Minimum Spanning Tree Based Bayesian Structural Learning's score value is higher than the other methods for all the cases. Moreover it has lowest score value, at the same time it has lowest processing time for all the cases (in Fig.2 and Table 3)

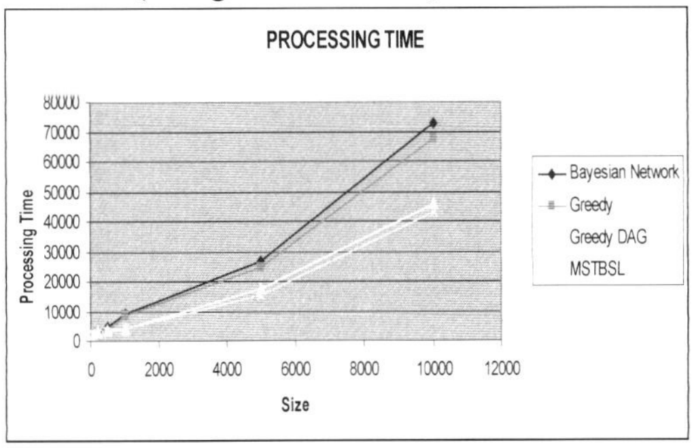


Fig.4. Comparing of the Bayesian Structural Learning Methods with MSTBSL in processing time values on Alarm data set

TABLE 3 Processing time values on alarm data set

| Size | Bayesian Network | Greedy | Greedy DAG | MSTBSL |
|---|---|---|---|---|
| 100 | 2682 | 2230 | 1962 | 1918 |
| 200 | 3012 | 2982 | 2736 | 2715 |
| 500 | 4562 | 3253 | 3432 | 3150 |
| 1000 | 9256 | 8857 | 4321 | 4252 |
| 5000 | 26852 | 24727 | 17543 | 15462 |
| 10000 | 72651 | 67538 | 45631 | 43262 |

## V. Conclusion

Bayesian network reflects the potential relationship among data and important tool for data mining and knowledge discovery. We proposed a new approach to perform Bayesian learning and clustering. We considered a method for alarm Bayesian networks from distributed database. It is based on minimum spanning tree based collective structure learning algorithm. Up to now, some heuristic approaches (greedy algorithm, ant colony algorithm etc.) are used for Bayesian network learning but minimum spanning tree algorithm is not suggested until now. In application, we demonstrate to how create and use the suggested model in real-world data with decision support system. Our heuristic algorithm provides to improve the Bayesian network classification and learning structure searching for dependencies among the attributes. The experimental results show that the minimum spanning tree algorithm for learning BNs with forward structure search steps performed really well, it even reaches a better performance. It is improved, and the search time greatly reduced.

Consequently our algorithm is able to solve learning Bayesian networks with large number variables from data. Also, the experimental results on the benchmark alarm data set shows that the new algorithm is more effective and efficient in large scale databases, and greatly enhances convergence speed compared to the original algorithm.

## VI. References

[1] Neapolitan, R.E. Learning Bayesian Networks, Prentice Hall, New York, NY, USA (2003)

[2] Lauria, E.J.M., Duchessi, P.J. A Bayesian belief network for IT implementation decision support Decision Support Systems, 42 (3) (December 2006), pp. 1573–1588

[3] Ahn, J.H., Ezawa, K.J., Decision support for real-time telemarketing operations through Bayesian network learning Decision Support Systems, 21 (1) (September 1997), pp. 17–27

[4] Kim, S.H., Stochastic ordering and robustness in classification from a Bayesian network Decision Support Systems, 39 (3) (May 2005), pp. 253–266
[5] Jensen, F.V. An Introduction to Bayesian Network University of College London Press (1996)
[6] Andreassen, S., Woldbye, M., Falck, B., Andersen, S., MUNIN: a causal probabilistic network for interpretation of electromyographic findings Proceedings of the Tenth International Joint Conference on Artificial Intelligence (1987), pp. 366–372
[7] Heckerman, D., Horvitz, E., Inferring informational goals from free-text queries: a Bayesian approach G.F. Cooper, S. Moral (Eds.), Proceedings of the Fourteenth Conference on Uncertainty in Artificial Intelligence, Morgan Kaufmann, Wisconsin (July 1998), pp. 230–237
[8] Wong, M.L., Lee, S.Y., Leung, K.S., Data mining of Bayesian networks using cooperative coevolution Decision Support Systems, 38 (3) (December 2004), pp. 451–472
[9] Huang, Z., Li, J., Su, H., Watts, G.S., Chen, H., Large-scale regulatory network analysis from microarray data: modified Bayesian network learning and association rule mining Decision Support Systems, 43 (4) (August 2007), pp. 1207–1225
[10] Heckerman, D., A Tutorial on Learning Bayesian Networks. Kluwer: Learning in Graphical Models, 1996. 301−354
[11] Campos, L. M., Huete, J. F. A new approach for learning belief networks using independence criteria. International Journal of Approximate Reasoning, 2000, 24(1): 11−37
[12] Cheng, J., Greiner, R., Kelly, J., Bell, D., Liu, W., Learning Bayesian networks from data: an information theory based approach. Artificial Intelligence, 2002, 137(1-2): 43−90
[13] Geman, S., Geman, D., Stochastic relaxation, Gibbs distributions and the Bayesian restoration of images IEEE Transactions on Pattern Analysis and Machine Intelligence, 6 (1984), pp. 721–742
[14] Heckerman, D., A tutorial on learning Bayesian networks. Technical Report MSR-TR-95-06, Microsoft Research Adv. Technol. Div., Redmond, WA, 1995.
[15] Ramoni, M., Sebastiani, P., Efficient parameter learning in Bayesian networks from incomplete databases Technical Report KMI-TR-41Knowledge Median Institute, The Open University (1997)
[16] Goroncy, A., Rychlik, T., Lower bounds on the expectations of upper record values, Journal of Statistical Planning and Inference, Volume 141, Issue 8, August 2011, Pages 2726-2737.
[17] Spirtes, P., Glymour, C., Scheines, R., Causation, Prediction, and Search (second ed.)MIT Press (2000)
[18] Lam, W., Bacchus, F., Learning Bayesian belief networks: an approach based on the MDL principle Computational Intelligence, 10 (1994), pp. 269–293
[19] Lauría, E. J.M., Duchessi, P.J., A Bayesian Belief Network for IT implementation decision support, Decision Support Systems, Iss. 342, 1573-1588, 2007.
[20] Chickering, D.M., Optimal Structure Identification with Greedy Search, Journal of Machine Learning Research 3 (2002) 507-554.
[21] Pearl, J., Verma, T., A theory of inferred causation, in: J. Allen, R. Fikes, E. Sandewall (Eds.), Principles of Knowledge Representation and Reasoning: Proceeding of the Second International Conference, Morgan Kaufmann, San Mateo, CA, 1991, pp. 441-452.
[22] Zhang, S.Z., Liu, L., MCMC Samples Selecting for Online Bayesian Network Structure Learning, Proceedings of the Seventh International Conference on Machine Learning and Cybernetics, Kunming, 12-15 July 2008.
[23] http://www.bayesnet.com (Online available, 2012, March 18)
[24] Ahuja, R., K., Magnanti, T.L., Orlin, J.B., Network Flows, Theory, Algorithms, and Applications, Prentice Hall, Upper Saddle River, New Jersey, 1993.
[25]Aguilera, P.A., Fernández, A., Reche, F., Rumí, R. Hybrid Bayesian network classifiers: Application to species distribution models, Environmental Modelling & Software 25 (2010) 1630- 1639
[26] Chow, C.K., Liu, C.N., Approximating Discrete Probability Distribution with Dependence Trees, IEEE Trans. Information Theory, vol.14, 1968
[27] Kevin Murphy (2012, February 10)[online]. Available: http://www.cs.ubc.ca/~murphyk/Software/BNT/bnt.html
[28] Chen, X.W., Anantha, G., and Lin, X., Improving Bayesian Network Structure Learning with Mutual Information-Based Node Ordering in the K2 Algorithm, IEEE Transactions On Knowledge And Data Engineering, Vol. 20, No. 5, May 2008

# A LARGE SCALE DESALINATION OF SEA WATER BY SOLAR ENERGY USING AN UNCONVENTIONAL SEAWATER COLLECTORS SCHEME

Ashry, Mohammed H.
College of Sciences
Shaqra University
Shaqra, Riyadh
Saudi Arabia

IEEE DOI
Paper ID #: IKE2056

**Abstract:** The future of the world's drinking water will someday depend on cheap accessible technology to produce it. Saudi Arabia is the world's leading nation in water desalination. Without desalination, Saudi Arabia's central regions may become uninhabitable within the foreseeable future. There are many advanced yet less costly seawater-desalination techniques. These methods can produce large amounts of desalinated water for less and without the costly maintenance. Assuming that the common problem associated with water desalination is the costly maintenance of the plants; the method suggested in this paper will reduce costs significantly. Harvesting solar energy through the direct heating of seawater is the most economically efficient and least technologically advanced method available to man. Depending on the number and size of the multi-stage flash (MSF) evaporator units used, up to 20 BG/yr of desalinated sweat water maybe produced. The cost of this process can be summed up as follows; 1. The initial installation and construction of the concrete-based seawater collectors and its tar-covered metal tops. 2. The MSF evaporator units, the concrete reservoirs accessing tidal waters to and from the plant's site and of course, the gas-fuel powered pumps used to pump sweet water to customers. This paper will project the amount of water produced over the next ten years, and provide a simple economic cost and benefit analysis of the project in comparison to a similar (in size of output) nuclear and fully-gas-powered plants.

**Index of Terms:**

Coriolis force.................. ..= force of earth rotation
Desalination......................= distillation of sea water
Heat transfer coefficient = the material's capacity to transmit heat
Laminar flow = slow moving water, usually on flat surfaces under normal conditions and room temperatures
Shear stress......................= a form of pressure usually between two different materials with different density
Specific heat = material capacity to absorb and store/contain heat
Thermal conductivity = material capacity to conduct heat
Tidal range...................... = differences between tides at their lowest and highest levels
Turbulent flow = violent moving water usually sloping surfaces and often under high temperatures

**Glossary of Terms:**

$A_{cs}$ =duct cross sectional area =Dh*Pw/4
$A_{sf}$= area of solar fields
A=L*hw=area of the reservoir wall
$C_D$ = the wind drag coefficient
C = the Chezzy coefficient
d&l =length and width of the duct
$f_{cx}$ =-qΩ (Coriolis) Earth rotation forces in x direction
$f_{cy}$ = pΩ (Coriolis)Earth rotation forces in y directions
g = gravitational acceleration,
ha = the aluminum heat transfer coefficient
hMx = (ht*hti*ha)/(ht*hti+ht*ha+hti*ha))
hSm= heat transfer coefficient of the surface material in series
ht = the tar heat transfer coefficient and
hti = the tin heat transfer coefficient and
h= hMx =the heat transfer coefficient of the surface materials in series.
h&d are height and random height of measured velocity respectively
h=reservoir depth
Kc/y= thermal conductivity and base thickness respectively

$M_{fr}$ = mass flow rate
$P_r$=Pressure
P = h*u = velocity fluxes in x direction,
q=h*ν = velocity fluxes in y direction,
$V_{ave}$ = average velocity
u = depth-averaged-flow-velocities in x direction,
u(r)= velocity profile (laminar and turbulent cases)
ν, = depth-averaged-flow-velocities in y direction,
$u_w$ = is the wind speeds in x and y directions
$\nu_w$ = is the wind speeds in x and y directions
$\rho_w$ = the density of the water,
ρ=density
$\rho_w$= water density
$\rho_a$ = the density of the air,
$\Delta T_s$= surface temperature difference between the surface and the temp inside the duct in Kelvin
Δt= time per heating cycle
$\tau_{bx} = \rho_w\, gp(p^2+q^2)^{1/2}/(C^2h^2)$ and
$\tau_{by} = \rho_w\, gq(p^2+q^2)^{1/2}/(C^2h^2)$,
$\tau_{sx} = \rho_a\, C_D\, u_w\, |U_{wind}|$,
$\tau_{sy} = \rho_a\, C_D\, \nu_w\, |U_{wind}|$.
$\tau_{bx}$, = bed friction stresses in x direction
$\tau_{by}$ = bed friction stresses in y direction
$\xi = h + h_y$ = water depth above the gradually sloping sea bottom,

# 1. Introduction

Solar energy and its water distillation applications have always been the subject of extensive studies and analyses (1), although, it has never been deployed on a large scale. Efforts have been limited to small-scale housing units, small size water purification or distillation units etc (2). The reasons for this are easily recognized for the following reasons: 1. Cost of the units are – for roof/floor type solar distillation units - up to $ 40/m² of basin area (3), near semi populated areas, considering the amount of distilled water produced, thus making large-scale deployment economically unattractive when compared to other means of desalination. 2. Difficulties in maintenance because of the fragility of the units' glass panels, subject to breakage, flushing of the basins, cleaning the surface of the panels due to sand accumulation from sand storms, and flow of distillate to centralized water collection reservoirs, not to mention other natural causes resulting from weather patterns and other accidents. Now, for electric solar cells, the cost is astronomical, considering the electrical energy produced. The method, assuming it utilizes solar energy to produce electricity for desalinating or demineralizing river waters; separates unwanted minerals in saline water using electric current and selective permeable membranes (4). As a result, other methods have received the lion share of commercial utilization, in conjunction with other conventional distillation plants. However, the solar energy collection systems in most of these schemes are conventional collectors which are very costly, making the schemes economically (because of the high cost of collectors) and technically (because of breakage of plastic covers, corrosion problems, damage to electrical components, membranes (5), and other maintenance, and desert-related issues) (6), problematic (7). Hence most of the existing large scale (with capacity greater than 400-500MG/yr ) desalination plants around the world are fossil fuel powered (such as coal, petroleum, and natural gas, nuclear power introduced lately), and the majority of them are multi-stage flash (high temperature) evaporation (MSF) systems. Fossil fuels are predicted to be depleted, probably, within our lifetime, not to mention that their prices are already spiraling almost out of control. As a result of increases in water demand, rising world population and cost of industrialization it is imperative to look for new methods of solar distillation. The system employed in this paper is robust, economical, and utilizes direct solar heat. With this in mind, I have devised a scheme (8), to be outlined in this paper for a large scale desalination of sea water using solar energy (9), hopefully to be implemented in the eastern desert of Saudi Arabia: The technical and economic feasibility of this scheme was the subject of research, by many. However, my focus, in this case, is to present preliminary technical and simple cost calculations.

# 2. The Approach

The approach takes place in four stages (Figure 1). Stage I stresses bringing water in large masses to continuously running, in succession, reservoirs near and/or around the location of the solar collectors' fields, without the use of mechanical pumps. Two reservoirs will be utilized for the following reasons, 1. Keep the water running during changes in sea-tides, 2. Avoid accumulation of desert sand, during sand storms in the solar field water ducts, which may lead to clogging up the ducts, 3. Expedite the process during maintenance periods. Stage II consists of two solar fields, each housing two thousand water heating ducts. Each duct is 90 cm wide, 10 cm high and 1000 meter long, with 10 cm separating the ducts. The water passes from Stage I, through the multi-stage flash (MSF) evaporators, in stage III, where it receives initial heating from the condensing vapor in the desalination plant's coolant tubes (condensers). The water then flows to stage II,
using gravity, where it is heated in the solar fields' ducts prior to going back to stage III's evaporators, where desalination takes place. Desalinated water flows to a special reservoir where it is pumped to customers. The excess sea-water flows to the outlet reservoir and on back to the sea through hydraulically controlled gates in stage IV. The water flowing into and out of the desalination plant will utilize sea tidal ranges in the area.

The approach emphasizes three main parameters: cost, amount of heating energy produced, and the scope of maintenance. A decision-making series of steps is used to determine the essential elements of this paper as follows:

1. Size and depth of the reservoirs are set as follows:
   a. For incoming water during high tide periods the two reservoirs must have the capacity to hold enough water for the daily amount required for desalination. The outlet reservoir has the capacity to hold the average amount processed in an entire daily cycle.
   i. For incoming water during high tide periods the two reservoirs must have the capacity to hold enough water for the daily amount required for desalination. The outlet reservoir has the capacity to hold the average amount processed in an entire daily cycle. The two solar fields are made up of 2000 rectangular ducts, each. (0.90) meter wide, (0.10) meter in height and 1000 meter in length.
   ii. The amount of water passing through the two solar fields per cycle (its duration to be determined later) is (.1*.9*1000*4000 = 360000 $M^3$ (cubic meter)/cycle ~ 95.101200 MG/cycle
   b. The depth, for the inlet reservoirs, must be at least one meter below the lowest low tide in the region, however, for the outlet reservoir it should be at the same height as the lowest tide.
      i. Simulation of the tidal ranges in the gulf (10, page 799), indicates certain aspects of the tides that can be used in favor of the plant's location (11), and ways to augment the tidal heights.
   c. The height of the inlet reservoir's walls must be at least one meter above the highest high tide, and as high as the desalination excess water level for the outlet reservoir.
      i. The referenced endnotes related to the low tides can be employed in enhancing the high tides
2. The water pressure-based four hydraulic gates must be designed to do the following (12):
   a. Control the flow of water
      i. From the sea to the feeding reservoirs,
      ii. From the feeding reservoirs to the solar fields through the evaporators
      iii. From the evaporators to the outlet-reservoirs and finally
      iv. From outlet-reservoirs to the sea.
   b. Be capable of holding the water mass of the reservoir at a base height equal to that of the low tide and as high as the reservoir's wall
   c. Must open and close at a pace that allows for the water flow-rate needed for the desalination process
   d. Must use mechanism that utilizes the water flow
      i. The fluctuation of water level and water weight
3. The material used to build the solar fields collectors, its surface-cover, and the solar-radiation heat-absorbing layer coating the surface should be selected with emphasis on:
   a. Cost effectiveness
   b. Availability and ease of manufacturing and fabrication
   c. Ease of maintenance and durability
   d. Resistance to corrosion and ruggedness to endure the extremes of the desert weather
      i. The floor of the collectors must consist of material that is resistant to corrosion and has a high heat capacity to endure the desert's temperature extremes
      1) A list of materials/elements are assessed in terms of the above characteristics
      a) Hard concrete was selected as it does meet, to a certain extent, all of the above attributes with the exception of the heat transfer rate/coefficient, where it is not a necessary requirement; since the floor and walls of the collectors will not be exposed to, or in contact with the source of the energy, the sun
      b) The cost effectiveness will be assessed, in more
      c) details, along with the materials selected for the surface layers
      d) The slope of the solar fields' ducts is determined through an analysis of the water velocity in a rectangular concrete duct:
      ✓ The analysis takes into account the assumption that the movement of water in a heated concrete-duct resembles the movement of water in a river
      ➢ The upward change in the duct's water temperature causes the water to move upward and as the water flows it reciprocates creating turbulence – added to the coarse concrete walls and surface-similar to that of a river's turbulent water flow because of the river's uneven and rough bed acting as resistance and creating turbulence
      ✓ The amount of time required for the water to reach its maximum seasonal

temperature is also a factor in both the water velocity and the solar ducts' sloping gradient

✓ The mathematical formulation employed takes into account the above factors

ii. The ceiling of the collectors must be made up of material that is resistant to corrosion with high specific-heat and heat transfer coefficient

1) The ceiling will be made up of three materials emphasizing absorptivity, conductivity, emissivity, radiation, convection, and transmission of heat

2) The material will be layered in accordance to the predisposed reactivity of the materials

a) The bottom of the surface layer is made up of a very thin layer of Tin laminate for its resistance to corrosion and its reasonably high thermal conductivity

b) The middle layer of the surface is Aluminum for its high heat capacity, and thermal conductivity

c) The upper layer is made up of thin Tar rolls for its high absorptivity and low emissivity

iii. The related theories of heat mass transfer, conductance, radiation, convection, absorbency, and admittance will be derived/formulated and employed with the above .

iv. The amount of heat energy transmitted to the water in the duct is calculated

4. The multi-stage flash (MSF) evaporators used for the desalination.

   a. The plant will be fitted with a set of multi stage flash evaporators capable of processing the volume of water heated by the solar fields

5. A simple cost analysis of the entire scheme is performed to evaluate the system as a future project

Figure 1: Sea water to condensers black arrows, sea water from condensers to water collectors red lines, heated sea water from collectors to evaporators blue lines, desalinated water to reservoir in yellow lines, and excess water to outlet reservoir where it flows back to sea through canals under sea water inlet during low tides (Outlet Reservoir)

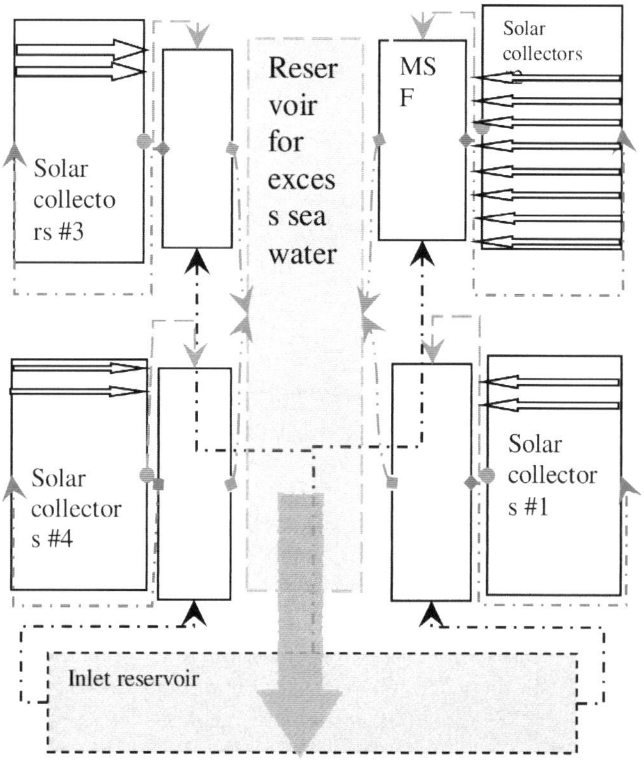


## 3. The Technical Analysis

### 3.1. Tidal Analysis:

The analysis of the tidal waves'-ranges in the eastern region of Saudi Arabia, west of the Persian Gulf can benefit from the relationship between tidal waves and shallow waters in the gulf. The tidal waves rotations are situated within pathways around amphidromic points where in shallower straits the tide elevate, kind of, as in the phenomenon called tsunami. Since the land in certain areas near the gulf is almost at sea level (13), the flow of water into the land during high tides requires the removal of no more than a few feet in depth of easily removable sand, for the plant's required area. The technical aspects can utilize the methodology applied By "Chwang, Lee, Leung" (14). These tides fluctuate throughout the year between 2 – 3 meters and may reach 5 meters, with human interference, as it approaches the straits between the islands on the seaside borders of Saudi Arabia between Bahrain and the location of the northern amphidromic point. Human interference can be used to influence both the tidal range and frequency through the establishment of man-made islands creating straits and shallow water channels (15). The main factors affecting the tidal ranges, in this case, have a lot to do with the movement of water around the amphidromic points. The water in the Persian Gulf circulates counter-clockwise, with Northward current along the Iranian shores and the southward current run along the Saudi shores, with the shoreline at the Iranian side shows a steep and narrow shoreline, while the Saudi side display a gradual slope with a wide intertidal zone (16). The water depth; its vector flux velocity, in x and y directions; Coriolis force, the force caused by the rotation of the earth and the moon's gravitational pull; the slope of the bottom of the sea, density of the water; and resistance to water movement so called the bed friction stresses of the water at sea bottom are the main factors impacting the tidal ranges. However, our objective is to increase the flux velocity and displacement in the x and y directions[1]. We know that the flux flow in the direction vertical to both earth rotation and the lunar gravitation force (in this case the z component) is negligible so our emphasis is to augment the water flow in a direction around the amphidromic point's semi-circular motion. The lunar gravitational force field creates a tidal flux flow that can be measured by incorporating simplified fluid dynamics schemes. the employment of the moon's gravitational pull along with the earth's rotation was, in my opinion, more successful with less mathematical complexity in describing the actual tidal fluctuations. Their analysis put more emphasis on the oceanic tidal fluctuation, and its effects on the occurrence and frequency of the major high tides in high and low seas(23).

### 3.2. Reservoirs Walls and Gates:

The reservoirs walls' structure should be within certain parameters and criteria to retain large amounts of water. It is expected to endure the weather extremes and salty waters for the lifetime of the project. The water weight and it's tidal pressure, the salty waters and the harsh environment are too intrusively abrasive; overtime, these combination will put a lot of stress on the walls and could cause major damage to the walls and the foundations, (17).

The water in the reservoirs and intake canals are almost always static, so the forces on the walls and foundations can be investigated in terms of the pressure applied (Figure 2); the
force formula is as follows:

$$F_r(h)= \rho_w * g * L * h_w * dh \quad (1)$$

$$Pr()\,(h)= \rho_w * g * dh \quad (2)$$

h=reservoir depth Pr=Pressure $\rho_w$= water density $A=L*h_w$=area of the reservoir wall Pressure increases as we go down the reservoir's wall (Figure 2)[2]

figure 2. water pressure on a wall 1

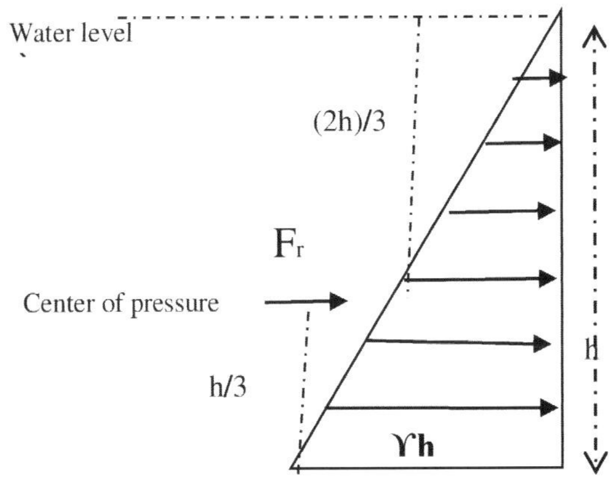


### 3.3. Water Velocity in Solar Fields Ducts (18):

The velocity calculation utilizes the law of conservation of mass where:

$$M_{fr}\text{[3]} = \rho * Vave * Acs = \int_{dl} \rho\, u(r) dAcs \quad (3)$$

Leads to

$$\hat{u}(r)= (M_{fr})(\rho * Acs)^{-1} \quad (4)$$

The volume flow rate can be employed to facilitate the calculation of the average velocity

$\dot{\upsilon} = V_{ave} * A_{cs} = M_{fr}/\rho$

Where the laminar and turbulent velocities are analyzed in terms of the roughness, friction factor, shear stress and Reynolds number where. The velocity of the water, although assumed to be laminar, may fluctuate during the hot summer days, however, it is approximated to be 0.065. It is possible for the water to flow at a faster pace during the summer as the temperature picks up and air density becomes lower.

$M_{fr}$ = mass flow rate, $\rho$=density, $V_{ave}$ = average velocity, Acs =duct cross sectional area $=D_h * P_w/4$,
u(r)= velocity profile (laminar and turbulent cases), d&l =length and width of the duct h&d are height and random height of measured velocity respectively, $D_h$= hydraulic diameter $P_w$=wetted parameter. Figure 3 presents a simplified image of the heat collectors.

(Figure 3): **The solar fields collectors' cross section**

---

[1] Discussion of the tidal technical aspects and further analysis is in appendix A

[2] Derivation and further analysis in appendix B

[3] Derivation and further analysis in terms of Reynolds and Prandt numbers in appendix C

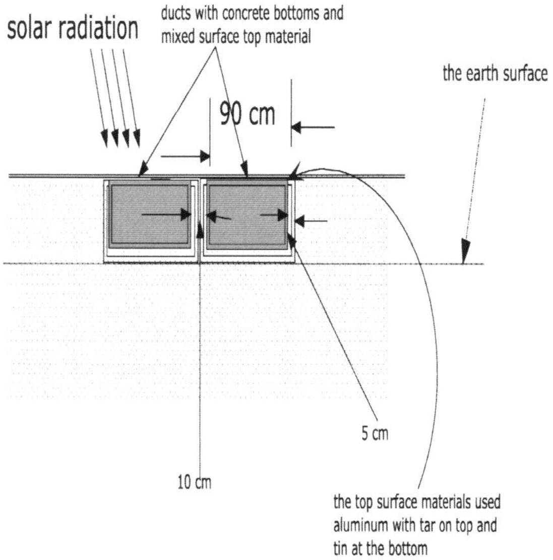


### 3.4. Heat Transfer Analysis:

The heat transferred to the water within the duct can be calculated in terms of the heat transmitted through the combination of materials used to cover the surface of the solar fields, namely the tar, the tin foil-rolls and the aluminum sheets in between[4]. The heat received from the concrete bottom of the solar fields is calculated using the temperature of the surface since the solar fields are laid flat on the desert floor[5]. The total heat transferred into the water is as follows: Heat from the surface of the ducts + heat from the bottom of the collectors (19) Where the time per heating cycle is approximated to be 4 hours, appropriate for the daily tidal rate of recurrence (diurnal phases)

$$Q_i = h_{Sm}*(\Delta T_s)*A_{sf}*(\Delta t)+(K_c/y)*(\Delta T_b)*A_{sf}*(\Delta t) \quad (5)$$

$$h_{Sm} =((1)/((1/h)+(M_x/K_x))) \quad (6)$$

(20),

$h_{Sm}$= heat transfer coefficient of the surface material in series -- $(\Delta T_s)$= surface temperature difference between the surface and the temp inside the duct in Kelvin, $A_{sf}$ is the area of solar fields $(\Delta t)$is time per heating cycle, $(K_c/y)$are thermal conductivity and base thickness respectively; $h_{Mx} = (h_t*h_{ti}*h_a)/(h_t*h_{ti}+h_t*h_a+h_{ti}*h_a))$ where $h_t$ is the tar heat transfer coefficient, and $h_{ti}$ is the tin heat transfer coefficient and $h_a$ is the aluminum heat transfer coefficient, h= $h_{Mx}$ =the heat transfer coefficient of the surface materials in series.

[4] Analysis and derivation of the surface heat energy produced is in appendix C

[5] Analysis and derivation of the concrete ducts' bottom is done in appendix C

The surface's temperature of the desert west of the Persian gulf fluctuates during the summer period from one year to another. A $50^0$+ C temperature was recorded for sixty days in a row in at least one summer during the first decade of this century in the Saudi desert, and that was in the shade, although it was not documented. However, I have measured the temperature of water in an aluminum pipe, one that is exposed to the sun throughout most of the day, during the last week of July, of 2010; the temperature was a whopping 83 $C^0$. The amount of energy transferred to the water for a 4 hr cycle is calculated to be

$Q_i$ = 2.961688 MJ/ $m^2$

Figure 4 presents a simple graph of the collector's shape for the water velocity and heat analysis

(Figure 4)coordinates and forces within the heat collectors

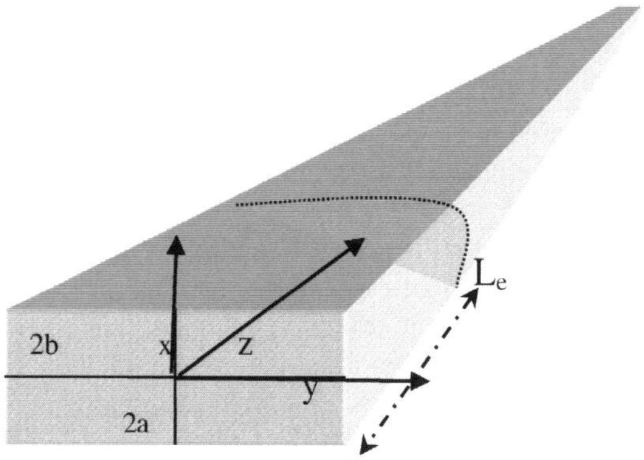


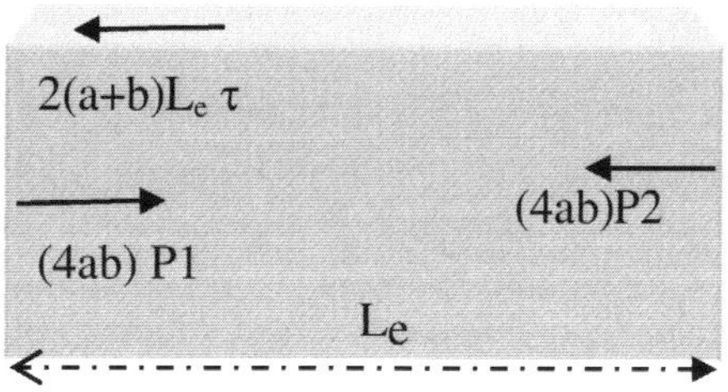


The sweet-water output of the distillation can be measured in many ways (21). In this case it is approximated using the following simple equation:

$W^6$ =E * Qi ( (MJ)* Asf )/ 2.3 *(hrs/cycle)(22)

(7)

W= 3.47676 $10^4 m^3$/hr ~ 9.1845679 MG/hr

The method used for calculating the desalination output emphasizes that the brine temperature out of the solar fields be >32 $C^0$ . The temperature of the sea water during the summer time is in that range, the solar fields

[6] Analysis of the system is in appendix D

collectors' temperature during the peak hours are estimated to exceed $70^0$ C. The new generation of multi stage flash evaporators are said to be 15-20 % more efficient than the old ones. The brine water pipes are smaller and sturdier with a higher heat transfer rate. The plant could maintain a productive cycle throughout the year (with the exception of January-February, where the water is more abundant, for maintenance and clean up of mostly sand and residuals in the MSF and solar fields' ducts respectively). In general, accurate estimates of the water produced will facilitate the manufacturing of better systems to evaporate and condense saline water. The complexity of such analysis maybe rewarded with better output, and eventually outcome for countries located in hydro-dynamically deficient territories(27). sea-water deposits.

### 3.5. Water and Cost:

Assuming a successful intake and output of water for the entire 3 summer months, the hottest months of the year, the plant utilizes over 64.8 X $10^7$ $M^3$/year to produce over 6.26 X $10^7$ $M^3$/year, the equivalent of approximately 16532.2 MG/year. The cost of the project is much lower when implemented on a large scale, the cost of the material is much higher when procured on retail basis. The method employs low technology in every aspect of the project and the material is easily accessible directly from the manufacturers within Saudi Arabia. The MSF units, the concrete material along with the elements used for the solar-field's surface are the most expensive elements in the entire project. A square meter, 2mm thick Aluminum sheet is \$1; a square meter, 1 mm thick Tar roll is \$0.4, a square meter, 0.1 mm thick roll of Tin/Aluminum foil is \$0.25. These are manufacturers' approximated prices, on large-stocks wholesale based-rates. Cement-based 1 square meter concrete slabs, 10.0 cm thick, cost on average \$3. Labor, in Saudi Arabia and specifically for a low-tech manual-labor effort is ~ \$ 4.0/$m^2$. Digging and tunneling of the plant's basin costs ~ \$ 4.0 /$m^2$, for each single cubic meter. On average, the project requires the basin to be 1-3 meters under ground-level, and above the low-tide level. The total area required is 6.0 X $10^6$ $m^2$. The plant is divided to four sections, reservoirs area, two parallel solar fields, each two kilometers long and one kilometer wide, and centrally located MSF evaporators-condensers units. The average cost of these units without the energy producing heaters/steamers and their electronic controls and pumps fluctuate. Companies, manufacturers and distributers provide limited data if the major elements are not included in the purchase. However, for the number and size of the units required to accommodate this large project \$600.0 is a close estimate (23). In addition to the cost of overhead; such as delivery, transportation and labor accommodations, and taking into account the fluctuating market prices, not to mention loan interests, the cost per square meter is estimated to reach \$150.0 /$m^2$. This stretches the project's total cost to \$900.0 million. This is 30-40 % cheaper than most MSF or reverse osmosis (RO) projects, largest of which produces over 50% less water, and requires continuous maintenance. One of the most important advantages of this project is its low cost and almost negligible maintenance-requirements. The two coldest months of the year are recommended for the plant's maintenance, for cleaning and removing precipitants and other sea-water deposits.

## 4. Conclusion:

The calculation above provides us with ample data indicating that seawater desalination using direct sun light is a very productive and profitable enterprise. The future world may be leaning towards modern and advanced methods of industry, however, the cost of such technology is also rising at an astronomical rate. Consequently, poor and technologically disadvantaged nations can employ such system to produce more water for less. Saudi Arabia is known for its vast and desolate desert. A project of this magnitude, and hopefully many more

## 5. References:


1. E. D. Howe and B. W. Tleimat, Solar Distillation at the University of California. *Solar Energy* **16**, 97 (1974).
2. Y. Assouad, Z. Lavan; "Solar Desalination With Latent Heat Recovery", J. Solar Energy Eng. ;(Feb 01, 1988) K. S. Spiegler, *Salt-Water Purification*, p 80 85, Plenum Press, New York (1977).
3. http://practicalactionpublishing.org/practicalanswers/product_info.php?cPath=22&products_id=165
4. Asghar Husain, Bushara , Ali El-Nashar and Aldil Alradif; PHYSICAL, CHEMICAL AND BIOLOGICAL ASPECTS OF WATER - Separation Phenomena in Desalination Processes
International Centre for Water and Energy Systems,
Abu Dhabi, UA
5. Asghar Husain, Bushara , Ali El-Nashar and Aldil Alradif; PHYSICAL, CHEMICAL AND BIOLOGICAL ASPECTS OF WATER - Separation Phenomena in Desalination Processes
International Centre for Water and Energy Systems, Abu Dhabi, UAE

6. D. B. Brice, Saline Water Conversion by Flash Evaporation Utilizing Solar Energy. *Adv. Chem. Ser* **38**, 99 (1963).
7. http://www.jubail-wildlife-sanctuary.info/pdf/physical_setting_detail.pdf
8. D. B. Brice, Saline Water Conversion by Flash Evaporation Utilizing Solar Energy. *Adv. Chem. Ser* **38**, 99 (1963).
9. C. N. Hodges *et al*. Solar Distillation Utilizing Multiple-Effect Humidification. *Final Rep*., Solar Energy Laboratory of the Institute of Atmospheric Physics, University of Arizona (1966).
10. Aghajanloo, Ameleh; Pirouz, Moharam Dolatshahi; Namin, Masoud Montazeri; Numerical Simulation of Tidal Currents in Persian Gulf; World Academy of Science, Engineering and Technology 58 2011.
11. www.jubail.wildlife.sanctuary.info/pdf/**physical_setting**_detail.pdf
12. Walski, Thomas M., "Water Distribution Systems Handbook"; Pennsylvania American Water Company, Wilkes-Barre, PA.
13. http://www.jubail.wildlife.sanctuary.info/pdf/physical_setting_detail.pdf
14. A.T. Chwang, J. H. W. Lee, D. Y. C. Leung; Hydrodynamics, Volume 1(pages 709-726); 1996 Balkema, Rotterdam.
15. www.jubail.wildlife.sanctuary.info/pdf/**physical_setting**_detail.pdf
16. www.jubail.wildlife.sanctuary.info/pdf/**physical_setting**_detail (pages 20-21).pdf
17. British Standard Institute (BSI), "Code of Practice for Design of Concrete Structures for Retaining Aqueous Liquids ";
18. Çengel, Yunus A.; Cimbala, John M. "FLUID MECHANICS: FUNDAMENTALS AND APPLICATIONS" Published by McGraw-Hill, a business unit of The McGraw-Hill Companies, Inc.,1221 Avenue of the Americas, New York, NY 10020. Copyright © 2006
19. E. R. G. Eckert and R. M. Drake, Jr., *Analysis of Heat and Mass Transfer*, McGraw-Hill, New York (1972).
20. D. B. Brice, Saline Water Conversion by Flash Evaporation Utilizing Solar Energy. *Adv. Chem. Ser* **38**, 99 (1963).
21. http://www.teriin.org/index.php?option=com_content&task=view&id=62
22. http://www.aquatech.com/technologies/Desalination/MultistageFlashMSF.aspx
    http://www.saltworkstech.com/
    http://www.doosan.com/doosanheavy/en/aboutus/see_doosan_at_work.page
23. Doan Mai-Linh, Brodsky, Emily E., Prioul, Romain, Signer, Claude; "Tidal analysis of borehole pressure A tutorial", (2006); University of California, Santa Cruz and and Schlumberger-Doll Research; December 20, 2006
24. Aghajanloo, Ameleh; Pirouz, Moharam Dolatshahi; Namin, Masoud Montazeri; Numerical Simulation of Tidal Currents in Persian Gulf; World Academy of Science, Engineering and Technology 58 2011
25. www.jubail.wildlife.sanctuary.info/pdf/**physical_setting**_detail (page 25).pdf
26. www.jubail.wildlife.sanctuary.info/pdf/**physical_setting**_detail (page 20-21).pdf
27. Yung, C. S., Lansing, F. L.; "Performance Simulation of the JPL Solar-Power Distiller, Part I. Quasi-Steady-State Conditions", DSN Engineering;


**Appendix A:**

Tidal Analysis

**Appendix B:**

Water velocity derivation and formulation

**Appendix C:**

Heat Analysis formula derivations and analysis

**Appendix D:**

Water output analysis

**Appendex E:**

The decision making fowchart

# SESSION

# POSTERS

## Chair(s)

### TBA

# An Investigation of Data Privacy and Utility Preservation using KNN Classification as a Gauge

**Kato Mivule[1] and Claude Turner PhD[2]**
[1]mivulek0220@students.bowiestate.edu,[2]cturner@bowiestate.edu
Computer Science Department, Bowie State University, Bowie, MD, USA

**Abstract –** It is obligatory that organizations by law safeguard the privacy of individuals when handling datasets containing personal identifiable information (PII). Nevertheless, during the process of data privatization, the utility or usefulness of the privatized data diminishes. Yet achieving the optimal balance between data privacy and utility needs has been documented as an NP-hard challenge. In this study, we investigate data privacy and utility preservation using KNN machine learning classification as a gauge.

**Keywords:** Data Privacy Preservation, Data Utility, Machine Learning, KNN Classification.

## I. Introduction

DURING the process of data privatization, the utility or usefulness of the privatized data diminishes. Yet achieving the optimal balance between data privacy and utility needs has been documented as an NP-hard challenge [1] [2]. In this study, we investigate data privacy and utility preservation using KNN machine learning classification as a gauge. As Cynthia Dwork succinctly and aptly stated [6]:

> "Perfect privacy can be achieved by publishing nothing at all, but this has no utility; perfect utility can be obtained by publishing the data exactly as received, but this offers no privacy".

In this study, we investigate data privacy and utility preservation using KNN machine learning classification as a gauge [4].

*Noise addition:* is a data privacy perturbative method that adds a random value, usually selected from a normal distribution with zero mean and a very small standard deviation, to sensitive numerical attribute values to ensure privacy [3] [8]. The general expression of noise addition as defined:

$$X + \varepsilon = Z \qquad (1)$$

Where $X$ is the original numerical dataset and $\varepsilon$ is the set of random values (noise) with a distribution $e \sim N(0, \sigma^2)$ that is added to $X$, and finally $Z$ is the privatized dataset.

This work was supported in part by the U.S. Department of Education HBGI Grant.

Claude Turner, PhD is an Associate Professor of Computer Science and Director for the Center for Cyber Security and Emerging Technologies at Bowie State University. (E-mail: cturner@bowiestate.edu).

Kato Mivule is a doctoral candidate, Computer Science Department, Bowie State University. (E-mail: mivulek0220@students.bowiestate.edu).

*K Nearest Neighbors (KNN):* is a classification method that matches items in the test data to those in the training data by measuring the distance between the two items. Any $k$ items that are closer to each other are then placed in the same class. The Euclidean distance is the normally used distance measure for KNN expressed as follows [5]:

$$distance(x, y) = \sqrt{\sum_{i=1}^{n}(x_i - y_i)^2} \qquad (2)$$

## II. Methodology

In the first stage of our approach, we apply a data privacy procedure, in this case, noise addition, on the Iris dataset for privacy [7]. The privatized Iris dataset is then sent to the KNN machine learning classifier for training and testing using 10 fold cross validation; the classification error is quantified. If the classification error is lower or equal to a threshold, then better utility might be achieved, otherwise, we adjust the data privacy parameters and re-classify the results.

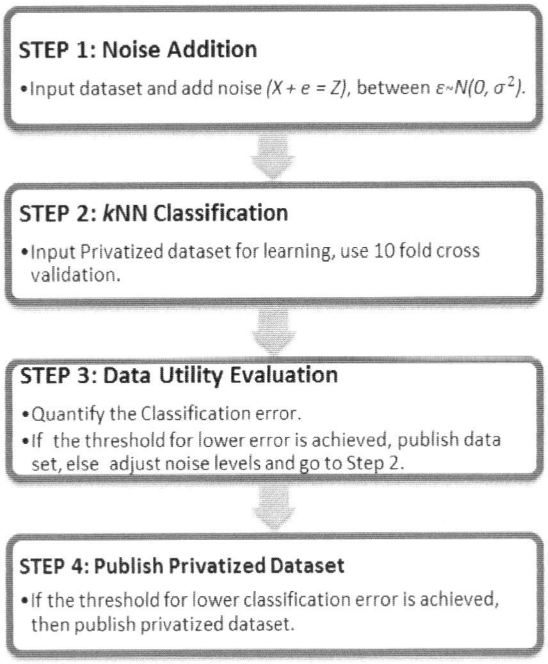


## III. Experiment

In our experiment, we used the Iris dataset from the UCI machine learning repository as our original dataset [9]. We then privatized the dataset by using the noise addition data privacy technique. We then used KNN classification and quantified the classification error. We adjusted the noise levels and run the privatized dataset through the KNN classifier after which we published the results. We used MATLAB for both noise addition and KNN classification.

## IV. Results

As shown in our initial results, only 4 percent of records from the original Iris dataset were misclassified. When noise addition was chosen between the mean and standard deviation for the privatized dataset, 32 per cent of records got misclassified. However, when noise addition was reduced to mean = 0 and standard deviation = 0.1 for the privatized dataset, 26 percent of records got misclassified, a 6 point reduction in classification error.

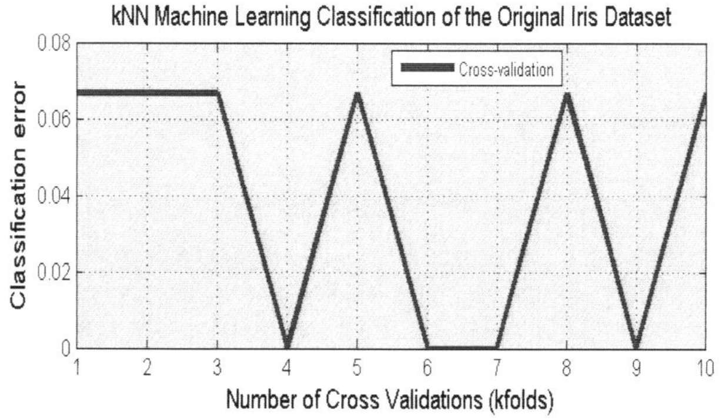


Fig 1: KNN classification of the original Iris dataset with classification error at 0.0400 (4 percent misclassified data)

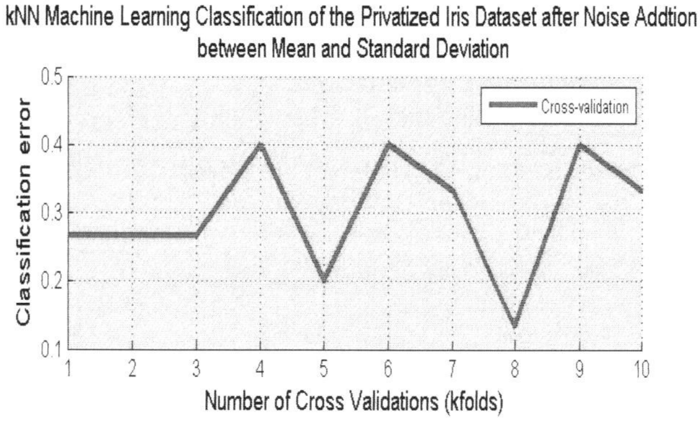


Fig 2: KNN classification of the privatized Iris dataset with noise addition between the mean and standard deviation.

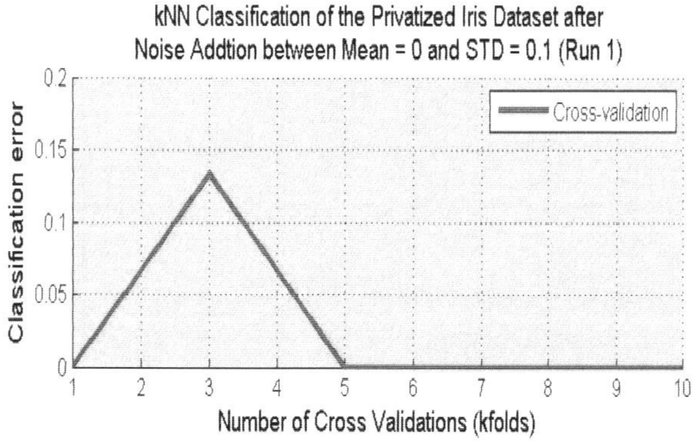


Fig 3: KNN classification of the privatized Iris dataset with reduced noise addtion between mean = 0 and standard deviation = 0.1

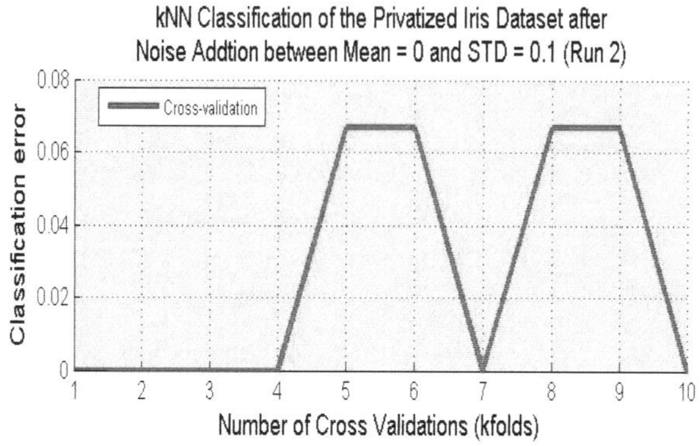


Fig 4: A second run of the *k*NN classification of the privatized Iris dataset with reduced noise addition between mean = 0 and standard deviation = 0.1.

## V. Conclusion and Discussion

The initial results from our investigation show that a reduction in noise levels does affect the classification error rate. However, this reduction in noise levels could lead to low risky privacy levels. Finding the optimal balance between data privacy and utility needs is still problematic.

## Acknowledgment

Special thanks to Dr. Claude Turner and the Computer Science Department at Bowie State University for making this work possible.

## References

[1] R. C.-W. Wong, A. W.-C. Fu, K. Wang, and J. Pei, "Minimality Attack in Privacy Preserving Data Publishing," Proceedings of the 33rd international conference on Very large data bases, pp. 543–554, 2007.
[2] A. Krause and E. Horvitz, "A Utility-Theoretic Approach to Privacy in Online Services," Journal of Artificial Intelligence Research, vol. 39, pp. 633–662, 2010.
[3] J. Kim, "A Method For Limiting Disclosure in Microdata Based Random Noise and Transformation," in Proceedings of the Survey Research Methods, American Statistical Association,, 1986, vol. Jay Kim, A, no. 3, pp. 370–374.
[4] M. Banerjee, "A utility-aware privacy preserving framework for distributed data mining with worst case privacy guarantee," University of Maryland, Baltimore County, 2011.
[5] B. Liú, Web Data Mining: Exploring Hyperlinks, Contents, and Usage Data, Datacentric Systems and Applications. Springer, 2011, pp. 124–125.
[6] C. Dwork, "Differential Privacy," in Automata languages and programming, vol. 4052, no. d, M. Bugliesi, B. Preneel, V. Sassone, and I. Wegener, Eds. Springer, 2006, pp. 1–12.
[7] K. Mivule, C. Turner, and S.-Y. Ji, "Towards A Differential Privacy and Utility Preserving Machine Learning Classifier," in Procedia Computer Science, 2012, vol. 12, pp. 176–181.
[8] K. Mivule, "Utilizing Noise Addition for Data Privacy, an Overview," in Proceedings of the International Conference on Information and Knowledge Engineering (IKE 2012), 2012, pp. 65–71.
[9] Frank, A., Asuncion, A. Iris Data Set, UCI Machine Learning Repository [http://archive.ics.uci.edu/ml/datasets/Iris]. Department of Information and Computer Science, University of California, Irvine, CA (2010).

# Building Energy Ontology for Energy Saving Based on Context-aware Reasoning

**Jinsoo Han, Youn-Kwae Jeong, and Ilwoo Lee**
Smart Green Life Research Department
Electronics and Telecommunications Research Institute, Daejeon, Republic of Korea

**Abstract** - *Ontology is very useful to represent knowledge as a set of concepts within a domain. A number of ontologies have been proposed and developed in many kinds of domain. Ontology can provide a method to model a specific domain and support reasoning capability. It can also provide context-awareness easily. Therefore, we propose the building energy ontology to save the building energy based on the context-aware reasoning. The proposed ontology is composed of six sub ontologies. We describe the building energy ontology model and explain its mechanism. The energy-wasting context information is reasoned based on the abstracted event data translated from the sensor data. The operation information is drawn based on the reasoned context information. The operation information is applied to the corresponding object to get rid of the energy-wasting context. The proposed ontology can contribute to the building domain energy saving through event-driven context-aware reasoning*[1].

**Keywords:** Ontology; Reasoning; Domain Knowledge; Energy Saving; Building Energy

## 1 Introduction

Ontology is a useful structural framework for organizing information and knowledge that represent the real world. In computer science and information science, ontology formally represents knowledge as a set of concepts within a domain, and the relationships between pairs of concepts [1]. These representational entities are able to be comprehended by human beings and come with machine-readable formats that are composed of the classes, the properties, and the relationships between classes [2]. Ontology can be used to model a domain and support reasoning about entities. It is widely used in artificial intelligence, the Semantic Web, systems engineering, software engineering, biomedical informatics, library science, enterprise bookmarking, and information architecture as a form of knowledge representation about the real world [1]. A number of ontologies have been developed in many kinds of domains: geographic information system (GIS) [3], cloud computing [4], project management system (PMS) [5], military intelligence [6], and health system [2]. Because ontology provides a method to model a domain and supports reasoning capability about entities, it can also be used to model a building energy domain as a new ontology domain and support the energy-saving reasoning based on the cumulative knowledge-base. Moreover, ontology is basically appropriate for context-awareness applications to describe the energy-wasting context.

In this paper, we propose the building energy ontology for energy saving based on context-aware reasoning to provide energy-saving measures drawn from the building conditions. We describes the building domain ontology architecture appropriate for building energy saving. The proposed ontology model and its mechanism are described.

[1] This work was supported by the MKE[20122010100060], Development of ICT-based Building Energy Consumption Diagnosis and Commissioning Technology.

## 2 Building energy ontology architecture

### 2.1 Building energy ontology Model

The building energy ontology is designed to describe a building energy condition and use a context-awareness from a lot of building information. It is composed of six sub ontologies: context, operation, event, time, object, and building description. Fig. 1 shows the structure of the proposed ontology model.

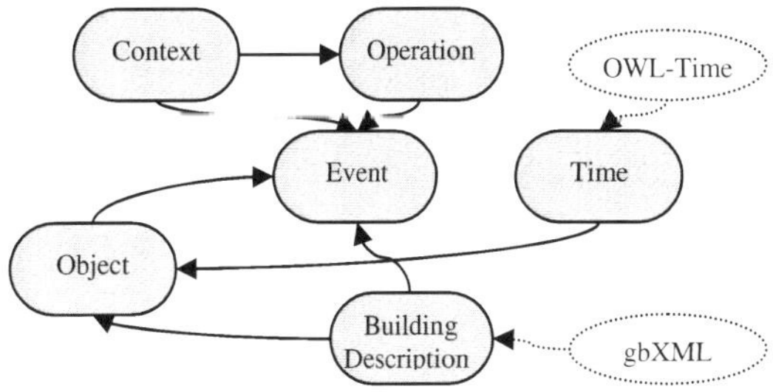


Fig. 1. Building energy ontology model structure

The object ontology contains object descriptions and objects' real-time status value. The building description ontology extends and draws abstract concepts about objects' location from the objects' status value and adopts the concepts of gbXML (green building XML). The time ontology extends and draws abstract concepts from the objects' sensing time and adopts the concepts of OWL time ontology. The event ontology describes the event instance information, and creates and stores abstract event information from building energy wasting events. The context ontology describes building energy-wasting context from the event information. The operation ontology describes objects' operations according to the energy-wasting contexts.

Fig. 2 shows the process flow of the event ontology. The event ontology creates event data semantically extended from quantitative sensor data. It creates the resource ontology instance by translating the sensor description and real-time sensor data. The created instance is connected to the event ontology through 'triggeredEvent' property. The time information of the real-time sensor data is connected to the time ontology through 'hasTime' property. The location of the sensor is connected to the spatial ontology through 'hasPosition' property. The weather data is connected to the spatial ontology through 'hasSpace' property and is connected to the time ontology through 'hasTime' property. The created basic data are connected to the event ontology through 'hasEventSpace', 'hasEventTemporal', hasEventWeather', and 'hasEventResource' properties. Each domain service is provided with one of these event ontology instances. Domain ontology is composed of context and service.

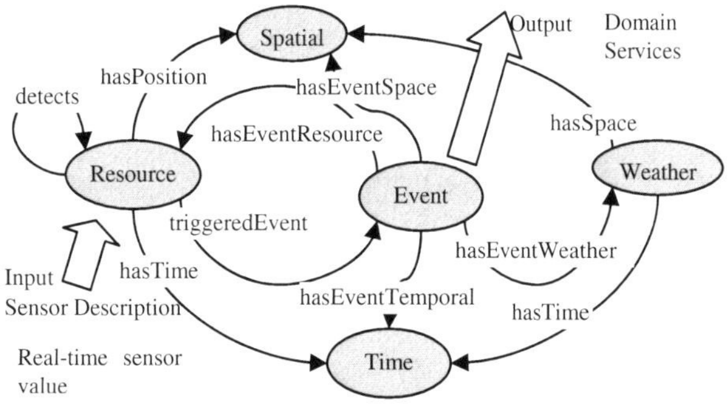


Fig. 2. Basic architecture of the event ontology

## 2.2 Mechanism of building energy ontology

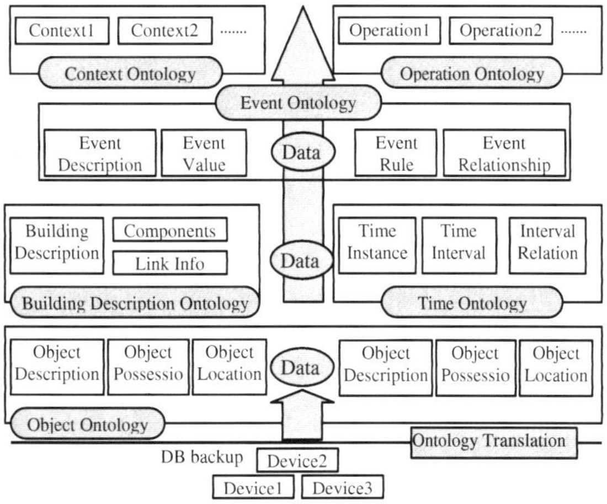


Fig. 3. Data flow of the building energy ontology model

The proposed ontology operates as shown in Fig. 3. The sensed status values of various devices are translated into resource description framework (RDF) data of the object ontology. The translated RDF data and the instance value of the object ontology are used as inputs. The proposed ontology extracts the abstracted event data from the status data of the objects by linking general knowledge independent of the specific service domain. The context information is reasoned based on the event data. It draws the energy-wasting context and the operation of the objects from the abstracted event data. The reasoned context information is used for services through operation ontology. The abstracted building energy context information and the objects' operation information are outputs of the ontology system.

# 3 Conclusions

We propose the building energy ontology to realize energy saving in buildings based on context-aware reasoning. We design building ontology model structure that contains six sub ontologies. Each ontology has its relationship with other ontologies. The process that the event data is obtained from the sensor description and real-time sensor value is described. The mechanism of the proposed ontology is illustrated from the device sensor data to the reasoned energy-wasting context and the final operation information. The proposed building energy ontology can be used to build the building energy saving knowledge-base system based on the context-awareness and reasoning. It can also contribute to the building domain energy saving through real-time event-driven context-aware reasoning.

# 4 References

[1] Ontology. Retrived April 18, 2013, from http://en.wikipedia.org/wiki/Ontology_(information_science)

[2] James N. K. Liu, et al, "A new method for knowledge and information management domain ontology graph model," *IEEE Trans. Syst., Man, Cybern.* vol.43, no.1, pp.115-127, Jan. 2013.

[3] Maojun Huan, "On the concept of geographic ontology-from the viewpoints of philosophy ontology, information ontology and spatial ontology," *Proceedings of 18th international conference on geoinformatics*, Jun. 2010, pp.1-5.

[4] Hong Zhou, Hongji Yang, and Andrew Hugill, "An ontology-based approach to reengineering enterprise software for cloud computing," *IEEE 34th annual computer software and applications conference*, Jul. 2010, pp.383-388.

[5] Sheng Lu, Zhongjian, and Tan Liu, "Study on ontology-based integration strategy and methods for PMS," *IEEE international conference on automation and logistics*, Sep. 2008, pp.1254-1259.

[6] Mei-ying Jia, Bing-ru Yang, De-quan Zheng, and Wei-cong Sun, "Research on domain ontology construction in military intelligence," *3th international symposium on intelligent information technology application*, Nov. 2009, pp.116-119.

# On-line Weighted Matrix Factorization for TV Program Recommendation

**Jin Jeon[1] and Munchurl Kim[2]**
[1, 2]Department of Electrical Engineering, Korea Advanced Institute of Science and Technology, Yuseong-gu, Daejeon, Korea

**Abstract** - *Matrix Factorization (MF) is known as an effective technique in collaborative filtering for recommendation. The MF approaches have often been applied for movie recommender systems which have user rating data. However, they cannot effectively be applicable for TV program recommender systems because (i) explicit rating values are not available; (ii) many TV programs are broadcast under single TV program titles such as News, Shows, Dramas etc.; and (iii) the preferences of TV viewers on TV programs are subject to change in time. Therefore, in this paper, we propose an MF technique that considers such problems, thus making the MF technique suitably applicable for TV domain. We also present experimental results to show the effectiveness of our proposed extended MF technique.*

**Keywords:** Matrix Factorization, Collaborative Filtering, TV Personalization

## 1 Introduction

As massive amounts of information for contents are available at users' sides, recommender systems have become popular to enhance user experience. The MF is known as an effective collaborative filtering which analyzes relationships between users and items. The MF models map both users and items to a joint latent factor vector in a multi-dimensional space as inner products of user-item interactions [1]. The MF models are based on the rating values which are not usually available in TV domain. Instead, the user watching history of TV programs can be used for TV recommender systems [2]. In TV domain, TV programs are often provided as TV program series such as News, Shows, Dramas, Sports etc. In this case, such individual TV programs cannot be dealt as different items such as movie items. Instead, the TV programs in the same series must be treated as single TV program titles in MF. The time-varying trend of user preference on TV programs must also be taken into account in MF [3]. In this paper, we consider these three facts in MF for TV program recommender systems.

The rest of the paper is organized as follows: In Section 2, we introduce a rating computation model for TV program recommender systems; Then, in Section 3, we proposed a hybrid MF model with both offline and online updates; We show the performance of the proposed MF model in Section 4; Finally, we conclude our works in Section 5.

## 2 A Rating Computation Model

To apply MF for TV program recommender systems, the most important data is the rating values of TV programs by users. Unlike the movies, the frequency of watching a TV program series is important to compute its rating value from the user's watching history. TV viewers are often likely to watch the TV programs in the same TV series which they watched before. Fig. 1 shows the probability of watching the TV programs in the same TV series versus the number watching weeks for four months.

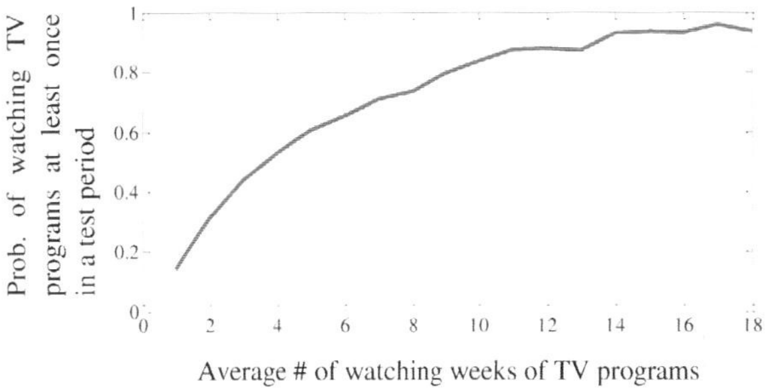


**Fig. 1** Probability of watching the same program again

As shown in Fig 1, the probability of watching TV programs at least once in a test period is moderately related with the average number of weeks for watched TV programs. Therefore, we propose a method of computing the implicit rating values of TV programs as

$$\bar{r}_{i,u} = \frac{\sum_j w_{i,u,j}}{t_{i,u} p_i} \alpha \left(1 - e^{-\lambda n}\right) \quad (1)$$

where $\alpha$ and $\lambda$ are constant values, and $w_{i,u,j}$ is the watching time of user $u$ who watched the episode $j$ of item (TV program) $i$. $t_{i,u}$ is the number of episodes of item $i$. The implicit rate computation in (1) by itself neither considers user preference nor reflects the changed user preference in time. The following section will address how to incorporate user preference changes into the proposed extended MF.

# 3 Hybrid Update Model

We propose an online update method that directly addresses the nature of user preference changes over time to improve a conventional MF model which is updated offline. For the proposed hybrid update method, the total training period is of four-month length where the periods of off-line and on-line training periods are of three-month and one-month lengths, respectively. The off-line MF training is performed with user's TV watching history of three months, and is followed by the on-line MF training of one month where the feature vectors of users and items from the off-line training are used as the initial feature vectors for the on-line MF training. Fig. 2 shows the proposed hybrid MF update model of off-line and on-line training. As shown in Fig. 2, after the first on-line update, the on-line update is further made three time in a row based on the feature vectors as the initial user and item feature vectors obtained from the previous on-line training period of one month. After the four-week on-line MF training, the prediction is perform for the following week which then becomes the testing period.

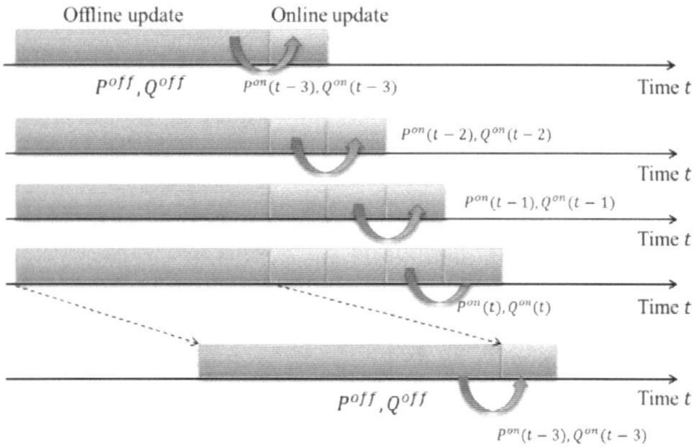


**Fig. 2** An example of hybrid update system framework

The on-line MF updates for item feature vector $q_i^{on}(t+1)$ and user feature vector $p_u^{on}(t+1)$ at time $(t+1)$ are given by

$$q_i^{on}(t+1) = q_i^{on}(t) + \alpha_q^{on} \Sigma \partial e(t) / \partial q_i^{on}(t) \quad (2)$$

$$p_u^{on}(t+1) = p_u^{on}(t) + \alpha_p^{on} \Sigma \partial e(t) / \partial p_u^{on}(t) \quad (3)$$

where $q_i^{on}(0) = q_i^{off}$ and $p_u^{on}(0) = p_u^{off}$ . $\alpha_q^{on}$ and $\alpha_p^{on}$ are learning parameters. The off-line MF update are

$$q_i^{off} = q_i^{off} + \alpha_q^{off} \Sigma_u \partial e_{i,u} / \partial q_{i,u}^{off} \quad (4)$$

$$p_u^{off} = p_u^{off} + \alpha_p^{off} \Sigma_i \partial e_{i,u} / \partial p_{i,u}^{off} \quad (5)$$

where $e_{i,u}$ is the difference between true and estimated rating values. $q_{i,u}^{off}$ and $p_{i,u}^{off}$ are the feature vectors of item $i$ and user $u$, respectively, in the off-line MF training. $\alpha_q^{off}$ and $\alpha_p^{off}$ are learning parameters.

# 4 Experimental Results

For the experiments to test the performance of the proposed recommendation scheme based on the extended MF, the TNmS Korea's TV usage history dataset of 1,742 people and 4,313 items is used which has been collected for 7 months from Jan. 1, 2011 to July. 31, 2011. We use the first 4 months for training and the remaining dataset for testing. The conventional MF is trained with 4 month data one time and the hybrid MF is trained with the first 3 months for off-line MF update and the remaining one month for the on-line MF update in a weekly basis. Table I shows the performance of the conventional MF and hybrid MF to the broadcast TV program contents.

**Table I**. Precision Comparison between the conventional MF and the hybrid MF.

| | Top-5 | Top-10 | Top-20 | Top-30 |
|---|---|---|---|---|
| conventional MF | 0.742 | 0.659 | 0.561 | 0.500 |
| hybrid MF | 0.807 | 0.726 | 0.623 | 0.548 |

The precision is defined as the ratio of how many watched items are in the Top-k list during the test period. The hybrid MF has higher precision than basic MF. For Top-5 recommendation, hybrid MF achieves 0.807 precision.

# 5 Conclusions

We studied an MF approach for TV program recommendation. We introduced an implicit rating model based on user watching time and incorporated it into a hybrid MF update model, making the MF applicable for TV program recommendation. The proposed method showed promising results, producing more accurate predicted performance than the conventional MF method.

**ACKNOWLEDGEMENT**

This research was supported by Basic Science Research Program through the National Research Foundation of Korea (NRF) funded by the Ministry of Education, Science and Technology (2012-01120197). This work was supported by the IT R&D program of MKE/KEIT. [10039161, Core UI technologies for improving Smart TV UX].

# 6 References

[1] Y. Koren, R. Bell and C. Volinsky, "Matrix factorization techniques for recommender systems," IEEE Comput. vol. 42, no. 8, pp. 30-37, Aug. 2009.

[2] E. Kim, S. Pyo, E. Park and M. Kim, "Automatic TV Program Recommendation for (IP)TV Personalization," IEEE Trans. on Broad., vol. 57, no. 3, pp. 674-684, Sept. 2011.

[3] S. Pyo, E. Kim and M. Kim, "Automatic and Personalized Recommendation of TV Program Contents using Sequential Pattern Mining for Smart TV User Interaction," Multimedia Systems, Published online, 19 Feb. 2013.

# SESSION

# LATE BREAKING PAPERS - INFORMATION RETRIEVAL, LEARNING METHODS, AND SOCIAL NETWORKS

## Chair(s)

**Prof. Hamid Arabnia**
**University of Georgia**

# Query Expansion using Association Matrix for Improved Information Retrieval Performance

**Jedsada Chartree**[1], **Ebru Celikel Cankaya**[2], **and Santi Phithakkitnukoon**[3]
[1]Department of Computer Science and Engineering, University of North Texas, Denton, TX 76207, USA
[2]Department of Computer Science, University of Texas at Dallas, Richardson, TX 75080, USA
[3]Computing Department, The Open University, Milton Keynes, United Kingdom

**Abstract**— *We propose a novel query expansion technique that employs association matrix to solve the problem of false positives: retrieving irrelevant documents, while missing actually required documents in a typical search engine environment. We present underlying infrastructure of our design, together with comparisons with existing query expansion algorithms and University of North Texas (UNT) Google search engine. Our results yield 14.3% improved Information Retrieval (IR) performance with more effective and precise retrievals than a conventional (non-expanded) search engine.*

**Keywords:** Query expansion, association matrix, information retrieval, relevance, mismatch, precision

## 1. Introduction

With the rapid growth of Internet technology, the number of online users is constantly on the rise, and so are their operations. *Information Retrieval (IR)*, being one of the most common operations that is used frequently by Internet users, may cause two problems: The search engine may retrieve *irrelevant* documents, and/or more importantly it may miss the *relevant* documents. These are the fundamental reasons why we get IR failures frequently. This paper proposes query expansion technique that employs association matrix to solve these two problems.

In recent years, the information content on the *World Wide Web* has been increasing in an amazing rate. This content overload introduces new challenges to the process of IR, such as delayed retrieval time, poor precision and recall rates, obscurity in word sense disambiguation, and difficulty in relevance feedback for the search engine [8, 13].

The essential problem with information retrieval is word mismatch, which typically occurs when users submit short and ambiguous queries. These queries most of the time result in retrieval of irrelevant documents, while missing the actually required (*relevant*) documents [8, 12, 13, 16]. To overcome this problem, a technique called *query expansion (QE)* has been proposed and is being widely used. The idea behind query expansion is to first add terms with close meaning to the original query to expand it, then reformulate the ranked documents to improve the relevant performance of the overall retrieval [6, 8, 11].

In this work, we improve the query expansion technique by integrating the *association matrix* concept. With this simple and fast expansion, we obtain better retrieval rates. We compare the relevance feedback results of the non-expanded (original) query implementation with that of the query expansion technique we propose by running two schemes separately. Moreover, we compare these two results with that of *UNT Google search engine*l.

The remainder of the paper is organized as follows. Section 2 reviews the background and motivation. Section 3 introduces the scheme we propose by explaining the search engine infrastructure that uses *Vector Space Model (VSM)* and query expansion with association matrix. We also describe the experimental setup in Section 3. Section 4 presents the results. The paper is concluded with a summary and an outlook on future work in Section 5.

## 2. Background and Motivation

Query formulation is one of the most important tasks, which has a direct impact on the relevance feedback rate in *Information Retrieval (IR)* systems [6, 8]. Many query expansion techniques have been proposed to improve the search performance, which are measured with *relevance feedback* and *pseudo-relevance feedback* values.

To obtain better retrieval rates, one can try expanding the original query. The majority of earlier work on query expansion concentrate on exploiting the term co-occurrences within documents. Unfortunately, most of the time queries are short, rendering this method inadequate. To improve this naive idea of query expansion, Gao et al. [9] propose expanding queries by mining user logs, namely by utilizing user interactions that are recorded in user logs. By analyzing the user logs, authors extract correlations between query terms and document terms. These correlations are then used to select high-quality expansion terms for new queries. Their method yields outperforming results over the current conventional search methods.

In [12], Li et al. propose a new approach to query expansion by combining thesauri and automatic relevance feedback methods. Using thesauri for query expansion is a very straightforward implementation: given a user query, the system performs a simple table look up for related terms from thesaurus and performs expansion accordingly. This technique comes with its obvious drawbacks: Most of the time, thesauri are built manually and hence they suffer from being too broad or on the contrary too concise. Moreover, building a thesaurus involves a thorough knowledge base analysis, which may get impractically slow, especially when dynamic updates are required frequently. And finally, human interaction in the preparation of the thesaurus makes it far from objective at most times. User feedback, as the name implies, is a cyclic feedback [2] that is obtained from actual users of the system, in the hope that they will help improve future retrieval efforts. Most of the time, user feedback may not perform well, due to the high rate of subjectivity involved in it. For this reason, a better approach called *automatic relevance feedback* is adopted. This technique eliminates the human factor by assuming that the top $n$ retrievals are the most relevant ones. Then, by using statistics, additional terms are selected from these $n$ documents. It is this statistical processing that makes automatic relevance feedback approach too complex and too slow to implement. By bringing together thesauri and automatic relevance feedback techniques, Li et al. shows better performance over traditional methods. Nonetheless, their implementation requires complex initial setup, and may involve significant latency in retrieval time.

Mining user logs for query expansion purposes is another common technique that is referred to by many scholar work. In [13], Peng and Ma expands this idea: They propose a theme-based query expansion scheme that extracts user intent through click-through data that is available on Web sites. This technique takes advantage of the classical search methods, e.g. Vector Space Model (VSM), and adds more features to them, such as close meaning terms and synonymous words.

Yue et al. propose using text classification as a means to obtain better query expansion in [17]. They first use text classification to classify the obtained document collection, then extract key phrases from each document head to eventually build a key phrase set. Their work yields promising precision against recall values with high retrieval rates. In our work, by introducing association matrix to the conventional Vector Space Model, we are able to get comparable rates by obtaining improved performance and reduced non-relevance feedback results.

In literature, there have been a number of works on query expansion that is applied to different source languages. For example, [10] designs and develops the query expansion scheme for answering document retrieval in the Chinese answering system. Their method extracts related words and expanded the query for a specific question. The study used the Vector Space Model and cosine similarity techniques. Their results show promising relevance feedback. There is, however, no performance comparisons with other existing techniques. In another work, Gao et al. [9] suggest techniques for cross-lingual query: retrieving results in languages other than the submitted query.

In another linguistic implementation of query expansion, Kannan et al. [11] use a different source language. They present a comparison between interactive and automatic query expansion techniques applied on Arabic language. According to their results, the automatic query expansion method gives much better relevance feedback than non-query expansion. In our work, we use English as the source language to evaluate our framework. This provides us the flexibility and generality in performance comparisons with similar work. Still, our work is a generic model that can be adopted by any source language.

Applying the standard technique of query expansion to data other than text retrieval is a straightforward and effective idea. As an example, Rahman et al. implement query expansion to improve image retrieval recall and precision values. In their work [14], they use Support Vector Machines (SVM) to generate a classification of images, which is similar to vocabulary classification of text.

# 3. Design

In this section, we describe our novel approach to query expansion, which provides a simple and fast means to achieve better information retrieval rates with higher precision. With our design, we also aim at alleviating, if not totally eliminating, the drawbacks of existing query expansion algorithms.

## 3.1 Search Engine Based On Vector Space Model

Vector Space Model is commonly used for finding the relevant documents as a result of a search engine query [5]. With this model, queries and documents are assumed as a vector in an $n$-dimensional space, where each dimension corresponds to separate terms or queries. The values of the vector represent the relevant documents. Basically, we compare the deviation of angles between each document and query vector. In practice, the Vector Space Model is considered as the cosine similarity between document vectors. The cosine similarity [11, 17] can be expressed as follows:

$$sim(d_i, d_k) = \frac{\sum_{i=1}^{n} w_{i,j}\, w_{i,k}}{\sqrt{\sum_{i=1}^{n} w_{i,j}^2}\sqrt{\sum_{i=1}^{n} w_{i,k}^2}} \quad (1)$$

where

$$w_{ij} = tf_{ij} idf_i \quad (2)$$

$$tf_i = \frac{f_{ij}}{max\{f_{ij}\}} \quad (3)$$

$$\begin{array}{c|cccc|} & w_1 & w_2 & w_3 \cdots\cdots & w_n \\ \hline w_1 & c_{11} & c_{12} & c_{13} \cdots\cdots & c_{1n} \\ w_2 & c_{21} & & & \\ w_3 & c_{31} & & & \\ \cdot & \cdot & & & \\ \cdot & \cdot & & & \\ w_n & c_{n1} & & & \\ \hline \end{array}$$

Fig. 1: Association Matrix

$$idf_i = log(\frac{N}{df_i}) \tag{4}$$

and $sim(d_i, d_k)$ is the cosine similarity between document $d_i$ and query $d_k$, where $w_{ij}$ is *tf-idf* weighting of term *i* in document *j*, $tf_{ij}$ is term frequency of term *i* in document *j*, $f_{ij}$ is frequency of term *i* in document *j*, $idf_i$ is the inverse document frequency of term *I*, *N* is the total number of documents, and $df_i$ is document frequency of term *i*.

## 3.2 Query Expansion Based On Association Matrix

In our proposal for the query expansion scheme, we combine two approaches to achieve better information retrieval performance: query expansion and association matrix. Query expansion is a technique that is used to expand a short query in order to obtain more relevant and more precise documents as a result of querying the search engine [8, 15, 17]. The expansion is achieved by adding other terms that are related to the original queries [6]. After query expansion, instead of the original query, the new expanded query is used in the Vector Space Model.

Association matrix is a 2-dimensional matrix, where each cell $c_{ij}$ represents the correlation factor between all terms in a query and the terms in documents (Fig. 1). This matrix is used to reformulate an original query to improve its retrieval performance [3].

Each correlation factor, denoted as $c_{ij}$ in Fig. 1, is calculated as follows:

$$c_{ij} = \sum_{d_k \in D} f_{ik} \times f_{jk}, \tag{5}$$

where $c_{ij}$ is the correlation factor between term *i* and term *j*, and $f_{ik}$ is the frequency of term *i* in document *k*. Additionally, these correlation values are used to calculate the normalized association matrix [9] as follows:

$$s_{ij} = \frac{c_{ij}}{c_{ii} + c_{jj} - c_{ij}}, \tag{6}$$

where $s_{ij}$ denotes normalized association score, and $c_{ij}$ represents the correlation factor between term *i* and term *j*.

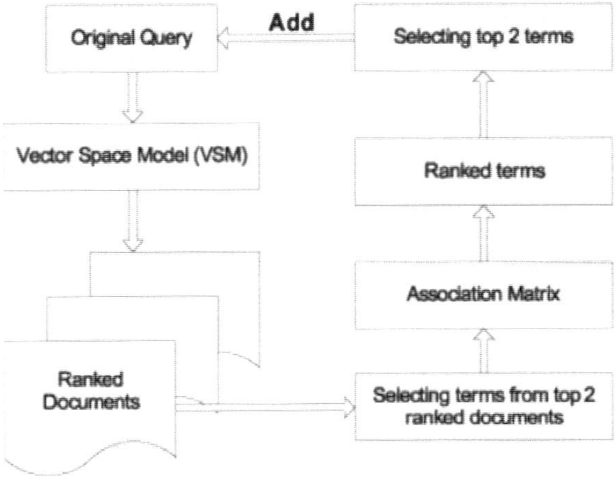


Fig. 2: The Association Matrix Query Expansion and Retrieval Framework

Higher normalized association score implies higher degree in correspondence with the original query. Thus, we choose several words, which have the highest association score, to add into the original query, then use this new query to calculate the cosine similarity instead of the original query.

## 3.3 Document Ranking

Fig. 2 illustrates the framework for our implementation: it brings together two main components for our design – the Vector Space Model and the association matrix. The Vector Space Model is used to re-represent a text document by applying the sequence of procedures as follows: Document indexing that is achieved by filtering out function words, etc., term weighting, and ranking the document with respect to the query according to a similarity measure. The association matrix is the 2-dimensional matrix that was explained in Section 3.2.

In the following subsections, implementation details for each component in Fig. 2 are described in more depth.

### 3.3.1 The Term-Weight Document

The term-weight document was used to calculate the cosine similarity value. It was generated by the following steps:

**i. Crawling Web pages module:** The crawling module of our program crawls 3000 Web pages of the University of North Texas (UNT) using *Breadth-First Search (BFS)* approach. This many number of web pages are good enough to be considered as part of a corpus system.

**ii. Preprocessing module:** This module is a combination of several tasks which includes removing SGML tags, tokenizing each word, eliminating stop words, and stemming each word using Porter Stemmer [7] to make it a root word.

**iii. Indexing module:** The indexing module calculates the term-weight of each word using Eq. (2). The results are stored as the term-weight document (text file), which was

Table 1: Example of Precision Values Obtained Query Expansion of the term "*career*" in different top pages and different top words

| #Pages / #Words | Precision | | | | | | | | |
|---|---|---|---|---|---|---|---|---|---|
| | 2 | 3 | 4 | 5 | 6 | 7 | 8 | 9 | 10 |
| 2 | 0.971 | 0.783 | 0.745 | 0.403 | 0.413 | 0.392 | 0.41 | 0.553 | 0.404 |
| 3 | 0.968 | 0.783 | 0.734 | 0.598 | 0.413 | 0.597 | 0.41 | 0.584 | 0.553 |
| 4 | 0.971 | 0.78 | 0.734 | 0.607 | 0.413 | 0.587 | 0.41 | 0.583 | 0.403 |
| 5 | 0.953 | 0.78 | 0.732 | 0.789 | 0.413 | 0.743 | 0.41 | 0.446 | 0.405 |
| 6 | 0.886 | 0.852 | 0.796 | 0.422 | 0.772 | 0.75 | 0.489 | 0.446 | 0.407 |
| 7 | 0.885 | 0.468 | 0.432 | 0.777 | 0.776 | 0.423 | 0.41 | 0.406 | 0.401 |
| 8 | 0.573 | 0.468 | 0.436 | 0.422 | 0.412 | 0.412 | 0.409 | 0.405 | 0.406 |
| 9 | 0.574 | 0.466 | 0.436 | 0.422 | 0.412 | 0.412 | 0.409 | 0.406 | 0.406 |
| 10 | 0.574 | 0.468 | 0.436 | 0.422 | 0.429 | 0.412 | 0.239 | 0.352 | 0.301 |

a combination of the Web pages (URLs), words, and *tf-idf* value.

### 3.3.2 The Web Interface Search Engine

The Web interface search engine module uses the Common Gateway Interface (CGI) protocol to achieve the following tasks:

1) Preprocess the query.
2) Calculate the cosine similarity between the query and the documents using the term-weight values in the term-weight document file that was built in Section 3.3.1.
3) Rank documents in descending order, based on the higher cosine similarity value from the previous step, and display the results on the Web browser.

### 3.3.3 The Query Expansion

This step is the intelligent part of the search engine that applies an association matrix algorithm to the search engine. To accomplish the desired query expansion, several tasks are executed as follows:

1) Choose the words from top two pages described by step 3 in Section. 3.3.2. to calculate the correlation factor between these words and the original query; this step uses Eq. (5).
2) Use the result from previous step to calculate the normalized association score with Eq. (6).
3) Rank these terms in descending order, based on the normalized association score.
4) Select the top two words from previous step as an expanding query and adding these words to the original query.
5) Use the new combination of these terms to calculate the cosine similarity as described in step 2 of Section 3.3.2.
6) Rank the documents as described in step 3 of Section 3.3.2 and display the results on the Web browser.

As an example, Table 1 shows precision values of the term "*career*" in different top pages and different top words.

# 4. Results

We first present the results of query expansion task from subsection 3.3.3 above as in Fig. 3, which shows that the pairs (*top 2 words, top 2 pages*) yield the highest average precision of ten sample queries. Note that while constructing the query expansion, choosing the number of pages (step 1 above) and selecting the number of words (step 4 above) directly affect the overall performance of our scheme due to the larger number of pages and the larger number of words will result in more irrelevant documents. Therefore, only the top two expansion terms from the top two pages are used to combine with the original query. We then compare the performance of our method (new query after expansion) to other two search engines: the original (without expansion) and UNT Google search engines. Figure 4 and Table 3 show the results from using ten sample queries in Table 2.

According to Fig. 4, the query expansion technique either improves or maintains the current retrieval performance, with

Table 2: Query terms of the ten user's queries

| User's queries | Query terms |
|---|---|
| Q1 | faculty |
| Q2 | career |
| Q3 | engineering |
| Q4 | gerontology |
| Q5 | computer lab |
| Q6 | mikler |
| Q7 | ieli |
| Q8 | admission |
| Q9 | orientation |
| Q10 | discovery |

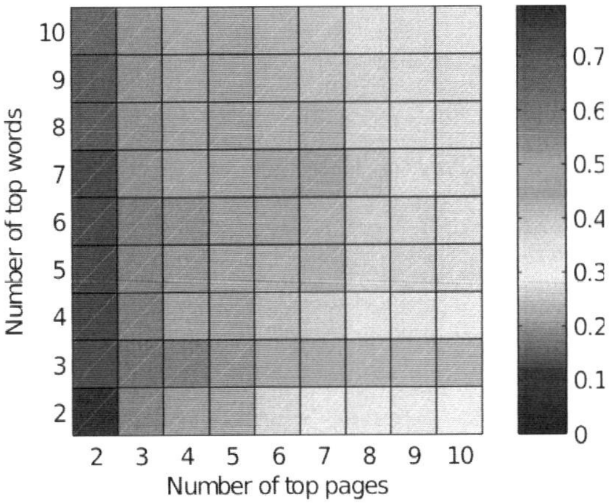


Fig. 3: Average Precision of 10 Sample Queries with the Number of Top Pages and Words Varying From 2 to 10.

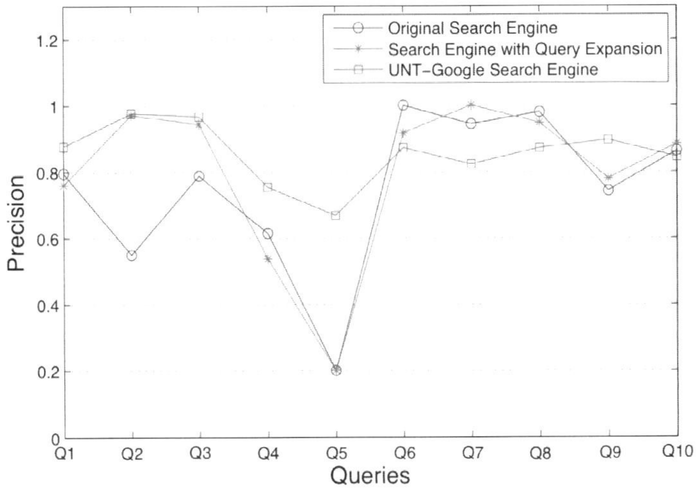


Fig. 4: The Comparison of Precision between Original Query, Query Expansion, and UNT Google Search Engine

the exception of query no. 1, 4, 6, and 8, but the precision values of these queries are very close the each corresponding query (between the original query and expansion query). This exception reminds us the fact that query expansion does not always guarantee better retrieval rates. Sometimes, it may even be the case that the unexpanded query is a better fit than its expanded counterpart.

In addition, the precision values of both the original and proposed search engines are less than the precision value of UNT Google search engine except the values of queries numbered 6, 7 ,8, and 10; this implies that sometimes the UNT Google search engine not always a better fit than the other two methods.

Overall, our proposed method (query expansion) improves the search engine's performance, particularly, it has better relevant feedback than the original search engine (without

Table 3: A Comparison of the Average Precision Rate of the Proposed Method with the Original and UNT Google Search Engines

| Methods | Average Precision Rate |
|---|---|
| Original Search Engine | 0.748 |
| UNT Google Search Engine | 0.855 |
| Proposed Search Engine with Query Expansion | 0.794 |

query expansion). Table 3 shows the average precision rate of 0.794 with query expansion and 0.748 without expansion. This indicates a 14.3% improvement on average. The UNT Google search however appears to outperform our proposed method with an average precision rate of 0.855.

To better explain the discrepancies in Fig. 4, we analyze each query in more detail. According to this analysis, we observe that query no.5 ("*computer lab*"), has a relatively low score. This may suggest that both of our search engines are not suitable for the queries that have more than one word; in fact, the search engines search the query that contains more than one word separately (as *computer* and *lab*), and there are many relevant feedbacks for both of them. This presumably causes the undesired low precision rate. Nevertheless, some other queries, such as queries numbered 6, 7, and 8, of both search engines (original search engine and search engine with query expansion) have higher precision values than the UNT Google search engine. This implies that both search engines work well for a person's first name (or last name) and abbreviation (*ieli* stands for Intensive English Language Institute). Especially for expanded query like query no. 6 (*mikler*) – it returns a new query contained both the first name and last name of a faculty member of UNT.

Furthermore, between the original queries and expanded queries, we notice that the expanded queries mostly return higher precision than unexpanded queries, and return relevant document differently. In fact, the ranked documents listed after applying query expansion are more relevant documents and are ranked higher towards the top of the ranking list as shown in Fig.5.

## 5. Conclusion and Future Work

The rapid growth of World Wild Web makes it more and more challenging for information retrieval to achieve desired performances, especially in obtaining relevant feedback for short queries. This work implements a query expansion by using association matrix to improve the retrieval performance. Our experimental results show a 14.3% performance improvement on average. Therefore, the results of these experiments indicate that query expansion using association matrix is provably efficient in improving the ranked relevant feedback of documents. Although our proposed search engine's performance is still slightly lower than the UNT

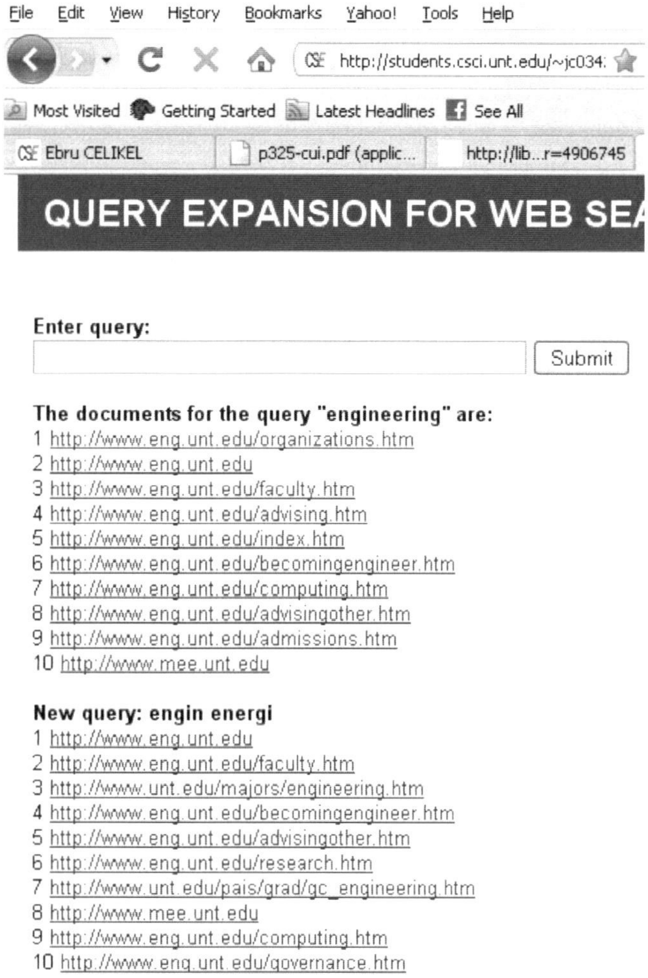


Fig. 5: The Results of Ranked Documents with query 6: "*engineer*"

Google search engine, it is not significant. This probably has to do with the different corpus that we use, i.e., for our search engines, we crawl only 3,000 webpages, and the UNT Google search engine use another corpus and another algorithm.

As our future work, we will continue to investigate the use of association matrix, as well as other techniques such as employing pseudo relevance feedback (PRF) [2, 4], or using genetic algorithm [1, 15] to improve the query expansion. An extensive comparison of these techniques will also be explored and studied in the future.

Moreover, we are planning to implement our scheme on different source languages to investigate how linguistic characteristics influence the performance of our scheme.

# References

[1] L. Araujo and J. R. Pï£¡rez-Aguera J. R., "Improving query expansion with stemming terms: a new genetic algorithm approach," in Proc. EvoCOP'08, 2008, pp. 182-193.

[2] K. Belhajjame, N. W. Paton, S. M. Embury, A. A. A. Fernandes, and C. Hedeler, "Feedback-based annotation, selection and refinement of schema mappings for dataspaces," in Proc. EDBT '10, 2010, pp. 573-584.

[3] A. M. Boutari, C. Carpineto, R. Nicolussi, "Evaluating term concept association measures for short text expansion two case studies of classification and clustering," in Proc. EDBT '10, 2010, pp. 163-174.

[4] M. Cartright, J. Allan, V. Lavrenko, A. McGregor, "Fast query expansion using approximations of relevance models," in Proc. CIKM '10, 2010, pp. 1573-1576.

[5] P. A. Chew, B. W. Bader, S. Helmreich, A. Abdelali, S. J. Verzi, "An information-theoretic, vector-space-model approach to cross-language information retrieval," Cambridge Natural Language Engineering, Vol. 17, pp. 37-70, Jan. 2011.

[6] P. D. Meo, G. Quattrone, and D. Ursino, "A query expansion and user profile enrichment approach to improve the performance of recommender systems operating on a Folkson," User Modeling and User-Adapted Interaction, 2010, pp. 41-86.

[7] F. N. Flores, V. P. Moreira, C. A. Heuser, "Assessing the impact of stemming accuracy on information retrieval," in Proc. PROPOR'10, 2010, pp. 11-20.

[8] L. Gan, S. Wang, M. Wang, Z. Xie, L. Zhang, and Z. Shu, "Query expansion based on concept clique for Markov network information retrieval model," in Proc. FSKD '08, 2008, pp. 29-33.

[9] W. Gao, C. Niu, J. Nie, M. Zhou, K. Wong, and H. Hon, "Exploiting query logs for cross-lingual query suggestions," ACM Transactions on Information Systems (TOIS), Vol. 28, May 2010.

[10] K. Jia, "Query expansion based on word sense disambiguation in Chinese question answering system," Journal of Computational Information Systems, Vol. 6, pp. 181-187, Jan. 2010.

[11] G. Kannann, R. Al-Shalabi, S. Ghwanmeh, and B. Bani-Ismail, "A comparison between interactive and automatic query expansion applied on Arabic language," in Proc. IIT '07, 2007, pp. 466–470.

[12] J. Li, M. Guo, and S. Tian, "A new approach to query expansion," in Proc. Machine Learning and Cybernetics, 2005, pp. 2302-2306.

[13] V. Oliveira, G. Gomes, F. Belem, W. Brandao, J. Almeida, N. Ziviani, and M. Goncalves, "Automatic query expansion based on tag recommendation," in Proc. CIKM '12, 2012, pp. 1985-1989.

[14] M. M. Rahman, S. K. Antani, and G. R. Thoma, "A query expansion framework in image retrieval domain based on local and global analysis," Information Processing and Management, vol. 47, pp. 676-691, Sep. 2011.

[15] V. Wood, "Improving query term expansion with machine learning," M. Sci. thesis, University of Otago, Dunedin, New Zealand, 2013.

[16] S. Wu "The weighted Condorcet fusion in information retrieval," Information Processing and Management, vol. 49, pp. 108-122, Jan. 2013.

[17] W. Yue, Z. Chen, X. Lue, F. Lin, and J. Liu, "Using query expansion and classification for information retrieval," in Proc. SKG '05, 2005, pp. 31-38.

# A New Adaptive Sampling Method for Scalable Learning

**Jianhua Chen and Jian Xu**
Division of Computer Science and Engineering
School of Electrical Engineering and Computer Science
Louisiana State University
Baton Rouge, LA 70803-4020
E-mail: jianhua@csc.lsu.edu, jxu1@lsu.edu

**Abstract**—*Scaling up data mining algorithms to handle huge data sets is an important issue in machine learning and knowledge discovery. Random sampling is often used to achieve better scalability in learning from massive amount of data.* Adaptive sampling *offers advantages over traditional batch sampling methods in that adaptive sampling often uses much lower number of samples and thus better efficiency while assuring guaranteed level of estimation accuracy and confidence. In this paper, we present a new adaptive sampling method for estimating the mean of a Bernoulli variable, along with preliminary theoretical studies of the method. We present empirical simulation results indicating that our method often use significantly lower sample size (i.e., the number of sampled instances) while maintaining competitive accuracy and confidence when compared with batch sampling method. We also briefly outline how to make use of this new sampling method to build a scalable ensemble learning algorithm by Boosting.*

**Keywords:** Adaptive Sampling, Sample Size, Chernoff-Hoeffding Bound, Scalable Learning, Boosting

## 1. Introduction

Random sampling is an important technique that is widely used in statistical analysis, computer science, machine learning and knowledge discovery. In machine learning, researchers use sampling to estimate the accuracy of learned classifiers or to estimate features from vast amount of data. In scalable data mining, in order to efficiently perform knowledge discovery from huge data sets, sampling could be used to draw a random subset from the entire data set and apply data mining algorithms to the more manageable random sample. Designing a suitable sampling method and applying it to derive an efficient learning and knowledge discovery algorithm is an important research issue in machine learning and data mining.

A key issue in designing a sampling scheme is to determine *sample size*, the number of sampled instances sufficient to assure the estimation accuracy and confidence. Conventional (batch) sampling methods are *static* in the sense that sufficient sample size is determined *prior to* the start of sampling, typically using well-known theoretical bounds such as the Chernoff-Hoeffding bound [1], [10]. Adaptive sampling, in contrast, draws samples in an online fashion and decides whether it has seen enough samples dependent on some measures related to the samples seen so far. This adaptive nature of sequential sampling method is attractive from both computational and practical perspectives. Clearly, it is desirable to keep the sample size small subject to the constraint of estimation accuracy and confidence. This would save not only computation time, but also the cost of generating the extra random samples when such costs are significant.

Efficient adaptive sampling has great potential applications to machine learning and data mining, especially when the underlying dataset is huge. For example, instead of using the entire huge data set for learning a target function, one can use sampling to get a subset of the data to construct a classifier. In Boosting, an ensemble learning method, the learning algorithm needs to select a "good" classifier with classification accuracy above $\frac{1}{2}$ at each boosting round. This would require estimating the accuracy of each classifier either exhaustively or by sampling. Watanabe and his colleagues recently showed [7], [8], [14] successful application of their adaptive sampling methods to Boosting.

Researchers in statistics and computer science have recently developed *adaptive sampling* schemes [7], [8], [14] that are of *non-asymptotic* nature for parametric estimation. Earlier works in Computer Science on adaptive sampling include the methods in [11], [12], [13] for estimating the size of a database query.

In [4], [5], an adaptive, multi-stage sampling framework has been proposed. The key idea in these works consists in formulating the coverage probability (and thus the stopping criterion for sampling) as a function of the "coverage tuning parameter" $\zeta$, and using computation to calculate the optimal value for $\zeta$ before sampling starts.

Inspired by the works in [4], [5], in our recent works, a new adaptive sampling method was proposed [3] and then applied to scalable data mining using Boosting [2]. The adaptive sampling method presented in [3] uses a stopping criterion function similar to the *Chernoff stopping rule* in [4], with an important difference that the parameter $\zeta$ is not needed. In contrast to [4], [5], the method in [3] does not require any computational efforts before sampling starts, and the criterion function is very simple to implement. Moreover, empirical studies in [3] showed that the method often uses much smaller samples compared with existing sampling methods. The work reported in [2] adapted the sampling scheme in [3] and applied it to build an efficient Boosting algorithm, in a fashion similar to the *Madaboost* work proposed in [7], [8]. Preliminary experimental results [2] showed that our Boosting via adaptive sampling method uses a much lower sample size while maintaining competitive prediction accuracy.

In this paper, we develop a new adaptive sampling method in the same spirit of the work in [3]. Here in the new sampling scheme, the stopping criterion function can be seen as an adaptation of the *Massart Stopping Rule* in [4] without using the parameter $\zeta$. The benefit of this approach is the simplicity of the implementation and the potential reduction in sample size as compared with other existing sampling methods such as that in [14]. We present a preliminary theoretical analysis of the new sampling technique, along with some results of simulation studies. Moreover we briefly outline how to apply this new sampling method to build an efficient Boosting learner, in the same spirit as in [2].

The rest of the paper is organized as follows. In Section 2, we present preliminary information about this research topic and related works. In Section 3, we present the new adaptive sampling method for controlling absolute error. Section 4 contains the method for relative error. The outline on applying the sampling method for scalable Boosting learning is presented in Section 5, followed by conclusions in Section 6.

## 2. Background

The basic problem tackled in this paper is to estimate the probability $p = \Pr(A)$ of a random event $A$ from observational data. This is the same as estimating the mean $\mathbb{E}[X] = p$ of a Bernoulli random variable $X$ in parametric estimation. We have access to i.i.d. samples $X_1, X_2, \cdots$ of the Bernoulli variable $X$ such that $\Pr\{X = 1\} = 1 - \Pr\{X = 0\} = p$. An estimator for $p$ can be taken as the *relative frequency* $\widehat{\boldsymbol{p}} = \frac{\sum_{i=1}^{\mathbf{n}} X_i}{\mathbf{n}}$, where $\mathbf{n}$ is the sample number at the termination of experiment. In the context of fixed-size sampling, the Chernoff-Hoeffding bound [1] asserts that, for $\varepsilon, \delta \in (0,1)$, the coverage probability $\Pr\{|\widehat{\boldsymbol{p}} - p| < \varepsilon\}$ is greater than $1 - \delta$ for any $p \in (0,1)$ provided that $\mathbf{n} > \frac{\ln \frac{2}{\delta}}{2\varepsilon^2}$. Here $\varepsilon$ is called the *margin of absolute error* and $1 - \delta$ is called the *confidence level*. Recently, an exact computational method has been established in [4], [6] to substantially reduce this bound. To estimate $p$ with a relative precision, it is a well-known result derived from the Chernoff bound that $\Pr\{|\widehat{\boldsymbol{p}} - p| < \varepsilon p\} > 1 - \delta$ provided that the pre-specified sample size $\mathbf{n}$ is greater than $\frac{3}{\varepsilon^2 p} \ln \frac{2}{\delta}$. Here $\varepsilon \in (0,1)$ is called the *margin of relative error*. Since this sample size formula involves the value $p$ which is exactly the one we wanted to estimate, its direct use is not convenient.

Chernoff-Hoeffding bounds have been used extensively in statistical sampling and Machine Learning. And in many cases, they are already quite tight bounds. However we are interested in doing even better than just using these bounds in the static way. We seek adaptive sampling schemes that allow us to achieve the goal of low sample size requirements without compromising accuracy and confidence. In adaptive sampling, we draw some number of i.i.d. samples and test certain stopping criterion after seeing each new sample. The criterion for stopping sampling (and thus the bound on sufficient sample size) is determined with a formula dependent on the prescribed accuracy and confidence level, as well as the samples seen so far. In this paper, we consider the problems of controlling absolute error and relative error in adaptive sampling:

**Problem 1: Control of Absolute Error:** Construct an adaptive sampling scheme such that, for *a priori* margin of absolute error $\varepsilon \in (0,1)$ and confidence parameter $\delta \in (0,1)$, the relative frequency $\widehat{\boldsymbol{p}}$ at the termination of the sampling process guarantees $\Pr\{|\widehat{\boldsymbol{p}} - p| < \varepsilon\} > 1 - \delta$ for any $p \in (0,1)$.

**Problem 2 – Control of Relative Error:** Construct an adaptive sampling scheme such that, for *a priori* margin of relative error $\varepsilon \in (0,1)$ and confidence parameter $\delta \in (0,1)$, the relative frequency $\widehat{\boldsymbol{p}}$ at the termination of the sampling process guarantees $\Pr\{|\widehat{\boldsymbol{p}} - p| < \varepsilon p\} > 1 - \delta$ for any $p \in (0,1)$.

The common practice for controlling absolute error in random sampling is *batch* sampling and the stopping criterion is computed *in advance* using the Chernoff bound:

$$If \ \ \mathbf{n} > \frac{\ln \frac{2}{\delta}}{2\varepsilon^2} \ \ Then \ \ \Pr\{|\widehat{\boldsymbol{p}} - p| < \varepsilon\} > 1 - \delta \tag{1}$$

In our recent work [3], a new adaptive sampling method for controlling absolute error was introduced. The new method is empirically shown to be much more sample-efficient while maintaining competitive estimation accuracy compared with batch sampling.

For estimating $p$ with margin of relative error $\varepsilon \in (0,1)$ and confidence parameter $\delta \in (0,1)$, Watanabe proposed in [14] to continue i.i.d. Bernoulli trials until $A$ successes occur and then take the final relative frequency $\widehat{\boldsymbol{p}}$ as an estimator for $p$, where

$$A > \frac{3(1+\varepsilon)}{\varepsilon^2} \ln \frac{2}{\delta}. \tag{2}$$

We will show (empirically) in this paper that our proposed method for controlling relative error uses much smaller number of samples while maintaining competitive accuracy and confidence as compared to the adaptive sampling scheme of [14].

## 3. The New Sampling Method: Controlling Absolute Error

In this section we present our sampling method. Let us define the function $\mathscr{U}_M(z, \theta)$ which will be useful for studying our sampling scheme.

$$\mathscr{U}_M(z,\theta) = \begin{cases} \frac{9}{2}\frac{(z-\theta)^2}{(z+2\theta)(z+2\theta-3)} & z \in [0,\ 1],\ \ \theta \in (0,\ 1) \\ -\infty & z \in [0,\ 1],\ \ \theta \notin (0,\ 1) \end{cases}$$

Let $0 < \varepsilon < 1$, $0 < \delta < 1$. The sampling algorithm $ABS_M$ for controlling absolute error using the Massart's rule is shown as follows.

**Algorithm** $ABS_M$**.**
Let $\mathbf{n} \leftarrow 0$
$X \leftarrow 0$ and $\widehat{\mathbf{p}} \leftarrow 0$.
While $\mathbf{n} < \frac{2\ln\frac{2}{\delta}}{\varepsilon^2}[1/4 - (|\widehat{\mathbf{p}} - 1/2| - \frac{2}{3}\varepsilon)^2]$
Do
**begin**
Draw a random sample Y with parameter $p$.
Let $X \leftarrow X + Y$,
$\mathbf{n} \leftarrow \mathbf{n} + 1$ and $\widehat{\mathbf{p}} \leftarrow \frac{X}{\mathbf{n}}$.
**end**
Output $\widehat{\mathbf{p}}$ and $\mathbf{n}$.

Algorithm $ABS_M$ was inspired by the multistage sampling scheme proposed in [4, Section 4.1.1, Version 20], which can be described as "continue sampling until $(|\widehat{\boldsymbol{p}_{\ell}} - 1/2| - \frac{2}{3}\varepsilon)^2 \geq 1/4 + \frac{\varepsilon^2 n_\ell}{2\ln(\zeta\delta)}$ at some sampling stage with index $\ell$, and then take the final relative frequency as the estimator for $p$", where $n_\ell$ and $\widehat{\boldsymbol{p}}_\ell$ are respectively the sample size and the relative frequency at the $\ell$-th stage. However there are several key differences between our method and the one in [4]. The one in [4] needs to use computation to find the optimal value for the parameter $\zeta$, which is not needed in our method. Moreover, the number of sampling stages $\tau$ and the sample sizes $n_\ell$ need to be fixed in advance in [4] but we do not have such a restriction.

**Preliminary Theoretical Analysis of the Algorithm** $ABS_M$**.** We have conducted a preliminary theoretical analysis on the properties of our sampling method.

First we note the *Massert's Inequality* which forms the basis of the stopping criterion function.

*Lemma 1:* Let $\boldsymbol{p_n}$ be the estimation of the Bernoulli parameter $p \in (0, 1)$ after seeing $n$ samples. For any $0 \leq z < p$, we have $Pr\{\boldsymbol{p_n} \leq z|p\} < e^{n\mathscr{U}_M(z,p)}$. For any $p < z \leq 1$, we have $Pr\{\boldsymbol{p_n} \geq z|p\} < e^{n\mathscr{U}_M(z,p)}$.

**Theorem 1.** Let

$$n_u = \max\{\lceil \frac{\ln\frac{\delta}{2}}{\mathscr{U}_M(p+\varepsilon,\ p+2\varepsilon)} \rceil,\ \lceil \frac{\ln\frac{\delta}{2}}{\mathscr{U}_M(p-\varepsilon, p-2\varepsilon)} \rceil\}.$$

Assume the true probability $p$ to be estimated satisfies $p \leq \frac{1}{2} - 2\varepsilon$. Then with a probability of no less than $1 - \frac{\delta}{2}$, Algorithm $ABS_M$ will stop with $\mathbf{n} \leq n_u$ samples and produce $\widehat{\mathbf{p}}$ which satisfies $\widehat{\mathbf{p}} \leq p+\varepsilon$. Similarly, if $p \geq \frac{1}{2}+2\varepsilon$, with a probability no less than $1-\frac{\delta}{2}$, the sampling algorithm will stop with $\mathbf{n} \leq n_u$ samples and produce $\widehat{\mathbf{p}}$ which satisfies $\widehat{\mathbf{p}} \geq p - \varepsilon$.

Here one can view $n_u$ as an upper-bound on the number of samples that the Algorithm $ABS_M$ would use in most cases.

The above theorem indicates that Algorithm $ABS_M$ would not use too many samples and is guaranteed to produce estimations that will not exceed the error bound $\varepsilon$ on one side. Showing the other half of the error bound turns out to be quite hard. However we present here some simulation results empirically showing that the new method indeed produce estimates with high accuracy and high confidence. Matlab is used for the experiment. In each experiment, random samples are drawn according to the pre-determined probability $p$ and the $ABS_M$ algorithm is applied to estimate the $\widehat{\mathbf{p}}$ and decide when to stop sampling. Each simulation performs 1000 experiments for each target probability $p$ value. Then we measure the max, min, and average of the $\widehat{\mathbf{p}}$ and $n$ for the simulation. The results are averaged over 10 simulations. See Table 1 (next page) for details. Figures 1 and 2 show histograms indicating the frequency of estimated values and the number of random samples used in one simulation which consists of 1000 experiments.

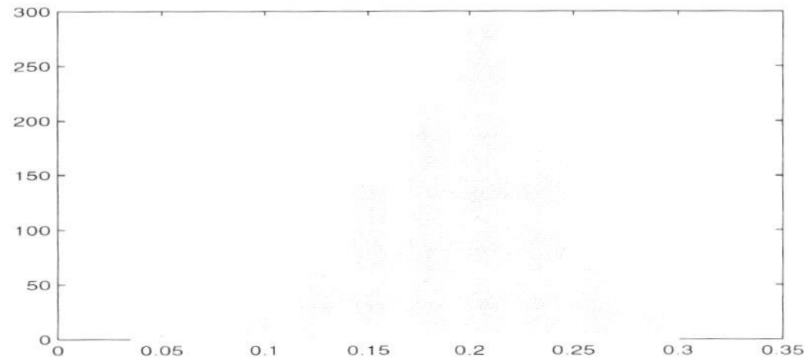


Fig. 1: Algorithm $ABS_M$, Histogram for the estimated $\widehat{\mathbf{p}}$ values. The horizontal axis indicates the estimated $\widehat{\mathbf{p}}$ values ($p$ = 0.2, $\varepsilon = \delta = 0.1$).

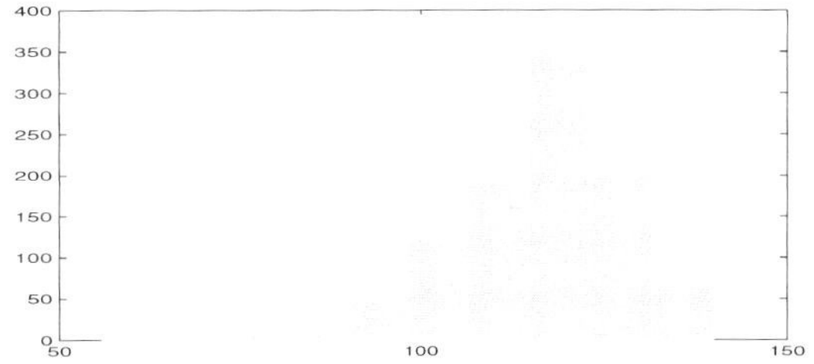


Fig. 2: Algorithm $ABS_M$, Histogram for the random variable $\mathbf{n}$, the number of samples needed in each trial. ($p$ = 0.2, $\varepsilon = \delta = 0.1$).

Table 1: Performance of Algorithm $ABS_M$ with $\varepsilon = \delta = 0.1$

| $p$ | 0.1 | 0.2 | 0.3 | 0.4 | 0.5 | 0.6 | 0.7 | 0.8 | 0.9 |
|---|---|---|---|---|---|---|---|---|---|
| $\widehat{\Pr}\{\lvert\widehat{\boldsymbol{p}} - p\rvert \geq \varepsilon\}$ | 0.001 | 0.012 | 0.012 | 0.014 | 0.015 | 0.012 | 0.010 | 0.010 | 0.000 |
| $\widehat{\boldsymbol{p}}$ mean | 0.097 | 0.197 | 0.299 | 0.400 | 0.500 | 0.601 | 0.703 | 0.804 | 0.906 |
| $\widehat{\boldsymbol{p}}$ max | 0.191 | 0.322 | 0.422 | 0.526 | 0.630 | 0.740 | 0.845 | 0.949 | 0.985 |
| $\widehat{\boldsymbol{p}}$ min | 0.015 | 0.048 | 0.167 | 0.264 | 0.364 | 0.474 | 0.573 | 0.691 | 0.802 |
| $\mathbf{n}$ mean | 81 | 116 | 138 | 148 | 149 | 148 | 138 | 116 | 81 |
| $\mathbf{n}$ max | 115 | 142 | 150 | 150 | 150 | 150 | 150 | 141 | 117 |
| $\mathbf{n}$ min | 48 | 61 | 108 | 133 | 147 | 132 | 104 | 63 | 48 |

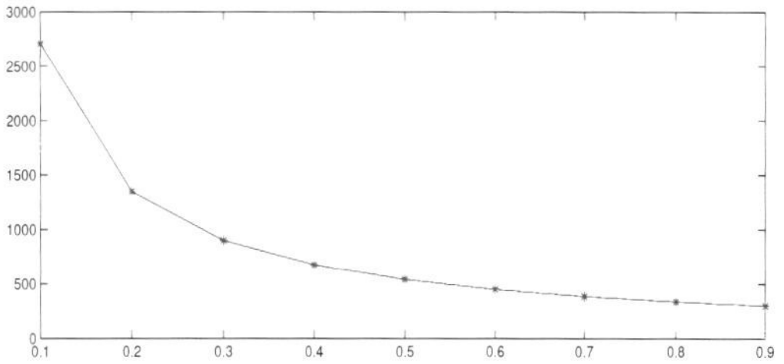


Fig. 3: Average sample size comparisons for controlling relative error. The top curve: Watanabe stopping rule; the lower curve: Algorithm $REL_M$. The horizontal axis indicates the target probability $p$ values, and the vertical axis indicates the average sample size.

## 4. The New Sampling Method: Controlling Relative Error

In this section, we present our sampling method for controlling relative error.

Given $0 < \varepsilon < 1$, $0 < \delta < 1$, the sampling method for controlling relative error proceeds as follows.

**Algorithm** $REL_M$**.**
Let $\mathbf{n} \leftarrow 0$, $X \leftarrow 0$ and $\widehat{\boldsymbol{p}} \leftarrow 0$.
While $\widehat{\boldsymbol{p}} = 0$ *or* $\mathbf{n} < \frac{\ln \frac{\delta}{2}}{\mathscr{U}_M(\widehat{\boldsymbol{p}}, \frac{\widehat{\boldsymbol{p}}}{1+\varepsilon})}$
Do
**begin**
Draw a random sample Y with parameter $p$.
Let $X \leftarrow X + Y$,
$\mathbf{n} \leftarrow \mathbf{n} + 1$ and $\widehat{\boldsymbol{p}} \leftarrow \frac{X}{\mathbf{n}}$.
**end**
Output $\widehat{\boldsymbol{p}}$ and $\mathbf{n}$.

**Preliminary Analysis of Algorithm** $REL_M$**.**
We can readily establish the following lemmas.

*Lemma 2:* Consider the functions $f_1(x) = \mathscr{U}_M(x, \frac{x}{1-\varepsilon})$ and $f_2(x) = \mathscr{U}_M(x, \frac{x}{1+\varepsilon})$. We have $f_1(x) \leq f_2(x)$ for $x \in (0, 1)$.

*Lemma 3:* The function $f(x) = \mathscr{U}_M(x, \frac{x}{1+\varepsilon})$ is monotonically decreasing for $x \in (0, 1)$. The function $g(x) = \mathscr{U}_M(x, \frac{x}{1-\varepsilon})$ is monotonically decreasing for $x \in (0, 1 - \varepsilon)$.

*Lemma 4:* Let $\hat{\boldsymbol{p}} \in (0, 1)$ be an estimate produced by Algorithm $REL_M$, and let $p$ be the true probability to be estimated. Then $p \in [\frac{\hat{\boldsymbol{p}}}{1+\varepsilon}, \frac{\hat{\boldsymbol{p}}}{1-\varepsilon}]$ if and only if $\hat{\boldsymbol{p}} \in [p(1 - \varepsilon), p(1 + \varepsilon)]$.

Let $N_1 = \max\{\lceil \frac{\ln \frac{\delta}{2}}{\mathscr{U}_M(p(1-\varepsilon), p)} \rceil, \lceil \frac{\ln \frac{\delta}{2}}{\mathscr{U}_M(p(1+\varepsilon), p)} \rceil\}$ and $N_2 = \lceil \frac{\ln \frac{\delta}{2}}{\mathscr{U}_M(p(1-\varepsilon), \frac{p(1-\varepsilon)}{1+\varepsilon})} \rceil$.

*Lemma 5:* Let $p$ be the true probability to be estimated. Let the number of Bernoulli trials $n$ satisfies $n \geq N_1$, then $\Pr\{\lvert\frac{\widehat{\boldsymbol{p}}_n - p}{p}\rvert \geq \varepsilon\} \leq \delta$.

*Lemma 6:* With probability of at lease $1 - \delta/2$, Algorithm $REL_M$ will stop with $n \leq N_2$.

Proof. First we notice $N_2 \geq N_1$. This is because $\mathscr{U}_M(p(1-\varepsilon), \frac{p(1-\varepsilon)}{1+\varepsilon}) > \mathscr{U}_M(p, \frac{p}{1+\varepsilon}) > \mathscr{U}_M(p(1+\varepsilon), p)$ by the monotonic decreasing property of $\mathscr{U}_M(x, \frac{x}{1+\varepsilon})$ shown in Lemma 3, and $\mathscr{U}_M(p(1-\varepsilon), \frac{p(1-\varepsilon)}{1+\varepsilon}) > \mathscr{U}_M(p(1-\varepsilon), \frac{p(1-\varepsilon)}{1-\varepsilon}) = \mathscr{U}_M(p(1-\varepsilon), p)$. Therefore when Algorithm $REL_M$ stops with $n \geq N_2$, we know that $n \geq N_1$, and thus by Lemma 5, the probability of $\widehat{\boldsymbol{p_n}} < p(1 - \varepsilon)$ is at least $1 - \frac{\delta}{2}$.

On the other hand, assume that the sampling by Algorithm $REL_M$ did not stop at $n = N_2$. This means, according to the algorithm, we have $\lceil \frac{\ln \frac{2}{\delta}}{\lvert\mathscr{U}_M(p(1-\varepsilon), \frac{p(1-\varepsilon)}{1+\varepsilon})\rvert} \rceil = N_2 < \lceil \frac{\ln \frac{2}{\delta}}{\lvert\mathcal{U}_M(p\hat{N}_2, \frac{p\hat{N}_2}{1+\varepsilon})\rvert} \rceil$. This shows $\mathscr{U}_M(\widehat{\boldsymbol{p_{N_2}}}, \frac{\widehat{\boldsymbol{p_{N_2}}}}{1+\varepsilon}) > \mathscr{U}_M(p(1-\varepsilon), \frac{p(1-\varepsilon)}{1+\varepsilon})$, and so by the monotonic decreasing property of $\mathscr{U}_M(x, \frac{x}{1+\varepsilon})$, we have $\widehat{\boldsymbol{p_{N_2}}} < p(1 - \varepsilon)$. From the argument in the previous paragraph, seeing $N_2$ samples and still producing $\widehat{\boldsymbol{p_{N_2}}} < p(1-\varepsilon)$ is an event with probability at most $\frac{\delta}{2}$. Thus, the opposite (sampling will stop with $n \leq N_2$) is true with probability of at least $1 - \frac{\delta}{2}$.

Based on the lemmas in this section, we have the following result:

**Theorem 2.** With probability of at least $1 - \frac{\delta}{2}$, Algorithm $REL_M$ will stop with $n \leq N_2$ and produce $\widehat{\boldsymbol{p}} \geq p(1 - \varepsilon)$.

We would desire to show that the Algorithm will stop between $N_1$ and $N_2$ steps with high probability. What remains to be proven is that with high probability, the algorithm will NOT stop too early and produce an estimate

$\widehat{p}$ which is bigger than $p(1+\varepsilon)$. Similar to the absolute-error case, this is not so easy to prove. However, we will show empirical results to support the conjecture that the algorithm indeed will stop after $N_1$ steps (most of the time). Moreover we will show simulation results comparing our method and the adaptive sampling method in [14].

In the following Table 2 (next page) we show the simulation results using $p = 0.1, 0.2, ..., 0.7$ with $\varepsilon = 0.2$ and $\delta = 0.1$ in these simulations. The columns labeled as "new" are results of using Algorithm $REL_M$, whereas the columns labeled as "Wata" are results of the method (Equation (2)) of Watanabe in [14]. As in the absolute error case, each simulation is a result of 1000 repeated experiments, and the numbers in the table are average results over 10 simulations.

The mean sample size comparison is also shown in the Fig. 3, which clearly shows the reduction in sample size of our method.

From the data in Table 2 (next page), it can be seen clearly that Algorithm $REL_M$ achieves competitive estimation accuracy as indicated by the mean of the $\widehat{p}$ while using much fewer samples as shown by the mean of $n$, when compared with the stopping rule (Equation (2)) in [14]. Of course, the Watanabe method has smaller variances which is obtained at the cost of using more samples.

# 5. A Scalable Boosting Learner by Sampling

In this section we briefly outline how to use the proposed new sampling method to construct an efficient ensemble learning method based on Boosting.

Boosting proceeds by constructing a sequence of hypotheses $h_1$, $h_2$, ..., $h_T$ in an iterative fashion such that the combination of these hypotheses will produce a strong classifier with high classification accuracy. The Adaboost [9] is perhaps the best-known boosting algorithm. Watanabe [7] proposed an adptive-sampling based boosting method *Madaboost* which uses sampling to obtain a subset $S_t$ of all samples, and select a best hypothesis $h_t$ from $S_t$ instead. This method is useful when the training dataset is huge. In [7], a stopping condition that adaptively determines the sample size for $S_t$ was proposed. Moreover theoretical analysis and experimental results were presented in [7] showing that Madaboost can generate classifiers with comparable accuracies and better efficiency.

We note that our adaptive sampling method could be readily applied to construct a new boosting algorithm. The idea is to adapt the criterion function in Algorithm $ABS_M$ for estimating the mean of a Bernoulli variable to estimate the prediction accuracy of a hypothesis in each boosting round. Given a fixed distribution $\mathscr{D}$ over a training dataset $D$, each hypothesis $h$ in the hypothesis space is associated with a Bernoulli random variable $V_h$ such that $Pr\{V_h = 1\} = \Sigma_{x \in S \,\wedge\, h(x)=c(x)} \mathscr{D}(x)$, where $c(x)$ denotes the correct classification of instance $x$. Namely, $V_h = 1$ if and only if hypothesis $h$ correctly classifies an instance $x$ drawn according to $\mathscr{D}$. Put $P_h = \Pr\{V_h = 1\}$. So $P_h$ is the prediction accuracy of $h$ according to distribution $\mathscr{D}$. Here we try to estimate $P_h$ from a sample $S$ of all training data $D$ via adaptive sampling.

When sampling is used to estimate the accuracy ($P_h$) of each hypothesis $h$, how do we determine, a "reasonable" sample size sufficient to guarantee with high confidence that the estimated accuracy $P_{h,S}$ based on sample $S$ is "close" enough to $P_h$, for each hypothesis $h$? Once that is decided, we can choose the hypothesis $h$ with the highest $P_{h,S}$ as a result for a boosting round, because $h$ should be close to the actual best hypothesis $h^*$ with high probability. There are various ways to define "closeness" between two hypotheses. The most important issue in Boosting is that at least the "weak" hypothesis selected at each round should have accuracy above $1/2$. So one very modest requirement of "closeness" between the selected hypothesis $h$ and the best one $h^*$ is that if $P_{h^*} > 1/2$, then $P_h > 1/2$. So we want our estimated probability $P_{h,S}$ and the true $P_h$ to fall on the same side of $1/2$.

This could be formulated as the problem to select a stopping rule on sample size $|S|$ such that

$$\Pr\{|\boldsymbol{P_{h,S}} - P_h| \geq \varepsilon|P_h - 1/2|\} \leq \delta.$$

The Algorithm $ABS_M$ for controlling absolute error can be adapted for the above problem. We will replace the $\widehat{p}$ in Algorithm $ABS_M$ by $P_{h,S}$ and the *fixed* $\varepsilon$ in Algorithm $ABS_M$ by $\frac{\varepsilon|P_{h,S}-1/2|}{1+\varepsilon}$.

We are currently conducting experimental studies on this new adaptive sampling based boosting learner and the results will be reported in a separate paper.

# 6. Conclusions and Future Work

In this paper we present a new adaptive sampling method for estimating the mean of a random Bernoulli variable based on Massart's rule inspired by the works in [4], [3]. A preliminary theoretical analysis is presented, along with empirical studies. The experimental results show that the new method often uses a much smaller sample size while maintaining competitive estimation accuracy. We also briefly outline how to utilize the new sampling method to build an efficient ensemble learning algorithm by Boosting.

The theoretical studies presented here are only preliminary and there is room for further analyzing the sampling schemes and proving its exact consistency. We would also like to conduct experimental studies on the ensemble boosting learner proposed here and compare the results with that of [2].

Table 2: Performance Comparison, Algorithm $REL_M$ and Watanabe method [14], $\varepsilon = 0.2$, $\delta = 0.1$, $\{err\} = \{|\widehat{\mathbf{p}} - p| \geq \varepsilon p\}$

| $p$ | 0.1 | | 0.2 | | 0.3 | | 0.4 | | 0.5 | | 0.6 | | 0.7 | |
|---|---|---|---|---|---|---|---|---|---|---|---|---|---|---|
| | new | Wata | new | Wata | new | Wata | new | Wata | new | Wata | new | Wata | new | Wata |
| $\widehat{\Pr}\{err\}$ | 0.010 | 0.002 | 0.008 | 0.001 | 0.009 | 0.001 | 0.009 | 0 | 0.009 | 0 | 0.009 | 0 | 0.010 | 0 |
| $\widehat{\mathbf{p}}$ mean | 0.100 | 0.100 | 0.201 | 0.201 | 0.302 | 0.301 | 0.403 | 0.401 | 0.503 | 0.501 | 0.605 | 0.601 | 0.708 | 0.701 |
| $\widehat{\mathbf{p}}$ max | 0.127 | 0.122 | 0.253 | 0.240 | 0.385 | 0.356 | 0.515 | 0.466 | 0.649 | 0.572 | 0.801 | 0.682 | 0.936 | 0.779 |
| $\widehat{\mathbf{p}}$ min | 0.083 | 0.083 | 0.162 | 0.169 | 0.243 | 0.256 | 0.325 | 0.346 | 0.407 | 0.436 | 0.498 | 0.531 | 0.585 | 0.611 |
| $\mathbf{n}$ mean | 1752 | 2707 | 788 | 1349 | 469 | 899 | 309 | 675 | 213 | 540 | 148 | 449 | 102 | 385 |
| $\mathbf{n}$ max | 2221 | 3247 | 1020 | 1601 | 619 | 1053 | 421 | 781 | 301 | 619 | 215 | 508 | 158 | 433 |
| $\mathbf{n}$ min | 1331 | 2232 | 588 | 1123 | 326 | 759 | 203 | 580 | 126 | 471 | 70 | 396 | 36 | 346 |

## Acknowledgment

We would like to thank Dr. Xinjia Chen for helpful discussions on topics related to this work. This work is partially supported by Louisiana Board of Regents under contract number LEQSF-EPS (2013)-PFUND-307.

## References

[1] H. Chernoff, "A measure of asymptotic efficiency for tests of a hypothesis based on the sum of observations," *Ann. Math. Statist.*, vol. 23, pp. 493–507, 1952.

[2] J. Chen, " Scalable ensemble learning by adaptive sampling", *Proceedings of International Conference on Machine Learning and Applications (ICMLA2012)*, Florida, December 2012.

[3] J. Chen and X. Chen, "A new method for adaptive sequential sampling for learning and parameter estimation," *Proceedings of International symposium on Methodologies for Intelligent Systems (ISMIS2011)*, Warsaw, Poland, June 2011.

[4] X. Chen, "A new framework of multistage estimation," arXiv.0809.1241 [math.ST].

[5] X. Chen, "A new framework of multistage parametric inference," *Proceeding of SPIE Conference*, vol. 7666, pp. 76660R1–12, Orlando, Florida, April 2010.

[6] X. Chen, "Exact computation of minimum sample size for estimation of binomial parameters," *Journal of Statistical Planning and Inference*, vol. 141, pp. 2622-2632, February 2011. Available at http://arxiv.org/abs/0707.2113.

[7] C. Domingo and O. Watanabe, "Scaling up a boosting-based learner via adaptive sampling," *Knowledge Discovery and Data Mining*, pp. 317–328, Springer, 2000.

[8] C. Domingo and O. Watanabe, "Adaptive sampling methods for scaling up knowledge discovery algorithms," *Proceedings of 2nd Int. Conference on discovery Science*, Japan, December 1999.

[9] Yoav Freund and Robert E. Schapire, "A decision-theoretic generalization of on-line learning and an application to boosting,"*Journal of Computer and System Sciences*, 55(1):119–139, 1997.

[10] W. Hoeffding, "Probability inequalities for sums of bounded variables," *J. Amer. Statist. Assoc.*, vol. 58, pp. 13–29, 1963.

[11] R. Lipton, J. Naughton, D.A. Schneider, and S.Seshadri, "Efficient sampling strategies for relational database operations," *Theoretical Computer Science*, vol. 116, pp. 195–226, 1993.

[12] R. Lipton and J. Naughton, "Query size estimation by adaptive sampling," *Journal of Computer and System Sciences*, vol. 51, pp. 18–25, 1995.

[13] J. F. Lynch, "Analysis and application of adaptive sampling," *Journal of Computer and System Sciences*, vol. 66, pp. 2-19, 2003

[14] O. Watanabe, "Sequential sampling techniques for algorithmic learning theory," *Theoretical Computer Science*, vol. 348, pp. 3–14, 2005

# Mining the Boundaries of Social Networks: Crawling Facebook and Twitter for BlogIntelligence

**Philipp Berger[1], Patrick Hennig[1], Thomas Klingbeil[2], Matthias Kohnen[2], Steffen Pade[2], and Christoph Meinel[3]**
Hasso-Plattner-Institute, University of Potsdam, Germany
[1]{philipp.berger, patrick.hennig}@hpi.uni-potsdam.de
[2]{thomas.klingbeil, matthias.kohnen, steffen.pade}@student.hpi.uni-potsdam.de
[3]office-meinel@hpi.uni-potsdam.de

**Abstract**— *Today's number of weblogs is higher than ever before and still growing. These blogs are interconnected by numerous links and other diverse connections, generating a series of notable patterns. Weblogs are not isolated and highly connected with other social networks like Facebook and Twitter. Thus, we analyze the references and investigate methods to gather data from the social platforms that are interconnected with weblogs. By analyzing the communication flow between weblogs, Facebook and Twitter, we observe that Facebook is mostly used for referencing real people instead of posts. In contrast, tweets are primarily used for information propagation and citation.*

**Keywords:**
Data Mining, Social Networks, Weblogs, Twitter, Facebook

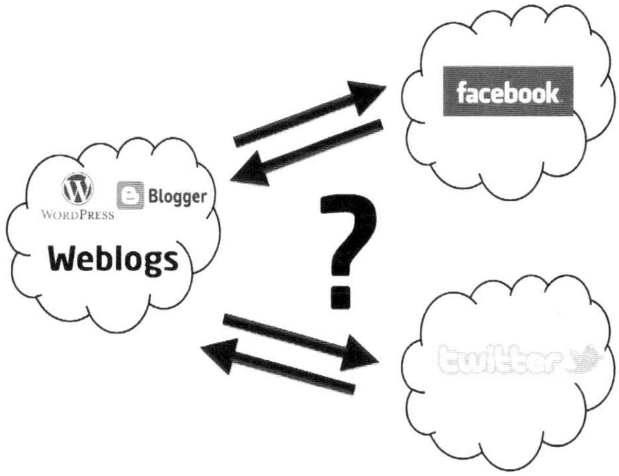


Fig. 1: How are weblogs and other social networks connected?

## 1. Platforms in the Social Web Have to Be Connected

Weblogs, called *blogs*, are one of the most popular "social media tools" of the World Wide Web (WWW) [1]. They are specialized, but easy-to-use content management systems. Blogs focus on frequently updated content, social interactions, and interoperability with other Web-authoring systems.

The actual power of blogs evolves through their common superstructure, i.e. a blog integrates itself into a huge think tank of millions of interconnected weblogs, called blogosphere that creates an enormous and ever-changing archive of open source intelligence [2].

The structure of the whole social web has undergone a huge shift within the last years. Instead of using a single social platform users tend to use multiple platforms in parallel.

Today's social web consists of a collection of these platforms like Facebook[1], news portals, weblogs and diverse other intercommunication websites like *Twitter*[2], *Pinterest*[3], and *Foursquare*[4]. Research around social networks focuses on one specific platform and investigates the communities, information flow, and social structure within this platform. One example is the BlogIntelligence[5,6] project. Within the scope of this project there have been several research efforts on structure, growth, and emergence of weblogs. Although blogs account for a major segment of the social web, different analyses show that weblogs extensively link to other social networks, especially Twitter and Facebook.

We observe that besides linking social profiles, bloggers use external platforms to announce posts, redirect discussions (instead of using comments), pickup controversial opinions or reference people. These observations in mind, we identify the need for a deeper analysis. Therefore, we need to collect data from these "external" sources, first, and secondarily put them into a semantic relation to the already gathered data from weblogs.

This leads to various new insights and at the very least offers a new perspective on how connections between the

[1] `http://facebook.com`
[2] `http://twitter.com`
[3] `http://pinterest.com`
[4] `http://foursquare.com`
[5] `http://blog-intelligence.com`
[6] `http://hpi.uni-potsdam.de/meinel/knowledge_tech/blog_intelligence`

different kinds of social web platforms are created and maintained (see Figure 1). Interesting research questions on this topic are for instance the differences in user activity between the platforms or how trends spread among them. The results of this research include analyses on how topics (especially high interest, popular trending topics) spread among the platforms or whether or not the platforms concentrate on different fields of topics. Are users of two or more of the platforms also talking about the same things on all of them? This and many more questions could be answered by these results. More details on what could also be of interest will be given in Section 5.

Within the scope of this paper we investigate methods and realize harvesting applications for Facebook and Twitter. Since BlogIntelligence is only focused on weblogs, we need to extract the connections to other social platforms from the existing data set to find links pointing to Facebook and Twitter.

The next section gives an overview of related work. Sections 3.1 and 3.2 focus on the crawling processes for Facebook and Twitter. The data retrieved by these processes is then analyzed in Section 4. This paper closes with recommendations for further research in Section 5 and a conclusion in Section 6.

## 2. Related Work

We distinguish two areas of related work. First, related approaches for harvesting the social networks in scope, e.g. Facebook and Twitter. Second, approaches towards mining of the interaction between social networks.

Under the name *TwitterEcho*, a research group has already developed an open source Twitter crawler [3]. Their work is using the REST API, as Twitter still allowed whitelisting during the time of their research, in order to increase the allowed number of requests per hour. As whitelisting is no longer possible, we had to focus on finding an algorithm, which intelligently uses the Streaming API to achieve our goals.

Another group from INRIA Sophia Antipolis has focused on acquiring a full overview of the user base of Twitter and drawing a graph of the way the users are connected [4]. For their work, they used a distributed platform, called PlanetLab. Their findings include information regarding user activity and the influence of Twitter policies and social conventions on the structure of that graph. In contrast to our work, their gathered data does explicitly not contain the content of the tweets.

The topic of the topological characteristics of the Twitter network has also been picked up by H. Kwak et al. from the Department of Computer Science, KAIST, Korea. They compared the way social networks work to characteristics of traditional human social networks. This research group also introduced a PageRank ranking algorithm for Twitter users. As a result of their research they presented that over 85% of Twitter posts are news-related content [5]. For us this means, that linking the information from Twitter to the information already gathered about the Blogosphere is an important step.

Apart from Twitter, also Facebook crawling has been conducted by other researchers at the University of Messina, Italy [6]. Again, they looked into the details of the connections and interactions between the participants of Facebook. They have used Breadth-first-search sampling, which means seed nodes have been employed at the beginning of the crawling phase. Instead of using the faster Graph API provided by Facebook, they used the deprecated Ajax interface.

Another important topic which needs to be considered is, how spam users can be detected and filtered from the data to be analyzed. Research in this field has been conducted by F. Benevenutu et al. from the Computer Science Department of the Universidade Federal de Minas Gerais Belo Horizonte, Brazil [7]. They presented an algorithm, which allows a precision of 70% while classifying spammers, which is based on detecting specific characteristics using machine learning techniques.

To the best of our knowledge the research concerning cross-platform social media mining experiences only little investigation in the community. Quandt et al. [8] relate social networks and traditional channels like newspapers and discuss the opinion towards the quality and usefulness of weblogs for journalism. Likewise, Hermida et al., [9] investigate the interaction between television and Twitter. From an architectural point of view, Pallis et al. [10] dive into the similarities of social networks with the goal to develop cross-platform services.

In contrast to related work, we explore the relations across online social networks and try to identify unknown connections, diffusion mechanisms, et cetera.

## 3. Social Network Harvesting

To mine different social networks and their boundaries we need to harvest the publicly available information and make them available offline. This enables us to run offline cross-network analyses. As mentioned above, the BlogIntelligence project already stores blog data that a tailor-made crawler downloads. Thus, we focus on finding referenced social networks in this data set and on developing adapted crawlers for Facebook and Twitter.

### 3.1 Facebook Crawling

Within the last years Facebook has grown to be the world's largest social network according to their active user groups. It has been of no surprise that the BlogIntelligence data contains a high number of references to Facebook pages, posts and user pages. Due to the structure of the filtered links and the structure of the social network itself, it needs to be considered that there are different instances of Facebook entities. Whereas the individual user pages are well-known, there are also pages of businesses, celebrities, groups and diverse other information sources. Due to the API, which will be explained in more detail in the next part of this section, the data preprocessing needs to identify these types of pages and decide how to crawl the source.

Further, the somewhat unclear terms of use of this API have led to uncertainty on what exactly an automated web crawler is allowed to do with Facebook. Since this uncertainties could not be cleared so far we have decided to continue gathering data in a smaller and cautious way by only running the application occasionally with lighter sets of data.

### 3.1.1 API and Restrictions

Although there is an old legacy REST API and the FQL (Facebook Query Language) API the only reasonable interface to use is the Facebook Graph API which allows for the execution of RESTful requests with JSON formatted data against their website. The structure of such a query is held quite simple and makes exact requests even for a single post possible.

With that in mind the filtered links pointing to Facebook had to be investigated on what exactly they are pointing to - a page, a user, etc. - and the according request had to be made. Unfortunately the terms and conditions[7] applying to the usage of the Facebook Graph API do only consider using this API for building a so-called Facebook app. This term describes an application that is either a stand-alone product connecting and authenticating a Face book user or a web application that can be accessed via the Facebook website. The automated data collection has only the requirement that the collector has to make the collected data searchable, collect data for purposes of search respectively. Since we will be able to visually represent the gathered data in our webportal we thus comply to this requirement by our integrated search functionality.

### 3.1.2 The Data Collection Process

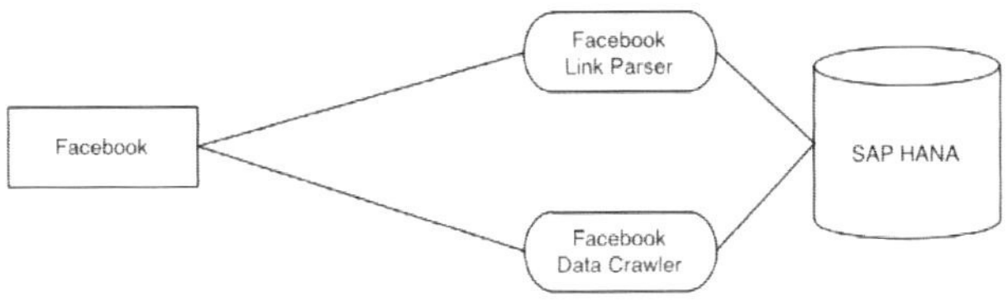


Fig. 2: Conceptual view on the Facebook crawling process

The data collection process consists of four steps:

1) filter and normalize links from BlogIntelligence data
2) select most active users
3) connect to Facebook
4) download and store information

[7]`http://www.facebook.com/apps/site_scraping_tos_terms.php`

**a) Step 1:** This step is the most challenging caused by the limited amount of requests and the relatively noisy data set. Hereby, we need to filter, prepare and understand the links within the BlogIntelligence data set.

As stated before, Facebook as a social network introduces different types of entities like users, groups, posts, and events. Since the focus of BlogIntelligence is mainly on tracking discussions of blog authors on the internet, the focus of this project was placed in the same manner. For that reason Facebook events and groups are excluded from the collection process. These URLs were filtered out as well as all the corporate Facebook pages like help pages, information pages and obviously the home page itself.

By analyzing the given set of links we empirically detect link patterns to distinguish between user pages and unusable links. Further, we normalize those links by removing all but the user identification alias. This excludes unwanted subpages and allows us to easily match links of different posts to the same user. The user alias is used to request all the posts of one user for a given time frame. Since there are no restrictions to the number of requests, this process can run in parallel for each user every day or even every couple of hours. Nevertheless, bandwidth and server time restrictions can dictate us to concentrate on a subset of all Facebook users.

**b) Step 2:** During our test period we ran this process two times within 30 days. Moreover, these two executions provided the chance to research user activity. This leads us to the prioritization of users depending on their activity on Facebook.

Therefore, we distinguish between "very active" and "less active" users by incorporating the posting frequency of users. We rank users according to their activity and only queue the top-k users for regularly updating.

To react to changes in user behavior only the last 30 days are taken into account. The evaluation of user activity is executed before every harvesting stage. With a growing dataset the ranking of users gets more and more accurate. Especially during the initial crawling the number of posts crawled for each user is quite low and there are also many users without any crawled posts. To deal with this issue the harvesting is restarted after quite short time frames to enable the collection of data for all users.

This distinction method works more satisfactory if a bigger number of posts is crawled and if for most of the users posts have been found.

**c) Step 3:** The connection to Facebook is mainly handled by an external library called *restfb*[8]. It encapsulates Facebook's Graph API into an easy-to-use Java interface. This library especially simplifies the authentication with Facebook.

[8]`http://restfb.com/`

**d) Step 4:** This step consists of downloading and storing the received data. Thus, we use restfb to request the wanted data. We translate the data into our own structures and store it using JDBC drivers into our relational database called *SAP HANA*[9].

## 3.2 Twitter Crawling

Regarding the number of active users, Twitter is Facebook's largest competitor. The BlogIntelligence data set reflects this by including also a high number of links to Twitter. Based on our observations, we like to crawl Twitter users because we assume that most of the Bloggers also maintain a Twitter account for publishing their posts and additional ideas. Nevertheless, the crawling of tweets of these users and of additional linked content is the logical next step.

The opportunities offered by Twitter's APIs are described in the next part of this section. Following this, we reflect on the implementation of the crawling process.

### 3.2.1 APIs and Restrictions

Twitter offers two different APIs with specialized capabilities. The *REST API* enables the access to all Twitter resources like tweets, user information, followship graphs and many more. The *Streaming API* provides the ability to retrieve a continuous stream of tweets for selected users.

During the year 2012 Twitter launched a new version of both APIs changing restrictions and methods. The old REST API version 1 allowed 350 requests to the REST API per hour and authenticated user. The new version 1.1 distinguishes between different REST API methods and restricts the number of requests depending on and per called method for each authenticated user. For some methods the restriction is set to 15 requests every 15-minute window. Nevertheless, the methods used by our Twitter crawler only have a restriction of 180 requests per 15 minutes. This allows 720 requests per hour with the API methods of version 1.1, which is more than twice the amount available with version 1.

Caused by this restriction we develop a method to combine both APIs to enable the best crawling performance by sticking to the restriction.

After identifying the Twitter user accounts within the BlogIntelligence data set, we use the REST API to gather all past tweets for this users. So, the REST API helps us to fill our tweet archive and collect the initial seed of tweets. Furthermore, this API is of high interest for time-discrete crawling of less active users. Thereby, we avoid to idle while waiting for new tweets of these users.

The coverage of highly active users tweeting many times a day or even per hour is very expensive in terms of requests to the REST API. This is exactly where the Streaming API is of crucial value. We use the full capacity of this API to observe our most active users. This enables us to continuously collect each new post of these users. The distinction into "less active" and "highly active" let us use each API to its limits and the crawler can gather tweets of identified users in the least possible time.

### 3.2.2 The Data Collection Process

The collection process of Twitter is similar to the Facebook crawling and consists of the same 4 steps (see Section 3.1.2):

1) filter and normalize links from BlogIntelligence data
2) select most active users
3) connect to Twitter
4) download and store information

**a) Step 1:** We empirically identify patterns for the Twitter link recognition. Hereby, we have to distinguish between links containing the screen name and links containing the user IDs. The screen names are human readable and necessary for user interfaces like a webportal. The user IDs are required for accessing the above mentioned APIs to crawl tweets, which are not directly linked.

**b) Step 2:** Within the process of crawling tweets from Twitter users, the same approach for distinguishing active and less active users for Facebook crawling is applied. This process was described in Section 3.1.2.

In contrast to Facebook, Twitter offers the Streaming API that enables us to get more frequent updates for a user group with a limited size of 5 000. Thus, for the most active users we use the Streaming API to retrieve continuous up-to-date tweets. The REST API allows for crawling tweets of the less active users. We conclude from the less frequent posting activity in the past that these users will continue to post in an infrequent manner. Thus, the REST API is sufficient to retrieve all tweets, even with the described limitations.

**c) Step 3:** To access the Twitter API we use *twitter4j*[10].

**d) Step 4:** Besides differences in the data structure, the storing process is the same as for Facebook.

# 4. Data Analyses

In this section, we show our first analysis results that directly result from a real life crawled data set obtained by BlogIntelligence. First, we present the key indicator of the base data. Following, the insights into the data collected from Facebook and Twitter.

[9] http://www.sap.com/hana/

[10] http://twitter4j.org/

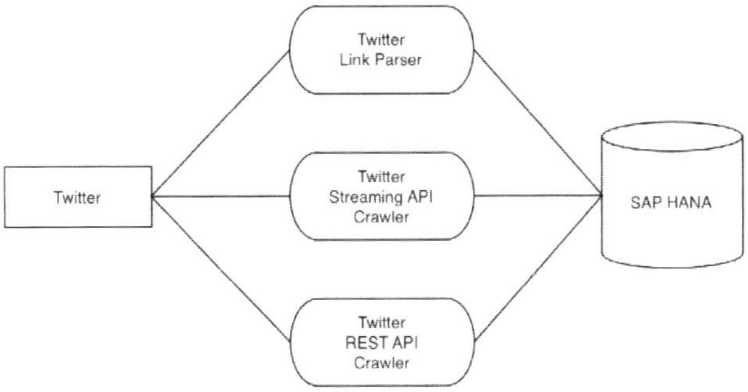


Fig. 3: Conceptual view on the Twitter crawling process

## 4.1 BlogIntelligence Data

The used data set of BlogIntelligence for this evaluation consists of 15 327 blogs with 818 865 posts. These posts consist of 200 000 000 links. This data set is the result of a 3-week-run from August 2012. Since we have integrated our crawling components into the BlogIntelligence Framework, we use this data as a basis.

## 4.2 Facebook and Twitter Data

We identify 554 962 links to Facebook users or posts of Facebook users. There are 31 825 distinct links. This implies that most users are linked multiple times. On average each user is referred to 17.4 times where 28 292 unique users can be extracted from the links.

The usage of Twitter is quite different because the 325 659 distinct links to Twitter users or tweets occur 1 425 244 times. Each link is used less often than Facebook link posts on weblogs (on average 4.4 times). Furthermore, only 13 589 unique Twitter users can be parsed from the links. A deeper analysis of the links shows that many times tweets are linked which are related to the topic of weblog posts. These numbers support the logical inference that links pointing into Facebook's social network are supposed to link to a Facebook user's profile and mainly inform about the existence of such a profile. Whereas, the linkage of tweets seems to link to a third-party source of information or to refer to a citation. This is also an indicator for the transient nature of tweets.

Posts and tweets crawled from Facebook and Twitter can also be analyzed to learn more about the structure of the data. Due to the afore-mentioned legal problems regarding the crawling of Facebook the main focus of this analysis is based on Twitter data.

From Facebook 96 317 posts were crawled during the short crawling periods. 64 353 of these posts contain a link to an external resource. Thus, over 60% of Facebook posts connect to other webpage that bring up new questions like "Do these links point to other weblogs?". Nevertheless, for more detailed insights this data set is too limited. Thus, we need to continue crawling to run deeper analyses.

Twitter was crawled for two weeks in February 2013. During this time 3 760 577 tweets were retrieved.

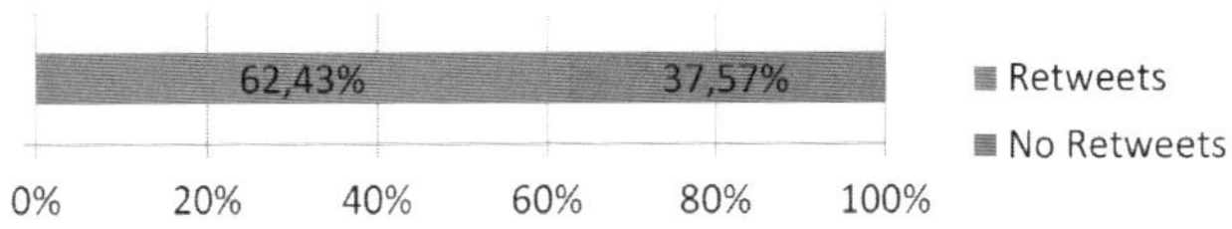


Fig. 4: Ratio of tweets being retweets to own tweets

One main feature of Twitter is the ability to retweet someone's tweet. This enables users to spread information and likewise show their appreciation for a tweet. As shown in Figure 4, 62.43% of all tweets are retweets of other tweets. This means that 2.3 million tweets are created just by the retweeting of an original tweet. The set of retweets references 216 911 tweets. The maximum retweet count of a single tweet in the data set is 30 888. This indicates the popularity of Twitter as a publishing channel that can rapidly spread information through its whole user base.

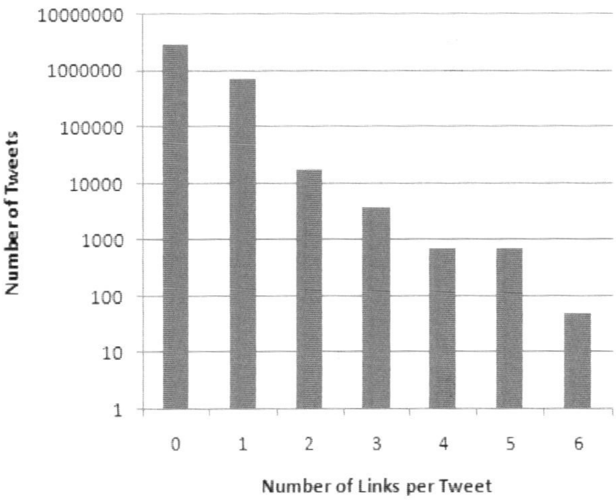


Fig. 5: Number of links occurring in one tweet, please mind the logarithmic scale

Many tweets are used to refer to other external websites by links. The analysis of the tweets, depicted in Figure 5, points out that most tweets, about three million, contain no links. About 740 000 tweets contain one link. The number of tweets with more than one link is quite small. This is also characteristic for the short messages of Twitter, but also indicates that the information flow does not stop in the referenced social network. It may also be doubtful whether tweets containing up to six different links have any relevant content.

Hashtags allow the Twitter users to give a short summary of the content of a tweet. This feature is widely used when posting about an event or discussing ongoing topics. This allows many different analyses to be performed on the data

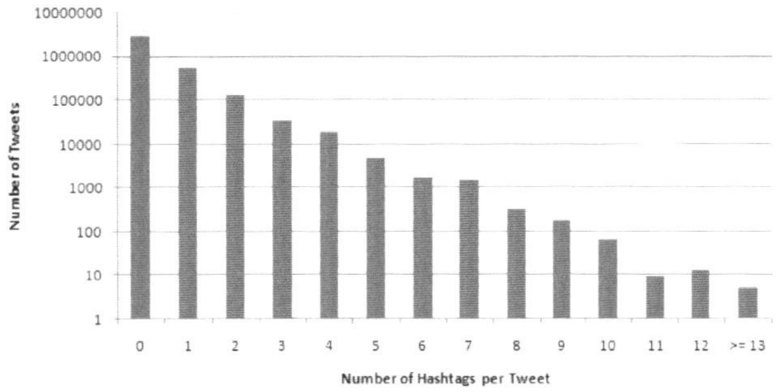


Fig. 6: Number of hashtags used in one tweet, please mind the logarithmic scale

like trend detection or clustering. The evaluation of the Twitter data regarding hashtags is quite similar to the analysis of links in the tweets, about three million tweets contain no hashtags, 550 000 tweets have one hashtag and two hashtags are assigned to 130 000 tweets. A higher number of hashtags is used less frequently and again it is questionable whether up to 18 hashtags contain any relevant information. The distribution of hashtags is shown in Figure 6.

## 5. Recommendations for Further Research

As described in Section 1 this project's goal was to implement the first step of a larger whole. Thus, only a limited result set is presented. The next step will be a more dedicated set of analyses on how weblogs and weblog networks interact with Facebook and Twitter by representing other types of social networks.

These analyses should aim to answer different questions of interest. In the scope of the present research activity within this project a next step will consider the relations between blogs, blog posts and the gathered tweets and Facebook posts respectively needs to be determined, which will then provide possibilities for investigating connections between the networks.

At this point there will be different fields to be regarded. A first interesting point will be how topics spread among the blogosphere and social networks when considering time and intensity. Upcoming interesting questions are:

- What time-gap lies between the first appearance of a topic and its encroaching to platforms of other types?
- Is there a platform (blogosphere / Facebook / Twitter) where new topics mostly appear the first time?
- Are main topics of one platform also main topics of all / one other platform?
- Which users are actively posting on all of the platforms?
- Which platforms are best synchronized concerning their main topics?
- Is a user who is active on two or more distinct platforms talking about the same things on all of them?

Answering these questions will give first indications on correlations between the blogosphere and Facebook and Twitter based on discussed topics and possible common or distinct user groups. Regarding the activities of users next steps will include some kind of an activity index calculated on possibly how often a user makes a post on one of the platforms or an activity index calculating how often new posts are made all over on one platform. These indexes in turn can give a metric to compare the platforms based on the activity of their members.

Furthermore, the gathered data from the social networks contains further links pointing to network internal and external resources. At this point the unanswered question is how much sense it would make to follow these references and include what they are pointing to into the data collection process. Whereas it was not considered for this project so far it might lead to new and more specific insights. When taking the second level links into account it will be necessary to distinguish them from the first level links originating in the blogosphere, especially their relevance to topic determination, trend detection or user activity. They have to be put into relation by weighing their importance against the large whole.

As a last point it should be mentioned that there are several other social networks out there. Since the follow-up step of this research project will also take them into consideration. The more data sources there are the more interesting and significant this project's results will be in the future.

## 6. Conclusion

We introduced the area of cross-platform social network analysis. Our work is based on the BlogIntelligence project and thus our starting social network is the blogosphere. By investigating the link structure of blogs we found numerous connections to other social networks especially Facebook and Twitter.

To investigate these connections we implement a harvesting application for both networks that makes the relations available for analyses. We conclude that even though gathering the data itself is easy, as comprehensible APIs are available from the providers, a lot of legal aspects need to be considered. Amongst others, this concerns the collection of personal data of users which even though publicly available, undermines certain rules. Additionally, the providers restrict the amount of data which can be retrieved within a specified amount of time. This makes it necessary to create intelligent algorithms which specify which data will be fetched at which point of time.

As a preliminary result of our research, we deduct that weblogs are strongly interconnected with the social networks Twitter and Facebook. These connections are bi-directional, as on the one hand blog posts are linked in Twitter and Facebook and on the other hand, weblog authors write about the content of tweets and Facebook pages. This advanced level of relationship analysis can lead to the creation of a whole new *meta network*, interconnecting parts of the traditional blogosphere and social networks.

We analyzed the characteristic of the connected Facebook links and observed that those are mostly used for referencing people instead of posts. In contrast, the Twitter links mostly refer to tweets and we observe that these tweets are primarily used for information propagation.

# References

[1] T. Cook and L. Hopkins, "Social media or, "how i learned to stop worrying and love communication"," September 2007. [Online]. Available: http://trevorcook.typepad.com/weblog/files/CookHopkins-SocialMediaWhitePaper-2007.pdf

[2] J. Schmidt, "Weblogs: eine kommunikationssoziologische studie," 2006.

[3] M. Boanjak and E. Oliveira, "TwitterEcho: a distributed focused crawler to support open research with twitter data," *Proceedings of the 21st ...*, pp. 1233–1239, 2012. [Online]. Available: http://dl.acm.org/citation.cfm?id=2188266

[4] M. Gabielkov and A. Legout, "The complete picture of the Twitter social graph," *Proceedings of the 2012 ACM conference on ...*, pp. 20–21, 2012. [Online]. Available: http://dl.acm.org/citation.cfm?id=2413260

[5] H. Kwak, C. Lee, H. Park, and S. Moon, "What is Twitter , a Social Network or a News Media?" *... of the 19th international conference on ...*, 2010. [Online]. Available: http://dl.acm.org/citation.cfm?id=1772751

[6] S. Catanese, P. D. Meo, and E. Ferrara, "Crawling facebook for social network analysis purposes," *arXiv preprint arXiv: ...*, pp. 0–7, 2011. [Online]. Available: http://arxiv.org/abs/1105.6307

[7] G. Magno and T. Rodrigues, "Detecting Spammers on Twitter," *Science*, pp. 1 – 9, 2010. [Online]. Available: http://www.nber.org/chapters/c2665

[8] T. Quandt and J. B. Singer, "Convergence and cross-platform content production," *Handbook of journalism studies*, pp. 130–144, 2009.

[9] A. Hermida, "From tv to twitter: how ambient news became ambient journalism," *Media/Culture Journal*, vol. 13, no. 2, 2010.

[10] G. Pallis, D. Zeinalipour-Yazti, and M. D. Dikaiakos, "Online social networks: status and trends," in *New Directions in Web Data Management 1*. Springer, 2011, pp. 213–234.

# SESSION

# DATA MINING, OPINION MANAGEMENT, SOFTWARE QUALITY ISSUES, BIOINFORMATICS, AND APPLICATIONS

## Chair(s)

**Prof. Hamid Arabnia**
**University of Georgia**

# DELAY-CFIM: A Sliding Window Based Method on Mining Closed Frequent Itemsets over High-Speed Data Streams

Chunkai Zhang, Yulong Hu, Lei Zhang
School of Shenzhen Graduate, Harbin Institute of Technology, Shenzhen, China

*Abstract*—*Closed frequent itemset mining plays an essential role in data stream mining. It could be used in business decisions, basket analysis, etc. Most methods for mining closed frequent itemsets store the streamlined information in compact data structure when data is generated. Whenever a query is submitted, it outputs all closed frequent itemsets. However, the online processing of existing approaches is so slow that those methods cannot deal with data streams generated at a high speed. In this paper, a novel method DELAY-CFIM for mining closed frequent itemsets is proposed to solve the problem of slow online processing. It divides the closed frequent itemset mining process over data streams into two steps. Firstly, when transactions are generated, it stores the frequency information of itemsets in a summary data structure. Then it mines closed frequent itemsets until a query is submitted. The method can improve the speed of online processing.*

*Keywords- closed frequent itemset, data stream, sliding window.*

## I. INTRODUCTION

Recently, data stream mining has been a hot topic in data mining. With the development of information technology, large amount of data streams are generated every day[1]. Different from the traditional static dataset, a data stream is a massive open-ended sequence of data elements continuously generated at a rapid rate. In order to play its role, the data streams need to be converted into useful information so that they could be applied in different applications. Frequent itemset mining is one of the most important types in data stream mining. It could be applied in many different domains, including network monitoring, market basket analysis, catalog design and cross-marketing, and customer shopping behavior analysis, etc[2].

The approaches for mining closed frequent itemsets over data streams are mostly based on the methods for mining traditional static dataset. To solve the problems caused by fast data streams and massive data, most of the algorithms maintain a summary data structure in memory. Due to time and memory constraints, it is impossible to monitor all the information of data streams in the summary data structure. Hence, window mechanisms are involved to deal with the data streams. According to the stream processing model[3], algorithms of frequent itemset mining over data streams could be divided into three categories: sliding window, landmark window and damped window. The algorithms based on sliding window try to mine the most recent frequent itemsets over data streams. A users' specified threshold *windowSize* is involved to limit the number of transactions in the sliding window. Algorithms based on landmark window not only concern about the information in current window, but also consider the history data. Because of the large amounts of data, it is impossible to store all the history data in the summary data structure. Hence these algorithms usually provide each itemset with an estimated frequency and ignore the itemsets whose estimated frequency is lower than the specified threshold. The algorithms based on damped window do not ignore the history data totally. Data is stored from the landmark time point. However, damped window algorithms give a weight to the obsolete data for decreasing the importance of them[4]. Therefore, damped window mechanism combines ideas of sliding window and landmark window and considers the contribution of recent windows is more than that of older ones.

Most methods for mining closed frequent itemsets are based on sliding window. In [5], Chi et al proposed the first one-pass algorithm-MOMENT Algorithm for mining closed frequent itemsets over data streams. MOMENT Algorithm maintains all closed frequent itemsets and several boundary itemsets in main memory based on a user specified threshold. But it wastes a mass of memory to maintain the boundary nodes and only outputs closed frequent itemsets whose supports are higher than the user specified threshold. In [6], Jiang et al presented an improved MOMENT Algorithm, CFI-Stream, which maintains all closed itemsets in a summary data structure and output closed itemsets with arbitrary value of support. However, due to the nature of the algorithm, it performs well when minimum support is low but much worse when minimum support turns higher. In [7], Ren et al proposed HCFI Algorithm. Different from MOMENT and CFI-Stream, it uses a vertical representation of itemsets and involves hash table to reduce the time overhead of closure detection. But it is only suitable for the data streams with a few items and applications with small window size. In [8], Yen et al shown CloStream Algorithm with list data structure to maintain closed itemsets. It performs well when the total number of items is not large.

However, these algorithms make closure detection for each frequent subset of a transaction, which leads to an exponential complexity of online processing. This paper focuses on the problem of mining closed frequent itemsets over data streams and proposes a method with a linear complexity of online processing. In the paper, a summary data structure (*OTT*) is designed to store the compact information of data streams. And a novel algorithm DELAY-CFIM is proposed to discover the closed frequent itemsets from *OTT*. DELAY-CFIM scans *OTT* once and generates the frequent itemsets by reinserting the suffix itemsets into *OTT*. Then it checks the closure feature for each frequent itemset on the closed frequent itemset tree (*CFIT*). Several efficient pruning strategies are proposed to reduce the time and space overhead of DELAY_CFIM. The algorithm is proposed based on sliding window for capturing changes of data streams in time. Different from the previous approaches for closed frequent itemset mining, DELAY_CFIM delays the mining procedure until a query is submitted. Hence, the online processing of DELAY_CFIM is much faster than the previous methods.

# II. PRELIMINARY

Closed frequent itemsets record complete and condensed information of frequent itemsets. And sliding window records the most recent complete information of data streams. Hence mining closed frequent itemsets over sliding window adapts rapidly to the change in data streams.

## A. Closed Frequent Itemsets

Define a threshold *s* called minimum support (*min_sup*), $0 < s \leq 1$ . Frequent itemset (*FI*) is an itemset whose *support* is not less than *s*.

An itemset *A* is called closed itemset only if there does not exist any superset *B* of *A* with the same support of *A*.

According to the definitions above, if an itemset is both frequent and closed in *D*, Which is defined as a database of transactions, it is closed frequent itemset which is abbreviated as *CFI* in this paper.

## B. Sliding Window

In Fig.1, a sliding window model is shown with *windowSize* = 4. Firstly, four transactions $T_1$ , $T_2$ , $T_3$ and $T_4$ are included in current window $w1$ . As transaction $T_5$ arrives, $T_1$ leaves the sliding window, window $w2$ becomes the current window with transactions $T_2$ , $T_3$ , $T_4$ and $T_5$ . According to the sliding window mechanism, when a query is submitted, only the transactions in current window need to be mined. Such as it is shown in the Fig.1, if there is a query submitted after $T_4$ 's arrival, only the transactions in $w1$ are mined, the mining result of *CFIS* is: $\{b,c\}$ , $\{b\}$ . However, if the query is submitted after $T_5$ 's coming, the current window changes to be $w2$, the mining result is: $\{b\},\{c\},\{d\}$ .

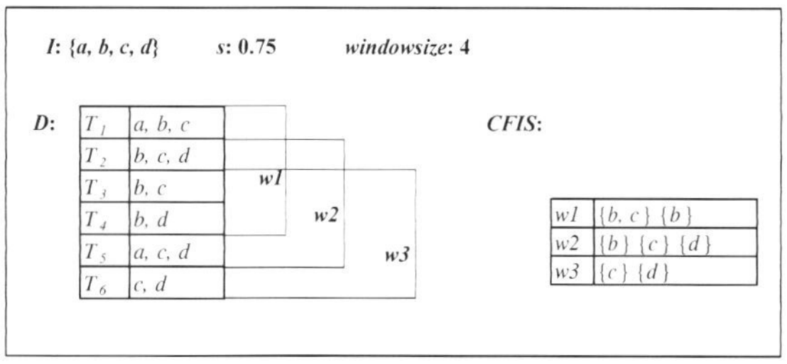


Fig.1. Sliding Window

# III. ORDERLY TRANSACTION TREE AND CLOSED FREQUENT ITEMSET TREE

## A. The Summary Data Structure-OTT

*Definition1.* An *Orderly Transaction Tree* (*OTT*) is a transaction-ordered and tree based data structure defined as follows:

*1)* *OTT* is composed of the transactions in the current sliding window. It maintains almost all the information in the current sliding window except the generated order of transactions. Each node *N* on *OTT* represents an itemset *I* including the items on the path from root to the node, and each child node of *N* represents an itemset which is obtained by adding a new item to *I*.

*2)* Each node on *OTT* consists of four data fields: *item_id*, *item_count*, *temp_count* and *fromTree_id*.

a) *item_id* identifies a unique id in *I*.

b) *item_count* registers the number of the transactions, which have their items sorted in ascending order, with the same prefix item sequence as the itemset represented by current node.

c) *temp_count* records the number of the temporary inserted itemsets in mining process. During construction and maintenance process of *OTT*, the value of *temp_count* assigned to a new node is 0.

d) *fromTree_id* records where the reinserted sub-tree comes from during mining process.

Fields *item_id* and *item_count* are maintained in the whole process including construction and maintenance of *OTT* and the mining process. Fields *temp_count* and *fromTree_id* only take effect in the mining operation.

*3)* Child nodes for each node on *OTT* are linked up in ascending order according to the field *item_id*. For example, if a node *N* includes four child nodes whose *item_id* are separately *d*, *b*, *c* and *a*, according to the definition, these nodes must be linked up in the order *a*, *b*, *c*, *d*. The ordered structure plays a key role in mining process.

## B. Construction and maintenance of OTT

*1)* Con*struction of OTT*

*OTT* is constructed from an empty tree. The construction scenario of *OTT* is described as follows:

a) When a transaction *T* arrives, sort the items of *T* in an ascending order. The ordered transaction is called *OT* in this thesis.

b) Insert *OT* into *OTT*. If the path covering *OT* exists, update the field *item_count* of each node on the path. Otherwise, construct a new path for *OT* and keep the ordered structure for *OTT* at the meantime.

*2)* Maintenance of *OTT*

As the transaction are generated, the total number of transactions will exceeds *windowSize*. Hence the outdated transactions must be removed from *OTT*. The maintaining process is described as follows:

Whenever a new transaction is generated, insert it into *OTT* as described in *OTT* construction process. Then delete the outdated transaction from *OTT* which have left the sliding window. During the process, if there are nodes whose *item_count* fields have been reduced to zero, delete the nodes.

Fig. 2 shows an example for maintenance of *OTT*. Fig. 2 a) outlines a transaction sequence in data stream and defines *windowSize* as 4. Fig. 2 b) ~ d) presents the changes of *OTT* with the sliding window moving on. In Fig. 2 c), transaction $T_5$ is generated and transaction $T_2$ becomes outdated. Hence, path $\{a,c,d\}$ is constructed for $T_5$, and nodes *b* and *c* are deleted from path $\{a,b,c\}$ as their *item_count* have decreased to zero.

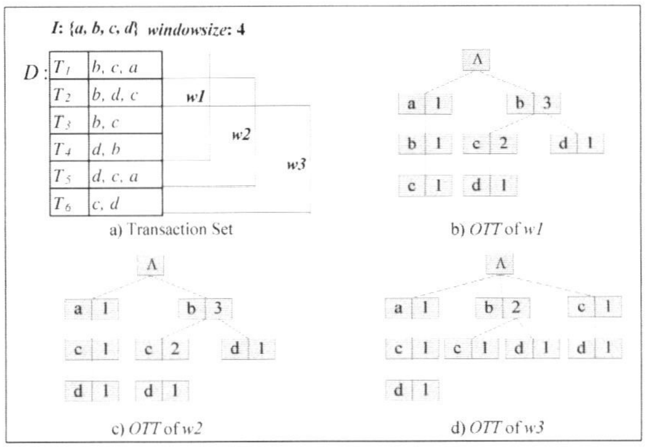


Fig.2. Maintain of *OTT*

## C. Closed Frequent Itemset Tree-CFIT

*Definition2.* A *Closed Frequent Itemset Tree* (*CFIT*) is an ordered structure for maintaining closed frequent itemsets, it is defined as follows:

*1)* A *Closed Frequent Itemset Tree* (*CFIT*) is composed of an *Itemset Tree* and an *Item List*. *Itemset Tree* maintains the closed itemsets generated so far. And *Item List* records the items appearing in *Itemset Tree*. Several *Special Link-List* structures (*SLL*) which begin with an *Item List* node followed by several *Itemset Tree* nodes are constructed among *Itemset Tree* and *Item List* nodes.

*2)* Each node on *Itemset Tree* consists of four fields: *item_id*, *treeItem_count*, *node_height* and *treeNextNode_pointer*.

a) *item_id* identifies a unique id in *I*.
b) *treeItem_count* records *frequency* of the itemset represented by the node. Each node, whose value of *treeItem_count* is unequal to its child nodes, represents a closed frequent itemset including the items from tree root to current node.
c) *node_height* registers height of the node on *OTT*.
d) *treeNextNode_pointer* links up the nodes with same *item_id* on *Itemset Tree*. The nodes which are linked up by *treeNextNode_pointer* compose the tail part of *Special Link-List* structure (*SLL*). All the nodes linked up together in the same *SLL* have an equal value of *item_id* and are sorted in descending order by the field *treeItem_count*.

*3)* Each node in *Item List* consists of three fields: *item_id*, *listItem_count* and *listNextNode_pointer*.

a) *item_id* identifies a unique id in *I*.
b) *listItem_count* records the largest value of *treeItem_count* of *OTT* nodes which are with the same *item_id* as current *Item List* node.
c) *listNextNode_pointer* links up the nodes with the same *item_id* on *OTT* and makes the node be head of a *SLL*.

*4)* The child nodes of each node on *Itemset Tree* are sorted in ascending order according by *item_id*.

*5)* The nodes in *Item List* are linked up in ascending order by *item_id*.

## D. Construction of CFIT

According to the definition of *CFIT*, the construction process of *CFIT* is described as follows:

*1)* When a new closed itemset *CI* is generated, firstly update the *Item List*.

a) If all items of *CI* are in the *Item List* and *frequency* of *CI* is larger than *listItem_count* of the corresponding nodes, update *listItem_count* with the *frequency* of *CI*.
b) Otherwise, if any item in *CI* does not exist in the *Item List*, create a new node for it and keep the correct order of the nodes in *Item List* in the meantime.

*2)* Then update the *Itemset Tree*.

a) If the path on *Itemset Tree* covering *CI* exists and the *treeItem_count* value of the corresponding node is smaller than the *frequency* of *CI*, update the field *treeItem _count* with the *frequency* of *CI*.
b) Otherwise, if the path does not exist, construct the path and assigned *CI frequency* to the field *treeItem_count* of each new node. In the insertion operation, the special structure of *Itemset Tree* and *Special Link-List* must be maintained.

# IV. ALGORITHM DELAY-CFIM

DELAY-Closed Frequent Itemset Mining (DELAY-CFIM), is introduced in this section. It is composed of two steps: frequent itemset generation and closure detection. Whenever a query is submitted, the algorithm generates all the frequent itemsets in the current window from *OTT*. Then closure detection is done on *CFIT* for each frequent itemset generated. The correctness of DELAY-CFIM is proved in this section and several effective pruning strategies are introduced at last.

## A. Frequent Itemset Generation

Based on the definition of *OTT*, all condensed frequency information of itemsets is maintained on it. Since the information has been aggregated and compressed, if it is made full use of, much time and memory space would be reduced. Algorithm 1 presents the pseudo code for generating the frequent itemsets from *OTT*.

```
Algorithm1.            Frequent itemset generation
Input: Root of OTT in current window (T)
       Current record path (p) // initialized by ∅
       Minimum support s
Output: A set of frequent itemsets
FIGeneration (T, p, s)
1.  if ( T -> children ≠ NULL ) then
2.    for each child node T_C of T do
3.        Reinsert( T_C , T )
4.        if ( T_C → item_count + T_C → temp_count ≥ s × windowSize ) then
5.              p' = p ∪ T_C
6.              FIGeneration ( T_C , p' , s )
7.              restore T_C
8.        end if
9.    end for
10. end if
11. if ( p ≠ ∅ )
12.   output p
13. end if

Algorithm2.            Reinsert
Input: Root of source tree T_S
       Root of destination tree T_D
Output: The result tree
Reinsert ( T_S , T_D )
1.  if ( T_S -> children ≠ NULL ) then
2.    for each child T_SC of T_S do
3.      if( T_SC → item_id = item_id of one child T_DC of T_D ) then
4.          T_DC → temp_count+ = T_SC → item_count + T_SC → temp_count
5.      else
6.          create T_DC with T_DC → item_count=0 and
7.          T_DC → temp_count+ = T_SC → item_count + T_SC → temp_count
8.      end if
9.      Reinsert ( T_SC , T_DC )
10.   end for
11. end if
```

Algorithm 1 is a depth-first procedure visiting *OTT* in post order. Before visiting a subtree $T_C$ on *OTT*, it first reinserts the subtrees of $T_C$ into $T_C$'s parent node $T$ (line 3). Then it compares $T_C$'s *support* with *min_sup s*. If $T_C$'s *support* is larger than $s$, it adds $T_C$ to the current path and recursively visits $T_C$. At last it restores whole structure of $T_C$ after visiting it (lines 4-7).

Algorithm 2 shows the pseudo code of reinsertion operation. If the destiny child node $T_{DC}$ to be inserted exists, it would update the *temp_count* field of $T_{DC}$ (lines 3-4). Otherwise, a new tree node would be created with *item _count* set to be zero (lines 5-7).

## B. Correctness Proof for Frequent Itemset Generation

*Lemma1.* Algorithm 1 generates all frequent itemsets for a given *OTT*.

*Proof.* We prove Lemma 1 in two steps:

*1)* Firstly we prove that Algorithm 1 generates all itemsets for *OTT* if without support condition (Line 4 in Algorithm 1).

*2)* Then we prove the infrequent itemsets have been pruned in the check of support condition.

For a given set of items $I = \{i_1, i_2, ..., i_n\}$, we sort the items in each subsets of $I$ in ascending order. Hence the subsets of $I$ are divided into n parts: subsets beginning with $i_1$, subsets beginning with $i_2$, … , subsets beginning with $i_n$. The generated sequence of frequent itemsets in Algorithm 1 is just following it, which means frequent itemsets beginning with $i_1$ are generated at first and frequent itemsets beginning with $i_n$ are generated at last. It is because *OTT* is an orderly tree, and algorithm 1 travels it in post order. According to the definition of *OTT*, the subtrees on *OTT* with root height equal to 2 are rooted at $i_1, i_2, ..., i_n$. Now, we will prove before mining frequent itemsets on a subtree of *OTT* which is rooted at $i_m$, all of the itemsets beginning with $i_m$ in current sliding window have been inserted into the subtree. An inductive method is used in the proof.

Firstly, considering of the case of $m = 1$, we check the feature of the subtree rooted at $i_1$. Since the items in each transaction have been sorted before inserting it into *OTT*, and all the itemsets including $i_1$ are beginning with $i_1$. Hence all the itemsets beginning with $i_1$ have been inserted into the subtree rooted at $i_1$ during *OTT* construction.

Then suppose the feature is matched when $m < k$. Consider the case: $m = k$. We divide the itemsets beginning with $i_k$ into two parts and check them separately.

*1)* Itemsets included by ordered transactions beginning with $i_k$. It is easy to prove that these itemsets have been inserted into the subtree rooted at $i_k$ during *OTT* construction.

*2)* Itemsets included by ordered transactions not beginning with $i_k$. Since items in each transaction have been sorted in ascending order, these transactions must begin with one of items $i_1$, $i_2$, … , $i_{k-1}$. And according to the assumption, before mining subtree rooted at $i_k$, the algorithm has traveled and reinserted those subtrees rooted at $i_1$, $i_2$, … , $i_{k-1}$. Hence, all subsets beginning with $i_k$ in these transactions have been reinserted into subtree rooted at $i_k$.

At last, according to the inductive method, all itemsets beginning with $i_m$ have been inserted into the subtree rooted at $i_m$ before it is visited.

Since Algorithm 1 is a recursive method, the feature introduced above is satisfied by any depth of the recursive process. Hence, when a path is outputted, all the frequency information of the itemsets in the path has been aggregated on it.

So far, proof of the first step has been finished. Then we prove that each itemset which Algorithm 1 outputs is frequent. In Algorithm 1, the condition shown in the Equation 2 is used to prune the subtrees whose *support*s are lower than *s*. According to the definition of *OTT*, the itemset represented by $T_C$ is a subset of that represented by $T_C$ 's child nodes. Hence the *support*s of nodes on the subtree rooted at $T_C$ must be not higher than *support* of $T_C$, which means all the itemsets pruned in Algorithm 1 are infrequent. And it is obvious that itemsets output by Algorithm 1 are frequent.

$$T_C \rightarrow item\_count + T_C \rightarrow temp\_count \geq s \times windowSize \quad (2)$$

In conclusion, Algorithm1 generates all the frequent itemsets for a given *OTT*.

## C. Closure Detection

According to the definition of *CFIT*, closed frequent itemsets could be maintained on it. Whenever a new frequent itemset $FI$ is generated, one scan on *CFIT* is processed to check whether there exists a superset of $FI$ with *support* equal to $FI$ 's *support*. If it is, $FI$ is not closed. Otherwise, it would be inserted into *CFIT*. Algorithm 3 presents the pseudo code for closure detection on *CFIT*.

```
Algorithm3.        Closure Detection
Input: A frequent itemset (FI)
        The frequency of FI (fFI)
        The Itemset Tree in CFIT (IT)
        The Itemset List in CFIT (IL)
Output: A Boolean value (isClosed)
                    // TRUE means FI is closed, FALSE means unclosed
bool closureDetection (FI, fFI, IT , IL )
1.  for each item (i) in FI do
2.     if ( i ∉ IL || fFI >(listItem_count of node with the same item_id as i))
    then
3.         insert FI into CFIT
4.         return TRUE
5.     else
6.         insert FI into Item List
7.         Record lastN as the IL node with the same item_id as the last item of
    FI
8.         break
9.  for each IT node ( ITNode ) in the SSI beginning with lastN do
10.    if (fFI = ITNode → treeItem_count ) then
11.        if the path from root node of IT to ITNode covers nFI then
12.            return FALSE
13. insert FI into CFIT
14. return TRUE
```

Algorithm 3 does closure detection in two steps:

*Step1*. Check the items of *FI* in the *Item List* (lines 1-8), if any item of *FI* is not included in *Item List* , *FI* is closed, Algorithm 3 inserts it into *CFIT* and terminates itself.

*Step2*. Then check the path on *Itemset Tree* which might cover *FI* (lines 9-14). If all of the possible paths do not cover it, *FI* is closed, Algorithm 3 inserts it into *CFIT* and terminates itself.

## D. Correctness Proof for Closure Detection

According to the description above, Algorithm 3 only checks supersets for a given frequent itemset on *CFIT*. That means Algorithm 3 is based on the hypothesis that the frequent itemsets generated after the current itemset (*FI*) cannot be the superset of *FI*. In this section, proof of the hypothesis is presented.

*Lemma2.* The frequent itemsets generated after *FI* in Algorithm 1 cannot be the superset of *FI*.

*Proof.* We divide the supersets of *FI* into two parts. Suppose:

$$FI = \{i_{f1}, i_{f2}, \dots i_{fk}\} \quad (i_{f1} \prec i_{f2} \prec \dots \prec i_{fk}) \quad (3)$$

Supersets in the first part begin with prefix-set *FI*:

$$FI_{super1} = \{i_{f1}, i_{f2}, \dots i_{fk}, i_{s1}, \dots i_{sm}\}$$
$$(i_{f1} \prec i_{f2} \prec \dots \prec i_{fk} \prec i_{s1} \prec \dots \prec i_{sm}) \quad (4)$$

The other supersets compose the second part. Take one of them for example:

$$FI_{super2} = \{i_{f1}, i_{f2}, \dots i_{f(j-1)}, i_{s1}, i_{fj}, \dots i_{fk}, i_{s2}, \dots i_{sm}\}$$
$$(i_{f(j-1)} \prec i_{s1} \prec i_{fj}) \quad (5)$$

As *OTT* has a special structure that the child nodes of each node have been sorted in ascending order, we can conclude:

*1)* The first part of the supersets must be generated when Algorithm 1 travels subtree with the pre-path *FI*. Since Algorithm 1 travels *OTT* in post order, all of the supersets in the first part are generated before *FI*.

*2)* According to the special structure of *OTT*, the second part of the supersets must be generated before visiting subtree with the pre-path *FI*. We take $FI_{super2}$ for example, the subtree with the pre-path $i_{f1}, i_{f2}, \dots i_{f(j-1)}, i_{s1}$ must be visited before the subtree with the pre-path $i_{f1}, i_{f2}, \dots i_{f(j-1)}, i_{fj}$ as $i_{s1} \prec i_{fj}$. Hence, $FI_{super2}$ must be generated before *FI*.

Hence, all the supersets of *FI* are generated before itself.

In Step2 of Algorithm 3, the *SSL* begins with the *Item List* node *lastN* has been scanned. And Algorithm 3 only checks the closed itemsets matching the conditions as follows:

*1)* Including the last item of *FI*.

*2)* With a *frequency* equal to *FI*.

According to the definition of the closed itemsets, it is easy to prove that the itemsets not including the last item of *FI* cannot be the superset of *FI*. Lemma 3 proves the correctness of the second condition.

*Lemma3.* The *frequency* of *FI*'s supersets on *CFIT* must equal to *FI*'s *frequency*.

*Proof.* Suppose there is a closed itemset $\overline{FI}$ which is the superset of *FI* and has a *frequency* $f\_\overline{FI}$ which is larger than *frequency* of *FI* (*f_FI*). Since $\overline{FI}$ is the superset of *FI*, the transactions in *D* including $\overline{FI}$ must include *FI*. According to the definition of *frequency*, there are $f\_\overline{FI}$ transactions in *D* including $\overline{FI}$ and they must include *FI* at the meantime. Hence *frequency* of *FI* is not less than $f\_\overline{FI}$ which is in contradiction with the assumption. Hence only the closed itemsets with *frequency* not larger than that of *FI* could be the superset of *FI*.

According to the definition of closed itemsets, closed itemset with a lower *frequency* than *FI* does not need to be checked. Hence, Algorithm 3 checks the closed itemsets with the same *frequency* as *FI* only.

In conclusion, Algorithm 3 checks the closure feature correctly for each frequent itemset generated in Algorithm 1.

## E. Pruning

All the frequent itemsets in the current sliding window are generated in Algorithm 1. But some of these itemsets can be determined to be not closed without closure detection.

The rules for maintaining *fromTree_id* are introduced as below:

*1)* In the process of *OTT* construction and maintenance, each node on *OTT* is created with $fromTree\_id = -1$.

*2)* In the reinserting operation, four cases are considered:

a) The field *fromTree_id* of destiny subtree equals to -1. It remains -1 after reinsertion.
b) If the source subtree and the destiny subtree are with the same value of *fromTree_id*, it would not be changed after reinsertion.
c) If the source subtree and the destiny subtree are with the different values of *fromTree_id*, after reinsertion, *fromTree_id* of destiny subtree would be assigned to -1.
d) If the destiny subtree does not exist, a new subtree should be created with the field *fromTree_id* being the parent node of the source node.

According to the analysis above, a pruning rule is proposed: In the process of Frequent Itemset Generation, only the subtrees with *fromTree_id* value equal to -1 are mined.

# V. EXPERIMENTAL RESULTS

In this Section, DELAY-CFIM is compared with CFI-Stream, a classic algorithm on closed frequent itemset mining over data streams.

## A. Datasets Used in Experiments

*1)* IBM quest market-basket synthetic data

The synthetic data sets used in this thesis are generated by IBM synthetic data generator[5]. It simulates the transactions in the retailing environment. Each item in the dataset represents a commodity in the retail stores maybe a super market. Each transaction in the dataset represents a sale record of customers. Then a frequent itemset represents the commodities which customers usually buy together.

The parameters of the data set are described as below:

a) *T* : Average transaction size.
b) *I* :Average size of maximal potentially frequent itemsets.
c) *N* : Number of items.
d) *D* : Number of transactions.

According to the definitions above, a dataset named *T*10.*I*5.*N*10k.*D*100k includes 100k transactions, the average number of items in each transaction is 10, the average size of maximal potentially frequent itemsets is 5, and the total number of items is 10k.

*2)* Real dataset BMS-WebView-2

BMS-WebView-2 is a real dataset containing several months' click stream data from an e-commerce web site. Each transaction in the dataset is a set of product detail pages which are clicked in a web session. This dataset has been used in KDDCUP 2000[9]. There are totally 77,512 transactions and 3,340 distinct items in BMS-WebView-2. Average transaction size of it is 5.

## B. Experiments on Sliding Window

*1)* Experiments on different *windowSize*

Fig. 3 a) shows the average online running time for each transaction in CFI-Stream and DELAY-CFIM for the dataset *T*5.*I*4.*N*1k.*D*100k. In the experiments, threshold *min_sup* has been set to 0.1%. In the figure, DELAY-CFIM consumes much less online processing time than CFI-Stream, because CFI-Stream needs to do closure detection for all subsets of each transaction, in this process it must scan the summary data structure for many times. However, DELAY-CFIM only inserts the transaction to the summary data structure *OTT*, which only scans *OTT* once. In the figure, the online running time of CFI-Stream is more sensitive for *windowSize* than that of DELAY-CFIM, as it needs to scan the current window during *CFI* maintaining, larger *windowSize* leads to a longer scanning time.

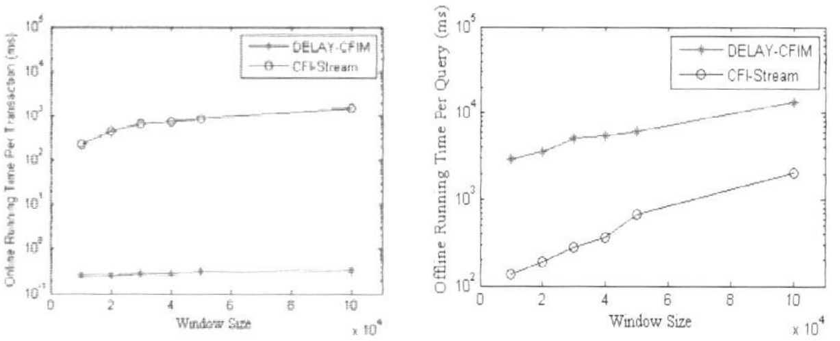


Fig.3. Performance with different *windowSizes* (*T*5.*I*4.*N*1k.*D*100k)

Fig. 3 b) shows the average processing time of a query for the dataset *T*5.*I*4.*N*1k.*D*100k. Threshold *min_sup s* is set to 0.1%. In the figure, as the *windowSize* increases, online processing time of both algorithms increase. However, DELAY-CFIM consumes much more offline processing time than CFI-Stream. That is the price of the less online processing time.

Fig.4 shows the number of nodes generated during the algorithms running. In the figure, more *OTT* nodes are created than *CFI* nodes, however, considering the node structure of them, each *CFI* node stores a whole itemset but each *OTT* node only records an item. At fact, they almost consume same amount of memory space.

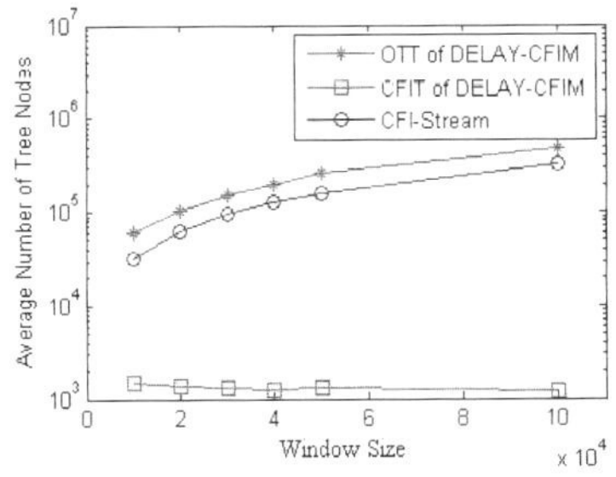


Fig.4 Memory usage performance with different *windowSizes* (*T*5.*I*4.*N*1k.*D*100k)

According to the analysis above, both DELAY-CFIM and CFI-Stream takes more time and space overhead as window size increases. But the online processing time of CFI-Stream is sensitive than DELAY-CFIM. As DELAY-CFIM delays the mining process until a query is submitted, it consumes less online running time but more offline processing time.

*2)* Experiments on different query frequencies

Fig.5 shows the average running time over 10k sliding windows with different query frequencies for real dataset BMS-WebView-2. Thresholds *min_sup* and *windowSize* are separately set to be 0.1% and 50k.

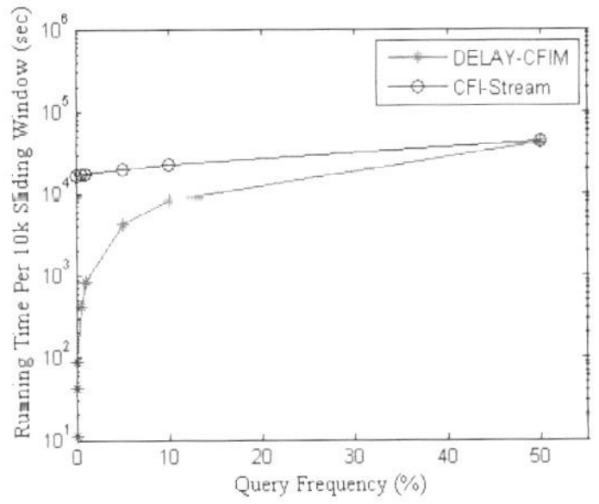


Fig.5. Running time performance with different query frequencies over 10k sliding windows (BMS-WebView-2)

In the figure, DELAY-CFIM performs much better than CFI-Stream when query frequency is low. And DELAY-CFIM is much more sensitive of query frequency than CFI-Stream. This is because CFI-Stream keeps all closed frequent itemsets in memory all the time, the offline processing time complexity of CFI-Stream is linear. Hence the offline processing time of DELAY-CFIM is larger than that of CFI-Stream. Therefore frequent queries lead to amount of total running time.

# VI. CONCLUSION

In this paper a novel algorithm, DELAY-CFIM, is proposed to maintain the compact information in the current data stream sliding window and output the closed frequent itemsets whenever a query is submitted. The algorithm offers a method to reduce the online processing time and delay mining closed frequent itemsets until a query is submitted. Experimental results show that DELAY-CFIM outperforms the representation algorithm CFI-Stream in time overhead, especially when query frequency is low.

In addition, the method proposed in this thesis is based on sliding window, which limits its applied fields. If the summary data structure OTT is modified to maintain information in landmark window or damped window, the algorithm could be applied in more occasions. Alhough this paper use the delay strategy to reduce the online processing time overhead, it consumes more time when queries are proposed, especially when the minimum support is low. Hence, more researches are required to speed up the mining procedure.

# REFERENCES

[1] K. I. Mouratidis. Data stream processing: An overview of recent research [D]. Hong Kong University of Science and Technology, 2003.

[2] R. Wong and A. Fu. Mining top-K frequent itemsets from data streams [J]. Data Mining and Knowledge Discovery, 13(2): 193-217, 2006.

[3] Y. Y. Zhu and D. Shasha. StatStream: Statistical monitoring of thousands of data streams in real time [C]. In Proceedings of the 28th VLDB Conference, 2002: 358-369.

[4] D. Lee and W. Lee. Finding maximal frequent itemsets over online data streams adaptively [C]. In Proceedings of the 5th IEEE International Conference on Data Mining (ICDM'05), 2005: 8-8.

[5] Y. Chi, H. X. Wang, P. S. Yu, et al. Moment: Maintaining closed frequent itemsets over a stream sliding window [C]. In Proceedings of the International Conference on Data Mining, 2004: 59-66.

[6] N. Jiang and L. Gruenwald. CFI-Stream: Mining closed frequent itemsets in data streams [C]. In Proceedings of the 12th ACM SIGKDD International Conference on Knowledge Discovery and Data Mining, 2006: 592-597.

[7] J. D. Ren and C. Huo. Mining closed frequent itemsets in sliding window over data streams [C]. In Proceedings of the 3rd International Conference on Innovative Computing Information and Control, 2008: 76-76.

[8] S. J. Yen, C. W. Wu, Y. S. Lee, et al. A fast algorithm for mining frequent closed itemsets over stream sliding window [C]. In Proceedings of IEEE International Conference on Fuzzy Systems, 2011: 996-1002.

[9] Z. Zheng, R. Kohavi and L. Mason. Real world performace of association rule algorithms [C]. In Proceedings of the 2001 International Conference Knowledge Discovery and Data Mining (SIGKDD'01), 2001: 401-406.

# Time Interval Sequential Sequence Mining in Large Database

Kiran R. Amin, *Member, IEEE and* J. S. Shah

***Abstract*—"Time interval sequential sequence mining" mines sequential sequence from database with efficient support counting. It is used to find frequent subsequences occur with minimum support value. The sequential sequence mining focuses on sequence of events occurred frequently in given dataset unlike simple association rule mining. The sequence of the items plays major role. We use the order dataset where all events stored in some particular order. The traditional sequential sequence mining doesn't care for the timing between the purchasing of items.**

**The goal of our research work is to develop and evaluate new Time interval sequential sequence mining algorithms of MySSM which efficiently produce sequential sequences in large database having significant improvement in execution Time and Memory.**

***KeyWords*--MySSM, GAS, CMEM and OUTR, Time Interval Sequential Sequence**

## I. INTRODUCTION

TRADITIONAL Association Rule Mining [10] works on transactional data. It considers various items to be purchased in single transaction of a particular customer. It doesn't care for the same customer purchases items in different transactions. The concept of sequential sequence mining arrived and it considers various items to be purchased in different transactions. It covers the idea regarding same customer purchases items in more than one transaction and in more than one time. However the current state-of-the-art techniques have limitations with the performance of Memory and Time which are focused by us.

In investment, a certain stock rises or falls is one of the important tasks that the stock investors wanted to know. Further, the owners are worried about the stock trend of their own businesses. Stockholders or Industry analysts also like to know the rise/fall of certain stocks, which is actually one of the useful information extractions from the time interval sequences of stock prices. The stock prices are recorded in every transaction which acts as a historical data. We may find the time interval stock sequences from the stock interval event database.

We have proposed time interval sequential sequence mining algorithms SYNTIM, MySSM, GCON, FS, GSGT, GAS, CMEM and OUTR.

The fundamental aim of our research is to study and develop a new sequential sequence mining technique that produces sequential sequences from the large database. It considers the time gap between successive items to be purchased by the customers. It produces the sequential sequences with reasonable amount of Time and Memory.

## II. SEQUENTIAL SEQUENCE MINING TECHNIQUES

Sequential sequence [7] is defined as: The data set is a set of sequences, named as data-sequences. Each data-sequence is a group of transactions. Each transaction is a set of literals, called items or events. Typically there is a transaction time associated with each transaction. The sequential sequence mining finds all sequential sequences with a user defined minimum support. Various sequential sequence mining techniques are discussed here.

### A. *Apriori-based Techniques*

The first and simplest family of sequential sequence mining algorithms is Apriori-based algorithms and their main characteristic is that they use Apriori principle [10]. The problem of sequential sequence mining was introduced along with other three Apriori-based algorithms (AprioriAll, AprioriSome and DynamicSome) [7]. At each step $k$, a set of candidate frequent sequences $C_k$ of size $k$ is generated by performing a self-join on $L_{k-1}$; $L_k$ consists of all those sequences in $C_k$ that satisfy a minimum support threshold. The efficiency of support counting was improved by using a hash-tree structure.

A similar approach, GSP (Generalized Sequential Patterns) was developed [6] that uses time constraints as well as the window constraints. This was proved to be more efficient than its predecessors.

The inefficient description of temporal information decreases the mining efficiency and the interpretability of the sequences[11]. They provided an efficient representation of spatio-temporal movements and proposed a new approach to discover spatio-temporal sequences in trajectory data. Their proposed method first finds spatio-temporal regions by using prefix-projection methods and extracts frequent spatio-temporal sequences.

Discovering all frequent sequential sequences in large databases was a very challenging task since the search space was large.

D. FricTer [20] proposed a sequential sequence mining

method to analyze multimodal data streams using a quantitative temporal approach. They presented a new temporal data mining method focusing on extracting exact timings and durations of sequential patterns extracted from multiple temporal event streams.

### B. *Tree-based Techniques*

A faster and more efficient candidate production can be attained by using a tree-like structure [12]. The traversal is made in a depth-first search manner. It is applied such that all the candidate sequences applying both subset infrequency and superset frequency pruning. Initially, the above idea was introduced for mining frequent itemsets, but then it was extended for sequential sequences. Ayres employed an efficient approach in SPAM [3].

### C. *Lattice-based Techniques*

Lattice structure was another class of sequential sequence mining algorithms was proposed a lattice based method to enumerate the candidate sequences efficiently. In fact, a lattice seems to be a "tree-like" structure where each node may have more than one parent node. A node on the lattice represents a sequence *s*, is connected to all the pairs of nodes on the previous level that can be joined to form *s*. This is shown in the example: let *s = {d, (bc), a}*, then all the following nodes should be connected to *s* on the lattice: *{(bc), a}*, *{d, b, a}*, *{d, (bc)}*, *{d, c, a}*, since all pairs of these subsequences can be joined to form *s*.

SPADE [4] used above structure to efficiently specify the candidate sequences. The basic characteristics of SPADE were

(1) Vertical representation of the database using id-lists, where each sequence is associated with a list of database sequences in which it occurs.

(2) Used lattice-based approach to decompose the original search space into smaller subspaces.

(3) Each sub-lattice, two different search strategies (breadth-first and depth-first search) were used for getting frequent sequences.

cSPADE was the extension of SPADE was proposed in [4], which allows a set of constraints to be placed on the mined sequences. These constraints are:

(1) Length and width constraints
(2) Gap and window constraints
(3) Item constraints
(4) Class constraints

GO-SPADE [13] was the similar algorithm proposed later on, where the idea of generalized occurrences was introduced. The aim behind GO-SPADE was that in a sequence database certain items may appear in a consecutive way. For reducing the cost of the mining process, GO-SPADE tried to compact all these consecutive occurrences by defining a generalized occurrence of a sequence p as a tuple (sid, [min, max]), where sid is the sequence id, and [min, max] used for the interval of the consecutive occurrences of the last event of p.

### D. *Regular Expression based Techniques*

Huge majority of the former algorithms focused the discovery of frequent sequential sequences based on only a support threshold, which limits the results to the most common. Thus, a lack of user controlled focus in the sequence mining process can be detected that may sometimes lead to great volume of useless sequences. A solution to this problem was proposed in [14], where the mining process was restricted by a support threshold and user-specified constraints modeled by regular expressions. Later on the series of SPIRIT [14] algorithms were introduced, where a set of constraints *C* was pushed into the mining process along with a sequence database. Therefore, the minimum support requirement and a set of additional user specified constraints were applied simultaneously which restrict the set of candidate sequences produced during the mining process. To fulfill this, two different types [14] of pruning techniques were used.

Fabian Moerchen[14] represented Temporal pattern mining for time point based and time intervals based methods. They distinguished time point-based methods and interval-based methods as well as univariate and multivariate methods.

They presented symbolic temporal data models and temporal operators that were used for pattern discovery in data mining research. They divided temporal data models such as time point v/s. time interval data, univariate v/s. multivariate data and numeric v/s. symbolic data.

### E. *Prefix-based Techniques*

Other techniques of sequential sequence mining algorithms include the prefix-based [15]. In this method, the database is projected with respect to a frequent prefix sequence and based on the outcome of the projection, new frequent prefixes are identified and used for further projections until the support threshold constraint is satisfied.

Chen [8] proposed a method for discovering time-interval sequential sequences in sequence databases. Dhany, Saputra [1] proposed improved version of prefixspan named as i-prefixspan.

W. Li [16] proposed novel concept of a frequent time interval association sequences. They used multiple gene sequences. Their algorithm has several advantages over traditional methods. A set of genes simultaneously show complex time item interval expression sequences recurrently across multiple microarray datasets. Such time interval signals are hard to recognize in individual microarray datasets, but become significant by their frequent occurrences across multiple datasets. They designed an efficient two-stage algorithm to identify FTAPs [16].

GSP & DynamicSome generate too many candidate items for low values of minimum support. Execution time of all the algorithms increases as the support decreases because of a large increase in the number of large sequences in the result. GSP & DynamicSome perform worse. DynamicSome generates and counts a much larger number of candidates in the forward phase & intermediate stages.

The efficiency [12] of all frequent sequence mining algorithms is provided by following way. With the minimum support threshold is $\sigma$ with $n = |C|$ different items in the item collection, $C$. For $| I |$ different possible existent itemsets, where $I$ is the powerset of $C$, and its value is given by equation 2.1.

$$| I |= \sum_{j=1}^{n} \binom{n}{j} - 1 = 2^n - 1$$

...Equation (2.1)

Let the database has sequences with at most $m$ itemsets and each itemset has at most one item. In this condition, there would be $nm$ possible different sequences with $m$ itemsets and different arbitrary length sequences. It is given in equation 2.2

$$\sum_{k=1}^{m} n^k = \frac{n^{m+1} - n}{n - 1}$$

...Equation (2.2)

Similarly, if each itemset has an arbitrary number of items, there exists $S_m$ with possible frequent sequences with $m$ itemsets, with the value of $S_m$ is given by equation 2.3.

$$S_m = | I |^m = (2^n - 1)^m$$

...Equation (2.3)

The $S$ sequences in general, as in equation 2.4.

$$S = \sum_{k=1}^{m} (2^n - 1)^k = \frac{(2^n - 1)^{m+1} - 2^n - 1}{2^n - 1} = \Theta\left(2^{nm}\right)$$

...Equation (2.4)

### *F. Prefixspan [9]*

This algorithm uses a pattern growth approach. It never generates the candidates which do not appear in the database. It uses optimization methods. For closed sequence, it is easy to extend it with other constraints for the closed sequences. It uses a divide and conquer technique. First it generates the projected database and then finds the frequent sequences.

To overcome this bottleneck of the FreeSpan, Jiaweihan and Jianpei developed new algorithms called PrefixSpan [2]. It outperforms both the Apriori and FreeSpan algorithms in almost all the fields like huge no of sequences, support. Different projection methods are used for PrefixSpan [2]: level-by-level projection, bi-level projection etc. The comparison is shown in Figure 2.1.

When the support threshold is high, it has a limited number of sequential sequences and the length of sequences is short, these methods are very near in terms of runtime. However, as the support threshold decreases, the time to generate the sequences become more. It clearly seems that FreeSpan and PrefixSpan overcome GSP. And also PrefixSpan methods are more efficient than FreeSpan.

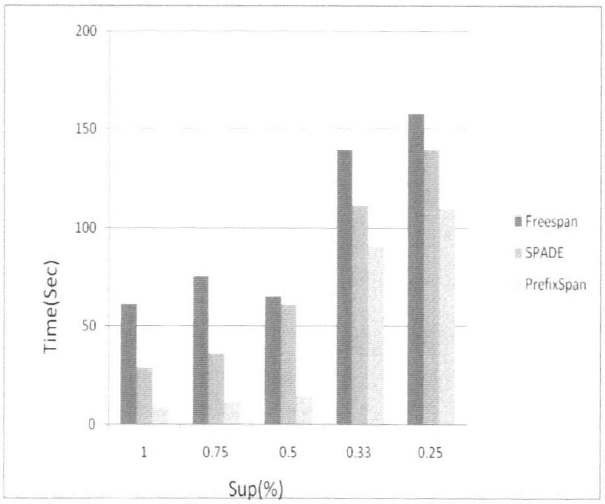


Figure 2.1: Comparison – Freespan, SPADE, PrefixSpan

## III. TIME INTERVAL SEQUENTIAL SEQUENCE MINING ALGORITHMS

Our time interval sequential sequence algorithms improve the performance and efficiency compared to various algorithms developed for sequential sequences like DynamicSome, GSP, AprioriSome, AprioriAll, SPAM, Prefixspan [2], I-prefixspan [8][1] etc. It generates various time interval sequences by using sequence generator table. Here we have analyzed various sequential mining techniques and compared them. Our algorithm outperforms other sequential sequence mining algorithms. More ever our algorithms have excellent scale-up properties.

Typical prefixspan [2] fails to provide sequences with time interval gap [8] between sequences, our algorithm gives the sequences by taking care of time interval between sequences.

We have proposed the series of MySSM algorithms. The first algorithm is proposed as a **SYNTIM** for synthetic data generation. It generates the synthetic data with different time intervals, different transactions and different items. This algorithm is given in Figure 3.1. Algorithm 2 reads the "config.dat" file. This proposed algorithm is called as a GCON. Algorithm 3 is proposed as a FS & GSGT which finds the *0*-sequence and also generates the sequence generator Table. Algorithm 4 is proposed to generate all frequent sequences. It is proposed as a GAS. Algorithm 5 is proposed as a CMEM which checks the memory. The 6$^{th}$ proposed algorithm is named as a OUTR, which generates the sequences in "output.dat" and also generates the "analysis.dat" file. The 7$^{th}$ proposed algorithm is a MYSSM. It is a Sequential Sequence Generation Algorithm. This algorithm is main algorithm which includes all algorithms. These algorithms are shown in Figure 3.1 to Figure 3.7.

### 3.1 Algorithm 1 : SYNTIM

**Algorithm** SYNTIM
**Input** Number of Customers, Number of Items
**Output** Datasct.dat,Datasetdetail.dat
**Begin**
**Open** dataset.dat file for writing
**for i** ← 0 to Last customer **do**
  **for j** ← 0 to No of Transaction
    **do** time ← random value
      item ← random value
  **end for**
**end for**
**Close** dataset.dat file
**Open** datasetdetail.dat file for writing
  Average items per transaction ←
  Total no of items/No. of transactions
Average number of transactions per customer ←Total number of transactions / Total no of customers
**Close** dataset detail file.
**End**

Figure 3.1 : SYNTIM

The SYNTIM algorithm generates the customers' transactions with various time intervals and items to be purchased. It generates the items based on number of transactions and number of items available. This detail is stored in "dataset.dat" file. Later on, it is used by MsSSM algorithm for the finding sequential sequence. It also generates the average items per transaction and average transactions per customer, which is stored in "datasetdetail.dat" file.

### 3.2 Algorithm 2: GCON

**Algorithm** GCON
**Input** Config.dat
**Output** Time interval, range, items, support
**Begin**
**Initialize** line, data
**Initialize** interval, range, item, customer, minsup
**Open** config.dat file for reading
 **for** line ← 1 to end of data **do**
  **if**(line==1)**then** interval ← data
  **else if**(line==2) **then** range ← data
  **else if**(line==3)**then** item ← data
  **else if**(linenum==4)**then** customer ← data
  **else if**(line==5)**then** minsup ← data
  **end if**
 **end for**
**Close file**
**End**

Figure 3.2 : GCON

GCON algorithm reads the "config.dat" file. It reads all the data from the file. It first reads the interval of time unit, range of time interval, items to be purchased, Number of customers & minimum support. These values are used by MySSM algorithm.

### 3.3 Algorithm 3: FS & GSGT

**Algorithm** FS & GSGT

**Input** dataset.dat
**Output** sequence generator table
**Begin**
**Initialize** datanum,indexno,i,item,time,count
**Open** dataset.dat
**Repeat** until end of file encountered
 **read** time index and item index
 Initialize counter, indexno
 **Repeat** until length of customer sequence
 Store the item index and time where the sequence occurs
 Generate sequence generator table
 Store using array index and time interval for each SID
 Read item occurred in all SIDs
 Increment the counter for the particular item occurred
 **If** the counter value is more than minimum support **then**
   add this item in large item list
 **else** ignore it
**end repeat**
**Close** file
**End**

Figure 3.3 : FS & GSGT

The FS & GSGT algorithm reads the "dataset.dat" file and generates the sequence generator table. The sequence generator table stores the values of item index and time. By using sequence generator table, it finds sequential sequences which occur frequently.

### 3.4 Algorithm 4: GAS

**Algorithm GAS**

**Input** sequence generator table
**Output** frequent sequential sequence
**Begin**
Declare the variables
Scan the sequence generator table
**Repeat** until end of file encountered
Scan the sequence generator table by Sequence ID
Scan the sequence generator table by item ID
Measure the repeated sequences with Time ID
**If** occurrence >= minimum support **then**
  Keep it
  **Else** ignore it
Check other combinations
**If** found **then** keep it
    **Else** ignore it
**End**

Figure 3.4 : GAS

The GAS algorithm scans the sequence generator table by using sequence Id, Item Id and Time ID. It generates all the frequent sequences occurred in the database whose support count is more than minimum support.

### 3.5 Algorithm 5: CMEM

**Algorithm CMEM**

**Input** dataset.dat, config.dat
**Output** sequential
Initialize maxMemory ← 0
**Begin**
Get total Memory during runtime
Get total Free Memory during runtime
current Memory = Total Memory - Free Memory
**If** current Memory >= maxMemory
**then** maxMemory = Current Memory
**Return** maxMemory in MB
**End**

Figure 3.5 : CMEM

The CMEM algorithm finds the maximum memory used during run time. First it finds the total memory during execution. The memory used during execution is found by making a difference between max memory and free memory.

### 3.6 Algorithm 6: OUTR

**Algorithm OUTR**

**Input** Sequence generated by GAS
**Output** output.dat, analysis.dat
**Begin**
**Open** the output.dat file for writing
Write minimum support
**Do while** sequences exist
Write 0-sequences
Write all desired sequences generated by GAS algorithm
  **End do**
**Close** file
**Open** analysis.dat file for writing
    Write Number of Time Intervals, Gap between
    Time interval, Minimum support
Write summary of all sequences generated by GAS
Write Total number of sequence generated
Write Execution time in MilliSeconds & MaxMemory in MB
**Close** file
**End**

Figure 3.6 : OUTR

The algorithm OUTR uses the sequences generated by GAS algorithm. It generates the "output.dat" file. It writes the minimum support along with 0-sequences and all frequent sequences generated by GAS algorithm in "output.dat" file. The OUTR algorithm generates the status of the execution process. It creates "analysis.dat" file in which, it writes the summary of the execution of the programs like, Number of Time Intervals, Gap between Time intervals, Minimum support, Total number of sequence generated, Execution time in MilliSeconds & MaxMemory in MB.

### 3.7 Algorithm 7: MySSM

**Algorithm MySSM**

**Input** dataset.dat, config.dat
**Output** sequential sequences, Execution time, Memory used

**Begin**
  Initialize time, range, item, support
  Initialize t1, t2, maxMemory
**Open** Dataset.dat and config.dat files
Initialize customer's sequence, counter
Initialize arraylist for finding index and time
   **Call** Procedure GCON()
    Read the parameters from config.sys
    t1 ← System.currentTimeMillis();
    **Call** procedure FS&GSGT()
      Generate all sequences onwards sequence-0
      Generate sequence generator table
   **Return** large sequence

  **Call** procedure CMEM()
  **Return** Memory used

**Call** procedure OUTR()
**Return** Time Interval, Gap, Min support, sequences
t2 ← System.currentTimeMillis() - t1;
**Return** sequential sequence
**Close** files
**End**

Figure 3.7 : MySSM

The algorithm MySSM reads the data from config.dat, dataset.dat files. It generates the large sequential sequences whose support count is greater than minimum support. It finds time and memory used during execution.

## IV. EMPIRICAL ANALYSIS

The scale-up properties with respect to these parameters are shown in Figure 4.1 and 4.2. Figure 4.1 shows the analysis graph of Number of customers v/s Memory in MB with number of time intervals are 3 and gap of time interval is 8, support in value is 0.3, Number of different items are 10, Number of transactions per customer are 11, Number of items per transaction are 3 for 500 to 1,20,000 customers. The graph linearly increase when Number of customers increase.

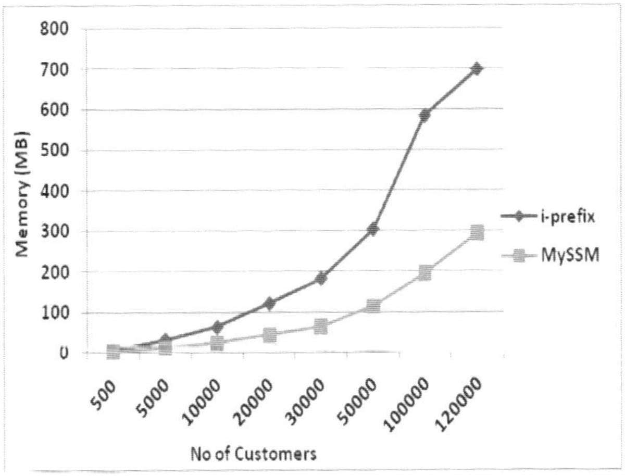


Figure 4.1: Number of Customers v/s Memory(MB)

Figure 4.2 shows the analysis graph of Number of customers v/s Time in Milliseconds with number of time intervals are 3 and gap of time interval is 8, support in value is 0.3, Number of different items are 10, Number of transactions per customer are 11, Number of items per transaction are 3 for 500 to 1,20,000 customers.

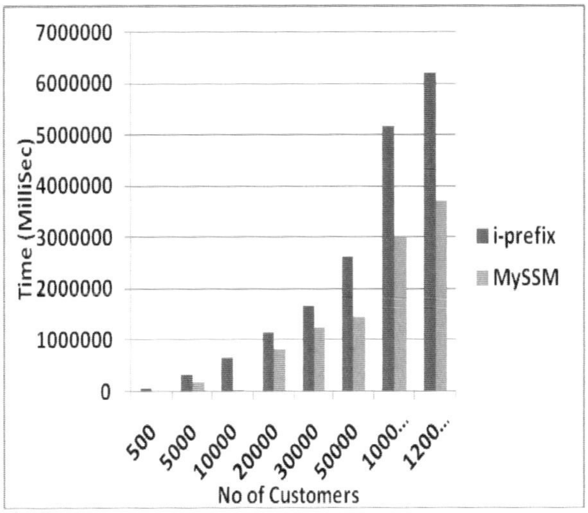


Figure 4.2 : Number of Customers v/s Time(Milliseconds

## V. CONCLUSION

We generated the synthetic dataset. We tested the scalability of MySSM in both runtime and memory usage using different parameters of matrix of evaluation such as different support, items per transaction and transactions per customer. MySSM shows a linear scalability in both the runtime and memory usage. We compared our results with i-prefixspan[1][8]. The empirically analysis shows that the performance of our algorithm MySSM is better than the i-prefixspan.

In typical I-prefixspan [1], the projection table is created every time while creation of every sequence, so it requires more Memory and Time while generating sequences. The database is kept in the Memory after use so this algorithm is less effective because of consumption of Memory. Our algorithms create sequence generator table from original database. The frequent sequences are created based on sequence generator table. Hence therefore, it requires less Memory, Time and very efficient compare to latest algorithms developed now a day.

ACKNOWLEDGEMENT

We acknowledge the dean and the faculty members of U. V. Patel College of Engineering for supporting the research work. We thank to the Ganpat University for providing support in all aspect to carry out this research.

REFERENCES

[1]. Dhany, Saputra and Rambli Dayang, R.A. and Foong, Oi Mean,"Mining Sequential Patterns Using I-PrefixSpan", World Academy of Science, Engineering and Technology, Dec., 2008.

[2]. J. Pei, J. Han, B. Mortazavi-Asl, H. Pinto, Q. Chen, U. Dayal and M.-C. Hsu, "Mining Sequential Patterns by Pattern-Growth: The PrefixSpan Approach", Transactions on

Knowledge and Data Engineering, Vol. 16, No. 11, Pages 1424-1440, 2004.

[3]. J. Ayres, J. Gehrke, T. Yiu, and J. Flannick, "Sequential Pattern Mining Using a Bitmap Representation", Proc. ACM SIGKDD Int'l Conf. Knowledge Discovery and Data Mining (SIGKDD '02), Pages 429-435, July 2002.

[4]. M. Zaki, "SPADE: An Efficient Algorithm for Mining Frequent Sequences", Machine Learning, Vol. 40, Pages 31-60, 2001.

[5]. J. Han, J. Pei, B. Mortazavi-Asl, Q. Chen, U. Dayal, and M.-C. Hsu., "Freespan: Frequent pattern-projected sequential pattern mining", In Proc. 2000, Int'l Conf. Knowledge Discovery and Data Mining (KDD'00), Pages 355–359, Aug. 2000.

[6]. R. Srikant and R. Agrawal, "Mining Sequential Patterns: Generalizations and Performance Improvements", Proc. Fifth Int'l Conf. Extending Database Technology (EDBT '96), Pages 3-17, Mar. 1996.

[7]. R. Agrawal and R. Srikant, "Mining Sequential Patterns", Proc. 1995 Int'l Conf. Data Eng. (ICDE '95), Pages 3-14, Mar. 1995.

[8]. Chen, Y.L., Chiang, M.C. and Ko, M.T., "Discovering time-interval sequential patterns in sequence databases", Expert Syst. Appl., Vol. 25, No. 3, Pages 343-354, 2003.

[9]. J. Pei, J. Han, B. Mortazavi-Asl, H. Pinto, Q. Chen, U. Dayal and M.-C. Hsu, "PrefixSpan: Mining Sequential Patterns Efficiently by Prefix-Projected Pattern Growth", Proc., Int'l Conf. Data Eng. (ICDE '01), Pages 215-224,2001.

[10]. R Agrawal, R Srikant, "Fast Algorithm for Mining Association Rules", Proc. 20th Int'l Conf. Very Large Data Bases, VLDB, Pages 487-499, 1994.

[11]. Juyoung Kang and Hwan-Seung, "Mining Spatio-Temporal Patterns in Trajectory Data", Journal of Information Processing Systems, Vol. 6, No.4, 2010.

[12]. Bayardo, R., Agrawal, R., and Gunopulos, D., "Constraint-based rule mining in large, dense databases", In Proc. of IEEE Int'l Conf. on Data Engineering (ICDE), Pages 188–197, 1999.

[13]. Leleu, M., Rigotti, C., Boulicaut, J., and Euvrard, G., "Go-spade: Mining sequential patterns over databases with consecutive repetitions", In Proc. of Int'l Conference on Machine Learning and Data Mining in Pattern Recognition (MLDM), Pages 293–306, 2003.

[14]. Garofalakis, M., Rastogi, R., and Shim, K.,"Spirit: Sequential pattern mining with regular expression constraints", In Proc. of Int'l Conf. on Very Large Databases (VLDB), Pages 223–234,1999.

[15]. M.C., "Prefixspan: Mining sequential patterns efficiently by prefixprojected pattern growth", In Proc. of IEEE Int'l Conf. on Data Engineering (ICDE), Pages 215–224, 2001.

[16]. Wenyuan Li, Min Xu, Xianghong Jasmine Zhou, "Unraveling complex temporal associations in cellular systems across multiple time-series microarray datasets", Journal of BI 43, Elsevier, ScienceDirect, Pages 550–559, 2010

[17]. Yan Huang, Liqin Zhang, and Pusheng Zhang, "A Framework for Mining Sequential Patterns from Spatio-Temporal Event Data Sets", IEEE Transactions on Knowledge and Data Engineering, Vol. 20, NO. 4, 2008.

[18]. Claudia Antunes and Arlindo L. Oliveira, "Sequential Pattern Mining Algorithms: Trade-offs between Speed and Memory", In 2nd Workshop on Mining Graphs, Trees and Seq, 2004.

[19]. Fabian Moerchen, "Temporal pattern mining for time points, time intervals, and semi-intervals", Siemens Corporate Research, January, 2011

[20]. Damian Fricker Hui Zhang Chen Yu, "Sequential Pattern Mining of Multi modal Data Streams in Dyadic Interactions", ICDL, 978-1-61284-990-4/11, IEEE, 2011.

# A METHOD FOR VR MANAGEMENT IN PUBLIC OPINION

**Jin Du, Yanhui Du**

Chinese People's Public Security University, Beijing
koaladj@126.com, dyh6889@126.com

## Abstract

Public opinion management system plays an important role on information management nowadays. Developing characteristics and rules of online public opinion are discussed by means of optimized model analyzing method in present paper. The public opinion was regarded as a 'resource' from which the conception of 'configuration' was proposed and its control model was developed as well. Based on that, correlation degree variables between 'social network' cluster nodes were dynamically introduced and general rules of public opinion between associated network cluster management were studied at the time. The 'public opinion resource' correlation optimized model which can regulate the relationship between VR management and verified by means of empirical research of sociology, journalism and psychology. At last, artificial intelligence and decision support can be supplied to relevant industries by instructing system design and management system by means of the study of public opinion.

**Keywords:** Public opinion management; Public opinion VR control model; VR resource configuration; Bayers theory.

## 1 Background

With the development of emerging online media, social networking cluster also accelerate the exchange. The discovery and management of the public opinion of a focus event is challenging in information management. If some of the public opinion, the improper development of the information, it is easy to cause serious public safety and social harm. Therefore, the public opinion management is an extremely important part of information management.

Currently, many scholars and institutions from different disciplinary perspectives and entry point for the mechanisms and laws of the events on the online public opinion research. Public opinion information has freedom, interactivity, immediacy, occult mass characteristics, and there is a certain evolution mechanism. Conduct the allocation of resources in the network environment, there is great difference, compared to the traditional approach. Network resource allocation to the appropriate method based Employment Computer Information talent it is valid, based on the optimize model validation. Therefore, by means of the use of computer and information technology, on the basis of the original proposed an optimization model for a reasonable configuration of the network resource of public opinion, is the focus of this study. [1]

## 2. IMPORTANCE OF VR RESOURCE CONFIGURATION ON PUBLIC OPINION MANAGEMENT

The VR resource configuration on public opinion management plays an extremely positive significance role on network. From the perspective of resource, only when reasonable configuration could make the values for management; only when reasonable configuration could improve efficiency; only when reasonable configuration method and model have improve harmony and progress. From the perspective of management, only when reasonable configuration could develop their potential and strengthen their positivity; only when reasonable configuration could make maximum effectiveness. [2]

## 3. MODEL OF VR RESOURCE CONFIGURATION ON PUBLIC OPINION MANAGEMENT

There are two methods about VR resource configuration on public opinion management. One is paying attention to measurement of ability on human capital. We make the standard for judging human capital values and setup measurement of ability model on human capital values according from human capital's marginal output effect theory. Another is designing two-way selection model and optimization model of VR resource configuration based on ability through researching the configuration about resource and methods to how to improve efficiency. They can't make the best model of VR resource configuration on public opinion management though the two models have their advantages and disadvantages. The research will judge configuration can be fit for position of demand from based on configuration status of job position, interesting and ability on public opinion management. The configuration of resource will be reasonable optimized and combined about its future on the basis of its status. So the writer tried to resolve the VR resource configuration problem based on information and Bayes theory. [3]

Based on the objective circumstances of rapid development of public opinion management and shortage of professional configuration, the writer researched some popular methods of VR resource configuration and tried to setup VR resource configuration model based on Bayes theory. Bayes theory is parametric probability density estimation. It is regarded parameter as a random variable. It estimates parameter according to the observation data and prior probability parameters. Based on application of Bayes theory, When observing an event x, it estimate and give its internal parameters θ, it shows the degree of happens about event x. When you need to select an optimal value to do prediction, we select the distribution P(θ| x) and get the value of θ to make P(θ| x) maximum as the parameters form P(θ| x), we get the degree of parameters. The optimization model of VR resource configuration indicated probability function can be qualified job position from configuration status (i.e. the configuration can be qualified on the most suitable for the job).The verification about model can be selected P(θ) as conjugate prior distribution of P(x |θ).If there can have the same form the normalized results of P(x |θ) multiply P(θ) and P(θ) meet P(θ) Conjugate to P(x |θ)('likelihood function'),that is to say the same form of posterior probability distribution and prior probability distribution can meet conjugate distribution verification.

### 3.1 Optimal estimation to VR resource configuration based on Bayes estimation

The essence of Bayes estimation is to get optimal estimation of parameter θ based on Bayes decision. It makes risk to minimization of total expectation. If selection of samples is qualified their job position, we will assume and estimate this following: Set $p(\theta)$ to priori probability density of estimated parameter θ and get values of θ relation with samples as shown in equation (1). Set the values of samples to parameters θ , set $\lambda(\hat{\theta},\theta)$ to $\hat{\theta}$ as loss function of estimated value $\theta$, we will get equation (2) and get equation (3) as minimization of total expectation:

$$\mathbf{X}=\{x_1,\cdots,x_n\}\ E^d \qquad (1)$$

$$\lambda(\hat{\theta},\theta)=(\hat{\theta}-\theta)^2 \qquad (2)$$

$$R=\int_{E^d}\int_{\Theta}\lambda(\hat{\theta},\theta)p(\theta|x)p(x)d\theta dx, \qquad (3)$$

Define conditions of risk based on sample x to equation (4) and get as shown in equation (5) using by simplification:

$$R(\hat{\theta}|x)=\int_{\Theta}\lambda(\hat{\theta},\theta)p(\theta|x)d\theta, \qquad (4)$$

$$R=\int_{E^d}R(\hat{\theta}|x)p(x)dx, \qquad (5)$$

Get the minimization values of $R$ as $R(\hat{\theta}|x)$ with nonnegative value of $R(\hat{\theta}|x)$ and get equation (6):

$$\theta^*=\arg\min R(\hat{\theta}|x), \qquad (6)$$

Get equation (7) with optimal estimation:

$$\theta^*=\int_{\Theta}\theta p(\theta|x)d\theta. \qquad (7)$$

### 3.2 Estimation of the samples probability density function as configuration be qualified for their job

We estimated parameters with the assumption that the sample probability density interval (the values of probabilities is 0 to 1) and directly get estimation of sample probability density function based on Bayes estimation with as shown in equation(8).

$$p(x|X)=\int_{\Theta}p(x|\theta)p(\theta|X)d\theta. \qquad (8)$$

From equation (8), we got $p(x|X)$ as posterior probability with weights of $\theta$ in case where all parameters got to weighted average values of sample probability density.

### 3.3 Analyze optimization model of VR resource configuration with calculation model

We got parameter θ to the status of configuration competence for their job with α(0.5<α ≤1 with a random variable) and got p （θ） to prior distribution with configuration competence . So we got the actual probability value: θ is the status of configuration, Dj is the numbers of job configuration, Dk is the observation results of status of configuration with the K-th. We got β(0<β≤1) to prior distribution of values of configuration competence for their job, the following ： p （θ） ≥β； P （θ） = p （θ1 .θ2 .θ3） ,p (θ1) ≥0.5， p (θ2) ≥0.5， p (θ3) ≥0.5；

We got modified survey equation (9)

$$\frac{p'(\theta_1)}{p'(\theta_2)} = \frac{w_1}{w_2} \cdot \frac{p(\theta_1)}{p(\theta_2)}; \quad \frac{p'(\theta_1)}{p'(\theta_3)} = \frac{w_1}{w_3} \cdot \frac{p(\theta_1)}{p(\theta_3)}; \quad p'(\theta_k) = p(\theta_k), k \in \{1,2,3\} \tag{9}$$

p (θ1), p (θ2) and p (θ3) are respectively as prior probability with configuration's competence for their job of the achievements of configuration at past or present, the interesting of configuration and ability of configuration. We defined p (θ1) ≥0.5,p (θ2) ≥0.5,p (θ3) ≥0.5 to reduce the times and costs of optimize resource configuration. That is to say the degree of supporting configuration competence for their job with the status of them at present is not less than 50 percent. p (θ1),p (θ2) and p (θ3) have different degree of influence to configuration's competence their job on w1+w2+w3=1 and gave them to different weights as w1,w2 and w3,w1+w2+w3=1.We use the method to check and correct prior probability.

Fortunately, we got the optimization model of VR resource configuration just like equation:

$$p(\theta_i|D_j) = \frac{p(\theta_i)p(D_j|\theta_i)}{\sum_{k=1}^{m} p(\theta_i)p(D_k|\theta_i)} \tag{10}$$

### 3.4 Method of analyzing data sample and building model

Got the Prior distribution $p(\theta)$ from $\theta$;

Got samples combined distribution from density distribution $p(x|\theta)$ of unknown x to equation (11):

$$p(X|\theta) = \prod_{n=1}^{N} p(x_n|\theta); \tag{11}$$

Got posterior distribution of $\theta$ from Bayes as shown in equation (12) :

$$p(\theta|X) = \frac{p(X|\theta)p(\theta)}{\int_{\Theta} p(X|\theta)p(\theta)d\theta}; \tag{12}$$

Got the optimization estimate of equation (13):

$$\theta^* = \int_{\Theta} \theta p(\theta|x)d\theta. \tag{13}$$

In the optimization model of VR resource configuration, we can optimize the degree of configuration competence for their job from calculating the prior probability, posterior probability of configuration based on Bayes theory and experimental samples which are determined to finish new job with new demand. (Figure 1)

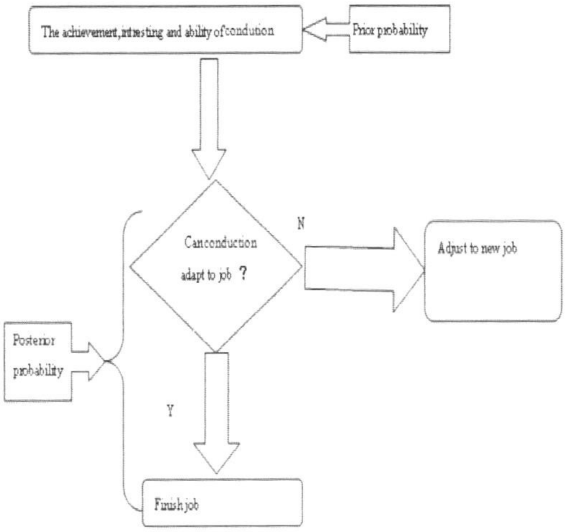


**Figure 1. The optimization model of VR resource configuration based on Bayes theory**

## 4. PUBLIC OPINION VR CONTROL MODEL OF RESOURCE CONFIGURATION

If an department could get estimation of sampling to configuration competence for their job using the conjugate prior distribution and data validation. They will get this following that the parameters of the probability is unlikeness; competent and incompetent results presents non-uniform distribution. We transferred parameter θ with Bernoulli model and got Distribution form of results (P(x |θ ) =θ x (1−θ )$^{1-x}$,their conjugate prior distribution conforms to beta. We made two parameters α and β to meet equation (14):

$$P(x|\alpha,\beta) = \frac{\theta^{\alpha-1}(1-\theta)^{\beta-1}}{\int_0^1 \theta^{\alpha-1}(1-\theta)^{\beta-1}d\theta} \tag{14}$$

θ is the probability of configuration competence for their job(0<θ<1).We observed the degree of belief of parameter θ after updating x as this equation to be normalized. We calculated P (θ | x) over passing the denominator of equation of normalized constant and normalized after calculating. We use α as times of configuration competence for their job and β as not configuration incompetence for their job, and to them as distribution parameter of beta. We got two conclusions: One is 6 times of configuration competence for their job, 14 times of not configuration incompetence for their job, when we tested 20 times. Another is 9000 times of configuration competence for their job, 21000 times of not configuration incompetence for their job, when we tested 30000 times. This conclusion clearly tested the degree of belief about this model.

It accorded with the maximum entropy principle of informational theory that the model tested distribution prior probability of configuration competence for their job based on their competence using with setting distribution prior probability as even distribution with information and Bayes theory.

## 5 Conclusions

By means of the modeling analysis, at the Public Sentiment normal distribution and network cluster associated premise, discuss the general regularity of public opinion information between the associated cluster organizations. Secondly, it is proposed that the association between the management and control of VR management. In turn can regulate the resource configuration of public opinion forming control or affect the extreme instance in the cluster, to reduce or enhance the relationship by the optimized model.

Targeted a specific event or phenomenon, factors affecting the formation of public opinion is often complex and changeable. There are many uncertainties in which, from the chaos of individual opinion to have a marked tendency in the emergence of public opinion, the information generated evolution exists for the study of the common models. Journalism, "the rule of the majority" in the theory and psychology "psychological resistance" phenomenon, with the study of the evolution of public opinion information to learn from each other, mutual authentication, and thus confirmed the model made with the establishment of reasonable.

## Acknowledgement

Supported by the Natural Science Foundation of China (Grant No. 71173199 and No. 09CZZ011).

## References

[1] Chinese Public opinion management research center.(2012.).http://wenku.baidu.com/

[2] view/cd397ded6294dd88d0d26bf4.html

[3] Liu xiao-hong ,Liu Fan ,Zhang Cai-juan.An optimization model of configuration setup based Bayes theory(2006).Journal of Southwest University for Nationalities .Natural Science Edition.32(5):992-996

[4] Sun jian-qian The research on resource configuration optimization configuration model and (2008).Technology and management.10(2):121-123

[5] WRIGHT PATRICK M.BOSWELL WENDY R. Desegregating HRM: A Review and Synthesis of Micro and Macro Human.Resource Management Research(2002).Journal of Management.28(3): 247-276.

[6]

[7] Wang Hongwei, He Yong, Petri net: a tool of visualization modeling support, Journal of Systems Engineering, 12(2), (1997) 73-78.

[8] Frederick E. Webster, Jr. and Yoram Wind. A general model for understanding organizational buying behavior. Journal of

[9] Petri C. Communication with automata. Technical Report RADC-TR-65-377, Rome Air Dev .Center, New York, NY,1966.

[10] Wang Hongwei, He Yong, Petri net: a tool of visualization modeling support, Journal of Systems Engineering, 12(2), (1997) 73-78.

[11] Michael K. Molloy(1982). Performance Analysis Using Stochastic Petri Nets . IEEE, Transactions On Computers, c-31(9):913-917

[12] Rachid H , Boualem B. A Pet ri net2based model for Web service composition/ / Proceedings of the 14t h Aust ralian Da2 tabase Conference on Database Technologies. Adelaide ,Sout h Aust ralia , 2003 : 1912200

[13] Hu Hao , Yin Qin , Lu Jian. Service behavior and quality consistency in virtualized computing environment . Journal of Software , 2007 , 18 (8) : 194321957 (in Chinese).

[14] Milner R. Communication and Concurrency. Upper Saddle River , NJ , USA : Prentice Hall , 1989.

[15] Foster H , Uchitel S , Kramer J et al . Compatibility verifica2 tion for Web service choreography/ / Proceedings of the IEEE International Conference on Web Services. San Diego , CA , USA , 2004 : 7382741.

[16] J ensen K. Coloured Pet ri Net s : Basic Concept s , Analysis Met hods and Practical Use. Vol . 1. Berlin , Heidelberg ,New York : Springer2Verlag , 1997.

# Bioinformatics Knowledge Transmission (training, learning, and teaching): overview and flexible comparison of computer based training approaches.

Etienne Z. Gnimpieba, Douglas Jennewein, Luke Fuhrman, Carol M. Lushbough
Computer Science Department, University of South Dakota, 414 E. Clark St. Vermillion, SD 57069, USA,
{Etienne.gnimpieba; Doug.Jennewein; Luke.Fuhrman, Carol.Lushbough}@usd.edu

**Corresponding author:** Etienne.gnimpieba@usd.edu, +1 605 223 0383.

~o~

**Abstract: The merger of computer science, mathematics, and life sciences has brought about the discipline known as bioinformatics. However, the transmission (e.g. training, learning, and teaching) of this knowledge becomes an important issue. Many tools have been developed to help the bioinformatics community with that transmission challenge. When selecting the best of these tools, called here BKTMS (Bioinformatics Knowledge Transmission Management Systems), there may be confusion. What makes a good BKTMS? How can we make this choice efficiently? These questions remain unanswered for many users (e.g. learner, teacher and student, trainer and trainee, administrator). This paper provides a critical review of 32 existing BKTMS and a flexible comparison. This review and evaluation will be used to gain insight into the tools, systems, and capabilities that will be added to or excluded from a new proposed model for the next generation of BKTMS, involving multidisciplinary, web semantic tools (e.g. web services, workflow) and standards like LOM, or SCORM.**

**Keywords:** bioinformatics, learning object, knowledge transmission, education, multidisciplinary.

## Introduction

Biolnformatics allowed creation of vast knowledge amounts based on data, tools, processes, and technology. Bioinformatics aims to use and create technologies for identification, manipulation, modification, and creation of life science data. Currently, the transmission of bioinformatics knowledge and skills is a difficult task to accomplish [1]. The growing mass of bioinformatics knowledge, data, and tools has led to a growing need for adequate knowledge transmission and collaborative tools.

The diversity of academic domains, student profiles, and skills requires the specialization and the personalization of bioinformatics training programs. Over the past ten years, higher education institutions have begun to offer courses in bioinformatics and computational biology [2]. A survey conducted by Messersmith et al. shows that about 30% of United States universities offered bioinformatics educational workshops as of 2011 [3]. Some high schools in the world have begun education in bioinformatics as well [4]. In addition, we are witnessing a growing development of tools for managing the transmission of knowledge using computer engineering, called computer-based training (CBT). Users are faced with the difficulties of choice and the good definition quality of the results. In the bioinformatics field, the complexities of the subjects (i.e. multidisciplinarity) and the diversity of training needs make a choice even more difficult. Indeed, most of the management tools for bioinformatics knowledge transmission that have been developed in recent years are related to proprietary needs or specific bioinformatics software (e.g. ExPASy, EBI, NCBI, ...). Other management tools try to adapt existing educational frameworks to facilitate standardization of their content (e.g. E-Biomics, EMBR, OpenHelix, etc.). Others tried to build new transmission strategies based on Bioinformatics knowledge networking (e.g. BTN, Biostar). However, it is difficult to select the appropriate

BKTMS from this panoply of BKTMS. An evaluation of these tools proves necessary.

For example, possessing statistics skills can qualify a person for several career profiles such as *systems biology* modeling, data analysis, or data modeling (data learning). This concept of knowledge transmission requires modularity of transmitted knowledge. In fact, to transmit the knowledge necessary for understanding complex concepts in bioinformatics and computational biology such as modeling of systems biology [5], [6], a BKTMS needs modularity to facilitate both transmitting and receiving. Standardization, modularity, reusability and flexibility prove to be important in the design criteria of BKTMS (Yusof, Mansur, & Othman, 2011; [8]. This paper presents a critique of 32 existing BKTMS and a flexible score-based comparison of these BKTMS with 8 generic Learning Management System (LMS).

## 1. Bioinformatics Knowledge Transmission Management System (BKTMS) overview

A BKTMS is a web portal that provides resources for learning, teaching, training, or helping with executing bioinformatics work/problems. It can be a learning object repository (LOR), learning management system (LMS), courses management system (CMS), virtual learning environment (VLE), computer based training (CBT) portal or a simple website. These portals intend to offer a service to different groups of users in order to facilitate an understanding of specific tools, databases, functions, exercises, bioinformatics processes, programs, skills, and career profile requirements. In many cases, this service is made available for educational purposes in order to advance knowledge and understanding in bioinformatics.

There are some existing portals. What are their flaws and benefits? Table 1 indicates a number of portals reviewed with a standard set of theoretical parameters. Some descriptive parameters and information can be found in the educational tools evaluation system literature (Landon, Henderson, & Poulin, 2006, [2]. Our selected features to describe tools are: tool identification (Portal name, Base Institution, contact/author, main Statement/Goals, URL/location, comments) and technical information (approach, login, freely downloadable accessible materials, updates clearly indicated, reviewing/ranking material option, searchable materials, trainer/contact information, information about training facilities, links to courses and events).

Using these features, Table 1 describes 32 BKTMS. With some BKTMS there was no clear approach in the design or learning strategy, but instead a presentation collection of training resources. Through the accessibility evaluation criteria, BKTMS are categorized as free, partially free (free for academic use for example), and paid systems. Free tools are preponderant. To the nature and organization of content, there is a low diversity of formats (usually slides, videos or text). The organization is usually related to owner activities. BKTMS are usually organized by topics, by subdomain, by tool (software, database), on application or case study (DNA sequence analysis). This organization diversity attests to the complexity of the bioinformatics domain, but reveals that standardization of the learning context should be evaluated for efficient bioinformatics knowledge transfer.

Many of the tools and portal aspects mentioned previously are required for a competent bioinformatics training portal; however, a few new integrations would be useful as well. Many portals include profiles and sign-in capabilities, but it seems that none use that function as effectively as they could. A portal that allows users to sign-in to a profile, and customize that profile, could be a useful resource. A function should be implemented that allows users to build and edit workflows or training lists and save them for future use. This would drastically increase the teaching utility of the bioinformatics portal. Users need to be able to communicate with one another, form groups, and share training lists with those groups. An educator could compose a list of training materials and share that list with a group of students. This would also be a useful resource when presenting bioinformatics workshops. An application that can assess a user's intention, skill level, and needs would be a beneficial application as well. A user could sign-in, take an assessment, and have a generated list of training materials available to complete their desired intentions. For example, consider a user who wants to learn to perform a sequence alignment. Their assessment would indicate this need and generate a list of resources including

"Introduction to BioExtract Server," "ClustalW Usage," and "Phylogenic Tree Creation Tutorial" for example. Since the content is aimed at the user, a rating system for content based on user background would be advisable. Suggested categories of rating could be: high school student, post-secondary student, educator, and researcher.

Table 1 allows us to understand the BKTMS tools diversity. The diversity is based on Bioinformatics sub-domains and Bioinformatics applications. This shows that evaluation criteria for managing knowledge transmission are not yet a priority in BKTMS tools. Indeed, these BKTMS lack the factors necessary for the establishment of a complete pedagogical method. We can cite the factors as course level, monitoring and evaluation of the receiver (e.g. trainee, student), and many others. We propose a more formal study of these critical tools to contribute to the improvement of the next generations of BKTMS tools.

## 2. BKTMS Tools comparison

### a) Comparison principle

We use criteria provide in [10] because of its pluridisciplinarity and flexibility (Figure1). We provide a comparison of our review BKTMS (Table 1). That comparison involves 8 other LMS from EduTools and is described in [11].

Based on this information and our exploration of these tools, a grade table was proposed with KTMS in the rows and criteria in the columns (Table 2). Each criterion was weighted based on its importance related to the BKTMS. Based on the calculated scores, the user can select appropriate tools or use radar or histogram chart visualization for more details. The graphic visualization provides a snapshot of each KTMS position for each criterion (Figure 1 and Figure 2).

For simplification and compliance needs, grades for all criteria are brought to a discrete evaluation scale [1...8]. The numeric value of the evaluation may be changed, but with greatly improved ability to compare tools. The comparison is based on our context and our need. Each user can specify the priorities and degrees of importance to each criterion function in its own context. That is to say each criterion may have a score of 1 to 8, and a weight to express its importance in the given context.

### b) Score calculation and comparison result visualization

Scores were calculated using the simple expert's (decision maker's) additive utility function [12] (Eq.5)

$$f(X) = \sum_{i=1}^{m} p_i f_i(X) \qquad \text{(Eq.5)}$$

where $f_i(X) = \{1,2,3,\dots,8\}$ is the rating grade of the criterion $i$ for each examined alternative BKTMS $X_j$, $m$ is the number of criteria, and $p_i$ is the weighted weight of a given criterion $i$ (weight i on the total weight).

### c) Grades, score calculation and score visualization.

Table 2 shows our BKTMS evaluation grades and scores. The first line contains the BKTMS name; lines 2 to 39 contain the KTMS grades for each criterion. The last line contains the score of each BKTMS weighting with the equation (Eq.5) formula. This table includes: grade for global criteria (white background) and detailed criteria (grey background), calculated score (black background) using equation (Eq.5), for global criteria (penultimate line) and detail criteria (last line). The first and second column contains the criterion name and its code, the third column contains the weight of the related criterion in our context. The remains columns contain the data related to each BKTMS. A high weight is put on pluridisciplinarity, collaboration, and networking criteria, given their predominance in bioinformatics.

Figure 2 shows radar chart visualization of KTMS global criteria scores (G) and detail criteria for each global criterion for more information: technical (T), pedagogy (P), interdisciplinary (I), communication (C), others (O) (related to Table 2).

## Conclusion

How can one choose an appropriate BKTMS? What BKTMS should be used for what goals? What training? What learning? What level? What is a bioinformatics program? We can continue the list indefinitely. Depending on one's involvement in the pluridisciplinary education world like bioinformatics, researcher can be looking for answers to some of these questions. This paper proposes some elements that can help in finding answers.

This study has primarily focused on providing a standardized critique of the existing BKTMS critics review. Even if the tools list was not exhaustive, it allowed us to present evidence of the strengths and failures of existing tools for bioinformatics knowledge transmission. Evaluation criteria were finally applied on the described BKTMS selected list.

Figure analysis has shown that the existing BKTMS has a relatively low score compared to the 8 selected LMS. And yet these BKTMS have high grades in multidisciplinary criteria. Through careful observation we noted that the grades for collaborativity, networking, and sharing criteria were low. Even strong weighting of the interdisciplinarity criteria could not compensate for this weakness.

This review and evaluation will be used to gain insight into the tools, systems, and capabilities that will be added to or excluded from a new proposed model for the next generation of BKTMS, involving web services and standards like SCORM, LOM, or IMS.

**Acknowledgments**: **Acknowledgments**: The authors would like to thank Dr. Doug Goodman and Jerry Prentice for their helpful corrections on this work.

**Funding**: This work was made possible by SD-INBRE Grant #P20RR016479-09 from the National Center for Research Resources (NCRR), a component of the National Institutes of Health (NIH). Its contents are solely the responsibility of the authors and do not necessarily represent the official views of NCRR or NIH. NSF Grant IOS-1126481 Integrating the BioExtract Server with the iPlant Collaborative.

**Terminologies:**

*LOs: Learning Objects*
*LORs: Learning Object Repository*
*CBT: Computer Based Training*
*LMS: Learning Management System*
*KTMS: Knowledge Transmission Management System*
*BKTMS: Bioinformatics Knowledge Transmission Management System*
*SCORM: Sharable Content Object Reference Model*
*VLEs: Virtual learning environments*
*CBTE: competence-based teaching education,*
*HBTE: humanistic-based teacher education,*
*IMS: instructional management system*
*LOM: learning object model*

## References

[1] S. Cattley and J. W. Arthur, "BioManager: the use of a bioinformatics web application as a teaching tool in undergraduate bioinformatics training.," *Briefings in bioinformatics*, vol. 8, no. 6, pp. 457–65, Nov. 2007.

[2] M. V Schneider, P. Walter, M.-C. Blatter, J. Watson, M. D. Brazas, K. Rother, A. Budd, A. Via, C. W. G. van Gelder, J. Jacob, P. Fernandes, T. H. Nyrönen, J. De Las Rivas, T. Blicher, R. C. Jimenez, J. Loveland, J. McDowall, P. Jones, B. W. Vaughan, R. Lopez, T. K. Attwood, and C. Brooksbank, "Bioinformatics Training Network (BTN): a community resource for bioinformatics trainers.," *Briefings in bioinformatics*, vol. 13, no. 3, pp. 383–9, Nov. 2011.

[3] D. J. Messersmith, D. a Benson, and R. C. Geer, "A Web-based assessment of bioinformatics end-user support services at US universities.," *Journal of the Medical Library Association : JMLA*, vol. 94, no. 3, pp. 299–305, E156–87, Jul. 2006.

[4] H. Gelbart and A. Yarden, "Learning genetics through an authentic research simulation in bioinformatics," vol. 40, no. 3, 2006.

[5] E. Z. Gnimpieba, D. Eveillard, J.-L. Guéant, and A. Chango, "Using logic programming for modeling the one-carbon metabolism network to study the impact of folate deficiency on methylation processes.," *Molecular Biosystems*, vol. 7, no. 8, pp. 2508–2521, 2011.

[6] I. Koch, W. Reisig, and F. Schreiber, Eds., *Modeling in Systems Biology*, vol. 16. London: Springer London, 2011.

[7] N. Yusof, A. B. F. Mansur, and M. S. Othman, "Ontology of moodle e-learning system for social network analysis," in *2011 IEEE Conference on Open Systems*, 2011, pp. 122–126.

[8] D. Gasevic, J. Jovanovic, V. Devedzic, and M. Boskovic, "Ontologies for reusing learning object content," in *Fifth IEEE International Conference on Advanced Learning Technologies (ICALT'05)*, 2005, pp. 944–945.

[9] B. Landon, T. Henderson, and R. Poulin, "Peer Comparison of Course/Learning Managemment Systems, Course Materials Life Cycle, and Related Costs," Massachusetts Institute of Technology, 2006.

[10] E. Z. Gnimpieba, D. Jennewein, L. Fuhrman, and C. M. Lushbough, "Multidisciplinarity in Knowledge Transmision Management System (KTMS) evaluation." in process, 2013.

[11] Edutools, "CMS evaluation report," 2012.

[12] E. Kurilovas and V. D. E, "Multiple Criteria Comparative Evaluation of E-Learning Systems and Components," vol. 20, no. 4, pp. 499–518, 2009.

## List of figures

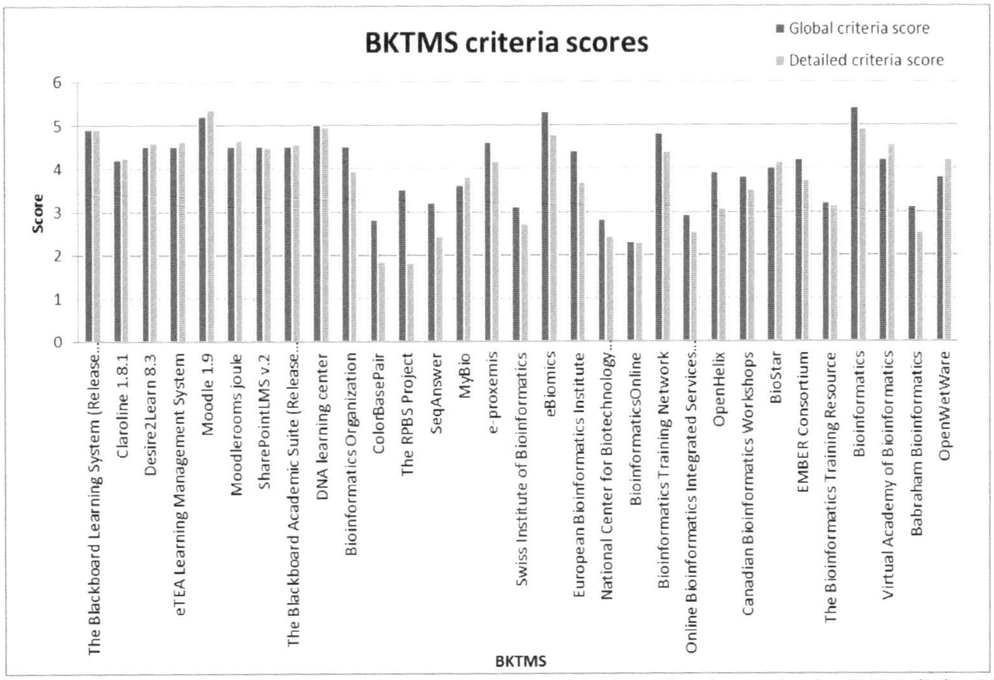


Figure 1: Score visualization histogram for BKTMS based on global evaluation criteria T,P,I,C,O (black), and detailed criteria (grey).

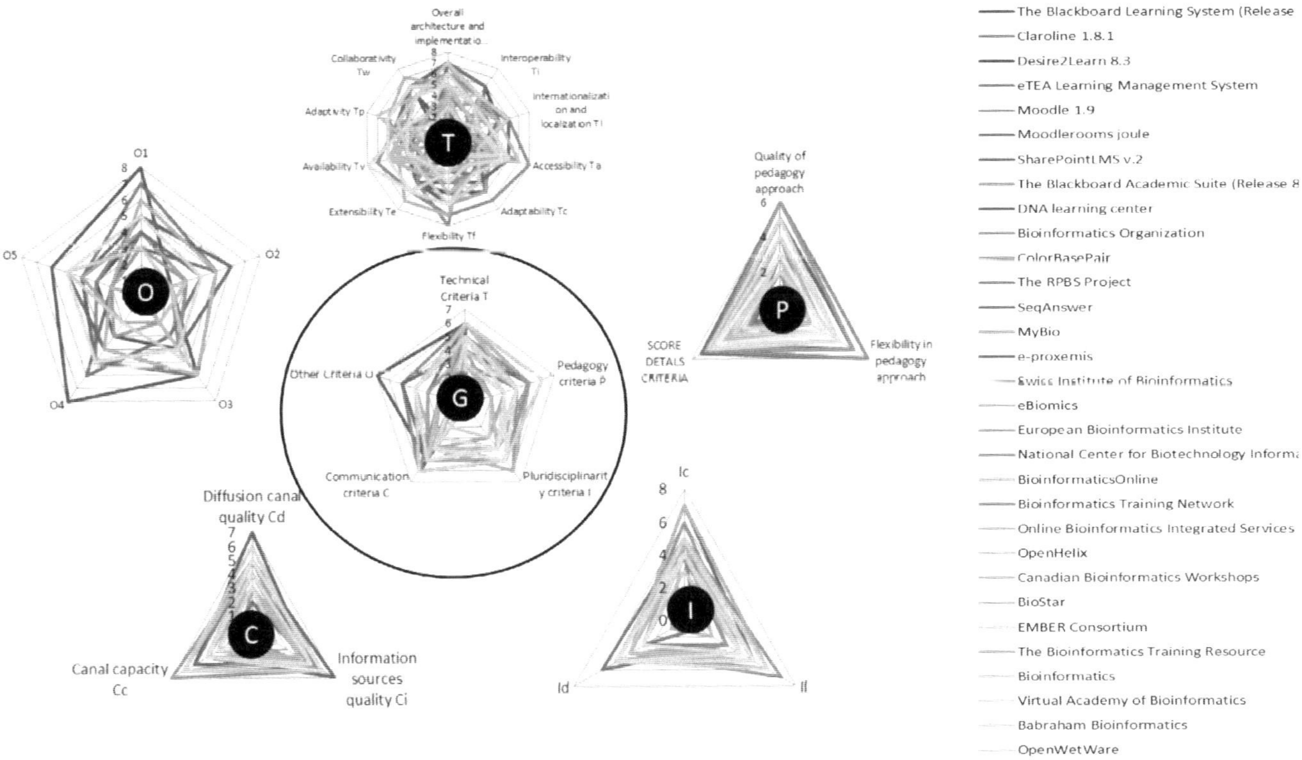


Figure 2: Score radar visualization of BKTMS based on global criteria (G). Zoom on detail criteria for each global criterion for more detail, technical (T), pedagogy (P), interdisciplinary (I), communication (C), others (O) (Table 4).

# List of tables:

## Table 1: BKTMS overview

| Portal Name | Base Institution | Contact/author | Main Statement/Goals | URL | Comments | Approach | Login | Freely download/ access materials | Updates clearly indicated | Reviewing/ranking material option | Materials searchable | Trainer/contact informat | Info about training facili | Links to courses and events |
|---|---|---|---|---|---|---|---|---|---|---|---|---|---|---|
| Bioinformatics Organization | Bioinformatics Organization, Incorporated | J.W. Bizzaro | The Bioinformatics Organization develop computational resources to facilitate world-wide communications and collaborations between people of all educational and professional levels. It provide and promote open access to the materials and methods required for, and derived from, research, development and education. | http://www.bioinformatics.org/ | Basic usage is free, Professionals has a cost. Uses Wikipedia as a base site or reference location. | Unclear | Yes, not required. | Yes | Yes | No | Yes | Yes | No | Yes |
| Compbiology | | Jennifer Steinbachs | A computer biology related news site. | http://compbiology.org/ | Seems abandoned. | Unclear | Yes, not required. | NA | Yes | No | No | No | No | No |
| BioPlanet | ISCB | - | Collection of bioinformatics training programm in the world and job search | http://www.bioplanet.com/ | | Unclear | No | NA | No | No | No | No | No | Yes |
| ColorBasePair | - | - | Provide bioinformatics resources such as bioinformatics news, bioinformatics jobs, bioinformatics books, bioinformatics tutorials, bioinformatics training | http://www.colorbasepair.com/ | | Unclear | No | Yes | Yes | NA | No | No | No | Yes |
| MyBio | Wikia | | BIO international event planing tool (see and be seen, networking, explore sessions event) | http://mybio.wikia.com/wiki/Tutorials_in_bioinformatics | | collection list | Yes | Yes | Unclear | NA | Yes | No | No | No |
| e-proxemis | SIB | | Bioinformatics learning portal for proteomics | http://e-proxemis.expasy.org | Display tools and offsite tools based on type of research [ex. sequence classification = PROSITE, Pfam, PRINTS, etc..). Has practice lab for tools such as BLAST | Try to fulfill resource requirements search by category of work being done. Similar for teaching tools | Yes | NA | Unclear | No | No | No | No | No |
| Swiss Institute of Bioinformatics | | Peter Malama | collection of bioinformatics resources (slides, video) organize in programms, workshops, practices labs | | Connexion between events and training courses. | Foccus based organisation of resources | No | Yes | Yes | No | Yes | Yes | Yes | Yes |
| SEQanswers | USA and Chinese Universities | | SEQanswers provides a real-time knowledge-sharing resource to address this need, covering experimental and computational aspects of sequencing and sequence analysis | http://seqanswers.com/ | - | integration, collaborativity, question based, wiki | Yes | Yes | Yes | Yes | Yes | NA | NA | No |
| Galaxy | The Huck Institutes of the Life Sciences, The Institute for CyberScience at Penn State, and Emory University | | Galaxy is an open, web-based platform for *accessible*, *reproducible*, and *transparent* computational biomedical research. | http://wiki.galaxyproject.org/ | Workflow based tools and related learning resources | topic based videos, wiki | Yes | Yes | No | No | Yes | Yes | NA | NA |
| eBiomics | NBIC / Wageningen / ULB / SDC | many persons | Devoted to workbench basedn training in bioinformatics. It is composed of several interconnected sections that can be accessed through different interactive activities. The purpose of eBiomics is to familiarise users with bioinformatics analysis flows in diverse -omics applications. | http://ebiomics.sdcinfo.com/ | For each database or tool, they have "how to use this" sections, and a link to the tool. | Try to fulfill resource requirements search by category of work being done. Similar for teaching tools. | Yes | Yes | Yes | No | Yes | Yes | Yes | Yes |
| Bioinformatics Resource Portal | | | providing resources | http://bioinformaticstools.webs.com/index.htm | Many tools and databases are provided. | | No | Yes | No | No | No | No | No | Yes |
| European Bioinformatics Institute | European Molecular Biology Laboratory | Janet Thornton | Provide advanced bioinformatics training to scientists at all levels, from PhD students to independent investigators. | http://www.ebi.ac.uk/ | | Primary database. Find resources and training tools by research category. | No | Yes | Yes | No | Yes | Yes | Yes | Yes |
| GATK forum | | | GATK is an industrial-strength infrastructure and engine that handle data access, conversion and traversal, as well as high-performance computing features | http://gatkforums.broadinstitute.org/ | | Primary database. Find resources and training tools by research category. | Yes | Yes | Yes | No | Yes | Yes | Yes | Yes |
| National Center for Biotechnology Information | NCBI | board of members | collection of learning resources for tools and databases use in NCBI portal | http://www.ncbi.nlm.nih.gov/guide/training-tutorials/ | | Primary database. Find resources and training tools by research category. | No | Yes | Unclear | No | No | No | No | No |
| BioinformaticsOnline | Bioinformatics Skill Development Programme | Jitendra Narayan | BioinformaticsOnline(BOL) is a bioinformatics education portal for the students of Bioinformatics and Biotechnology and specifically designed to help research scientist, working on various project. The aims at bringing together research scientists interested in Bioinformatics and allied fields and to support develop and spread Bioinformatics in a scientific, academic, technologic and industrial environment in India and abroad. | http://www.bioinformaticsonline.com/ | | Separate by tools, databases, career, training, companies, etc... (not based off of discipline or anything) | Yes | Yes | No | NA | Yes | Yes | No | Yes |
| Bioinformatics Training Network | EMBL-EBI based maintainers | EMBL-EBI | The BTN is a community-based project aiming to provide a centralised facility to share materials, to list training events (including course contents and trainers), and to share and discuss training experiences. You are welcome to browse the site, and we encourage you to join us to share (license) information and materials – please register. | http://www.biotnet.org/ | Devoted to the teachers/professors/trainers | Provide teaching resources based off of research category (proteomics, nutrigenomics, etc.), also list available workshops, and list training facilities. | Yes | Yes | Yes | Yes | Yes | Yes | Yes | Yes |
| Online Bioinformatics Integrated Services (iBIS) | University of Miami and OpenHelix | University of Miami | iBIS is UM's online Bioinformatics Integrated Services portal. iBIS was developed particularly for biologists and medical researchers- it is a user-friendly, (fairly) comprehensive, customizable portal which includes education materials to guide you through your bioinformatics experience. The idea is that your saved workspace in iBIS contains links to all your frequently used bioinformatics databases, tools, or UM services. | http://bio.ccs.miami.edu/ibis/UMIBIS.jsp | Student resources available through OpenHelix. | Use of widgets to allow easy access of tools, databases, etc. Allows users to "save workspace" or list of tools present for certain research or training resources | Yes | No) | No | No | Yes | Yes | Yes | Yes |
| Bioportal RENCI | | Stan Ahalt | We bring the latest cyber tools and technologies to bear on pressing problems. We work with scientists who study critical issues from climate change to the causes of cancer. We form research teams that involve faculty members at universities across North Carolina and the U.S. and that are positioned to bring major research projects to North Carolina. We partner with North Carolina government agencies so they are able to better serve the state's citizens. | http://www.renci.org/ | | More private group advancing computational technology. | No | NA | Yes | NA | NA | Yes | Yes | Yes |
| Bioinformatics Institute of India (BII) | - | - | Teaching for money | http://www.bii.in/ | | Pay to train or learn bioinformatics | Yes | No | No | Yes | Yes | Yes | Yes | Yes |
| Oslo Bioportal | University of Oslo | - | The Bioportal at University of Oslo is a web-based portal for phylogenomic analysis, population genetics and high-throughput sequence analysis. The main advantage of Bioportal lies in an access to a parallel computational resource that enables demanding computations. Therefore, this resource is designed for large, time consuming computations rather than for an interactive use. | http://www.bioportal.uio.no/ | | Have some tools and instructions for use for phylogenomic analysis. Based off of tool name. | No | Yes | Yes | No | Yes | Yes | Yes | Yes |
| OpenHelix | own company | Mary E. Mangan | OpenHelix empowers researchers by providing a search portal to find the most relevant genomics resource and training on those resources; distributing extensive and effective tutorials and training materials on the most powerful and popular genomics resourcs; contracting with resource providers to provide comprehensive, long-term training and outreach programs. | http://www.openhelix.com/ | Must pay for training resources. | Based off of ABC order of tool or database names. Have some free resources. | No | Partially | Yes | No | Yes | No | No | No |
| Canadian Bioinformatics Workshops | bioinformatics.ca and supporters | Michelle Brazas | Provide workshops | http://www.bioinformatics.ca/ | Have won many education awards, Might have to pay to attend workshops | Host workshops around Canada and British Columbia on different bioinformatics topics. Such as: cancer genomics, metabolomics, thorough sequencing, microarray data analysis. | No | NA | Yes | NA | No | Yes | No | Yes |
| eusol | European Commission | Dr. R.M. Klein Lankhorst | The distributed bioinformatics platform aims at making state-of-the-art bioinformatics data and analyses available to all EU-SOL partners, which will be offered training in utilizing this resource for their research. | http://www.eu-sol.net/science/bioinformatics/portal-overview | Tomatoes information based. | Provide tools, training of those tools, and databases related to bioinformatics on tomatoes. | Yes | Yes | No | NA | Yes | Yes | Yes | Yes |
| BioStar | Unclear | Parnell Lindenbaum | is site's focus is bioinformatics, computational genomics and biological data analysis. We welcome posts that are detailed and specific, written clearly and simply, of interest to at least one other person somewhere | http://www.biostars.org/show/questions/ | Question answers rating forum | More of a question forum for bioinformatics. | Yes | NA | No | NA | Yes | Yes | NA | NA |
| ExPASy | SIB | SIB | ExPASy is the SIB Bioinformatics Resource Portal which provides access to scientific databases and software tools (i.e., resources) in different areas of life sciences including proteomics, genomics, phylogeny, systems biology, population genetics, transcriptomics etc. On this portal you find training resources from many different SIB groups as well as external institutions. | http://expasy.org/ | | | No | Yes | Yes | NA | Yes | No | Yes | Yes |
| EMBER Consortium | EMBER | | online practical training resources designed to introduce a range of bioinformatics services, databases and software available on the Web | http://www.ember.man.ac.uk | | Course, Question, QUIZZ | Yes | Yes | NA | NA | Yes | Yes | Yes | NA |
| The Bioinformatics Training Resource | BTR | | BTR is an organized collection of links to online tutorials, online courses, essays, book chapters, course syllabi, glossaries, bibiliographies of key papers, etc. In short everything that interested scientists need in order to train themselved in the emerging discipline of bioinformatics. | http://www.med.nyu.edu/rcr/rcr/btr/ | | | No | Yes | No | No | Yes | Yes | Yes | Yes |
| Bioinformatics | | | professional development courses for continuing scientific education. | http://www.bioinformatics.org/edu/ | use Moodle LMS tools | use Moodle site based tools | Yes | No | No | Yes | Yes | Yes | Yes | Yes |
| Virtual Academy of Bioinformatics | BioInfoBank | | Bioinformatics master degree programs collection of courses (and lectures inside courses) built around a subject. | http://lib.bioinfo.pl/programs/view/1 | | Formal academic course approach | Yes | Yes | No | No | Yes | Yes | Yes | Yes |
| Babraham Bioinformatics | Babraham Institute | | Collection of courses related to 30 bioinformatics research teams collaboration | http://www.bioinformatics.babraham.ac.uk/training.html | | Research topic focus tutorial | No | yes | No | No | Yes | Yes | Yes | No |
| OpenWetWare | Collaborative effort | | OpenWetWare is an effort to promote the sharing of information, know-how, and wisdom among researchers and groups who are working in biology & biological engineering | http://openwetware.org/wiki/ Wikiomics | | Wiki and collaborative | Yes | Yes | Yes | No | Yes | Yes | Yes | No |
| DNA Learning Center | | | The DNA Learning Center (DNALC) is the world's first science center devoted entirely to genetics education and is an operating unit of Cold Spring Harbor Laboratory, an important center for molecular genetics research. | http://www.dnalc.org/about/ | | cognitive teaching, 3D course | Yes | No | Yes | Yes | Yes | Yes | Yes | NA |

Table 2: BKTMS table for evaluation grades and scores calculation.

| Criteria | | | The Blackboard Learning System) - | Claroline 1.8.1 | | System | Moodle 1.9 | Moodlerooms joule | | | | | | The RPBS Project | | | e-proxemis | | | | | | | | Op | Canadian Bioinformatics | | | | | | | |
|---|---|---|---|---|---|---|---|---|---|---|---|---|---|---|---|---|---|---|---|---|---|---|---|---|---|---|---|---|---|---|---|---|---|
| | To | 1 | 7 | 6 | 7 | 7 | 7 | 7 | 5 | 7 | 6 | 6 | 3 | 2 | 4 | 5 | 7 | 3 | 7 | 5 | 4 | 4 | 6 | 4 | 5 | 4 | 6 | 6 | 3 | 7 | 5 | 3 | 5 |
| Interoperability | Ti | 1 | 5 | 5 | 6 | 4 | 5 | 5 | 4 | 5 | 5 | 5 | 0 | 1 | 1 | 4 | 6 | 4 | 4 | 3 | 3 | 2 | 5 | 5 | 3 | 5 | 4 | 4 | 2 | 5 | 4 | 2 | 4 |
| | Tl | 1 | 6 | 5 | 5 | 6 | 6 | 6 | 5 | 5 | 6 | 2 | 0 | 0 | 0 | 3 | 3 | 3 | 4 | 4 | 2 | 2 | 4 | 3 | 3 | 3 | 5 | 4 | 2 | 6 | 4 | 3 | 3 |
| | Ta | 1 | 3 | 4 | 4 | 3 | 8 | 3 | 3 | 4 | 6 | 7 | 4 | 5 | 4 | 5 | 3 | 2 | 5 | 5 | 3 | 4 | 5 | 4 | 2 | 6 | 7 | 6 | 5 | 3 | 6 | 5 | 6 |
| | Tc | 1 | 6 | 4 | 6 | 6 | 7 | 5 | 5 | 6 | 5 | 2 | 0 | 1 | 1 | 3 | 4 | 3 | 3 | 3 | 1 | 2 | 4 | 4 | 2 | 3 | 2 | 3 | 3 | 5 | 3 | 2 | 4 |
| Flexibility | Tf | 1 | 5 | 5 | 5 | 6 | 7 | 6 | 4 | 6 | 6 | 8 | 0 | 0 | 1 | 7 | 3 | 3 | 3 | 2 | 1 | 2 | 4 | 5 | 1 | 4 | 3 | 3 | 3 | 6 | 4 | 3 | 6 |
| | Te | 1 | 5 | 5 | 5 | 5 | 6 | 5 | 5 | 5 | 5 | 5 | 0 | 0 | 4 | 7 | 4 | 4 | 4 | 3 | 4 | 2 | 4 | 3 | 2 | 3 | 3 | 6 | 4 | 4 | 3 | 3 | 6 |
| | Tv | 1 | 3 | 4 | 3 | 3 | 7 | 4 | 4 | 4 | 4 | 2 | 4 | 0 | 4 | 5 | 4 | 4 | 4 | 2 | 2 | 6 | 6 | 5 | 2 | 6 | 3 | 8 | 6 | 4 | 4 | 2 | 6 |
| | Tp | 1 | 5 | 5 | 5 | 5 | 5 | 5 | 6 | 5 | 5 | 4 | 2 | 2 | 4 | 6 | 3 | 2 | 4 | 5 | 1 | 3 | 4 | 3 | 4 | 4 | 7 | 4 | 3 | 5 | 4 | 3 | 6 |
| | Tw | 5 | 6 | 5 | 6 | 5 | 6 | 6 | 6 | 5 | 5 | 3 | 1 | 1 | 2 | 7 | 2 | 2 | 5 | 2 | 0 | 2 | 6 | 3 | 0 | 3 | 5 | 3 | 3 | 5 | 5 | 2 | 6 |
| | Li | 1 | 5 | 5 | 5 | 6 | 6 | 5 | 4 | 5 | 4 | 2 | 0 | 0 | 2 | 3 | 3 | 2 | 5 | 3 | 1 | 1 | 3 | 2 | 3 | 5 | 6 | 3 | 2 | 6 | 3 | 3 | 6 |
| | Lc | 1 | 6 | 6 | 6 | 5 | 7 | 4 | 4 | 6 | 4 | 1 | 2 | 2 | 1 | 6 | 8 | 5 | 4 | 2 | 4 | 3 | 5 | 3 | 4 | 4 | 3 | 5 | 2 | 4 | 4 | 3 | 6 |
| | Ll | 1 | 5 | 5 | 5 | 4 | 4 | 5 | 5 | 5 | 5 | 3 | 3 | 3 | 4 | 2 | 3 | 2 | 3 | 3 | 2 | 3 | 3 | 1 | 2 | 4 | 5 | 3 | 3 | 6 | 6 | 1 | 6 |
| | La | 1 | 3 | 4 | 4 | 4 | 6 | 4 | 3 | 4 | 4 | 5 | 3 | 3 | 3 | 5 | 3 | 1 | 5 | 5 | 4 | 4 | 5 | 3 | 2 | 6 | 6 | 5 | 5 | 3 | 4 | 2 | 6 |
| | Lp | 1 | 6 | 5 | 5 | 5 | 6 | 6 | 4 | 5 | 5 | 5 | 1 | 1 | 1 | 3 | 6 | 3 | 4 | 4 | 2 | 2 | 4 | 2 | 5 | 5 | 4 | 6 | 3 | 5 | 4 | 3 | 4 |
| LO Design and usability | Lu | 1 | 6 | 4 | 5 | 5 | 5 | 5 | 4 | 5 | 5 | 4 | 1 | 2 | 4 | 3 | 7 | 3 | 4 | 6 | 3 | 2 | 4 | 2 | 4 | 4 | 4 | 5 | 4 | 7 | 5 | 2 | 4 |
| | Ls | 1 | 4 | 5 | 5 | 5 | 6 | 5 | 5 | 5 | 6 | 2 | 1 | 1 | 2 | 2 | 3 | 2 | 4 | 6 | 4 | 3 | 4 | 1 | 3 | 3 | 7 | 4 | 3 | 6 | 5 | 3 | 3 |
| | Lv | 1 | 6 | 5 | 5 | 5 | 5 | 5 | 4 | 5 | 4 | 3 | 1 | 1 | 0 | 2 | 5 | 3 | 6 | 6 | 5 | 3 | 6 | 4 | 5 | 4 | 5 | 5 | 4 | 5 | 6 | 4 | 6 |
| | Lt | 1 | 6 | 5 | 6 | 6 | 5 | 5 | 5 | 6 | 5 | 4 | 0 | 0 | 0 | 1 | 5 | 1 | 5 | 4 | 2 | 1 | 6 | 3 | 2 | 2 | 6 | 3 | 2 | 6 | 4 | 1 | 4 |
| LO Retrievability | Lr | 1 | 5 | 5 | 5 | 5 | 6 | 5 | 5 | 5 | 5 | 2 | 4 | 4 | 4 | 3 | 6 | 3 | 4 | 3 | 3 | 3 | 4 | 1 | 4 | 4 | 4 | 3 | 2 | 4 | 5 | 1 | 4 |
| | Ld | 4 | 4 | 4 | 4 | 4 | 4 | 4 | 4 | 4 | 7 | 6 | 3 | 3 | 3 | 4 | 5 | 2 | 4 | 3 | 3 | 2 | 3 | 1 | 3 | 2 | 4 | 3 | 3 | 5 | 6 | 1 | 4 |
| **Technical Criteria** | **T** | 1 | **6** | **5** | **5** | **5** | **6** | **5** | **4** | **5** | **6** | **4** | **3** | **3** | **3** | **5** | **6** | **4** | **6** | **4** | **3** | **3** | **5** | **3** | **4** | **5** | **6** | **5** | **3** | **6** | **5** | **3** | **5** |
| Quality of pedagogy approach | Pa | 1 | 5 | 5 | 5 | 5 | 6 | 5 | 5 | 5 | 6 | 4 | 3 | 3 | 3 | 3 | 4 | 2 | 6 | 4 | 3 | 2 | 5 | 3 | 4 | 3 | 2 | 4 | 3 | 5 | 4 | 3 | 3 |
| | Pf | 6 | 5 | 5 | 5 | 5 | 6 | 5 | 5 | 5 | 6 | 3 | 1 | 1 | 2 | 3 | 3 | 2 | 5 | 2 | 1 | 1 | 4 | 2 | 3 | 3 | 4 | 3 | 3 | 4 | 4 | 3 | 3 |
| | **P** | 3 | **5** | **5** | **5** | **5** | **5** | **5** | **5** | **5** | **6** | **4** | **3** | **4** | **3** | **3** | **4** | **2** | **5** | **4** | **2** | **2** | **5** | **2** | **4** | **3** | **4** | **4** | **3** | **6** | **4** | **3** | **3** |
| | Ic | 5 | 4 | 5 | 4 | 4 | 4 | 4 | 4 | 5 | 7 | 5 | 4 | 4 | 4 | 4 | 5 | 4 | 7 | 5 | 4 | 3 | 6 | 5 | 4 | 4 | 5 | 5 | 4 | 5 | 4 | 4 | 4 |
| | Il | 4 | 4 | 4 | 4 | 4 | 5 | 4 | 4 | 4 | 5 | 7 | 1 | 1 | 3 | 4 | 3 | 3 | 6 | 6 | 3 | 4 | 4 | 2 | 4 | 5 | 4 | 5 | 5 | 6 | 4 | 4 | 5 |
| Dominant idea definition | Id | 5 | 4 | 3 | 3 | 3 | 5 | 3 | 3 | 3 | 4 | 4 | 3 | 3 | 3 | 3 | 6 | 4 | 4 | 4 | 5 | 3 | 4 | 1 | 5 | 5 | 4 | 4 | 4 | 5 | 5 | 3 | 5 |
| | **I** | 4 | **4** | **4** | **4** | **4** | **5** | **4** | **4** | **4** | **5** | **6** | **3** | **4** | **4** | **4** | **5** | **4** | **6** | **5** | **4** | **3** | **5** | **4** | **4** | **5** | **4** | **5** | **4** | **5** | **4** | **4** | **5** |
| ty | Cd | 1 | 5 | 5 | 5 | 5 | 5 | 5 | 5 | 5 | 7 | 4 | 3 | 2 | 2 | 5 | 4 | 4 | 3 | 5 | 3 | 1 | 5 | 4 | 5 | 4 | 4 | 3 | 3 | 6 | 5 | 3 | 4 |
| | Ci | 1 | 7 | 6 | 6 | 6 | 6 | 6 | 7 | 6 | 5 | 5 | 6 | 6 | 5 | 6 | 6 | 5 | 4 | 4 | 2 | 2 | 6 | 4 | 6 | 5 | 5 | 5 | 5 | 5 | 6 | 2 | 5 |
| Canal capacity | Cc | 1 | 4 | 4 | 4 | 4 | 5 | 4 | 4 | 4 | 5 | 3 | 1 | 2 | 2 | 3 | 4 | 3 | 4 | 6 | 3 | 2 | 7 | 3 | 6 | 3 | 3 | 3 | 3 | 6 | 4 | 3 | 4 |
| **ication criteria** | **C** | 1 | **5** | **5** | **5** | **5** | **6** | **5** | **5** | **5** | **6** | **4** | **4** | **4** | **4** | **5** | **5** | **4** | **4** | **5** | **3** | **2** | **6** | **3** | **5** | **4** | **4** | **4** | **4** | **6** | **5** | **3** | **4** |
| | O1 | 1 | 8 | 0 | 4 | 7 | 5 | 3 | 5 | 4 | 0 | 0 | 0 | 0 | 0 | 0 | 4 | 1 | 6 | 3 | 0 | 0 | 0 | 0 | 0 | 0 | 0 | 0 | 0 | 3 | 5 | 0 | 0 |
| Student Tracking | O2 | 1 | 2 | 1 | 3 | 5 | 6 | 5 | 6 | 3 | 0 | 2 | 0 | 0 | 0 | 0 | 4 | 1 | 5 | 3 | 0 | 0 | 3 | 0 | 3 | 0 | 0 | 2 | 0 | 2 | 4 | 0 | 0 |
| - | O3 | 1 | 6 | 1 | 4 | 6 | 4 | 6 | 4 | 2 | 0 | 4 | 0 | 0 | 0 | 3 | 3 | 1 | 6 | 2 | 0 | 0 | 4 | 0 | 2 | 0 | 6 | 0 | 0 | 5 | 4 | 0 | 0 |
| Automated Testing Management | O4 | 1 | 8 | 0 | 3 | 5 | 5 | 4 | 5 | 2 | 0 | 0 | 0 | 0 | 0 | 0 | 6 | 1 | 4 | 3 | 0 | 0 | 0 | 0 | 0 | 0 | 0 | 0 | 0 | 2 | 5 | 0 | 0 |
| - | O5 | 1 | 6 | 1 | 3 | 4 | 3 | 5 | 4 | 4 | 0 | 0 | 0 | 0 | 0 | 2 | 2 | 1 | 2 | 2 | 0 | 0 | 2 | 2 | 0 | 0 | 0 | 0 | 0 | 5 | 5 | 0 | 0 |
| | **O** | 1 | **7** | **1** | **4** | **4** | **5** | **4** | **5** | **4** | **0** | **1** | **0** | **0** | **0** | **1** | **3** | **1** | **4** | **3** | **0** | **0** | **2** | **1** | **2** | **0** | **2** | **1** | **0** | **4** | **4** | **0** | **0** |
| | | **10 57** | | | | | | | | | **5** | | | | | | | | | | | | | | | | **4** | | | | | | |

# A Micro-Level Analysis of Energy Consumption within ICT Organisations: A Holistic Perspective

*Girish Bekaroo*[†], *Suraj Juddoo*[†], *Chandradeo Bokhoree*[‡] *& Colin Pattinson*[‡‡]

[è] School of Science and Technology,
Middlesex University (Mauritius Branch Campus)

[H] School of Sustainable Development and Tourism,
University of Technology, Mauritius

[Å] Faculty of Arts, Environment & Technology,
Leeds Metropolitan University, UK

***Abstract*— The ICT industry has been growing at a fast rate down the previous years in different countries around the world. As a matter of fact, the energy consumption of this industry accounts for 2% of the world's carbon emission. Consequently, this has led to an adverse impact on the global environment, mainly in the form of climate change. As such, it is becoming increasingly important to properly manage our energy consumption. To be able to optimize energy consumption within the ICT industry, it is of utmost importance to understand where and how energy is consumed within organizations in the sector. Accordingly, this paper holistically focuses on the key areas of energy consumption within ICT organizations. It also addresses key features towards green practices, for example, in the business process and green technology applications.**

***Keywords*— Micro-Level Analysis, Green ICT Organisations, Sustainable Energy Consumption***

## I. INTRODUCTION

In recent years, the Information and Communications Technology (ICT) industry has been one of the fastest growing industries in several countries around the world [1]. Businesses today are dependent on the use of ICT resources in the main forms of computing and networking technologies in routine business operations due to the various advantages provided by their adoption [2]. However, it has been estimated that during a normal working day within companies, computers are in use for around 4 hours and idle for another 5.5 hours on average [3]. Similarly, energy consumed in un-optimized business processes can also contribute to energy consumption within the same organization [4]. A typical example involves an employee having to travel in order to meet a supplier to get a quotation, where a simple phone conversation could have been more energy efficient.

As such, energy inefficiency due to the unsustainable use of resources within such organizations directly impacts the environment negatively, mainly in the form of climate change which is currently being experienced in several countries around the world. Studies have estimated that ICT accounts for 2% of worldwide carbon emissions which is the same level of $CO_2$ emissions as the airline industry [5]. In order to determine the key steps towards improvement of energy efficiency within ICT organizations, it is of utmost importance to gain a holistic understanding of a typical ICT organization's energy consumption. This paper presents a study made on the different key areas of energy consumption within ICT organizations identified in a previous work [34]. The study focuses on ICT organizations which refer to companies whose profit making revolves around ICT, even though such organizations may vary in terms of different parameters including size, location, type of organization and internal processes [34]. Examples of ICT organizations include software development companies, business process outsourcing companies, call centers, telecommunications companies and computer shops.

## II. ANALYSIS OF KEY ENERGY CONSUMPTION AREAS

Within ICT organizations, the different key areas of energy consumption include equipments consuming power, business processes, the building, business products and employee operation [34]. An analysis on how energy is consumed within each identified key area is made as follows:

### *A. Equipments Consuming Power*

In Physics, the terms energy and power are closely related, where energy is defined as the total amount of work done during a time period and power is defined the rate at which a system carries out the work [6]. Both power and energy are measured in watts. Within ICT organizations, several electrical and electronic devices are present which consume energy. Among ICT resources within data centers in general, most power is consumed in four main categories namely ICT load, cooling system, power conversion (e.g. from power distribution sources) and hostelling (including lighting and other overheads) as depicted in Fig. 1 [7,8].

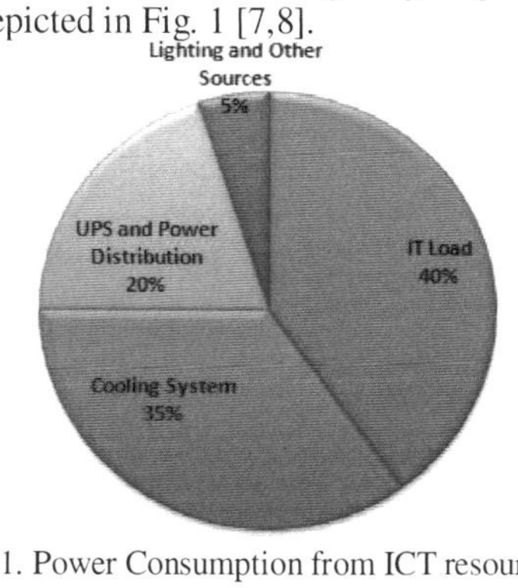


Fig. 1. Power Consumption from ICT resources

These different categories are better described as follows:

1. *Critical computational systems*

A big percentage of the energy consumed in this category is from ICT load, which accounts for around 40% of overall consumption involving use of servers, computers, networks and storage devices. In this category, most of the energy, representing 62% of this category's total energy, is spent on computers, servers and monitors [7]. Servers, which need to be in constant waiting mode in order to service requests from clients, consume a lot of power via their memory and processors. Even though server processors are controlling and restricting their power usage, the amount of memory used within a server is continuously growing and this growth adversely increases power consumption by computer memory [9,10]. The approximate percentage of power consumption by the different sub categories in critical computational systems are better depicted in Fig. 2.

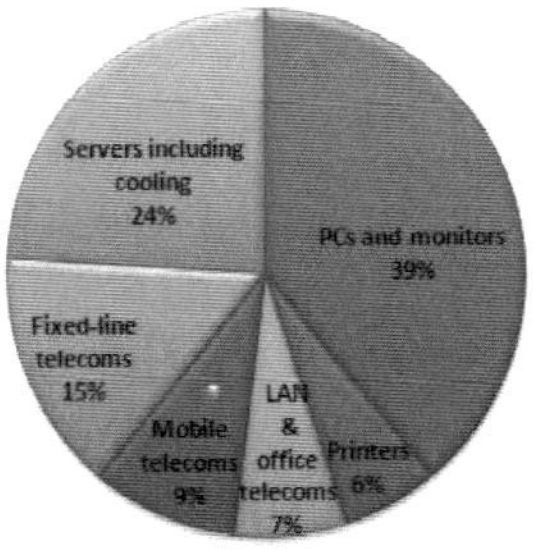


Fig. 2. Power Consumption from ICT equipments

Likewise, networking is a big source of power consumption representing 31% of the total power consumed from ICT equipments, as shown in Fig. 2. Most ICT organizations have got their Local Area Network (LAN), interconnected by different networking devices including hubs, routers, switches, and bridges; and interlinked by different transmission media where the most common one being the copper-based twisted pairs cabling [11]. Among the networking devices within a LAN, the network switch is considered as most power hungry device [12]. This is because network switches conduct different network infrastructure tasks and in the process, a considerable amount of power is used. Finally, among ICT equipments, a significant 6% of total power consumption is by printers. Different types of printers are used in organizations including laser printers, inkjets and thermal printers [12]. These devices consume power during the production of hard copies of output.

Now, in terms of the power breakdown across different components of a computer, studies based on a laptop computer connected wirelessly to the Internet and sharing data [13], showed that the central processing unit (CPU) and network adapters consume most of the power (34%). The CPU consumes power during processing while the wireless network card is responsible for providing the networking capabilities of the computer. Other important sources of power consumption on the same chart is from the Liquid Crystal Display (LCD) backlight for display, 3D or graphics card for enhanced display, power supply for power provision and conversion, the hard disk for secondary storage, and memory in the form of random access memory (RAM) and read only memory (ROM). The complete power breakdown is shown in Fig. 3.

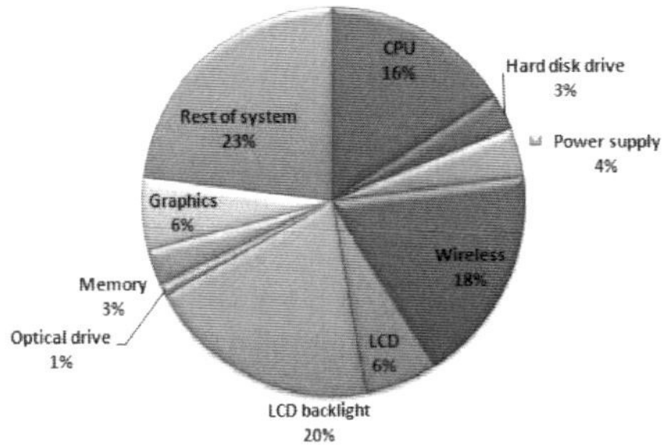


Fig. 3. Laptop Power Consumption Breakdown

Besides power consumption from devices, a computer system involves continuous processing of instructions fed to the machine, which contributes to power and energy consumption. The set of instructions to perform a specific task is known as a software and different software having the same aim (for example, web browser and movie player) utilize different amount of energy especially in two ways, namely when running a workload and while being idle [14]. Workload energy is when active computation is being performed and idle energy is when no useful work is being done by the software. This is similar to energy consumption by devices where both during processing and when being idle, power is consumed. The difference in software energy consumption is due to several reasons where some of the most common ones being the platform used for software development, middleware used as the operating system, coding style of the software engineer and complexity of the features within the program [15].

2. *Cooling systems*

Virtually every watt expended in computer processing, power supplies, lighting, among others, is eventually turned into heat and an organization must make arrangements to remove that heat. Cooling, which is the removal of waste heat generated by these electronic equipments usually consumes around 35% of the overall power consumed in data centers [8]. Determination of the power consumed from cooling within energy intensive environment is difficult because of external factors, including the outside air temperature. For instance if the outside air temperature is higher than that within the organization's building, then a considerable amount of energy is needed to dump large quantities of heat outside. Other factors affecting energy consumption from cooling systems include [8]:

ð method of cooling used
ð effectiveness of the design and installation
ð level of maintenance applied to installation
ð solar gain of the organization's building
ð use of air or water economizers that take advantage of cooler conditions

3. *Power conversion*

This category includes UPS and power distribution units and accounts for around 20% of power consumption within organizations [8]. Electric current is conveyed to a computer system in two stages. In the first stage, power is supplied to the computer case from electrical wall socket via the power cord to the computer. Today, due to high competition in the market, suppliers are selling different types of power conversion units with different price ranges and energy efficiency [16]. However, several companies tend to go for cheaper and inefficient power supplies, which inefficiently convert alternating current (AC) to direct current (DC) thereby increasing power consumption.

The UPS consumes a big amount of electricity during power conversion [17]. The most popular power conversion type used by such devices is the online double conversion method, which takes in the mains voltage and converts it to direct DC in order to charge standby mode batteries within the UPS. This DC current is then fed into an inverter, which presents clean mains voltage to the IT load. The reason why this method is popular is because it fully segregates the load from the incoming supply and the direct connection of the inverter to the batteries, meaning that the supply is never interrupted at all. However, the negative consequence is that the AC to DC conversion, followed by a DC to AC conversion and the output transformer is very inefficient leading to 12 to 15% of the power is lost as heat in the UPS [8]. This heat dispersed to the air is also to be handled by cooling techniques. For smaller systems, transformer-less version of UPS is recommended, which run more efficiently with only 3% of losses.

*4. Hostelling*

This includes everything else that do not form part of the above categories. This category accounts for the remaining 5% of power consumption and cater for lighting and all the different building overheads in the organization, such as consumption by smoke detectors and alarms, among others [7, 8]. Good lighting is extremely important within organizations since it provides a comfortable visual working environment to employees. This becomes even more important if the building hosting the company has not been sustainably designed to use sunlight for lighting purposes.

*B. The Building*

In the world, buildings are considered as one of the biggest consumers of energy, accounting for 25% to 33% of all energy use and a comparable amount of GHG emissions [18]. Also, buildings account for approximately 16.7% of the world's fresh water withdrawals, 25% of its wood harvest, and 40% of its material [19]. In addition to power consumed within buildings as described in the previous section, building hosting an organization in itself is a source of energy consumption. Previous studies showed that buildings account for 33% of total energy use in Canada, 17% of total energy use in Mexico and 40% of total energy use in the U.S [20,21].

The placement, design, and construction materials used can affect the energy efficiency of buildings . For instance, during a sunny working day, the amount of heat absorbed by the building is high, which raises the internal temperature and energy consumed of the building and as such, more powerful cooling techniques have to be adopted to reduce the heat within the building. Similarly, the positioning of the building has an effect on its energy flow and is important to consider during building design in order to make most out of the sunlight and wind energy [22,23]. In the past, much emphasis was not put on sustainability factors during building construction. The energy consumption of unsustainable buildings is higher and poses the following major negative consequences to organizations:

1. higher expenses from utility bills (water, electricity, gas, etc) thus affecting the profit after tax of organizations
2. does not raise awareness on `going green_
3. reduced productivity of employees

Not adhering to sustainable building construction techniques can lead to energy loss from different resources including water, sunlight, air, etc. For example, instead of using lights within buildings, glass panes can be used to allow natural lighting of office areas. Likewise, instead of cooling via fans or air conditioners within a building, natural airflow can be used similar to rainwater or recycled water, which can be re-used for irrigation or cleaning [23].

*C. Business Processes*

The collection of tasks designed in order to produce a specific output is referred to as a business process, which is another source of energy consumption within organizations [4]. Example of business processes include logistics process, accountability process or procurement process. Business Process Management (BPM) refers to the theories, methods, and techniques which support the design, composition, enactment, assessment, and supervision of business processes [24,25]. During a business process, work is done in order to accomplish goals and in the process, energy is consumed. However, the amount of energy consumed relies on the amount of work done. For example, consider the supplier payment process where an accountant within an organization has to get money transferred to another organization. If this process is done traditionally as depicted in Fig. 4, there is the involvement of a messenger who has to physically move (drive or via some other transport means) to the bank and then after performing the transfer, move back to the office.

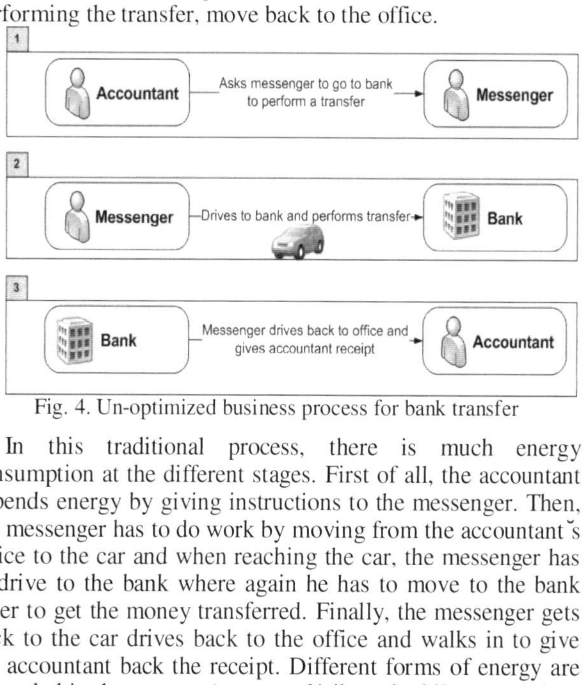


Fig. 4. Un-optimized business process for bank transfer

In this traditional process, there is much energy consumption at the different stages. First of all, the accountant expends energy by giving instructions to the messenger. Then, the messenger has to do work by moving from the accountant`s office to the car and when reaching the car, the messenger has to drive to the bank where again he has to move to the bank teller to get the money transferred. Finally, the messenger gets back to the car drives back to the office and walks in to give the accountant back the receipt. Different forms of energy are expended in the process (e.g. petrol/oil used while commuting) where the business process could have been optimized as shown in Fig. 5. This is one among the various examples of un-optimized business processes which are present within ICT organizations.

Fig. 5. Optimized business process for bank transfer

In general, ICT is deemed to have positive effects on the environment, where through the use of ICT resources, energy efficiency can be increased via automation, monitoring and management, dematerialization, and travel substitution [26]. In this money transfer scenario, if the organization has access to internet banking facilities, the accountant can himself login to the bank's website via the internet and then transfer the money within a few minutes. Much energy is saved in the process which is quicker and environmental friendly at the same time. Furthermore, even today, very few organizations have defined business processes that contain definitions for energy management. For instance, if the business practices of an organization are depleting a finite resource over a short period of time, then the organization is not expected to be around for long [27]. In this context, resources refer to supplies used over time to operate a business and these include energy, cash, water, lighting, staffs, among others. Unsustainable business processes can be in the form of bad or improper production planning and organization, incorrectly using equipments, excessively consuming paper, inappropriate document shipping, un-optimized travelling and logistics, insufficient automation, among others. These inefficiencies contribute to increasing energy costs while at the same time affecting the environment [28]. However, there is a lack of experimental validation on how much energy is consumed or wasted from these different business processes.

### D. *Business Products and Services*

The product(s) of an organization is result of an act or a process established by the organization which it commercializes in order to make money. In organizations, products are in the form of goods, software solutions, hardware and services provided to clients. In the design and manufacturing phase of a product, it is essential to consider its life cycle. A product's lifecycle consists of all the different activities that go into the fabrication, transportation, usage and disposal of the product. In other words, the life cycle of a product consists of a different phases starting from raw materials extraction, through design and creation, processing, fabrication, packaging, use, re-use, recycling to finally end with disposal as waste [29]. During each of the above phases of the life cycle of a product, from its cradle to grave, work is done and also energy is consumed. The energy consumed during the different phases of the product life cycle for different types of products can be in different forms, ranging from thermal energy involved during the manufacturing process, to mechanical energy involved during the usage of the product until its disposal. The energy hidden through the life cycle of products is also referred to as grey energy. As an example, consider the manufacturing stages of a Laptop within a company specialized in the manufacturing of laptops as shown in Fig. 6.

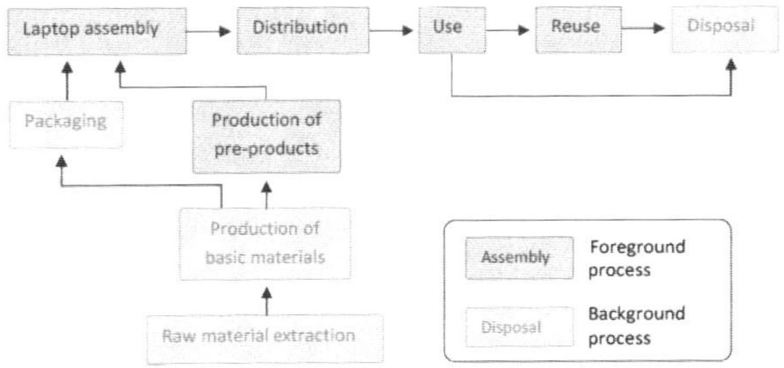


Fig. 6. Life cycle of a laptop [28]

A considerable amount of energy and resources is needed for the building up of a laptop [30,31]. In the manufacturing process of a laptop, energy is consumed at all the different stages starting from the raw material extraction, to the production of the basic materials, packaging, assembly, distribution, use and reuse, before finally being disposed. A study found that the manufacturing process of an average desktop computer with a monitor needs approximately 1.8 tons of total raw materials and other natural resources [32]. Furthermore, the production process of the same needs 22 kg of chemical products, 240 kg of fossil fuels and 1,500 kg of water. Upon the end of the lifecycle of the product, many parts which needed a big amount of energy in the fabrication process (e.g. semiconductors) are destroyed during the end of product life, in the recycling process. These destroyed parts are never recovered back again. As such, it is very important to efficiently use such products and if possible, re-use existing products of same type via product upgrade or recycling.

Likewise, energy is consumed during work done while providing services by a particular business [33]. Providing services to clients contributes to profit making by businesses, similar to the selling of business products. During the complete lifecycle of a particular service, energy is consumed when work is done at the different stages of the service life-cycle including planning, delivery, operation and management. Even at the end of the life-cycle, materials used (e.g. paper, CDs, etc) in the early stages have to be disposed or reused and again this contributes to the overall energy consumption by the organization.

### E. *Employee Operation*

By doing work within organizations, energy is consumed by all the employees [38]. For example, a software engineer writing codes on a computer system during a particular working day has to use his hands and brains for writing and thinking respectively. Similarly, a cleaner moves from one place to another in the office in order to clean the floor and the office facilitator commuting in order to purchase office supplies. The amount of energy consumed to do a piece of work varies according to the amount of work done as well as some internal and external factors to the employee. Internal factors relate to the personal characteristics of the employee and these include working experience, skill set, motivation level, and age, among others [34]. External factors originate from the external or working environment and these include building room temperature, amount of light available, and noise level of the environment. Similarly, different employees within the same organization can take different amount of time to do the same allocated task or piece of work, affected by the above discussed internal and external factors. By putting in different amount of effort or by consuming different amount of time to do an allocated task, this implies different employee also consume different amount of energy to do the same piece of work.

Furthermore, employees are critical in cutting down energy waste within organizations. Recent studies have shown that employees could save UK organizations £500 million and 2 million tonnes of $CO_2$ where each individual employee˘s efforts can help to reduce 220 kg of $CO_2$ emissions [35]. Similarly, the European Environment Agency showed that between 2005 and 2009, the electricity consumption per employee showed an annual growth at a rate of 1.3% during the same period due to the increased use of air conditioning and of ICT and electronic equipments [36]. Also, in a survey conducted on 300 respondents [37], ICT managers were asked to deduce the awareness level for the other employees of their organizations towards energy efficiency. Results showed that less than one fifth of organizations monitor how employees reduce their energy consumptions.

## III. Towards Sustainable Energy Consumption

As a potential solution to reduce energy consumption in each key energy consumption area within ICT organizations, green technologies and green ICT best practices can be adopted [39, 40]. Typical examples of green ICT best practices include switching off devices after use, adoption of computer power management techniques, using energy efficient devices and printing minimization [41]. Furthermore, green building techniques, green business process design practices and green manufacturing techniques can be adopted to improve the energy efficiency of buildings, business processes and products respectively. Some common green building design practices include optimized building orientation in order to minimize solar heat gains, rainwater drainage systems to collect rain water for reuse in toilets and for irrigation and use of solar panels to supplement power consumption within the building. As discussed earlier, employees are critical in cutting down energy waste within organizations. To improve employee awareness in :going green˘, green education, in the form of training on environmental or sustainability topics can help employees see why being environmentally conscious is important and how it helps both themselves and the company.

## IV. Future Works

As described in the paper, there is still lack of experimental validation on the different key areas of energy consumption within ICT organizations. The micro-level analysis conducted in this study helped to further break down these identified key areas in order to facilitate experimentation. The energy consumed within each key area can now be experimentally verified in order to answer the following main questions on:

1. the energy consumption breakdown of the key areas (in terms of percentage),
2. energy consumption optimization for each key area,
3. the identification of which energy consumption area has more negative consequences on the environment,
4. compatibility of the identified key energy consumption areas with varying types of ICT organizations.

However, before the experimentation process, the energy consumption metrics and measurement techniques to be used within each key area have to be identified. With the resources available (e.g. metrics, devices and tools), experimentation can then be conducted in varying types of ICT organizations in order to confirm the above questions. Furthermore, a holistic dynamic framework can be created with the aim to optimize energy consumption within ICT organizations based on the previous work [34], complemented with the micro-level analysis in this paper. The framework will also help towards energy efficiency improvement and cost reduction within ICT organizations.

## V. Conclusion

In order to reduce energy consumption within ICT organizations, it is of utmost importance to understand the key sources of energy consumption within such organizations. This paper holistically breaks down and discusses the key areas of energy consumption within ICT organizations in terms of its electrical and electronic devices, business processes, building, business products and employee operation. It also identifies avenues for different works to be conducted in the area of green technologies.

## VI. References

[1] KPMG, (2006), "Information Technology" [online], A report by KPMG for IBEF, DAVOS 2006, Accessed on: 10 Feb 2013, Available at: http://www.arc.unisg.ch/

[2] B. Choudhuri, S. Maguire, and U. Ojiako, (2009), "Revisiting learning outcomes from market led ICT outsourcing", Business Process Management Journal, Vol. 15 Iss: 4, pp.569 - 587

[3] MILLER School of Medicine University of Miami, (2008), "Computer power management "[online], Accessed on: 13 Feb 2013, Available at: http://it.med.miami.edu/x1159.xml

[4] B. Unhelkar , (2011), "Green IT Strategies and Applications: Using Environmental Intelligence", CRC Press

[5] Gartner, (2007), "Gartner Estimates ICT Industry Accounts for 2 Percent of Global CO2 Emissions" [online], Accessed on: 12 Dec 2012, Available at: http://www.gartner.com/it/page.jsp?id=503867

[6] A. Beloglazov, R. Buyya., Y. Lee, and A. Zomaya, (2011), "A Taxonomy and Survey of Energy-Efficient Data Centers and Cloud Computing Systems", Advances in Computers, vol. 82 , 48-111.

[7] L. Curtis, (2008), "Environmentally Sustainable Infrastructure Journal", The Architecture Journal , pp. 2-8.

[8] G. Sauls, (2008), "Measurement of data centre power consumption", Falcon Electronics Ltd, Accessed on: 15 Jan 2013, Available at: https://learningnetwork.cisco.com/servlet/JiveServlet/previewBody/3736-102-1-10478/measurement%20of%20data%20centre%20power%20consumption.pdf

[9] L. Minas, B. Ellison, (2009), "Energy Efficiency for Information Technology: How to Reduce Power Consumption in Servers and Data Centres (Computer System Design)" [Paperback], Intel Press.

[10] A. Chandrakasan, and R. Brodersen, (1995), "Minimizing Power Consumption in Digital CMOS Circuits", Proceedings of the IEEE, Vol.83, No. 4 , 498-523.

[11] R. Winkelman, (2012), Cabling, University of South Florida, Accessed on: 12 Mar 2013, Available at:
http://fcit.usf.edu/network/chap4/chap4.htm

[12] N. Chilamkurti, S. Zeadally, and F. Mentiplay, (2009), "Green Networking for Major Comp4onents of Information Communication Technology Systems", EURASIP Journal onWireless Communications and Networking.

[13] A. Mahesri, and V. Vardhan, (2004). "Power Consumption on a Modern Laptop". Workshop on Power Aware Computing Systems, 37th International Symposium on Micro-architecture (PACS).

[14] B. Steigerwald, C. Lucero, A. Chakravarthy, and A. Agrawal, (2012), "Energy Aware Computing - Powerful Approaches for Green System Design". Intel Press.

[15] C. Wilke, S. Gotz, S. Cech, J. Waltsgott, and R. Fritzsche, (2011), "Aspects of Software˘s Energy Consumption", Institut fur Software und Multimediatechnik.

[16] PCGuide, (2001), "Power" [online], Accessed on: 18 Feb 2013, Available at: http://www.pcguide.com/ref/power/index.htm

[17] R.L. Sawyer, (2004), "Calculating Total Power Requirements for Data Centers", American Power Conversion

[18] W. Hong, M. Chiang, R. Shapiro, and M. Clifford, (2007), "Building Energy Efficiency - Why Green Buildings are key to Asia's Future", Asia Business Council.

[19] D. Roodman, N. Lessen, (1995), "A Building Revolution: How Ecology and Health Concerns are Transforming Construction", Worldwatch Paper 124 (pp. 5), Washington, DC: Worldwatch Institute.

[20] Canada Green Building Council, (2007), "Green Building Toolkit", Accessed on: 25 Feb 2013, Available at: http://www.cagbc.org/

[21] Commission for Environmental Cooperation, (2008), "Green Building in North America - Opportunities and Chellenges", Accessed on: 26 Feb 2013, from: http://www.cec.org/Storage/61/5386_GB_Report_EN.pdf

[22] UNEP. (2011). "Building for the future. Nairobi" from United Nations Environment Programme.

[23] E. Tay, (2011), "Adding the green touch with technology", Accessed on: 2 Mar 2013, Available at: http://www.greenbusinesstimes.com/2011/04/26/adding-the-green-touch-with-technology-news/

[24] A. Nowak, F. Leymann, and D. Schumm, (2011), "The Differences and Commonalities between Green and Conventional Business Process Management", Proceedings of the International Conference on Cloud and Green Computing (pp. 569-576), IEEE Computer Society.

[25] M. Weske, (2007), "Business Process Management: Concepts, Languages", Berlin Heidelberg: Springer-Verlag.

[26] J.J. Berleur, M.D. Hercheui, and L.M. Hilty, (2010), "What Kind of Information Society? Governance, Virtuality, Surveillance, Sustainability, Resilience", IFIP Advances in Information and Communication Technology (pp. 236-247), New York: Springer.

[27] M. Blake, (2011), "What makes a business 'unsustainable'?", Accessed on: 12 Mar 2013, available at: http://thegreenasiagroup.com/2011/12/01/what-makes-a-business-un-sustainable/

[28] A. Bashir, (2010), "The Energy Efficient Enterprise", Accessed on: 14 Mar 2013, available at: http://www.worldenergy.org/documents/congresspapers/240.pdf

[29] A. Jensen, L. Hoffman, B. Møller, A. Schmidt, (1997), "Life Cycle Assessment (LCA) - A guide to approaches, experiences and information sources", Environmental Issues Series.

[30] A. Hoang, (2009), "Life Cycle Assessment of a laptop computer and iIts contribution to Greenhouse Gas Emissions", San Diego National Uni.

[31] A. Ciroth, and J. Franze, (2011), "LCA of an Ecolabeled Notebook - Consideration of Social and Environmental Impacts Along the Entire Life Cycle", Accessed on: 12 Mar 2013, available at: http://www.greendeltatc.com/uploads/media/LCA_laptop_final.pdf

[32] E. Williams, (2004), "Energy Intensity of Computer Manufacturing: Hybrid Assessment Combining Process and Economic Input-Output Methods", Environmental Science Technology, Volume 38.

[33] Rixon, C. (2009), "How to Cut IT Energy Consumption Using Business Service Management", Accessed on: 19 Mar 2013, Available at: http://www.eweek.com/c/a/Green-IT/How-to-Cut-IT-Energy-Consumption-Using-Business-Service-Management/

[34] G.Bekaroo, C. Bokhoree, and C.Pattinson, (2012), "Towards Green IT Organisations: A Framework for Energy Consumption and Reduction", International Journal of Technology, Knowledge, and Society, Vol 8.

[35] The Guardian, (2012), "Employees could save UK organisations £500m and 2 million tonnes of $CO_2$", Accessed on: 20 Mar 2013, Available at: http://www.guardian.co.uk/sustainable-business/employee-engagement-cut-carbon-save-money

[36] European Environment Agency, (2012), "Energy intensity in the service sector (ENER 024)", Accessed on: 20 Mar 2013, Available at: http://www.eea.europa.eu/data-and-maps/indicators/energy-intensity-in-the-service-sector/assessment-2

[37] C. Kogelman, (2011), "CEPIS Green ICT Survey - Examining Green ICT Awareness in Organisations: Initial Findings", The European Journal for the Informatics Professional, 6-10.

[38] T. Schwartz, C. McCarthy, (2007), "Manage Your Energy, Not Your Time", Harvard Business Review, Accessed on: 18 Mar 2013, Available at: http://hbr.org/2007/10/manage-your-energy-not-your-time

[39] S. Murugesan, (2008), "Harnessing Green IT: Principles and Practices", IT Professional, 24-33.

[40] G. Sissa, (2011), "Utility Computing: Green Opportunities and Risks", The European Journal for the Informatics Professional, 16-21.

[41] M. Bluejay, (2011), "How much electricity do computers use?", Saving Electricity, Accessed on: Apr 14, 2013, Available at: http://michaelbluejay.com/electricity/computers.html

# The Interpretation of Maintainability Quality Attribute into Assessed Requirements

Mona Mohamed Abd Elghany
Assistant Professor in FAD department
Arab Academy for Science & Technology
Egypt
E-mail: mabdelghany2000@gmail.com

Nermine Mohamed Khalifa
Assistant Professor in BIS department
E-mail: nerminek@gmail.com

Marwa Mohamed Abd Elghany
Assistant Professor in BIS department
E-mail: marwam@aast.edu

*Abstract*— **Maintainability denotes the ease of a defect correction or software changes that is extremely dependent on how simple the software can be understood and tested. The flexibility of a system is strongly linked to the maintainability of a system. High maintainability is essential for systems that are to go through periodical revisions and for products that are developed quickly. Most of the researchers do not have the adequate knowledge to define how maintainability quality factor should be assessed. This paper aims to claim the entities to be used in placing maintainability requirements and describe them into metrics. Then the main contribution of the proposed manuscript is the interpretation of the vague external maintainability quality attribute or in other words the imprecise non-functional requirements into specific structured functional requirements for implementation in the software system project.**

*Keywords— Maintainability Attribute; Software Maintenance; Maintainability Metrics; Maintainability Requirements.*

## I. Introduction

With the upraising trend in products' complexity and size, software maintenance tasks have turned to be more and more problematic. Developing high quality software should be one of the main targets of any software engineering process independent of the development paradigm in use [1]. In software engineering, quality characteristics are typically categorized as internal or external. That is, the design of any software product is said to possess a number of measurable internal characteristics having a causal effect on external quality characteristics, such as maintainability.

Maintainability is a critical quality attribute that requires providing significant resources (human, technical, financial) during software lifetime. Software maintenance ought not to be a design second thought. Maintainable software products and fielded software should be updated hence enhanced much more rapidly and at a lesser cost and also should be reused thus alleviating costly update time. As well, faults diagnosis and correction reduces system downtime, ensures system availability and helps in meeting delivery schedules.

Studies conducted by the Standish Group Report of period, between 2002 and 2004, indicate that more than 70% of software projects were totally collapsed, exceeding the estimated delivery due and did not meet user requirements or even cancelled before issuing the software [2]. Since hundreds of software applications alternatives exist, more focus, effort and resource on software maintenance is needed for that. The effort needed for maintaining software after its issue might exceed 70% of overall effort spent in development [3]. In terms of financial resources needed, more than 80% of estimated funds might be directed to maintenance. Accordingly, early prediction of maintainability is desirable given that software maintenance has long been regarded as one of the most resource-consuming development phases. For example, reference [4] and [5] previously suggested that over 60 percent of the total lifetime cost of a system is spent on maintenance.

Various development artefacts, such as requirements, design and code documents have disclosed the majority of software faults prior to testing and enhanced the ability to make meaningful assessments and predictions of software product quality. Quality assessment is indeed problematic and the puzzling problem is to identify what is meant by users' demand of a robust, reliable, efficient and maintainable system [6]. Reference [7], for instance, provides a definition for software quality but does not give clues for assessment; the machine learning approach outlines an assessment nevertheless not so clear to quality definition. The software quality assessment became a vital aspect in software development. Continuous computer application could not be broadly employed without controlling efficient maintainable software. The software quality assurance for both developers and users is essential. Nevertheless, it is not easy to assess software quality in software engineering field.

Previous quality models provide more like characteristics of an art rather than an engineering discipline. There occur no common acceptable guidelines for quality assessment. Several quality frameworks have been suggested in the literature, though no one has been broadly practised in software industry or even appeared as a potential standard. Quality criteria are expressed in terms of abstractions with no detailed specification. It is difficult to operationalize in practice. Further, reference [8] ensured that standardisation of concepts and terminology is missing in the software quality research, conveying the disjointed nature of the research area. Also, there exist very few references concerning software quality or quality management literature in addition to inconsistency with relevant international standards in software quality such as reference [7].

Current approaches for software quality assessment depend on the measurement of time and effort to accomplish tasks associated with the software quality attribute. These approaches generate objective measures but do not provide the representation condition of assessment for the quality attribute. Most of the existing models adopted for software development process use the result of design, implementation and test phases; whereas the assessment of the software desired characteristics in the early phase of software development process would better support risk management and effort estimation associated with software projects.

Robert Charette states that *"satisfying the non-functional requirements is often more vital than satisfying the functional requirements in terms of the system's perceived success or failure in real world environment"* [6]. Therefore, it is crucial to fulfill not only the functional requirements or services that the system should serve, but also the characteristics representing the non-functional requirements that influence the quality of the global system architecture [9]. The selection of an appropriate architecture for a software system is an open research problem that has been extensively tackled in the literature [10]. Accordingly, dealing with quality attributes in the shape of non-functional requirements does not provide developers with enough information about what kind of artefacts to use to satisfy such requirements. The features represent particular functionalities that can be built into a software system. Since functional requirements describe the functions that the software is to execute, these functional requirements need to be explicitly specified, just like any other functionality. Consequently, the proper description of these functionalities in the requirements specification leads to the expected built-in into the system.

## II. Overview on Maintainability Practice

Software maintenance is the doings of faults correction in the software system, to adapt it to environment changes. Maintenance takes from 40 up to 80 percent of software costs hence it is possibly the most vital phase of the software life cycle [11], [12], [13]. Reference [14] emphasized that systems built with modern development methods, such as analysis, prototyping and computer-aided software engineering are more reliable than others. Reference [12] views maintenance as the way for constructing something slightly different from what has been constructed before. The software quality attribute which is referring to maintenance is maintainability that is the ease of software system maintenance performance. It is crucial to discuss the maintainability quality in software system development and how common requirements on maintainability are expressed. The maintainability practice corresponds with theories in literature that are categorizing the maintainability requirements into requirements' specifications as briefly presented in the following.

Maintainability is a key attribute in the dependability matrix bounded by [15]. In some cases, the maintenance activities could be handled by software users while commonly the vendor may take such responsibilities. In rare cases, both may contribute side by side to diagnose and undertake appropriate actions. Built-in features could automate a request delivery of maintenance needed. Enhancing the maintainability of software would affect the software quality positively. McCall (1977) proposed a matrix for quality attributes and investigated the different software phases of application development, adaptation and maintenance as cited in reference [3]. McCall highlights the importance of simple software, modular applications, well-documented software and tools usage as key enablement of smooth maintenance. A number of limitations were pointed out for such matrix such as neglecting the complexity of some applications and how to trace system function in structured programs.

Maintainability is the cost of allocating and fixing errors [16]. Reference [17] updated McCall's definition and expressed maintenance as the non-operational costs associated with a product after a successful user acceptance test. Without a proper system product documentation the cost rises and the maintainability drops [17]. According to reference [18] maintainability is an attributes' set carrying the effort required to perform specified modifications. The ISO 9126-1 Quality Model defined maintainability as the ability of the software product to be modified including corrections, improvements or adaptations of the software to environment's changes as cited in [19]. Maintainability or modifiability or extensibility deals with the ability to add unspecified future functionality. Then maintainability is the extent to which updating the software is facilitated to satisfy new requirements without affecting the operability of the software system, i.e. activities such as changing functions, correcting functions, adding and deleting functions must be easy to accomplish. This requires the following questions to be answered when measuring this attribute: Has a reserved memory capacity kept for future extension? Does the software allow for a change in its modular tasks? So as the maintainable software product should be well-documented.

The term maintainability could be categorized into "corrective, adaptive and perfective maintenance" [20]. Corrective maintainability can be outlined as the ability to undertake certain type of maintenance activities for corrective or evolving purpose. The adaptive maintenance might take place in order to align the application with operational setting of environment that can be referred to change in hardware or database management system. Other cases of adaptive maintenance might be related to applying change in the software itself such as limited functionalities. Sometimes, maintenance may intend to optimize the software performance, update to newer version or enhance its interface and system acceptance. And perfective is concerned with improvements performed for users' fulfillment.

Reference [21] defined maintainability from two different perspectives: reparability and evolvability. Reparability is more related to repairing software by dealing with errors raised and consequences resulting from such errors. The evolvability perspective deals with managing the ultimate change of user requirements and needs for more features and function to be embedded in the existing software. More involvement of human factors within different phases of software development would save evolving effort that might be needed in further stages. Evolvability is related to systems modularity that should rely on clear system specification so system maintenance could address the targeted modules with accurate and precise amendments.

Additionally, reference [22] classified maintainability as general and specific. General denotes the adoption of software engineering principles which are supposed to provide high maintainability. Specific denotes the ease of changes that could be done. The standard IEEE 830-1998, IEEE Recommended Practice for Software Requirements Specifications [23] outlines a proposal for software requirements specifications which endorses that maintainability has to specify software attributes related to the ease of software maintenance itself such as requirements for modularity, interface, complexity, etc. Reference [24] describes software quality requirements like maintainability as generally specified instead of poorly specified in industrial requirement specifications.

From ISO/IEC 9126-1:2001 perspective, the quality characteristic of maintainability is defined as the level of effort required for modifying the software product and can be sub-divided into four measurable sub-characteristics: analysability, changeability, stability and testability. These sub-characteristics are defined in [18] as:

- Analysability: is the software product ability to diagnose failures' causes for the parts to be amended;
- Changeability: is the software product ability to specify modifications to be applied;
- Stability: is the software product ability to avoid unanticipated impacts from modification;
- Testability: is the software product ability to validate the modified software.

## III. Maintainability Metrics

The ISO 9126-1: 2001 [18] suite of maintainability metrics included:

- Analysability Metric: Failure Analysis Efficiency (FAE) that is equal to Sum (T)/N, where T is the time taken to analyse each cause of failure (or time taken to locate a software fault) and N is the number of failures;
- Changeability Metric: Modification Complexity (MC) that is equal to Sum (T) =N, where T is the work time spent on each change and N is the number of changes;
- And Stability Metric: Modification Impact Localization (MIL) that is equal to A/B; where A is the number of emergent adverse impacts (failures) in the system after modifications and B is the number of modifications made.

The ISO/IEC 14764:2006 maintenance standard states that a modification request can be classified as either a correction (corrective and preventive activities) or enhancement (adaptive and perfective activities). This is because software products typically include a large number of business rules and associated business processes, which have been shown to be the most unstable part of software applications [25]. This suggests a potential increase in the rate and number of corrective and perfective tasks required to keep up with rapidly changing business requirements [26]. Corrective maintenance refers to modifications necessitated by errors (that is defects) in a software product [27]. Perfective maintenance refers to modifications performed to provide new functionality or improvements for users [27].

On the whole, maintainability requirements are typically expressed in terms of a time metric, such as mean repair time, mean maintenance time, or administrative and logistics delay time; and a physical aspect, such as the replaceable items that must be available and modular [28]. Maintainability involves all restoring actions, not just hardware but as well consistent with the software maintenance. Reference [29] claimed that this concept includes two levels: the first level entails immediate problem resolution and the second entails software modifications for corrective or perfective maintenance. Mean time to repair (MTTR) applies to first level maintenance and is categorized as a quantitative requirement that is concerned with the restoration of the system back to its action, whereas modularity does cover the second level of software maintainability and could be considered as a qualitative requirement that tackles design and coding practices.

Moreover, reference [29] addressed the software maintainability requirements at the first level as follows:

- system monitoring capabilities;
- problem cause diagnosis;
- ease of installation;
- operator control capabilities for corrective actions;
- success detection possibility and service restoration;
- restoration time display to convey affected software components.

And at the second level, requirements should be addressing [27]:

- code readability and conformance to coding standards and conventions;
- documenting design;
- abstraction and modularity;
- analysis and ability of support systems detection such as simulators and drivers.

## IV. Adopted Methodology

The authors' main objective is to identify the maintainability quality attributes affecting the software project in an organization; this necessitates the need to use a mixture of methods to collect data: from IT professionals and project managers through the conduction of semi-structured interviews, from official documents and through direct observation, to obtain a complete picture about a real maintainable software project and its essential role in the organization. The design of the conducted interviews was based mainly on the extensive literature review and guidance from the authors and their content was pre-tested with practitioners and academic experts. Minor alterations were made as a result of this pre-test. Interviews were conducted with a relatively small sample size of around 40 project managers (including requirements' engineers, system designers, software developers, system operational support, software maintenance specialists, testers, etc.) whom currently and previously were engaged in managing software development projects from the Information and Documentation Centre and also staff members of the Computing & Technology Faculty, due to their expertise in programming and analysis, within the collaborating institution.

Any ambiguity on part of the interviewees during the pilot test was subsequently transcribed into the final questionnaire version. The study dealt with a concrete construct of particular importance to the surveyed individuals. Participants were asked simple questions; both questionnaires and interviews used similar schedules, leading to good alignment between research methods. The interviews were semi-structured, with the interviewer designing uptake questions based on interviewees' responses. The core interview schedule included questions like the following:

1. Please give example(s) of an assessment activity you used recently in your development in accordance to the concerned attribute.

2. Describe the purpose of the assessment activity you have just mentioned.

3. Illustrate other development practices that could be considered for usage?

4. What do you think is the best way to assess the attribute of interest?

Also, in order to ensure that all participants directly addressed the above four conceptions, at the end of the semi-structured interview about assessment and its purposes, participants were asked to indicate the extent to which they agreed or disagreed with the suggested prompts taken directly from the questionnaire, relating to each conception. Potential responses to each interview question were recorded to ensure that each question sought sufficient and appropriate data. The resultant list of questions was reviewed and modified to respond to comments. In most cases, the participant's answer to the questionnaire prompt matched the researcher's holistic judgment of the interview data. Then for next stage, project managers would be asked to rate each question according to its relevant importance to the attribute under investigation. The type of system being developed impacts the project management methods i.e. commercial systems development differ from medical systems and would differ again from an internet based accounting application. Maintainability is a crucial factor in web-based applications.

The highly structured questionnaire method and the semi-structured interview provided evidence of consensus between methods. The questionnaire generally took participants approximately 20 minutes to complete, the interviews usually lasted for about an hour, giving more time to expose the variabilities and inconsistencies within human thinking as advised by reference [30] in (2005), and [31] in (1992). The questionnaire means scores for these related factors averaged out multiple constructs. The authors tried to fulfill the following in the conduction of this mixed method; structured questionnaire and data interview obtained from practitioners to examine their conceptions of assessment and ascertain the degree to which methodological artefacts impact on the attribute of concern which is maintainability,

1. Structured and similar interview prompts and questionnaire items.

2. Separate data collection through a short time period.

3. Concrete presentation of the object of interest.

4. Anchoring participants' responses to a common context.

5. Focusing on simple internal structure and avoiding hierarchical & complex structures.

6. Using consensus and consistent procedures.

The main advantage of using mixed method research is that data gained through different methods complement each other, overcoming weaknesses in individual methods. Pairing structured interviews with structured questionnaires would create methodological richness [32]. The mixed method demonstrate that triangulation through distinctly different methods can lead to confirmation and explanation of the circumstances of occurrence.

Produced questionnaire, shown below in Table I, was employed after the modification of the questions according to the conducted interviews and was put into its final form until the authors felt confident that the questionnaire could be used for the intended survey which is to explore the maintainability requirements that have not yet been fully discovered.

TABLE I. PRODUCED QUESTIONNAIRE FROM THE CONDUCTED INTERVIEWS

| **Question Element** | | **Importance Degree** | | | | |
|---|---|---|---|---|---|---|
| **First: Questions relating to Corrective Maintainability** | NA | 1 | 2 | 3 | 4 | 5 |
| 1. Verifies the program output and sequential order of instructions for debugging purpose. | | | | | | |
| 2. Enables operator control capabilities for corrective actions like add, delete and modify. | | | | | | |
| 3. Records the time taken to repair a defect. | | | | | | |
| 4. Provides time limit for debugging and error correction. | | | | | | |
| 5. Able to define time period between maintenance operations. | | | | | | |
| 6. Capable of reporting problem diagnosis with its affected software components. | | | | | | |
| 7. Offers system monitoring capabilities. | | | | | | |
| **Second: Questions relating to Perfective Maintainability** | | | | | | |

| Questions relating to Architecture and Design | NA | 1 | 2 | 3 | 4 | 5 |
|---|---|---|---|---|---|---|
| 8. Provides independent modules and separate specified program functions to be performed individually to ease plug in and reduces redundant coding. | | | | | | |
| 9. Indicates the sequence, dependency and functionalities of software modules as well as the data structure and its control flow. | | | | | | |
| 10. Identifies the number of (modules, comment lines, total lines of code, decision points, variables and processors used to indicate the degree of complexity). | | | | | | |
| 11. Provides factory abstraction pattern and template throughout the system. | | | | | | |
| 12. Indexing the software documents and its functions to facilitate the tracing task. | | | | | | |
| 13. Offers a suite of regression test cases to accompany the system can be a way to reduce the risk of introducing faults. | | | | | | |
| **Questions relating to Documentation** | **NA** | **1** | **2** | **3** | **4** | **5** |
| 14. Indicates ownership agreement to make it legal for the user to use and modify. | | | | | | |
| 15. Provides complete software documentations with precise description of software module, system functionalities, design, used programming language and software operational setting. | | | | | | |
| 16. States critical success factors of software implementation. | | | | | | |
| 17. Mentions the type of amendments that had been applied previously. | | | | | | |
| 18. Utilizes one set of coding standards: flowchart construction, input/output processing, error processing, module interfacing and naming of modules and variables. | | | | | | |
| 19. Delivers documentation in English language and in paper based form as well as in a unified mark-up language. | | | | | | |
| 20. Delivers documentation on the database schema in form of entity-relationship diagrams and the diagrams containing attributes and operations of the classes as well as the relations between them. | | | | | | |
| 21. Follow naming standardization encompass the systematic assignment of mnemonic terms chosen to suggest their own interpretation and one-to-one correspondence between variable names throughout the program. | | | | | | |
| 22. Defines global variables in a common glossary with their names the same in all routines to provide consistency. | | | | | | |
| 23. Follow presentation style standardization such as: (1) Indentation and spacing; (2) Use of capitalization; (3) Use of headers; (4) Source code listings; (5) Conditions under which comments are provided and format to be used; (6) And size of code aggregated. | | | | | | |
| **Third: Questions relating to Adaptive Maintainability** | **NA** | **1** | **2** | **3** | **4** | **5** |
| 24. Entails automated request delivery for maintenance. | | | | | | |
| 25. Specifies a time limit indicating how long a version change may take. | | | | | | |
| 26. Enables update that can be made without interruption. | | | | | | |
| 27. Requires specific process steps being performed. | | | | | | |

## V. CONCLUSION

A large number of researchers admitted that quality attributes such as maintainability can hardly be defined precisely or measured quantitatively despite the existence of several publications proposing systems for assessing and estimating the effort needed for software maintenance. Most of these studies focus on the determinants that enable maintenance such as software documentation, capabilities of technical and development team and so on.

For instance, published papers produce predictive systems for maintenance effort (i.e. maintainability) such as that of reference [33]. Any maintenance effort measurement is affected by the time needed to perform a maintenance activity using a specific set of factors like the documentation available, the maintenance engineers, the testing extent made after maintenance and the expertise of the maintenance team. Yet, maintainability remains an unspecified measure of the maintenance ease and maintenance effort should be measured through a specific set of activities that should be performed on any given system. The assessment of the maintainability requirements in a software project system can be obtained from the research field questionnaire conducted to date. Software developers are capable of getting tangible specification for the maintainability software quality attribute that is simple to be achieved through the proposed procedures presented in the questionnaire. The maintainability improvements should leverage the initial expenditure and decrease the total lifetime cost of the system. Moreover, it is expected that improvements in maintainability will be more pronounced in industrial scale systems containing large services and requiring more complex maintenance tasks.

This paper demonstrates a scientific relation between an abstracted software artefacts (maintainability features) and the external quality attribute (maintainability). Despite the fact that such demonstration needs the experts' opinion for the assessment of the quality attribute yet it is different than the expert assessments employed to acquire quantified criteria for validation like that existed in references [34] and [35]. The content validity of the structured questionnaire has been assessed through reviewing pertinent literature related to maintainability quality attribute and the conduction of semi-structured interviews with projects managers' experts. As well, criterion based validity has been assessed by relating associated quality attribute features. Then the developed questionnaire could be useful for both researchers and practitioners in grasping the critical related features of software maintainability attribute in order to obtain the needed software system quality, the business is looking for. Hence, it provides a road-map for improving software quality as well. Specifically, a manager could inspect the software project periodically, assess changes and consequently take appropriate action to ensure continuous improvement in software quality

Furthermore, this questionnaire can be so helpful to define if a set of questions assumed to be associated with a specific subjective attribute, actually do relate to this attribute. This could be done next through measuring the difference in variance between the responses to the questions; using an ordinal scale value. Then statistics could be used to express the relevance assessment of questions to the attribute of interest and denote the attribute with respect to a measurement theory. Cronbuch alpha is to be used in the statistical analysis to provide score values for the entity's subjective attribute. The results that would be obtained from the true classes of the entities can be employed to develop an independent and unbiased assessment of a predictive system for a quality attribute to give definitive values for the quality attribute of software entities. Moreover, it should be taken into account to continue the evaluation of software quality attributes through other assessment methods and iterated refinement cycles. In any case, the selected quality attribute and its associated features provide a starting point in cases where argumentation is needed for further improvement.

## ACKNOWLEDGMENT

Sincere gratitude goes to the colleagues and staff members in the College of Management & Technology and in the College of Computing Science in the Arab Academy for Science & Technology, as well as practitioners in the Office and Documentation Center for their participation and consultations in the adopted approach.

## REFERENCES

[1] N.E. Fenton, and S.L. Pfleeger, Software Metrics: A Rigorous and Practical Approach, second ed. Course Technology, 1998.

[2] Maria Haigh, "Software quality: non-functional software requirements and IT-business alignment," Software Quality Journal, (18) 361–385, DOI 10.1007/s11219-010-9098-3, (2010).

[3] Roger S. Pressman, Software Engineering: A Practitioner's Approach, 7/e, R. S. Pressman & Associates, Inc., McGraw-Hill, ISBN: 0073375977, 2010.

[4] H. Zuse, A Framework of Software Measurement, Walter de Gruyter, Berlin, (1998).

[5] R.S. Pressman, Software Engineering: A Practitioner's Approach, 6th ed., McGraw-Hill, (2005).

[6] K. Weigers, Software Requirements, Redmond, Wash: Microsoft Press, (1999).

[7] ISO/IEC-9126, Software Engineering - Product Quality Model, International Organization for Standardization, Geneva (Switzerland), (2004).

[8] R. Maier, Organisational concepts and measures for the evaluation of data modelling, in: S. Becker (Ed.), Developing Quality Complex Database Systems: Practices, Techniques and Technologies, Idea Group Publishing, Hershey, USA, (2001).

[9] Francisca Losavio, Ledis Chirinos, and Maria A. Pérez, "Quality Models to Design Software Architecture," Proceedings of the technology of Object-Oriented Language and System, (2001).

[10] M. Shaw, and D. Garlan, Software Architecture: Perspectives on an Emerging Discipline, Upper Saddle River, N.J.: Prentice Hall, New Jersey, (1996).

[11] J. Foster, Cost Factors in Software Maintenance, in Computer Science Department: University of Durham, NC, (1993), available at: http://www.jsjf.demon.co.uk/thesis/Thesis.html

[12] R.L. Glass, Facts and Fallacies of Software Engineering, Addison-Wesley, (2002).

[13] B.P. Lientz, , E.B. Swanson, and G.E. Tompkins, Characteristics of Application Software Maintenance, Communications of the ACM, vol. 21, pp. 466-471, (1978).

[14] S.M. Dekleva, "The Influence of the Information Systems Development Approach on Maintenance," MIS Quarterly, vol. 16, pp. 355-372, (1992).

[15] J.C. Laprie, "Dependability: Basic Concepts and Terminology, Dependable Computing and Fault-Tolerant Systems," Vol. 5, J.C. Laprie, (ed.), New York: Springer-Verlag, 1992.

[16] J.A. McCall, P.K. Richards, and G.F. Walters, Factors in software quality, Vols. I-III, Rome Air Development Centre, Italy, AD/A-049-014/015/055, Nat'l Tech. Information Service, Springfield, (November 1977).

[17] Roman Fitzpatrick, Software Quality: Definitions and Strategic Issues, School of Computing Report, Advanced Research Module, Staffordshire University, (April 1996).

[18] ISO/IEC 9126-1:2001 Software Engineering: Product Quality - Quality Model, International Organisation for Standardisation/ International Electro-technical Commission, (2001).

[19] F. Losavio, L. Chirinos, A. Matteo, N. Levy, and A. Ramdane-Cherif, "ISO quality standards for measuring architectures", the Journal of Systems and Software, Vol. 72, pp.209-223, (2004).

[20] Mario Barbacci, Mark H. Klein, Thomas A. Longstaff, and Charles B. Weinstock, Quality Attributes, Technical Report of Software Engineering Institute ESC-TR-95-021, Carnegie Mellon University Pittsburgh, Pennsylvania, (1995).

[21] Khairuddin Hashim, and Elizabeth Key, "A Software Maintainability Attributes Model," Malaysian Journal of Computer Science, Vol. 9, No. 2, pp. 92-97, 1996.

[22] L. Bass, P. Clements, and R. Kazman, Software Architecture in Practice, Reading, Mass.: Addison-Wesley, (1998).

[23] IEEE Std. 830-1998, IEEE Recommended Practice for Software Requirements Specifications, (1998).

[24] J. Bosch, Design & Use of Software Architectures, Addison Wesley, 2000.

[25] W. Wan Kadir, and P. Loucopoulos, "Relating Evolving Business Rules to Software Design," Journal of Systems Architecture: The EURO-MICRO J., vol. 50, no. 7, pp. 367-382, (2004).

[26] T. Erl, SOA: Principles of Service Design, Prentice Hall, (2007).

[27] ISO/IEC/IEEE, ISO/IEC 14764:2006, IEEE Std. 14764-2006: Software Engineering: Software Life Cycle Processes - Maintenance, International Organisation for Standardisation, (2006).

[28] John D. Parr, and Patrick C. Larter, Standardisation of Reliability/Maintainability/Availability Metrics for USAFSCN Common User Element, Proc. Ann. Reliability & Maintainability Symp., (Jan 1999).

[29] Myron Hecht, Karen Owens, and Joanne Tagami, "Reliability-Related Requirements in Software-Intensive Systems," IEEE, pp.155-160, (2007).

[30] F. Marton, & W.Y. Pong, "On the unit of description in phenomenography, Higher Education Research and Development," 24(4), 335-348, (2005).

[31] M.F. Pajares, " Teachers' beliefs and educational research: Cleaning up a messy construct," Review of Educational Research, 62(3), 307-332, 1992.

[32] C. Antaki, & M. Rapley, "Questions and answers to psychological assessment schedules: Hidden troubles in 'quality of life' interviews, " Journal of Intellectual Disability Research, 40(5), 421-437, (1996).

[33] L. Yu, S. R. Schach, K. Chen, & J. Offutt, "Categorization of common coupling and its application to the maintainability of the linux kernel, " IEEE Transactions on Software Engineering, 30(10), 694–706, (2004).

[34] D. Coleman, D. Ash, D. Lowther, & P. Oman, "Using metrics to evaluate software systems maintainability," IEEE Computer, 27(8), 44–49, (1994).

[35] A. Melton, D. Gustafson, J. Bieman, & A. Baker, "A mathematical perspective for software measures research," IEE/BCS Software Engineering Journal, 5(5), 246–254, (1990).

# Using Graph Theoretic Approach to Digital Steganography


Nasreddin Bashir El Zoghbi
Dean, Dept. of Computer Science & I.T
Tripoli University
Tripoli, Libya
nzoghobi@yahoo.com

P.G.V.Suresh Kumar
Dept. of Computer Science & I.T
Adama Sci&Tec University
Adama, Ethiopia
pendemsuresh@gmail.com

Getahun Mekuria
Deputy Scientific Director
Addis Ababa Institute of Technology
Addis Ababa, Ethiopia
getahun4433@gmail.com



**Abstract**— Steganography literally means secret writing. The technique has been used in various forms for 2500 years or long. It has found its application in various fields including military, diplomatic, personal and intellectual property applications. Briefly stated, Steganography is the term applied to any number of processes that will hide a message within an object, where the hidden message will not be apparent to an observer. The paper describes the concept of finding natural relationship between a digital cover and a message. The relationship can be used to hide the information in cover without actually replacing or distorting any useful bits of the cover. It introduces a concept called sustainable embedding of message in a cover using natural relationship and representing it using graph theoretic approach.



**Keywords- Extra bytes, graph theoretic approach, pure steganography, secret key steganography, sustainable, natural embedding, spatial resource, bipartite graph, maximum bipartite matching, steganalysis.**


## I. INTRODUCTION

Steganography is the art of invisible communication. Its purpose is to hide the very presence of communication by embedding messages into innocuous-looking cover objects. Each steganographic communication system consists of an embedding algorithm and an extraction algorithm. To accommodate a secret message in a digital cover, the original cover is slightly modified by the embedding algorithm. The result is modified cover object that contains the secret message and it is called stego object. The important requirement for a steganographic system is its detectability by an attacker with probability not better than random guessing, given the full knowledge of the embedding algorithm, including the statistical properties of the source of cover object. Of course the stego key is not revealed. The most commonly used steganographic method is the Least Significant Bit (LSB) replacement. It works by embedding message bits as the LSBs of randomly selected pixels. A secret stego key shared by the communicating parties usually determines pixel selection.

The popularity of LSB embedding is due to its simplicity as well as the false belief that modifications of LSBs in randomly selected pixels are undetectable because of the noise commonly present in digital images of natural scenes. However, flipping the bits of the LSB plane does not occur naturally. The even pixel values are either unmodified or increased by one, while odd values are either decreased by one or left unchanged. This imbalance in the embedding distortion is utilized to mount successful attacks. The image in figure 1(a) is modified to embed "Graph Theoretic Approach" to get stego in figure 1(b). Through the naked eye, it is nearly impossible to detect any difference but any steganalysis tool can very easily find the presence of some message in the cover, given the cover 1(a).

(a) (b)

Figure 1

The image is of size 100x100 pixels and 24 bit color, so there are total of

100x100x3 + 54 bytes = 30,054 bytes in the

file. Even using LSB replacement technique, roughly

$$\frac{30054}{8} \cong 3756\,bytes$$

are available to hide a message of 3756 characters. There are a few extra bytes also available in any image. Can it be utilized for the purpose? Can a message be hidden in a cover without replacing any useful bits? These are few questions that we try to answer through this paper by introducing a graph theoretic approach to steganography. Before explaining the concept let us have a brief description of types of Steganography in use today.

## II. TYPES OF STEGANOGRAPHIC METHODS

The Steganography technique used today can be broadly classified into three categories: Pure Steganography, Secret Key Steganography and Public Key Steganography.

### PURE STEGANO GRAPHY

It is defined as a Steganographic system that does not require the exchange of a cipher such as a stego-key. This method of secret communication is treated as least secure means of communication. The sender and receiver rely upon the presumption that no other parties are aware of this secret mes s age. But the amateur hackers who are working 24x7, can scan the cover (stego) using various tools available

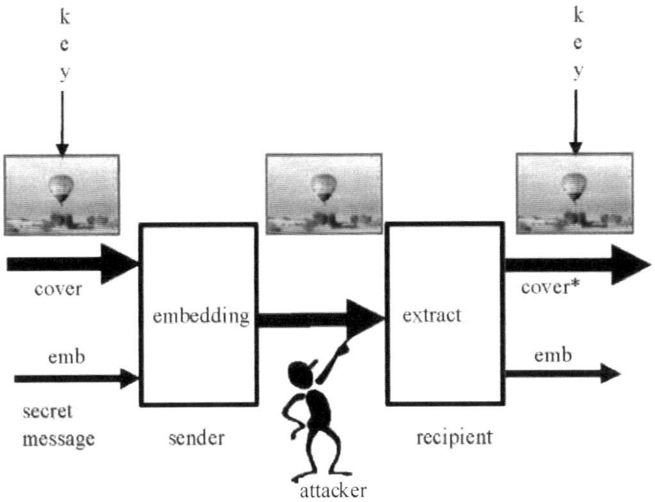


Figure 2

today to guess the presence of a possible secret message and can either alter or destroy it on the way.

### SECRET KEY STEGANOGRAPHY

It is a method that involves exchange of stego-key pre or post communication of secret message steganographically. Secret Key Steganography takes a cover message and embeds the secret message inside of it by randomized technique. The random key that forms the secret key is also called stego-key. Only the communicating partners know the stego key and can reverse the process and read the secret message. Secret key steganography is more secure than pure steganography because only those parties who know the secret key can extract the secret message.

### PUBLIC KEY STEGANOGRAPHY

It uses the concepts of public key cryptography [13]. Public key steganography is defined as a steganographic method that uses a public key and a private key to secure the communication between the parties wanting to communicate secretly. The sender will use the public key during the encoding process and the private key, which has a direct mathematical relationship with the public key, can decipher the secret message. Public key Steganography provides a more robust way of implementing a steganographic system because it can utilize a much more robust and researched technology in Public Key Cryptography. Before any unwanted parties could intercept the secret message they have to first suspect the use of s teganography and then they have to find a way to crack the algorithm used by the public key system. In this way it provides multiple layers of security.

The schematic diagram shown in the figure 2 explains the secret key steganography. Despite the security provided to steganographic method by stego key, bits replacement incorporated in cover file provides enough statistics to the hacker to guess the presence of message and classifying the med ia as stego.

To overcome this limitation of Steganography, a graph theoretic approach is suggested where message is treated as naturally embedded without either replacing or exchanging the useful color bits of a cover file.

## III. GRAPH THEORETIC APPROACH

A graph theoretic approach can be described combining meanings of three different words: graph, theoretic and approach. 'Graph' is a branch of mathematics dealing with the properties of diagrams to study the arrangements of objects and relationships between objects. 'Theoretic' is concerned primarily with theories or hypothesis rather than practical considerations; called "Theoretical science". Setting aside this classical definition of theoretic, this term may be taken in this context as "concept of data structures used to store a graph in Computer science". An 'approach' is described as a method used or steps taken in setting about a task, problem, etc. When the three words are combined, we may interpret "graph theoretic approach" as "a method that uses graph data structure in principle to solve a problem." When it is used to solve a steganographic problem, it is called "Graph theoretic approach to Steganography". There are two ways of using graph theoretic concept in digital steganography.

(i) Find relationship (if required) between smallest data unit of message and a group of such smallest unit of cover object and represent the relationship using a graph. If required, hide the relationships in the zero bytes of cover.

(ii) Use a graph as cover object and find redundancy in its feature like node or segment or its attributes and embed secret message in it.[9]

In the case of (ii) a data structure for storing graph has to be used so that features like node, segment and points constituting a segment should be stored [9]. In case of (i) it is explored to find association between bits string in cover and bit string in secret message. In case such association is found then following issues need to be addressed to implement the graph theoretic approach to digital steganography.

(i) What data structure should be used to represent such association?
(ii) And how this data can be embedded or assumed to be embedded in the cover?
(iii) What stegokey can be used between the communicating partners?

In the following sections of the paper, possible approach is described. Authors of the paper are working in this area.

## IV. FINDING RELATIONSHIP

In digital world, every cover media like image, video, audio, speech etc can be treated as collection of data units. Each data unit is nothing but string of bits. Say the size of data units be k bits. Thus a cover can be treated as an array of such data units. Similarly a secret message to be embedded in the cover, may be treated as an array of data units each of size k bits. Let size of message array is n. The size k can be adjusted in a way to avoid any padding. An embedding factor can be defined as ratio

$$m = \frac{\text{size of cover array}}{\text{size of message array}}$$

It means that potentially **m** data units are available in cover for one data unit of secret message. Thus cover data units may be arranged in two-dimensional array of size n x m. A maximum bipartite matching can be found using the natural presence of secret message in cover. Detail is given in the next section while finding a way to embed the relationship in cover.

For example, if m = 4 and k = 2, then one of the data unit "01" of message is said to be naturally present in the corresponding m data units of cover "10 00 01 10" at $3^{rd}$ place. Also, if we take additional modulo 4 of " 10 00 01 10" then it is also equal to 01 and hence it can be concluded that the part of secret message is naturally present in the corresponding part of the cover. There can be many other ways to find such relationship. If such correspondence is achieved for every data unit of the secret message then the message is embedded without any replacement of bits in the cover. But such ideal situation is rarely available.

In case some mismatch is found then it may be explored that $i^{th}$ data unit may corresponds to some combinations of $j^{th}$ block of m data units of cover file. If it is found, then the association can be represented as an arc (i, j). There may be one to many associations because one data unit may correspond to multiple m data units of cover file. At the end there may be some data units in message that are not associated to any of the block in cover. Thus, there are three possibilities:

(i) Direct relationship is found between $i^{th}$ data unit of message and $i^{th}$ block of cover.

(ii) Cross relationship is found between $i^{th}$ data unit of message and $j^{th}$ block of cover.

(iii) Some mismatched data unit of message say (some $k^{th}$) data units.

After formulating the concept of finding relationships between bit patterns in message and that in cover, it is time to formulate a way to use the relationship to hide message in cover in such a way that no or very little modification of color bits of cover is required.

## V. EMBEDDING THE RELATIONSHIP

The method is computation intensive. We first define a bipartite graph G = (V, E) taking every data unit of message as a node in the set L (left). Similarly every block of m data units from cover is taken as node in the set R (right). A bipartite graph is a graph G whose vertex set V can be partitioned into two non empty disjoint sets L and R in such a way that every edge of G joins a vertex in L to a vertex in R. Using the direct relationship and cross relationship, as described in the previous section, we find a maximum bipartite matching.

A matching of G is a subset M of the set E of edges of G, with the property that no two edges in M have a common vertex. Thus no left vertex is incident to more than one edge of the matching, and no right vertex is incident to more than one edge of the matching. The matching associates, or matches, some of the left vertices to some of the right vertices in a one-to-one way. Matchings are an important area of study in graph theory because many practical problems can be seen as requiring the discovery of an optimal matching in a bipartite graph.

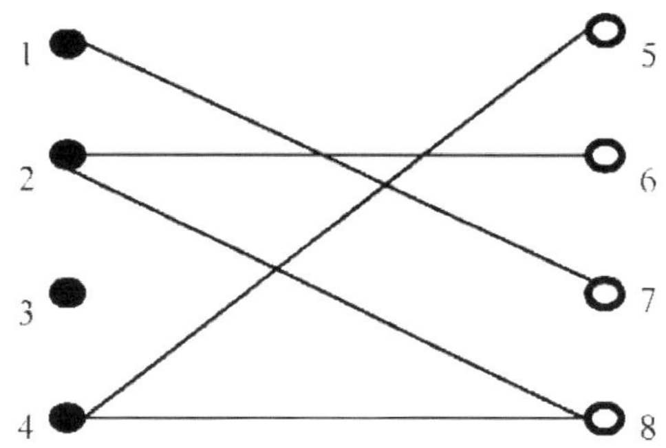


Figure 3

A matching is a collection of edges. Each edge in the matching is a confirmation that data unit of secret message is naturally embedded in the block of data units of cover image and there is no need to flip any bits of the cover to hide that part of message. Clearly the best matching we can obtain would have three edges. M = {(1, 7), (2, 8), (4, 5) } is one such matching. There are a few others in the graph. A matching having a maximal number of edges is called a max-matching. How to use this concept to embed secret message in cover?

Let us take an example to illustrate it. Suppose four data units, denoted as node 1, 2, 3, and 4 in the bipartite graph of figure 3, of secret message are to be embedded in the four blocks of data units of cover image, denoted as node 5, 6, 7, and 8 in the graph. Node 1 cross matches with only one node 7. Node 2 directly match to node 6 and cross matches to node 8. Similarly node 4 directly matches to node 8 and cross matches to node 5. After scanning it found that data units 2 and 4 have direct relationship with corresponding blocks in cover and that part of secret message is naturally embedded. Nothing needs to be done to hide these parts of secret message. Node 1 cross matches with 7 so hiding (1,7) in the cover in the extra byte s hall achieve the following:

(i) No color bits of cover is flipped to accommodate the message, and

(ii) In stead of writing message part, its indexes and cover block index is stored only.

Next the unmatched part i.e. node 3 is embedded as (M, 3, <message part>) in extra byte. Extra bytes are those parts in a image that are padded and kept to maintain a fixed predefined file format of the image. It needs to be explored in a cover before applying this approach. We have explored a few file formats including BMP to get presence of extra bytes.

At the end, a secret key is generated that contains <Size of the message, Data unit size>. The size of the message and data unit size together determines array size of message. The size of the image received at the recipient side and this information is used to find embedding factor. Once the information from the extra bytes, if any, is retrieved, it conveys how many are naturally embedded in the image and then the secret message can be reconstructed from image data itself.

## VI. STEGANALYSIS

Discussion of steganography necessarily leads to discussion of steganalysis. Steganalysis is the art of discovering the presence or transmission of stego content in the communication channel. From information security point of view it is crucial to thwart any attempt of stego communication. It is a probabilistic science. A steganalysis algorithm generally output a number within a given range to indicate the likelihood that stego was actually used on the input file. Steganalysis is a rapidly advancing science, and will continue to develop as long as steganographic algorithms are being created and used.

There are two approaches to the problem of steganalysis, one is specific to a particular steganographic algorithm. The other is developing techniques completely independent of the s teganographic algorithm to be analyzed. Each of the two approaches has it's own advantages and disadvantages. A steganalysis technique specific to an embedding method would give very good results when tested only on that embedding method and in all possibility it fails on other steganographic algorithm. However an independent steganalysis method may perform less accurately but it is capable to provide acceptable result on any new embedding algorithm. When the embedding algorithm is based on a graph theoretic approach that either does not change/replace any color bits of cover or changes very few colors bit, a general steganalysis algorithm can not work. In fact associations in the maximum bipartite matching takes care of the embedding process.

In general, the number of unmatched vertices is an upper bound on the number of changes to first-order statistics. An experimental result has shown that sufficiently good matching (< 3% unmatched) can be reached for natural cover data. This makes a graph theoretic approach practically undetectable by tests that look only at first-order statistics. It would be interesting to run a blind steganalysis scheme against this implementation to compare its detectability to the other tested algorithms. Adding a restriction to the set of edges could easily extend this graph theoretic approach and make it more secure against any general steganalysis algorithm. However in the approach presented the steganography totally depends on the key pairs consisting of size of message and data unit size. To the third party none of the information is known and hence given the arbitrariness of message size and data unit size for any message, it is simply Herculean for any body to guess and extract the message.

Today, a fairly large numbers of downloadable steganographic programs are available on the Internet that is based on the Least Significant Bit (LSB) embedding technique. A few examples are: Steganos II, S-Tools 4.0, Steghide 0. 3, Contraband Hell Edition, Web Stego 3.5, EncryptPic 1.3, StegoDos, Winstorm, Invisible Secrets Pro, and many others.

## CONCLUSION

A graph theoretic approach to steganography in an image as cover object helps in retaining all bits that participate in the color palette of image. The method is based on exploring maximum natural embedding and then finding relationship that conveys the presence of message in cover without either replacing or exchanging any bits of cover. This way the technique achieves sustainability. Sustainable steganography can be described as a method of hiding in such a way that no color bit is altered. Today various digital data formats are used in steganography. Most popular among them are bmp, doc, gif, jpeg, mp3, txt and wav because of the relative ease by which redundant or noisy data can be removed from them and replaced with a hidden message. BMP image is found to be more suitable because of presence of some redundant bytes at the quad word boundary. Since every digital cover file is simp ly stream of bits, an algorithm that treats cover as stream of bits, can be applied to any image/audio format with a little modification in finding zero bytes and header information. The concept presented in this paper for natural embedding can be further improved by using variable embedding factor k for adjusting its value whenever maximum natural embedding is achieved.

## FUTURE SCOPE

Steganographic research is primarily driven by the lack of strength in the cryptographic systems on its own and the desire to have complete secrecy in an open-systems environment. Redundancy is not always useless. A lot of research is required to evolve techniques to naturally embed message in digital cover media. It can be used for the benefit of the society as well as for better administrative management by keeping any secret information secret and beyond the reach of spoiler by maintaining its utmost privacy. The rich resources of spatial data available under national spatial database project by many governments around the world may also be used for the purpose of steganography using graph-theoretic approach to steganography. "A successful steganography is one that neither disturbs nor replaces any useful bits of cover. A successful steganalysis is one that retrieves message from stego without any clue about it."

## ACKNOWLEDGEMENT

We acknowledge our sincere thanks to Pendem Padmaja, India and Dr. Nune Srinivas Asst. Professor, Addis Ababa University who co-operated a lot from beginning to end to bring the paper to the present form. We are thankful to my friends and well-wishers whose encouragement to prepare the paper is Well worthy. Inspiration comes from many sources. In fact it is always there. One has to look around to know the presence of something worth noticing. The paper is result of the present potential threat that the wide spread information exchange through network is facing from amateur hackers. The open world today wishes to exchange information using a public network infrastructure but in secured manner. Thankfully, the situation provides an opportunity to think about. We are also very grateful to all those who have been constantly encouraging us to go for such scientific research work besides the regular work which we are doing in our respective departments.

## REFERENCES

[1]. Anderson R., F. Petitcolas, 1998, On the Limits of Steganography, IEEE Journal on Selected Areas in Communications, 16(4):474-481.

[2]. Bender W., D. Gruhl, N. Morimoto, A. Lu, 1996, Techniques for Data Hiding, IBM Systems Journal 35 (3&4):313-336.

[3]. Cole, Eric: Hiding in Plain Sight: Steganography and the Art of Covert Communication, Wiley Publishing, Inc, (2003).

[4]. David Kirkby (G8WRB), "BMP Format", http://atlc.sourceforge.net/bmp.html

[5]. Gonzalez, R.C. , Woods, R.E.: Digital Image Processing. Addison-Wesley. Reading, MA, (1992)

[6]. Johnson, N.F., Jajodia, S. : Exploring Steganography: Seeing the Unseen. IEEE Computer. February (1998) 26-34.

[7]. Johnson, Neil F., "Steganography", 2000, URL: http://www.jjtc.com/stegdoc/index2.html

[8]. Krinn, J., "Introduction to Steganography", 2000,URL: http://rr.sans.org/covertchannels/steganography.php

[9]. Kumar, V. and Muttoo, S. K. „A data structure for graph to facilitate hiding information in a graph's segments -A Graph Theoretic Approach to Steganography', Int. J. Communication Networks and Distributed Systems.

[10]. Neil F. Johnson, Zoran Duric, Sushil Jajodia, 2001, Information Hiding: Steganography and Watermarking - Attacks and Countermeasures, Kluwer Academic Publishers.

[11]. Noto, M., "MP3Stego: Hiding Text in MP3 files", 2001, URL: http://rr.sans.org/covertchannels /mp3stego.php

[12]. Petitcolas, Fabien A.P., "Information Hiding: Techniques for Steganography and Digital Watermarking.", 2000.

[13]. Stallings, W.: Cryptography & Network Security: Principles and Practice, Prentice Hall, (1999).

[14]. Stefan Hetzl and Petra Mutzel, "A Graph-Theoretic Approach to Steganography", CMS 2005, LNCS 3677, pp 119-128.

[15]. StegoArchive, "Steganography Information, Software and News to enhance your Privacy", 2001, URL: www. StegoArchive.com

[16]. The WEPIN Store, "Steganography (Hidden Writing)", 1995, URL: http://www.wepin.com/pgp/stego.html.

[17]. Weiss, I. 1993, Review - Geometric Invariants and Object Recognition, International Journal of Computer Vision, 10:207-231.

# Named Entity Recognition of Indian Origin Names in English Documents

Chaitanya Gupta, Deepanshu Sood, Mahua Bhattacharya*

ABV-Indian Institute of Information Technology & Management
Morena Link Road Gwalior 474010, India
*Corresponding author e-mail: bmahua@hotmail.com*

***Abstract***: Named Entity Recognition (NER) is the task of identifying and classifying all proper nouns in a document as person names, organization names, location names, date & time expressions and miscellaneous. There has been a growing interest in this field since early 1990s. Earlier, work has been done on NER taking English language as the medium. Apart from that some researchers have also tried their hands on Hindi and regional languages such as Telugu. The objective of our project is to identify names of Indian origin in English documents. The idea is to cover cross-linguistic aspects of text while performing NER on Indian names. The proposed project mainly distinguishes persons, organizations, locations and contact numbers in a document. The approach adopted is mainly unsupervised learning based on the feature space. Gazetteers are also used to improve the results of the experiment. The application is developed in C#.NET using the IDE of Visual Studio 2008.

*Keywords*: *NER, Indian names, Text mining, Hindi names in English documents.*

## 1. INTRODUCTION

The objective of NER is to classify all tokens in a text document into predefined classes such as person, organization, location, miscellaneous. In evaluations at the Message Understanding Conferences of the 1990s, it became clear that in order to reasonably extract information from documents, it is useful to first identify certain classes of information referred to in the text. They therefore established the Named Entity Task, where systems attempted to identify dates, times, numerical information and names [1]. At the time, MUC was focusing on IE tasks wherein structured information on company and defense-related activities are extracted from unstructured text, such as newspaper articles. In defining IE tasks, people noticed that it is essential to recognize information units such as names including person, organization, and location names, and numeric expressions including time, date, money, and percentages. Identifying references to these entities in text was acknowledged as one of IE's important sub-tasks and was called "Named Entity Recognition (NER)." Before the NER field was recognized in 1996, significant research was conducted by extracting proper names from texts. A paper published in 1991 by Lisa F. Rau [2] is often cited as the root of the field. Named Entity Recognition has remained an essential component of Information Extraction (IE) and related NLP tasks. NER also finds application in question answering systems and machine translation. NER is an essential subtask in organizing and retrieving biomedical information [3]. NER can be treated as a two step process

- identification of proper nouns.
- classification of these identified proper nouns.

A large number of techniques have been developed to recognize named entities for different languages. Some of them are Rule based and others are Statistical techniques. The rule based approach uses the morphological and contextual evidence of a natural language and consequently determines the named entities. This eventually leads to formation of some language specific rules for identifying named entities. The statistical techniques use large annotated data to train a model (like Hidden Markov Model) and subsequently examine it with the test data.

In its canonical form, the input of an NER system is a text and the output is information on boundaries and types of NEs found in the text. This work is about the creation of an autonomous NER system, which based on some rules and feature space will be able to recognize Indian origin names in English documents.

We may list some tasks related to NER. These tasks revolve around the notion of rigid designation, whereby the direct goal is not to recognize the named things from documents. We also thoroughly survey fifteen years of research—from 1991 to 2006—in a systematic review published in a special issue of

*Linguisticae Investigationes*[4].

**Personal name disambiguation** [5] is the task of identifying the correct referent of a given designator. For example, it may consist of identifying whether *Sachin Bansal* is the race driver, the film editor, or the Flipkart founder in a given context. Corpus-wide disambiguation of personal names has applications in document clustering for information retrieval. In the work of Mann and Yarowski [5], it is used to create biographical summaries from corpora.

**Named entity translation** [7][8] is the task of translating NEs from one language to another.

**Analysis of name structure** [9] is the identification of the parts in a person name. For example, the name "Doctor Saurav R. Sharma" is composed of a person title, a first name, a middle name, and a surname. It is presented as a preprocessing step for NER and for the resolution of co-references to help determine, for instance, that "APJ Abdul Kalam" and "President Kalam" are the same person, while "APJ Abdul Kalam" and "Shahid Kalam" are two distinct persons.

**Acronym identification** [10] is described as the identification of an acronym's definition (e.g., "ACM" stands for "Association for Computing Machinery") in a given document. The problem is related to NER because many organization names are acronyms (GE, NRC, etc.). Resolving acronyms is useful, again, to build co-reference networks aimed at solving NER. On its own, it can improve the recall of information retrieval by expanding queries containing an acronym with the corresponding definition.

**Record linkage** [11] is the task of matching named entities across databases. It involves the use of clustering and string matching techniques [28] in order to map database entries having slight variations (e.g., Sachin Tendulkar and S. *Tendulkar*). It is used in database cleaning and in data mining on multiple databases.

**Case restoration** [12] consists of restoring expected word casing in a sentence. Given a lower case sentence, the goal is to restore the capital letters usually appearing on the first word of the sentence and on NEs. This task is useful in machine translation, where a sentence is usually translated without capitalization information.

*1.3 Earlier Research:* Computational research aiming at automatically identifying NEs in texts forms a vast and heterogeneous pool of strategies, methods, and representations. One of the first research papers in the field was presented by Lisa F. Rau [2] at the 7$^{th}$ IEEE Conference on Artificial Intelligence Applications. Rau's paper describes a system to "extract and recognize [company] names." It relies on heuristics and handcrafted rules. From 1991 to 1995, the publication rate remained relatively low. It accelerated in 1996, with the first major event dedicated to the task: MUC-6[19]. It has not decreased since, with steady research and numerous scientific events: HUB-4[20]; MUC-7 and MET-2[1]; IREX [22]; CONLL [21]; and HAREM [23].

A good proportion of work in NER research is devoted to the study of English, but a possibly larger proportion addresses language independence and multilingualism problems. German is well studied in CONLL-2003 and in earlier works. Similarly, Spanish and Dutch are strongly represented, and were boosted as the focus of a major conference: CONLL-2002. Japanese has been studied in the MUC-6 conference, the IREX conference, and other works. Chinese is studied in abundant literature [24], and so are French [25], Greek [14], and Italian [6].

## 2. PROBLEM STATEMENT

As discussed in earlier section, a lot of work has been done on English and other languages such as German as well. Hindi in its pure form witness a lot of challenges as Hindi is a kind of unstructured language where subject can come early or later to predicate.

People have considered phoneme-based approach for finding named entities in Hindi language in past. However, the case we consider in this thesis is when a document covers Hindi names and places in an English document, i.e., addressing cross-linguistic issues while extracting information from a document.

English is the third most spoken language in the world and most of the countries have adopted it and created their own form of spoken English. In India also, most of the print media have adopted Hinglish (Hindi+English) as a common notion of information sharing.

Since most of the text and information on internet and print media is available in English language, it is important to come up with an approach that can effectively extract information available in Hindi language from those documents.

Our main focus would be to extract names, locations, organizations and contact numbers from the documents.

## 3. METHODOLOGY

While early studies were mostly based on handcrafted rules, most recent ones use supervised machine learning (SL), as a way to automatically induce rule-based systems or sequence labeling algorithms, starting from a collection of training examples.

*3.1 Supervised Learning:* The current dominant technique for addressing the NER problem is supervised learning. SL techniques include Hidden Markov Models (HMM), Decision Trees, Maximum Entropy Models (ME), Support Vector Machines (SVM), and Conditional Random Fields (CRF). These are all variants of the SL approach, which typically feature a system that reads a large annotated corpus, memorizes lists of entities, and creates disambiguation rules based on discriminative features.

*3.2 Semi Supervised Learning:* The term "semi-supervised" (or "weakly supervised") is relatively recent. The main technique for SSL is called "bootstrapping" and involves a small degree of supervision, such as a set of seeds, for starting the learning process. For example, a system aimed at "disease names" might ask the user to provide a small number of example names. Then, the system searches for sentences that contain these names and tries to identify some contextual clues common to the five examples. Then, the system tries to find other instances of disease names appearing in similar contexts. The learning process is then reapplied to the newly found examples, so as to discover new relevant contexts. By repeating this process, a large number of disease names and a large number of contexts will eventually be gathered.

*3.3 Unsupervised Learning:* The typical approach in unsupervised learning is clustering. For example, one can try to gather NEs from clustered groups based on context similarity. Basically, the techniques rely on lexical resources, on lexical patterns, and on statistics computed on a large corpus.
The approach we would be adopting is a blend of Semi-supervised and Unsupervised learning with the help of a feature space. Firstly, machine analyses the document based on patterns or features present. If features clearly indicate word to be name or place, then it is categorized as such, else gazetteer would be looked into and based on list look-up for a particular word, rules would be derived.

*3.4 Feature Space:* Features are describers or characteristic attributes of words designed for algorithmic consumption. The system has two types of rules:

- a recognition rule ( for example, capitalized words are entity candidates)
- a classification rule ( for example, the type of entity candidates of length greater than or equal to 3 words is organization)

The features that we will be using in identifying names, location, organizations are listed as follows:

TABLE 1: Feature space for identifying names (PER)

| | |
|---|---|
| Case | Name begins with Capital letter |
| Length | More than or equal to 3 characters |
| Titles | Dr., Mr., Mrs. |
| Part of Speech | Use of 'he', 'she', 'I' relates to a person |
| Morphology | Common ending. Examples: 'esh' in Rakesh and Suresh. |
| Punctuations | Presence of apostrophe s ('s) |
| Grammar | Next character such as 'is' denotes an entity. |
| Frequency of occurrence | A Person's name does not occur too frequently in a document. |

TABLE 2: Feature space for identifying locations (LOC)

| | |
|---|---|
| Case | Name begins with Capital letter |
| Length | More than or equal to 3 characters |
| Morphology | Common ending. Examples: 'ore' in Bangalore and Mangalore. |
| Punctuations | Presence of apostrophe s ('s) |
| Grammar | Use of 'in' or 'at' before the entity refers to a location |
| Frequency of occurrence | A Place's name does not occur too frequently in a document. |

TABLE 3: Feature space for identifying organizations (ORG)

| | |
|---|---|
| Case | Name begins with Capital letter, All letters capital or mixed case |
| Length | More than or equal to 3 characters |
| Frequency of occurrence | An organization's name does not occur too frequently in a document. |
| Punctuations | Use of '-'or '.' In between or at the end of the entity or special characters such as '&'. |

There are many challenges that might come across in this model. For example, after encountering an entity with initial capital letter, we mark it as PER, what if other entity starts from the second word again with a capital letter. It actually denotes that the first entity didn't end and second entity is a part of the first entity like a last name of a person.

So we use B-PER for first entity encountered and E-PER to denote that it is a part of previously found B-PER entity.

Similarly, we can resolve the same issue for organizations by using B-ORG and I-ORG.

Based on the above feature-space discussed, we will differentiate if an entity is a person, organization or a location.

*3.5 Proposed algorithm*

1. Application fulfills the purpose of Named Entity Recognition in two ways: by simply entering the text on home screen or by uploading a word document.
2. The text is read from the textbox or from the document and read word by word.
3. Let's say we pick up a word, X at a time.
4. We check if X starts from a number or '+'? If yes, then jump to next step else go to step 6.
5. Call a routine to check if X fulfills the criteria to be called a contact number.
6. Check if X has first letter capital? If no, then pick up next word and go back to step 4, else go to next step.
7. Check if X is not an article or interrogative forms (The, These, They, Are, Is, Was, When, Why etc.)? If yes, go to next step else pick up next word and go back to step 4.
8. Check if X is a title (Mr., Mrs., Dr. etc.)? If yes, then mark X as 'PER' and look for B-PER in next word and I-PER next to that, else go to next step.
9. Check for X in all possible feature space, i.e. for Name, Place and Organization.
10. For whichever feature space, X satisfies the highest ratio of features classifies into that feature-set.

*3.6 Flowchart*

The flowchart shows various modules of the application and the flow of the application. The entities once recognized are checked for features against different feature-space of name, place or organization/miscellaneous. Contact numbers are identified separately in the beginning only depending on the occurrence of the digits in a word.

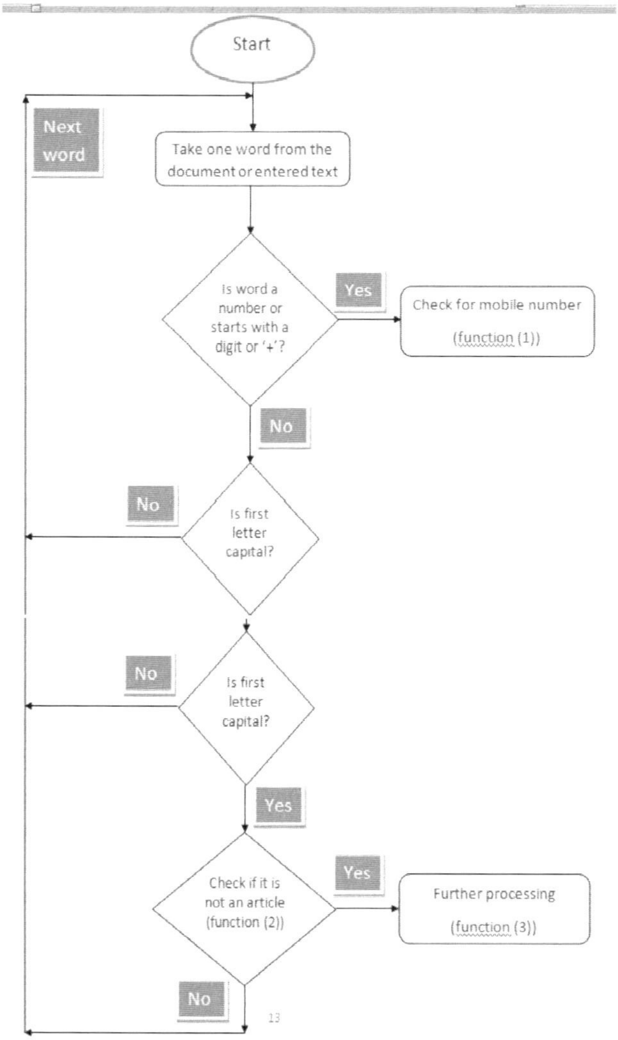

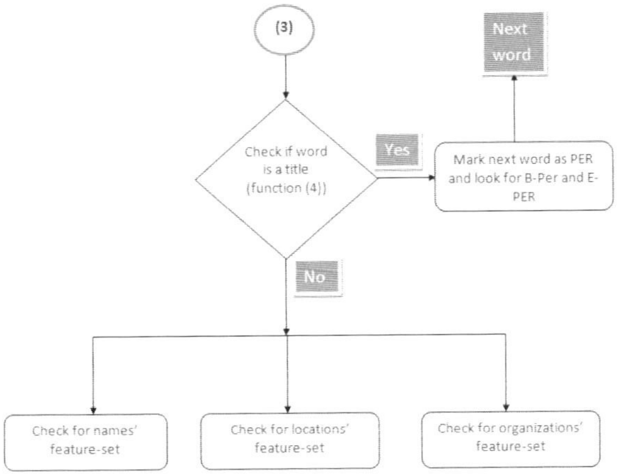


## 4. OBSERVATIONS AND RESULTS

The two basic parameters to judge the output are: Precision and Recall.

$$Recall = \frac{\text{Number of NEs detected by the system}}{\text{Number of NEs present in the gold standard test set}} \times 100\%$$

$$Precision = \frac{\text{Number of detected NEs that are correct}}{\text{Number of NEs detected by the system}} \times 100\%$$

We will test the application on some random excerpts of data and calculate the recall and precision for them.

Some screenshots have been pasted for example:

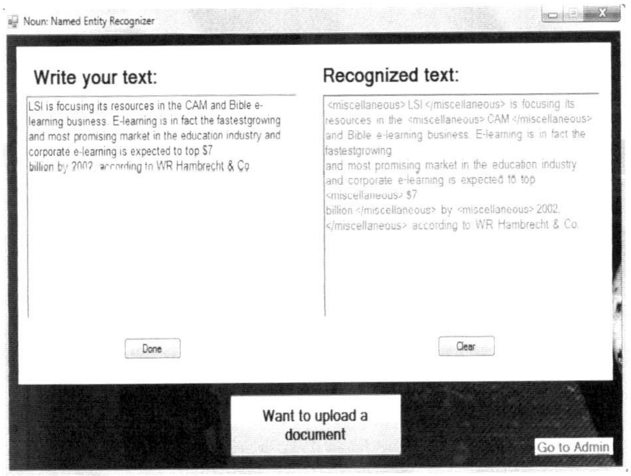


Recall = 80%, Precision = 75%, f-score = 77.42%

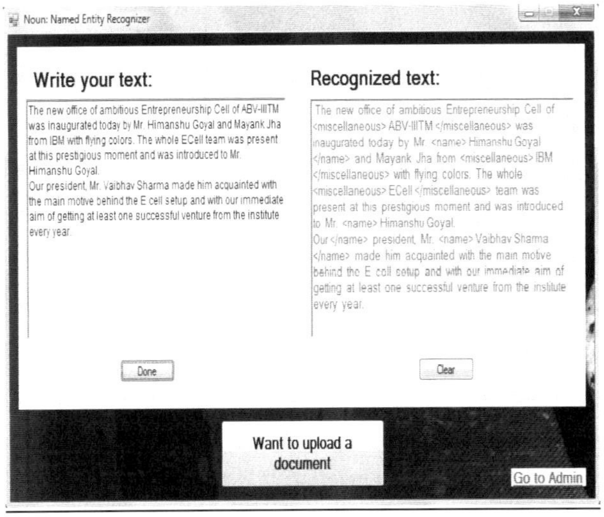


Recall = 75%, Precision = 83%, f-score = 78.797%

On an average, including many other test cases performed on this application, the Recall came to be more than 83% and Precision is around 90%.

Gazetteer is being improvised to enhance the results of the application.

## 5. CONCLUSION AND FUTURE WORK

The limitation with this model is that it never gives 100% accurate result but the results can be improved. Most of the previous works have achieved a precision of about 80%. To improve the result, A Gazetteer might also be used but will be an over-head on the complexity of the system and processing time.

Till now, based on the results obtained while testing the application, it can be said that application is able to give a satisfactory performance but efforts are being made to improve the result and reach a Recall and Precision of almost 100% if not exactly 100%.

Also, once named entities have been recognized from a given text, relations can be derived based on the context. This can be the further step in the project once best results from this application have been achieved in extracting named entities.

REFERENCES


[1] Chinchor, Nancy, "Overview of MUC-7/MET-2", Proc. Message Understanding Conference *MUC-7*, 1999.

[2] Rau, Lisa F., "Extracting Company Names from Text", Proc. Conference on Artificial Intelligence Applications of IEEE, 1991.

[3] Tzong-Han Tsai, Richard; Wu S.-H.; Chou, W.-C.; Lin, Y.-C.; He, D.; Hsiang, J.; Sung, T.-Y. and Hsu, "Various Criteria in the Evaluation of Biomedical Named Entity Recognition", vol. 6, *BMC Bioinformatic, 2006*.

[4] Nadeau, David and Sekine, S., "Named Entities: Recognition, classification and use", Special issue of Lingvisticæ Investigationes, vol. 30/1, pp. 3-26, 2007.

[5] Yarowsky, David and Florian, R., "Evaluating Sense Disambiguation across Diverse Parameter Spaces", Journal of Natural Language Engineering, vol. 8, pp. 293-310, 2002.

[6] Cucchiarelli, Alessandro and Velardi, P., "Unsupervised Named Entity Recognition Using Syntactic and Semantic Contextual Evidence", *Computational Linguistics,* vol. 27, no. 1, pp. 123-131, 2001.

[7] Fung, Pascale, "A Pattern Matching Method for Finding Noun and Proper Noun Translations from Noisy Parallel Corpora", Association for Computational Linguistics, vol. 21, no. 3, pp. 159-17, 1995.

[8] Huang, Fei, "Multilingual Named Entity Extraction and Translation from Text and Speech", Ph.D. Thesis, Carnegie Mellon University, 2005.

[9] Charniak, Eugene, "Unsupervised Learning of Name Structure from Coreference Data", Meeting of the North American Chapter of the Association for Computational Linguistics, vol. 27, no. 2, pp. 110-107, 2001.

[10] Nadeau, David and Turney, P., "A Supervised Learning Approach to Acronym Identification", Proc. Canadian Conference on Artificial Intelligence, 2005.

[11] Cohen, William and Richman, J., "Learning to Match and Cluster Entity Names", Proc. International ACM SIGIR Conference on Research and Development in Information Retrieval, 2001.

[12] Agbago, Akakpo; Kuhn, R. and Foster, G., "Truecasing for the Portage System", Proc. International Conference on Recent Advances in Natural Language Processing, 2006.

[13] Smith, David A., "Detecting and Browsing Events in Unstructured Text", Proc. ACM SIGIR Conference on Research and Development in Information Retrieval, 2002.

[14] Boutsis, S., Demiros, I. , Giouli, V. , Liakata, M. , Papageorgiou, H. and Piperidis, S., "A system for recognition of named entities in Greek" Proc. International Conference on Natural Language Processing, 2000.

[16] Pasca, Marius, "Acquisition of Categorized Named Entities for Web Search", Proc. Conference on Information and Knowledge Management, 2004.

[17] Wang, Lee, Wang, C., Xie, X., Forman, J., Lu, Y., Ma, W.-Y. and Li, Y., "Detecting Dominant Locations from Search Queries", Proc. International ACM SIGIR Conference, 2005.

[18] Sánchez, David and Moreno, A., "Web Mining Techniques for Automatic Discovery of Medical Knowledge", Conference on Artificial Intelligence in Medicine, 2005.

[19] Grishman, Ralph and Sundheim, B., "Message understanding conference - 6: A brief history", Proc. International Conference on Computational Linguistics, 1996.

[20] Chinchor, Nancy; Robinson, P. and Brown, E., "Hub-4 Named Entity Task Definition", DARPA Broadcast News Workshop, 1998.

[21] Tjong Kim Sang, Erik. F. and De Meulder, F., "Introduction to the CoNLL-2003 Shared Task: Language-Independent Named Entity Recognition", Proc. Conference on Natural Language Learning, 2003.

[22] Sekine, Satoshi and Isahara, H., "IREX: IR and IE Evaluation project in Japanese", Proc. Conference on Language Resources and Evaluation, 2000.

[23] Santos, Diana; Seco, N.; Cardoso, N. and Vilela, R., "HAREM: An Advanced NER Evaluation Contest for Portuguese", Proc. International Conference on Language Resources and Evaluation, 2006.

[24] Wang, Liang-Jyh; Li, W.-C. and Chang, C.-H., "Recognizing Unregistered Names for Mandarin

Word Identification", Proc. International Conference on Computational Linguistics, 1992.

[25] Poibeau, Thierry, "The Multilingual Named Entity Recognition Framework", Proc. Conference on European chapter of the Association for Computational Linguistics, 2003.

# Author Index